MW01014653

Information Technology and Law Series

Volume 35

More information about this series at https://link.springer.com/bookseries/8857

Bart Custers · Eduard Fosch-Villaronga
Editors

Law and Artificial Intelligence

Regulating AI and Applying AI in Legal Practice

Editors
Bart Custers
eLaw - Center for Law and Digital
Technologies
Leiden University
Leiden, The Netherlands

Eduard Fosch-Villaronga
eLaw - Center for Law and Digital
Technologies
Leiden University
Leiden, The Netherlands

ISSN 1570-2782   ISSN 2215-1966 (electronic)
Information Technology and Law Series
ISBN 978-94-6265-522-5   ISBN 978-94-6265-523-2 (eBook)
https://doi.org/10.1007/978-94-6265-523-2

Published by T.M.C. ASSER PRESS, The Hague, The Netherlands www.asserpress.nl
Produced and distributed for T.M.C. ASSER PRESS by Springer-Verlag Berlin Heidelberg

This T.M.C. ASSER PRESS imprint is published by the registered company Springer-Verlag GmbH,
DE part of Springer Nature.
The registered company address is: Heidelberger Platz 3, 14197 Berlin, Germany

Acknowledgements

This book comes as a result of a magnificent collective effort that mostly took place during the COVID-19 pandemic, perhaps one of the most turbulent times of contemporary history. These few lines try to summarize our dearest *thank you* to those behind this effort.

First, we thank all the authors that participated in this volume, which could not have come into existence without their fantastic contributions. All authors have shared their time and thoughts, and delivered outstanding scholarship, providing insights into their research on how law shapes AI and vice versa.

Second, we thank all the reviewers who ensured the academic quality of the contributions of this book. The pool of reviewers was formed by several of the authors that contributed to the book. Other scholars did a phenomenal job helping us with the review process, and we would like to thank them personally. Thank you Linda Louis, Lexo Zardiashvili, Henrik Skaug Sætra, Desara Dushi and Nertil Berdufi, Alejandro Zornoza Somolinos, Anne Kjersti Befring and Vibeke Vallevik, Tomás Gabriel García-Micó, and Yorick van Benten for your time and help in reviewing the contributions.

Third, a special thank you to Hadassah Drukarch for her immense work in helping us with all the not-that-fun and behind-the-scenes logistics that come with a large volume like this one. Hadassah was working at the time as a research assistant at the eLaw Center for Law and Digital Technologies at Leiden University when, apart from contributing to the book as an author, she also contributed to ensuring we kept to the deadlines, and assisted us in the communication with the authors, the reviewers, and the publishing house.

Last but not least, we would like to thank the people in the SAILS project, Leiden University's interdisciplinary AI research program, and eLaw, the Leiden Law School's Centre for Law and Digital Technologies, for facilitating, encouraging, and supporting this book and our work in the field of Law and Digital Technologies.

Leiden, The Netherlands   Bart Custers
May 2022   Eduard Fosch-Villaronga

Contents

About the Editors

Prof. Bart Custers Ph.D. M.Sc. LLM is a (full) professor of Law and Data Science and the director of eLaw, Center for Law and Digital Technologies at Leiden University, the Netherlands. He has a background in both law and physics and is an expert in the area of law and digital technologies, including topics like profiling, big data, privacy, discrimination, cybercrime, technology in policing, and artificial intelligence. As a researcher and project manager, he acquired and executed research for the European Commission, NWO (the National Research Council in the Netherlands), the Dutch national government, local government agencies, large corporations, and SMEs. Until 2016, he was the head of the research department on Crime, Law enforcement and Sanctions of the scientific research center (WODC) of the ministry of security and justice in the Netherlands. Before that, he worked for the national government as a senior policy advisor for consecutive ministers of justice (2009–2013) and for a large consultancy firm as a senior management consultant on information strategies (2005–2009). On behalf of the Faculty of Law, he is the coordinator of the SAILS project. This project, funded by the Executive Board of Leiden University, deals with the societal and legal implications of artificial intelligence.

He published three books on profiling, privacy, discrimination, and big data, two books on the use of drones, and one book on the use of bitcoins for money laundering cybercrime profits. On a regular basis, he gives lectures on profiling, privacy and big data and related topics. He has presented his work at international conferences in the United States, Canada, China, Japan, Korea, Malaysia, Thailand, the Middle East, and throughout Europe. He has published his work, over a hundred publications, in scientific and professional journals and in newspapers.

Dr. Eduard Fosch-Villaronga is an Assistant Professor at the eLaw Center for Law and Digital Technologies at Leiden University (NL) where he investigates legal and regulatory aspects of robot and AI technologies, with a special focus on healthcare. He is currently the Principal Investigator of PROPELLING (2021–2022), an FSTP from the H2020 Eurobench project, a project using robot testing zones to support evidence-based robot policies. He is also the co-leader of the project Gendering Algorithms, an interdisciplinary pilot project aiming to explore the functioning, effects, and governance policies of AI-based gender classification systems.

Eduard published the book "Robots, Healthcare, and the Law. Regulating Automation in Personal Care" with Routledge and is interested in human–robot interaction, responsible innovation, and the future of law. He was the PI of LIAISON (2020–2021), an FSTP from the H2020 COVR project that aims to link robot development and policymaking to reduce the complexity in robot legal compliance. He was also the co-leader of the Ethical, Legal, and Societal Aspects Working Group at the H2020 Cost Action 16116 on Wearable Robots and participates actively at the Social Responsibility Working Group at the H2020 Cost Action 19121 GoodBrother. In 2020, he served the European Commission in the Sub-Group on Artificial Intelligence (AI), connected products and other new challenges in product safety to the Consumer Safety Network (CSN) to revise the General Product Safety directive.

Previously, he was the recipient of a personal Marie Skłodowska-Curie Postdoctoral Researcher under the COFUND LEaDing Fellows at the eLaw Center for Law and Digital Technologies at Leiden University (NL) (Jan 2019–Dec 2020). He also was a postdoc at the Microsoft Cloud Computing Research Center at Queen Mary University of London (the UK, 2018) investigating the legal implications of cloud robotics; and at the University of Twente (NL, 2017) as a postdoc, exploring iterative regulatory modes for robot governance. He holds an Erasmus Mundus Joint Doctorate (EMJD) in Law, Science, and Technology coordinated by the University of Bologna (IT, 2017), an LL.M. from University of Toulouse (FR, 2012), an M.A. from the Autonomous University of Madrid (ES), and an LL.B. from the Autonomous University of Barcelona (CAT, 2011). He is also a qualified lawyer in Spain, fluent in Catalan, Spanish, English, Italian and French.

Part I
Introduction

Chapter 1
Humanizing Machines: Introduction and Overview

Bart Custers and Eduard Fosch-Villaronga

Contents

Abstract This chapter provides an introduction to this book (Law and Artificial Intelligence: Regulating AI and Applying it in Legal Practice) and an overview of all the chapters. The book deals with the intersection of law and Artificial Intelligence (AI). Law and AI interact in two different ways, which are both covered in this book: law can regulate AI and AI can be applied in legal practice. AI is a new generation of technologies, mainly characterized by being self-learning and autonomous. This means that AI technologies can continuously improve without (much) human intervention and can make decisions that are not pre-programmed. Artificial Intelligence can mimic human intelligence, but not necessarily so. Similarly, when AI is implemented in physical technologies, such as robots, it can mimic human beings (e.g., socially assistive robots acting like nurses), but it can also look completely different

B. Custers (✉) · E. Fosch-Villaronga
eLaw Center for Law and Digital Technologies, Leiden University, Leiden, The Netherlands
e-mail: b.h.m.custers@law.leidenuniv.nl

E. Fosch-Villaronga
e-mail: e.fosch.villaronga@law.leidenuniv.nl

© T.M.C. ASSER PRESS and the authors 2022
B. Custers and E. Fosch-Villaronga (eds.), *Law and Artificial Intelligence*,
Information Technology and Law Series 35,
https://doi.org/10.1007/978-94-6265-523-2_1

3

if it has a more functional shape (e.g., like an industrial arm that picks boxes in a factory). AI without a physical component can sometimes be hardly visible to end users, but evident to those that created and manage the system. In all its different shapes and sizes, AI is rapidly and radically changing the world around us, which may call for regulation in different areas of law. Relevant areas in public law include non-discrimination law, labour law, humanitarian law, constitutional law, immigration law, criminal law and tax law. Relevant areas in private law include liability law, intellectual property law, corporate law, competition law and consumer law. At the same time, AI can be applied in legal practice. In this book, the focus is mostly on legal technologies, such as the use of AI in legal teams, law-making, and legal scholarship. This introductory chapter concludes with an overview of the structure of this book, containing introductory chapters on what AI is, chapters on how AI is (or could be) regulated in different areas of both public and private law, chapters on applying AI in legal practice, and chapters on the future of AI and what these developments may entail from a legal perspective.

Keywords Artificial Intelligence · autonomy · self-learning technologies · robots · cyber-physical systems · legal practice

1.1 The Rise of Artificial Intelligence

Peter is an engineer who has recurring nightmares in which he dreams about aliens attacking the planet. Due to these nightmares, his relationship with his wife Alice and his daughters Hanna and Lucy is under pressure. When he visits a clinic to receive psychiatric help, he meets another patient who reveals having the same visions.

One night, invading spaceships enter the skies and start attacking the city where Peter and his family live. They manage to flee and seek shelter, but an explosion injures his wife, Alice. One of the heavily armoured alien soldiers from the spaceships follows them, however. When this soldier removes his helmet, he turns out to be human.

A medic examines Alice, but informs Peter he cannot save her. To his surprise, Peter is told that Alice is synthetic, not a human being. She is a robot based on Artificial Intelligence (AI), as are Peter and his daughters. It turns out that the alien invaders are humans from Mars, who have been living there for 50 years and now want to take back their planet.

This is the plot of the 2018 movie *Extinction*, directed by Ben Young and written by Spenser Cohen and Brad Kane. Admittedly, the general public thinks it is not a great movie, receiving somewhere around two out of five stars on review sites like

Moviemeter[1] and Rotten Tomatoes.[2] According to critics, it has a muddled plot and a frustrating pacing.[3] From a scientific point of view, it is hard to consider the narrative realistic.

The fight between humans and machines is the topic of many science fiction movies[4] and novels and has immensely shaped the narratives surrounding robots and AI.[5] What is interesting is how the roles of the good guys and the bad guys are reversed in this movie. Usually, the humans of flesh and blood are the creatures we (i.e., a human audience) can easily relate to, with actions and emotions we can recognize. Enemy machines of cold steel are usually pictured as things to be destroyed (rather than killed, as they are considered to be without life).

In the movie Extinction, this is reversed. The synthetics are androids (anthropomorphic robots designed to resemble human beings), presented as human beings, living their lives, having families, jobs, and pets, and experiencing the full range of human emotions. They are presented as humans, but of another kind, perhaps another race. It is the humans that are to some extent depicted as the bad guys, killing the androids and the planet. After fearing that the android workers might rise against humans, the military attacked the unarmed synthetics. The synthetics fought back and eventually drove all humans off the planet. Peter's nightmares are memories of this war, but most of the synthetics chose to wipe their memories of the war and live as humans, unaware of their nature or history.

The image pictured in Extinction raises philosophical questions about how artificial intelligence could actually become a new form of life, a new species, something that the European Institutions have been discussing intensely.[6] If such forms of AI are not only intelligent, but also able to experience emotions, learn new things, and be creative, they may be worthy of protection and eligible for having rights and obligations.[7] Human brains are based on carbon, but AI brains based on silicon may function equally well, maybe even better. If AI can make decisions and alter the world, maybe society wants to regulate that. But Extinction also works as a mirror that reflects human action; a dystopian reality that allows the spectator to be in the shoes of the synthetic beings and see, in a different context, how humans treat this

---

[1] See https://www.moviemeter.nl/film/1117116.

[2] See https://www.rottentomatoes.com/m/extinction_2018.

[3] See https://www.rottentomatoes.com/m/extinction_2018/reviews?intcmp=rt-what-to-know_r ead-critics-reviews.

[4] Some prominent examples include the *Terminator* franchise (starting in 1984), Ridley Scott's *Blade Runner* (1982), and Stanley Kubrick's 1968 film *2001: A Space Odyssey*.

[5] A prominent example includes the Butlerian Jihad in the Dune series by Frank Herbert, starting with Herbert 1963.

[6] See for instance the draft report on Civil Law Rules that the EU Parliament discussed back in 2016, available at https://www.europarl.europa.eu/doceo/document/JURI-PR-582443_EN.pdf, which proposed the creation of a legal status of an "electronic person" for "autonomous", "unpredictable" and "self-learning" robots and that started an outrage among the legal community leading to an open letter being published against it, See: http://www.robotics-openletter.eu/.

[7] Darling 2017.

world. This shifts back the attention to humans and to the need to regulate their actions to ensure future societies are not endangered, even more, by human actions.

The current state of the art technology in the area of AI is nowhere near the technology shown in the movie Extinction. However, given the rapid pace with which technology is currently evolving, it may be a good idea to further reflect on how the technologies we are developing may impact society and, therefore, how these should look like, to avoid disastrous consequences for humanity. The best way to avoid any future wars between humans and machines is perhaps to build these machines in ways that align with the needs, preferences, and interests of humans. Or, alternatively, if these machines are also to have their own needs, preferences and interests, to try to align these with those of humans. Given the current state of affairs, an open question remains who will decide[8] and what is in the best interest for society.

Since the future starts today, it makes sense to look at current technologies, examine where technological developments are heading and investigate in which directions we should steer them. This is where regulation comes in and where this book starts. With the help of regulation, it is possible to avoid the development of particularly harmful technologies (or at least mitigate the risks involved) and facilitate the development of technologies beneficial for society. In other words, some technologies and some applications of technology may be ok and desirable (e.g., lower-limb exoskeletons that help wheelchair users walk again), others are not (e.g., some autonomous weapon systems),[9] and regulation could play a role in promoting or stopping certain developments. Since we are still in the early stages of the development of AI technology, we can still adjust where things are going. However, since technology growth is exponential,[10] there is no time to waste.

Although it is interesting to reflect on future AI technologies and science fiction can be a good instrument to speculate about possible futures, this book primarily deals with AI technologies currently in use—only at the very end the future of AI is examined. Current-day AI is mostly not about androids or gynoids.[11] Despite some prominent examples like Sofia, a social humanoid robot developed by Hanson Robotics,[12] most robots do not resemble human beings. In fact, most forms of AI do not even have a physical embodiment that serves any specific function. Instead, the majority of the technologies called AI are machine learning applications that run on computers.

---

[8] Including who will decide who will decide, see Zuboff 2019.

[9] See for instance the campaign against 'killer robots' that is pushing for an international treaty similar to the one for field mines: https://www.stopkillerrobots.org/.

[10] Teeuw et al. 2008.

[11] Humanoids can resemble men or women. *Android* comes from the ancient Greek word ἄνδρος which means 'man'. *Gynoid* (also *fembot*) is the female cyborg version and comes from the Greek word γυνή and was first used by Isaac Asimov in an editorial in 1979, See https://sfdictionary.com/view/2481/gynoid.

[12] Greshko 2018. See also https://www.hansonrobotics.com/sophia/.

The European Commission defines *Artificial Intelligence* as 'systems that display intelligent behavior by analyzing their environment and taking actions—with some degree of autonomy—to achieve specific goals.'[13] These systems fall on a spectrum between physical devices and virtual applications.[14] If the task is to identify patterns, make predictions, and learn over time, the system will probably be software-based. However, sometimes the task (e.g., to perform surgery) requires the support of sophisticated physical instrumentation on top of the processing of vast amounts of information. Those types of AI with a physical or hardware component are usually referred to as cyber-physical systems (CPS).[15] Typical examples of CPS are drones or unmanned aerial vehicles (UAV),[16] autonomous vehicles systems, including trucks and cars and delivery robots,[17] and industrial control systems (systems monitoring and controlling industrial processes, such as in chemical plants or in car manufacturing). Other examples of CPS are robots in the healthcare domain, including surgery, physical and socially assistive robots, and service robots;[18] and also those for farming assistance and agriculture.[19]

Examples of types of software-based AI without many physical components are virtual smart assistants, face and speech recognition systems, image analysis software, search engines, and natural language processing (NLP) tools.[20] These systems usually work in a three-step process: (1) collect the data through various means, including sensors, (2) reason and process such information iteratively to create models, and (3) derive insights from these models and make future predictions on similar data in the real world.[21] Many of these systems are functioning without the user being aware of their presence.[22] In other words, users only see the front end and hardly anything of the underlying technology (as is the case with smart assistants and NLP tools) or nothing at all (as is the case with many online profiling tools). These processes, that could more accurately be described as *opaque,* raise questions on information asymmetries between on the one hand those who can see and

---

[13] HLEG on AI 2019.

[14] Fosch-Villaronga and Millard 2019.

[15] STOA 2016.

[16] Custers et al. 2015.

[17] Viscelli 2018. See also the delivery robots being tested by Albert Heijn, one of the largest Dutch supermarkets, https://www.dutchnews.nl/news/2019/07/albert-heijn-trials-driverless-robot-that-delivers-groceries-to-your-door/.

[18] Fosch-Villaronga and Drukarch 2021.

[19] The Digital Innovation Hub on Agrobofood has its headquarters at Wageningen University in the Netherlands and builds the European ecosystem for the effective adoption of robotics technologies in the European agricultural food sector, See https://www.wur.nl/en/project/agROBOfood-Towards-a-European-network-and-effective-adoption-of-robotics-technologies.htm.

[20] HLEG on AI 2019.

[21] IBM 2021.

[22] See the third entry of the definition of transparent by the Oxford dictionary: https://www.lexico.com/definition/transparent.

understand the processed information and on the other hand the end users or auditing agencies that may not have enough knowledge to understand the inner workings of the systems, and thus call for more robust transparency and explainability mechanisms to empower users.[23]

1.2 So What is New About This?

1.2.1 A New Technology

Compared to the previous generation of information technologies, two things are novel about these new technologies. Firstly, these new technologies are capable of *self-learning*, i.e., a process by which a system takes the initiative without the assistance of humans to identify patterns, discover new information, and predict future events with similar data. In this sense, AI is often referred to in one breath with technologies like algorithms, data mining, and machine learning. However, there are some important distinctions between these technologies. Data mining focuses mostly on knowledge discovery in databases. In machine learning, the focus is more on how a system can learn tasks and optimize them over time. E.g., a model is iteratively trained to result in a maximum or minimum function evaluation.[24] Both data mining and machine learning make use of algorithms, but in machine learning these can improve automatically with experience. Generally, an algorithm is a sequence of computations or instructions. As such, it can be applied to data for performing calculations, data processing, or automated reasoning. In itself, an algorithm is not smart or self-learning—the same input will always yield the same output.[25] Data mining technologies focusing on regression, clustering, and classification to find patterns in large datasets usually make use of algorithms, but these algorithms do not evolve automatically.[26] However, the algorithms can also be designed in such a way that they autonomously improve themselves through learning processes. There are three approaches to this: supervised learning, unsupervised learning, and reinforcement learning, which will be further explored in Chap. 2, along with the major disciplines within the field of AI.

Secondly, and related to the self-learning characteristic, AI can act with a certain level of *autonomy*.[27] This means that AI systems can make decisions themselves, decisions that are not preprogrammed. Typical examples are drones and autonomous vehicles that can use evasive maneuvers to avoid collision with unexpected objects

---

[23] Felzmann et al. 2019.

[24] Secherla 2018.

[25] Or the same kind of output: where random or pseudo-random components are used, the output is not exactly the same. Nevertheless, this is not self-learning technology.

[26] Calders and Custers 2013.

[27] Fosch-Villaronga et al. 2021.

(like animals crossing their paths) or maintain flight stability despite lost connection.[28] Here, the trajectory that is followed is not preprogrammed. It depends on the AI system's decision in a particular situation. Higher levels of autonomy usually involve that the technology is assigned with a specific task and can choose the optimum strategy to execute that task. In the example of evasive maneuvers, drones or autonomous vehicles can be programmed to avoid collisions, but can decide autonomously on the best strategy to do this. As a result, the optimum strategy can be different in each specific situation. In fact, AI may have learned a better strategy after some time, which means that the next time it is confronted with the same situation it may choose a different strategy, In theory, an even higher level of autonomy would involve AI that can autonomously determine optimum strategies to fulfill specific tasks or achieve certain goals, and even set its tasks and goals—but that kind of technology is currently in its infancy.[29]

Taking these aspects of self-learning and autonomy together, we call these technologies intelligent technologies, or more precisely, *Artificial Intelligence*. *Artificial* because they are human-made and not alive in the biological sense. And *intelligent* because these technologies may perform tasks that humans consider intelligent.[30] They can mimic human or animal intelligence, but not necessarily so. They can be intelligent in one specific area, such as drones and autonomous vehicles because they are capable of processing information and avoiding collisions, or smart assistants because they recognize instructions when users talk to them in real time. In some of these areas, this intelligence may easily exceed human intelligence, for instance, when processing or memorizing large amounts of data. Some of these systems that beat human intelligence are well known examples, such as Deepblue that beat world chess champion Kasparov (in 1996),[31] Google's AlphaGo beating Go world champion Lee Sedol (in 2016),[32] or IBM's Watson beating human TV quiz Jeopardy champions (in 2010).[33] If AI is able to learn any intellectual task that a human being can learn, this is referred to as Artificial General Intelligence (AGI). However, AGI currently does not (yet) exist (cf. Chap. 26).

This is also where, due to different connotations, different terminology comes in. In this book, we refer to AI, AI systems, and AI technology. However, some people refer to 'an AI', which usually means they have a personified entity in mind, a form of AGI that acts and perhaps looks like a human being. However, since such AI technology does not yet exist, talking about 'an AI' is not appropriate unless it

---

[28] Custers 2016.

[29] These technologies are being explored in the field of AI for board of directors, see Fox et al. 2019. For autonomous surgeries, see Shademan et al. 2016.

[30] We understand that one of the shortcomings of this approach is that intelligence is not a concept that has an agreed definition among scholars and that it usually involves a pretty anthropo-centric vision of what intelligence is.

[31] Higgins 2017.

[32] Metz 2016.

[33] Thompson 2010.

concerns distant-future technology. This book contains several chapters on the future of AI that will focus on this (Part V of this book), but for the most part, the focus is on current and near-future AI technology.

1.2.2 A New Need for Regulation

AI is rapidly and radically changing the world around us. AI helps us to understand complex and vast amounts of data in many different areas, such as drug discovery, human speech recognition,[34] legal documents interpretation,[35] stock markets prediction,[36] human behavior regulation, and even the creative industry,[37] that could not be done before. Developments in AI are essential for the realization of autonomous vehicles, accurate diagnosis, and sophisticated language translation technologies. As such, AI is often thought to be a great promise to make this world a better place.

However, as the saying goes, *the road to hell is paved with good intentions.* Automating society, particularly when introducing highly sophisticated autonomous technologies, can result in disadvantages, undesirable side-effects, and unforeseen new applications. This may call for regulation, for instance, to offer sufficient protection to citizens and to reflect specific norms and values in the design of such new technologies. Since we are still in the early stages of the development of AI technology, we can still relatively easily adjust where things are going. However, once the technology has developed further, adjusting this may be much more challenging.

Also, the more autonomous and self-learning these machines are, the more the roles and responsibilities of the creators of these technologies change,[38] and the need to regulate these new behaviors may become more evident. Imagine, for instance, that in the future, AI will develop its own will.[39] Similar to how children after years of parental care may at some point follow their own path in life, it is not hard to imagine that AI technology may find its own ways of doing so. The case of AlphaGo is an illustrative example of such a case, a historical moment in which the AI system started doing Go moves that had never been performed by humans before.[40]

Most probably, AI will evolve beyond our limited human-centered vision of the world and perhaps resemble the emergence or 'origin' of a new species, not an animal or a species that is cognitively less developed than humans, but a species that evolved differently. At some point, perhaps not so far in the future, it may be less relevant how we think of AI, but all the more relevant how AI thinks of us. For instance, many technologies, including AI, are designed to do dull, dangerous, or dirty tasks

---

[34] Sathya et al. 2017.

[35] Kauffman and Soares 2020.

[36] Ferreira et al. 2021.

[37] de Cock Buning 2018.

[38] Fosch-Villaronga et al. 2021; Yang et al. 2017.

[39] Totschnig 2020.

[40] Gibney 2016.

because humans prefer not to do these things. However, at some point, an intelligent search and rescue robot may decide to be no longer willing to risk being crushed in an earthquake or avalanche, a sex robot may decide to serve the needs of others no longer, but to enjoy its own sexual preferences, and an intelligent classification system may develop its own moral standards for non-discrimination and privacy. All this may raise competing interests between the meaningful control that humans and machines have over reality.[41] This requires careful regulatory attention, as humanizing machines might dehumanize people and encourage poor human decision-making in allocating resources and responsibility.[42]

However, even if AI technologies are only used to serve humans, there can be competing interests. For instance, in the scenario that autonomous vehicles equipped with AI technology drive safer than human drivers, human drivers may become obsolete and perhaps even prohibited. If human drivers are the more dangerous alternative in transport, that may be sufficient reason to prohibit them from driving. These scenarios are increasingly realistic, also in other domains, such as healthcare (e.g., where AI-powered robot surgeons help perform less invasive procedures), economy (e.g., AI in online pricing and in stock trading) and the military (e.g., AI in drones and autonomous weapon systems).[43] These developments may also raise questions with regard to access to these technologies. If they are exclusively accessible to wealthy people, they may cause or contribute to inequality and social segregation.

If AI is applied in the legal domain, several of these issues deserve further attention. For instance, AI technologies are increasingly used by litigating parties in courts, as they may be able to predict a positive outcome, decide on the best negotiation or litigation strategy, or settle disputes. Typically, AI can be helpful in preparatory legal research and in predicting court rulings.[44] However, if not all parties have access to the same technologies in lawsuits, this may interfere with the principle of equality of arms during litigation.

Things may become even more complicated when discussing computer judges, i.e. AI that can provide a ruling in particular cases.[45] For instance, in the case of AI in transport or medicine, it is relatively easy to set goals (e.g., less traffic incidents or less complications during surgery) and determine how the use of AI contributes to such goals. In the case of computer judges, both determining the goal (what is a fair ruling?) and the extent to which a goal was reached (to what extent is the ruling fair?) can be extremely complicated—even without the use of AI, there are often no conclusive answers, but certainly many questions, for instance, regarding whether AI is used in courts will ensure or hamper the right to a fair trial.[46]

---

[41] Santoni de Sio and Van den Hoven 2018.

[42] Bryson 2010.

[43] Yang et al. 2017; Ferreira et al. 2021; Asaro 2012.

[44] Custers and Leeuw 2017.

[45] Nakad-Weststrate et al. 2015.

[46] Ulenaers 2020.

1.2.3 A New Book

Over the last years, several books and papers have been written about regulating AI[47] and applying AI in legal practice.[48] So it is a fair question to ask what this book adds to all this knowledge already available.

First, many of the existing papers and journals address only one issue or only one application of AI, whereas this book provides a comprehensive overview of developments across all of the most relevant areas of law, both in public law and private law. In a moment of regulatory turmoil in which many pieces of legislation are being updated, including the General Product Safety Directive, the Machinery Directive, and laws are being put forward to frame AI development,[49] having such an overview facilitates crossing over different areas of law relatively easily, which enables learning from developments and lessons in other areas.

Second, many of the existing books are either mostly technical or mostly legal in nature. This book is based on contributions of authors from all kinds of disciplines, including scholars with a background in law and technology, but also experts in philosophy, psychology, computer science, and economics. As a result, this book considers developments in law and AI from many different perspectives.

Third, many of the existing books take a national perspective, whereas this book has a broad, international perspective. Instead of focusing on how AI is regulated in a specific jurisdiction, this book mostly focuses on how AI could or should be regulated, regardless of any specific jurisdiction. As such, the focus is much more on regulatory issues regarding AI than on specific legislation. This favors problem-solving thinking based on lesson-learned. Having said that, many of the contributions to this book focus on the EU and this may offer only a partial picture of how AI is being regulated or applied worldwide. Still, many examples from different jurisdictions are used to illustrate particular developments and issues, or to present best practices.

Fourth, this book deals with state-of-the-art technologies, an advantage over earlier books simply because they were published earlier. Developments are so fast that they merit new publications with new insights every few years and this book contributes to keep the discussion going in the field of law and AI by offering the most recent knowledge available and produced by leading scholars in the field. We realize this also means that part of this book may be outdated within a few years, especially

---

[47] de Bruyne and Vanleenhove 2021; Barfield and Pagallo 2020; Passchier 2021; Gellers 2020; Guihot and Bennett Moses 2020; Fosch-Villaronga 2019; Calo et al. 2016.

[48] Katz et al. 2021; Legg and Bell 2020; Ashley 2017.

[49] For the most recent developments, follow the Proposal for a Regulation of the European Parliament and of the Council on machinery products, https://ec.europa.eu/docsroom/documents/45508; The revision of the General Product Safety Directive, https://ec.europa.eu/info/business-economy-euro/product-safety-and-requirements/product-safety/consumer-product-safety_en; and the Proposal for a Regulation of the European Parliament and of the Council laying down harmonised rules on Artificial Intelligence (Artificial Intelligence Act), https://eur-lex.europa.eu/legal-content/EN/TXT/?uri=CELEX%3A52021PC0206.

with respect to technological advances. However, we hope that the discussions and reflections here presented remain perennial in future discussions on how to regulate contemporary technologies among scientists and scholars.

1.3   What This Book is About

This book provides information about AI technologies in order to better understand the scope of this book and the issues that AI technologies may cause (which may need to be regulated), but it does not primarily have a technological focus. This book deals with the intersection of law and AI as described here below.

1.3.1   The Novelty of This Book

Law and AI intersect in two different ways. Firstly, AI may require regulation. As mentioned earlier, it may be expected that AI will bring significant changes in several sectors of society, including transport (e.g., self-driving cars), healthcare (e.g., automated drug discovery, predicting virus outbreaks[50]), education (e.g., adaptive virtual tutors catering to personalized individual needs), and language (e.g., real-time translations of conversations). Applying AI may offer all kinds of benefits that range from safer roads to more effective surgeries, but there may also be risks involved that cause direct or indirect harm to society–holistically understood.[51] In order to offer sufficient protection to people, some kind of regulation or regulatory guidance may be required. Several aspects are already regulated in the EU, for instance, via legislation, such as the processing of personal data (covered by the EU General Data Protection Regulation),[52] intellectual property (covered by IP Law),[53] and product liability (covered by the liability for defective products).[54] However, these legal instruments are often technology-neutral and lack field knowledge, which may be a problem for enforcement and compliance.[55] Acknowledging the existence of such a disconnect between policy and enforcement, in April 2021, the EU issued a draft regulation directed explicitly at AI, particularly high-risk AI.[56] However, as shown

---

[50] Custers 2005.

[51] Amodei et al. 2016.

[52] General Data Protection Regulation 2016.

[53] AI systems are mainly protected as trade secrets because copyright and patent laws encounter application difficulties. For instance, algorithms are excluded from protection under the EU Software Directive. See Foss-Solbrekk 2021.

[54] Liability of defective products regime at https://ec.europa.eu/growth/single-market/goods/free-movement-sectors/liability-defective-products_en.

[55] Fosch-Villaronga and Heldeweg 2018.

[56] Artificial Intelligence Act 2021.

throughout this book, most of the existing legislation may at times be challenging to apply to AI. In particular situations, the protection of people may be insufficient and at some points legislation simply may not even (yet) exist to frame such novel developments.[57]

Part II and Part III of this book contain chapters on regulating AI in different areas of law. Part II focuses on areas in public law, such as non-discrimination law, labour law, humanitarian law, constitutional law, immigration law, criminal law, and tax law. Part III focuses on areas in private law, such as liability law, intellectual property law, corporate law, competition law, and consumer law. Section 1.5, at the end of this chapter, provides a more detailed overview of the structure of this book.

Secondly, law and AI may interact in the sense that AI may also offer many opportunities when applied in the legal domain, i.e., in legal research and legal practice.[58] AI offers opportunities particularly with regard to (1) predictions, e.g., predictions of outcomes of litigation, (2) searching, structuring, selecting, and analysing large amounts of data, particularly legal big data,[59] and (3) decision-making and empirical legal research, e.g., taking over the decision-making of courts or law-making of legislators.[60] Quantitative legal predictions increasingly play a role in decisions on whether to take a case to court. Robust quantitative prediction models already exist for the US Supreme Court[61] and the European Court of Human Rights.[62] It may be expected that such models will soon be available for lower courts and perhaps even individual judges unless that will be prohibited, such as in France, where quantitative legal predictions for individual judges are not allowed.[63]

AI contributing to the processing of large amounts of data, including collecting, structuring, and analysing such data, is already common practice in many law firms. Tools like Ravellaw[64] quickly visualise all available case law in any given area. However, it may be expected that future AI technology will also take over (parts of) legal decision-making, like dispute resolution and even court rulings. Several online platforms already have technology that can partially or fully take over online dispute resolution.[65] However, AI taking over the roles of judges ('robojudges') is usually approached with much more reluctance–similar to fully autonomous and pilotless airplanes. Most people seem to adhere to the *cognitive computing paradigm*, assuming that although technology can certainly assist judges in structuring and analysing data when they have to rule in specific cases, this will always require uniquely human qualities like ethical considerations, intuition, and creativity.[66]

---

[57] Drukarch et al. 2021.
[58] Custers 2018.
[59] Custers and Leeuw 2017.
[60] Nakad-Weststrate et al. 2015.
[61] Katz et al. 2014.
[62] Aletras et al. 2016.
[63] Szczudlik 2019.
[64] Eckholm 2015.
[65] Lodder and Thiessen 2003.
[66] Arafat et al. 2019; Coccoli et al. 2017.

However, this may be hard to sustain in light of the impressive advancements in information processing and decision-making that systems like IBM Watson offer in many applications. Future doctors and judges may be unable to review and check the output of AI systems that process information that would take them ten days in just two microseconds?[67] Although ethical values and creativity seemed once reserved for humans uniquely (and hardly seem to exist in the animal kingdom), it may well be that such a human-centered vision is just too narrow to capture human and artificial intelligence. There already exists AI-generated music[68] (cf. Chap. 17) and AI-generated art that ('blindfolded') experts considered more esthetic, profound, and innovative than works of art created by humans.[69] Time will tell how far the role of AI in legal research and legal practice will develop, but some scholars argue that AI will profoundly change the legal field and the work of lawyers.[70]

AI may constitute an important contribution and radical transformation to legal practice and legal scholarship as it may provide novel, unexpected insights and considerably increase efficiency (fewer resources, more results) and effectiveness (more accurate and reliable results) of legal research, both in legal practice and legal scholarship. This may, among other things, result in improved legal services, new business models, new knowledge, and a more solid basis for evidence-based policies and legislation. Part IV of this book contains several chapters on these and other applications of AI in the legal domain.

1.3.2 Readership and Target Audience

This book is mainly addressed to people that want to equip themselves with a deeper understanding of the latest developments in the field of law and Artificial Intelligence. This book offers a deep dive into the technological workings of AI that can be instrumental to an audience without a background in technology. It also offers rich reflections and provocative thoughts that can be extremely valuable to lawyers interested in the latest developments in AI and how these developments most profoundly affect the legal domain they work in, either in academia or in legal practice, including lawyers, judges, and lawmakers. Also, this book is of value to lawyers interested in how AI-based legal technologies can transform their way of working and how their work may look like in the future. In this sense, they may find this book a roadmap to the journey their law firm may take to adapt to current times and develop services to clients in a more efficient and effective way. Apart from lawyers, this book may provide valuable insights into the field of law and AI useful for academics in other disciplines, such as ethics, sociology, politics, and public administration, as well as to

---

[67] See IBM Watson Discovery https://www.ibm.com/nl-en/cloud/watson-discovery.

[68] Johnson 1997.

[69] BBC 2018.

[70] Susskind 2013.

future generations studying law and AI and related disciplines in which more knowledge on law and technology is essential. Lastly, other people who may be confronted with the use of AI in their work, including policymakers, judges, and people working at supervisory authorities and government agencies may find in this book insights on how to start getting ready for the AI revolution.

Due to the speed of many technological developments, it may sometimes be difficult for people without a technological background to understand how these technologies work and what their impact is. This book attempts to explain and discuss the latest technological developments with regard to AI in plain language to ensure it is intelligible for a broad audience. People with a background in technology, for instance, engineers designing and developing AI technology may find this book helpful because it provides further guidance on how technologies can be developed in ways that are by default legally compliant and that foster high levels of user acceptance and can count on broad public support. These are essential elements for preventing adverse consequences when technology is widely adopted.

1.4 Leiden University and the SAILS Project

In many countries, large amounts of funding have been made available for further research on AI.[71] Also in the Netherlands, research on AI is gaining momentum.[72] In 2019, the executive board of Leiden University decided to fund a four-year cross-faculty research program on AI, called the SAILS project.[73] With a budget of approximately 5 million euros, research positions for assistant and full professors and PhD candidates were created across all faculties of Leiden University and the Leiden University Medical Centre to advance the contemporary understanding of AI.

The SAILS project aims to forge links between the different disciplines at Leiden University and to initiate new academic partnerships. This includes research in fields such as innovative medical imaging, the hunt for candidate drugs, and the use of algorithms for decision-making in public administration, the judiciary or corporations. The research results of this project are also implemented in the education programs that Leiden University offers.

The motto of the SAILS project is 'The Future of AI is Human', which shows a clear focus on the interdisciplinary approach to AI, combining insights and expertise from both science and the humanities. The synergy flowing from this collaboration brings about new creativity, funding and inspiration. Perhaps more importantly, it helps to address the social, political, legal and ethical questions that AI may raise.

---

[71] Rosemain and Rose 2018; Harper 2021. Also many countries worldwide are thinking about developing policies for AI, see Jobin et al. 2019.

[72] See, for instance, the Netherlands AI Coalition, https://nlaic.com and the innovation funding schemes of the 'Groeifonds', https://nos.nl/artikel/2376036-vier-miljard-euro-uit-groeifonds-ver deeld-ai-quantumtechnologie-en-groene-waterstof.

[73] SAILS stands for Society, Artificial Intelligence, and Life Sciences. See https://www.universit eitleiden.nl/sails.

Thanks to the SAILS project, technology experts like data scientists, computer scientists, and mathematicians are working together with psychologists, linguists, medical doctors, archeologists, lawyers, and philosophers.

This book originated in the SAILS project and has been curated within eLaw, the Leiden Law School's Centre for Law and Digital Technologies, which is located at Leiden University, in the Netherlands. eLaw is a multi-disciplinary institute that brings together a unique set of expertise on the legal, philosophical and social implications of the information society. eLaw conducts fundamental and applied research on the Internet's legal, social, and technological regulation and other technologies. Several chapters in this volume are authored by scholars affiliated to the SAILS project, eLaw, or both.

Apart from this starting point, this book also welcomed scholars from around the globe to contribute in this endeavor. We started with an open call for papers that was disseminated online via social media platforms and via the different networks of our research groups, including the above-mentioned SAILS project. Furthermore, authors in the areas of AI and law and digital technology were contacted via a targeted approach. As a result, a total of 67 abstracts were received.[74] After careful consideration, the editors invited the authors of 42 abstracts to submit a full chapter and rejected 25 abstracts. After the conditional acceptance of their abstract, a total of nine proposals for chapters were withdrawn by their authors, most of them indicating that due to the situation caused by the COVID-19 pandemic, they were unable to submit a full chapter. The 33 full chapters submitted to the editors went through two reviews: an editorial review and an external double-blind peer review. If one of the editors was also the author or co-author of a chapter, the other editor performed the editorial review and the peer review was single-blind. This review process resulted in minor or major revisions of some chapters and rejection of other chapters. Another round of editorial review plus double-blind peer review was performed for those reviews that initially resulted in a major revision. As can be seen in the table of contents, in the end a total of 26 chapters were accepted, which follow after this chapter. This comes down to an acceptance rate of almost 40%. As per the timeline, the call for papers opened in the autumn of 2020 and the final manuscript was ready in the autumn of 2021.

1.5 The Structure of This Book

This book contains five different parts, in which the chapters are organized according to their topic:

- **Part I** contains introductory chapters, like this chapter which provides an introduction to and an overview of the structure of this book. The other chapters in this part provide an introduction to intelligence and to AI technology respectively.

---

[74] This first chapter was written after all chapters were completed and is not included in these numbers and was not part of the review process described here.

- Part II and III focus on regulating AI from public law and private law perspectives, respectively. **Part II** focuses on areas in public law, such as non-discrimination law, labour law, humanitarian law, constitutional law, immigration law, criminal law, and tax law.
- **Part III** focuses on areas in private law, such as liability law, intellectual property law, corporate law, competition law, and consumer law.
- **Part IV** focuses on applying AI in legal practice. Here, the focus is mostly on legal technologies, such as AI in legal teams, law-making, and legal scholarship.
- Finally, **Part V** focuses on the future of AI. Whereas Parts II, III and IV focus on current AI technology, Part V focuses on future technological developments and what these may entail. Here, the focus is on topics like human enhancement, general AI (AGI, see Sect. 1.2.1) and future AI law.

The following subsections provide a more detailed chapter-by-chapter introduction for each part of this book:

1.5.1 Part I: Introduction

In Chap. 2, **De Kleijn** contrasts artificial intelligence with human intelligence. He argues that it is necessary to take inspiration from the human brain to create human-level intelligence successfully. In this chapter, several ways are illustrated in which this approach has led to improvements in artificially intelligent systems for both symbolic and subsymbolic forms of AI.

In Chap. 3, **Häuselmann** examines what AI is and how it works, setting the stage for the debate on legal and ethical issues of the developments in AI, which are discussed in-depth in the other parts of this book. He outlines that AI is an exciting, challenging, and complex domain, covering a broad range of disciplines, approaches, and techniques. Five major AI disciplines relevant to lawyers are discussed: Machine Learning, Automated Reasoning, Computer Vision, Affective Computing, and Natural Language Processing.

1.5.2 Part II: Public Law

In Chapter 4, **Morondo Taramundi** explores discriminatory effects in AI-based decision-making and to what extent the notion of indirect discrimination can address this. Indirect discrimination is focused on the effects rather than on the sensitive characteristics that produce discrimination. The application of indirect discrimination to algorithm-based decisions is determined by elements and requirements developed in EU anti-discrimination law and the EU Court of Justice's case law. Limitations of indirect discrimination include limitations regarding the relevant comparator, the working of objective justification, or the exhaustive list of protected grounds. Technical tools need to be developed that can improve the performance of anti-discrimination mechanisms and anti-discrimination legal reasoning.

In Chap. 5, **López Belloso** takes a feminist and intersectional approach towards AI-based decision-making, arguing that regulatory frameworks can play a relevant role in combating and reducing AI biases and protecting vulnerable groups. Normative processes from transformative and ambitious perspectives are required to achieve this, guarantee respect for fundamental rights, and provide "situated" proposals by incorporating feminist and intersectional approaches. These approaches can contribute to the use of AI for responding to the needs of women, LGBTQ+ groups, and ethnic and racial minorities.

In Chap. 6, **Fosch-Villaronga and Poulsen** explore what diversity and inclusion mean in the context of AI. Discrimination and bias in AI derive from limited datasets that do not fully represent society as a whole or from the AI scientific community's western-male configuration bias. This chapter reviews the literature on diversity and inclusion in AI to unearth the underpinnings of the topic and identify key concepts, and provide concrete examples of usually overlooked communities in the development of AI, such as women, the LGBTQ+ community, senior citizens, and disabled persons. Gendering algorithms, more diverse design teams, and more inclusive and explicit guiding policies are proposed. By integrating diversity and inclusion considerations, AI systems can be more attuned to all-inclusive societal needs, respect fundamental rights, and represent contemporary values in modern societies.

In Chap. 7, **Alexiadou** investigates AI in employment, particularly how awareness can empower persons with disabilities in accessing a labour market. Realizing the full potential of AI technologies within employment settings is challenging from a disability rights perspective. Essentially, AI technologies framed as a matter of equity and in consistency with human rights principles have the potential to unlock unlawful discriminatory barriers that persons with disabilities systematically experience in accessing the labour market. Incorporating a disability rights approach to AI in employment will make the experiences and concerns of persons with disabilities an integral component of the design, development, training, deployment, and assessment of AI. This can improve workplace accessibility, diversity, and inclusivity.

In Chap. 8, **Chiappini** looks into humanitarian law to investigate accountability issues in developing and deploying Lethal Autonomous Weapon Systems ("LAWS"). These systems may cause grave breaches of international humanitarian law, mainly because their target selections are highly unpredictable. Under current international criminal law, criminal responsibility can only be attributed when there is at least intent and knowledge of a crime. The mere likelihood of a breach taking place is insufficient to hold operators or programmers responsible for a war crime committed by LAWS. Commander responsibility appears to be the most suitable mode of liability, provided that these weapons are deployed under a specialized command structure. The command structure should include a team with technical expertise to test and monitor the weapon systems' functioning constantly.

In Chap. 9, **Longo** analyzes how the democratic arena is changing and deteriorating due to the impact of the power of social media platforms. Personalized forms of information and digital affordances can produce online information cocoons (or filter bubbles), limiting the range of political ideas people encounter. As such, filter bubbles lack transparency and can harm media pluralism. This poses threats to democracy and liberty, which are discussed.

In Chap. 10, **Laupman, Schippers and Gagliardi** examine the role of AI in immigration law. AI is increasingly used in migratory procedures, for instance, to evaluate visa applications, determine the stay and deportation of people, and even to analyze the probability that an asylum seeker can be recognized as a refugee. However, the AI systems used can sometimes lead to biased decisions due to compromised data or because data were collected or registered by biased or prejudiced individuals. As a consequence, decisions in migratory procedures can directly interfere with the lives of individuals. The risks related to bias are exacerbated in the case of marginalized people (migrants in general), especially in particularly vulnerable people (refugees and asylum seekers).

In Chap. 11, **Custers** investigates the increasing role of AI in criminal law. Both criminals and law enforcement are increasingly making use of the opportunities that AI may offer. From a substantive criminal law perspective, AI can contribute to existing and new types of crime. AI can also play a role in assessing the effectiveness of sanctions and other justice-related programs and practices. From a procedural criminal law perspective, AI can be used as a law enforcement technology, for instance, for predictive policing or as a cyber agent technology. AI can play a role in securing, analyzing, and assessing evidence. Focus areas for further legal research, needed to understand and regulate these developments, are proposed.

In Chap. 12, **Bal** focuses on the use of AI in tax law. STIR is a data analytics tool implemented by the Polish National Revenue Administration to detect VAT fraud in nearly real-time. STIR operates as a black-box AI algorithm from the taxpayer's perspective because the fraud risk indicators are not disclosed to the general public. Despite concerns about STIR's compliance with the principle of proportionality and the right to explanation, both of which are mandated under the EU data protection regulation and human rights legislation, the objective of combating tax fraud and the safeguards provided by the Polish law could justify STIR's operation.

1.5.3 Part III: Private Law

In Chap. 13, **De Conca** discusses AI in the context of liability law. She draws attention to what happens when an AI system causes harm to an individual. Using hypothetical scenarios, she shows how contractual and extra-contractual redress mechanisms are challenged by AI's technological and commercial features. This might lead to unsatisfactory results (liability gaps) for the damaged party, mitigating or fragmenting the liability among the various AI producers, operators, and users. A guiding principle to design solutions to the liability gaps could focus legislation more on protecting damaged individuals, particularly their dignity, rights, and interests. This principle aligns with the values underlying other EU legislation (consumer protection, privacy protection). It would mitigate the power imbalance between producers and damaged parties and stimulate the development of safer and more trustworthy AI.

In Chap. 14, **De Graaf and Wuisman** turn to the contractual liability of a company using an AI system to perform its contractual obligations. From Dutch and EU law perspectives, three defenses against contractual liability are discussed, which a company can put forward in case of a breach. These three defenses are (1) the AI system was state-of-the-art when deployed, (2) the user had no control over the AI system, and (3) an AI system is not a tangible object, and its use in the performance of contractual obligations can thus not give rise to strict liability under Dutch liability.

In Chap. 15, **Prifti, Stamhuis and Heijne** examine the liability of operators of AI systems in healthcare. This idea stems from a legislative proposal of the European Parliament. A legal analysis of this proposed legislation shows that the proposal leads to considerable inconsistencies and disruptions of the legal liability regime in the EU. This is because it does not address the product/service dichotomy present in EU liability law and the doctrinal inconsistency in the level of control needed for operators of AI systems to fall under strict liability. Moreover, economic considerations show that, while a new actor is required for the liability framework due to the shift in context factors, affording strict liability rules to this new actor would lead to either bypassing attempts or a chilling effect. The chapter offers directions for further research.

In Chap. 16, **Bertolini and Arian** investigate patient rights in the context of AI in healthcare. After classifying AI-based applications in the care of frail individuals pursuant to the function they serve, they distinguish the constitutional right of the elderly to care from the right to cure. Based on this presented, different types of assistance offered by social robots for elderly care are investigated. They argue that the use of companion robots does not meet the criteria in national and international legal standards for the right to care. Considering that the overall well-being of older adults to socialization, autonomy, and dignity is at the heart of caring, some applications may be deemed to violate the right of the elderly to meaningful care and dignity. Hence, they argue, a deontological approach in which human dignity is an external and objective criterion that limits freedom of self-determination and prevents people from being manipulated (in their emotions), instrumentalized, or isolated is needed.

In Chap. 17, **Smits and Borghuis** investigate intellectual property law in the context of AI that generates music. The use of generative AI in creative domains, such as music, could lead to an abundance of individually customized content, where works are generated for a particular user in a specific situation and presented once, perhaps never to be repeated. These developments challenge core concepts of intellectual property rights, like "authorship" and "work." Under current copyright law, autonomous AI systems cannot be considered authors, and the content they generate cannot be considered a work. Although different ideas are being developed to extend intellectual property rights to cover AI-generated works, they currently fall in the public domain. At the same time, generative AI systems, even those with a high degree of autonomy, can be considered instruments and, as such, protected under existing IP law.

In Chap. 18, **Drukarch and Fosch-Villaronga** explore AI in corporate law, particularly the role and legal implications of autonomy in AI-driven boardrooms. AI-driven boardrooms bring about legal challenges within the field of corporate law, mainly due to the expanding autonomy and capabilities AI has to support corporate decisions. Recurrent legal questions revolve around the attribution of legal personhood to autonomous systems and who is responsible if something goes wrong due to AI-based decisions. By introducing autonomy levels for AI in the boardroom, potential legal and regulatory challenges can be identified and discussed from a corporate law frame of reference. The authors conclude that the more autonomous and powerful AI systems become, the more decision-making processes shift from human-based to AI-powered, which have ulterior consequences for liability allocation.

In Chap. 19, **Van Duijvenvoorde** explores AI in competition law. The interactions between algorithms, the vast amount of available data, and the online platforms challenge competition law. These interactions lead to a discussion on the effectiveness of competition law, a revival of the concept of fairness, and the introduction of harmonization regulation. Qualifying a fair market under competition law requires weighing the pro-competitive and anti-competitive effects on markets. Fairness principles are market-oriented and have their limitations due to choices made in the system in competition law. New harmonization regulation aims to regulate online platforms, algorithms, and data via a competition-based approach. This has less flexibility in assessing the pro-competitive aspects regarding innovation than competition law and could entail risks for the development of digital markets and potentially for fairness in the long term.

In Chap. 20, **Owens** investigates personalized algorithmic pricing and the application of Article 102(c) TFEU to this phenomenon. She argues that competition law contains the necessary flexibilities to resolve this new form of price discrimination. However, further clarification is needed, as the lack of tangible criteria for determining equivalent transactions makes it difficult for competition authorities to meet the increased burden of proof to sanction instances of personalized pricing. The ambiguous welfare effects of personalized algorithmic pricing require the case-by-case enforcement offered by competition law. However, concerns may arise concerning data protection and consumer protection law. Cooperation with other legislative areas is necessary to form cohesive artificial intelligence policies that ensure consumer protection from algorithmically personalized prices.

1.5.4 Part IV: Legal Practice

In Chap. 21, **Weinstein** examines the use of AI in legal teams. He investigates lawyers' perceptions on the use of AI in their legal work through a meta-synthesis of published large-scale surveys of the legal profession completed in 2019 and 2020 in the UK, US, and EU. This reveals a dissonance between hype and reality: while some lawyers see that AI and machine-learning-driven legal tech innovation can transform aspects of legal practice, others have little awareness of its existence. There appears to be a first-mover advantage for some legal practitioners to incorporate innovative legal tech tools into their business models. However, few metrics can help legal teams evaluate whether such legal tech tools provide a sustainable competitive advantage to their legal work. Further research in semi-structured interviews is necessary to give additional nuance and depth to the perceptions reflected in the large-scale surveys.

In Chap. 22, **Meuwese and Drahmann** explore AI in lawmaking. They investigate a broad range of AI applications in lawmaking processes and simultaneously draw lessons from the Dutch experience with 'digitization of lawmaking' in the case 'Digital System Environment and Planning Act.' Exploring three dimensions of such applications (i.e., technique, process, and monitoring) makes a case for incremental development of IT systems parallel to new legislation. They suggest that the most promising use of AI in lawmaking concerns applications that do not use personal data, such as legal textual data or geodata connected to regulations instead.

In Chap. 23, **Zarra** investigates AI in legal scholarship. She explores the current legal debate on AI employing unsupervised machine learning on articles published in legal journals from 1982 to 2020. The results show three critical functions of AI in legal research. First, owing to substantial advancements in the computational power of machines, AI has become instrumental in digital forensics, evidence discovery, and cryptography. Second, legal informatics has established itself as a leading sub-field over the years. Third, owing to recent scandals (e.g., Cambridge Analytica) involving the breach of personal data by powerful online players and the concomitant urge to regulate automated decision-making with new laws (e.g., the EU GDPR), data protection features as one of the key topics in the legal scholarly community. Other highly debated topics are the regulation of AI applications, online platforms, social media, ethics, and robots' legal personhood. These results provide an exploratory understanding of the main trends in legal research, depicting the field's evolution over time while offering some preliminary guidance for researchers interested in specific sub-fields.

1.5.5 Part V: The Future of AI

In Chap. 24, **Verheij** considers AI as law. The progress of AI is so inspiring that legal professionals also experience its benefits and have high expectations of the capabilities AI offers in this domain. At the same time, the powers of AI have been rising so strongly that it is no longer evident that AI applications (whether in the law or elsewhere) help promote a good society; in fact, they are sometimes harmful. Safeguards are needed for AI to be trustworthy, social, responsible, humane, and ethical. A starting point for establishing proper safeguards for AI is to consider the problems and solutions studied in AI & Law, which are considered in this book chapter. The chapter explains that already for decades, AI & Law has worked on the design of social, explainable, responsible AI aligned with human values, addressed the hardest problems across the breadth of AI (in reasoning, knowledge, learning, and language), and inspired new solutions (argumentation, schemes, and norms, rules and cases, interpretation). Now, more than ever, this scholarship needs to be considered to develop responsible AI.

In Chap. 25, **Biber and Capasso** focus on human enhancement and the philosophical and legal debate on the right to mental integrity. Although the right to mental integrity has been recognized in international and European human rights law, its meaning and scope have remained unclear. To fill this gap, they focus on two specific AI-cognitive human enhancement technologies (brain-computer interfaces and intelligent personal assistant) and engage with the issue of an adequate form of cognitive integration with these technologies. Due to their unprecedented capabilities, AI-cognitive human enhancement technologies may not be entirely or sufficiently integrated with human cognitive processes and therefore not serve the mental integrity of individuals. Hence, it is necessary to introduce absolute protection to mental integrity in conjunction with mental privacy to protect the individual from any intrusion of mental states.

In Chap. 26, **Mahler** discusses Artificial General Intelligence (AGI). He examines to what extent ongoing EU policymaking on AI is relevant for AGI. AGI is typically contrasted with narrow AI, which excels only within a specific given context. Although many researchers are working on AGI, there is uncertainty about the feasibility of developing it. If achieved, AGI could have cognitive capabilities similar to or beyond humans' and may be able to perform a broad range of tasks. There are concerns that such AGI could undergo recursive circles of self-improvement, potentially leading to superintelligence, which could be a significant power factor in society. However, dystopian superintelligence scenarios are highly controversial and uncertain. Moreover, it is doubtful whether the approaches for AGI regulation discussed in the literature would be effective or even feasible.

In Chap. 27, **Liu and Sobocki** examine the future of AI law and policy through five frames (influence, immersion, intensity, integration, and interaction. They argue that we currently have an overly narrow model of AI which unnecessarily constrains the palette of law and policy responses to AI. They suggest a more integrated and open-minded approach towards AI, which focuses on different types of human relationships with AI, drawing attention to the legal and policy implications of engaging in AI-influenced worlds and currently underexplored AI problems in the literature. The frames are discussed from the perspective of harm to reveal the challenges of adopting them and the biases present in extant law and policy, which can be overly narrow and too path dependent. New types of harm may dilute or elude legal protection.

References

Aletras N, Tsarapatsanis D, Preoțiuc-Pietro D, Lampos V (2016) Predicting judicial decisions of the European Court of Human Rights: A natural language processing perspective. PeerJ Computer Science, 2, e93.

Amodei D, Olah C, Steinhardt J, Christiano P, Schulman J, Mané D (2016) Concrete problems in AI safety. https://arxiv.org/abs/1606.06565.

Arafat S, Aljohani N, Abbasi R, Hussain A, Lytras M (2019) Connections between e-learning, web science, cognitive computation and social sensing, and their relevance to learning analytics: A preliminary study. Computers in Human Behavior, Vol. 92, pp. 478–486, https://doi.org/10.1016/j.chb.2018.02.026.

Asaro P (2012) On banning autonomous weapon systems: human rights, automation, and the dehumanization of lethal decision-making. International review of the Red Cross, 94(886), 687–709.

Ashley K D (2017) Artificial intelligence and legal analytics: new tools for law practice in the digital age. Cambridge University Press.

Barfield W, Pagallo U (2020) Advanced Introduction to law and artificial intelligence. Edward Elgar, Cheltenham, UK.

BBC (2018) Portrait by AI program sells for $432,000. BBC News, 25 October 2018. https://www.bbc.com/news/technology-45980863.

Bryson J J (2010) Robots should be slaves. Close Engagements with Artificial Companions: Key social, psychological, ethical and design issues. Artificial Models of Natural Intelligence, 8, 63–74.

Calders T, Custers BHM (2013) What is data mining and how does it work? In: Custers BHM, Calders T, Schermer B, Zarsky T (eds) Discrimination and Privacy in the Information Society, no. 3. Springer, Heidelberg.

Calo R, Froomkin AM, Kerr I (eds) (2016) Robot law. Edward Elgar Publishing.

Coccoli M, Maresca P, Stanganelli L (2017) The role of big data and cognitive computing in the learning process. Journal of Visual Languages & Computing, 38, 97–103.

Custers BHM (2005) The Risks of Epidemiological Data Mining. In: Tavani H (ed) Ethics, Computing and Genomics: Moral Controversies in Computational Genomics. Jones and Bartlett Publishers, Inc., Boston.

Custers BHM (2016) Drones. Here, There and Everywhere: Introduction and Overview. In: Custers BHM (ed) The Future of Drone Use: Opportunities and Threats from Ethical and Legal Perspectives. T.M.C. Asser Press, The Hague.

Custers BHM (2018) Methods of data research for law. In: Mak V, Tjong Tjin Tai E, Berlee A (eds) Research Handbook in Data Science and Law. Edward Elgar, Cheltenham, pp. 355–377.

Custers BHM, Leeuw F (2017) Legal big data. Nederlands Juristenblad, afl. 34, pp. 2449–2456.

Custers BHM, Oerlemans J, Vergouw S (2015) Het gebruik van drones, Een verkennend onderzoek naar onbemande luchtvaartuigen. Boom Lemma, The Hague.

Darling K (2017) 'Who's Johnny?' Anthropomorphic framing in human-robot interaction, integration, and policy. Anthropomorphic Framing in Human-Robot Interaction, Integration, and Policy. In: Lin P, Abney K, Jenkins R (eds) (2017) Robot ethics 2.0: From autonomous cars to artificial intelligence. Oxford University Press.

de Bruyne J, Vanleenhove C (2021) Artificial Intelligence and the Law: A Belgian Perspective. Intersentia, Cambridge, UK.

de Cock Buning M (2018) Artificial Intelligence and the creative industry: New challenges for the EU paradigm for art and technology by autonomous creation. In: Barfield W, Pagallo U (eds) (2018) *Research handbook on the law of artificial intelligence*. Edward Elgar Publishing.

Drukarch H, Calleja C, Fosch-Villaronga E (2021) An iterative regulatory process for robot governance. Data for Policy 2021 Conference, 14–16 September 2021, available at https://zenodo.org/record/5211103#.YRtZKdMzY_U.

Eckholm E (2015) Harvard Law Library Readies Trove of Decisions for Digital Age. New York Times, 28 October 2015.

EU Parliament (2016) Civil Law Rules on Robotics, available at https://www.europarl.europa.eu/doceo/document/JURI-PR-582443_EN.pdf.

Felzmann H, Fosch-Villaronga E, Lutz C, Tamò-Larrieux A (2019) Transparency you can trust: Transparency requirements for artificial intelligence between legal norms and contextual concerns. Big Data & Society, 6(1), 2053951719860542.

Ferreira FG, Gandomi AH, Cardoso RT (2021) Artificial intelligence applied to stock market trading: A review. IEEE Access, 9, 30898–30917. https://ieeexplore.ieee.org/stamp/stamp.jsp?tp=&arnumber=9350582

Fosch-Villaronga E (2019) Robots, healthcare, and the law: Regulating automation in personal care. Routledge.

Fosch-Villaronga E, Drukarch H (2021) On Healthcare Robots: Concepts, definitions, and considerations for healthcare robot governance. available at https://arxiv.org/abs/2106.03468.

Fosch-Villaronga E, Khanna P, Drukarch H, Custers BHM (2021) A human in the loop in surgery automation. Nature Machine Intelligence, 3, pp. 368–369. https://doi.org/10.1038/s42256-021-00349-4.

Fosch-Villaronga E, Heldeweg M (2018) "Regulation, I presume?" said the robot–Towards an iterative regulatory process for robot governance. Computer law & security review, 34(6), 1258–1277.

Fosch-Villaronga E, Millard C (2019) Cloud robotics law and regulation: Challenges in the governance of complex and dynamic cyber–physical ecosystems. Robotics and Autonomous Systems, 119, 77–91.

Foss-Solbrekk K (2021) Three routes to protecting AI systems and their algorithms under IP law: The good, the bad and the ugly. Journal of Intellectual Property Law & Practice, 16(3), 247–258.

Fox J, North J, Dean J (2019) AI in the boardroom: Could robots soon be running companies? Governance Directions, 71(10), 559–564.

Gellers J C (2020) Rights for Robots: Artificial Intelligence. Animal and Environmental Law. Routledge.

Gibney E (2016) Google AI algorithm masters ancient game of Go. Nature News, 529(7587), 445.

Greshko M (2018) Meet Sophia, the Robot That Looks Almost Human. National Geographic, 18 May 2018, retrieved from https://www.nationalgeographic.com/photography/article/sophia-robot-artificial-intelligence-science. See also https://www.hansonrobotics.com/sophia/.

Guihot M, Bennett Moses L (2020) Artificial intelligence, robots and the law. LexisNexis Butterworths.

Harper J (2021) Federal AI Spending to Top $6 Billion. National Defense Magazine, 10 February 2021, https://www.nationaldefensemagazine.org/articles/2021/2/10/federal-ai-spending-to-top-$6-billion.

Herbert F (1963) Dune. Chilton Books, New York.

Higgins C (2017) A brief history of Deep Blue, IBM's chess computer. Mental Floss, 29 July, https://www.mentalfloss.com/article/503178/brief-history-deep-blue-ibms-chess-computer.

High-Level Expert Group (HLEG) on Artificial Intelligence (AI) (2019) A definition of Artificial Intelligence: main capabilities and scientific disciplines. European Commission. Available at https://digital-strategy.ec.europa.eu/en/library/definition-artificial-intelligence-main-capabilities-and-scientific-disciplines.

IBM (2021) AI done right. Retrieved from https://www.ibm.com/downloads/cas/YE6N4XRV.

Jobin A, Ienca M, Vayena E (2019) The global landscape of AI ethics guidelines. Nature Machine Intelligence, 1(9), pp. 389–399.

Johnson G (1997) Undiscovered Bach? No, a Computer Wrote It. New York Times, 11 November 1997. https://www.nytimes.com/1997/11/11/science/undiscovered-bach-no-a-computer-wrote-it.html.

Katz DM, Bommarito II MJ, Blackman J (2014) Predicting the behavior of the Supreme Court of the United States: A general approach. arXiv preprint arXiv:1407.6333.

Katz DM, Dolin R, Bommarito MJ (2021) Legal Informatics. Cambridge University Press, Cambridge, UK.

Kauffman ME, Soares MN (2020) AI in legal services: new trends in AI-enabled legal services. Service Oriented Computing and Applications, 14, 223–226.

Legg M, Bell F (2020) Artificial Intelligence and the Legal Profession. Hart Publishing.

Liability of defective products regime at https://ec.europa.eu/growth/single-market/goods/free-mov ement-sectors/liability-defective-products_en.

Lodder A, Thiessen E (2003) The role of artificial intelligence in online dispute resolution. In: Workshop on Online Dispute Resolution at the International Conference on Artificial Intelligence and Law. Edinburgh, UK.

Metz C (2016) Google's AI wins first game in historic match with Go champion. Wired, 3 September, https://www.wired.com/2016/03/googles-ai-wins-first-game-historic-match-go-champion/.

Nakad-Weststrate HWR, van den Herik HJ, Jongbloed AWT, Salem ABM (2015) The Rise of the Robotic Judge in Modern Court Proceedings. International Journal of Digital Society, 6(4), 1102–1112.

Passchier R (2021) Artificiële Intelligentie en de rechtsstaat. Boom Juridisch, The Hague.

Proposal for a Regulation of the European Parliament and of the Council on machinery products, https://ec.europa.eu/docsroom/documents/45508.

Proposal for a Regulation of the European Parliament and of the Council laying down harmonised rules on Artificial Intelligence (Artificial Intelligence Act), https://eur-lex.europa.eu/legal-con tent/EN/TXT/?uri=CELEX%3A52021PC0206.

Regulation (EU) 2016/679 of the European Parliament and of the Council of 27 April 2016 on the protection of natural persons with regard to the processing of personal data and on the free movement of such data, and repealing Directive 95/46/EC (General Data Protection Regulation) (text with EEA relevance).

Revision of the General Product Safety Directive, https://ec.europa.eu/info/business-economy-euro/ product-safety-and-requirements/product-safety/consumer-product-safety_en.

Rosemain M, Rose M (2018) France to spend $1.8 billion on AI to compete with US, China. 29 March 2018, Reuters, https://www.reuters.com/article/us-france-tech/france-to-spend-1-8-bil lion-on-ai-to-compete-with-u-s-china-idUKKBN1H51XP.

Santoni de Sio F, Van den Hoven J (2018) Meaningful human control over autonomous systems: A philosophical account. Frontiers in Robotics and AI, 5, 15.

Sathya R, Pavithra M, Girubaa G (2017) Artificial intelligence for speech recognition. International Journal of Computer Science & Engineering Technology (IJCSET); ISSN, 2229–3345.

Science and Technology Options Assessment Panel (STOA) (2016) Ethical Aspects of Cyber-Physical Systems. Scientific Foresight study. Retrieved from https://www.europarl.europa.eu/ RegData/etudes/STUD/2016/563501/EPRS_STU(2016)563501_EN.pdf.

Secherla S (2018) Understanding Optimization Algorithms in Machine Learning. Medium, https:// towardsdatascience.com/understanding-optimization-algorithms-in-machine-learning-edfdb4 df766b.

Shademan A, Decker RS, Opfermann JD, Leonard S, Krieger A, Kim PC (2016) Supervised autonomous robotic soft tissue surgery. Science translational medicine, 8(337), 337ra64–337ra64.

Susskind RE (2013) Tomorrow's Lawyers: An Introduction to Your Future. Oxford University Press, Oxford.

Susskind RE (2019) Online courts and the future of justice. Oxford University Press.

Szczudlik K (2019) AI must not predict how judges in France will rule. newtech.law, 14 June 2019, https://newtech.law/en/ai-must-not-predict-how-judges-in-france-will-rule/.

Teeuw WB, Vedder AH, Custers BHM, Dorbeck-Jung BR, Faber ECC, Iacob SM, Koops B-J, Leenes RE, de Poot HJG, Rip A, Vudisa JN (2008) Security Applications for Converging Technologies: Impact on the constitutional state and the legal order. O&B 269. WODC, The Hague.

Thompson C (2010) Smarter than you think: What is IBM's Watson? New York Times, 16 June 2010.

Totschnig W (2020) Fully Autonomous AI. Sci Eng Ethics, 26, pp. 2473–2485. https://doi.org/10.1007/s11948-020-00243-z.

Ulenaers J (2020) The Impact of Artificial Intelligence on the Right to a Fair Trial: Towards a Robot Judge? Asian Journal of Law and Economics, 11(2).

Viscelli S (2018) Driverless? Autonomous trucks and the future of the American trucker. The National Academies of Science, Engineering, Medicine. Retrieved from https://trid.trb.org/view/1540733.

Yang GZ, Cambias J, Cleary K, Daimler E, Drake J, Dupont PE, Taylor RH (2017) Medical robotics—Regulatory, ethical, and legal considerations for increasing levels of autonomy. Science Robotics, 2(4), 8638.

Zuboff S (2019) The age of surveillance capitalism: The fight for a human future at the new frontier of power. Profile Books.

Bart Custers PhD MSc LLM is (full) professor of Law and Data Science and director of *eLaw, Center for Law and Digital Technologies* at Leiden University, the Netherlands. He has a background in both law and physics and is an expert in the area of law and digital technologies, including topics like profiling, big data, privacy, discrimination, cybercrime, technology in policing and artificial intelligence. As a researcher and project manager, he acquired and executed research for the European Commission, NWO (the National Research Council in the Netherlands), the Dutch national government, local government agencies, large corporations and SMEs. Until 2016 he was the head of the research department on Crime, Law enforcement and Sanctions of the scientific research center (WODC) of the Ministry of Security and Justice in the Netherlands. Before that, he worked for the national government as a senior policy advisor for consecutive Ministers of Justice (2009–2013) and for a large consultancy firm as a senior management consultant on information strategies (2005–2009). On behalf of the Faculty of Law, he is the coordinator of the SAILS project. This project, funded by the Executive Board of Leiden University, deals with the societal and legal implications of Artificial Intelligence. Bart Custers published three books on profiling, privacy, discrimination and big data, two books on the use of drones and one book on the use of bitcoins for money laundering cybercrime profits. On a regular basis he gives lectures on profiling, privacy and big data and related topics. He has presented his work at international conferences in the United States, Canada, China, Japan, Korea, Malaysia, Thailand, the Middle East and throughout Europe. He has published his work, over a hundred publications, in scientific and professional journals and in newspapers.

Eduard Fosch-Villaronga is an Assistant Professor at the *eLaw Center for Law and Digital Technologies* at Leiden University (The Netherlands), where he investigates legal and regulatory aspects of robot and AI technologies, with a special focus on healthcare, diversity, governance, and transparency. Currently, he is the PI of PROPELLING, an FSTP from the H2020 Eurobench project, a project using robot testing zones to support evidence-based robot policies. Previously, Eduard served the European Commission in the Sub-Group on Artificial Intelligence (AI), connected products and other new challenges in product safety to the Consumer Safety Network (CSN) and was the PI of LIAISON, an FSTP from the H2020 COVR project that aimed to link robot development and policymaking to reduce the complexity in robot legal compliance. In 2019, Eduard was awarded a Marie Skłodowska-Curie Postdoctoral Fellowship and published the book *Robots, Healthcare, and the Law* (Routledge). Eduard holds an Erasmus Mundus Joint Doctorate in Law, Science, & Technology, coordinated by the University of Bologna (Italy, 2017), an LL.M. from University of Toulouse (France, 2012), an M.A. from the Autonomous University of Madrid (Spain), and an LL.B. from the Autonomous University of Barcelona (Catalonia, Spain, 2011). Eduard is also a qualified lawyer in Spain.

Chapter 2
Artificial Intelligence Versus Biological Intelligence: A Historical Overview

Roy de Kleijn

Contents

Abstract The discipline of artificial intelligence originally aimed to replicate human-level intelligence in a machine. It could be argued that the best way to replicate the behavior of a system is to emulate the mechanisms producing this behavior. But whether we should try to replicate the human brain or the cognitive faculties to accomplish this is unclear. Early symbol-based AI systems paid little regard to neuroscience and were rather successful. However, since the 1980s, artificial neural networks have become a powerful AI technique that show remarkable resemblance to what we know about the human brain. In this chapter, we highlight some of the similarities and differences between artificial and human intelligence, the history of their interconnection, what they both excel at, and what the future may hold for artificial general intelligence.

Keywords artificial intelligence · symbolic AI · connectionism · artificial neural networks

2.1 Introduction

Humans are still considered to be smarter than machines, despite impressive progress in the field of artificial intelligence, with computers outperforming humans on several benchmark tasks. The big question that unites the fields of artificial intelligence and

R. de Kleijn (✉)
Cognitive Psychology Unit, Leiden University, Leiden, The Netherlands
e-mail: kleijnrde@fsw.leidenuniv.nl

© T.M.C. ASSER PRESS and the authors 2022
B. Custers and E. Fosch-Villaronga (eds.), *Law and Artificial Intelligence*,
Information Technology and Law Series 35,
https://doi.org/10.1007/978-94-6265-523-2_2

cognitive science remains unsolved: what makes humans so intelligent? It is surely not unreasonable to think that whatever it is that makes humans intelligent could be implemented in a computer system to make it as intelligent as a human. Unfortunately, we do not have a complete understanding yet of the origins of human intelligence, but we do have some ideas based on both empirical evidence as well as some educated guesses.

First of all, we know that our cognitive faculties are physically implemented in the brain. This is a cantaloupe-sized mass of ~1300 grams consisting of 10^{11} nerve cells called neurons, which are interconnected by around 10^{15} synapses. Neurons can transmit signals to other neurons, which can then send that signal to other neurons, et cetera, generating interneuronal communication. Information can then propagate through this network of interconnected neurons.[1] Simplified, a neuron receives a signal from other neurons, integrates these signals, and sends a signal when the sum of its received signals reaches a certain threshold. Depending on the strength of the synapse, such a signal can excite or inhibit other neurons. Computationally, what neurons do can be seen as a floating-point operation,[2] of which the human brain can carry out 10^{18} per second.[3] The highest performing modern (as of 2021) personal computers can perform around 10^{14} floating-point operations per second, which makes them four magnitudes of order slower than a human brain. As such, whatever the brain *computationally* does in one minute could be performed on such a computer in a week. But, impressive as this may be, is it unlikely that it is simply the brain's speed of floating-point operations that enable it to produce intelligence. The fact that we do not actually know *how* to simulate a minute's worth of full human cognition, even given all the computing power in the world, suggests that we may need to understand more than mere floating-point operations in order to understand human intelligence.

But, even if we start with this, floating-point operations do not exist in a vacuum, they require *operands*. It is still unclear what the operands of the computations that produce the human mind are. On a neural level they may be the activation values of neurons, but the relationship between neural activity and the mind is everything but clear. To create intelligent systems, some argue we should aim to recreate the brain, others argue we should recreate the mind, and others believe we can do a better job than either. Several different schools of thought have dominated the field of artificial intelligence and cognitive science over the past century, but for the purpose of this chapter will divide them into symbolic and subsymbolic approaches of intelligence.

We will first discuss how the fields of artificial intelligence and cognitive science both emerged as new disciplines from the same fundamental questions about the

---

[1] Although it should be noted that it is unknown how anything but the most trivial information (e.g. stimulus intensity) is represented by neurons.

[2] Simplified, a floating-point operation (FLOP) is an arithmetic operation (such as addition or multiplication) involving two real numbers. This is arguably what neurons and synapses do as well: multiplying incoming activation with the strength of the synapse.

[3] Every synapse carrying out floating-point operations at 1000 Hz; McClelland 2009; Zador 2019.

nature of cognition. We will then explain the first steps taken using symbolic representations of intelligence, an assumption shared between the two disciplines at least in the 1960s and 1970s. Lastly, we will discuss artificial neural networks, an approach based on the neural foundations of the brain.

2.2   The Beginnings of Artificial Intelligence and Cognitive Science

The origins of modern artificial intelligence cannot be seen separate from the origins of the field of cognitive science, which emerged from the ashes of the then-dominant psychological school of behaviorism.[4] In what is now known as the *cognitive revolution*, emphasis shifted from studying behavior to studying the computations producing it.[5] Moving beyond stimulus-response associations, concepts like reasoning and representations became the topic of study for the new fields of cognitive science and cognitive psychology. This new generation of researchers used models of mental processes to study the mind and behavior. Around the same time, a group of researchers interested in the idea of implementing intelligence in machines organized what is now known as the birthplace of the field of artificial intelligence: the Dartmouth Conference of 1956.[6] Although many topics were discussed in this two-month(!) meeting, one of the most direct outcomes of the Dartmouth Conference was the rise of symbolic artificial intelligence.

2.3   Symbolic AI and Physical Symbol Systems

Allen Newell and Herbert Simon, two cognitive scientists who participated in the Dartmouth Conference, suggested that human intelligence is essentially symbol manipulation. And if humans are intelligent by virtue of their symbolic representation and manipulation, it could perhaps be possible to endow computer systems with this same capability. This position is now known as the *physical symbol system hypothesis* and was strengthened by the success of their computer programs *Logic*

---

[4] At least, then-dominant in the United States. Behaviorism posits that psychology should limit itself to observing and predicting *behavior*, in contrast to *convictions* and *beliefs*, as only behavior could be a source of objective evidence. This behavior was regarded as the learned product of the interactions between an organism and its environment.

[5] It could be argued that Chomsky's 1959 *Review of B. F. Skinner's Verbal Behavior* kickstarted the cognitive revolution. In this critique, Chomsky argued against the concept of language as purely learned behavior. For example, children are able to understand sentences they have never been exposed to before.

[6] Attendees included Marvin Minsky, Claude Shannon, Allen Newell, Herbert Simon, W. Ross Ashby, and Ray Solomonoff, researchers who would become known as founders of the field.

Theorist[7] and *General Problem Solver*.[8] Using manipulation of high-level symbols, the first could reason, and generate proofs for mathematical theorems, even improving on some proofs found by humans, while the second was a more general program to solve logical problems.

Newell and Simon's General Problem Solver would use means-end analysis to solve problems similar to how humans were thought to solve them, a paradigm that has been referred to as *reasoning as search*. How exactly humans solve unfamiliar problems was not well known, but Newell and Simon hypothesized that means-end analysis would be involved. Accordingly, they implemented this assumed human problem-solving technique into a computer system. Given a well-defined problem, it would cast it in terms of an initial state, a goal state, and operators that define the transition between two states. It would then solve the problem using heuristic search, narrowing the search space to make the search tractable.[9] First, it would evaluate the difference between the current state and the goal state. Second, it would find a transformation leading to a subgoal that reduces the difference between the current state and the goal state. It would then check if the transformation can be applied to the current state, and if not, would find another transformation. By iteratively transforming the symbolic representation of the initial state, the program could then find a solution to the problem. Newell and Simon demonstrated that their program could solve the *Towers of Hanoi* and *missionaries and cannibals*[10] problems, although it could be applied to any well-defined problem. Although immensely influential in cognitive psychology, some argue that the General Problem Solver failed as a psychological theory or as an explanation of human problem solving as the idea that problem solving relies on a general mechanism does not seem to hold.[11] But even today, some concepts from the General Problem Solver are still used in some cognitive architectures that try to model human cognition, such as the Soar cognitive architecture.[12]

In the 1970s, progress was made in the field of *expert systems*. These systems attempted to implement the knowledge and decision making of human experts. In line with the physical symbol system hypothesis, knowledge would be represented symbolically in a *knowledge base* and reasoned with using an *inference engine*. A well-known example is MYCIN, an expert system developed in the early 1970s at Stanford. With a knowledge base of around 600 rules, it was designed to diagnose blood infections using a physician as an intermediate. The physician would be presented with a series of questions (e.g. "What is the form of the individual organisms visible

---

[7] Newell et al. 1957.

[8] Newell and Simon 1961.

[9] Avoiding exhaustive search that would be computationally prohibitive for anything but very small state spaces.

[10] Or any of the river-crossing puzzles such as the related *jealous husbands problem* or the identical *foxes and chickens problem*.

[11] Ohlsson 2012.

[12] Laird 2012.

in the blood?") and the system would then produce a list of possible diagnoses with certainty factors. Although the quality of MYCIN's prescribed antimicrobials was as least as good as human faculty specialists,[13] the system was never used in medical practice. Ethical and legal issues surrounding liability and reliability of such a novel technique in medical practice, most of which have not been solved as of yet and are in fact still relevant today, detracted from its usefulness.

To develop an expert system, knowledge from human experts needs to be extracted and represented in its knowledge base and inference engine, a process known as *knowledge acquisition*. In other words, it requires the transfer of symbolic knowledge from the human mind to an artificial system. In its earliest form, this would consist of finding a group of domain experts and interviewing them to try to represent their most relevant knowledge, which itself was acquired from textbooks and other experts in a system of rules and symbols.[14] Modern approaches to knowledge acquisition include automated analysis of natural language in for instance user manuals or textbooks and storing the acquired knowledge in (general-purpose) ontologies: databases that describe relevant concepts and the relationships between them, e.g. "a bird *is a type of animal*".[15] As such, the principle of transferring symbolic knowledge from humans to artificial systems has not changed, but attempts are made to automate the transfer.

Modern ontologies play a significant role in allowing robots to perform actions in real-world environments. One of the problems in creating general-purpose robots is that the tasks they should perform are often greatly underspecified.[16] For example, a cooking robot trying to follow a recipe may encounter the instruction to "add a cup of water to the pan." While this is trivial for any human to follow, it requires knowledge about where to find water, where to get a cup from, and not to add the cup itself to the pan, but merely its contents. This common-sense knowledge that is so self-evident to humans is not usually available to robots. However, attempts have been made to use online accessible ontologies such as Cyc for the structuring of common-sense knowledge in a symbolic, structured format available to other robots and computer systems.[17]

2.4 Artificial Neural Networks

However powerful symbolic AI had shown to be, by the end of the 1960s it became clear that there were some forms of human intelligence that it could not even begin to

---

[13] Yu et al. 1979.

[14] Russell and Norvig 2010.

[15] Sowa 2012.

[16] de Kleijn et al. 2014.

[17] Lenat et al. 1990.

replicate. Interestingly, these seemed to be skills that humans would perform effort-lessly, such as object recognition, walking, or having a conversation.[18] As psychol-ogist Steven Pinker noted: "The main lesson of thirty-five years of AI research is that the hard problems are easy and the easy problems are hard."[19] The tasks that AI research had concentrated on thus far were tasks that humans found particularly diffi-cult, such as logic, symbolic algebra, and playing chess, which were seen as good indicators of intelligence. It was thought that if those problems were solved, the "easy" problems like vision would be solvable as well, an optimism well-illustrated by Herbert Simon's 1960 prediction that "machines will be capable, within twenty years, of doing any work a man can do."[20] As we now know, this would prove to be more difficult than expected. In 1973, reporting to the British Science Research Council, mathematician James Lighthill criticized the progress made in the field of AI in what is now known as the Lighthill report.[21] The report specifically mentioned that many of the problems that AI systems of the time could solve were solvable only for small toy problems, turning out to be computationally intractable when scaled to real-world problems.[22] Also, it was unclear how problems such as vision, motor control, and noisy measurements such as encountered in robotics would be represented symbolically.

Some of these more difficult problems seemed to be particularly well-suited for an approach to AI other than the symbolic approach, namely *connectionism*, with *artifi-cial neural networks (ANNs)* as a prominent example architecture. In these systems, information is not represented symbolically, but subsymbolically as activation values distributed over a network of elementary units with no intrinsic meaning.[23] Similar to neurons, which receive activity in the form of electrochemical signals through their dendrites and send activity along their axons, these units receive activation from other units, and send activation as a function of their input activation. Such networks are parameterized by the weights of the connections between the units and their activation functions, comparable to synapse strength and activation thresholds in the human brain. Although research into the mathematical modeling of neurons and their computational capability dates back to the 1940s when neuroscientists Warren

---

[18] The observation that computers perform tasks that humans find difficult such as reasoning or playing chess very quickly and accurately, but have great difficulty performing tasks that humans find trivial such as walking or face recognition, is known as *Moravec's paradox*. Moravec 1990 argues that the difficulty for a computer system to solve a problem is proportional to the time evolution has had to optimize solving it in humans.

[19] Pinker 1994, p. 192.

[20] Simon 1960, p. 38.

[21] Lighthill 1973.

[22] These problems turned out to be most likely solvable only in exponential time where the required time to solve grows exponentially with input size, which is only acceptable for very small input sizes such as the toy problems AI was concerned with.

[23] Although it could be argued that localist representations of the input and output layers of some connectionist models are symbolic in nature.

McCulloch and Walter Pitts studied the implementation of logical functions in artificial neurons, it took almost half a century for artificial neural networks to take off.[24] In the 1980s, David Rumelhart and James McClelland published their now-standard collection *Parallel Distributed Processing*, in which they showed that artificial neural network models could account for a range of psychological phenomena, suggesting that the computational techniques they use are similar in nature. Such a network of artificial neurons can be used as a classifier, where it can take an input (such as an image), process it, and return an output such as a category label (is it a dog or a cat?). However, in order for it to do so, the network needs to be trained. Training a neural network to classify dogs and cats is often done using *supervised learning*, in which a large, correctly labeled dataset is presented to the network with a learning algorithm adjusting the network weights until it is able to correctly classify novel inputs.

At the start of the 2010s, deep neural networks reached or even surpassed human performance in certain image classification tasks, the start of a *deep learning* revolution.[25] Using a deep neural network and a training set of almost 40,000 images of 43 different German road signs,[26] researchers demonstrated a recognition accuracy of 99.46%, where humans scored 98.84%. At the same time, the same researchers showed 99.77% accuracy on the benchmark MNIST handwritten digit recognition dataset, which is close to human performance at 99.8%.[27] More recently, an ensemble of three deep neural networks trained to predict breast cancer from mammograms exceeded the average performance of six certified radiologists. In another study, the researchers showed that in a so-called *double-reading process*, a process used in the UK for screening mammograms using two independent interpretations, the second reader's workload can be reduced by 88% without compromising the standard of care.[28] With these artificial neural networks reaching or even surpassing human-like performance, looking at the similarities between this type of artificial intelligence and its biological counterpart becomes even more interesting.

Human brains are not just 10^{11} neurons randomly crammed together in a skull, they are structured into a specific topology with some groups of neurons more densely connected than others. As mentioned earlier, the biological inspiration for artificial neural networks arose from the concept of a network of elementary units (neurons in humans), connected through weighted links (synapses in humans). These units are arranged in layers: an input layer representing the input to the network, an output layer representing the output, and one or more hidden layers. But determining how many layers we actually *need* to solve a certain problem is an art as well as a science. From a science perspective, some fundamental limitations have become clear. It was

---

[24] This is not to say that no important discoveries were made during the period in between, as important research into the power and limitations of neural networks was done by e.g. Minsky and Papert at MIT, and Rosenblatt at Cornell.

[25] The *deep* in *deep learning* refers to the number of layers (depth) in an artificial neural network, see below for an explanation.

[26] The German Traffic Sign Recognition Benchmark (GTSRB) dataset containing more than 50,000 traffic sign images was used; Stallkamp et al. 2011.

[27] Cireşan et al. 2012.

[28] McKinney et al. 2020.

shown in 1969 that at least one hidden layer is necessary to learn some complex patterns, and sufficient to learn arbitrarily complex patterns.[29] However, the deep learning revolution that accompanied an impressive increase in the performance of artificial neural networks showed that adding more layers to a network can increase its performance. In these deep networks, higher layers represent more abstract features such as faces or letters, while lower layers represent more raw features such as edges or orientation. A similar architecture can be seen in the human visual cortex, where neurons in lower layers specifically respond to location and orientation while neurons in higher layers respond to faces or objects. In fact, the representations learned by deep networks show similarities to the representations developed in the primate visual system.[30] Such a hierarchical topology greatly increases representational power for a given number of parameters, both in biological and artificial neural networks.

When training ANNs using supervised learning (see Chap. 3), network weights are usually optimized using a technique known as *backpropagation.* The backpropagation algorithm computes the gradient of the error function[31] with respect to the network weights at the output layer, which is then propagated back to previous layers. This gradient information can then be used to adjust network weights, e.g., using gradient descent. While a powerful technique for supervised learning of network weights, as a model of brain function backpropagation was quickly criticized for being biologically implausible.[32] Biological neurons do not seem capable of transmitting information about the error gradient backwards along the axon, or any information at all for that matter. This is not to say that there are no return pathways in the brain, as there clearly are, but units or pathways that compare the output of a neuron to its required output and propagate it across layers to cause changes in synaptic strength have not been discovered.[33] Not only is the biological plausibility of backpropagation controversial, the entire supervised learning process could be argued to be implausible. Humans are simply not provided with thousands of correctly labeled training data[34] for every object or concept they encounter, something that is required for the successful training of a deep network. Instead, humans seem to learn through trial-and-error: trying different actions and learning about their outcomes.

---

[29] More specifically, it was shown that learning non-linearly separable functions such as XOR requires at least one hidden layer, and that this is enough to approximate any continuous function; Minsky and Papert 1969; Cybenko 1989.

[30] Yamins and DiCarlo 2016.

[31] The error function defines the error between the actual output of the network and the required output of the network for a set of input-output pairs. For classification problems (a popular use of ANNs) cross entropy is often used.

[32] And not only backpropagation, but the entire endeavor of connectionist modeling, see e.g. Crick 1989 for a scathing commentary.

[33] It should be noted that the biological plausibility of backpropagation is controversial, and by no means a solved question. For example, there is evidence to suggest that when an action potential travels through an axon, it can cause a retrograde signal being sent to the presynaptic neuron through the dendrites. However, this is still far from actually propagating an error signal back across several neurons. See e.g. Stuart et al. 1997; Bogacz et al. 2000.

[34] Training data in supervised learning consists of an input (e.g., a picture of a cat) and a desired output (e.g. the label "cat"), see Chap. 3.

This process, also known as *operant conditioning* or *reinforcement learning* (see Chap. 3) has been a topic of research in psychology since the early 1900s and has shown to be a successful paradigm in machine learning as well. Modern deep reinforcement learning models use deep neural networks to approximate the expected outcome of possible actions to be taken, with impressive results.

In the animal visual cortex, neurons respond to the activation of other neurons in a specific area, known as the receptive field.[35] Convolutional neural networks are inspired by architecture of the animal visual cortex. Whereas in traditional artificial neural networks the units in each layer are connected to all the units in the previous layer,[36] in convolutional neural networks the units in a layer are connected to a *subset* of units in the previous layer. This greatly reduces the number of parameters of the network, reducing overfitting,[37] allowing for deeper networks, and reducing training time. Not only are convolutional neural networks successful classifiers, they can predict large-scale activation of human brain regions and the firing patterns of neurons, suggesting similar mechanisms and computational principles between the two.[38]

While deeper networks are more powerful, they are also harder to train and can suffer from the *vanishing gradient problem*.[39] Residual neural networks (ResNets) are inspired by the architecture of pyramidal cells in the cerebral cortex. In fully connected artificial neural networks, all units in a layer are connected to all units in the next layer. As such, there are no connections between units in layer x and layer $x+2$ or beyond, only to layer $x+1$. In a residual neural network, these connections *are* allowed, effectively skipping one or more layers when propagating activation (see Fig. 2.1). It has been shown that for extremely deep networks, residual neural networks are easier to train, allow more layers, and perform better than non-residual networks given a specific network complexity.[40]

As said earlier in this section, artificial neural networks can now outperform human intelligence on certain specific tasks using techniques inspired by neurological principles. But even the types of networks that can outperform humans appear to have some idiosyncrasies that are remarkably different from human performance. So-called *adversarial examples* are inputs to a classifier that are slightly modified so that they are misclassified even though a human observer may see no difference.[41] It

---

[35] Hubel and Wiesel 1959.

[36] This is referred to as a *fully connected* network.

[37] *Overfitting* refers to the phenomenon where a network is trained to the point in which it can correctly classify the training data it has seen, without being able to generalize to novel instances. For example, it would be able to correctly classify its 10,000 training images as a cat, but fails to correctly classify a new picture of a cat.

[38] Zhou and Firestone 2019.

[39] The vanishing gradient problem occurs when the gradient of the error function becomes so small that network weights are no longer being updated. This is more likely to happen with very deep networks as the gradient decreases exponentially with the number of layers.

[40] He et al. 2016.

[41] Although it should be noted that there are adversarial examples that fool both time-limited humans and computers, see e.g., Elsayed et al. 2018; Goodfellow et al. 2015.

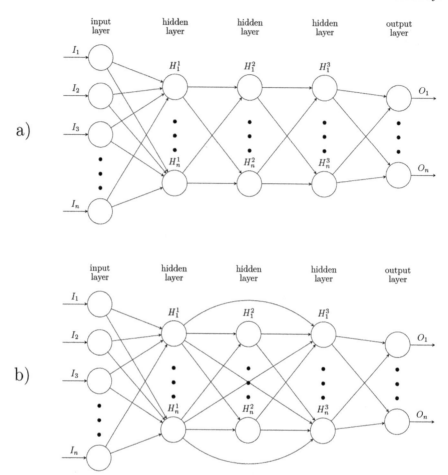

Fig. 2.1 A regular deep neural network **a** compared to a residual neural network **b**. Note that in **b** there are connections between units in layer H^1 and H^3, effectively skipping layer H^2 [*Source* The author]

has recently been shown that the modification can be as small as a single pixel,[42] and does not have to be directly applied to the input data directly, but can also be applied to a real-world object that indirectly serves as an input, such as an object that is photographed.[43] These misclassifications can be quite stunning to a human observer, for instance when a clear image of an elephant is being classified as a baseball, or a car as a milk can. Although interesting from a machine learning perspective, these findings are perhaps even more interesting from the perspective of human intelligence. Adversarial examples are often indistinguishable from their originals to humans, but

---

[42] Su et al. 2019.
[43] Kurakin et al. 2017.

are able to fool deep networks causing them to misclassify them. And not only that, deep networks assign high confidence ratings to their incorrect classification. This phenomenon casts doubt on the alleged similarity between deep neural networks and human object recognition mechanisms. However, some authors[44] have argued that these differences may not be caused by a qualitative difference between artificial and biological object recognition mechanisms and computational principles, but by the limitations of the human visual system which cannot perceive the perturbations used in adversarial examples. In other words, the existence of adversarial examples may not tell us anything about the high-level mechanisms of object recognition, but the low-level architecture of the visual system.[45] Perhaps the difference between human and computer intelligence in object recognition can be best illustrated with an analogy.[46] Human cognition allows us to distinguish between objects *appearing to be like* something and objects *being* something, for instance when distinguishing between a cloud that looks like a dog and an actual dog. Deep networks have no such luxury, and instead are forced to pick the label that is most likely.

2.5 Conclusion

The fields of artificial intelligence and the study of human intelligence have been intertwined, and devoting only one book chapter can hardly be enough. We limited ourselves here to two central forms of knowledge representation, symbolic and subsymbolic. The first approach represents knowledge symbolically, and reasons using these symbols. Problem solving can be seen as symbol manipulation, according to this view. And knowing what we know about human cognition, it seems that at least part of our reasoning is symbolic in nature, not to speak of human symbolic communication.[47] On the other hand, it is also clear that many of the tasks we perform, such as vision and walking do not lend themselves well to symbolic representation. Artificial neural networks have found inspiration in the biological brain in many forms, not only the function of individual neurons, but also topological constraints such as deep, convolutional, and residual neural networks.

The idea of artificial neural networks is appealing. We know that the human brain produces some very intelligent behavior, so trying to emulate its mechanisms seems like an appropriate course of action. But opinions differ on whether brain-inspired artificial intelligence holds the key to creating *truly* intelligent artificial systems. It could be that although neuroscience has inspired ANN research, we have already

---

[44] For example Zhou and Firestone 2019.

[45] Although any evidence that the low-level architecture of the visual system is different for humans and computers should not come as a surprise; see Zhou and Firestone 2019.

[46] Analogy taken from Zhou and Firestone 2019.

[47] We have purposefully refrained from discussing human language (well, with the exception of one Chomsky reference) in this book chapter due to space constraints. Discussing it in the context of artificial intelligence would open up a can of worms that no single book, let alone a chapter, could do justice to.

reached the limits of what can be learned from brain research.[48] Although there are many commonalities between human intelligence and its artificial implementations, the one dimension on which they differ greatly is domain-specificity. While expert systems and deep networks can show better-than-human performance on several tasks, these remain very specific and are limited to the tasks these systems were designed or trained for. Although progress has been made in transfer learning and other areas, generalizability remains a puzzle and these developments have not yet been scaled to true out-of-domain performance. A computer system implementing artificial *general* intelligence[49] remains elusive, and although it has been the topic of research for decades, no big leaps in progress have been reported. The question remains whether human-level artificial intelligence—if ever achieved—will be the result of incremental progress on deep supervised, unsupervised and reinforcement learning, or that a paradigm shift is needed for artificial general intelligence. Meanwhile, the mechanisms causing human intelligence are not any less elusive. It seems that the one thing that is absolutely clear is that both the fields of artificial intelligence and cognitive science have a lot of work ahead of them. With the already impressive success of biologically inspired techniques, it is inevitable that new discoveries about the human brain and mind will further advance the state of artificial intelligence.

References

Bogacz R, Brown MW, Giraud-Carrier C (2000) Frequency-based error back-propagation in a cortical network. Proceedings of the IEEE-INNS-ENNS International Joint Conference on Neural Networks 2:211–216.

Chomsky N (1959) A review of B. F. Skinner's *Verbal Behavior*. Language 35:26–58.

Cireşan D, Meier U, Schmidhuber J (2012) Multi-column deep neural networks for image classification. Proceedings of the 2012 IEEE Conference on Computer Vision and Pattern Recognition (CVPR), pp. 3642–3649.

Crick F (1989) The recent excitement about neural networks. Nature 337:129–132.

Cybenko G (1989) Approximation by superpositions of a sigmoidal function. Mathematics of Control, Signals, and Systems 2:303–314.

de Kleijn R, Kachergis G, Hommel B (2014) Everyday robotic action: Lessons from human action control. Frontiers in Neurorobotics 8:13.

Elsayed GF, Shankar S, Cheung B, Papernot N, Kurakin A, Goodfellow I, Sohl-Dickstein J (2018) Adversarial examples that fool both computer vision and time-limited humans. arXiv:1802.08195.

Goodfellow I, Shlens J, Szegedy C (2015) Explaining and harnessing adversarial examples. Proceedings of the 2015 International Conference on Learning Representations.

He K, Zhang X, Ren S, Sun J (2016) Deep residual learning for image recognition. Proceedings of the 2016 IEEE Conference on Computer Vision and Pattern Recognition (CVPR), pp. 770–778.

Hubel DH, Wiesel TN (1959) Receptive fields of single neurons in the cat's striate cortex. Journal of Physiology 148:574–591.

Kurakin A, Goodfellow I, Bengio S (2017) Adversarial examples in the physical world. arXiv:1607.02533v4.

---

[48] Zador 2019.

[49] Artificial general intelligence (AGI) refers to a hypothetical type of AI that would be able to learn any task that humans can perform.

Laird JE (2012) The Soar Cognitive Architecture. MIT Press.

Lenat DB, Guha RV, Pittman K, Pratt D, Shepherd M (1990) Cyc: Toward programs with common sense. Communications of the ACM 33:30–49.

Lighthill J (1973) Artificial intelligence: A general survey. In: Artificial intelligence: a paper symposium. Science Research Council.

McClelland JL (2009) Is a machine realization of truly human-like intelligence achievable? Cognitive Computation 1:17–21.

McKinney SM, Sieniek M, Godbole V et al (2020) International evaluation of an AI system for breast cancer screening. Nature 577:89–94.

Minsky M, Papert S (1969) Perceptrons: An introduction to computational geometry. MIT Press, Cambridge, MA.

Moravec H (1990) Mind children: The future of robot and human intelligence. Harvard University Press.

Newell A, Simon HA (1961) GPS, a program that simulates human thought. In: Billing H (ed) Lernende Automaten. R. Oldenbourg, pp. 109–124.

Newell A, Shaw JC, Simon HA (1957) Empirical explorations with the logic theory machine. Proceedings of the Western Joint Computer Conference 15:218–239.

Ohlsson S (2012) The problems with problem solving: Reflections on the rise, current status, and possible future of a cognitive research paradigm. Journal of Problem Solving 5:101–128.

Pinker S (1994) The language instinct: The new science of language and mind. William Morrow, New York.

Russell SJ, Norvig P (2010) Artificial intelligence: A modern approach, 3rd edn. Prentice Hall, Upper Saddle River, NJ.

Simon HA (1960) The new science of management decision. Harper & Brothers, New York.

Sowa JF (2012) Knowledge representation: Logical, philosophical, and computational foundations. Course Technology, Boston, MA.

Stallkamp J, Schlipsing M, Salmen J, Igel C (2011) The German traffic sign recognition benchmark: A multi-class classification competition. Proceedings of the 2011 International Joint Conference on Neural Networks: 1453–1460.

Stuart G, Spruston N, Sakmann B, Häusser M (1997) Action potential initiation and backpropagation in neurons of the mammalian CNS. Trends in Neurosciences 20:125–131.

Su J, Vargas DV, Sakurai K (2019) One pixel attack for fooling deep neural networks. IEEE Transactions on Evolutionary Computation 23:828–841.

Yamins DLK, DiCarlo JJ (2016) Using goal-driven deep learning models to understand sensory cortex. Nature Neuroscience 19:356–365.

Yu VL, Fagan LM, Wraith SM, Clancey WJ, Scott AC, Hannigan J, Blum RL, Buchanan BG, Cohen SN (1979) Antimicrobial selection by a computer: A blinded evaluation by infectious diseases experts. JAMA 242:1279–1282.

Zador AM (2019) A critique of pure learning and what artificial neural networks can learn from animal brains. Nature Communications 10:3770.

Zhou Z, Firestone C (2019) Humans can decipher adversarial images. Nature Communications 10:1334.

Roy de Kleijn Holds graduate degrees in Cognitive Neuroscience and Computer Science. He received his PhD from Leiden University for his dissertation on robotic action control. As an assistant professor at Leiden University, with a research focus on (deep) reinforcement learning and evolutionary robotics, he teaches in both the psychology and computer science programs.

Chapter 3
Disciplines of AI: An Overview of Approaches and Techniques

Andreas Häuselmann

Contents

Abstract This chapter provides an introduction to AI for people without a background in technology. After examining different definitions of AI and a discussion of the scope of the concept AI, five different disciplines of AI are discussed: Machine Learning, Automated Reasoning, Computer Vision, Affective Computing and Natural Language Processing. For each discipline of AI, approaches and techniques are discussed.

Keywords Artificial Intelligence · Machine Learning · Computer Vision · Natural Language Processing · Affective Computing · Automated Reasoning

---

[1] See for example https://www.independent.co.uk/topic/artificial-intelligence, https://www.youtube.com/results?search_query=Artificial+intelligence, https://www.reddit.com/r/artificial/, accessed 10 September 2021.

A. Häuselmann (✉)
eLaw—Center for Law and Digital Technologies, Leiden University, Leiden, The Netherlands
e-mail: a.n.hauselmann@law.leidenuniv.nl

© T.M.C. ASSER PRESS and the authors 2022
B. Custers and E. Fosch-Villaronga (eds.), *Law and Artificial Intelligence*,
Information Technology and Law Series 35,
https://doi.org/10.1007/978-94-6265-523-2_3

3.1   Introduction

Artificial Intelligence has recently received tremendous attention beyond the research community.[1] However, because people with different backgrounds are now making use of the technological terminology, the terminology is increasingly used in different ways than originally intended, beyond its technological meaning. In order to understand the debate on legal and ethical issues of AI, a proper understanding of what AI is and how it works is required. For better understanding of the chapters that follow, this chapter examines what AI is (and what it is not), the technology of AI and the terminology used. This chapter is not written as a technological chapter, but as a chapter explicitly intended for readers without a background in technology, particularly for lawyers.

This chapter starts with discussing existing definitions of AI (Sect. 3.2), followed by an overview of the disciplines of AI (Sect. 3.3). Whereas AI covers a very broad range of disciplines, concepts and terms, this chapter focuses on AI disciplines most relevant for law and lawyers. These disciplines include Machine Learning (Sect. 3.3.1), Natural Language Processing (Sect. 3.3.2), Computer Vision and Face Recognition (Sect. 3.3.3), Affective Computing (Sect. 3.3.4) and Automated Reasoning (Sect. 3.3.5). For each of these disciplines, relevant approaches and techniques are discussed. Section 3.4 completes the chapter with a conclusion.

3.2   Definitions of AI

There exists no universally agreed definition of Artificial Intelligence (AI). AI covers a broad range of concepts and terms, which makes it difficult to define. Available definitions often involve ambiguous terms such as "thinking", "learning" and "intelligence". In 1968, Marvin Minsky, a mathematician, computer scientist, and pioneer in the field of AI, defined AI as "the science of making machines do things that would require intelligence if done by men".[2] Bellman defined AI in 1978 as "the automation of activities that we associate with human thinking, activities such as decision-making, problem solving, learning, creating, game playing, and so on".[3] More recently, Nilsson described AI as "activity devoted to making machines intelligent, and intelligence is that quality that enables an entity to function appropriately and with foresight in its environment."[4] Russell and Norvig organise definitions of AI into four categories: thinking humanly, acting humanly, thinking rationally and acting rationally.[5] According to Munakata, AI entails abilities such as "inference based on knowledge, reasoning with uncertain or incomplete information, various forms of

---

[2] Minsky 1968.

[3] Bellman 1978, p. 3.

[4] Nilsson 2010, preface xiii.

[5] Russell and Norvig 2016, p. 2.

perception and learning, and applications to problems such as control, prediction, classification, and optimization".[6]

The field of AI may be divided into narrow and general AI. Narrow AI refers to systems which are capable of solving a specific problem or of performing a specific task. A typical example of a narrow AI system is IBM's "Deep Blue" chess playing computer. Deep Blue defeated the reigning world champion in chess, Garry Kasparov, in 1997.[7] This example shows that computers can perform better than humans do. However, this holds only true for a narrow domain, such as playing chess. General AI aims to build machines that perform generally on a human level and have a "human-level" skillset. In order to achieve this goal, such a system must be able to mimic the functioning of the human brain in every aspect.[8] Unlike narrow AI, general AI arguably has not been achieved yet because there are many open challenges. Although AI found its "birth" at the Dartmouth Summer Research Project on AI in the summer of 1956 in New Hampshire,[9] AI appears to still be in its infancy. According to Shi, AI research is still in its first stage since no breakthrough progresses have been achieved for some key challenges such as common-sense knowledge representation and uncertain reasoning.[10] Therefore, current AI systems must be considered as examples of "narrow" AI. However, computing power has become more affordable; computers became faster and contain larger memories. This led to the "summer of AI"[11] and it seems reasonable to expect major developments in the field of AI.

In his famous paper called 'Computing Machinery and Intelligence',[12] Alan Turing, a brilliant mathematician and computer pioneer, proposed the 'Imitation Game' which has later become known as the 'Turing Test'.[13] Turing offered his test as a sufficient condition for the existence of AI.[14] This test involves three actors, namely A a machine, B a human and C another human called the interrogator (see Fig. 3.1). The human interrogator C stays in a room apart from the other two actors A and B. The human interrogator knows the machine A and human B by labels X and Y[15] and thus does not know which actor is A or B.[16] The object of the test is for the interrogator C to determine which of the other two actors is the human and which is the machine[17] by means of asking X and Y questions which they must

---

[6] Munakata 2008, p. 2.

[7] https://www.livescience.com/59065-deep-blue-garry-kasparov-chess-match-anniversary.html, accessed 10 September 2021.

[8] Warwick 2012, p. 65.

[9] Kline 2011, pp. 4–5, see also Chap. 2.

[10] Shi 2011, p. 18.

[11] In the second decade of the twenty-first century, AI has morphed into a full-fledged summer with significant growth see Franklin 2014, p. 28.

[12] Turing 1950, pp. 433–460.

[13] Bernhardt 2016, p. 157.

[14] Franklin 2014, p. 17.

[15] Turing 1950, pp. 433–460.

[16] Bernhardt 2016, p. 157.

[17] Turing 1950, pp. 433–460.

Fig. 3.1 Illustration of the Turing test [*Source* The author]

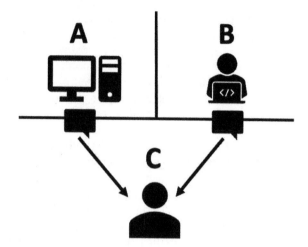

answer.[18] In other words, the human interrogator engages in conversation with either a human or an AI natural language program[19] which are both hidden from view. If the human interrogator cannot reliably distinguish between the human and the program/machine, (artificial) intelligence is ascribed to the program.[20]

But what exactly is required in order to pass the Turing test? Turing himself envisaged that computers pass the test if they "play the imitation game so well that an average interrogator will not have more than 70 per cent chance of making the right identification after five minutes of questioning."[21] Despite its notoriety, the Turing test does not seem to be the most appropriate test to evaluate AI because it is neither gradual nor factorial and it can be gamed by non-intelligent chatbots.[22] This criticism, however, does not mean to discard the idea of evaluating AI by human judges or comparing it with humans. There are many variants of the Turing test, and one of them is being used widely. We all know the Completely Automated Public Turing test to tell Computers and Humans Apart (CAPTCHA) which is said to be the "reverse Turing test" and used today in order to ensure that an action (e.g. registering a for a service, accessing a service) is indeed performed by a human.[23]

There are plenty of definitions for AI, entailing ambiguous terms such as the ones already mentioned above. In this chapter, AI refers to adaptive machines that can autonomously execute activities and tasks which require capabilities usually associated with cognitive skills of humans. "Autonomously" in this sense means that the machine has the ability to make its *own* decisions and execute tasks on

---

[18] Bernhardt 2016, p. 157.

[19] See Sect. 3.3.2 below.

[20] Franklin 2014, pp. 17, 18.

[21] Turing 1950, p. 442.

[22] Hernández-Orallo 2017, p. 405; for more objections and criticism on the Turing test, see <https://plato.stanford.edu/entries/turing-test/> accessed 10 September 2021.

[23] Hernández-Orallo 2017, p. 405.

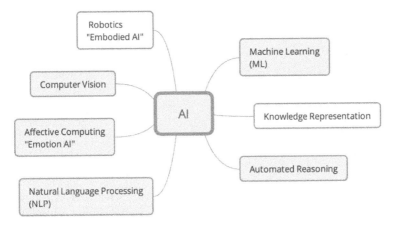

Fig. 3.2 Illustration created by the author outlining the disciplines of AI inspired by Russel/Norvig[28] and slightly adjusted by adding the field of Affective Computing [*Source* The author]

the designer's behalf.[24] "Adaptive" refers to the capability of the machine to learn from, and adapt to, its environment in order to preserve its autonomy in dynamic environments.[25] Adaptivity is very important since only a machine that *learns* will succeed in a vast variety of environments.[26] Learning in this context corresponds to "adapt" the performance according to previously made experiences based on statistics and probability calculations.[27]

3.3 Disciplines of AI

AI is commonly considered to consist of seven major disciplines, shown in Fig. 3.2. Since AI covers a broad range of concepts, this chapter focuses on AI disciplines most relevant for law and lawyers. These disciplines of AI are coloured blue in Fig. 3.2.[29] The remaining two disciplines not coloured blue (Robotics "Embodied AI" and Knowledge Representation) will not be discussed in this chapter. Embodied AI includes approaches such as driverless vehicles, surgical robots and companions and we expect that the reader is familiar with these applications. The discipline of

---

[24] Alonso 2014, pp. 235, 236.

[25] Ibid., 235.

[26] Russell and Norvig 2016, p. 39.

[27] Strauß 2018, p. 7.

[28] Russell and Norvig 2016, pp. 2, 3.

[29] This figure shall not be considered as a complete overview of all disciplines of AI, but serves as an illustrative overview for this chapter.

AI commonly referred to as Knowledge Representation focuses on the computers capabilities to store what it knows and hears.[30] Research in the field deals with conceptual issues[31] not necessarily relevant for this book. The other disciplines are discussed in the following subsections.

3.3.1 Machine Learning

Machine learning may be considered as a major discipline (or one of the tools) of AI.[32] In this chapter, we consider it as a discipline of AI. Computer science has traditionally aimed to manually program computers. The aim of machine learning however, is that computers program themselves based on experience.[33] In other words, the goal of machine learning is to adapt to new circumstances and to detect and extrapolate patterns.[34] Murphy defines machine learning as "a set of methods that can automatically detect patterns in data, and then use the uncovered patterns to predict future data, or to perform other kinds of decision making under uncertainty".[35] Machine learning can simply be described as the set of computational methods using experience to improve its performance or to make accurate predictions.[36] This is achieved by using machine learning algorithms, i.e. algorithms that learn from experience.[37] Experience refers to data available to the algorithm for analysis.[38] Learning in this context is about making computers modify or adapt their performance (actions) so that these actions get more *accurate*.[39] Machine learning uses data-driven methods, combining fundamental concepts in computer science with approaches from statistics, probability and optimisation.[40] In fact, the probabilistic approach in machine learning is closely related to the field of statistics, but differs slightly in terms of its emphasis and terminology. The probabilistic approach is particularly helpful to handle ambiguous cases.[41] The main goal of machine learning is to generate accurate predictions for unseen data and to design efficient algorithms to produce these predictions.[42]

---

[30] Russell and Norvig 2016, p. 2.

[31] E.g. the issue of whether or not represent knowledge, Franklin 2014, pp. 24, 25.

[32] Kotu and Bala 2019, p. 2.

[33] Mitchell 2006, p. 1.

[34] Russell and Norvig 2016, p. 2.

[35] Murphy 2012, p. 1.

[36] Mohri et al. 2012, p. 1.

[37] Goodfellow et al. 2016, p. 97.

[38] Mohri et al. 2012, p. 1.

[39] Marsland 2015, Chapter 1.2.1.

[40] Mohri et al. 2012, p. 1.

[41] Murphy 2012, pp. 1, 4.

[42] Mohri et al. 2012, p. 2.

Before a specific type of machine learning called Deep Learning (DL) is discussed, some of the most widely used machine learning methods will be elaborated on first. These methods are called supervised, unsupervised and reinforcement learning. In practice, the distinction between supervised and unsupervised learning is not always clear-cut. Therefore, semi-supervised learning creates a continuum between supervised and unsupervised learning: the algorithm is provided with a few labelled examples (supervised learning) but also has the task to uncover hidden patterns and structures in the data (unsupervised learning).[43] Another method deployed in machine learning is Reinforcement Learning. The latter is becoming increasingly relevant, particularly in Natural Language Processing, a discipline of AI which aims to enable computers to process human language.

3.3.1.1 Supervised Machine Learning

Supervised machine learning aims to learn a mapping from input x to output y given a labelled set of input-output pairs called the *training set* or training data. It can be used to make predictions on *new* input through generalisation.[44] Generalisation refers to the ability of the algorithm to categorise new examples that differ from the ones used during the training phase.[45] In the supervised machine learning approach, the learning algorithm receives a number of examples, each *labelled* with the correct label (training data). Consider for example several labelled pictures with different animals (lions, horses, and cows). The goal is that the algorithm automatically recognises the correct label for the training data and *predicts* the value of unseen (unlabelled) input.[46] In other words, the aim is that the algorithm *generalises* accurately by producing a model that can classify input *not seen* during training.[47] The user who provides the correct labels to the algorithm is the teacher, knowing for each input the correct output. Therefore, this is called "supervised" learning: the algorithm learns under the supervision and guidance of the teacher.[48] To measure the accuracy of the model generated by the algorithm, the teacher provides the algorithm with a test set of examples that are *different* from the training set.[49] Hence, the teacher feeds the algorithm with new pictures containing lions, horses and cows and evaluates the accuracy of the model, namely whether the algorithm recognised the animals correctly. The algorithm learns by adjusting the relevant parameters so that the model makes the most accurate predictions on the data.[50]

---

[43] Russell and Norvig 2016, p. 695.

[44] Murphy 2012, p. 3.

[45] Bishop 2006, p. 2.

[46] Mohri et al. 2012, p. 7.

[47] Alpaydin 2016, p. 39.

[48] Munakata 2008, p. 38.

[49] Russell and Norvig 2016, p. 695.

[50] Alpaydin 2016, p. 39.

There are basically two techniques used for supervised machine learning: classification and regression.[51] As indicated by its name, classification refers to situations where the predicted attribute is categorical and regression applies to situations where the predicted attribute is numeric.[52] Classification orders data into exhaustive and exclusive groups or classes on the basis of their similarity. Consequently, all data can only be assigned to one class.[53] The example above with the animal referred to the technique of classification. Regression is suitable when the prediction to be made by the algorithm should be a numerical value. Regression could be described as a statistical approach which is used to identify the relationship between variables.[54] Hence, the technique of regression could be used to predict the number of people likely to click on an online advertisement based on the ad content and the user's previous browsing history. Other real-world examples using regression are predicting stock market prices given current market conditions, or predicting the age of a viewer watching a given video on YouTube.[55]

3.3.1.2 Unsupervised Machine Learning

Unlike supervised machine learning, the algorithm in unsupervised learning only receives *un*labelled training data.[56] That means that the algorithm is not told what the desired output is for each form of input. Unsupervised machine learning does not require a human expert to manually label the data.[57] Due to the fact that there is no external comparison between actual and ideal output by the teacher, this approach is called unsupervised: there are no correct answers available.[58] Hence, the algorithm tries to discover patterns in the input even though no explicit feedback is supplied.[59] The goal of unsupervised machine learning is to identify the associations and patterns among a set of input data[60] and categorise them together accordingly.[61] It can be difficult to quantitatively evaluate the performance of the model since there are no labelled examples available.[62] Two branches of techniques used for unsupervised learning are clustering and dimensionality reduction.[63]

---

[51] Usuelli 2014, p. 155.

[52] Usuelli 2014, p. 154.

[53] Calders and Custers 2013, p. 32.

[54] However, note that decision tree regression would not be considered as traditional statistics.

[55] Murphy 2012, p. 9.

[56] Mohri et al. 2012, p. 7.

[57] Murphy 2012, p. 9.

[58] Munakata 2008, p. 38.

[59] Russell and Norvig 2016, p. 694.

[60] Hastie et al. 2008, p. xi.

[61] Marsland 2015, chapter 1.3

[62] Mohri et al. 2012, p. 7.

[63] Usuelli 2014, p. 164.

Clustering in this context means to divide detected patterns into groups or clusters. Similar patterns are placed in the same group while all others are put in different groups.[64] Simply put, clustering refers to the partition of unlabelled items into homogeneous regions.[65] Clusters may overlap, whereas classifications do not. Clustering is particularly performed in order to analyse very large datasets. A common example is to use clustering in the context of social network analysis, where the clustering algorithm tries to identify "communities" within large groups of people.[66] The same applies to e-commerce, where users are clustered into groups based on their purchasing or online behaviour, which enables online shops to send customised targeted ads to each group.[67]

Dimensionality reduction aims to represent data with fewer dimensions[68] and is useful to project high dimensional data to a lower dimensional subspace in order to capture the "essence" of the data.[69] By reducing the dimensions, *hidden patterns* and *structures* in the data may be observed and noninformative features are discarded. Dimensional representations often produce *better predictive accuracy* because they focus on the essence of the object and filter nonessential features out.[70] Dimensionality reduction is commonly applied in Natural Language Processing (see Sect. 3.3.2 below), e.g. for acoustic signals[71] and used to pre-process digital images in computer vision tasks[72] (see Sect. 3.3.3 below).

3.3.1.3   Reinforcement Learning

Reinforcement learning is a distinct method in machine learning which differs from supervised and unsupervised machine learning approaches. In reinforcement learning, the algorithm interacts with its environment and the method is inspired by behavioural psychology.[73] Reinforcement learning algorithms modify or acquire new behaviours incrementally and use *trial-and-error* experience without requiring complete knowledge or control of the environment.[74] Unlike supervised learning, reinforcement learning learns with a "critic" who does not instruct the algorithm what to do, but rather provides it with feedback in the form of a reward or punishment.[75] The reward depends on the correctness of the decision (the performed action

---

[64] Munakata 2008, p. 72.

[65] Mohri et al. 2012, p. 2.

[66] Mohri et al. 2012, p.

[67] Murphy 2012, p. 11.

[68] Alpaydin 2016, pp. 115, 116.

[69] Murphy 2012, p. 11.

[70] Ibid., 12.

[71] Murphy 2012, p. 11.

[72] Mohri et al. 2012, p. 2.

[73] Goodfellow et al. 2016, p. 104.

[74] François-Lavet et al. 2018, pp. 2, 15.

[75] Alpaydin 2016, p. 127.

by the agent).[76] In reinforcement learning, the decision-maker is called the agent who interacts with everything outside the agent, called the environment. Agent and environment interact continuously: the agent selects actions and the environment responds to those actions and presents new situations to the agent.[77] The agent has no prior knowledge of what action to take, it learns from interaction with the environment.[78] The object of the agent is to maximise its reward over a course of interactions with the environment.[79] Hence, the agent uses the received feedback to update its knowledge so that it learns to perform actions which return the highest reward.[80] An illustrative example is a machine (agent) that learns how to play chess. The chessboard is the environment of the agent which has to decide over a sequence of actions, namely "moves" on the chessboard (environment) in order to achieve a certain goal, in this case winning the game. In reinforcement learning, the agent evolves and learns while analysing consequences of its actions with the feedback received from the environment.[81] This is different to the unsupervised machine learning approach, where no feedback is distributed. Reinforcement learning also differs from supervised machine learning because the agent does not learn from the initially labelled training data, but from the interaction with the environment based on feedback in the form of a punishment or reward.[82] Combining it with deep learning techniques (see below) has made "deep RL" increasingly successful in addressing challenging sequential decision-making problems such as mastering the game Go or beating the world's top professionals at Poker. Its adaptive capabilities make reinforcement learning very suitable for interactive applications. For example, deep reinforcement learning is applied in dialogue systems and conversational agents, particularly digital assistants and chatbots.[83] Deep reinforcement learning seems to possess promising potential for real-world applications such as robotics, self-driving cars, finance and smart grids.[84] Current machine learning applications based on the supervised method for natural language processing and speech recognition (see Sect. 3.3.2) require vast amounts of labelled training data. This issue could be eliminated by applying deep reinforcement learning methods.[85]

---

[76] Engelbrecht 2007, p. 83.

[77] Shi 2011, p. 365

[78] Engelbrecht 2007, p. 83.

[79] Mohri et al. 2012, p. 8.

[80] Alpaydin 2016, p. 126.

[81] Shi 2011, p. 362.

[82] Das et al. 2015, pp. 31, 32.

[83] Serban et al. 2017, p. 1.

[84] François-Lavet et al. 2018, p. 3.

[85] Deng and Liu 2018a, b, p. 316.

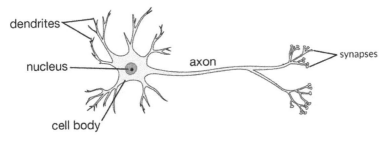

Fig. 3.3 Biological neuron illustrated by Singh Gill[88] [*Source* Singh Gill 2019]

3.3.1.4 Artificial Neural Networks and Deep Learning

The human brain consists of a very large number of processing units called neurons.[86] These neurons have an output fibre called axon and a terminal called synapse. Axons split up and connect to several dendrites, which are the input paths of other neurons through the junction terminal synapse.[87] Because the neurons of the human brain are connected, it is called a neural network. Figure 3.3 shows a typical biological neuron.

Although it is not entirely clear how the neural network of human brains actually works, it is considered to be the fundamental functional source of intelligence, which includes perception, learning and cognition.[89] The characteristic of a neural network is that the neurons operate in parallel and transfer information among themselves over the synapses so that the neurons are connected and influence each other.[90] The brain is believed to learn by examples, experience and to be highly capable to adapt to external changes.[91]

A single biological neuron would be too simple to make decisions like humans do. Similarly, a single artificial neuron would not be able to cope with challenging decision-making and prediction processes. Hence, to unleash the full potential of artificial neurons, they must operate in parallel and transfer information among themselves. That is why researchers such as Rumelhart and others in 1986 attempted to design Artificial Neural Networks (ANN) with the aim to allow an arbitrarily connected neural network to develop an internal structure that is appropriate for a particular task.[92] ANN can be simply described as an abstract model that is inspired by the knowledge of the inner workings of the human brain that can be programmed in a computer. ANNs consist of artificial neurons and interconnections similar to

---

[86] Alpaydin 2016, p. 86.

[87] Chow and Cho 2007, p. 2.

[88] Singh Gill 2019, Overview of Artificial Neural Networks and its application <https://www.xen onstack.com/blog/artificial-neural-network-applications/> accessed 10 September 2021.

[89] Munakata 2008, p. 7.

[90] Alpaydin 2016, p. 86.

[91] Chow and Cho 2007, p. 2.

[92] Rumelhart et al. 1986, p. 533.

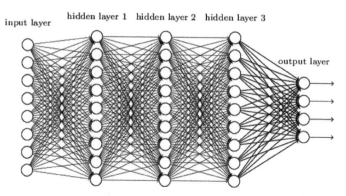

Fig. 3.4 Example of a deep Artificial Neural Network illustrated by Michael Nielsen[96] [*Source* Nielsen 2015]

the human brain. The network receives input, performs internal processes such as the activation of the neurons and finally yields output.[93] However, ANNs are not generally designed to be realistic models of the human brain.

The neural perspective on deep learning is motivated by two main ideas; firstly, that the brain provides an example that intelligent behaviour is possible, and secondly, to create machine learning models that shed light on the principles of the brain and human intelligence.[94] The pattern of connections between the artificial neurons is called the architecture or topology of the ANNs and consists of distinct layers of neurons. The layers depend on the model that is used.[95] Each of the layers has a certain number of neurons which is usually determined by a specific application problem the model aims to solve. An example of a Deep ANN is given in Fig. 3.4.

Generally, there is one input layer and one output layer and *any number* of hidden layers. Neurons of the input layer are connected to the neurons of the hidden layer through edges, and the neurons of the hidden layer(s) are connected to the output layer. A weight is associated to each edge. The input layer (see on the left side of Fig. 3.4) consists of neurons that receive their input directly from the data and its function is to merely send out input signals to the hidden layer neurons; it does not compute anything.[97] The hidden layer then applies computation methods to the input received, depending on the model used for the neural network, transforming the received input to something the output layer can use. Hidden means that the values in these layers are not given in the data, but the model has the task to determine which concepts are useful for explaining the relationships in the observed data.[98] It then sends its output to the next layer, in this case to hidden layer 2, which sends it

---

[93] Munakata 2008, pp. 3, 7.

[94] Goodfellow et al. 2016, p. 13.

[95] Munakata 2008, p. 9.

[96] Nielsen 2015, chapter 5.

[97] Munakata 2008, p. 10.

[98] Goodfellow et al. 2016, p. 6.

to the hidden layer 3 and subsequently to the output layer (see on the right side of Fig. 3.4). Subsequently, the role of the output layer is to produce the output of the whole network. The output of ANNs can then be used to extract a prediction or a decision.

Deep learning is a particular kind of machine learning that represents the world as a nested hierarchy of concepts[99] and can be used for supervised, unsupervised and reinforcement learning methods. The human brain seems to execute many levels of processing with increasing levels of abstraction.[100] Deep learning seems to resemble this by computing more abstract concepts in terms of less abstract ones.[101] Most of the models used for supervised and unsupervised machine learning have a simple two-layer architecture.[102] This is different with deep learning models, which use many different layers. Approaches in deep learning feed a large set of input data into the ANN that produces successive transformations of the input data where each hidden layer combines the values in its preceding layer and learns more complicated functions of the input.[103] Then, the final transformation predicts the output.[104] The deep learning approach avoids that the human operator has to specify all the knowledge which the computer requires. Deep learning solves this by enabling the computer to build complex concepts out of simpler concepts. When illustrating the approach in a graph by building the concepts on top of each other, that graph is deep with many layers. This is why the approach is called deep learning (see Fig. 3.3 above).[105] Deep learning draws inspiration from many fields, especially from linear algebra and probabilistic statistics. Interestingly, all achievements in modern deep learning have been made with an astonishingly small number of neurons contained in the ANNs when compared with neural networks of the human brain. Although today's ANNs are considered quite large from a computational perspective, they are smaller than neural networks of relatively primitive animals like frogs. Some scholars predict that ANNs will not reach the same number of neurons as the human brain possesses before the 2050s unless new technologies enable faster scaling.[106]

However, most of the current deep learning models lack reasoning and explanatory capabilities, which makes them vulnerable to produce unexplainable outcomes. Despite the recent success of deep learning, deep learning methods based on ANN generally lack interpretability.[107] Interpretability remains a challenge due to the hierarchical and nonlinear structure of ANNs and the central concept in deep learning called connectionism. In deep learning models, each artificial neuron works *independently* by computing a relatively simple task and therefore *partially* contributes

---

[99] Ibid., p. 8.
[100] Murphy 2012, p. 95.
[101] Goodfellow et al. 2016, p. 8.
[102] Murphy 2012, p. 995.
[103] Alpaydin 2016, p. 104.
[104] Goldberg 2017, p. 2.
[105] Goodfellow et al. 2016, pp. 1, 5.
[106] Goodfellow et al. 2016, pp. 16, 21, 25.
[107] Deng and Liu 2018a, b, pp. 11, 12.

to the output produced by the ANNs.[108] ANNs produce output based on the central concept in deep learning called *connectionism,* where the idea is that a large number of simple computational units (artificial neurons) achieve intelligent behaviour when networked together.[109] Consequently, combining the characteristic of artificial neurons to work independently with the concept of connectionism leads to a situation where thousands or hundreds of thousands of artificial neurons work in parallel in an ANN with hidden layers to jointly calculate certain output.[110] Hence, it seems neither possible to understand which artificial neuron contributed to a distinct part of the output nor to understand what happened in the intermediate (hidden) layers of the ANN.[111] In other words, it is not possible to extract any underlying rules which may be implied by the deep learning model.[112] This holds even true for deep learning algorithms using the supervised learning method where the algorithm cannot learn without providing it with correct sample patterns. So even if an ANN has successfully been trained to perform its goal, the many numeric values of the weights produced by the model do not have a meaning to the supervisor.[113] Differently put, the model is parameterised by all those weights, but it remains unclear how these weights have been calculated and to which extent the various input variables contributed to the outcome. ANNs in use can be *updated dynamically* as new data is fed into the network.[114] Subsequently, this updates the weights produced by the model because they learn by experience. These updates contribute to further challenges concerning the interpretability of deep learning approaches.[115] Deep learning is well suited to situations in which the data corresponds to complex sensor data such as input from cameras and microphones that proved to be difficult to process when using conventional computational methods.[116] This applies in particular to cognitive tasks which include natural language processing and speech recognition or face recognition, which are discussed below.[117]

Current research in deep learning attempts to decode speech directly from the human brain. Such approaches record the activity in the cortex to decode characteristics of produced speech.[118] State of the art deep neural network models arguably contribute to an improved overall accuracy in speech reconstruction from neural recordings in the human auditory cortex.[119] The short-term goal of these research

---

[108] Munakata 2008, p. 44.

[109] Goodfellow et al. 2016, p. 16.

[110] Alpaydin 2016, p. 155.

[111] Ibid.

[112] Munakata 2008, p. 44.

[113] Ibid., pp. 12, 25, 35.

[114] A production model has fixed weights after training. To continuously update weights is possible, but by no means necessary.

[115] De Laat 2017, p. 14.

[116] Chow and Cho 2007, pp. 1–2.; Mitchell 2006, p. 95.

[117] Chow and Cho 2007, p. 2.

[118] Moses et al. 2019, p. 10.

[119] Yang et al. 2015, p. 1124.

projects is to help individuals that are not able to communicate due to injuries or neurodegenerative disorders by creating a synthesized version of their voice that can be controlled by the activity of their brain's speech centres.[120] However, the long term goal of this could be much broader, and very different. Facebook announced that it wants to "build a non-invasive, wearable device that lets people type by simply imagining themselves talking."[121]

3.3.2 Natural Language Processing

Natural Language Processing (NLP) aims to give computers the ability to process human language. This interdisciplinary field comprises many concepts and methods like speech and language processing, human language technology, natural language processing, computational linguistics, and speech recognition and synthesis.[122] Natural language processing includes both the generation and understanding of natural language.[123] From an engineering perspective, natural language processing intends to develop novel practical applications to facilitate the interactions between computers and human languages.[124] Current natural language processing systems require large amounts of labelled data.[125] Speech recognition is a typical application of natural language processing and its aim is to *automatically transcribe* the sequence of spoken words. It may be defined as the process of converting a speech signal to a sequence of words by means of an algorithm implemented by a computer program.[126] Notably, speech recognition does not concern *understanding,* but is merely responsible to *convert* language from spoken words to text form. [127] The observable "physical" signal of natural language is called text in a symbolic form, and its counterpart is the speech signal, namely the continuous correspondence of spoken texts.[128] Speech recognition relies on the acoustic signal captured by a microphone as input. The classes are the words that can be uttered. A word is considered to be a sequence of phonemes, which are the basic speech sounds.[129] Hence, speech recognition converts phonemes (i.e. the speech signal) into text. A specific challenge

---

[120] Weiler N (2019) Breakthrough device translates brain activity into speech, https://www.univer sityofcalifornia.edu/news/synthetic-speech-generated-brain-recordings. Accessed 10 September 2021.

[121] Tech@Facebook (2020) Imagining a new interface: Hands-free communication without saying a word https://tech.fb.com/imagining-a-new-interface-hands-free-communication-without-saying-a-word/. Accessed 10 September 2021.

[122] Jurafsky and Martin 2014, p. 1.

[123] Franklin 2014, p. 26.

[124] Deng and Liu 2018a, b, p. 1.

[125] Deng and Liu 2018a, b, p. 316.

[126] Abhang et al. 2016, p. 13.

[127] Tur et al. 2018, p. 24.

[128] Ibid., p. 24.

[129] Alpaydin 2016, p. 67.

in speech recognition is that different people pronounce the same word differently due to factors related to age, gender or accent, which makes it more difficult to recognise the words.[130]

Speech signals cannot only reveal the intended message, but also the identity of the speaker. The ways in which prosodic characteristics such as rhythm and intonation are manifested in speech disclose important information regarding the identity of the speaker.[131] Prosody refers to the study of the intonational and rhythmic aspects of language.[132] Systems in the domain of speaker verification are capable of using the voice of an individual in order to identify an unknown person (speaker identification), verify the identity of a person (speaker verification) and classify specific characteristics like age or gender (speaker classification).[133] The text-based verification of an individual by means of voice analysis is technically possible with a very short text such as "Ok Google", which takes approximately 0,6 seconds if uttered by an individual.[134] Hence, a speaker's identity is embedded in his or her voice and can be recognised using automatic speaker recognition systems, which apply deep learning approaches.[135]

Current research in speech recognition focuses on how speech is modulated when a speaker's emotion changes from neutral to another emotional state. For example, it has been observed that speech in anger or happiness shows longer utterance duration and higher pitch and energy value with deep length.[136] Speech emotion recognition may be used for various areas, such as call centres, smart devices or self-driving cars.[137]

3.3.3 Computer Vision and Face Recognition

Computer vision is a discipline of AI devoted to perceive objects,[138] i.e. the automated understanding of visual images and comprises many fields of applications.[139] The goal of object detection is to detect all instances of objects from a known class, such as people, cars, or faces in an image.[140] Computer Vision may also be described as the science and technology of machines that "see", where the latter refers to the ability of

---

[130] Alpaydin 2016, p. 67.

[131] Mary 2019, p. 1, 8.

[132] Jurafsky and Martin 2014, p. 238.

[133] Hourri and Kharroubi 2020, p. 123.

[134] Heigold et al. 2015, p. 1.

[135] Mary 2019, p. 7.

[136] Abhang et al. 2016, pp. 14, 105.

[137] See services of the company audeering: https://www.audeering.com/ Accessed 10 September 2021.

[138] Russell and Norvig 2016, p. 3.

[139] Franklin 2014, p. 26.

[140] Amit et al. 2021, p. 875.

the machine to extract information from an image that is necessary to solve a task.[141] It aims to infer properties from the observed visual data, which originates from a variety of sensors such as cameras, laser scans etc.[142] Computer vision algorithms reconstruct the properties of one or more images, such as shape, illumination and colour distributions. Researchers develop mathematical techniques for recovering the three-dimensional shape and appearance of objects in imagery.

Real-world applications include Optical Character Recognition (OCR) for automatic number plate recognitions (of vehicles), medical imaging for pre-operative and intra-operative imagery, automotive safety to detect unexpected obstacles such as pedestrians on the street, surveillance to monitor intruders and fingerprint recognition for automatic access authentication.[143] Techniques from the domain of computer vision are currently also used to identify individuals based on their gait, i.e. the manner in which an individual walks. Biometric research implies that the gait constitutes a unique identifier like fingerprints and iris.[144] Biometrics necessary for gait identification may be captured at public places and from a distance in a rather ubiquitous manner. Methods used for identification are model based approaches which consider the human body or its movements to acquire gait parameters (e.g. step dimensions, cadence, human skeleton, body dimensions) as well as model free approaches that acquire gait parameters by relying on gait dynamics and the measurement of geometric representations such as silhouettes.[145]

Another real-world example is Amazon Go. Amazon Go is a checkout-free grocery store which is equipped with state-of-the-art cameras and sensors. Amazon Go is powered by computer vision, deep learning and sensor fusion[146] in order to track shoppers and their purchases. Sensor fusion exploits the best features of sensors (e.g. cameras and small Bluetooth radio transmitters called 'beacons') installed in a given environment. It is particularly helpful in situations where the sensors themselves are not self-sufficient to achieve a certain goal, for instance comprehensive and precise tracking of shoppers.[147] In Amazon Go stores, shoppers enter by scanning an Amazon Go smartphone app and sensors track items that the shoppers take from the shelves. Once picked up, the items are automatically charged to the Amazon accounts of the shoppers when they leave the store.[148] Where Amazon Go's inventory system

[141] Yoshida 2011, p. vii.

[142] Jampani 2017, p. 1.

[143] Szeliski 2011, pp. 3, 5.

[144] Sokolova and Konushin 2019, p. 213.

[145] Kovač et al. 2019, pp. 5621, 5622.

[146] See https://www.amazon.com/b?ie=UTF8&node=16008589011 and Mavroudis and Veale 2018, p. 6.

[147] For example, cameras offer a high level of precision, but might be too expensive to cover the whole shop. Beacons are not self-sufficient to provide tracking data for customer analysis, but can cover a wider operational range. Combined by means of sensor fusion, the sensors allow precise consumer path tracking. See Sturari et al. 2016, pp. 30, 31, 40.

[148] Carey and Macaulay (2018) Amazon Go looks convenient, but raises huge questions over privacy, https://www.techworld.com/business/amazon-go-looks-amazing-but-at-what-cost-3651434/. Accessed 10 September 2021.

cannot detect the object the user removed from the shelf, this system "may consider past purchase history" of the user.[149]

Face recognition is one of the applications of computer vision. Face recognition refers to the technology capable to identify or verify the identity of subjects in images or videos based on biometric data.[150] It is one of the major biometric technologies and has become increasingly relevant due to the rapid advances in image capture devices and the availability of huge amounts of face images on the web.[151] Unlike other biometric identification methods such as iris recognition (which requires individuals to get significantly close to a camera), face recognition can be used from a distance and in a covert manner.[152] Hence, the range of potential applications for face recognition is wide because it can be easily deployed.[153]

Face recognition systems operate with a face verification (authentication) and/or face identification (recognition) mode. The former involves a one-on-one match that compares a query face image of the person whose identity is claimed (e.g. for self-serviced immigration clearance using E-passports). The latter involves one-to-many matching which compares a query face image against multiple face images in a database to associate the identity of the query face. Usually, finding the most similar face is not sufficient and a confidence threshold is specified. Hence, only those faces whose similarity score is above the threshold are reported.[154] Face recognition systems are usually built on four building blocks:

1. Face detection, which finds the position of a face in an image;
2. Face normalisation, which normalises the face geometrically and photometrically;
3. Face feature extraction, performed to extract salient information which is useful to distinguish faces such as reference points located at fixed locations in the face (e.g. position of eyes, nose, lips); and
4. Face matching, where extracted features from the input face are matched against one or many of the enrolled faces in the database.[155]

The facial features used for building block 3 may be grouped into two classes: continuous and discrete features. Continuous features are real valued numbers and are extracted using distances and angles between facial landmarks, such as forehead height, eyebrows length, nose height, chin height, ears length, mouth length etc. Discrete features represent a finite number of categories, for example the shape of the eyebrow or nose root width.[156] Figure 3.5 provides an example of such features.

---

[149] Kumar et al. 2019, Detecting item interaction and movement, US Patent Number US 10268983 (Assignee: Amazon Technologies, Inc.) https://patentimages.storage.googleapis.com/01/0b/6e/de5 7009f5670ae/US20150019391A1.pdf Accessed 10 September 2021.

[150] Trigueros et al. 2018, p. 1.

[151] Li and Jain 2011, p. 1.

[152] Ibid.; Trigueros et al. 2018, p. 1.

[153] Trigueros et al. 2018, p. 1.

[154] Li and Jain 2011, p. 3.

[155] Ibid., 4; Trigueros et al. 2018, p. 1

[156] Tome et al. 2015, pp. 271, 273.

Fig. 3.5 Face layout illustrated by Tome et al.[157] with examples of facial features extracted by using distances and angles between facial landmarks such as eyebrows, eyes, nose and lips. [*Source* Tome et al. 2015]

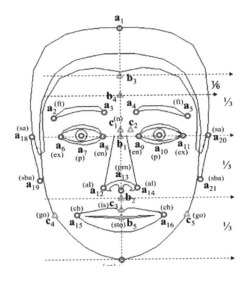

Current face recognition applications use deep learning methods based on convolutional neural networks (CNN) which are trained with very large datasets.[158] A CNN is a specific kind of neural network for processing data which has a known grid-like typology. For example, image data can be thought of as a 2D grid of pixels. As the name indicates, CNN employs a mathematical operation called convolution, which is a specialised kind of linear operation.[159] Notably, the performance of a face recognition system largely depends on a variety of factors such as illumination, facial pose, expression, age span, hair and motion.[160] Whereas the building blocks of face recognition systems and the general architecture of the ANNs are predetermined by the developer of the system, the ANN itself decides how to create the optimal score for determining similarity in the face matching building block mentioned above. Hence, it remains often unclear how the similarity score is calculated by the ANN, even to the developer of the system.[161] Another issue is that face recognition systems perform poorly in recognising individuals of different ethnicities. For example, face recognition software of Hewlett Packard could not recognise dark-coloured faces as faces.[162] A "passport robot" in New Zealand rejected the passport picture of an Asian man because the "subject's eyes are closed" although his eyes were open.[163]

---

[157] Tome et al. 2015, pp. 271, 273.

[158] Trigueros et al. 2018, p. 1.

[159] Goodfellow et al. 2016, p. 326.

[160] Li and Jain 2011, p. 3.

[161] Welinder and Palmer 2018, p. 104.

[162] Zuiderveen Borgesius 2019, p. 17.

[163] Regan J (2016) New Zealand passport robot tells applicant of Asian descent to open eyes, https://www.reuters.com/article/us-newzealand-passport-error/new-zealand-passport-robot-tells-applicant-of-asian-descent-to-open-eyes-idUSKBN13W0RL. Accessed 10 September 2021.

Face recognition systems are widely used in commercial applications and consumer products with built-in AI capabilities. Examples are cars with on-board cameras to deploy biometric identification and monitor driving behaviour or connected retail spaces. Furthermore, there is a trend to enhance face recognition systems with capabilities to monitor and analyse the emotions of the individuals in real-time based on extracted biometric data and facial expressions. The gained knowledge is then used to build specific customer profiles.

3.3.4 Affective Computing

Affective Computing (AC), sometimes called "emotion AI", is computing that relates to, arises from or influences emotion. It is a scientific and engineering endeavour inspired by psychology, neuroscience, linguistics and related areas.[164] Emotions form an important part of human intelligence and daily live, be it for decision making, social interaction, perception or learning. In other words, emotions play a pivotal role in functions considered essential to intelligence.[165] Picard, the pioneer in the field of affective computing, therefore concludes that if computers shall be genuinely intelligent, they too should have emotional capabilities. In this chapter, the focus lies on affect detection from facial expressions and speech since they may be easily deployed compared to more invasive approaches including measurement of physiological factors such as measurement of skin conduction or heart rate in order to determine anxiety.

3.3.4.1 Facial Expressions

Facial expressions are likely the most natural way how humans express their emotions.[166] Due to the developments in technology, it is possible to detect facial information automatically in real-time. However, automatic detection of emotions derived from facial expressions and their interpretation is not simple and context-driven.[167] The leading approach to detect and classify emotions from facial expressions is the Facial Action Coding System (FACS) developed to measure facial activity and to classify its motions into the six basic emotions.[168] Facial expressions and hypothesised 'basic emotions' are illustrated in Fig. 3.6.

FACS describes facial activity in terms of anatomically based Action Units (AUs)[169] such as "Inner Brow Raiser", "Chin Raiser", "Lip Corner Puller" and are

---

[164] Calvo et al. 2015, p. 2.

[165] Picard 1997, p. 47.

[166] Calvo 2015, p. 4.

[167] Marechal et al. 2019, pp. 314, 315.

[168] Kanjo et al. 2015, pp. 1197, 1204.

[169] Cohn and De La Torre 2015, p. 132.

Fig. 3.6 Facial movements and hypothesised 'basic' emotion categories illustrated by Barret et al. [170] [*Source* Barrett et al. 2019]

Emotion	Example photo	Action units	Physical description
Fear	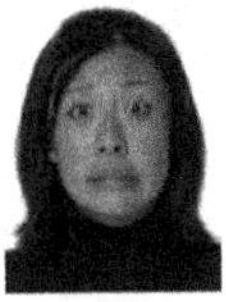	$1+2+4+5+7+20+25$	Eyebrows raised and pulled together, upper eyelid raised, lower eyelid tense, lips parted and stretched
Happiness		$6+7+12+25+26$	Duchenne display

Fig. 3.7 Facial expression examples for basic emotions 'fear' and 'happiness', the corresponding FACS action units and physical descriptions for each expression illustrated by Keltner et al. [171] [*Source* Keltner et al. 2019]

classified into emotion categories by matching facial events with emotional events coded from previous empirical studies.[172] Figure 3.7 provides some examples of AUs.

Computer scientists use computer vision and graphics to automatically analyse and synthesise facial expression in Automated Face Analysis (AFA) systems. AFA systems seek to detect emotions by typically following four steps: face detection, face registration, feature extraction and classification or regression.[173] Most of the current approaches use supervised learning,[174] with a tendency to also make use of Deep Learning and ANN methods.[175] Fully automatic FACS coding systems use state-of-the-art machine learning techniques that arguably can recognise any facial action.[176]

---

[170] Barrett et al. 2019, pp. 1, 19.

[171] Keltner et al. 2019, pp. 133, 142.

[172] Rosenberg 2005, pp. 14, 16.

[173] Valstar 2015, p. 144.

[174] Cohn and De La Torre 2015, p. 137.

[175] Tzirakis et al. 2015, p. 1.

[176] Bartlett et al. 2005, p. 395.

Real world examples include the Emotion Analysis API[177] of the company Kairos[178] which is offered to casinos, restaurants, retail merchants and companies in the hospitality sector.[179] The Amazon 'Rekognition' API offers similar image and video analysis for the purpose of emotion detection.[180] A notable EU funded research project concerning an automated border control system called iBorderCtrl "analyses the micro-gestures of travellers to figure out if the interviewee is lying".[181] Lie detector systems are essentially based on affective computing technology.[182] HireVue's video interview software analyses the emotions a candidate portrays during the video-assessment[183] based on affective computing and AFA components.

It must be noted that this approach is problematic since the meaning of an expression depends on the context. For example, smiles accompanied by cheek raising express enjoyment, the same smile combined with head lowering and turning to the side convey embarrassment. Furthermore, facial expressions may be posed or faked.[184]

3.3.4.2 Speech in Affective Computing

Emotions of a person may be measured and quantified by observing speech signals of this person. This is exactly what speech-based emotion recognition systems aim at. Such systems are based on insights gained from research that investigates the emotional speech production mechanisms.[185] Research in emotion recognition has shown that emotions in speech are related to prosody features,[186] such as pitch and

---

[177] A set of functions and procedures allowing the creation of applications that access features or data of an operating system, application or other service, see https://www.lexico.com/definition/api. Accessed 3 August 2020.

[178] See https://www.kairos.com/docs/api/#get-v2media. Accessed 10 September 2021.

[179] Pascu L (2019) New Kairos Facial Recognition Camera Offers Customer Insights, https://www.biometricupdate.com/201909/new-kairos-facial-recognition-camera-offers-customer-insights. Accessed 10 September 2021.

[180] See https://aws.amazon.com/about-aws/whats-new/2019/08/amazon-rekognition-improves-face-analysis/. Accessed 10 September 2021.

[181] Note that the system is only a research project funded by the EU under the H2020 programme and it remains to be seen whether it will be used at the border in the future. European Commission (2018), Smart lie-detection system to tighten EU's busy borders, https://ec.europa.eu/research/infocentre/article_en.cfm?artid=49726 Accessed 10 September 2021.

[182] Chen A and Hao K (2020) Emotion AI researchers say overblown claims give their work a bad name, https://www.technologyreview.com/2020/02/14/844765/ai-emotion-recognition-affective-computing-hirevue-regulation-ethics// Accessed 10 September 2021.

[183] Mondragon N et al. (2019) The Next Generation of Assessments, http://hrlens.org/wp-content/uploads/2019/11/The-Next-Generation-of-Assessments-HireVue-White-Paper.pdf. Accessed 10 September 2021.

[184] Cohn and De La Torre 2015, p. 132.

[185] Lee et al. 2015, p. 171.

[186] For prosody, see Sect. 3.3.2 above.

energy.[187] Research has demonstrated specific associations between emotions such as fear, anger, sadness and joy, and measures of pitch, voice level and speech rate.[188] Pitch is a perceptual property of a signal. The pitch of a sound is the mental sensation of fundamental frequency. If a sound has a higher frequency, it is generally perceived as having a higher pitch.[189] The pitch of speech associated with emotions such as anger or happiness is higher than the pitch of speech associated with emotions such as sadness or disappointment.[190] In terms of speech rate, it has been shown that if the person who speaks is in an emotional state of anger or fear, his or her speech is normally faster. If the person is bored or sad, then the speech is typically slower. Hence, effects of emotion tend to be present in features such as average pitch, pitch range and pitch changes, speech rate, voice quality and articulation.[191] Approaches in affective computing extract these acoustic signal features that characterise emotional speech. Machine learning algorithms map the automatically derived acoustic features described before to the desired emotion representations.[192] Research in this field aims to extract features from the voice to detect depressive people[193] or candidates stress levels during job interviews by means of machine learning and ANN.[194] Also recent methods applied to speech emotion recognition involve deep learning approaches.[195]

3.3.5 Automated Reasoning

Automated reasoning aims to develop computers that can use stored information to answer questions and to draw new conclusions.[196] It may be described as the science of developing methods that intend to replace human reasoning by procedures that perform individual reasoning automatically.[197] Automated reasoning is devoted to answering questions from diverse data without human intervention and also includes decision making. As a form of reasoning, decision making focuses on an autonomous agent trying to fulfil a task for a human.[198] Reasoning problems are of practical significance, they arise naturally in many applications that interact with the world, for example reasoning about knowledge in science or natural language processing. Furthermore, reasoning algorithms form the foundation of theoretical

---

[187] Calix et al. 2012, pp. 530, 531.

[188] Sobin and Alpert 1999, p. 347.

[189] Jurafsky and Martin 2014, p. 238.

[190] Chuang and Wu 2004, pp. 45, 62.

[191] Picard 1997, pp. 179, 180.

[192] Lee et al. 2015, p. 173, 177.

[193] Zbancioc and Feraru 2015, p. 1.

[194] Tomba et al. 2018, p. 560.

[195] Fayek et al. 2017, p. 60.

[196] Russell and Norvig 2016, p. 2.

[197] Jebelean 2009, p. 63.

[198] Eyal 2014, p. 191.

investigations into General AI (human level AI).[199] Reasoning is the process of obtaining new knowledge from given knowledge, in which certain transformation rules are applied that depend only on knowledge and which can be done exclusively in the brain without involving senses.[200] Research in automated reasoning focuses on logical reasoning, probabilistic reasoning and common sense reasoning.[201] Logical reasoning attempts to avoid any unjustified assumptions and confine itself to inferences that are infallible and beyond reasonable dispute.[202] Probabilistic reasoning deals with uncertainty about knowledge and belief. Uncertainty may be approached by applying tools from probability theory and statistics. Research in probabilistic reasoning focuses on the representation of different types of uncertainty and uncertain knowledge, reasoning with these types of knowledge, and learning them. It facilitates the development of applied systems of practical importance, such as machine vision, medical diagnosis and natural language processing. Probabilistic reasoning models are close to machine learning and serve as a medium between machine learning and automated reasoning.[203] For a very long time, scientists and philosophers have tried to understand and formalise human reasoning and whether reasoning methods may be automated.[204] Common sense reasoning constitutes a central part of human behaviour and is a precondition for human intelligence. Unsurprisingly, the creation of systems that exhibit common sense reasoning is a central goal towards achieving general AI. The history of AI has proven that it is more difficult to develop systems with common sense reasoning capabilities compared to systems that solve explicit reasoning problems, such as chess-playing programs or expert systems that assist in clinical diagnosis. Part of this difficulty is due to the all-encompassing aspect of common-sense reasoning: it requires many different kinds of knowledge. Furthermore, most common-sense knowledge is implicit and therefore difficult to explain and compute, unlike expert knowledge which is usually explicit. Hence, implicit common-sense knowledge has to be made explicit in order to develop common-sense reasoning systems.[205] Common-sense reasoning capabilities are still a challenge in AI applications, as the AI Index 2018 indicates.[206] According to Etzioni, who oversees the Allen Institute for Artificial Intelligence, AI "is devoid of common sense".[207] Hence, to acquire common sense from massive amounts of data and implementing it in intelligent systems appears to be the next frontier in AI.[208]

[199] Ibid.

[200] Jebelean 2009, p. 63.

[201] Eyal 2014, p. 193.

[202] Harrison 2009, p. 1.

[203] Eyal 2014, p. 201.

[204] Gavanelli and Mancini 2013, p. 113.

[205] Davis and Morgenstern 2004, p. 1.

[206] Shoham et al. 2018, p. 64.

[207] Metz P (2018) Paul Allen Wants to Teach Machines Common Sense, https://www.nytimes.com/2018/02/28/technology/paul-allen-ai-common-sense.html. Accessed 10 September 2021.

[208] Tandon et al. 2017, p. 49.

3.4 Conclusion

This chapter outlined that AI covers a broad range of disciplines, approaches and techniques. In this chapter, we focused on five major AI disciplines relevant for lawyers: Machine Learning, Automated Reasoning, Computer Vision, Affective Computing and Natural Language Processing.

As a major discipline of AI, machine learning is focused on computers that program themselves based on experience. Machine learning can be applied by means of several methods, ranging from supervised to unsupervised to reinforcement learning. Deep learning is a very promising kind of machine learning considering that the achievements in the field have been reached with automated neural networks (ANNs) comprising an astonishingly small number of neurons when compared with neural networks of the human brain. By means of natural language processing, machines can process human language. Natural language processing significantly contributes to improved interactions between machines and humans. Computer vision facilitates the automated understanding of visual images and thus enables machines to see. Face recognition, which is one of the applications of computer vision, empowers machines to identify or verify the identity of humans in images or videos based on biometric data. Because emotions form an important factor of human intelligence and daily life, affective computing aims to equip machines with emotional capabilities. Approaches in affective computing to derive emotions from facial expressions and speech may be easily deployed and widely used. Efforts in the discipline of automated reasoning strive to perform individual reasoning automatically.

This chapter demonstrates that AI is an exciting, challenging and complex domain. Artificial Intelligence develops at a tremendous pace. However, these exciting developments inevitably lead to legal, ethical, and societal issues, which are examined in-depth in the following chapters.

References

Abhang P et al (2016) Introduction to EEG- and speech-based emotion recognition. Elsevier Inc, London.

Alonso E (2014) Actions and agents. In: Frankish K, Ramsey W (eds) The Cambridge Handbook of Artificial Intelligence. Cambridge University Press, Cambridge.

Alpaydin E (2016) Machine Learning: The New AI. MIT Press, Cambridge.

Amit Y et al (2021) Object Detection. In: Ikeuchi K (ed) Computer Vision—A Reference Guide. Springer, Boston.

Barrett LF et al (2019) Emotional Expressions Reconsidered. Psychological Science in the Public Interest 20(1):1–68.

Bartlett M et al (2005) Toward Automatic Recognition of Spontaneous Facial Actions. In: Ekman P, Rosenberg E (eds) What the Face Reveals. OUP, Oxford.

Bellman R (1978) An Introduction to Artificial Intelligence: Can computers think? Boyd & Faser, San Francisco.

Bernhardt C (2016) Turing's Vision: The Birth of Computer Science. MIT Press, Cambridge.

Bishop C (2006) Pattern Recognition and Machine Learning. Springer, New York.

Calders T, Custers B (2013) What is Data Mining and How Does it Work? In: Custers B et al (eds) Discrimination and Privacy in the Information Society. Springer, Berlin.

Calix R et al (2012) Detection of Affective States from Text and Speech For Real-Time Human-Computer Interaction. Human Factors and Ergonomics Society 54(4):530–545.

Calvo R et al (2015) Introduction to Affective Computing. In: Calvo R et al (eds) The Oxford Handbook of Affective Computing. OUP, Oxford.

Chen A, Hao K (2020) Emotion AI researchers say overblown claims give their work a bad name. https://www.technologyreview.com/2020/20/14/844765/ai-emotion-recognition-affective-computing-hirevue-regulation-ethics//. Accessed 10 September 2021

Chow T, Cho SY (2007) Neural Networks and Computing: Learning Algorithms and Applications. Imperial College Press, London

Chuang Z, Wu C (2004) Multi-Modal Emotion Recognition from Speech and Text. (2004) Vol. 9 No. 2 Computational Linguistics and Chinese Language Processing 9(2):45–62.

Cohn J, De La Torre F (2015) Automated Face Analysis for Affective Computing. In: Calvo R et al (eds) The Oxford Handbook of Affective Computing. OUP, Oxford.

Das S et al (2015) Applications of Artificial Intelligence in Machine Learning: Review and Prospect. 15), IJCA 115(9):31–41.

Davis E, Morgenstern L (2004) Introduction: Progress in formal commonsense reasoning. Artificial Intelligence 153:1–12.

De Laat P (2017) Algorithmic Decision-Making based on Machine Learning from Big Data: Can Transparency restore Accountability. Philos. Technol 31(4):525–541.

Deng L, Liu Y (2018) A Joint Introduction to Natural Language Processing and Deep Learning. In: Deng L, Liu Y (eds) Deep learning in natural language processing. Springer, Singapore.

Deng L, Liu Y (2018) Epilogue: Frontiers of NLP in the Deep Learning Era. In: Deng L, Liu Y (eds) Deep learning in natural language processing. Springer, Singapore.

Engelbrecht A (2007) Computational Intelligence – An Introduction. John Wiley & Sons, Hoboken.

Eyal A (2014) Reasoning and decision making. In: Frankish K, Ramsey W (eds) The Cambridge Handbook of Artificial Intelligence. Cambridge University Press, Cambridge.

Fayek H et al (2017) Evaluating deep learning architectures for Speech Emotion Recognition. Neural Networks 92:60–68.

François-Lavet V et al (2018) An Introduction to Deep Reinforcement Learning. Foundations and Trends in Machine Learning 11 (3-4):2–140.

Franklin S (2014) History, motivations, and core themes. In: Frankish K, Ramsey W (eds) The Cambridge Handbook of Artificial Intelligence. Cambridge University Press, Cambridge.

Gavanelli M, Mancini T (2013) Automated Reasoning. Intelligenza Artificiale 7(2):113–124.

Goldberg Y (2017) Neural Network Methods in Natural Language Processing. Morgan & Claypool Publishers, San Rafael.

Goodfellow I et al (2016) Deep Learning. MIT Press, Cambridge www.deeplearningbook.org Accessed 10 September 2021.

Harrison J (2009) Handbook of Practical Logic and Automated Reasoning. Cambridge University Press, Cambridge.

Hastie T et al (2008) The Elements of Statistical Learning. Springer, New York.

Heigold G et al (2015) End-to-End Text-Dependent Speaker Verification. https://arXiv.org/pdf/1509.08062.pdf Accessed 10 September 2021.

Hernández-Orallo J (2017) Evaluation in Artificial Intelligence: from task-oriented to ability-oriented measurement. Artificial Intelligence Review 48:397–447.

Hourri S, Kharroubi J (2020) A deep learning approach for speaker recognition. International Journal of Speech and Technology 23(1):123–131.

Jampani V (2017) Learning Inference Models for Computer Vision. https://publikationen.uni-tuebingen.de/xmlui/handle/10900/76486 Accessed 10 September 2021.

Jebelean T et al (2009) Automated Reasoning. In: Buchberger B et al (eds) Hagenberg Research. Springer, Berlin.

Jurafsky D, Martin J (2014) Speech and Language Processing. Pearson Education Limited, New Jersey.

Kanjo E et al (2015) Emotions in context: examining pervasive affective sensing systems, applications, and analyses. Pers Ubiquit Comput 19:1197–1212.

Keltner D et al (2019) Emotional Expression: Advances in Basic Emotion Theory. Journal of Nonverbal Behaviour 43(2):133–160.

Kline R (2011) Cybernetics, Automata Studies, and the Dartmouth Conference on Artificial Intelligence. IEEE 33(4):5–16.

Kotu V, Bala D (2019) Data Science. Elsevier, Cambridge.

Kovač V et al (2019) Frame-based classification for cross-speed gait recognition. Multimedia Tools and Applications 78:5621–5643.

Kumar D et al (2019) Detecting item interaction and movement US Patent Number US 10268983. https://patentimages.storage.googleapis.com/01/0b/6e/de57009f5670ae/US2015001 9391A1.pdf Accessed 10 September 2021.

Lee C et al (2015) Speech in Affective Computing. The Oxford Handbook of Affective Computing. OUP, Oxford.

Li St, Jain A (2011) Introduction. In: Li S, Jain A (eds) Handbook of Face Recognition. Springer, London.

Marechal C et al (2019) Survey on AI-Based Multimodal Methods for Emotion Detection. In: Kołodziej J, González-Vélez H (eds) High-Performance Modelling and Simulation for Big Data Applications. Springer, Cham.

Marsland S (2015) Machine Learning: An Algorithmic Perspective. Chapman & Hall, Boca Raton.

Mary L (2019) Extraction of Prosody for Automatic Speaker, Language, Emotion and Speech Recognition. Springer International, Cham.

Mavroudis V, Veale M (2018) Eavesdropping Whilst You're Shopping: Balancing Personalisation and Privacy in Connected Retail Spaces. https://doi.org/10.1049/cp.2018.0018.

Metz P (2018) Paul Allen Wants to Teach Machines Common Sense. https://www.nytimes.com/ 2018/02/28/technology/paul-allen-ai-common-sense.html. Accessed 10 September 2021

Minsky M (1968) Semantic Information Processing. MIT Press, Cambridge.

Mitchell T (2006) The discipline of Machine Learning. http://www.cs.cmu.edu/~tom/pubs/Machin eLearning.pdf Accessed 10 September 2021.

Mohri M et al (2012) Foundations of Machine Learning. MIT Press, Cambridge.

Moses D et al (2019) Real-time decoding of question-and-answer speech dialogue using human cortical activity. Nature Communication 10:1-14.

Munakata T (2008) Fundamentals of the New Artificial Intelligence. Springer, London.

Murphy K (2012) Machine Learning: A Probabilistic Perspective. MIT Press, Cambridge.

Nielsen M (2015) Neural Networks and Deep Learning. Determination Press, http://neuralnetwor ksanddeeplearning.com/chap5.html Accessed 10 September 2021.

Nilsson N (2010) The Quest for Artificial Intelligence: A History of Ideas and Achievements. Cambridge University Press, Cambridge.

Pascu L (2019) New Kairos Facial Recognition Camera Offers Customer Insights. https://www. biometricupdate.com/201909/new-kairos-facial-recognition-camera-offers-customer-insights. Accessed 10 September 2021

Picard R (1997) Affective Computing. MIT Press, Cambridge.

Regan J (2016) New Zealand passport robot tells applicant of Asian descent to open eyes. https:// www.reuters.com/article/us-newzealand-passport-error/new-zealand-passport-robot-tells-applic ant-of-asian-descent-to-open-eyes-idUSKBN13W0RL. Accessed 10 September 2021

Rosenberg E (2005) Introduction: The Study of Spontaneous Facial Expressions in Psychology. In: Ekman P, Rosenberg E (eds) What the Face Reveals. OUP, Oxford.

Rumelhart D et al (1986) Learning representations by backpropagating errors. Nature 323:533–536.

Russell S, Norvig P (2016) Artificial Intelligence: A Modern Approach. Pearson Education Limited, Essex.

Serban I et al (2017) A Deep Reinforcement Learning Chatbot, https://arXiv.org/pdf/1709.02349. pdf Accessed 10 September 2021.

Shi Z 2011 Advanced Artificial Intelligence World Scientific Singapore 2011.

Shoham Y et al (2018) The AI Index 2018 Annual Report. https://hai.stanford.edu/sites/default/files/2020-10/AI_Index_2018_Annual_Report.pdf Accessed 10 September 2021.

Sobin C, Alpert M (1999) Emotion in Speech: The Acoustic Attributes of Fear, Anger, Sadness, and Joy. Journal of Psycholinguistic Research 28(4):347–365.

Sokolova A, Konushin A (2019) Methods of Gait Recognition in Video. Programming and Computer Software 45(4):213–220.

Strauß S (2018) From Big Data to Deep Learning: A Leap Towards Strong AI or Intelligentia Obscura. BDCC 2(3):2–16.

Sturari M et al (2016) Robust and affordable retail customer profiling by vision and radio beacon sensor fusion. Pattern Recognition Letters 81:30–40.

Szeliski R (2011) Computer Vision: Algorithms and Applications. Springer, London.

Tandon N et al (2017) Commonsense Knowledge in Machine Intelligence. SIGMOD Record 46(4):49–52.

Tomba K et al (2018), Stress Detection Through Speech Analysis. ICETE 1:394–398.

Tome P et al (2015) Facial soft biometric features for forensic face recognition. Forensic Science International 257:271–284.

Trigueros D et al (2018) Face recognition: From Traditional to Deep Learning Methods. https://arXiv.org/pdf/1811.00116.pdf Accessed 10 September 2021.

Tur G et al (2018) Deep Learning in Conversational Language Understanding. In: Deng L, Liu Y (eds) Deep learning in natural language processing. Springer, Singapore.

Turing A (1950) Computing Machinery and Intelligence. Mind LIX(236):433–460.

Tzirakis P et al (2015) End-to-End Multimodal Emotion Recognition using Deep Neural Networks. Journal of Latex Class Files 14(8):1–12.

Usuelli M (2014) R machine learning essentials. Packt Publishing, Birmingham.

Valstar M (2015) Automatic Facial Expression Analysis. In: Mandal M, Awasthi A (eds) Understanding Facial Expressions in Communication. Springer, New Delhi.

Warwick K (2012) Artificial Intelligence: The basics. Routledge, New York.

Welinder Y, Palmer A (2018) Face Recognition, Real-Time Identification, and Beyond. In: Selinger E et al (eds) The Cambridge Handbook of Consumer Privacy. Cambridge University Press, Cambridge.

Yang M et al (2015) Speech Reconstruction from Human Auditory Cortex with Deep Neural Networks. https://www.isca-speech.org/archive_v0/interspeech_2015/papers/i15_1121.pdf Accessed 10 September 2021.

Yoshida S (2011) Computer Vision. Nova Science Publisher Inc, Lancaster.

Zbancioc M, Feraru S (2015) A study about the automatic recognition of the anxiety emotional state using Emo-DB. DOI: https://doi.org/10.1109/EHB.2015.7391506.

Zuiderveen F (2019) Discrimination, artificial intelligence, and algorithmic decision-making. https://rm.coe.int/discrimination-artificial-intelligence-and-algorithmic-decision-making/168 0925d73 Accessed 10 September 2021.

Andreas Häuselmann is an external PhD candidate at eLaw, Center for Law and Digital Technologies at Leiden University. Next to his external PhD research, Andreas forms part of the Privacy and Cybersecurity practice at an international law firm located in Amsterdam. He holds a Master of Laws (LL.M.) in Information and Communication Technology Law from the University of Oslo and a Master of Laws (LL.M.) in Information Technology and Intellectual Property Law from the Leibniz University Hannover. Andreas is particularly interested in the legal and ethical issues of AI, with a focus on privacy and data protection law. One of his favourite topics is Affective Computing and the new class of data ('emotional data') it creates, and the question how such data is and should be protected under EU data protection law.

Part II
Public Law

Chapter 4
Discrimination by Machine-Based Decisions: Inputs and Limits of Anti-discrimination Law

Dolores Morondo Taramundi

Contents

Abstract The use of algorithm-based decisions is quickly expanding. These decisions have been shown to have a differentiated impact on traditional discrimination grounds such as sex, race and disability. Technical complexity, together with proprietary interest and economic calculations, make it very difficult to understand exactly how algorithms discriminate. Yet, anti-discrimination law has a specific category, namely, indirect discrimination, which focuses on discriminatory effects rather than on discriminatory treatment, and would seem applicable to algorithmic discrimination. The application of indirect discrimination to algorithm-based decisions is determined by how certain elements and requirements have been developed in EU anti-discrimination law and in the European Union Court of Justice's case law. It is argued that the assessment of these elements and requirements might offer useful insights for a critical theory of anti-discrimination law.

Keywords algorithmic discrimination · EU anti-discrimination law · indirect discrimination · structural discrimination · stereotyping · transparency

4.1 Introduction

Automated and semi-automated decisions are increasingly frequent in all areas of life. Both public administrations and private companies use algorithms designed to assist in, or substitute for, human decision makers. Algorithm-based solutions can be

D. Morondo Taramundi (✉)
Human Rights Institute, University of Deusto, Bilbao, Spain
e-mail: dolores.morondo@deusto.es

© T.M.C. ASSER PRESS and the authors 2022
B. Custers and E. Fosch-Villaronga (eds.), *Law and Artificial Intelligence*,
Information Technology and Law Series 35,
https://doi.org/10.1007/978-94-6265-523-2_4

found in education and in the labour market, including in the selection of students by universities or recruitment processes to fill vacancies[1]; in the social services sector, in making decisions regarding applications for subsidies or benefits, or determining social protection needs[2]; and even in very sensitive areas of government power, such as when the police must establish the credibility of a complaint or the likelihood that victims of domestic violence will be attacked again, in terms of giving them access to adequate preventive and protection measures.[3] Algorithm-based solutions promise to curb the arbitrariness and inconsistency of human decision makers, assess volumes of data in timeframes which would be impossible for human minds, and all at a much lower cost. Automated decision-making is thus presented as a tool for increasing accuracy and efficiency, both in terms of the content and quality of the decisions (better decisions, data-based and consistent throughout the set), and in terms of the decision-making process (faster, more economical, better informed, free of human error or negligence, arbitrariness, or prejudice).

Algorithms are mathematical sets of instructions aimed at solving a class of problems or perform calculations. The scientific literature has elaborated on the description and classification of different kinds of algorithms and related IT techniques that might interact with human decision-makers.[4] Rule-based algorithms, for example, have been studied by legal philosophers since the 1980s in the hope of easing or helping with adjudication-related tasks. The failure of early attempts to achieve significant practical results has been explained by arguing that the Law and legal decisions have important semantic and pragmatic dimensions that are different from algorithmic models, which are based on the logical functions of language.[5] The techniques of natural language processing have sought to close this gap so that current expert systems can operate with multiple functions that allow for automating data and documents and providing intelligent assistance.[6] Still greater potential is to be

---

[1] For example Köchling and Wehner 2020. The impact of algorithmic decision-making in the labour market has been assessed in reports commissioned by the International Labour Organisation (De Stefano 2018) and the European Commission (Wood 2021); regarding the use of algorithmic decision-making in higher education, Prinsloo 2020.

[2] In *Automating Inequality*, Virginia Eubanks investigates three cases of automated and semi-automated decision making in access to social benefits in the USA (Eubanks 2018).

[3] For example, the VioGén system used by the Spanish Police, gathers personal, social, police and judicial information for each case of intimate partner violence, makes predictions as to the level of risk of the victims, establishes the protection measures related to the risk level and alerts of relevant information (for example, when the aggressor gets out of prison).

[4] See, for example, the results of the project e-SIDES (Ethical and societal impacts of data science), available at https://e-sides.eu/ (Accessed 5 July 2021).

[5] Martino 2019.

[6] See, for example, PROMETEA, an Artificial Intelligence (AI) expert system created by the Public Prosecutor's Office in Buenos Aires, Argentina (https://mpfciudad.gob.ar/institucional/2020-03-09-18-42-38-innovacion-e-inteligencia-artificial). Performance results of PROMETEA indicate that the Public Prosecutor's Office has increased its processing rate by 275% between 2017 and 2018,

found with machine-learning algorithms. Machine-learning systems define their own sets of rules based on data outputs. In contrast to deterministic rule-based systems, data-driven machine learning systems are probabilistic and try to solve problems by detecting information patterns in big data analysis.

Algorithm-based decisions—as any other decision—might affect human rights and fundamental freedoms in a number of ways. A recent Dutch court decision,[7] for example, stopped the algorithm-based Dutch Welfare fraud surveillance system on grounds of bias and human rights violations. In comparison to biased decisions made by human beings on their own, automated and semi-automated decisions based on discriminatory criteria pose a problem of scale, since they apply decisions faster and to a larger number of individuals, reducing the likelihood of identifying and addressing the problem in a timely manner. Machine-learning algorithms may also discriminate on a large scale through solutions that reproduce inequality patterns embedded in the data from which they learn.[8]

As political concern about the ethical implications of the use of AI increases, the scientific scholarship on the subject is also expanding, with interdisciplinary contributions from practitioners from various fields (IT, Engineering, and Law). Although most of the scholarship focuses on violations of rights (such as privacy or criminal law general principles) that occur in the use, misuse or fraudulent use of IT, algorithmic discrimination has started to attract attention. So far, most of the research on algorithms and discrimination has focused on the US context,[9] and only more recently has attention been paid to EU anti-discrimination law.[10]

This chapter investigates the EU's anti-discrimination response to algorithmic discrimination. Based on a critical theory of anti-discrimination law, the objective of the chapter is to examine how indirect discrimination applies to algorithmic discrimination. Section 4.2 briefly introduces the concept of indirect discrimination in EU law. Section 4.3 examines the potential and the shortcomings of this category to address algorithmic discrimination; and Section 4.4 presents some conclusions drawn from this discussion, which could feed back into a critical theory of anti-discrimination law.

---

as using PROMETEA means that a file can be processed in 5 days instead of 3 months. See Solar Cayón 2020.

[7] Judgment of The Hague District Court of 5 February 2020, ECLI:NL:RBDHA:2020:1878.

[8] Xenidis and Senden 2020.

[9] Barocas and Selbst 2016; Gillis and Spiess 2019, and the bibliography cited there.

[10] Hacker 2018; Zuiderveen Borgesius 2020; Xenidis and Senden 2020. To be noted also the reports commissioned by the Council of Europe (Zuiderveen Borgesius 2018) and by the European Commission (Gerards and Xenidis 2020).

4.2   Indirect Discrimination

EU law, the European Convention of Human Rights, and constitutional law across European countries prohibit discrimination.[11] Discrimination is generally understood as a violation of the principle of equal treatment and is, therefore, equated with less beneficial or disadvantageous treatment given to some individuals on the basis of prohibited grounds, such as sex, race or ethnic origin, religious affiliation, sexual orientation, and disability.

When assessing discrimination by algorithms, a number of reactions can be found which point at the difficulties in establishing the relationship between anti-discrimination law and algorithm-based decisions. It is sometimes argued that algorithms do not discriminate[12]: they cannot do so because they are only mathematics, they just collect and process data; an argument that has been graphically expressed as 'garbage in, garbage out'.[13] The differentiated impact along prohibited discrimination lines such as sex, race or ethnic origin, disability and age, which algorithmic-based decisions have been shown to have,[14] is thus blamed on structural inequalities embedded in the data used by algorithms. It has been argued that the training samples used for machine-learning systems may be biased, or the data to which the system has access reflects engrained social hierarchies, mis- or under-representation of certain social groups, unequal distribution of goods, opportunities and burdens, and so on. It could also happen that designers and developers of AI models introduce their own biases and prejudices (of which they may be unaware). They may unintentionally incorporate these when they design models or prepare training samples. In any case, it seems too difficult to prove any of this: biases and stereotypes might be unintended, or if intentional, they might be hidden or masked in very complex coding. Algorithms may yield discriminatory results for some groups, not by using a prohibited category as a variable, but through proxies and correlations established within the context of big data, and thus very difficult—if not impossible—to trace back or review. Algorithm models are frequently termed 'black boxes' both because the complexity of their coding impedes transparency and accessibility, and because they are products protected by intellectual property law, so developers and clients are generally uninclined to open them up to the public gaze.

The existing literature considers it unlikely that elements such as sex or other forbidden grounds of discrimination could be used in the algorithm coding, thus

---

[11] For the purposes of this chapter, references to domestic law are limited to Spain. For a broader view of anti-discrimination law in different European countries, country reports and comparative reports of the European network of legal experts in gender equality and non-discrimination can be consulted at https://www.equalitylaw.eu/.

[12] The tendency to believe computers has been sometimes called "automation bias", Zuiderveen Borgesius 2018.

[13] Xenidis and Senden 2020, p. 157.

[14] Köchling and Wehner 2020; Barocas and Selbst 2016.

creating cases of direct discrimination.[15] Unlike US anti-discrimination law, discriminatory intent is irrelevant in EU anti-discrimination law; consequently, intentional and implicit biases by developers or decision-makers would play no role in qualifying the situation as direct discrimination. Direct discrimination occurs when protected characteristics are used to grant differentiated treatment.

In the context of algorithmic decision-making, especially in the case of machine-learning, a decision would be unlikely to be made on the basis of a protected characteristic, since solutions usually take into account a multitude of factors and variables statistically correlated across large volumes of data.[16] It has been noted that risk is exactly the opposite, that discrimination becomes more 'fine-grained' and highly intersectional, and exceeds the limited number of protected categories.[17] Furthermore, the proof that an algorithm was based on protected characteristics and thus discriminated directly would be hindered by the lack of transparency of algorithmic models, due both to their complexity and to the unwillingness of the firms to disclose the codes of the algorithmic models they are using. Although the signal sent out by the CJEU in *Meister*[18] fell short of supporting transparency, other EU organs[19] and domestic Courts[20] have stressed that transparency is an integral part of the obligations enshrined in the prohibition of discrimination.

However, anti-discrimination law has a specific category, i.e., indirect discrimination, which focuses on the *effects* of norms, criteria and practices that might not be prima facie discriminatory (as they apply to everyone indistinctly), but they have a differentiated effect on individuals of protected groups. The category of indirect discrimination was introduced into EU anti-discrimination law by the CJEU in the mid-1970s and early 1980s, in relation to nationality and sex. In the latter case, it was held that indirect discrimination occurred because of the less beneficial treatment of part-time workers and of workers with parental responsibilities. In particular, this indirectly affected women who, because of the sexual division of labour and care work, constituted most of the part-time workforce and of the workers that took parental leave. Under Article 2(1)(b) of Directive 2006/54/EC,[21] indirect discrimination is defined as the situation 'where an apparently neutral provision, criterion or

---

[15] For example, Hacker 2018.

[16] Hacker 2018, p. 1151.

[17] Xenidis and Senden 2020, p. 163.

[18] In *Meister*, the CJEU ruled that a right to recruitment information does not exist vis-à-vis the employer. CJEU Judgement of 19 April 2012, *Meister*, ECLI:EU:C:2012:217.

[19] The European Commission Recommendation on equal pay of 2014, for example, established a right of access to information for workers to know salary levels segregated by sex and category through workers' representatives. European Commission Recommendation of 7 March 2014 on strengthening the principle of equal pay between men and women through transparency, https://eur-lex.europa.eu/legal-content/EN/TXT/PDF/?uri=CELEX:32014H0124&from=EN. Accessed 2 April 2021.

[20] Judgment of the Spanish Supreme Court, of 18 July 2011, ECLI:ES:TS:2011/5798.

[21] Directive 2006/54/EC of the European Parliament and of the Council of 5 July 2006 on the implementation of the principle of equal opportunities and equal treatment of men and women in matters of employment and occupation (recast). There are similar definitions in Council Directive 2000/43/EC of 29 June 2000 implementing the principle of equal treatment between persons

practice would put persons of one sex at a particular disadvantage compared with persons of the other sex, unless that provision, criterion or practice is objectively justified by a legitimate aim, and the means of achieving that aim are appropriate and necessary'.

By shifting the focus from treatment to effects, indirect discrimination makes it possible to bypass the problems related to the 'black-box' effect mentioned earlier. When the criteria for the correlations made by machine-learning models cannot be known because their structure is too complex, or because the firm or the developer is unwilling to disclose them, a case of indirect discrimination can still be made. Indirect discrimination does not focus on whether protected categories had a role in the results offered by the algorithm; rather, it focuses on the effects that the algorithm-based decision had on certain groups. The proof of indirect discrimination does not require assessing the criteria or the variables that the algorithmic model uses, but ascertaining the disadvantage or the differentiated impact that the application of the algorithmic model has on members of protected groups.

This focus on the effects makes indirect discrimination suitable also for those situations in which algorithms use proxies for establishing correlations with protected groups, when biased training data are used, or when there is an 'unequal truth ground', that is when the available data mis- or under-represents certain social groups. In these cases, indirect discrimination is also established by showing that the application of the algorithm has a discriminatory impact even without knowing how the bias was introduced into the model.

4.3   Addressing Algorithmic Discrimination Through Indirect Discrimination: Potential Shortcomings

While indirect discrimination might seem straightforwardly applicable to algorithmic discrimination, there are a number of technical issues which should be considered more closely.

To start with, it may be difficult even to establish a prima facie case of indirect discrimination. In the context of algorithmic discrimination (as in many other instances of indirect discrimination) group disadvantage may not be easy to prove. The CJEU has ruled that indirect discrimination does not require a comparison of 'similarly situated groups',[22] since the neutral rule produces disparate impacts precisely because groups are not similarly situated. However, in order to argue that a seemingly neutral rule or criterion causes a disadvantage, the disadvantaged group has to be identified and a pool of suitable comparators needs to be established. As

irrespective of racial or ethnic origin and Council Directive 2000/78/EC of 27 November 2000 establishing a general framework for equal treatment in employment and occupation, which covers the grounds of religion or belief, disability, age and sexual orientation.

[22] CJEU Judgment of 10 March 2005, *Vasiliki Nikoloudi* v *Organismos Tilepikoinonion Ellados*, ECLI:EU:C:2005:141; CJEU Judgment of 17 July 2014, *Leone*, ECLI:EU:C:2014:2090.

noted earlier, algorithmic discrimination might create refined and highly intersectional categories which make the identification of a disadvantaged group linked to a protected category much more difficult. EU law and many domestic jurisdictions do not have specific provisions for multiple or intersectional discrimination, and this further aggravates the position of members of 'finer-grained' categories to argue that they are representative of a protected category.[23]

The pool of suitable comparators and the frames of reference[24] are also affected by the scope and the volume of data on which algorithm-based decisions are made. Even if comparators can be hypothetical, the determination of the disadvantage is sometimes impaired by the comparison level. In part-time work cases, for example, the percentage of women working part-time at national level might not be considered relevant for establishing the disadvantage of women working part-time in an industrial sector, in a given firm, or in a specific job category within the firm.[25]

Here again the lack of access to relevant information for individual claimants appears to play a fundamental role. The lack of information for establishing the disadvantage in the case of algorithmic information has much in common with cases of indirect discrimination. These commonalities point to the shortcomings that individual litigation-based strategies have when it comes to challenging indirect discrimination. In Spain, for example, there are almost no cases of indirect discrimination affecting structural issues such as labour market sex segregation and the gender salary gap. Victims of indirectly discriminatory practices are not, generally, in a position to understand the (economic, social, legal) processes that have put them in a disadvantaged position, let alone to gather evidence and resources (time, knowledge, money) to bring forward legal claims.

It is therefore necessary that cases with a significant collective dimension are tackled by public policy. This can be done by establishing monitoring bodies and mechanisms that assess the effects of algorithm-based decisions on the rights and opportunities of different groups; by granting legal standing to interest associations, public authorities and trade unions to bring cases before the courts; or by exerting public pressure on designated authorities (such as equality institutes, data protection agencies, labour inspectorates, trade unions, consumer protection offices) to produce statistics and information that might be used by victims in court and to prosecute cases on their own. Universities also have a role to play in research and knowledge dissemination on ethical issues regarding AI. If we do not have data and assessments on how AI affects fundamental rights and social justice, it might appear that AI is objective, natural or unavoidable, that it is impossible to have or ask for different, non-discriminatory algorithms.

A second problematic issue is that the definition of indirect discrimination has an exception clause. Indirect discrimination prohibits neutral rules or practices which have a disadvantageous effect on members of protected groups, *unless* the rule or practice can be objectively justified.

---

[23] MacKinnon 2013, pp. 1021–1023.

[24] Mulder 2020, p. 125.

[25] CJEU Judgment of 8 May 2019, *Villar Láiz*, ECLI:EU:C:2019:382.

Objective justification is fraught with difficulties. The concept has changed over the years in the CJEU's case law.[26] Initially, it required the employer to show that the apparently neutral rule or practice that had a disadvantageous impact on members of protected groups was based on reasons unrelated to discrimination. This requirement seemed to refer to what was known as 'covert discrimination', in that the employer could keep the rule or practice in place if it could be shown that the rule was not a means to bypass the prohibition of discrimination by using a proxy with practically the same effect as the protected ground would have had, even if it produced a disadvantageous effect on members of protected groups.

Over time, the objective justification requirement has been structured by the CJEU as a proportionality test with a three-step assessment: the measure must serve a legitimate aim, it must be appropriate, and it must be necessary.

The opportunities offered by objective justification undermine the effort to categorise algorithmic discrimination as indirect discrimination.[27] Some authors have argued that the predictive function of algorithmic decision-making would in itself provide a legitimate aim (such as the measurement of job performance or credit worthiness) and appear as appropriate to that aim.[28] Even the proportionality test, the requirement to show that the algorithm model used was necessary and that a less harmful model was not available (using less biased data or less discriminatory proxies), is considered relatively easy to overcome. In addition, judges will have a hard task running a proportionality test to strike a balance between the highly technical explanations in relation to the algorithmic model and the trade-offs in terms of costs, predictive accuracy and potential biases in alternative models.[29]

Notwithstanding both the weight of these arguments and the CJEU's case law, which has often failed to address structural issues of inequality through indirect discrimination,[30] there are some arguments around objective justification which should be closely regarded.

Firstly, it must be noted that algorithms' 'predictive accuracy' is equivalent to probabilistic estimation. Regardless of how complex machine-learning algorithms might be from a technical point of view, their solutions are based on probability. There are numerous debates on the margin of error of these calculations when they are based on data that is biased, does not represent groups equally, or is not applicable outside the controlled setting in which the model was developed; on the technical difficulties to detect these errors[31]; and on the design of tools to address them.[32] Beyond these debates, it is necessary to examine the idea that businesses and administrations adopt algorithmic decision-making to cut costs and reduce time and effort. And this is not

---

[26] Tobler 2005, p. 183; Ellis and Watson 2012, p. 169; Collins 2018, p. 258 ff.

[27] Hacker 2018, p. 1161; Xenidis and Senden 2020, p. 182.

[28] Hacker 2018, pp. 1161–1162.

[29] Hacker 2018, p. 1161; Xenidis and Senden 2020, p. 182.

[30] CJEU Judgment of 15 December 1994, *Helmig*, ECLI:EU:C:1994:415; CJEU Judgment of 14 September 1999, *Gabriele Gruber*, ECLI:EU:C:1999:405.

[31] Hacker 2018.

[32] Hajian et al. 2015; Hajian and Domingo i Ferrer 2013.

necessarily a legitimate aim in terms of justifying indirect discrimination. The CJEU has rejected purely financial aims within the context of objective justification,[33] and even if the prohibition of indirect discrimination does not amount to a duty to ensure substantive equality by employers, it might hold them accountable to the extent that they exploit or benefit from structural inequalities.[34]

Secondly, the burden of proof is on the decision-maker that has chosen to deploy an automated system. Questions related to responsibility will be examined next, but when a decision-maker is identified, the burden of proof for objective justification is on them, and the CJEU has ruled that what the employer has to provide objective justification for is the difference between those who consider themselves discriminated against and the comparators.[35]

Thirdly, another development in the case law of the CJEU that might be of importance in understanding objective justification of algorithmic discrimination is anti-stereotyping jurisprudence. The fact that solutions by data-driven algorithms are probabilistic and that they reflect structural inequalities might bring these cases close to the reasoning of stereotypes, where individuals are evaluated through characteristics they have in common with others, regardless of their pertinence to the individual situation. Correlations play an important role both in stereotypes and in algorithms, as does analogous reasoning. The CJEU's approach to gender stereotyping is fragmentary and inconsistent,[36] but it has shown that it has some potential to disrupt stereotyped justifications.[37]

A third problematic issue in the application of anti-discrimination law to algorithmic decisions is the difficulty in establishing who is responsible for the eventual discriminatory effects of the decisions. It is sometimes argued that algorithms do not discriminate, because they are only mathematics.[38] This is a non-technical understanding of discrimination, which equates discrimination with discriminatory intent (which algorithms certainly do not have), but, as has already been discussed, it is beside the point in EU anti-discrimination law and, especially, in relation to indirect discrimination. However, even if it is not intent that determines responsibility, the CJEU has ruled that there must be a link between the acts of an employer and the effects in order to establish responsibility.[39]

In this regard, there are various solutions available. In existing case law on indirect discrimination in job promotion, for example, the Spanish Supreme Court has ruled that a system of promotion that lacked even minimal transparency constituted

---

[33] CJEU Judgment of 17 October 1989, *Danfoss*, ECLI:EU:C:1989:383 paras 18–22.

[34] Schiek 2007, pp. 441–443.

[35] CJEU Judgment of 28 February 2013, *Kenny and Others*, ECLI:EU:C:2013:122 para 38–41.

[36] Timmer 2016.

[37] CJEU Judgment of 30 September 2010, *Roca Álvarez*, ECLI:EU:C:2010:561; CJEU Judgment of 16 July 2015, *Maistrellis*, ECLI:EU:C:2015:47.

[38] See supra note 12.

[39] CJEU Judgment of 17 September 2002, *Lawrence and Others*, ECLI:EU:C:2002:498; CJEU Judgment of 13 January 2004, *Allonby*, ECLI:EU:C:2004:18.

indirect discrimination, as women were under-represented in the higher positions.[40] The lack of transparency would prevent the employer/decision-maker from giving a satisfactory justification for the decision.

Responsibility can also be attributed separately from the elements in the definition of indirect discrimination. The Guidelines of the Spanish Data Protection Agency,[41] for example, include the concept of proactive responsibility or accountability, which involves the obligation for the client/decision-maker to run a risk-based analysis, specifically concerning the risks to rights and freedoms, including the risks of bias in automated decision-making and algorithmic discrimination. Furthermore, these guidelines have established that any person that adopts a decision related to the use of AI cannot argue that they have insufficient information or technical knowledge to avoid responsibility; responsibility cannot be allocated to the developer or provider of the tool, and even less to the AI system itself. It is the client who is responsible for testing and auditing the treatment that is produced by the AI-based system.

4.4   Conclusions

Indirect discrimination can be applied to situations of algorithmic discrimination or discrimination produced by the use of automated or semi-automated decision-making. At the operational level, however, there are difficulties in applying anti-discrimination categories to real-life cases of algorithm-based decisions. Beyond the more technical aspects of how algorithms work, it is also important to address conceptual questions that these issues raise in relation to our understanding of discrimination and the function of anti-discrimination law.

One commonality between indirect discrimination and algorithmic discrimination is their relationship to structural patterns of inequality, social hierarchies which are embedded in every social arrangement, and the collective dimensions of disadvantages and privileges. Indirect discrimination has been argued to be different from direct discrimination, even a sui generis form of anti-discrimination law, precisely because it has the ability to reveal or to make evident structural forms of inequality.[42] It could also give impetus to anti-discrimination law and a potential mechanism for transforming inequality structures, rather than only addressing single instances of invidious treatment.[43]

---

[40] Judgment of the Spanish Supreme Court, of 18 July 2011, ECLI:ES:TS:2011/5798.

[41] Spanish Data Protection Agency (2020) Adecuación al RGPD de tratamientos que incorporan Inteligencia Artificial [Adaptation of treatments that incorporate Artificial Intelligence to the GDPR], www.aepd.es/sites/default/files/2020-02/adecuacion-rgpd-ia.pdf. Accessed 1 April 2021.

[42] Collins 2018.

[43] Fredman 2018.

The structural dimension of inequality at the basis of both indirect discrimination and algorithmic discrimination calls for questioning the limitations of the individualised litigation model which is the main tool in the implementation of the anti-discrimination directives.[44] The limitations to transparency and accessibility are a major operational hurdle in assessing algorithmic discrimination. Very specific technical issues hinder a proper understanding of structural inequalities and the harm they cause. As a result, many members of disadvantaged groups are left with no access to redress. Furthermore, addressing structural inequality issues through individualised litigation of indirect discrimination has led to notorious double blinds and paradoxes.[45]

The multiplicity of correlations made by algorithmic solutions emphasises and scales up a problem that critical anti-discrimination theory had already identified as troublesome, i.e., the shortcomings and limitations of anti-discrimination models based on a limited number of protected grounds. However, structural inequality shows patterns of disadvantage and privilege which combine fluidly across multiple and intersectional combinations of factors. A correct understanding of proxies as a category is equally important for indirect discrimination and for algorithmic discrimination. This leads to the need to further assess the role of the mechanisms involved in indirect discrimination which algorithmic discrimination shows with greater clarity, including stereotypes, correlations, associations, and analogy.

The study of algorithmic discrimination has much to offer towards a critical theory of anti-discrimination law aimed at strengthening the transformative potential of indirect discrimination. Beyond theoretical assessment and conceptual fine-tuning, research into algorithmic discrimination might also offer technical tools to improve the performance of anti-discrimination mechanisms and of anti-discrimination legal reasoning through, for example, the design of de-biasing tools and anti-stereotyping firewalls.[46]

It is evident that current AI technologies need to avoid gender and other biases in their learning and decision-making processes. More research and data are necessary to understand and curb existing biases and control mechanisms should be implemented to avoid losing rights and guarantees.

---

[44] McCrudden 2011.

[45] There is abundant commentary regarding these effects in relation to child-care responsibilities or part-time work. See, for example, Mulder 2020.

[46] In the field of data mining there are already some antidiscrimination techniques (Hajian et al 2015; Hajian and Domingo i Ferrer 2013; Calders and Custers 2013), but there is also ongoing research on further possibilities of antidiscrimination intervention (Custers 2018; Žliobaitė and Custers 2016).

References

Barocas S, Selbst D (2016) Big Data's Disparate Impact. California Law Review, https://doi.org/10.15779/Z38BG31

Calders T, Custers B (2013) What is Data Mining and How Does it Work? In: Custers B et al (eds) Discrimination and Privacy in the Information Society. Springer, Heidelberg, pp 27–42

Collins H (2018) Justice for Foxes: Fundamental Rights and Justification of Indirect Discrimination. In: Khaitan T, Collins H (eds) Foundations of Indirect Discrimination Law. Hart Publishing, Oxford, pp 249–278

Custers B (2018) Methods of Data Research for Law. In: Mak V et al (eds) Research Handbook in Data Science and Law. Edward Elgar, Cheltenham, pp 355–377

De Stefano V (2018) 'Negotiating the Algorithm': Automation, artificial intelligence and labour protection. https://www.ilo.org/wcmsp5/groups/public/---ed_emp/---emp_policy/docume nts/publication/wcms_634157.pdf Accessed 5 July 2021

Ellis E, Watson P (2012) EU Anti-Discrimination Law. Oxford University Press, Oxford

Eubanks V (2018) Automating Inequality. How high-tech tools profile, police, and punish the poor. Picador, New York

Fredman S (2018) Direct and Indirect Discrimination: Is There Still a Divide? In: Khaitan T, Collins H (eds) Foundations of Indirect Discrimination Law. Hart Publishing, Oxford, pp 31–56

Gerards J, Xenidis R (2020) Algorithmic discrimination in Europe: Challenges and opportunities for gender equality and non-discrimination law. www.equalitylaw.eu/downloads/5361-algorithmic-discrimination-in-europe-pdf-1-975 Accessed 2 April 2021

Gillis T B, Spiess J L (2019) Big Data and Discrimination. University of Chicago Law Review 86:459–488

Hacker P (2018) Teaching fairness to artificial intelligence: Existing and novel strategies against algorithmic discrimination under EU law. Common Market Law Review 55:1143–1185

Hajian S, Domingo i Ferrer J (2013) A Methodology for Direct and Indirect Discrimination Prevention in Data Mining. IEEE Transactions on knowledge and data engineering, https://doi.org/10.1109/TKDE.2012.72

Hajian S et al (2015) Discrimination- and privacy-aware patterns. Data mining and knowledge discovery, https://doi.org/10.1007/s10618-014-0393-7

Köchling A, Wehner M C (2020) Discriminated by an algorithm: a systemic review of discrimination and fairness by algorithm decision-making in the context of HR recruitment and HR development. Business Research, https://doi.org/10.1007/s40685-020-00134-w

Mackinnon C (2013) Intersectionality as Method: A Note. Signs: Journal of Women in Culture and Society 38:1019-1030

Martino A (2019) Inteligencia artificial y Derecho. Acerca de lo que hay [Artificial Intelligence and Law. What is out there]. Revista de Ciencia de la Legislación [Online] 6

McCrudden Ch (2011) Introduction. Thinking the Unthinkable? European Gender Equality Law 1:3–5

Mulder J (2020) Indirect sex discrimination in employment. Theoretical analysis and reflections on the CJEU case law and national application of the concept of indirect sex discrimination. www.equalitylaw.eu/downloads/5362-indirect-discrimination-in-employment-pdf-1-434-kb Accessed 2 April 2021

Prinsloo P (2020) Of 'black boxes' and algorithmic decision-making in (higher) education – A commentary. Big Data and Society, https://doi.org/10.1177/2053951720933994

Schiek D (2007) Indirect Discrimination. In: Schiek D et al (eds) Cases, Materials and Text on National, Supranational and International Non-Discrimination Law. Hart Publishing, Oxford, pp 323–375

Solar Cayón J I (2020) La inteligencia artificial jurídica: nuevas herramientas y perspectivas metodológicas para el jurista [Legal artificial intelligence: New tools and methdolological prospects for lawyers]. Revus, https://doi.org/10.4000/revus.6547

Timmer A (2016) Gender Stereotypes in the Case Law of the EU Court of Justice. European Equality Law Review 1:37–46

Tobler C (2005) Indirect Discrimination. Intersentia, Antwerp

Wood A J (2021) Algorithmic Management. Consequences for Work Organisation and Working Conditions. https://ec.europa.eu/jrc/sites/default/files/jrc124874.pdf Accessed 5 July 2021

Xenidis R, Senden L (2020) EU non-discrimination law in the era of artificial intelligence: Mapping the challenges of algorithmic discrimination. In: Bernitz U et al (eds) General Principles of EU law and the EU Digital Order. Kluwer Law International, Alphen aan den Rijn, pp 151–182

Žliobaitė I, Custers B (2016) Using sensitive personal data may be necessary for avoiding discrimination in data-driven decision models. Artif Intell Law, https://doi.org/10.1007/s10506-016-9182-5

Zuiderveen Borgesius F J (2018) Discrimination, artificial intelligence, and algorithmic decision-making. https://rm.coe.int/discrimination-artificial-intelligence-and-algorithmic-decision-making/1680925d73 Accessed 2 April 2021

Zuiderveen Borgesius F J (2020) Strengthening legal protection against discrimination by algorithms and artificial intelligence. The International Journal of Human Rights, https://doi.org/10.1080/13642987.2020.1743976

Dolores Morondo Taramundi is the Principal Investigator at the Human Rights Institute of the University of Deusto (Bilbao, Spain). She holds a PhD in Law from the EUI with a thesis on feminist legal theory. She has taught courses on legal philosophy, history and philosophy of human rights, and international protection of human rights. She is a member of the European network of legal experts in gender equality and non-discrimination. Her main areas of research and publication include antidiscrimination law, legal critical theories, especially feminist legal theory, human rights and legal methodology.

Chapter 5
Women's Rights Under AI Regulation: Fighting AI Gender Bias Through a Feminist and Intersectional Approach

María López Belloso

Contents

Abstract AI (Artificial Intelligence) introduces a wide range of benefits including more access to education (and more personalised education), the prediction of natural disasters or chatbots and systems to assist women victims of gender based violence. However, these systems have the potential to perpetuate and amplify different types of biases. A particular problem worldwide is the impact of gender biases that propagate in AI. These biases usually result from: (i) the lack of diversity in the discipline; (ii) the poor quality and lack of representativeness of the data that feed the algorithms; (iii) and the discrimination produced and exacerbated by the algorithms themselves on vulnerable groups. To solve the adverse effects these biases can have on specific groups, gender mainstreaming has been gaining ground on the international agenda and is gradually being incorporated into policy and regulatory processes. This chapter examines the role that different normative proposals to regulate the use of AI can reduce the impact of these biases and promote the protection of women and other vulnerable groups. It argues that incorporating feminist and intersectional approaches

M. López Belloso (✉)
Social Sciences and Humanities Faculty, University of Deusto, San Sebastian, Spain
e-mail: mlbelloso@deusto.es

© T.M.C. ASSER PRESS and the authors 2022
B. Custers and E. Fosch-Villaronga (eds.), *Law and Artificial Intelligence*,
Information Technology and Law Series 35,
https://doi.org/10.1007/978-94-6265-523-2_5

can effectively protect these groups from the risks of biases exposing them and have transformative potential for promoting and promoting their human rights.

Keywords Gender Equality · Intersectionality · Biases · Regulatory Frameworks · Human Rights

5.1   Introduction

There is no doubt that Artificial Intelligence represent both an excellent opportunity to promote progress, prosperity and to achieve sustainable development goals (SDGs)[1] and a challenge to the achievement of some of them.[2] These SDGs are a shared call for action to end poverty, foster wellbeing, and gender equality[3] and protect the planet and the technical possibilities of AI and related technologies have been acknowledged as a key tool to achieve these goals.[4]

Scientific and technological progress has historically been a driver for regulatory advancement.[5] However, despite the call for regulation of technological progress since the 1970s, it is recently that different initiatives have been launched to regulate the use of new technologies. The approach to regulating these tools will determine their potential to achieve the goals set out in the 2030 Agenda, and therefore requires a regulatory focus that enables their appropriate use in the service of development and peace, and at the same time, protects fundamental rights.

Adequate regulation must protect both men's and women's rights and ensure that these technologies are used to promote and defend both men and women's needs.[6] Despite a growing interest in diversity and inclusion in AI regulatory actions, the lack of diversity in technological disciplines and Artificial Intelligence[7] makes it difficult to adequately integrate gender and women's rights perspectives in such initiatives. As in social sciences, the failure to incorporate women both as the object and subject of AI and related technologies hinders the adequate treatment of women's human rights violations and accentuates the biases of such technologies.[8] This chapter will explore the potential contribution to the emerging regulatory framework for AI for the protection of women and other vulnerable groups such as LGTBIQ+ or ethnic minorities to respect their fundamental rights and protect them from any adverse effect these developments may cause them.

---

[1] Vinuesa et al. 2020; Montes et al. 2021.

[2] Ibid.

[3] Kostoska and Kocarev 2019.

[4] Secretary-General's Strategy on New Technologies, 2018. Retrieved from: https://www.un.org/en/newtechnologies/images/pdf/SGs-Strategy-on-New-Technologies.pdf Last accessed 29 June 2021.

[5] Picker 2001.

[6] López Belloso 2021.

[7] Stathoulopoulos 2019; Houser 2019.

[8] Adam 1993; Adam 1995; Silvestre Cabrera et al. 2020.

5.2   Gender Biases in AI Development

5.2.1   The Challenges of Missing Sex and Gender Considerations in Algorithms

Since the emergence of AI in the mid-20th century, its exponential development and growing role in today's society have prompted extensive analysis of its qualities, attributes, and implications for ethics and human rights.[9] One of the aspects that have attracted most interest because of its impact on fundamental rights, especially of vulnerable groups, is the biases AI can have. These biases can repeat and exacerbate existing biases or create new ones resulting from the very construction of the discipline[10] or the data processing. One example is the race and gender bias of face recognition systems, that result in a misidentification of dark-skinned females.[11]

The literature has intensively analysed the biases related to the lack of diversity and data quality, constituting perhaps the most studied component of AI gender biases[12] The belief that large volumes of data representativeness make them more objective has been disproved by authors such as Kate Crawford, who speaks of the "hidden biases of data".[13] As Srinivassan and Chandler explain, biases in the data can occur at different points: during data collection, while classifying/labelling data, and during the data processing.[14] Consequently, data bias can appear either in (multimodal) data through sensitive features and their causal influences, or through under/over-representation of certain groups, such as women,[15] and especially black women, because this group is mis- or underrepresented at the collection, at the labelling, or at the data processing.[16] The aforementioned example of gender bias in facial recognition systems illustrates this.

AI can not only exacerbate existing data biases but also create new ones.[17] These algorithmic biases[18] can occur through the so-called sample "selection biases" (for example, selecting gender stereotyped features in the selection criteria, as in the Amazon recruitment algorithm[19]) or "confounding biases" (when algorithms do not consider all the information of the dataset, as for example biases of algorithms in

---

[9] For more on the ethical implications of AI see: Floridi 2018; Winfield 2019; Mittelstadt 2019; Siau 2020.

[10] Roselli 2019; Silberg and Manyika 2019; Nelson 2019.

[11] EC 2020, p. 30.

[12] Gebru et al. 2018; Roselli 2019; p. 540, Ntoutsi 2020.

[13] Crawford 2013.

[14] Srinivasan and Chander 2021, p. 48.

[15] Ntoutsi 2020, p. 4.

[16] Buolamwini and Gebru 2018.

[17] Bolukbasi et al. 2016; Gebru 2020, p. 11, Leavy et al. 2020; Hooker 2021.

[18] Barocas et al. 2019; Gutierrez 2021; Fosch-Villaronga et al. 2021.

[19] Dastin 2018.

Medicine school resulting in gender discrimination[20]). Another algorithmic bias known as "design-related biases", linked to algorithms' limitations[21] These algorithmic biases can result in different threats to gender related human rights such as the wrong gender classification in social networks,[22] algorithmic moderation resulting in Instagram's censorship,[23] or the "algorithmic oppression" to marginalised people.[24]

Beyond algorithms, gender biases can also be found in embodied AI, such as robots[25] or AI Virtual Personal Assistants.[26] AI systems reproduce social gender stereotypes when using female voices for specific tasks, for instance for caring purposes. Also, when embodied AI uses submissive language or female bodies and can also derive in biased devices that threaten specific vulnerable groups, such as women, when dealing with gender-based violence, ethnicity or xenophobia.[27] An example can be found with the experience of Microsoft TAY chatbot deployed in the wild that resulted in the bot's shut down only 2 hours after its launch due to its offensive, sexist and fascist messages.

5.2.2 Scholarly Approaches to Mitigate AI Gender Biases

The growing importance of analysing the implications of gender inequality on the global agenda, thanks to the struggle of the feminist movement, has also led to an increase in studies that address the gender biases of AI.[28] According to Bunch, a feminist transformation of human rights has excellent transformational potential to address human rights violations. It first looks at the violations of women's rights and then challenges the human rights concept to make it "more responsive to women"[29] This approach is clearly in line with feminist epistemology, and more specifically of Standpoint Theory.[30] Applied to the field of Artificial Intelligence, the incorporation of this approach involves reflecting on what knowledge is represented in the area (composition of the discipline), what kind of knowledge is reflected in the applications (what needs it responds to) and what implications it has for the applicability of these systems.[31] Following this approach, to understand the impact of gender bias of AI in human rights, it is necessary to identify the consequences of

---

[20] Schwartz 2019.

[21] Srinivasan and Chander 2021; Gutierrez 2021.

[22] Fosch-Villaronga et al. 2021, p. 25.

[23] Are 2020, p. 742.

[24] Noble 2018.

[25] Tay et al. 2014; Alesich and Rigby 2017.

[26] Adams and Ní Loideáin 2019.

[27] Karnouskos 2021.

[28] Haraway 1995; Wellner and Rothman 2020; Gutierrez 2021; Tannenbaum et al. 2019.

[29] Bunch 1990, p. 496.

[30] Harding 1989.

[31] Adam 1995, p. 409.

these gender biases in women's lives to then challenge the AI itself. This way of addressing women's human rights violations is connected with the intersectional approach promoted by feminists[32] As Sarah Ciston argues, intersectionality is a practical approach to analysing AI's "biases and problems" and "uncover alternative ethics from its counter-histories".[33] As argued by Smriti Parsheera, it is necessary to begin by analysing the biases of the discipline itself, as the translation of human biases to artificial intelligence systems is evident.[34] According to this author, the limited representation of women and vulnerable groups is translated in the "under-representation" of their ideas in the AI Agenda and the replication of existing gender stereotypes in AI technologies.[35] To overcome these biases, she draws on Abbasi et al.'s "fairness by design"[36] that highlights the need to adopt debiasing techniques of AI tools and diversifying the discipline in terms of gender, race, ethnicity and sexual orientation. To do this, she also proposes fostering collaboration between disciplines, particularly with social sciences.[37] Marie Hicks and Timnit Gebru have also described the "hostility" of the IA environment,[38] but as the latter explains, the biases of AI are also related to other aspects such as the datasets and the algorithms themselves.

To mitigate and avoid these biases Adams and Ni Loideain call for more exhaustive social analysis and interdisciplinary expertise along with the AI life systems.[39] Buolamwini and Gebru stress the need for intersectional tests to address different identities and power relations to overcome these biases (Buolamwini and Gebru 2018).

As Roselli et al. state, despite the robust literature on the problems caused by biases in AI, less work has addressed methodologies for dealing with such biases[40] Alan Digman argues that the major challenge is not identifying AI problems and biases but public governance response.[41] In this regard, regulatory framework can play an important role in governing AI[42] Recently, different regulatory initiatives have been launched. Given the importance of AI's gender biases, in the next section this chapter will analyse them from a gender perspective to check if the protection of women's rights is protected or even considered through main AI regulatory proposals.

---

[32] Crenshaw 1991.

[33] Ciston 2019, p. 39.

[34] Parsheera 2018.

[35] Ibid., p. 3.

[36] Abbasi 2018.

[37] Parsheera 2018, p. 5.

[38] Hics 2017, Gebru 2020.

[39] Adams and Ní Loideáin 2019.

[40] Roselli 2019, p. 542.

[41] Dignam 2020.

[42] Mazzini 2019; Gasser and Almeida 2017.

5.3 Increased Attention to Diversity and Inclusion in the Development of AI from the Regulatory Perspective

There is an increasing agreement on the need to construct a suitable regulatory framework for AI that can guarantee the protections of ethics[43] values[44] or human rights.[45] Indeed, some authors affirm that:

> Without an agreed framework of norms that clearly identifies and articulates the relevant ethical standards which AI systems should be expected to comply with, little real progress will be made towards ensuring that these systems are in practice designed, developed and deployed in ways that will meet widely accepted ethical standards.[46]

In this section, we pay particularly attention to UNESCO Recommendation, Toronto Declaration and EU existing regulatory proposals for AI and related technologies. These three instruments represent a set of regulatory initiatives coming from different actors and regional contexts and are a clear indication of the growing interest on the regulation of AI. Moreover, we argue that human rights provide a shared grounding on values reflected in different universal, regional and national regulations that provide an adequate framework to deal with and try to limit the impact of AI biases to fundamental rights. In the different proposals to regulate these technologies, the principle of non-discrimination, equality, and diversity occupies a relevant place. Existing human rights framework of laws and international standards for the protection and advancement of equality and non-discrimination should be incorporated to AI regulatory process to ensure that these regulatory proposals do not infringe existing equality and non-discrimination framework.

Below, this work analyses how the three main proposals for regulating AI and related technologies address this issue and their potential contribution for a better protect women's and vulnerable groups' rights.

5.3.1 UNESCO Recommendation on Guiding Principles for AI

UNESCO's recommendation for the regulation of AI aligns with the UN policy on new technologies and other existing initiatives to regulate these technologies.[47] UNESCO is aware of the existing gender gap in AI and related technologies and expressed it in the recommendations made during the UNESCO Global

---

[43] Goldsmith and Burton 2017; Floridi 2018; Hagendorf 2020.

[44] Dignum 2017.

[45] Yeung and Howes 2019; Aizenberg and Van den Hoven 2020.

[46] Yeung and Howes 2019, p. 79.

[47] Secretary-General's Strategy on New Technologies (2018). See note 3.

Dialogue 2020, which resulted in a specific report on gender equality and AI[48] This gender awareness has also informed the work on the proposed *Recommendation on Guiding Principles for AI* presented in 2020, and that expects its approval in November 2021, where gender equality and non-discrimination are included in a cross-cutting way throughout the text. From the preamble of the Recommendation, there are constant references to equality and diversity[49] Gender equality and non-discrimination inform UNESCO´s approach and are included among the values and principles that actors involved in AI must respect, such as human dignity, gender equality and non-discrimination,[50] respect and protection of diversity[51] or fairness and non-discrimination.[52]

Furthermore, the more relevant aspect regarding gender and diversity issues is the inclusion of the promotion of gender equality among the recommendation objectives, and a gender specific policy area (6).[53] In this Policy area's definition, the recommendation states that:

[m]ember States should ensure that digital technologies and artificial intelligence fully contribute to achieving gender equality; and that the rights and fundamental freedoms of girls and women, including their safety and integrity are not violated at any stage of the AI system life cycle.[54]

This statement aligns with the promotion of equality through the use of AI to protect and promote the rights of girls and women. The wording, instead of focusing on risk prevention or non-discrimination with the use of technologies, shows commitment to use of these advances for the advancement of equality, which can be a very relevant tool to boost the use of AI for the protection of the human rights of women and girls.

5.3.2 Toronto Declaration

The particularity of the *Toronto declaration* is that it results from a shared discussion and co-creative process of different stakeholders and practitioners in AI, so it should

---

[48] UNESCO 2020, p. 9.

[49] "Convinced that the standard-setting instrument presented here, based on international law and a global normative approach, focusing on human dignity and human rights, as well as gender equality (…)Convinced that the standard-setting instrument presented here, based on international law and a global normative approach, focusing on human dignity and human rights, as well as gender equality (…) UNESCO Recommendation on Guiding Principles for AI. SHS/BIO/AHEG-AI/2020/4 REV.2 Paris, 7 September 2020, p. 1.

[50] UNESCO'S Recommendation on Guiding Principles for AI, para 13.

[51] Ibid., para 19.

[52] Ibid., para 28.

[53] Ibid., paras 89–94.

[54] Ibid., para 89.

be analysed concerning similar initiatives.[55] This instrument is led by Amnesty International and Access Now and has been widely endorsed by the global human rights community.[56] It builds on the framework of international human rights law, as human rights are defined and protected by law, what can be an added value to overcome the vagueness of abstraction of ethical principles. It also mainstreams gender along the full text of the declaration, as it understands that right to equality is a human right that underpins all other rights. The preamble places the right to equality and non-discrimination at the centre of the approach. It links these fundamental rights with the protection of related rights that could be affected by the use of AI, such as "the right to privacy and data protection, the right to freedom of expression and association, to participate in cultural life, equality before the law, and access to an effective remedy".[57] This prioritisation and focus on gender and inclusion are reflected in the text, which, unlike the UNESCO recommendation, opts for a preventive approach to the possible harm these technologies can cause to women and other vulnerable groups.[58] This vision of human rights, and specifically the right to equality and non-discrimination, nevertheless limits the capacity of the use of these technologies for the protection of women's human rights, as it focuses on the non-generation of harm and its eventual reparation, instead of assessing the potential use of these technologies to improve the situation of women.[59] Even though the Declaration calls for a diverse and intersectional AI, its focus on human rights as regulatory proposal do not suggest concrete mechanisms to promote the use of AI for the protection of diversity and non-discrimination, but focuses on mitigating the biases.[60]

---

[55] These initiatives include, for example, IEEE's Global Initiative on Ethics of Autonomous and Intelligent Systems and its work on Ethically Aligned Design; the World Economic Forum's "Global Technology Governance: A Multistakeholder Approach" (World Economic Forum 2019); the UNI Global Union's "Top 10 Principles for Ethical Artificial Intelligence" (UNI Global Union 2019); the Montreal Declaration for a Responsible Development of AI; the Harmonious Artificial Intelligence Principles (HAIP), unveiled by Université de Montréal, in collaboration with the Fonds de recherche du Québec; and the *Tenets* of the Partnership on AI.

[56] Endorsers of this Declaration can be found here: https://www.torontodeclaration.org/community/endorsers/ (last accessed 14 September 2021). It is worth noticing that most endorsers come from the civil society.

[57] UNESCO'S Recommendation on Guiding Principles for AI, *vid supra* note 42, para 6.

[58] Toronto Declaration para 14–17. Toronto declaration can be accessed here: https://www.torontodeclaration.org/declaration-text/english/#humanrights Late accessed 29 June 2021.

[59] "Governments have obligations and private sector actors have responsibilities to proactively prevent discrimination to comply with existing human rights law and standards. When prevention is not sufficient or satisfactory, and discrimination arises, a system should be interrogated and harms addressed immediately", Toronto Declaration para 14.

[60] Ibid, paras 47–49.

5.3.3 European Approach to AI Regulation

Last April, the European Commission (EC) released its proposal for a regulatory framework on Artificial Intelligence.[61] This proposal addresses the risks stemming from the different uses of AI systems, while at the same time aims to promote innovation in the field of AI. It represents an ambitious regulatory attempt, applying to private and public sector actors, providers and/or users of an AI system.

This proposal was informed by previous initiatives, such as proposal for a Regulation on Ethical Principles for the development, deployment and use of AI, robotics and related technologies,[62] and is framed within a clear EC strategy to boost the EU's role in the sector. This strategy is marked by a distinctive EU brand based on upholding ethical principles and fundamental values.[63]

AI Act would apply to AI and related technology that is "developed, deployed or used in the Union" (Article 2). Although it is committed to ensuring compliance with ethical principles and protecting fundamental values, AI Act has omitted to two explicit mentions to gender included in the previous European Parliament´s proposal[64]: non-bias and non-discrimination (Article 9 EP proposal) and social responsibility and gender equality (Article10). While article 9 focused on ensuring that these technologies do not involve discrimination, with a detailed description of the aspects included in the definition of "non-discrimination", article 10 advocated for the use of AI and related technologies that do not impinge or impact on rights with genders and social justice implications, such as workers' rights, education or intellectual property. On the contrary the proposal for AI Act refers to non-discrimination framing the regulatory proposal within consistency with existing Union legislation, such as EU Charter of Fundamental Rights and the existing secondary Union legislation on data protection, consumer protection, non-discrimination and gender equality.

Despite the significant advances that this regulatory proposal means, some civil society stakeholders[65] have already highlighted its limits to tackle discrimination.

---

[61] Proposal for a regulation of the European Parliament and of the Council laying down harmonised rules on artificial intelligence (Artificial Intelligence act) and amending certain union legislative acts (COM/2021/206 final).

[62] European Parliament resolution of 20 October 2020 on a framework for the ethical aspects of artificial intelligence, robotics and related technologies, 2020/2012(INL). Available at: https://oeil.secure.europarl.europa.eu/oeil/popups/ficheprocedure.do?lang=en&reference=2020/2012(INL).

[63] Thus, this proposal is framed in the European Strategy for AI and European Strategy for Gender Equality (https://digital-strategy.ec.europa.eu/en/policies/strategy-artificial-intelligence Late accessed 29 June 2021); and already existing documents guiding the use and implementation of AI in Europe, such as the White Paper On Artificial Intelligence—A European approach to excellence and trust—the Guidelines for Trustworthy AI or the Assessment List for Trustworthy AI.

[64] Proposal for a regulation of the European Parliament and of the Council laying down harmonised rules on artificial intelligence. See Note 60.

[65] EDRI 2021.

For example, the risk-based system does not require legal limits on developing "problematic uses of AI" such as surveillance or predictive policing, nor asks for sufficient safeguards from deployers of "high risk" AI[66] Therefore, this proposal fails to provide protection and remedies for people likely to endure harm due to AI.

5.4   The Promise of AI through Diversity and Inclusion Lenses

While the attention to sex and gender considerations is slowly getting more prominent in regulatory initiatives, AI offers the possibility to promote these goals on itself. However, lack of attention to women's rights has resulted in a limited analysis of the contribution that new technologies can make to protect and safeguard women's and vulnerable groups´ rights. Undoubtedly, there is a direct link between the lack of interest in this potential application and women's scarcity in the scientific and technological sector.[67] The lack of women in the field hinders not only the aforementioned situated knowledge of women as subjects and objects of the discipline,[68] but also a restructuring of the power dynamics in the discipline.[69] The location of knowledge, though, is not acquired per se, due to social belonging, but it is necessary to acquire it through critical reflection.[70] This critical reflection will ease the development of initiatives aligned to women and vulnerable group's needs. Indeed, there are already different initiatives that can contribute to promoting and protecting women's rights.[71] Based on the intersection of gender equality (SDG5) with other discrimination axes and SDGs, this work identifies existing technologies and initiatives that promote women's protection of human rights in the following lines.

Table 5.1 below summarises some of the initiatives that can protect women's rights from an intersectional approach and how AI contributes to this protection.

This table shows that there are currently several initiatives that contribute to the protection of women's human rights. For these applications to be truly effective, they must respond to women's own needs, as Bunch said, by identifying the problems they face,[72] and seeking solutions in which women's human rights are not only the object of study, but women are also subject in the field of AI[73]

As we have seen in Sect. 5.2, biases in AI are largely related to the absence of women and other groups (minority groups, LGTBIQ) in the discipline itself (subjects), but there are also biases in the "object" (algorithms, bots, robots…).

---

[66] Ibid.

[67] Adam 1995.

[68] Harding 1989; Haraway 1995.

[69] Ciston 2019.

[70] Willie 2003, p. 31.

[71] López Belloso and Stockhem 2021.

[72] Bunch 1990.

[73] Adam 1995, p. 414.

Table 5.1 Contribution of AI and related technologies to women's human rights

Gender dimension	Related human rights	The potential contribution of AI and New Technologies to protect women's rights	Relevant initiatives to protect women's rights
Human trafficking. Human trafficking is often considered as new slavery.[74]	Freedom from slavery or involuntary servitude	The use of technologies to fight human trafficking has recently increased at the level of investigation and prosecution, especially regarding sexual exploitation,[75] fostering a shift towards using technology "from a liability into an asset"[76] in the fight against sexual exploitation. Tech giants such as Microsoft, Google or Palantir have joined the combat against trafficking alongside law enforcement stakeholders, mobilising the last data analytics and artificial intelligence (AI) techniques to identify "hotspots of risk".[77]	Counter-Trafficking Data Collaborative[78] Minerva[79] Spotlight[80]

(continued)

---

[74] Allain 2018.

[75] OSCE (2020), p. 25.

[76] OSCE (2018).

[77] Latonero 2014.

[78] Counter-Trafficking Data Collaborative https://www.ctdatacollaborative.org/about-us accessed 10 March 2021.

[79] Minerva: https://socialinnovationexchange.org/insights/data-social-good-case-study-global-emancipation-network, accessed 10 March 2021.

[80] Spotlight: https://digitalreasoning.com/resources/thorn-case-study/ accessed 10 March 2021.

Table 5.1 (continued)

Gender dimension	Related human rights	The potential contribution of AI and New Technologies to protect women's rights	Relevant initiatives to protect women's rights
			Traffic Analysis Hub[81]
Online harassment and gender-based hate speech	Freedom of opinion and expression	The role of AI-based systems regarding the protection of freedom of expression and opinion has been highly contested for these systems' risks.[82] However, new technologies can also play an essential role in promoting freedom of expression. They provide new communication options and can assist vulnerable groups, such as women or LGTBI group, in communicating human rights abuses, such as online violence and harassment[83]	Blacklists[84]
			NLP initiatives[85]
			Content Moderation[86]

(continued)

[81] Traffic Analysis Hub https://www.traffikanalysis.org/ Accessed 10 March 2021.

[82] The impact of the use of automated technologies for dissemination on the right to freedom of expression for instance has been noted by OHCHR especially linked to the use of bots or troll armies (Kaye 2018). See also: http://www.ohchr.org/EN/Issues/FreedomOpinion/Pages/ContentRegulationInTheDigitalAge.aspx Accessed 13 February 2021.

[83] Amnesty International https://www.amnesty.org/en/latest/campaigns/2017/11/what-is-online-violence-and-abuse-against-women/ Accessed 13 February 2021.

[84] The use of blacklists as a content moderation mechanism has been highlighted by Jhaver et al. as an effective means to protect hate speech and online harassment (Jhaver 2018).

[85] Some initiatives have also been developed based on Natural language processing mechanisms to identify and prevent hate speech against women: Violentometro: https://violentom etro-online.herokuapp.com Accessed 13 February 2021.

[86] Existing tools can contribute to assessing trends and patterns of hate speech against women and vulnerable groups and therefore contribute to ensuring that women can access digital platforms and social media "equally, freely and without fear" (Amnesty International 2017, p. 3).

Table 5.1 (continued)

Gender dimension	Related human rights	The potential contribution of AI and New Technologies to protect women's rights	Relevant initiatives to protect women's rights
Unconscious biases in recruitment	Right to work and protection against unemployment	The growing use of AI-based recruitment systems in the work environment has relevant implications for non-discrimination and gender equality[87] These implications are linked to the unconscious biases reflected in the data set used to train the algorithms and training itself.[88] Some existing technological tools can contribute to reduce or minimise the aforementioned unconscious biases	Textio[89] / Gender bias decoder[90] / Algorithmic analysis of applicants' skills[91]

(continued)

[87] Servoz 2019, p. 102.

[88] A study performed by Cheong et al. proves how human gender biases that limit recruitment opportunities for women are mimicked and exacerbated by artificial intelligence (AI) used for sorting resumés (Cheong 2020). A clear example of these biases is the one of Amazon's recruiting tool: https://www.reuters.com/article/us-amazon-com-jobs-automation-insight/amazon-scraps-secret-ai-recruiting-tool-that-showed-bias-against-women-idUSKCN1MK08G Accessed 13 March 2021.

[89] https://textio.com/ Accessed 13 March 2021.

[90] This tool is based on a research paper (Gaucher et al. 2011) which showed job adverts that included different kinds of gender-coded language to men and women and recorded how appealing the jobs seemed and how much the participants felt that they 'belonged' in that occupation.

[91] Information available at https://www.recruitercentral.io/best-tools-for-writing-a-non-bias-job-description/ Accessed 13 March 2021. Other interesting uses of AI tools in gender-neutral recruitment are linked to the use of neuroscience-based games that measure cognitive and behavioural traits on a technological platform and then analyse the results by algorithms comparing the applicants' results with current employees' skills. A relevant example is one of Unilever's, where candidates applying for a job in the company via LinkedIn, play some games provided by technology company Pymetrics. Then, results are analyzed by algorithms that compare applicants' skills with those of employees https://www.businessinsider.com/unilever-artificial-intelligence-hiring-process-2017-6 Accessed 13 March 2021.

Table 5.1 (continued)

Gender dimension	Related human rights	The potential contribution of AI and New Technologies to protect women's rights	Relevant initiatives to protect women's rights
Under-examination of women's health issues.	Right to the standard of living adequate for the health and well-being of self and family	AI and New technologies could play a crucial role, as the amount of data generated by different health apps and tools could significantly affect women's understudied diseases. This potential has led to the so-called "Femtech"[92]	Period and fertility tracking apps[93]

(continued)

[92] "Femtech" is commonly understood as software, diagnostics, products and services, that use technology to support women's health. The term was originally coined by Ida Tin, the founder of Clue, a period tracking app, who used the term while she was discussing it with investors.

[93] Information available at: https://codeit.us/blog/women-health-apps-development Accessed 13 March 2021.

Table 5.1 (continued)

Gender dimension	Related human rights	The potential contribution of AI and New Technologies to protect women's rights	Relevant initiatives to protect women's rights
Gender violence against women		Women's well-being is related to health and relevant topics such as gender-based violence, including harassment and domestic violence.[94] Given the extended use of mobile phones and the internet,[95] digital applications can provide a space where women can exchange information on violence or provide victims and survivors safe environments to discuss their experiences and ask for help	*Take Back the Tech*[96] *HarrassMap*[97] *Together*[98] *MyAmbar*[99]
Access to education. Ad hoc training and mentoring	Right to education	An inclusive learning system can harness technology to create tools that efficiently serve the feminist transformation of human rights.	*Squirrel AI Learning*[100] *IMPACT EdITEch*[101]

Source The author

---

94 Baker 2018.

95 See: https://datareportal.com/global-digital-overview, Accessed 16 January 2021.

96 See: https://womanity.org/take-back-the-tech-has-always-been-a-celebration-of-women-and-tech/ Accessed 16 January 2021.

97 See: https://harassmap.org/en/, Accessed 16 January 2021.

98 See: https://gender-works.giz.de/an-application-to-prevent-and-fight-violence-against-women-una-app-para-prevenir-y-combatir-la-violencia-contra-las-mujeres/ Accessed 16 January 2021.

99 See: https://www.thehindubusinessline.com/info-tech/vodafone-idea-foundation-nasscom-foundation-launch-myambar-app-for-women-safety-in-india/article32925416.ece Accessed 16 January 2021.

100 Squirrel AI Learning uses AI to provide personalised learning and mentoring: See http://squirrelai.com Accessed 16 January 2021.

101 IMPACT EdTech: (tackling gender inequality in education) aims to foster greater gender equality in education and increase women's access to learning opportunities: http://www.eun.org/news/detail?articleId=4904219, 6 March 2020, Accessed 16 January 2021.

In order not only to combat these biases, but also to promote tools such as those mentioned in Table 5.1, it is necessary to raise awareness of the importance of guaranteeing equality and non-discrimination, and for this, the regulatory instruments of AI can play a fundamental role.

5.5 Reflections and Discussion

Gender equality and the protection of vulnerable groups have become increasingly important in political and legal discourses. For this reason, throughout the previous sections, this chapter has compiled the different factors that affect gender biases of artificial intelligence and how different existing regulatory proposals include equality, gender perspective and diversity in their respective approaches. Regulatory frameworks play an important role in creating incentives, fostering the identification by companies of unjust systems and creating reparation mechanisms.[102] In order to do this, policy approaches can opt for either gender mainstreaming in their drafts or the creation of specific standards to ensure the protection of women and vulnerable groups. This dichotomy is one of the great debates underlying feminism.[103] However, it seems to have been resolved in favour of mainstreaming, probably because of the consolidation of this approach in international policy.[104] As shown, this mainstreaming of gender has been adopted by the three regulatory proposals examined as gender is included among the principles and values. However, the three proposals also include specific sections (policy area 6 in the *UNESCO Declaration*, Art. 12, 13, 18 in the *Toronto Declaration* and art. 9 and 10 in the *European Parliament Resolution)* to ensure that biases do not result in gender and vulnerable group discrimination.

Nevertheless, the three documents and the recently published European AI Act proposal focus on a risk-based approach, paying attention to the impact and harm that biased AI could cause in different rights (discrimination or privacy). This approach to the regulation of AI limits the transformation potential that law can play in promoting women's and vulnerable groups' rights because it adopts a risk-based approach rather than banning High-risk AI systems. This risk-based approach fails then to protect human rights, as promised in AI Act p. 11 para 3.5.). Adopting a feminist approach to AI regulation would also contribute to Bunch's feminist transformation of human rights by identifying specific violations of rights that could be addressed through AI regulation.[105]

The need for a feminist approach to AI also stresses that regulatory proposals should increase the number of explicit references to gender and incorporate it to all dimensions in the study of gender and technology and target specific issues related

---

[102] Gutierrez 2021, p. 452.

[103] Scott 1996.

[104] Charlesworth 2005, p. 5.

[105] Bunch 1990.

to AI and gender,[106] as seen in Sect. 5.4. In order to foster the role of AI in the promotion and protection of women's and vulnerable group's rights, it is necessary to identify the areas where these groups still need to receive increased attention and protection so AI technologies can be developed and deployed to improve these groups' situation. As stated by feminist scientists such as Donna Haraway, situated knowledge is needed to avoid technology perpetuating global inequalities.[107] This situated knowledge, Hampton affirms, needs to answer questions such as "who is creating AI, for whose benefit and at whose expense".[108]

These three questions are linked to the different aspects resulting in biased AI addressed in Sect. 5.2. Despite its important role, regulatory frameworks will not solve all the issues mentioned above, and other measures will be needed to complement legal contribution. For example, the lack of females in the AI sector should be addressed through different policies to increase diverse participation in the AI field. More technology diversity will help solve the problem but not other issues related to algorithmic biases. Training and awareness-raising about the consequences of biases in particularly vulnerable groups are also necessary.[109] Regarding the biases related to data issues, feminist and intersectional approaches clearly state that data biases are not only solved by increasing or diversifying datasets[110] but need to incorporate counter-hegemonic narratives and "decode and critique" power structures behind AI systems.

By incorporating these elements into the different phases of the AI process, feminist and intersectional approaches can work to destabilise and deconstruct gender biases. Moreover, adding these approaches to AI could, for example, help to identify and inform about new or changing forms of gender-related discrimination (both direct and indirect).[111]

5.6 Conclusions

AI shows a clear potential to contribute not only to the achievement of the 2030 Agenda, but also to other sectoral agendas, such as the European Agenda for Gender Equality. The biases of this technology, however, limit its transformative potential if it is not approached from diversity and inclusion.

Regulatory frameworks, as has been pointed out, can play a relevant role in combating and reducing these biases and in protecting vulnerable groups. But these normative processes have to be approached from transformative and ambitious approaches, which guarantee not only respect for fundamental rights, but also

---

[106] Guevara-Gómez et al. 2021.

[107] Haraway 1995.

[108] Hampton 2021.

[109] Ferrando 2014.

[110] Ciston 2019.

[111] Berendt and Preibusch 2014, p. 181.

provide "situated" proposals through the incorporation of feminist and intersectional approaches that contribute to the use of AI for respond to the needs of women, LGTBIQ + groups and ethnic and racial minorities.

References

Abbasi A et al (2018) Make "fairness by design" part of machine learning. Harvard Business Review: https://hbr.org/2018/08/make-fairness-by-design-part-of-machine-learning Accessed 10 June 2021

Adam A (1993) Gendered knowledge—Epistemology and artificial intelligence. AI & Society, 7(4), 311–322

Adam A (1995) A Feminist Critique of Artificial Intelligence. European Journal of Women's Studies, 2(3), 355–377

Adams R, Ní Loideáin N (2019) Addressing indirect discrimination and gender stereotypes in AI virtual personal assistants: the role of international human rights law. Cambridge International Law Journal, 8(2), 241–257

Aizenberg E, Van den Hoven J (2020) Designing for human rights in AI. Big Data & Society, 7(2), 1–14

Alesich S, Rigby M (2017) Gendered robots: Implications for our humanoid future. IEEE Technology and Society Magazine, 36(2), 50–59

Allain J (2018) Genealogies of human trafficking and slavery. In: Piotrowicz R (ed) Routledge Handbook of Human Trafficking. Routledge, New York, pp. 3–12

Amnesty International (2017) Content regulation in the digital age. Amnesty International submission to United Nations Special Rapporteur on the promotion and protection of the right to freedom of opinion and expression, TIGO IOR/2017. 066, Amnesty International. Available at : https://www.ohchr.org/Documents/Issues/Opinion/ContentRegulation/Amnesty.pdf Accessed 3 March 2021

Are C (2020) How Instagram's algorithm is censoring women and vulnerable users but helping online abusers. Feminist Media Studies, 20(5), 741–744

Baker S (2018) We want that for ourselves': how girls and young women are using ICTs to counter violence and demand their rights. Gender & Development, 26(2), 283–297

Barocas S, Hardt M, Narayanan A (2019) Fairness and Machine Learning. Limitations and Opportunities. Fairmlbook.org. https://fairmlbook.org/pdf/fairmlbook.pdf Accessed 16 June 2021

Berendt B, Preibusch S (2014) Better decision support through exploratory discrimination-aware data mining: foundations and empirical evidence. Artificial Intelligence and Law, 22(2), 175–209

Bolukbasi T, Chang K-W, Zou J, Saligrama V, Kalai A (2016) Man is to computer programmer as woman is to homemaker? Debiasing word embeddings. Adv. Neural Inf. Process. Syst, 4349–4357

Bunch C (1990) Women's rights as human rights: Toward a re-vision of human rights. Hum. Rts. Q. 12, 12(4), 486–498

Buolamwini J, Gebru T (2018) Gender shades: Intersectional accuracy disparities in commercial gender classification. Conference on fairness, accountability and transparency. PMLR, pp. 77–91

Charlesworth H (2005) Not waving but drowning: Gender mainstreaming and human rights in the United Nations. Harv. Hum Rts. J., 18, 1–19

Cheong M et al (2020) Ethical Implications of AI Bias as a Result of Workforce Gender Imbalance. University of Melbourne, Melbourne. https://about.unimelb.edu.au/__data/assets/pdf_file/0024/186252/NEW-RESEARCH-REPORT-Ethical-Implications-of-AI-Bias-as-a-Result-of-Workforce-Gender-Imbalance-UniMelb,-UniBank.pdf Accessed 11 March 2021

Ciston S (2019) Imagining Intersectional AI. xCoAx: Conference on computation, Communication, Aesthetics, Milan, pp. 39–48

Crawford K (2013) The hidden biases in big data. Harvard business review. Harvard Business Review. https://hbr.org/2013/04/the-hidden-biases-in-big-data Accessed 15 June 2021

Crenshaw K (1991) Mapping the margins: intersectionality, identity politics, and violence against women of color. Stanford Law Review, 43, 1241–1299

Dastin J (2018) Amazon scraps secret AI recruiting tool that showed bias against women. Reuters. https://www.reuters.com/article/us-amazon-com-jobs-automation-insight-idU SKCN1MK08G Accessed 12 September 2021

Dignam A (2020) Artificial intelligence, tech corporate governance and the public interest regulatory response. Cambridge Journal of Regions, Economy and Society (13), 37–54

Dignum V (2017) Responsible artificial intelligence: designing AI for human values. ITU Journal: ICT Discoveries, 1–8

European Commission (EC) (2020) Gendered Innovations 2: How Inclusive Analysis Contributes to Research and Innovation (Policy Review), Publications Office of the European Union, Luxembourg. https://ec.europa.eu/info/publications/gendered-innovation-2-how-inclusive-analysis-con tributes-research-and-innovation_en. Accessed 12 September 2021

EDRI (2021) EU's AI proposal must go further to prevent surveillance and discrimination. EDRI: https://edri.org/our-work/eus-ai-proposal-must-go-further-to-prevent-surveillance-and-discrimination/ Accessed 12 September 2021

Ferrando F (2014) Is the post-human a post-woman? Cyborgs, robots, artificial intelligence and the futures of gender: a case study. European Journal of Futures Research, 2(1), (43)1–17

Floridi L et al (2018) AI4People—an ethical framework for a good AI society: opportunities, risks, principles, and recommendations. Minds and Machines, 28(4), 689–707

Fosch-Villaronga E, Søraa RA, Custers B (2021). Gendering algorithms in social media. ACM SIGKDD Explorations Newsletter, 23(1), 24–31

Gasser U, Almeida VA (2017) A layered model for AI governance. IEEE Internet Computing, 21(6), 58–62

Gaucher D, Friesen JP, Kay AC (2011) Evidence That Gendered Wording in Job Advertisements Exists and Sustains Gender Inequality. Journal of Personality and Social Psychology, 101(1), 109–128

Gebru T (2020) Race and Gender. In: Dubber M, [author, insert surname second editor] S (eds) The Oxford handbook of ethics of AI. Oxford University Press, New York, pp. 251–269

Gebru T et al (2018) Datasheets for Datasets. Proceedings of the Fifth Workshop on Fairness, Accountability and Transparency in Machine Learning, pp. 1–16. https://www.microsoft.com/en-us/research/uploads/prod/2019/01/1803.09010.pdf). Accessed 17 June 2021

Goldsmith J, Burton E (2017) Why teaching ethics to AI practitioners is important. Proceedings of the AAAI Conference on Artificial Intelligence, pp 4836–4840

Guevara-Gómez AO, de Zárate-Alcarazo L, Criado J I (2021) Feminist perspectives to artificial intelligence: Comparing the policy frames of the European Union and Spain. Information Polity, 26(2), 173–192

Gutierrez M (2021) New Feminist Studies in Audiovisual Industries| Algorithmic Gender Bias and Audiovisual Data: A Research Agenda. International Journal of Communication, 15, 439–461

Hagendorf T (2020) The Ethics of AI Ethics: An Evaluation of Guidelines. Minds and Machines, 30, 99–120

Hampton L M (2021) Black Feminist Musings on Algorithmic Oppression. Conference on Fairness, Accountability, and Transparency (FAccT´21) (pp. 1-12). Virtual event, Canada. ACM, New York

Haraway D (1995) Ciencia, cyborgs y mujeres. La reinvención de la Naturaleza. Cátedra, Madrid

Harding S (1989) Feminism & Science. In: Tuana N (ed) Is there a Feminist Method? Indiana University Press, Bloomington/Indianapolis, pp. 18–32

Hics M (2017) Programmed inequality: How Britain discarded women technologist and lost its edge in computing. MIT Press, Cambridge, MA/London, UK

Hooker S (2021) Moving beyond "algorithmic bias is a data problem. Patterns, 2(4), 100241

Houser K A (2019) Can AI Solve the Diversity Problem in the Tech Industry: Mitigating Noise and Bias in Employment Decision-Making. Stan. Tech. L. Rev, 22, 290–354

Jhaver S E et al (2018) Online harassment and content moderation: The case of blocklists. ACM Transactions on Computer-Human Interaction (TOCHI), 25(2), 1–33

Karnouskos S (2021) Symbiosis with artificial intelligence via the prism of law, robots, and society. Artificial Intelligence and Law, 1–23

Kaye D (2018) Mandate of the Special Rapporteur on the promotion and protection of the right to freedom of opinion and expression (OL OTH 41/2018). OHCR, Geneva

Kostoska O, Kocarev L (2019) A Novel ICT Framework for Sustainable Development Goals. Sustainability, 11(7), 1961, 1–31

Latonero M E (2014) Technology and Labor Trafficking Project: Framing document. University of Southern Carolina

Leavy S, Meaney G, Wade K, Greene D (2020) Mitigating Gender Bias in Machine Learning Data Sets. In: Boratto L, Faralli S, Marras M, Stilo G (eds) Bias and Social Aspects in Search and Recommendation. Springer, Cham, pp. 12–26

López Belloso M (2021) Nuevas tecnologías para la promoción y defensa de los derechos humanos. Revista Española de Derecho Internacional, 73(1), 137–164

López Belloso M, Stockhem O (2021) The Contribution of New Technologies to the Feminist Transformation of Women's Rights. In: ICGR 2021 4th International Conference on Gender Research (p. 163). Academic Conferences Inter Ltd

Mazzini G (2019) A system of governance for artificial intelligence through the lens of emerging intersections between AI and EU law. In: De Francheschi A, Schulze R (eds) Digital Revolution –New Challenges for Law. Data Protection, Artificial Intelligence, Smart Products, Blockchain Technology and Virtual Currencies. Verlag C. H. Beck, Munich, pp. 245–296

Mittelstadt B (2019) Principles alone cannot guarantee ethical AI. Nature Machine Intelligence, 1(11), 501–507

Montes R et al (2021) Inteligencia Artificial y tecnologías Digitales para los ODS. Real Academia de la Ingeniería

Nelson G S (2019) Bias in artificial intelligence. North Carolina Medical Journal, 80(4), 220–222

Noble SU (2018) Algorithms of Oppression: How Search Engines Discriminate? NYU Press, New York

Ntoutsi E (2020) Bias in data-driven artificial intelligence systems—An introductory survey. Wiley Interdisciplinary Reviews: Data Mining and Knowledge Discovery, 1–14

Parsheera S (2018) A gendered perspective on artificial intelligence. ITU Kaleidoscope: Machine Learning for a 5G Future, 1–7

Picker CB (2001) A view from 40,000 feet: International law and the invisible hand of technology. Cardozo L. Rev., 23, 149–178

Roselli D M (2019) Managing bias in AI. In . Companion Proceedings of The 2019 World Wide Web Conference, (pp. 539–544)

Schwartz O (2019) Untold History of AI: Algorithmic Bias Was Born in the 1980s IEE Spectrum: https://spectrum.ieee.org/untold-history-of-ai-the-birth-of-machine-bias Accessed 13 September 2021

Scott JW (1996) Only Paradoxes to Offer: French Feminists and the Rights of Man. Harvard University Press

Servoz M (2019) AI, The future of work, work of the future.: European Commission. Brussels https://ec.europa.eu/digital-single-market/en/news/future-work-work-future Accessed 10 March 2021

Siau K A (2020) Artificial intelligence (AI) ethics: ethics of AI and ethical AI. Journal of Database Management (JDM), 31(2), 74–87

Silberg J, Manyika J (2019) Notes from the AI frontier: Tackling bias in AI (and in humans). McKinsey Global Institute. https://www.mckinsey.com/~/media/McKinsey/Featured%20Insights/Artificial%20Intelligence/Tackling%20bias%20in%20artificial%20intelligence%20and%20in%20humans/MGI-Tackling-bias-in-AI-June-2019.pdf Accessed 5 June 2021

Silvestre Cabrera M, López Belloso M, Royo Prieto R (2020) The application of Feminist Standpoint Theory in social research. Investigaciones feministas, 11(2), 307–318

Srinivasan R, Chander A (2021) Biases in AI Systems: A survey for practitioners. Queue, 19(2), 45–64

Stathoulopoulos K (2019) Gender Diversity in AI Research. London: NESTA. https://ssrn.com/abstract=3428240 or http://dx.doi.org/https://doi.org/10.2139/ssrn.3428240. Accessed 5 March 2021

Tannenbaum C et al (2019) Sex and gender analysis improves science and engineering. Nature, Vol. 575, pp. 137–146

Tay B, Younbo J, Taezoon P (2014) When stereotypes meet robots: the double-edge sword of robot gender and personality in human–robot interaction. Computers in Human Behavior, 38, 75–84

UNESCO (2020) Artificial Intelligence And Gender Equality: Key findings of UNESCO's Global Dialogue. United Nations Educational, Scientific and Cultural Organization, Paris

UNI Global Union (2019) Top 10 Principles for ethical artificial intelligence. UNI Global Union, Nyon

Vinuesa R et al (2020) The role of artificial intelligence in achieving the Sustainable Development Goals. Nat Commun, 11, 233,https://doi.org/10.1038/s41467-019-14108-y

Wellner G, Rothman T (2020) Feminist AI: Can we expect our AI systems to become feminist? Philosophy & Technology, 33(2), 191–205

Winfield A (2019) Ethical standards in robotics and AI. Nature Electronics, 2(2), 46–48

World Economic Forum (2019) Global Technology Governance: A multistakeholder approach. World Economic Forum, Geneva

Wyllie A (2003) Why standpoint theory. In: Figueroa R, Harding S (eds) Science and Other Cultures: Issues in Philosophies of Science and Technology. Routledge, New York, pp. 26–48

Yeung K, Howes A G (2019) AI governance by human rights-centred design, deliberation and oversight: An end to ethics washing. In: Markus FP, Dubber D (eds) The Oxford Handbook of AI Ethics. Oxford University Press, Oxford, pp. 77–107

María López Belloso is an Associated Lecturer at the Social Sciences and Humanities Faculty at the University of Deusto. She holds a degree in Law from the University of Deusto and earned her PhD in Human Rights at the same university. She has a solid background in research, both in scientific production and in research management. Her thesis on truth, justice, and reparation processes for victims of forced disappearance in Western Sahara received the Brunet Award in 2017. Her research focuses on the emerging possibilities and potential application of new technologies to the promotion and advocacy of Human Rights. She has coordinated the Cluster on Human Rights and New Technologies in the EMA MA in the Global Campus (Lido) and has worked for several years with the international projects at the Engineering Faculty at the University of Deusto. She bets on an interdisciplinary approach to improve protection systems and to develop innovative human rights protection tools.

Chapter 6
Diversity and Inclusion in Artificial Intelligence

Eduard Fosch-Villaronga and Adam Poulsen

Contents

Abstract Discrimination and bias are inherent problems of many AI applications, as seen in, for instance, face recognition systems not recognizing dark-skinned women and content moderator tools silencing drag queens online. These outcomes may derive from limited datasets that do not fully represent society as a whole or from the AI scientific community's western-male configuration bias. Although being a pressing issue, understanding how AI systems can replicate and amplify inequalities and injustice among underrepresented communities is still in its infancy in social science and technical communities. This chapter contributes to filling this gap by exploring the research question: what do diversity and inclusion mean in the context of AI? This chapter reviews the literature on diversity and inclusion in AI to unearth

E. Fosch-Villaronga (✉)
eLaw Center for Law and Digital Technologies, Leiden University, Leiden, The Netherlands
e-mail: e.fosch.villaronga@law.leidenuniv.nl

A. Poulsen
Charles Sturt University, Bathurst, New South Wales, Australia
e-mail: apoulsen@csu.edu.au

© T.M.C. ASSER PRESS and the authors 2022
B. Custers and E. Fosch-Villaronga (eds.), *Law and Artificial Intelligence*,
Information Technology and Law Series 35,
https://doi.org/10.1007/978-94-6265-523-2_6

the underpinnings of the topic and identify key concepts, research gaps, and evidence sources to inform practice and policymaking in this area. Here, attention is directed to three different levels of the AI development process: the technical, the community, and the target user level. The latter is expanded upon, providing concrete examples of usually overlooked communities in the development of AI, such as women, the LGBTQ+ community, senior citizens, and disabled persons. Sex and gender diversity considerations emerge as the most at risk in AI applications and practices and thus are the focus here. To help mitigate the risks that missing sex and gender considerations in AI could pose for society, this chapter closes with proposing gendering algorithms, more diverse design teams, and more inclusive and explicit guiding policies. Overall, this chapter argues that by integrating diversity and inclusion considerations, AI systems can be created to be more attuned to all-inclusive societal needs, respect fundamental rights, and represent contemporary values in modern societies.

Keywords Artificial Intelligence · Gender · Diversity · Inclusion · LGBT · AI Act

6.1   Introduction

Artificial Intelligence (AI) technologies help automate industrial, retail, and farming sectors and, lately, healthcare, education, and public service. While AI can increase resource efficiency and productivity, automating parts of society reserved once only to humans is nonetheless straightforward and raises particular ethical, legal, and societal concerns.[1] A growing global concern is that AI systems may exacerbate and reinforce existing biases that different societies have with respect to gender, age, race, and sexual orientation.[2] For instance, face recognition systems having difficulty recognizing dark-skinned women and content moderator tools may automatically flag how drag queens use language as *toxic* and prevent them from freely communicating online.[3]

   These outcomes may derive from limited datasets that do not fully represent the society[4] or from the AI scientific community's structural and systematic configuration biases.[5] Still, they are very influential.[6] For instance, there is an exponential growth of social robots and voice assistants that can socially interact with users. A common feature of these artefacts is that many of them are given female names, have female voices, and usually display a servile personality engineered to please users all the time.[7] The use of female voices for serviceable contexts reinforces

---

[1] Schönberger 2019; Wisskirchen et al. 2017; Righetti et al. 2019.

[2] Noble 2018; Raji and Buolamwin 2019; Fosch-Villaronga et al. 2021.

[3] Raji and Buolamwini 2019; Gomes et al. 2019.

[4] Zhao et al. 2017.

[5] Roopaei et al. 2021.

[6] Willson 2017; Noble 2018; Ito 2019.

[7] Liu 2021; Giger et al. 2019.

gender stereotypes about the role women should (or should not) play in society.[8] And these are usually biases rooted in oppressive gender inequalities that have existed throughout history and are typically exacerbated by the lack of diversity of the technical teams developing algorithms which usually work in companies with significant gender disparities in their board of directors.[9] Similar concerns are found in other AI applications, namely in algorithms for medical applications,[10] gender classifiers for marketing, social media platforms or recruiting practices, resulting in disparities in hiring.[11] Likewise, sex robotics often target straight males and objectify women's bodies.[12]

The scientific community broadly supports the narrative that integrating gender and sex factors in research makes better science.[13] However, many disciplines struggle to account for diversity. Authors continuously report that 'inequality and a lack of gender diversity still exist in medicine, especially in academia and leadership;'[14] and that 'when we look to the diversity in immunology research labs, overwhelmingly, women, people of color and LGBTQIA+ scientists are underrepresented among the laboratory head and top leadership roles.'[15] The AI community is no different in this respect, as highlighted by recent studies that explored gender biases in the community, i.e., 'our results indicate a huge gender disbalance among authors, a lack of geographical diversity (with no representation of the least developed countries and very low representation of African countries).'[16] Missing sex and gender considerations in the development of AI, however, can lead to adverse consequences for society that range from exacerbating existing biases and stereotypes (which are prohibited by law)[17] to safety concerns if misgendering a person in health-related applications.[18]

Although being a pressing issue, understanding how AI systems can replicate and amplify inequalities and injustice among underrepresented communities is still in its infancy in social science and technical communities. This chapter contributes to filling this gap by exploring the research question: what do diversity and inclusion mean in the context of AI? To address this question, this chapter reviews the literature on diversity and inclusion in AI to unearth the underpinnings of the topic. We identify key concepts, research gaps, and evidence sources to inform practice and

---

[8] Danielescu 2020.

[9] West et al. 2019; Rahman and Billionniere 2021.

[10] Cirillo et al. 2020.

[11] Park and Woo 2019.

[12] Richardson 2016.

[13] Schiebinger 2014; Tannenbaum et al. 2019.

[14] Ekmekcioglu 2021.

[15] Groom 2021.

[16] Freireç et al. 2020.

[17] See Article 5 of the Convention on the Elimination of All Forms of Discrimination against Women and Article 8(1)(b) of the Convention on the Rights of Persons with Disabilities.

[18] Cirillo et al. 2020.

policymaking in this area. As the most salient diversity and inclusion concerns in AI, sex and gender considerations are the focus here.

This chapter is structured as follows. First, three different levels of the AI development process where diversity and inclusion could be addressed are identified in Sect. 6.2: the technical, the community, and the target user level. Then, the implications of missing diversity and inclusion in AI affecting the target user level are expanded upon in Sect. 6.3, focusing on usually overlooked communities, namely women, the LGBTQ+ community, senior citizens, and disabled persons. This is done by examining four AI application case studies: social robots and gendered voices, algorithms for medical applications, gender classifiers for marketing, social media platforms, or recruiting practices, and sex robotics and gender-specific target market. In Sect. 6.4, mitigation strategies to account for missing sex and gender considerations in AI are proposed, including gendering algorithms, more diverse design teams, and more inclusive and explicit guiding policies. After that, this chapter closes with concluding remarks in Sect. 6.5.

6.2 Diversity and Inclusion in Artificial Intelligence

Like many concepts, such as intelligence, personality, or emotions, there are many ways to define, experience, and legalize diversity and inclusion. The dictionary defines diversity as 'the practice or quality of including or involving people from a range of different social and ethnic backgrounds and of different genders, sexual orientations.'[19]

In the context of AI, those at Google Research define diversity and inclusion as follows:[20]

- *Diversity*: Variety in the representation of individuals in an instance or set of instances, with respect to sociopolitical power differentials (gender, race, etc.). Greater diversity means a closer match to a target distribution over socially relevant characteristics.
- *Inclusion*: Representation of an individual user within an instance or a set of instances, where greater inclusion corresponds to better alignment between a user and the options relevant to them in an instance or set.

Given these definitions, diversity and inclusion in AI have ramifications at three different levels on which we expand here. The first one is the technical level, in which questions around the diversity of algorithms, techniques, and applications are centred around: are the algorithms taking into account all the necessary variables? Are these algorithms classifying users in discriminatory ways? The second level is the community surrounding the configuration, development, and deployment of such techniques and the questions revolving around their practices and how inclusive and

---

[19] *See* Lexico's definition at https://www.lexico.com/definition/diversity.
[20] Mitchell et al. 2020.

diverse they are: does the team have enough female representation? Are all the team members from the same background? The third level refers to the target user and focuses on questions about the person with whom the system will be interacting and affecting and often respond to questions around Responsible Research and Innovation (RRI): was the project conducted by taking all the stakeholders into account? Did the research include the users for feedback?

6.2.1 Technical Level

Algorithms are human-made and are likely to replicate human-like biases.[21] At the technical level, algorithms usually work in binary terms (e.g., yes/no, black/white, move/doesn't move) as if the world were a simple classification problem to be solved. However, the world is not black or white; it is not masculine or feminine. Think for instance the case of gender classifiers whose algorithms usually take *sex* as a primary point of reference when tasked with classifying users gender-wise: male or female. Gender Classification Systems (GCS) are trained using a training dataset (or corpus) of structured and labelled data. These labels categorize data, and the features within, as either masculine or feminine.

However, *sex*, *gender*, and *sexuality* are different concepts although they are often used in overlapping ways:[22]

- "*Sex*" usually refers to the assigned gender at birth based on sex characteristics (e.g. genitalia, chromosomes and hormones), usually 'male' or 'female.'—and in some cases 'indeterminate' for persons with intersex characteristics, in some places (e.g., New Zealand[23]). As one part of many gender-affirmation healthcare actions, medical transition can be engaged to accord sex characteristics with one's gender identity.[24]
- "*Gender*" is both a "person's internal, deeply held sense of their gender," also called *gender identity*[25]—also tied to social, cultural, and legal factors.
- "*Sexuality*" is taken to mean the 'physical, romantic, and/or emotional attraction to another person.'[26]

By using a binary understanding of *sex* as basis for algorithms, inferred data may lead to inaccuracies, e.g., systems can misclassify users whose *gender* differs from their *sex*.[27] Not classifying users correctly in gender terms can lead to bias and unfair decisions and may lead to self-fulfilling prophecies, a phenomenon well-known in

---

[21] O'Neil 2016; Caliskan et al. 2017.

[22] Fosch-Villaronga et al. 2021.

[23] *See* https://www.legislation.govt.nz/act/public/1995/0016/latest/DLM359369.html.

[24] *See* https://www.acon.org.au/wp-content/uploads/2019/07/TGD_Language-Guide.pdf.

[25] *See* https://www.glaad.org/reference/transgender.

[26] Ibidem.

[27] Fosch-Villaronga et al. 2021.

profiling.[28] These effects may amplify inequality, reinforce binarism, exacerbate gender stereotyping, and further push people into categories that are hard to break out.[29] This is particularly important because gender stereotyping is not only 'a generalized view or preconception about attributes or characteristics, or the roles that are or ought to be possessed by, or performed by, women and men.'[30] Gender stereotypes also affect members of the LGBTQ+ community, who often are subsumed under these roles too, e.g., gay men perceived to be feminine would map onto traditional 'warm but less competent' female stereotypes.[31] It also adversely affects the non-binary and transsexual communities, as it essentializes the body as the source of gender and cannot be accurately classified.[32]

6.2.2 Community Level

The AI community is not very diverse. As shown in a recent study reporting the lack of diversity amongst participants in top international AI conferences[33] or in the lack of gender balance ratio among the editors of AI journals (see Fig. 6.1), the AI community has been and continues to be male-based:

Historically, technological development seemed to refuse to acknowledge the existence of women and the LGBTQ+ community in science, as if science was only reserved to men.[34] Being queer was criminalized or devalued in many societies, and women were restricted to caring for the family and children upbringing. Not that long ago, in the 1950s, countries prosecuted homosexual scientists, as the United Kingdom famously did with Alan Turing. Elsewhere in the 1950s, Germany's opinion of the scientific community supported criminalizing homosexuality, defending the anti-gay paragraph 175 of the German criminal code.[35] Although Alan Turing was pardoned in 2013 and paragraph 175 of the German criminal code has since been abolished, the available data suggests it will take much more effort before diversity is a reality for this community in science.[36]

The same applies to the role women play in science. In the Netherlands, for instance, women accounted for only 24% of professors in 2018.[37] As a result, current research is shaped by heteronormative standards that tend to overlook essential elements that may affect women more negatively. For instance, not considering

[28] Custers 2013.

[29] O'Neil 2016; Hamidi et al. 2018.

[30] *See* https://www.ohchr.org/en/issues/women/wrgs/pages/genderstereotypes.aspx.

[31] Sink et al. 2018.

[32] Burdge 2007; Howansky et al. 2019.

[33] Freire et al. 2020.

[34] Cech and Waidzunas 2021; Tao 2018.

[35] Whisnant 2012.

[36] Gibney 2019.

[37] Rathenau Institute 2021.

Fig. 6.1 Screenshot taken 15 September 2021, of the Artificial Intelligence Journal (AIJ) editorial board webpage[38]

gender and diversity issues in automotive engineering can lead to more significant injuries in accidents; or in biomedical research, failing to use female cells and tissues can pose more health risks to women.[39] The lack of diversity and inclusion in AI practices, ranging from datasets that represent only a portion of broader society, binary algorithms, and structural and systematic bias in the AI scientific community prevents the understanding of how these systems affect a big part of society and puts vulnerable communities at risk.[40] A more inclusive and diverse workforce could on the contrary promote the exploration of questions and the addressing of problems beyond the narrow slice of humanity that much science currently represents.[41]

6.2.3 Target User Level

Gender and power relations mediate the development of technology and technologies also impact our understanding of gender and human-technology relations,[42] which

---

[38] *See* https://www.journals.elsevier.com/artificial-intelligence/editorial-board.

[39] Schiebinger 2014.

[40] Poulsen et al. 2020.

[41] Nature Editorial 2018.

[42] Haraway 2006; Bray 2007; Wajcman 2007.

often goes beyond the male-female binary understanding.[43] Unfortunately, other attributes such as sexuality are often not taken into consideration in the development of technology (see, e.g., O'Riordan and Phillips[44]). Users of technology, however, constitute an extensive entanglement of social constructions, relations, and practices with technology because they "consume, modify, domesticate, design, reconfigure, and resist technological development".[45]

When framing technology in a traditional white straight male hegemony seen throughout science, technology, engineering and mathematics (STEM),[46] where inclusion reduces to binary mainstreaming strategies (e.g., the quantitative counting of some women/men),[47] one risks different forms of exclusion. Oudshoorn et al. 2004 warn how 'configuring the user as "everybody"' runs the risk of making it work for the majority, while effectively excluding minorities.[48] For instance, women, senior citizens, persons with disabilities, and the LGBTQ+ communities have not been traditionally considered in society as equal to straight men. As a consequence, there has been much technological development without taking into consideration these communities. For instance, bicycles are designed without taking into consideration women's bodies, resulting in back seat pain, and female sex toys are often created by men.[49]

Persons with disabilities have also been historically marginalized throughout technological progress, usually preventing them systematically from enjoying the same opportunities and resources as the abled population. For instance, consider the slow progress to remove some architectural barriers for people with disabilities, which remains a problem in some nations.[50] Still, much of the work investigating bias in AI centres on the racial and gender discriminatory power these systems have but does not consider how algorithmic systems may also affect the disabled communities.[51] Various are the examples in which technology has been developed for a specific community with a disability but without really engaging with it, e.g., in the case of deaf populations.[52] In this way, science and technology fields have failed to observe a key principle amongst the disabled community and its advocates about participation and co-design: 'nothing about us without us'.[53] In the case of sexual rights, although there have been international efforts towards realizing their sexual rights from institutions like the United Nations,[54] after nearly 30 years of discussion, this

---

[43] Faulkner 2001.

[44] O'Riordan and Phillips 2007.

[45] Oudshoorn and Pitch 2003.

[46] Page 2009.

[47] Vida 2020.

[48] Oudshoorn et al. 2004.

[49] MoMa 2021.

[50] Moscoso-Porras 2019.

[51] Whittaker et al. 2019.

[52] Bragg et al. 2019.

[53] Goggin and Newell 2003.

[54] United Nations 1993.

remains an unfinished agenda for the disabled[55] as if they failed to recognize people with disabilities as sexual beings.[56] In this respect, technology that could empower persons with disabilities to engage with their sexual rights is not mainstream and disregarded as an opportunity.[57]

If AI applications disregard the LGBTQ+ community, this is not necessarily a deliberate decision, but it could be due to lack of visibility of this community comparable to the inequitable experiences LGBTQ+ researchers in STEM fields.[58] One study points out significant biases that context-less online content moderation with AI-driven technology can have concerning online content produced by the LGBTQ+ community. The authors show that Perspective, an AI-driven tool used to measure the toxicity levels of text developed by Google's Jigsaw, could potentially impact drag queens and the LGBTQ+ community online.[59] After analysing several drag queen Twitter accounts, results show that the content produced by drag queens is flagged as having higher levels of toxicity than typically contentious profiles, such as Donald Trump and white supremacists. By failing to understand the LGBTQ+ perspective, the online moderator tool fails to discern that some members of the LGBTQ+ community reclaim derogatory language aimed at this community in a socially valuable way. Whether this is a result of sample bias, that is using a limited dataset to train the system which lacks LGBTQ+ voices, or due to exclusion bias, that is due to human-made decisions that tag certain content in the training dataset as derogatory at the time of data labelling, this leads to prejudicial and algorithmic bias. These biases unfairly alienate an already vulnerable community further and entrench rigid social expectations into systems. Advancing diversity and inclusion in AI could be a step towards creating practices and systems that are informed by the social context in which they occur, and not informed by context-blind training datasets.

6.3   Implications of Missing Diversity and Inclusion in AI

As the primary stakeholders and direct casualties of biased AI systems, such as drag queens using online social media being banned for language use in the example above on how AI-powered content moderator tools may silence the LGBT community, target users are most at risk of being affected by the lack of diversity and inclusion in AI. To show the broader implications of missing diversity and inclusion in AI, this section highlights the typically overlooked target user groups affected: women, the LGBTQ+ community, senior citizens, and disabled persons. Furthermore, this is done by framing and examining these implications in four AI application case studies:

---

[55] Temmerman et al. 2014.

[56] Maxwell et al. 2006; Roussel 2013.

[57] Fosch-Villaronga and Poulsen 2021.

[58] Cech and Waidzunas 2021.

[59] Gomes et al. 2019.

Sect. 6.3.1 gendered social robots: the mechanization of women, Sect. 6.3.2 Binary gender classifiers: guessing objectively what is subjective; Sect. 6.3.3 Algorithms for medical applications: gender as a safety parameter; and Sect. 6.3.4 Sex robotics: able-bodied and male-dominated markets.

6.3.1 Gendered Social Robots: The Mechanization of Women

Social robotics research does not fail to account for gender and sex considerations entirely. Instead, it is one-sided, with women being the primary target for objectification in social robotics. The ideal Stepford-wife image and social role, which presents women as subservient, dutiful, and pleasant, is commonplace in social robotics.[60] For instance, the digital social robot Azuma Hikari[61] presents a stereotypical image of women emerging from the Japanese social context, exacerbating existing prejudice towards women.[62] The developer's website describes Azuma Hikari as 'your personal bride' and in traditional, stereotypically feminine language, such as soothing and hard-working, closing with a quote from Azuma Hikari: 'I look forward to living with you, master!'[63] This approach to social robotics perpetuates a biased representation of women as having to be "young, sexy, soothing, and hard-working in housework" in service of a male master-like husband user.[64]

The stereotype of perfect womanhood in social robots[65] is observed globally. The service robot Sona 2.5,[66] developed in India in response to the COVID-19 pandemic and used in hospitals for food delivery, appears to have breasts and be wearing a skirt, neither of which fulfils any task (see Fig. 6.2). Instead, these aspects are an aesthetic design choice, ultimately reinforcing the biased view that caregiving is a woman's role. Other social robots, including Xiaoice,[67] Siri,[68] and Google Assistant,[69] all come with female voices out of the box.[70] Social robotics needs a 'feminist reboot'[71] at least and, at best, wider and fairer stakeholder engagement to ensure diversity and inclusion.

---

[60] Strengers and Kennedy 2020.

[61] *See* https://www.gatebox.ai/en/hikari.

[62] Liu 2021.

[63] *See* https://www.gatebox.ai/en/hikari.

[64] Liu 2021.

[65] Giger et al. 2019.

[66] *See* https://clubfirst.org/product/sona-2-5-covid-19-robot/.

[67] *See* http://www.xiaoice.com/.

[68] *See* https://www.apple.com/au/siri/.

[69] *See* https://assistant.google.com/.

[70] Liu 2021.

[71] Strengers and Kennedy 2020.

Fig. 6.2. Service robot Sona 2.5, with breasts and a skirt. Screenshot of a video uploaded to YouTube by India Times[72]

6.3.2   Binary Gender Classifiers: Guessing Objectively What is Subjective

Automated Sensitive Traits Recognition alludes to the use of inference classification systems that are, in part, trained to look for sensitive traits that stereotypically identify users as a certain type of person. One of the traits these systems infer is gender via GCS technology which attempts to identify and compare elements in novel input (e.g., word usage or images) to known data labelled by gender (e.g., stereotypical feminine or masculine words or imagery) and classify it by gender. These systems exacerbate existing stereotypes because they take 'sex' as a parameter. In this sense, these technologies usually build on 'male' and 'female' categories that exclude the intersex community.[73] For instance, a study by Park and Woo 2019 trained a system to identify women using a dataset that paired gender with the frequency of sentiment-driven words.[74] During training, the system learned that content produced by women tended to use the words 'thank', 'bless, 'scary,' and 'illness' about twice as often as men. At the same time, men used the words 'accurate,' 'important,' 'issue,' and 'aches' twice as often as women.[75] The algorithmically produced assumption that a person with sensitive traits, such as one who might more frequently use words like 'thank' and

---

[72] *See* India Times 2020 Covid-19: Jaipur Hospital Turns To Robots To Take Care Of Coronavirus Patients https://navbharattimes.indiatimes.com/video/news/covid-19-jaipur-hospital-turns-to-robots-to-take-care-of-coronavirus-patients/videoshow/74818092.cms.

[73] Fosch-Villaronga et al. 2021.

[74] Park and Woo 2019.

[75] Park and Woo 2019.

'bless,' is probably a woman, perpetuates stereotypical feminine-masculine societal roles which do not fully represent society.

Popular training datasets for GCS technology are significantly gender-biased, associating female names more often with family words than career words and with arts more than mathematics and science.[76] As a result, 'models trained to perform prediction on these datasets amplify the existing gender bias when evaluated on development data.'[77] For example, the verb 'cooking' is heavily biased towards women in a classifier trained using the imSitu dataset, amplifying existing gender stereotypes.[78] The same gender biases have been shown in natural language processing,[79] another method used to support gender classifiers.[80]

Algorithms perform poorly in recognizing objectively internal and subjective aspects tied to social and cultural factors, including gender and emotions.[81] Given that biases can propagate throughout AI models,[82] these systems may misclassify users. In the context of GCS, these systems can misgender users, which has adverse implications that go from reinforcing gender binarism to undermining autonomy. Also they can be a tool for surveillance that can threaten someone's safety.[83] To be misgendered reinforces the idea that society does not consider or recognize a person's gender as real, causing rejection, impacting self-esteem and confidence, feeling authenticity, and increasing one's perception of being socially stigmatized.[84]

However, the main problem is that gender identity is primarily subjective and internal, which completely opposes the idea that gender can be recognized automatically, at least with state-of-the-art GCS technology.[85] The same applies to emotional recognition systems aimed at recognizing user emotions: emotional AI follows a procrustean design, in which emotions are reduced to physiological parameters only.[86] In this line of thought, it is not hard to imagine that misclassifications can occur. If used to support ulterior decision-making processes, such misclassification may lead to adverse effects for the users, ranging from mere discomfort to a chilling effect or even harm.[87]

---

[76] Nosek et al. 2002a; Caliskan et al. 2017; Nosek et al. 2002b.

[77] Zhao et al. 2017.

[78] Zhao et al. 2017.

[79] Sun et al. 2019; Zhou et al. 2019.

[80] Campa et al. 2019.

[81] Dupré et al. 2020; Fosch-Villaronga et al. 2021.

[82] Buolamwini and Gebru 2018; Font and Costa-jussà 2019; McDuff et al. 2019; Torralba and Efros 2011.

[83] Hamidi et al. 2018.

[84] Keyes 2018; Fosch-Villaronga et al. 2021.

[85] Fosch-Villaronga et al. 2021.

[86] Fosch-Villaronga 2019a, b.

[87] Hamidi et al. 2018; Büchi et al. 2020; Nišević et al. 2021.

6.3.3 Algorithms for Medical Applications: Gender as a Safety Parameter

If failing to account for sex and gender considerations in algorithmic systems is a point of concern in AI-driven social media practices (e.g., using GCS technology), failing to do so in sensitive domain applications like healthcare, where these considerations are essential in determining patient safety and healthcare outcomes, is a salient concern. Despite clear evidence to the contrary, science holds on to the promise that these systems will help deliver safer care.[88,89]

The persistent phenomena of failing to support diversity and inclusion has especially gained ground in the context of rising inequities and bias in healthcare today, which does not provide adequate care for all, explicitly excluding minority groups in society like the transgender and the intersex communities. Intertwined with this concern of exacerbating pre-existing inequities, including gender inequalities, is embedded bias present in many algorithms due to the lack of inclusion of minorities in datasets.[90] For example, AI used in dermatology to diagnose melanoma lacks the inclusion of skin colour.[91] Another example is the corpus of genomic data, which so far has seriously underrepresented minorities.[92] In the context of AI for medicine, such crucial differences in sex and gender can be vital when it comes to critical conditions and directly impact patient safety.

These findings indicate that much work is still needed in the area of diversity in AI for medicine to eradicate embedded prejudice in AI and strive for medical research that provides a true representative cross-section of the population.[93] Algorithms should be designed to look at specific features from an intersectional point of view, like gender as a non-binary characteristic, which may prevent discrimination for this community. Also, developers should only use sensitive information relating to gender, sex, or race in specific and regulated applications where it is proven they matter.[94] On the contrary, and as far as possible, AI could also use gender-neutral biomarkers for decision-making, a practice that could be more in line with the data minimization principle enshrined in EU data protection law. Alternatively, developers could design discrimination-aware or privacy-preserving algorithms, also in the context of medicine.[95] In this way, biases could be eliminated from the data used to train the AI and ensure an equal representation of examples.

---

[88] Yu et al. 2018; Ahuja 2019.

[89] Cirillo et al. 2020.

[90] Topol 2019.

[91] Esteva et al. 2017.

[92] Wapner 2018.

[93] Topol 2019.

[94] Fosch-Villaronga et al. 2021.

[95] Kamiran et al. 2013; Cirillo et al. 2020.

6.3.4 Sex Robotics: Able-Bodied and Male-Dominated Markets

Sex robots are service robots that perform actions contributing directly to increase in the satisfaction of the sexual needs of a user.[96] These robots often target young, able-bodied, and typically straight men, both in the way they are marketed and designed.[97] Given the widespread views and narratives concerning sex and sexuality, sex robots are commonly not targeted to people with disabilities, a group which might benefit the most from sex robot intervention to help fulfil unmet sexual needs.[98]

Through a broader lens, the lack of wider inclusion of different user groups leads sex robotics to have intimate connections with misogyny, child sexual exploitation, male violence, and the idea that women are programmable.[99] The results of a systematic exploratory survey on public opinion on sex robots reveal that, in general, men find sex robots more acceptable than women.[100] On the expected capabilities of sex robots, the statistics also show that women, more than men, prefer robots to be instructed and obey orders.[101] This may suggest that sex robots increase the objectification of the person, regardless of gender, and that, more research is needed to understand how the interplay between diversity and inclusion could affect sex robot development.[102]

Engaging with diversity and inclusion could help open new avenues for the sex robot industry and potentially help create counternarratives that favour new developments in this area. For instance, sex robots have many sexual characteristics and capabilities that might prove helpful in fulfilling the sexual desires of those in disability care. However, for the most part, sex robotics research excludes persons with disabilities as crucial stakeholders.[103] Also, some research on sex robots addresses sex offenders as users, exploring these artefacts' use to reduce poor sexual behaviour.[104] Yet, studies show that sex offenders are less likely to perceive sex robots as adequate deterrents for sexual violence against persons.[105] Hence, not engaging with the right communities more inclusively may create wrong and inconsiderate technology and prevent parts of the population from enjoying the benefits technology offers.

---

[96] Fosch-Villaronga and Poulsen 2021.

[97] Fosch-Villaronga and Poulsen 2021.

[98] Jecker 2020.

[99] Richardson 2016.

[100] Scheutz and Arnold 2016.

[101] Scheutz and Arnold 2016.

[102] Fosch-Villaronga and Poulsen 2021.

[103] Fosch-Villaronga and Poulsen 2021.

[104] Behrendt 2018.

[105] Zara et al. 2021.

6.4 Addressing Diversity and Inclusion in AI

Mitigation strategies are needed to account for the implications of sex and gender considerations in AI, such as those explored above. This section proposes three holistic approaches to advance diversity and inclusion in AI that align with current legislation and are more attuned to societal needs. These are gendering algorithms, more diverse design teams, and more inclusive and explicit guiding policies.

6.4.1 Diversity in Algorithms: Gendering Algorithms

At the technical level, data collection practices could be more diverse and inclusive. For instance, consider the use of AI in medicine via clinical decision support algorithms, which are trained using large datasets of electronic health records. These datasets may contain an unbalanced representation of sex and gender factors, resulting in algorithmic bias emerging during training.[106] Ultimately, considering the impact of sex and gender on human health (e.g., through opportunities for therapeutic discovery and the frequency and magnitude of adverse health events), missing these considerations in AI-driven medicine is of concern.[107] In this case, a push towards more diverse and inclusive AI practices could be to make an effort towards reducing and eliminating biases from datasets by ensuring there is an equal representation of sex and gender differences.[108] The same practice could be used in GCS research to the same end. Furthermore, similar advances towards equal representation in the realisation of others systems could also reduce bias and improve diversity, particularly in social and sex robotics through fairer stakeholder engagement.

The exclusion of diverse gender and sex considerations in AI puts vulnerable communities at risk. Digital identity and participatory culture play a significant role in the sense of self in the modern world and there could be more efforts to realize diversity and inclusion in the online world[109] to not perpetuate the normative view that particular groups of people, such as trans or non-binary people, do not exist.[110] For instance, gender classifiers could be developed using a more accurate understanding of gender to represent contemporary society fully. For instance, algorithms can be designed to look at certain features from an intersectional point of view, like gender as a non-binary characteristic. As far as possible, gender-neutral biomarkers could also be used by AI for decision-making. In this way, biases can be eliminated from the data used to train the AI by ensuring there is an equal representation of examples, and diversity can be better accounted for[111] Having a GCS that accounts for diversity

---

[106] Cirillo et al. 2020.

[107] McGregor 2016.

[108] Cirillo et al. 2020.

[109] Jenkins et al. 2016.

[110] Keyes 2018.

[111] Kamiran et al. 2013.

and inclusion would help reduce bias in systems in which gender inferences flow, including search and recommendation systems, which similarly need to be fairness-aware (i.e., data handling is guided by ethical, social, and legal dimensions).[112]

6.4.2 Diverse Teams, Organizations, and Design

Accounting for stakeholder values, promoting positive value impact, and eliminating and mitigating adverse effects requires teams designing, developing, and implementing AI to have diverse configurations, administration, and design thinking. Diverse groups have more accurate discussions, cite more facts, make fewer mistakes, and are more willing to discuss sensitive topics such as racism.[113] Diverse teams also contribute to radical innovation processes[114] and although they are less confident and perceive group interactions as less effective, they perform better than more homogeneous groups.[115] In short, people from diverse backgrounds can help improve group thinking. Given that AI can affect individuals and society at large, thinking of ways to increase diversity in the teams building AI systems can prove beneficial in the long term.

To avoid replicating bias in AI, considering the values of vulnerable communities, such as people with disabilities, the LGBTQ+ community, or women, is crucial. Participatory, user-centred design methods that centre on diverse human values and include the voice of the user in the realization of an artefact, such as value sensitive design,[116] are the best way forward to account for diversity and inclusion in AI. Furthermore, adopting holistic inclusion strategies and diverse teams in robotics and AI could ease the understanding of the challenges around discrimination and bias experienced by vulnerable communities.[117] Noteworthy outlier initiatives which have embraced these approaches and are pushing for diversity and inclusion in robotics and AI include Pride@CSIRO[118] and Queer in AI.[119] Both these initiatives seek to foster inclusive environments in AI research, recruit diverse and talented people, and engage grand technology challenges with a diversity of the minds and lived experiences.

Digital identity and participatory culture play a determinant role in the sense of self in the modern world. In this sense, there could be more efforts towards realizing diversity and inclusion in the online world[120] to not perpetuate the normative

---

[112] Geyik et al. 2019.

[113] Sommers 2006; Rock and Grant 2016.

[114] Díaz-García et al. 2013.

[115] Phillips et al. 2009.

[116] Friedman and Hendry 2019; Friedman et al. 2006.

[117] Poulsen et al. 2020.

[118] CSIRO 2019.

[119] Queer in AI 2019.

[120] Jenkins 2016.

view that certain collectives such as trans or non-binary do not exist.[121] Holistic inclusion strategies on multiple levels, e.g., how these communities and the individuals can benefit from robot technology, could combat this issue. More research is needed to create knowledge about how different communities, such as women, LGBTQ+, and persons with discapacities, engage with and value technologies to identify how to better include them in all levels of the design, creation, and implementation process. An essential recommendation is that these users are included thoroughly in the design-implementation-use lifecycle of AI through participatory, user-centred design methods, such as value sensitive design,[122] as these could positively or adversely impact these user groups' lives.

6.4.3 More Inclusive Guidelines, Policies, and Regulation

Designers play a significant role in shaping technology to meet the needs of users and the goals of regulators.[123] However, robot developers are not always in a position to foresee the potential risks that their creations may have because they are usually too intent on solving a particular problem. Users may also be more concerned with the practical benefits that they gain from employing the technology than reflecting on whether it is beneficial for them or not.[124] Branching across and above the technical, community, and target user levels, policy operates on a meta-level that could help strengthen diversity and inclusion in AI throughout the other levels. AI designers, for instance, need to respect the EU Charter of Fundamental Rights (EU CFR), including its Articles 1 on dignity, 7–8 on private life and protection of personal data, 21 on non- discrimination, 23 on equality between women and men. There are also two international human rights treaties that include explicit obligations relating to harmful and wrongful stereotyping. These articles translate into direct obligations for AI designers to develop systems that are safe, respect user privacy, do not discriminate, and do not generate or reinforce stereotypes.

Still, AI developers may struggle to implement these human rights in their teams or their designs because the current legal framework is fragmented, lacks concrete guidance, and strives to account for diversity and inclusion.[125] For instance, sex and gender considerations have not been traditionally considered sensitive or essential aspects in related EU legal frameworks, such as the General Data Protection Directive (GDPR), the Medical Device Regulation, or the Safety Machinery Directive.[126]

---

[121] Keyes 2018.

[122] Friedman and Hendry 2019; Friedman et al. 2006.

[123] Fosch-Villaronga and Özcan 2019.

[124] Carr 2011.

[125] Jobin et al. 2019.

[126] Martinetti et al. 2021. *See* Regulation (EU) of the European Parliament and of the Council of 27 April 2016 on the protection of natural persons with regards to the processing of personal data and on the free movement of such data; Regulation (EU) 2017/745 of the European Parliament and

In April 2021, the European institutions released a proposal for a regulation laying down harmonized rules on AI (also called draft AI Act).[127] The draft AI Act bases its wording on the idea that AI designers need to respect the principles of data protection, consumer protection, non-discrimination and gender equality. The draft AI Act complements existing EU law on non-discrimination that lays down specific requirements to minimize the risk of algorithmic discrimination, especially concerning the design and the quality of data sets used for AI systems and the obligations for testing, risk management, documentation, and human oversight throughout the AI systems' lifecycle.

The draft AI Act also identifies those 'AI systems that pose significant risks to the health and safety or fundamental rights of persons' as 'high-risk'. However, the AI Act does not have an intersectional approach for algorithmic discrimination of certain groups. Gender equality is only mentioned once, and although it is clear that the AI Act stresses that algorithms can discriminate against age groups, persons with disabilities, or persons of specific racial or ethnic origins or sexual orientation, this is in the context of work-related matters. However, failing to acknowledge that algorithms and AI can discriminate against society in general, including women, senior citizens, persons with disabilities, the LGBTQ+ community, or communities from different religions, is failing society. A more inclusive, diverse, and intersectional approach to AI regulation is deemed necessary if the EU expects to ensure that AI is of, by, and for the people.

Amidst this regulatory turmoil, the notion of responsible research and innovation (RRI) has emerged as an overarching concept that captures crucial aspects concerning what researchers can do to ensure that science, research, and innovation have positive, socially acceptable, and desirable outcomes.[128] The RRI approach provides a suitable framework to guide all the social actors involved in research and innovation (R&I) processes towards this aim. The European Commission defines RRI as "an approach that anticipates and assesses potential implications and societal expectations concerning research and innovation, intending to foster the design of inclusive and sustainable research and innovation."[129] Through the lens of RRI, the principles of inclusion, anticipation, reflection, and responsiveness typically guide the research and innovation (R&I) processes and could prove to be instrumental in achieving more inclusive and diverse AI—at least in transition times.

---

of the Council of 5 April 2017 on medical devices; and the Directive 2006/42/EC of the European Parliament and of the Council of 17 May 2006 on machinery.

[127] AI Act 2021.

[128] Stahl and Coeckelbergh 2016.

[129] European Commission 2012.

6.5   Conclusion

Social inequalities recreated as AI bias result from the lack of diversity and inclusion in AI practices. For instance, by failing to account for the socially valuable use of LGBTQ+ speech aiming to reclaim derogatory language within that community, AI-driven content moderator tools automatically flag online posts of drag queens using reclaimed language as *toxic* and prevent them from freely communicating online.[130] These kinds of biases emerge from a range of inequities preserved in AI practices, from limited datasets that do not fully represent society[131] to structural and systematic biased configurations of the AI scientific community.[132] At risk is the amplification of stereotypes, alienation of minority and silent communities, and entrenchment of rigid social expectations in systems.[133]

Although there is increasing attention from robotics, the Human-Robot Interaction and AI communities to address diversity, particularly biased and discriminatory algorithms,[134] biases persist, and vulnerable communities remain mainly invisible and at risk.[135] This calls for action toward the redefinition of inclusion and exclusion, the boundaries and limitations of diversity for the robotics and AI community.[136] Advancing diversity and inclusion in AI, therefore, could be a step towards creating practices and system output that are informed by the social context in which they occur, and not informed by a select few in a research laboratory or by context-blind trained systems.[137]

---

[130] Raji and Buolamwini 2019; Gomes et al. 2019.

[131] Zhao et al. 2017.

[132] Roopaei et al. 2021.

[133] Mitchell et al. 2020.

[134] Raji and Buolamwini 2019.

[135] Willson 2017; Noble 2018; Ito 2019.

[136] Some initiatives have started to explore these topics in the Netherlands. Check for instance the 'Gendering Algorithms' initiative started at Leiden University (*see* https://www.genderingalgori thms.org/) or the 'Diversity and Inclusion for Embodied AI' initiative started by the 4TU Federation and Leiden University (*see* https://www.dei4eai.com/).

[137] Mitchell et al. 2020.

References

Addlakha R et al (2017) Disability and sexuality: Claiming sexual and reproductive rights. Reproductive Health Matters https://doi.org/10.1080/09688080.2017.1336375

Ahuja A S (2019) The impact of artificial intelligence in medicine on the future role of the physician. Peer J, 7, e7702

Behrendt M (2018) Reflections on moral challenges posed by a therapeutic childlike sexbot. In: Cheok A, Levy D (eds) LSR 2017: Love and Sex with Robots. Springer, Cham, pp 96–113

Bragg D et al (2019) Sign language recognition, generation, and translation: An interdisciplinary perspective. In: Proceedings of the 21st International ACM SIGACCESS Conference on Computers and Accessibility. ACM, New York, pp 16–31

Bray F (2007) Gender and technology. Annu. Rev. Anthropol. https://doi.org/10.1146/annurev.ant hro.36.081406.094328

Büchi M, Fosch-Villaronga E, Lutz C, Tamò-Larrieux A, Velidi S, Viljoen S (2020) The chilling effects of algorithmic profiling: Mapping the issues. Computer law & security review 36, 105367

Burdge B J (2007) Bending gender, ending gender: Theoretical foundations for social work practice with the transgender community. Social work 52:243–250

Buolamwini J, Gebru T (2018) Gender shades: Intersectional accuracy disparities in commercial gender classification. In: Proceedings of the First Conference on Fairness, Accountability and Transparency. PMLR, pp 77–91

Caliskan A et al (2017) Semantics derived automatically from language corpora contain humanlike biases. Science https://doi.org/10.1126/science.aal4230

Campa S et al (2019) Deep & machine learning approaches to analyzing gender representations in journalism. https://web.stanford.edu/class/archive/cs/cs224n/cs224n.1194/reports/custom/157 87612.pdf

Carr N (2011) The Shallows: What the Internet is doing to our brains

Cech E A, Waidzunas T J (2021) Systemic inequalities for LGBTQ professionals in STEM. Science Advanceshttps://doi.org/10.1126/sciadv.abe0933

Cirillo D et al (2020) Sex and gender differences and biases in artificial intelligence for biomedicine and healthcare. NPJ Digital Medicine https://doi.org/10.1038/s41746-020-0288-5

Commonwealth Scientific and Industrial Research Organisation (CSIRO) (2019) Diversity & inclusion at the robotics and autonomous systems group. https://research.csiro.au/robotics/diversity-inclusion-at-the-robotics-and-autonomous-systems-group/

Custers B (2013) Data dilemmas in the information society: Introduction and overview. In: Custers B et al (eds) Discrimination and Privacy in the Information Society. Springer, Berlin, pp 3–26

Danielescu A (2020) Eschewing gender stereotypes in voice assistants to promote inclusion. In: Torres M I et al (eds) Proceedings of the 2nd Conference on Conversational User Interfaces. ACM, New York, pp 1–3

Di Nucci E (2017) Sex robots and the rights of the disabled. In: Danaher J, McArthur N (eds) Robot Sex: Social and Ethical Implications. MIT Press, Cambridge, pp 73–88

Díaz-García C, González-Moreno A, Saez-Martinez FJ (2013) Gender diversity within R&D teams: Its impact on radicalness of innovation. Innovation, 15(2), pp. 149–160

Döring N et al (2020) Design, use, and effects of sex dolls and sex robots: Scoping review. Journal of Medical Internet Research https://doi.org/10.2196/18551

Dupré D, Krumhuber EG, Küster D, McKeown GJ (2020) A performance comparison of eight commercially available automatic classifiers for facial affect recognition. PloS one 15(4):e0231968

Ekmekçioğlu O et al (2021) Women in nuclear medicine. Eur. J. Nucl. Med. Mol. Imaging https://doi.org/10.1007/s00259-021-05418-9

European Commission (2012) Options for strengthening responsible research & innovation. Retrieved from https://ec.europa.eu/research/science-society/document_library/pdf_06/options-for-strengthening_en.pdf

Esteva A et al (2017) Dermatologist-level classification of skin cancer with deep neural networks. Naturehttps://doi.org/10.1038/nature21056

Faulkner W (2001) The technology question in feminism: A view from feminist technology studies. Women's Studies International Forum https://doi.org/10.1016/S0277-5395(00)00166-7

Font J E, Costa-jussà M R (2019) Equalizing gender bias in neural machine translation with word embeddings techniques. In: Costa-jussà M R et al (eds) Proceedings of the 1st Workshop on Gender Bias in Natural Language Processing. Association for Computational Linguistics, Stroudsburg, pp 147–154

Fosch-Villaronga E (2019a) Robots, healthcare, and the law: Regulating automation in personal care. Routledge, Abingdon

Fosch-Villaronga E (2019b) "I love you," said the robot: Boundaries of the use of emotions in human-robot interactions. In: Ayanoğlu H, Duarte E (eds) Emotional design in human-robot interaction. Springer, Cham, pp 93–110

Fosch-Villaronga E, Özcan B (2020) The progressive intertwinement between design, human needs and the regulation of care technology: the case of lower-limb exoskeletons. International Journal of Social Robotics, 12(4), 959–972

Fosch-Villaronga E, Poulsen A (2020) Sex care robots. Paladyn, Journal of Behavioral Robotics https://doi.org/10.1515/pjbr-2020-0001

Fosch-Villaronga E, Poulsen A (2021) Sex robots in care: Setting the stage for a discussion on the potential use of sexual robot technologies for persons with disabilities. In: Companion of the 2021 ACM/IEEE International Conference on Human-Robot Interaction. ACM, New York, pp 1–9

Fosch-Villaronga E et al (2021) A little bird told me your gender: Gender inferences in social media. Information Processing & Management https://doi.org/10.1016/j.ipm.2021.102541

Freire A et al (2020) Measuring diversity of artificial intelligence conferences. arXiv preprint. https://arxiv.org/abs/2001.07038

Friedman B, Hendry D G (2019) Value sensitive design: Shaping technology with moral imagination. MIT Press, Cambridge

Friedman B et al (2006) Value sensitive design and information systems. In: Zhang P, Galletta D (eds) Human-computer interaction and management information systems: Foundations. M. E. Sharpe, New York, pp 348–372

Gartrell A et al (2017) "We do not dare to love": Women with disabilities' sexual and reproductive health and rights in rural Cambodia. Reproductive Health Matters https://doi.org/10.1080/09688080.2017.1332447

Geyik S C et al (2019) Fairness-aware ranking in search & recommendation systems with application to LinkedIn talent search. In: Proceedings of the 25th ACM SIGKDD International Conference on Knowledge Discovery & Data Mining. ACM, New York, pp 2221–2231

Gibney E (2019) Discrimination drives LGBT+ scientists to think about quitting. Nature. https://www.nature.com/articles/d41586-019-02013-9

Giger J-C et al (2019) Humanization of robots: Is it really such a good idea? Hum. Behav. & Emerg. Tech. https://doi.org/10.1002/hbe2.147

Goggin G, Newell C (2003) Digital disability: The social construction of disability in new media. Rowman & Littlefield, Lanham

Groom J R (2021) Diversity in science requires mentoring for all, by all. Nat. Immunol. https://doi.org/10.1038/s41590-021-00999-x

Gomes A et al (2019) Drag queens and artificial intelligence: Should computers decide what is 'toxic' on the internet? Internet Lab. http://www.internetlab.org.br/en/freedom-of-expression/drag-queens-and-artificial-intelligence-should-computers-decide-what-is-toxic-on-the-internet/

Hamidi F et al (2018) Gender recognition or gender reductionism? The social implications of embedded gender recognition systems. In: Proceedings of the 2018 CHI Conference on Human Factors in Computing Systems. ACM, New York, pp 1–3

Hao K (2019) Facebook's ad-serving algorithm discriminates by gender and race. MIT Technology Review. https://www.technologyreview.com/2019/04/05/1175/facebook-algorithm-discriminates-ai-bias/

Haraway D (2006) A cyborg manifesto: Science, technology, and socialist-feminism in the late 20th century. In: Weiss J et al (eds) The International Handbook of Virtual Learning Environments. Springer, Dordrecht, pp 118–158

Higgins A et al (2006) Sexual health education for people with mental health problems: What can we learn from the literature? Journal of Psychiatric and Mental Health Nursing https://doi.org/10.1111/j.1365-2850.2006.01016.x

Holder C et al (2016) Robotics and law: Key legal and regulatory implications of the robotics age (part II of II). Computer Law & Security Review https://doi.org/10.1016/j.clsr.2016.05.011

Howansky K et al (2021) (Trans)gender stereotypes and the self: Content and consequences of gender identity stereotypes. Self and Identity https://doi.org/10.1080/15298868.2019.1617191

International Federation of Robotics (2018) Executive summary world robotics 2018 service robots. https://ifr.org/downloads/press2018/Executive_Summary_WR_Service_Robots_2018.pdf

Ito J (2019) Supposedly 'fair' algorithms can perpetuate discrimination. MIT Media Lab. https://www.media.mit.edu/articles/supposedly-fair-algorithms-can-perpetuate-discrimination/

Jecker N S (2020) Nothing to be ashamed of: Sex robots for older adults with disabilities. Journal of Medical Ethics https://doi.org/10.1136/medethics-2020-106645

Jenkins H et al (2016) Participatory culture in a networked era: A conversation on youth, learning, commerce, and politics. Polity Press, Cambridge

Jobin A, Ienca M, Vayena E (2019) The global landscape of AI ethics guidelines. Nat Mach Intell 1(9):389–399

Kamiran F et al (2013) Techniques for discrimination-free predictive models. In: Custers B H M et al (eds) Discrimination and Privacy in the Information Society. Springer, Heidelberg, pp 223–239

Keyes O (2018) The misgendering machines: Trans/HCI implications of automatic gender recognition. Proceedings of the ACM on Human-Computer Interaction https://doi.org/10.1145/3274357

Liu J (2021) Social robots as the bride? Understanding the construction of gender in a Japanese social robot product. Human-Machine Communication https://doi.org/10.30658/hmc.2.5

Martinetti A, Chemweno PK, Nizamis K, Fosch-Villaronga E (2021) Redefining safety in light of human-robot interaction: A critical review of current standards and regulations. Front Chem Eng 32

Maxwell J et al (2006) A health handbook for women with disabilities. Hesperian, Berkeley

McCann E (2003) Exploring sexual and relationship possibilities for people with psychosis – A review of the literature. Journal of Psychiatric and Mental Health Nursing https://doi.org/10.1046/j.1365-2850.2003.00635.x

McDuff D et al (2019) Characterizing bias in classifiers using generative models. In: Wallach H et al (eds) Proceedings of the 33rd Conference on Neural Information Processing Systems. Curran Associates, New York, pp 1–12

McGregor A J et al (2016) How to study the impact of sex and gender in medical research: A review of resources. Biol. Sex Differ. https://doi.org/10.1186/s13293-016-0099-1

Mitchell M et al (2020) Diversity and inclusion metrics in subset selection. In: Proceedings of the AAAI/ACM Conference on AI, Ethics, and Society. ACM, New York, pp 117–123

MoMa (2021) Design innovations for women. Design store. https://store.moma.org/design-innovations-for-women.html

Moscoso-Porras M et al (2019) Access barriers to medical facilities for people with physical disabilities: The case of Peru. Cadernos de Saúde Pública https://doi.org/10.1590/0102-311x00050417

Nature Editorial (2018) Science benefits from diversity. Nature, 558, 5–6, https://www.nature.com/articles/d41586-018-05326-3

Nišević M et al (2021) Understanding the legal bases for automated decision-making under the GDPR. In: Kostas E, Leenes R (eds) Research Handbook on EU Data Protection. Hart Publishing, Oxford [forthcoming]

Noble S U (2018) Algorithms of oppression: How search engines reinforce racism. NYU Press, New York

Nosek B A et al (2002a) Harvesting implicit group attitudes and beliefs from a demonstration web site. Group Dynamics: Theory, Research, and Practice https://doi.org/10.1037/1089-2699. 6.1.101

Nosek B A et al (2002b) Math = male, me = female, therefore math ≠ me. Journal of Personality and Social Psychology https://doi.org/10.1037/0022-3514.83.1.44

Ntoutsi E et al (2020) Bias in data-driven artificial intelligence systems—An introductory survey. Wiley Interdisciplinary Reviews: Data Mining and Knowledge Discovery https://doi.org/10.1002/widm.1356

O'Neil C (2016) Weapons of math destruction: How big data increases inequality and threatens democracy. Crown, New York

O'Riordan K, Phillips D J (2007) Queer online: Media technology & sexuality. Peter Lang Publishing, Bern

Oudshoorn N, Pinch T (2003) How users matter: The co-construction of users and technology. MIT Press, Cambridge

Oudshoorn N et al (2004) Configuring the user as everybody: Gender and design cultures in information and communication technologies. Science, Technology, & Human Values https://doi.org/10.1177/0162243903259190

Page M et al (2009) The blue blazer club: masculine hegemony in science, technology, engineering, and math fields. Forum on Public Policy Online v2009:1–23

Park S, Woo J (2019) Gender classification using sentiment analysis and deep learning in a health web forum. Applied Sciences https://doi.org/10.3390/app9061249

Perry B L, Wright E R (2006) The sexual partnerships of people with serious mental illness. Journal of Sex Research https://doi.org/10.1080/00224490609552312

Phillips KW, Liljenquist KA, Neale MA (2009) Is the pain worth the gain? The advantages and liabilities of agreeing with socially distinct newcomers. Personality and Social Psychology Bulletin, 35(3), 336–350

Poulsen A et al (2020) Queering machines. Nature Machine Intelligence https://doi.org/10.1038/s42256-020-0157-6

Prince A E, Schwarcz D (2020) Proxy discrimination in the age of artificial intelligence and big data. Iowa Law Review 105:1257–1318

Quinn C, Browne G (2009) Sexuality of people living with a mental illness: A collaborative challenge for mental health nurses. International Journal of Mental Health Nursing https://doi.org/10.1111/j.1447-0349.2009.00598.x

Queer in AI (2019) Queer in AI. https://sites.google.com/view/queer-in-ai/

Rahman F, Billionniere E (2021) Re-entering computing through emerging technology: Current state and special issue introduction. ACM Trans. Comput. Educ. https://doi.org/10.1145/344 6840

Raji I D, Buolamwini J (2019) Actionable auditing: Investigating the impact of publicly naming biased performance results of commercial AI products. In: Proceedings of the 2019 AAAI/ACM Conference on AI, Ethics, and Society. ACM, New York, pp 429–435

Rathenau Institute (2021) Women in Academia. https://www.rathenau.nl/en/science-figures/personnel/women-science/women-academia

Richardson K (2016) The asymmetrical 'relationship' parallels between prostitution and the development of sex robots. ACM SIGCAS Computers and Society https://doi.org/10.1145/2874239. 2874281

Righetti L et al (2019) Unintended consequences of biased robotic and artificial intelligence systems [ethical, legal, and societal issues]. IEEE Robotics & Automation Magazine https://doi.org/10.1109/MRA.2019.2926996

Rock D, Grant H (2016) Why diverse teams are smarter. Harvard Business Review, 4(4), 2–5

Roopaei M et al (2021) Women in AI: barriers and solutions. In: Proceedings of the 2021 IEEE World AI IoT Congress (AIIoT). IEEE, New York, pp 0497-0503

Roussel S (2013) Seeking Sexual Surrogates. The New York Times. https://www.nytimes.com/video/world/europe/100000002304193/seeking-sexual-surrogates.html [video]

Schwalbe N, Wahl B (2020) Artificial intelligence and the future of global health. The Lancet https://doi.org/10.1016/S0140-6736(20)30226-9

Scheutz M, Arnold T (2016) Are we ready for sex robots? In: Proceedings of the 11th ACM/IEEE International Conference on Human-Robot Interaction. IEEE, New York, 351–358

Schiebinger L (2014) Scientific research must take gender into account. Nature 507, 9.https://doi.org/10.1038/507009a

Schönberger D (2019) Artificial intelligence in healthcare: A critical analysis of the legal and ethical implications. International Journal of Law and Information Technology https://doi.org/10.1093/ijlit/eaz004

Servais L (2006) Sexual health care in persons with intellectual disabilities. Mental Retardation and Developmental Disabilities Research Reviews https://doi.org/10.1002/mrdd.20093

Sink A, Mastro D, Dragojevic M (2018) Competent or warm? A stereotype content model approach to understanding perceptions of masculine and effeminate gay television characters. Journalism & Mass Communication Quarterly, 95(3), 588–606

Sommers SR (2006) On racial diversity and group decision making: identifying multiple effects of racial composition on jury deliberations. Journal of personality and social psychology, 90(4), 597

Søraa R A (2017) Mechanical genders: How do humans gender robots? Gender, Technology and Development https://doi.org/10.1080/09718524.2017.1385320

Sparrow R (2021) Sex robot fantasies. Journal of Medical Ethics https://doi.org/10.1136/medethics-2020-106932

Stahl BC, Coeckelbergh M (2016) Ethics of healthcare robotics: Towards responsible research and innovation. Robotics and Autonomous Systems, 86, 152–161

STOA (2018) Assistive technologies for people with disabilities. https://www.europarl.europa.eu/RegData/etudes/IDAN/2018/603218/EPRS_IDA(2018)603218_EN.pdf

Strengers Y, Kennedy J (2020) The smart wife: Why Siri, Alexa, and other smart home devices need a feminist reboot. MIT Press

Sun T et al (2019) Mitigating gender bias in natural language processing: Literature review. In: Korhonen A et al (eds) Proceedings of the 57th Annual Meeting of the Association for Computational Linguistics. Association for Computational Linguistics, Stroudsburg, pp 1630–1640

Tannenbaum C, Ellis RP, Eyssel F, Zou J, Schiebinger L (2019) Sex and gender analysis improves science and engineering. Nature 575(7781):137–146

Tao Y (2018) Earnings of academic scientists and engineers: Intersectionality of gender and race/ethnicity effects. American Behavioral Scientist https://doi.org/10.1177/0002764218768870

Temmerman M et al (2014) Sexual and reproductive health and rights: A global development, health, and human rights priority. The Lancet https://doi.org/10.1016/S0140-6736(14)61190-9

Topol E J (2019) High-performance medicine: The convergence of human and artificial intelligence. Nature Medicine https://doi.org/10.1038/s41591-018-0300-7

Torralba A, Efros A A (2011) Unbiased look at dataset bias. In: Proceedings of the Conference on Computer Vision and Pattern Recognition (CVPR). IEEE, New York, pp 1521–1528

United Nations (1993) Standard rules on the equalization of opportunities for persons with disabilities. https://www.un.org/disabilities/documents/gadocs/standardrules.pdf

United Nations (2007) Convention on the Rights of Persons with Disabilities and Optional Protocol. https://www.un.org/development/desa/disabilities/convention-on-the-rights-of-persons-with-disabilities.html

Urry K, Chur-Hansen A (2020) Who decides when people can have sex? Australian mental health clinicians' perceptions of sexuality and autonomy. Journal of Health Psychology https://doi.org/10.1177/1359105318790026

Vaughan C et al (2015) W-DARE: A three-year program of participatory action research to improve the sexual and reproductive health of women with disabilities in the Philippines. BMC Public Health https://doi.org/10.1186/2Fs12889-015-2308-y

Vida B (2021) Policy framing and resistance: Gender mainstreaming in Horizon 2020. European Journal of Women's Studies https://doi.org/10.1177/1350506820935495

Wajcman J (2007) From women and technology to gendered technoscience. Information, Community and Society https://doi.org/10.1080/13691180701409770

Wapner J (2018) Cancer scientists have ignored African DNA in the search for cures. Newsweek. https://www.newsweek.com/2018/07/27/cancer-cure-genome-cancer-treatment-africa-genetic-charles-rotimi-dna-human-1024630.html

Weber J (2005) Helpless machines and true loving care givers: A feminist critique of recent trends in human-robot interaction. Journal of Information, Communication and Ethics in Society https://doi.org/10.1108/14779960580000274

West M et al (2019) I'd blush if I could: Closing gender divides in digital skills through education. UNESCO. https://unesdoc.unesco.org/ark:/48223/pf0000367416.page=1

Willson M (2017) Algorithms (and the) everyday. Information, Communication & Society https://doi.org/10.1080/1369118X.2016.1200645

Wisskirchen G et al (2017) Artificial intelligence and robotics and their impact on the workplace. IBA Global Employment Institute

Wheeler A P, Steenbeek W (2021) Mapping the risk terrain for crime using machine learning. Journal of Quantitative Criminology https://doi.org/10.1007/s10940-020-09457-7

Whisnant C J (2012) Male homosexuality in West Germany. Palgrave Macmillan, London

Whittaker M et al (2019) Disability, bias, and AI. AI Now Institute. https://wecount.inclusivedesign.ca/uploads/Disability-bias-AI.pdf

World Health Organization (2015) Sexual health, human rights and the law report. https://apps.who.int/iris/bitstream/handle/10665/175556/9789241564984_eng.pdf

Yu KH, Beam AL, Kohane IS (2018) Artificial intelligence in healthcare. Nature biomedical engineering, 2(10), 719–731

Zara G et al (2021) Sexbots as synthetic companions: Comparing attitudes of official sex offenders and non-offenders. International Journal of Social Robotics https://doi.org/10.1007/s12369-021-00797-3

Zhao J et al (2017) Men also like shopping: Reducing gender bias amplification using corpus-level constraints. In: Palmer M et al (eds) Proceedings of the 2017 Conference on Empirical Methods in Natural Language Processing. Association for Computational Linguistics, Stroudsburg, pp 2979–2989

Zhou P et al (2019) Examining gender bias in languages with grammatical gender. In: Padó S, Huang R (eds) Proceedings of the 2019 Conference on Empirical Methods in Natural Language Processing and the 9th International Joint Conference on Natural Language Processing (EMNLP-IJCNLP). Association for Computational Linguistics, Stroudsburg, pp 5279–5287

Eduard Fosch-Villaronga is an Assistant Professor at the eLaw Center for Law and Digital Technologies at Leiden University (The Netherlands), where he investigates legal and regulatory aspects of robot and AI technologies, with a special focus on healthcare, diversity, governance, and transparency. Currently, he is the PI of PROPELLING, an FSTP from the H2020 Eurobench project, a project using robot testing zones to support evidence-based robot policies. Previously, Eduard served the European Commission in the Sub-Group on Artificial Intelligence (AI), connected products and other new challenges in product safety to the Consumer Safety Network (CSN) and was the PI of LIAISON, an FSTP from the H2020 COVR project that aimed to link robot development and policymaking to reduce the complexity in robot legal compliance.

In 2019, Eduard was awarded a Marie Skłodowska-Curie Postdoctoral Fellowship and published the book Robots, Healthcare, and the Law (Routledge). Eduard holds an Erasmus Mundus Joint Doctorate in Law, Science, & Technology, coordinated by the University of Bologna (Italy, 2017), an LL.M. from University of Toulouse (France, 2012), an M.A. from the Autonomous University of Madrid (Spain), and an LL.B. from the Autonomous University of Barcelona (Catalonia, Spain, 2011). Eduard is also a qualified lawyer in Spain.

Adam Poulsen is a computer scientist and researcher at Charles Sturt University in New South Wales, Australia. His research covers human-robot interaction, healthcare and social robotics, value sensitive design, computer ethics, care ethics, and LGBTQ+ aged care. At present, Adam primarily focuses on exploring the value sensitive design of robots to assist in, or enhance, the provision of care. Through his research, Adam has developed a novel value sensitive design approach, values in motion design, to model social robots for members of the older LGBTQ+ community experiencing loneliness. It is his hope that such robots can be helpful in the self-care of this vulnerable, under surveyed population and others in the future. Adam holds a Ph.D. and graduated 1st Class Honours of a Bachelor of Computer Science from Charles Sturt University (AU). This work has been partly funded by the Global Transformation and Governance Challenges Seed Grant from Leiden University.

Chapter 7
Artificial Intelligence in Disability Employment: Incorporating a Human Rights Approach

Elisavet Athanasia Alexiadou

Contents

Abstract Persons with disabilities experience high levels of unemployment, job insecurity, tightly bound with persistent socioeconomic aspects such as poverty, social isolation and marginalization. Such worrisome developments tend to magnify and reproduce the inequality and discrimination this vulnerable group faces in the field of employment with long-lasting effects on their life course and on economic development in general. At the same time, in an increasingly unequal world Artificial Intelligence (AI) technologies have rapidly emerged from the shadows to become a priority in the global market as well as to advance people's lives. Against this backdrop, the opportunities and challenges in harnessing AI technologies (i.e., applications/smart devices amplifying human capability) to reasonably accommodate the needs of persons with disabilities in the labour market are examined in this chapter. Undoubtedly, realizing the full potential of AI technologies within employment settings from a disability rights perspective is particularly challenging. To this end, a human rights approach brings into play established frameworks of legal obligations and tools so as to regulate and evaluate the performance of AI technologies with the immediate and ultimate goal the benefit of the whole society. Looking ahead, as a way of facilitating employment opportunities for persons with disabilities this chapter concedes that AI should be framed as a matter of equity and in consistency with human rights principles and standards for achieving optimum workplace accessibility and inclusivity.

Keywords Artificial Intelligence · Disability · Human rights · Employment · Inequality · Discrimination

E. A. Alexiadou (✉)
Aristotle University of Thessaloniki, Thessaloniki, Greece

© T.M.C. ASSER PRESS and the authors 2022
B. Custers and E. Fosch-Villaronga (eds.), *Law and Artificial Intelligence*,
Information Technology and Law Series 35,
https://doi.org/10.1007/978-94-6265-523-2_7

7.1 Introduction

Globally, more than one billion people -nearly 15% of the world's population- is estimated to be living with some type of disability (temporary or permanent impairment), representing "the world's largest minority" as acknowledged by the United Nations.[1] Admittedly, persons with disabilities worldwide constitute one of the most vulnerable and marginalized population groups facing multiple and disproportionate barriers to the full enjoyment of their rights and to their inclusion in society in comparison to the general population.[2] Throughout history, societies have attached negative connotations to persons with disabilities, often perceived as inferior relative to persons without disabilities.[3] Persons with disabilities constantly experience prejudice, discriminatory attitudes and stigma with long-lasting detrimental effects on their life course.[4] Essentially, such disability-based discrimination pervades every aspect of their public-social life undermining their job prospects, incomes and independent living arrangements, affronting their dignity and ultimately perpetuating inequality. At the same time, in an increasingly unequal world Artificial Intelligence (AI) technologies have rapidly emerged from the shadows to become a priority in the global market as well as to advance people's lives.[5] Crucially, AI technologies have been brought to the fore of disability agendas at the International and European levels to foster new ideas and solutions on amplifying human capability and effectively addressing current and future inequalities experienced by persons with disabilities in the labour market.[6]

This chapter sets out to examine the use and application of AI technologies in the employment domain from a disability rights perspective. In addition to this brief introduction, the chapter is divided into two main sections. Section 7.2 focuses on the potential added value of AI technologies towards bridging the gap between disability and the labour market and paving the way for the development of inclusive, accessible and diverse workplaces. Following that, Section 7.3 uses a human rights lens through which to identify principal standards that set forth a legal framework which can be used to regulate and evaluate the performance of AI technologies towards ensuring equal employment opportunities for persons with disabilities. Finally, Section 7.4 sums up the main findings of the chapter and offers some concluding thoughts.

The overall aim of this chapter is to inform human rights scholars, civil society, technology providers and other stakeholders about the real opportunities in harnessing AI technologies to reasonably accommodate the needs of persons with

---

[1] World Health Organization and World Bank 2011. United Nations undated. World Health Organization 2020a.

[2] World Health Organization and World Bank 2011.

[3] Ibid. See generally Rembis et al. 2018.

[4] Ibid. See also Broderick and Ferri 2019, p. 28.

[5] See generally International Telecommunication Union 2019. Human Rights Council 2020, p. 2.

[6] See, for instance, Employer Assistance and Resource Network on Disability Inclusion 2019. See also Outline for the Draft preparation of a General Comment on Article 27 of the CRPD (the right to work and employment). Human Rights Council 2020, p. 2. European Disability Forum 2020.

disabilities in the labour market in order to benefit the whole society. Indeed, as will be further discussed, a focus on the potential power of AI technologies as an equalizer for persons with disabilities in the labour market—under certain conditions—can have profound human rights repercussions for persons with disabilities and their families in today's world that leads to their social disadvantage through hindering their access to social protection schemes and entitlements that other segments of the society may take for granted.[7] And attention to the potential dynamics of AI technologies in society, primarily as a crucial condition for human well-being and for people's ability to actively participate in the economy may produce considerable lasting change within society;[8] persons with disabilities will have the opportunity to offer their full potential, function as productive members of the society and contribute to their families and local communities in a meaningful way, while breaking the vicious cycle of marginalization and poverty.[9] In turn, this will help changing the way society views disability with positive society-wide outcomes, involving human capital development, increased productivity, innovation, and ultimately long-term (economic) prosperity.[10]

7.2 AI Technologies: Towards Bridging the Gap Between Disability and the Labour Market

Persons with disabilities are not a homogeneous group, but constitute a diverse population group confronted with different types of impairments and requiring distinct assistive and support services.[11] Most notably, within the United Nations (UN) human rights system, disability is acknowledged as an "evolving concept" and it is explicitly stressed that "persons with disabilities include those who have long-term physical, mental, intellectual or sensory impairments which in interaction with various barriers may hinder their full and effective participation in society on an equal basis with others".[12] Obviously, as is well established, disability stems predominantly from the failure of the wider social environment to accommodate the needs and aspirations of persons with impairments and to facilitate their full and active participation in society

---

[7] World Health Organization and World Bank 2011.

[8] See generally Tomašev et al. 2020, pp. 1–6; Floridi et al. 2018, pp. 689–707.

[9] UN Department of Economic and Social Affairs 2019, p. 150. See in relation Buckup 2009.

[10] World Bank 2020. Employer Assistance and Resource Network on Disability Inclusion 2019. International Labour Office (ILO) 2011, pp. 5–6.

[11] World Health Organization and World Bank 2011, p. 245. United Nations 2020, p. 4.

[12] See Preamble recital (e) and Article 1, UN Convention on the Rights of Persons with Disabilities, UN Doc A/RES/61/106. https://www.ohchr.org/en/hrbodies/crpd/pages/conventionrightspersonsw ithdisabilities.aspx Accessed 27 February 2021; Human Rights Council 2008. In a nutshell, it is of note that four main theoretical models of disability are identified in literature: the medical model (known also as the "charity" or "individual" model), the social model, the human rights model and the capabilities approach. For an analysis of the theoretical models of disability, see Broderick and Ferri 2019, pp. 18–26. See also Siebers 2008, p. 25.

and economic activities on an equal basis with others.[13] The first World Report on Disability, prepared jointly by the World Health Organization (WHO) and the World Bank (WB), in fact, emphasizes that persons with disabilities experience structural discrimination in all areas of daily life, such as in employment, on the grounds of their disability tightly bound with persistent socioeconomic aspects such as poverty, social isolation and marginalization, thereby increasing the impact of disability.[14]

Importantly, in terms of employment, the International Labour Office (ILO) highlights that the unemployment rate among persons with disabilities is extremely high, almost reaching 80% in some countries.[15] Additionally, evidence indicates that inaccessible workplaces, negative systematic societal attitudes and misconceptions about the working capacity of persons with disabilities play a significant role in undermining and limiting the employment opportunities for those persons.[16] Indeed, data from eight geographical regions across the world on the situation of persons with disabilities in employment reveal that on average 36% of persons with disabilities of working age (aged 15+) are employed compared to 60% for persons without disabilities.[17] Furthermore, the WHO and WB joint report affirms that a persistent wage gap exists in the labour market as regards to persons with disabilities, in that even when persons with disabilities manage to find paid employment, they often encounter wage discrimination owed to a perceived reduced capacity for work.[18] For instance, in 2012 in the United States persons with disabilities who worked full-time earned 14% less than persons without disabilities.[19] Nevertheless, such worrisome developments, which primarily lack a rights perspective, tend to reinforce and reproduce societal inequalities and persistent patterns of exclusion and disadvantage that deny, inter alia, equal employment opportunities to persons with disabilities with far-reaching repercussions on the well-being of persons with disabilities and their families as well as on economic development in general (e.g., excessive financial pressure on social security systems).[20]

Given this precarious reality it is asserted that "*an enterprise culture*" encompassing workplace inclusion and accessibility is required to counter or at least significantly mitigate the adverse impacts and to promote the right to work and employment

---

[13] Waddington and Broderick 2018, p. 37. See, Preamble, recital (e) and Article 1, UN Convention on the Rights of Persons with Disabilities, UN Doc A/RES/61/106. https://www.ohchr.org/en/hrbodies/crpd/pages/conventionrightspersonswithdisabilities.aspx Accessed 27 February 2021.

[14] World Health Organization and World Bank 2011.

[15] United Nations Factsheet on Persons with Disabilities.

[16] UN Department of Economic and Social Affairs 2019, p. 150. World Health Organization and World Bank 2011, p. 240.

[17] UN Department of Economic and Social Affairs 2019, p. 152.

[18] World Health Organization and World Bank 2011, pp. 239–240. See also UN Committee on Economic, Social and Cultural Rights, General comment No. 23 on the right to just and favourable conditions of work (article 7 of the International Covenant on Economic, Social and Cultural Rights), UN Doc. E/C.12/GC/23, 27 April 2016, para 47 (c).

[19] UN Department of Economic and Social Affairs 2019, p. 158.

[20] See Sainsbury and Coleman-Fountain 2014, p. 2. Buckup 2009.

of persons with disabilities.[21] From a practical perspective, this requires the development and adoption of active labour market policies that address discriminatory and negative attitudes towards persons with disabilities in the employment domain with much attention paid to the constructive engagement of (public and private) employers in attempts to bring persons with disabilities into the labour market.[22] Such suggestion rests on the proposition that workplace inclusivity and accessibility will depend upon the development and implementation of those measures and tools considered to be most assistive and effective in terms of enabling persons with disabilities to perform their job duties. Within this context, it is now widely recognized that AI technologies have a prominent role to play in facilitating workplace inclusivity and accessibility for persons with disabilities.[23] In fact, it is notable that 12% of all AI patent applications engage with the field of life.[24]

At this stage, it is essential to elucidate what AI encompasses as its deployment for meeting the needs of persons with disabilities in the employment field is at the forefront of this chapter's analysis. Arguably, while the existing definitions of AI may vary in literature, AI can be broadly conceptualized as computer algorithms that simulate human cognitive functions and capabilities, such as perceiving the environment, gaining information to act and then enhancing these actions based on machine learning.[25] In a similar vein, the European Commission in its Communication on AI stresses that "Artificial intelligence (AI) refers to systems that display intelligent behaviour by analyzing their environment and taking actions—with some degree of autonomy—to achieve specific goals. AI-based systems can be purely software-based, acting in the virtual world (e.g. voice assistants, image analysis software, search engines, speech and face recognition systems) or AI can be embedded in hardware devices (e.g. advanced robots, autonomous cars, drones or Internet of Things applications)."[26]

In recent years, several technology providers in cooperation with civil society organizations and academia have launched a number of AI applications on disability to be used in the employment domain towards bridging existing gaps between disability and labour market.[27] The development, adoption and implementation of these applications is structured around one central objective, which is to help persons with disabilities overcome physical and cognitive challenges so as not to be left out of job opportunities and society at large.[28] AI is a relatively new—albeit rapidly

---

[21] See Broderick and Ferri 2019, p. 217.

[22] Ibid. International Labour Office (ILO) 2011, p. 5–6. European Parliament 2017, para T.

[23] See, for instance, ILO Global Business and Disability Network and Fundación ONCE 2019.

[24] World Trade Organization, World Health Organization, World Intellectual Property Organization 2020, p. 89.

[25] World Trade Organization, World Health Organization, World Intellectual Property Organization 2020, p. 89. For existing definitions of AI, see also High-Level Expert Group on Artificial Intelligence 2019.

[26] European Commission 2018, p. 1.

[27] See for instance, World Business Council for Sustainable Development 2020. ILO Global Business and Disability Network and Fundación ONCE 2019, pp. 19–20.

[28] See generally Employer Assistance and Resource Network on Disability Inclusion 2019.

developing—concept to the world of labour market and at first glance, some stake-holders, involving employers, may wonder about the added value, let alone necessity, of incorporating AI into the workplace as a solution to pressing employment issues and challenges encountering persons with disabilities in the labour market. Nonetheless, technology providers develop AI based systems in the form of smart devices and AI powered communication systems that can assist persons with disabilities to see, hear, understand and freely act, thereby leading productive, independent and dignified lives. Examples include AI-based applications that recognize and describe images, texts and objects for persons who are blind, visually impaired as well as help speech recognition, captioning, sign language recognition and creation for persons with auditory and speech impairments.[29] Importantly, AI technologies in the form of smart devices/assistants that improve the functioning and independence of persons with disabilities must become front and centre on every employer's list of solutions so that persons with disabilities can participate actively in the labour market and offer their full potential. Therefore, it must be conceded that AI technology initiatives must be dominated by efforts that pay attention to the intersection between disability and employment towards making inclusive and diverse labour markets, which provide mutually practical benefits to employers and employees, involving persons with disabilities, such as increased productivity, creativity and enhanced workplace morale among employees.[30]

Last but not least, it is essential to mention that despite the proliferation and newfound popularity of AI technologies as a critical part of human welfare, a number of significant challenges, involving primarily regulatory issues, are raised due to the multifaceted nature of AI technologies.[31] Arguably, this technological innovation has the potential to meaningfully enhance the employment opportunities for persons with disabilities but equally to undermine them.[32] Nowadays, private corporations are increasingly deploying AI technologies in job applicants screening programmes for selecting and recruiting employees.[33] Particularly, AI-powered interview software is used to screen the candidates, namely to analyse and assess their facial expressions, posture, word choice, speech capability and other aspects of their personality

---

[29] World Business Council for Sustainable Development 2020, pp. 3–5. Here, it is essential to note that the above mentioned examples of AI serve as a representative illustration of AI tools and activities on disability carried out by technology providers. For a comprehensive account of AI tools and activities on disability, see, e.g., Employer Assistance and Resource Network on Disability Inclusion 2019, pp. 4–5.

[30] Employer Assistance and Resource Network on Disability Inclusion 2019. International Labour Office (ILO) 2011, pp. 5–6.

[31] As regards to the multifaceted nature of AI, see for instance Zardiashvili and Fosch-Villaronga 2020, p. 45.

[32] See, for instance, World Business Council for Sustainable Development 2020, p. 5. ILO Global Business and Disability Network and Fundación ONCE 2019, p. 18.

[33] Employer Assistance and Resource Network on Disability Inclusion 2019, p. 3. European Disability Forum 2020, p. 5.

in order to produce a score that can be compared to an existing data set that determines the right candidate.[34] However, in some cases those corporations tend to use AI based software with non-transparently programmed and even biased algorithms in employment recruitment processes that might reflect (intentionally or unintentionally) discriminatory biases, thereby leading to the exclusion of qualified candidates on the grounds of their disability, and ultimately to a possible backlash on the deployment of advanced technologies, like AI technologies, due to decreased social acceptance.[35] To put simply, when an algorithmic system is trained on non-inclusive or even biased data, it tends to adopt a "one-size-fits-all" approach across diverse groups of job applicants for the assessment of their skills and qualifications.[36] Clearly, the design and deployment of such AI programmes carry significant human rights implications for persons with disabilities in that they can lead to screen out or, even if not overtly, to the discrimination against "non-traditional" applicants, involving persons with disabilities.[37] Indeed, they could adversely affect employment opportunities for candidates with intellectual and other forms of disabilities and ultimately may lead to unlawful discriminatory decisions against those persons on the part of employers who employ this algorithmic system in decision-making processes.[38] Importantly, in increasingly diverse societies the EU General Data Protection Regulation (GDPR) takes an explicit stance against such disturbing developments and states in Article 22 para 1 ("automated individual decision-making, including profiling") that "the data subject shall have the right not to be subject to a decision based solely on automated processing, including profiling, which produces legal effects concerning him or her or similarly significantly affects him or her".[39]

On the basis of the preceding practices it is plausible to discern that without simplifying the challenges, AI technologies are, in principle, not contrary to the right of persons with disabilities to work and employment. It is the unregulated deployment of AI technologies in a non-disability inclusive way that affronts the dignity of persons with disabilities and poses considerable threats and obstacles to their access to the labour market. Hence, it is pointedly argued in literature that new technologies, such as AI, have the power to bring both benefits and risks to the enjoyment of human rights.[40] Crucially, from a disability rights perspective a pressing question remains as to how the benefits for persons with disabilities from the application and use of AI technologies in the labour market can be maximized

---

[34] Ibid. Employer Assistance and Resource Network on Disability Inclusion 2019.

[35] ILO Global Business and Disability Network and Fundación ONCE 2019, p. 18. World Business Council for Sustainable Development 2020, p. 5. See also Outline for the preparation of a General Comment on Article 27 of the CRPD (the right to work and employment). European Disability Forum 2020, pp. 5–8. World Business Council for Sustainable Development 2020, p. 5.

[36] Nugent et al. 2020, pp. 11–12. Employer Assistance and Resource Network on Disability Inclusion 2019, p. 4.

[37] Ibid.

[38] Ibid.

[39] European Parliament and Council of the European Union 2016.

[40] See generally Land and Aronson 2018, p. 1.

while the concerns and threats to the employment of those persons are minimized along the way.

7.3 Applicable Human Rights Standards

Since the adoption of the United Nations Convention on the Rights of Persons with Disabilities (CRPD) the rights of persons with disabilities are increasingly recognised in a world that is full of human rights challenges and tensions and a system of legal obligations is developed in virtue of which State conduct and domains beyond the State, involving advanced technologies (e.g., AI), can be regulated and evaluated over time.[41] Indeed, the legal basis that is the most standard setting concerning the rights of persons with disabilities is the CRPD.[42] The CRPD has been rapidly ratified by most of the countries worldwide, indicating the global interest in protecting *per se* the rights of persons with disabilities.[43] Most notably, Article 1 CRPD underscores that the purpose of the Convention is "to promote, protect and ensure the full and equal enjoyment of all human rights and fundamental freedoms by all persons with disabilities, and to promote respect for their inherent dignity".[44] As regards to the employment domain, the right to work and employment of persons with disabilities on an equal basis with others is recognized in Article 27 CRPD, which read in conjunction with Article 5 CRPD mandates states parties to safeguard and promote its realization by taking appropriate steps towards ensuring, inter alia: (i) the prohibition of discrimination on the basis of disability in recruitment, hiring and employment procedures, (ii) the promotion of equal opportunities for persons with disabilities in the labour market, and (iii) the provision of reasonable accommodation to persons with disabilities in the workplace by public and private entities in the form of assistive technologies and services.[45] Admittedly, Article 27 CRPD constitutes a significant provision given its contribution and interrelation to other substantive rights and principles enshrined in CRPD, involving the right to live independently and being included in the community (Article 19), accessibility (Article 9), equality and non-discrimination (Article 5).[46]

---

[41] See generally Broderick 2015.

[42] UN Convention on the Rights of Persons with Disabilities, UN Doc A/RES/61/106.

[43] Of note, currently 182 countries are parties to the CRPD (status as at 28 February 2021).

[44] UN Convention on the Rights of Persons with Disabilities, UN Doc A/RES/61/106.

[45] Ibid. Of note, the right to work is also recognised in other international human rights treaties, such as in Articles 6 and 7 of the International Covenant on Economic, Social and Cultural Rights (1966), in Article 32 of the Convention on the Rights of the Child (1989). For a definition of reasonable accommodation see Article 2 CRPD according to which reasonable accommodation means "necessary and appropriate modification and adjustments not imposing a disproportionate or undue burden, where needed in a particular case, to ensure to persons with disabilities the enjoyment or exercise on an equal basis with others of all human rights and fundamental freedoms".

[46] Broderick and Ferri 2019, p. 217.

Meanwhile, in 2020 the Human Rights Council adopted a resolution on the right to work of persons with disabilities which affirms that advanced technologies, including AI, have the potential to contribute to higher productivity, job creation, better services and well-being, while at the same time entailing challenges that may have broader implications for jobs, skills, wages and the nature of work itself.[47] Therefore, it must be conceded that caution must be paid in the design, development and application of AI technologies for persons with disabilities in the labour market. Indeed, in its General Comment 27 the Committee on the Rights of Persons with Disabilities, the oversight body for the CRPD, broadly underlines the significance of ensuring that the design and use of assistive technologies (AT) leave no space for potential abuse and exploitation of persons with disabilities.[48] Essentially, such an approach requires that equality and non-discrimination principles, well-embedded in Article 5 CRPD and further elucidated by the Committee on the Rights of Persons with Disabilities, should become integral components of AI technologies, thereby contributing to inclusive and accessible workplaces and ultimately to equal employment opportunities for persons with disabilities in the labour market.[49] For instance, the design and development of AI technologies, involving recruitment software and non-transparently programmed (even biased) algorithms, must not be discriminatory and these technologies should not be misused at the expense of persons with disabilities, leading those persons to exclusion from the labour market.[50]

At the same time, the Committee on the Rights of Persons with Disabilities explicitly stresses that in accordance with Articles 4 para 1 (f)-(g) and 20 CRPD assistive technologies (AT), such as AI technologies, are required to be accessible, affordable, available, transparent and of quality as to their actual operation, so as to achieve the full inclusion and participation of persons with disabilities in their respective communities.[51] At this point, it is essential to mention that the CRPD and its Committee have devoted considerable attention to the notion of accessibility which is firmly enshrined in Article 9 CRPD.[52] In fact, in the context of employment accessibility to assistive technologies in workplaces, involving AI, virtual assistance, constitutes a crucial

---

[47] Human Rights Council 2020, p. 2.

[48] UN Committee on the Rights of Persons with Disabilities, General Comment No 5 (2017) on living independently and being included in the community, UN Doc CRPD/C/GC/5, 27 October 2017, para 83.

[49] See UN Committee on the Rights of Persons with Disabilities, General Comment No. 6 on equality and non-discrimination, UN Doc. CRPD/C/GC/6, 26 April 2018.

[50] See in relation Outline for the preparation of a General Comment on Article 27 of the CRPD (the right to work and employment).

[51] UN Committee on the Rights of Persons with Disabilities, UN Doc CRPD/C/GC/5, para 84. See in relation Outline for the preparation of a General Comment on Article 27 of the CRPD (the right to work and employment).

[52] Pursuant to Article 9 CRPD accessibility refers to the access of persons with disabilities "on an equal basis with others, to the physical environment, to transportation, to information and communications, including information and communications technologies and systems, and to other facilities and services open or provided to the public, both in urban and in rural areas". See also UN Committee on the Rights of Persons with Disabilities, General Comment No. 2 on Article 9: Accessibility, UN Doc. CRPD/C/GC/2, 22 May 2014.

prerequisite for the fulfilment of employment rights of persons with disabilities on an equal basis with others.[53] Significantly, added to the non-discrimination, equality and accessibility requirements, pursuant to Article 16 CRPD accountability mechanisms for overseeing and coordinating the performance of AI technologies must be developed so as to prevent occurrence of any form of exploitation, abuse and unlawful discrimination against persons with disabilities.[54] Equally important, persons with disabilities and their representative organizations should actively participate in all processes related to the design, development, implementation, monitoring and evaluation of AI technologies, given their knowledge of the disability-related needs and the barriers in accessing the labour market.[55]

Within this context, the human rights framework can enable decision-makers in the labour market to effectively and timely identify, assess and respond to existing and potential risks contained in AI based systems to the benefit of persons with disabilities. To this end, at a practical level human rights impact assessments can be used as a tool for assuring that AI technologies operate in a manner consistent with human rights principles. In fact (public and private) employers and AI actors in general should be encouraged to conduct human rights impact assessments to evaluate the human rights implications of AI technologies and particularly of AI employment-related software in disability employment from its conception—during the design and development phase- to its deployment.[56] In essence, this two-stage procedure for undertaking human rights impact assessments would set in place an appropriate system of checks and balances prior and during the deployment phase in order: (i) to identify and modify at an early stage blind spots—effectiveness gaps—problematic processes and issues of AI based systems which were overlooked or unanticipated during the design phase, but are essential to their effective operation, consistent with human rights requirements; (ii) to uncover, respond and eliminate biases during the deployment phase; and (iii) to detect and remedy potential human rights violations at the deployment phase, while ultimately ensuring that AI actors take human rights considerations into account at all stages.[57]

All in all, keeping in mind that human rights must be "guiding action",[58] the human rights framework offers valuable guidance for developing a robust regulatory framework for the design and deployment of AI technologies in the labour market to the benefit of persons with disabilities and the whole society. Its incorporation constitutes an essential step towards ensuring that no one is left behind in the era of AI. Crucially, without a human rights approach to AI technologies, persons with

---

[53] See World Health Organization 2020b. Of note, according to the WHO, access to assistive technology constitutes a fundamental human right in that its primary purpose is to maintain and/or enhance an individual's functioning and independence, while enabling the user to have better access to employment opportunities and to fully participate in society in general.

[54] See Article 16 CRPD.

[55] See Article 4 para 3 CRPD.

[56] See generally McGregor et al. 2019, p. 330.

[57] Ibid.

[58] Beitz 2009, p. 46.

disabilities will remain at risk of abuse and marginalization as well as they will continue to face considerable barriers in accessing the labour market.

7.4 Conclusions

This chapter seeks to raise awareness about the key opportunities of AI technologies for empowering persons with disabilities in accessing the labour market. Nevertheless, not all potential paths to the development and application of AI technologies in the labour market are consistent with human rights requirements. Simply expanding the use and application of AI in employment procedures without due attention to equity and inclusive considerations in its design and implementation is not sufficient from a human rights perspective. Hence, the incorporation of a human rights approach to AI technologies can be a powerful statement of commitment on the part of responsible stakeholders, if accompanied by clear objectives and monitoring systems. Within this context, a framework for action, encompassing non-discrimination, equity, accountability, transparent and participatory decision-making, which will constitute a roadmap towards building a solid legal basis for the deployment of AI technologies to the actual benefit of persons with disabilities, needs to be developed. Without doubt, the implementation of such a framework requires constant regulation, continuous oversight, coordination and vigilance in terms of setting up an inclusive enabling environment for persons with disabilities under which workplace inequality and discrimination against those persons do no longer generate, when it comes to the design and use of advanced technologies, such as AI.

Essentially, the performance of AI technologies in the employment domain and particularly its adherence to human rights standards constitute a critical determinant of promoting equal employment opportunities for persons with disabilities in the labour market. AI technologies framed as a matter of equity and in consistency with human rights principles have the potential to unlock the unlawful discriminatory barriers that persons with disabilities systematically experience in accessing the labour market. Indeed, incorporating a disability rights approach to AI in employment will make the experiences and concerns of persons with disabilities an integral component of the design, development, training, deployment and assessment of AI technologies with the ultimate goal optimum workplace accessibility, diversity and inclusivity. All in all, (public and private) employers and other stakeholders should use the power of AI technologies as an equalizer for persons with disabilities in the labour market. As the International Labour Office pointedly argues "… the future of work is what we will make it. The challenge is to make it the one we want."[59]

---

[59] International Labour Office (ILO) 2015, p. 7.

References

Beitz Ch R (2009) The Idea of Human Rights. Oxford University Press, Oxford

Broderick A (2015) The Long and Winding Road to Equality and Inclusion for Persons with Disabilities: The United Nations Convention on the Rights of Persons with Disabilities. Intersentia, Cambridge/Antwerp/Portland

Broderick A, Ferri D (2019) International and European Disability Law and Policy: texts, cases and materials. Cambridge University Press, Cambridge

Buckup S (2009) The price of exclusion: the economic consequences of excluding people with disabilities from the world of work (employment working paper: no. 43). International Labour Office, Geneva

Employer Assistance and Resource Network on Disability Inclusion (2019) Use of artificial intelligence to facilitate employment opportunities for people with disabilities. www.askearn.org/wp-content/uploads/2019/06/AI_PolicyBrief-A.pdf Accessed 27 February 2021

European Commission (2018) Communication from the Commission to the European Parliament, the European Council, the Council, the European Economic and Social Committee and the Committee of the Regions – Artificial Intelligence for Europe. COM (2018) 237 final. https://eur-lex.europa.eu/legal-content/EN/TXT/?uri=COM%3A2018%3A237%3AFIN Accessed 27 February 2021

European Disability Forum (2020) EDF position on the European Commission's White Paper on Artificial Intelligence – A European Approach to excellence and trust. https://www.edf-feph.org/content/uploads/2021/02/edf_position_on_ec_ai_white_paper_06.2020.pdf%20link Accessed 28 February 2021

European Parliament (2017) European Parliament resolution of 30 November 2017 on implementation of the European Disability Strategy (2017/2127(INI)). OJ C 356/110, 4.10.2018. https://eur-lex.europa.eu/legal-content/EN/TXT/?uri=CELEX%3A52017IP0474 Accessed 27 February 2021

European Parliament and Council of the European Union (2016) Regulation (2016) 2016/679 of the European Parliament and of the Council of 27 April 2016 on the protection of natural persons with regard to the processing of personal data and on the free movement of such data, and repealing Directive 95/46/EC (General Data Protection Regulation), L 119/1 4.5.2016

Floridi L et al (2018) AI4People – An Ethical Framework for a Good AI Society: Opportunities, Risks, Principles, and Recommendations. Minds and Machines 28: 689–707

High-Level Expert Group on Artificial Intelligence (2019) A definition of AI: Main capabilities and scientific disciplines. European Commission https://digital-strategy.ec.europa.eu/en/library/definition-artificial-intelligence-main-capabilities-and-scientific-disciplines Accessed 28 February 2021

Human Rights Council (2008) Resolution 7/9. Human rights of persons with disabilities (A/HRC/RES/7/9). https://ap.ohchr.org/documents/E/HRC/resolutions/A_HRC_RES_7_9.pdf Accessed 15 February 2021

Human Rights Council (2020) Resolution adopted by the Human Rights Council on 19 June 2020 – Right to Work, A/HRC/RES/43/7. https://documents-dds-ny.un.org/doc/UNDOC/GEN/G20/158/54/PDF/G2015854.pdf?OpenElement Accessed 28 February 2021

International Labour Office (ILO) (2011) Disability in the Workplace: Employers' organizations and business networks (Working paper No 6). https://www.ilo.org/wcmsp5/groups/public/@ed_emp/@ifp_skills/documents/publication/wcms_167204.pdf Accessed 26 February 2021

International Labour Office (ILO) (2015) The future of work centenary initiative - Report I, International Labour Conference, 104th Session. https://www.ilo.org/wcmsp5/groups/public/---ed_norm/---relconf/documents/meetingdocument/wcms_369026.pdf Accessed 27 February 2021

ILO Global Business and Disability Network and Fundación ONCE (2019) Making the future of work inclusive of persons with disabilities. https://www.ilo.org/global/topics/disability-and-work/WCMS_729457/lang--en/index.htm Accessed 25 February 2021

International Telecommunication Union (2019) United Nations Activities on Artificial Intelligence (AI). www.itu.int/dms_pub/itu-s/opb/gen/S-GEN-UNACT-2019-1-PDF-E.pdf Accessed 27 February 2021

Land M K, Aronson J D (2018) The Promise and Peril of Human Rights Technology In: Land M K, Aronson J D (eds) New Technologies for Human Rights Law and Practice. Cambridge University Press, Cambridge, pp 1–20

McGregor L et al (2019) International Human Rights Law as a Framework for Algorithmic Accountability. ICLQ 68: 309–343

Nugent S et al (2020) Recruitment AI has a Disability Problem: questions employers should be asking to ensure fairness in recruitment. Institute for Ethical Artificial Intelligence, UK. https://doi.org/10.31235/osf.io/emwn5

Rembis M et al (eds) (2018) The Oxford Handbook of Disability History. Oxford University Press, Oxford

Sainsbury R, Coleman-Fountain E (2014) Diversity and change of the employment prospects of persons with disabilities: the Impact of redistributive and regulatory provisions in a multilevel framework. https://doi.org/10.13140/RG.2.2.30219.90408

Siebers T (2008) Disability Theory. University of Michigan Press, Ann Arbor

Tomašev N et al (2020) AI for social good: unlocking the opportunity for positive impact. Nature Communications 11(1): 1–6

UN Department of Economic and Social Affairs (2019) Disability and Development Report – Realizing the SDGs by, for and with persons with disabilities. www.un.org/development/desa/dspd/2019/04/un-disability-and-development-report-realizing-the-sdgs-by-for-and-with-persons-with-disabilities/ Accessed 27 February 2021

United Nations (2020) Policy Brief: A Disability-inclusive Response to Covid-19. https://unsdg.un.org/sites/default/files/2020-05/Policy-Brief-A-Disability-Inclusive-Response-to-COVID-19.pdf Accessed 15 February 2021

United Nations (undated) Factsheet on Persons with Disabilities. www.un.org/development/desa/disabilities/resources/factsheet-on-persons-with-disabilities.html Accessed 15 February 2021

Waddington L, Broderick A (2018) Combatting disability discrimination and realizing equality: A comparison of the UN Convention on the Rights of Persons with Disabilities and EU equality and non-discrimination law. Publications Office of the European Union, Luxembourg

World Bank (2020) Human Capital and Disability: Why It's Important to Invest in All People. https://documents1.worldbank.org/curated/en/919461591037705842/pdf/Human-Capital-and-Disability-Why-Its-Important-to-Invest-in-All-People.pdf Accessed 4 October 2021

World Business Council for Sustainable Development (2020) Empowering people with disabilities through AI – Microsoft case study. https://futureofwork.wbcsd.org/wp-content/uploads/2020/02/WBCSD-FoW-Case-Study_Microsoft_2020_final.pdf Accessed 25 February 2021

World Health Organization and World Bank (2011) World Report on Disability. WHO, Geneva. https://www.who.int/disabilities/world_report/2011/report.pdf Accessed 9 February 2021

World Health Organization (2020a) Disability and Health. https://www.who.int/news-room/fact-sheets/detail/disability-and-health Accessed 9 February 2021

World Health Organization (2020b) Policy Brief: Access to assistive technology. https://apps.who.int/iris/rest/bitstreams/1278953/retrieve Accessed 29 June 2021

World Trade Organization, World Health Organization, World Intellectual Property Organization (2020) Promoting Access to Medical Technologies and Innovation: Intersections between public health, intellectual property and trade, 2nd edn. https://www.wto.org/english/res_e/booksp_e/who-wipo-wto_2020_e.pdf Accessed 28 February 2021

Zardiashvili L, Fosch-Villaronga E (2020) AI in Healthcare through the Lens of Human Dignity. In: Fathisalout Bollon M, Berti Suman A (eds) Legal, Social and Ethical Perspectives on Health & Technology. Savoie Mont Blanc University Press, Chambery, pp 45–64

Other Documents

Outline for the preparation of a General Comment on Article 27 of the CRPD (the right to work and employment). https://www.ohchr.org/Documents/HRBodies/CRPD/GC/Outline_Gene ralComment_EN.docx Accessed 27 February 2021

UN Committee on Economic, Social and Cultural Rights, General comment No 23 on the right to just and favourable conditions of work (article 7 of the International Covenant on Economic, Social and Cultural Rights), UN Doc E/C.12/GC/23, 27 April 2016

UN Committee on the Rights of Persons with Disabilities, General Comment No 2 on Article 9: Accessibility, UN Doc CRPD/C/GC/2, 22 May 2014

UN Committee on the Rights of Persons with Disabilities, General Comment No 5 (2017) on living independently and being included in the community, UN Doc CRPD/C/GC/5, 27 October 2017

UN Committee on the Rights of Persons with Disabilities, General Comment No 6 on equality and non-discrimination, UN Doc CRPD/C/GC/6, 26 April 2018

UN Convention on the Rights of Persons with Disabilities, UN Doc A/RES/61/106. https://www.ohchr.org/en/hrbodies/crpd/pages/conventionrightspersonswithdisabilities.aspx Accessed 27 February 2021

Elisavet Athanasia Alexiadou holds an LL.M. degree in International and European Legal Studies with a specialisation in Public International Law (with distinction), an LL.M. degree in Medical Law and a M.Sc. degree in Healthcare Administration. In 2016 she received her Ph.D. degree in Law from the Faculty of Law, Leiden University, The Netherlands. Currently, she is conducting postdoctoral research at the Faculty of Law, Aristotle University of Thessaloniki funded by a two-year research grant from the State Scholarships Foundation (IKY Greece) through the Operational Programme «Human Resources Development, Education and Lifelong Learning» in the context of the project "Reinforcement of Postdoctoral Researchers - 2nd Cycle". She is a lawyer at the Supreme Court, Greece and an adjunct faculty member at the International Hellenic University and at Hellenic Open University. She is a Fellow at the Global Health Law Groningen Research Centre of the University of Groningen.

Chapter 8
Prosecuting Killer Robots: Allocating Criminal Responsibilities for Grave Breaches of International Humanitarian Law Committed by Lethal Autonomous Weapon Systems

Valeria Chiappini Koscina

Contents

Abstract The fast-growing development of highly automated and autonomous weapon systems has become one of the most controversial sources of discussion in the international sphere. One of the many concerns that surface with this technology is the existence of an accountability gap. This fear stems from the complexity of holding a human operator criminally responsible for a potential failure of the weapon system. Thus, the question on who is to be held criminally liable for grave breaches to international humanitarian law when these crimes are not intentional arises. This chapter explains how we will need to rethink the responsibilities, command structure, and everyday operations within our military when engaging in the use of fully autonomous weapon systems to allow our existing legal framework to assign criminal responsibility. For this purpose, this chapter analyses the different types of criminal responsibilities that converge in the process of employing lethal autonomous weapons and determine which of them is the most appropriate for grave breaches of international humanitarian law in this case.

V. Chiappini Koscina (✉)
Cerro La Parva 980 A, dept. 216, Las Condes, Santiago, Chile
e-mail: vac66@cornell.edu

© T.M.C. ASSER PRESS and the authors 2022   149
B. Custers and E. Fosch-Villaronga (eds.), *Law and Artificial Intelligence*,
Information Technology and Law Series 35,
https://doi.org/10.1007/978-94-6265-523-2_8

Keywords Lethal autonomous weapon systems · International criminal responsibility · Recklessness · Grave breaches of international humanitarian law · Command responsibility · *Dolus eventualis*

8.1 Delineating the Accountability Problem

The fast-growing development of highly automated and autonomous weapons has become one of the most polemic sources of discussion in the international sphere. The complexity of the technology and the limitless possibilities have rendered many, to say the least, sceptical of the ability of our current international legal system to confront the many unanswered questions this technology poses.

Among these, is the question of criminal accountability. One of the many fears that arise with this technology—and that has led its detractors to use it as an argument for its ban[1]—is the alleged difficulty to allocate in a human operator the responsibility for a potential failure of the weapon systems or for a violation of the norms that govern armed conflicts.

Those who advocate for this position argue that due to the complexities of these weapon systems, our current legal mechanisms for allocating criminal responsibility are inadequate to deal with the perils and threats these weapon systems pose,[2] and hence, any potential unlawful act committed by these weapons would have no human commander or operator who could be held directly responsible for the weapon's wrongful actions.[3]

However, if we consider that regardless of the level of autonomy a weapon achieves, there will always be some degree of human involvement in its operation;[4] and that the autonomous weapon—as any other—will only be the instrument of the criminal act,[5] there is no reason to assume any sort of accountability gap will exist.

This chapter argues that the legal accountability framework that exists today is sufficient to address the responsibility issues that may arise from the use of autonomous weapons, provided the deployment of Lethal Autonomous Weapon Systems ("LAWS") is overseen by a specialized command structure and accompanied by proper protocols.

For this purpose, Sect. 8.2 provides a brief description of LAWS, and the characteristics that raise the accountability concerns. Section 8.3 discusses the different crimes that could be committed using these weapon systems, analyses the different types of international criminal responsibilities that converge in the process of employing LAWS, and determines which of them is the most appropriate to address

---

[1] Human Rights Watch and IHRC 2015, p. 4.

[2] Human Rights Watch and IHRC 2015, p. 2.

[3] Human Rights Watch and IHRC 2015, p. 2.

[4] Human Rights Watch and IHRC 2015, p. 2. See also Sassóli 2014, p. 323; and Schmitt and Thurnher 2013, p. 235.

[5] Henderson et al. 2017, p. 359. See also Ohlin 2016, pp. 2–3.

grave breaches of international humanitarian law. Lastly, Sect. 8.4 provides a brief conclusion of the main arguments made throughout this chapter.

8.2 Lethal Autonomous Weapon Systems

Weapon systems are all the components required for the operation of a machine intended to injure, damage, destroy or disable military personnel or property.[6] Autonomous Weapon Systems are weapon systems that adapt their operational mode in response to the challenges and circumstances in the environment in which they are deployed.[7] The focus of this chapter is on Autonomous Weapon Systems designed to lethally attack[8] or that are equipped with lethal capabilities, namely Lethal Autonomous Weapon Systems.

Regretfully, there is no unified definition of LAWS available.[9] However, since the focus of this chapter is on the accountability issue relating to them, the following three categories of LAWS based on the amount of human involvement in their actions,[10] are suitable to understand the problem:

- Human-in-the-Loop Weapons: Robots that can select targets and deliver force only with a human command;
- Human-on-the-Loop Weapons: Robots that can select targets and deliver force under the oversight of a human operator who can override the robots' actions; and
- Human-out-of-the-Loop Weapons: Robots that can select targets and deliver force without any human input or interaction.[11]

Regarding the first category, "human-in-the-loop", the human operator is making all the decisions in relation to target selection and the use of force, therefore, there is no current issue of accountability. In this case, any grave breach of international humanitarian law while employing this type of LAWS, if performed with the requisite mental element, will be attributed to the operator, and potentially to its commander, through commander responsibility, as addressed in Sect. 8.3.2.

The last two categories, however, encompass weapons that can make targeting decisions on their own, without the need of any human participation. It is this lack of human involvement that raises concerns of accountability in situations where the LAWS operation causes grave breaches of international humanitarian law. These

---

[6] Mull 2018, p. 475.

[7] Sassóli 2014, p. 308 (quoting International Committee of the Red Cross, *International Humanitarian Law and the Challenges of Contemporary Armed Conflict: Report Prepared for the 31st International Conference of the Red Cross and Red Crescent* 39 (2011)).

[8] Mull 2018, p. 476.

[9] E.g., ICRC 2016, p. 1 (defines AWS as "[a]ny weapon system with autonomy in its critical functions. That is, a weapon system that can select [i.e., search for or detect, identify, track, select] and attack [i.e., use force against, neutralize, damage or destroy] targets without human intervention.").

[10] Human Rights Watch and IHRC 2012, p. 2.

[11] Human Rights Watch and IHRC 2012, p. 2.

types of LAWS use artificial intelligence to learn. Namely, the feedback, and data available from the environment in which it is deployed, permits the learning element of the LAWS to modify and improve its performance in future situations.[12]

The main advantage of employing artificial intelligence systems is that they outperform humans in data analysis and pattern identification tasks.[13] In the context of armed conflict, this means that LAWS are capable of processing information from several different sources simultaneously,[14] allowing them to make more informed target selections,[15] in less time.[16] Furthermore, since LAWS are devoid of human feelings, they can make more informed and unbiased decisions,[17] as well as take more feasible precautions than a human when engaging a target.[18]

Nevertheless, since LAWS' targeting decisions are based on algorithms and machine learning,[19] without any moral component that may guide them, they are unable to contain the required mental element to commit any war crime.[20] Hence, the problem is that even if they can process the information more effectively, "they lack understanding of the actual meaning and context behind the phenomena."[21]

Additionally, to be able to function autonomously, LAWS require millions of lines of code that cannot be written by just one person.[22] Thus, in their coding process, a team of programmers are involved.[23] This means that none of them knows the entire program and, as a result, no one can predict how it will respond to any given stimulus.[24] Therefore, the more autonomous the LAWS becomes, the harder it will be to predict or anticipate its future behaviour.[25]

Consequently, the main accountability concern in the employment of LAWS is not with situations in which they have been employed by the commander or operator purposefully in a way that breaches international humanitarian law. The answer in these circumstances is obvious, since the mental element for war crimes, as will be addressed in Sect. 8.3, is present. But rather with situations in which the LAWS

---

[12] Russel 1996, pp. 89–90 and 129. See also Crootof 2016, p. 1367.

[13] Krupiy 2018, p. 48.

[14] Sparrow 2016, p. 97.

[15] Bills 2014, p. 186.

[16] Bills 2014, p. 184.

[17] See Bills 2014, p. 183; Crootof 2016, p. 1372; Sassóli 2014, p. 310; and U.N. Human Rights Council, *Report of the Special Rapporteur on extrajudicial, summary or arbitrary executions, Christof Heyns*, para 54, U.N. Doc. A/HRC/23/47 (9 April 2013).

[18] Sassóli 2014, p. 336. See also U.N. Human Rights Council 2013, para 69.

[19] Margulies 2012, p. 415.

[20] See Cass 2015, p. 1019; and Crootof 2016, p. 1377.

[21] Krupiy 2018, p. 50. See also U.N. Human Rights Counci 2013, para 56.

[22] Cass 2015, p. 1052. See also Egeland 2016, p. 111.

[23] Cass 2015), p. 1052. See also Krupiy 2018, p. 67.

[24] Cass 2015, p. 1052. See also Egeland 2016, p. 112; and U.N. Human Rights Council 2013, para 79.

[25] Geiß and Lahmann 2017, p. 393. See also Davison 2017, p. 15.

perform in an unforeseen or unreliable manner,[26] without giving any opportunity to the human operator to override its course of action. This can certainly happen with Human-out-of-the-Loop types of LAWS, but also with Human-on-the-Loop types of weapons in cases where, due to the speed in which the weapon reacts to a particular stimulus, the operator is unable to react in time to the targeting decision.[27]

For a LAWS to be operational it must first comply with international humanitarian law. This means that when selecting a target, it must apply the principles of necessity,[28] distinction,[29] and proportionality,[30] and it must take all feasible precautions before engaging.[31] LAWS that can function and comply with international humanitarian law with complete autonomy from a human operator do not yet exist.[32] However, given the current state of technological advancement,[33] it is a matter of "when" and not "if" these weapon systems will become available. For this reason, the following section tries to answer the question of who can be held criminally responsible for any breaches of international humanitarian law that is caused by the unforeseen operation of these types of LAWS.

8.3 Criminal Responsibilities

International criminal law is predicated upon the notion of culpability, without which it seems unjust to criminally punish a person.[34] Therefore, to establish the commission of a crime a tribunal must examine if the corresponding elements of the crime are met. Those elements are the *actus reus* or objective element of the crime, which encompasses the typical action or omission punished by the crime; and the *mens rea* or mental element, which deals with the intention of the perpetrator.

However, unlike with the use of any other weapon, when it comes to LAWS, the decision to deploy lethal force falls onto the machine.[35] Hence, because a machine cannot have the intention to commit a war crime,[36] there are concerns regarding the

---

[26] Krupiy 2018, p. 50.

[27] Henderson et al. 2017, p. 362. See also Halajová 2020, p. 145.

[28] Convention (IV) relative to the Protection of Civilian Persons in Time of War art. 147, 12 August 1949, 75 U.N.T.S. 287.

[29] Protocol Additional to the Geneva Conventions of 12 August 1949 and relating to the Protection of Victims of International Armed Conflicts arts. 48, 51(2) and 52(2), 8 June 1977, 1125 U.N.T.S. 609 (Additional Protocol I).

[30] Additional Protocol I, arts. 51(5)(b) and 57.

[31] Additional Protocol I, art. 57.

[32] Sassóli 2014, p. 390.

[33] Crootof 2015, p. 919.

[34] See Werle and Jeßberger 2005, p. 36; Human Rights Watch and IHRC 2015, p. 23; Geiß and Lahmann 2017, p. 394; Egeland 2016, p. 115; Halajová 2020, p. 150.

[35] Cass 2015, p. 1019.

[36] Cass 2015, p. 1019.

accountability for grave breaches of international humanitarian law caused by the operation of LAWS.

These apprehensions are not present in cases where (a) an individual intentionally programs a LAWS to commit a serious violation of international humanitarian law; (b) an operator intentionally deploys a LAWS incapable of discriminating between lawful and unlawful targets in an urban area; or (c) a commander orders for a LAWS to be used inappropriately.[37] In these cases, there is no question as to the appropriate application of international criminal responsibility, because the mental element of war crimes is clearly present.

The problem arises when, due to their "inherent unpredictability and their destructive capacity",[38] LAWS breach international humanitarian law without anyone acting intentionally.[39] Thus, the question that arises is who, if anyone, should be held criminally responsible for the deadly consequences of LAWS unanticipated actions.

To address this question, the following subsections analyse the different types of criminal responsibilities and determine which of them is the most appropriate for grave breaches of international humanitarian law. It must be noted that because of the nature of LAWS, they are more likely to commit war crimes.[40] In particular, the crimes of killing or wounding civilians not taking direct part in hostilities or combatants that are *hors de combat*, the destruction of civilian and protected property, and causing severe damage to the natural environment.[41]

8.3.1   Individual Criminal Responsibility

As delineated above, the problem with attributing criminal responsibilities for the unpredictable actions of LAWS is that their targeting decisions cannot include the requisite mental element for an international crime to take place. Therefore, the decisions that need to be scrutinized are those of the persons involved in its deployment.[42]

---

[37] Crootof 2016, pp. 1376–1377. See also Henderson et al. 2017, pp. 359–360.

[38] Crootof 2016, p. 1373. See also Wagner 2014, p. 1409; and Hammond 2015, p. 662.

[39] Crootof 2016, p. 1366.

[40] Under international criminal law there are four types of international crimes: (1) genocide, (2) crimes against humanity, (3) war crimes, and (4) crime of aggression. Because of the nature of LAWS, war crimes are more likely to be committed by their deployment because they do not require a special intent, like genocide; or to be part of a widespread or systematic attack, like crimes against humanity. Furthermore, to attribute responsibility for the crime of aggression a person must be "in a position effectively to exercise control over or to direct the political or military action of a State." (Rome Statute of the International Criminal Court art. 25(3bis), 17 July 1998, 2187 U.N.T.S. 38544) Therefore, except in cases of command responsibility, discussed in Sect. 8.3.2, unpredictable actions by LAWS will rarely fall within this category.

[41] Rome Statute of the International Criminal Court art. 8, 17 July 1998, 2187 U.N.T.S. 38544 (Rome Statute).

[42] See Cass 2015, pp. 1017, 1020, 1021, 1058, and 1065–1066; Sassóli 2014, p. 323; Henderson et al. 2017, p. 358.

The current state of the law for the accidental death of protected persons or the damage to protected property is that there is no criminal accountability.[43] In this sense, unpredictable actions by LAWS are no different than a mistake made by a human combatant operating another weapon,[44] so there is no reason to treat a LAWS malfunction differently. The question then, is how do we deal with cases in which a LAWS is deployed, and the operator, commander, or programmer knows there is a high risk of an accident occurring.

These situations seem to fall within the concept of recklessness or *dolus eventualis*. The concept of *dolus eventualis* is not quite the same as recklessness,[45] but for the purposes of this chapter they will be used indistinctively, as entailing the awareness of the perpetrator "of the substantial likelihood that a criminal act or omission would occur as a consequence of his conduct",[46] and the acceptance of those consequences.[47] In this sense, the deployment of LAWS with the knowledge that there is high risk of a breach of international humanitarian law, would fall under this category.

8.3.1.1 Intent and Knowledge

Whether war crimes can be committed with *dolus eventualis* and/or recklessness is a matter of debate.[48] As such, for those who believe that at least some international crimes, specifically war crimes, can be committed with *dolus eventualis*,[49] the operation of a LAWS with the knowledge that there is a substantial likelihood of an international humanitarian law breach could entail criminal responsibility.[50] It follows that if an operator, programmer, or commander is (1) aware of a LAWS malfunction and the possibility of illegal deaths, injuries, or damages to protected

---

[43] Ohlin 2016, p. 361.

[44] Henderson et al. 2017; p. 361. See also Bo 2021, p. 24.

[45] Badar and Porro 2015, p. 657; Finnin 2012, pp. 159–160; Ambos 2013, pp. 277–278.

[46] *Prosecutor v. Kvočka et al.*, Case No. IT-98-30/1-T, Trial Chamber Judgement, para 251 (Int'l Crim. Trib. for the Former Yugoslavia, 2 November 2001); and *Prosecutor v. Milomir Stakić*, Case No. IT-97-24-T, Trial Judgement, para 587 (Int'l Crim. Trib. for the Former Yugoslavia, 31 July 2003). See also Werle and Jeßberger 2014, pp. 178–179.

[47] *Prosecutor v. Milomir Stakić*, Case No. IT-97-24-T, Trial Judgement, para 587 (Int'l Crim. Trib. for the Former Yugoslavia, 31 July 2003); *Prosecutor v. Blaškić*, Case No. IT-95-14-A, Appeals Chamber Judgement, para 42 (Int'l Crim. Trib. for the Former Yugoslavia, 29 July 2004). See also Prosecutor v. *Kordić and Čerkez*, Case No. IT-95-14/2-A, Appeals Chamber Judgement, para 30 (Int'l Crim. Trib. for the Former Yugoslavia, 17 December 2004); *Prosecutor v. Galić*, Case No. IT-98-29-A, Appeals Chamber Judgement, para 152 (Int'l Crim. Trib. for the Former Yugoslavia, 30 November 2006); Martinez 2007, p. 645; Finnin 2012, p. 158.

[48] See Finnin 2012, p. 176; Werle and Jeßberger 2005, pp. 43–44; Ohlin 2013, pp. 100–101; Schabas 2016, p. 629; Badar and Porro 2015, p. 666.

[49] See Ohlin 2013, pp. 104–105; Werle and Jeßberger 2005, p. 45; Werle and Jeßberger 2014, pp. 191–192; Bo 2021, p. 4, 11–12.

[50] Henderson et al. 2017, p. 363. See also Ohlin 2016, p. 22; Bo 2021, p. 18.

persons or property,[51] (2) accepts these risks, and (3) continues its use, they could be prosecuted for the commission of war crimes.[52]

However, it is arguable that *dolus eventualis* or recklessness is an acceptable form of intent for the attribution of criminal responsibility. Even though there's jurisprudence from the *ad hoc* criminal tribunals that support its inclusion,[53] state practice seems to indicate differently. Indeed, the first drafts of the Rome Statute of the International Criminal Court ("the Rome Statute") originally included a paragraph in the mental element provision that recognized the possibility of committing a crime with recklessness,[54] but later opted to delete it.[55] This exclusion shows their intention of eliminating the concepts of recklessness and *dolus eventualis* as a possible mental element for the commission of international crimes.[56]

Furthermore, the jurisprudence of the *ad hoc* tribunals are not examples of state practice, so they cannot create customary norms.[57] Particularly considering that the State delegates who participated in drafting the Rome Statute were uncomfortable with liability based on recklessness or *dolus eventualis*,[58] and ultimately these notions were dismissed by consensus.[59]

Additionally, the whole purpose of creating a universal International Criminal Court was to liberate international criminal law "from its customary origins in favour of a stringent and rigorous codification process that met the demands of the principle

---

[51] Geiß and Lahmann 2017, p. 393.

[52] See Sassóli 2014, p. 325; see Geiß and Lahmann 2017, p. 393.

[53] E.g., *Prosecutor v. Milomir Stakić*, Case No. IT-97-24-T, Trial Chamber Judgement, para 587 (Int'l Crim. Trib. for the Former Yugoslavia, 31 July 2003); *Prosecutor v. Kvočka et al.*, Case No. IT-98-30/1-T, Trial Chamber Judgement, para 251 (Int'l Crim. Trib. for the Former Yugoslavia, 2 November 2001); *Prosecutor v. Blaškić*, Case No. IT-95-14-A, Appeals Chamber Judgement, para 42 (Int'l Crim. Trib. for the Former Yugoslavia, 29 July 2004); *Prosecutor v. Kordić and Čerkez*, Case No. IT-95-14/2-A, Appeals Chamber Judgement, para 30 (Int'l Crim. Trib. for the Former Yugoslavia, 17 December 2004); *Prosecutor v. Galić*, Case No. IT-98-29-A, Appeals Chamber Judgement, para 152 (Int'l Crim. Trib. for the Former Yugoslavia, 30 November 2006); *Prosecutor v. Delalić et. al*, Case No. IT-96-21-T, Trial Chamber Judgement, para 432 (Int'l Crim. Trib. for the Former Yugoslavia, 16 November 1998) (*Čelebići* case); and *Prosecutor v. Kayishema and Ruzindana*, Case No. ICTR-05-1-T, Trial Chamber Judgement, para 146 (21 May 1999).

[54] U.N.G.A., Rep. of the Ad Hoc Comm. on the Establishment of an Int'l Crim. Ct., 59, U.N. Doc. A/50/22 (1995).

[55] See U.N.G.A., Rep. of the Preparatory Comm. on the Establishment of an Int'l Crim. Ct., Vol I, 45, U.N. Doc. A/51/22 (1996); U.N.G.A., Rep. of the Preparatory Comm. on the Establishment of an Int'l Crim. Ct., Vol. II, 92, U.N. Doc. A/51/22 (1996); U.N. Dipl. Conf. of Plenipotentiaries on the Establishment of an Int'l Crim. Ct., Rep. of the Preparatory Comm. on the Establishment of an Int'l Crim. Ct., Add. 1, 56, U.N. Doc. A/CONF.183/2/Add.1 (14 April 1998); and U.N. Dipl. Conf. of Plenipotentiaries on the Establishment of an Int'l Crim. Ct., Rep. of the Working Group on General Principles of Crim. L., Corr. 1, U.N. Doc. A/CONF.183/C.1/WGGP/L.4/Corr.1 (19 June 1998).

[56] Ohlin 2013, pp. 101, 103. See also Schabas 2016, p. 630; Ambos 2013, p. 276.

[57] Ohlin 2013, p. 108.

[58] Clark 2008, p. 525.

[59] Clark 2008, p. 529.

of legality."[60] Therefore, without clear state practice and *opinio juris*[61] that differ from the Rome Statute and the Elements of Crime—that were negotiated by State Parties[62]—*dolus eventualis* can hardly be considered an acceptable form of intent for war crimes.

Thus, under Article 30 of the Rome Statute, unless otherwise provided, war crimes can only be committed with intent and knowledge. Intent requires that a person means to engage in the conduct, and cause the consequence, or is at least aware that said consequence will occur in the ordinary course of events; and knowledge requires that the person is aware of the relevant circumstances and that a consequence will occur in the ordinary course of events.

The International Criminal Court has interpreted that the phrase "will occur in the ordinary course of events" includes only situations in which the perpetrator does not intend for a particular consequence to occur, but knowing it will happen, it accepts it (*dolus directus* in the second degree).[63] On the contrary, some argue that the requirement of knowledge includes the strictest definition of *dolus eventualis* in which the perpetrator knows there is a "high risk" of a consequence occurring.[64]

Nevertheless, the inclusion of the word "will", as opposed to "might", demands that a particular consequence is virtually certain to occur. Therefore, the awareness of a substantial likelihood of a breach of international humanitarian law is not enough to attribute individual criminal responsibility to the programmer, operator, or commander. In particular, because such likelihood, albeit high, is a mere probability or possibility of the consequences occurring.[65]

Consequently, under the general rules of individual criminal responsibility, programmers, operators, and commanders cannot be held liable for deploying LAWS in the knowledge that there is a high risk of the machine malfunctioning, because they will never have the required certainty that a war crime will ensue.

---

[60] Ohlin 2013, pp. 107–108.

[61] The International Court of Justice has recognized that state practice and *opinion juris* are the two elements that need to be present for a custom to emerge (North Sea Continental Shelf, Judgment, I.C.J. Reports 1969, p. 3.).

[62] Ohlin 2013, p. 109.

[63] *Prosecutor v. Bemba*, Case No. ICC-01/05-01/08, Decision Pursuant to Article 61(7)(a) and (b) of the Rome Statute on the Charges of the Prosecutor Against Jean-Pierre Bemba Gombo, para 360 (15 June 2009).

[64] Bo 2021, pp. 18–20.

[65] E.g., *Prosecutor v. Bemba*, Case No. ICC-01/05-01/08, Decision Pursuant to Article 61(7)(a) and (b) of the Rome Statute on the Charges of the Prosecutor Against Jean-Pierre Bemba Gombo, para 360 (15 June 2009); *Prosecutor v. Lubanga*, Case No. ICC-01/04-01/06, Judgment pursuant to Article 74 of the Statute, para 1011 (14 March 2012); Werle and Jeßberger 2014, pp. 180–181; Werle and Jeßberger 2005, p. 41; Badar 2009, pp. 441, 443; Badar and Porro 2015, p. 654; Finnin 2012, pp. 166, 169, 176; Ohlin 2013, p. 106; Schabas 2016, p. 630; Van der Vyver 2004, p. 66; Ambos 2013, pp. 276–277.

Nonetheless, it has been accepted[66] that the phrase "unless otherwise provided"[67] in Article 30 of the Rome Statute allows for the general standard of intent and knowledge to be lowered,[68] increased,[69] or complemented with a specific intent.[70] In this regard, Article 8 of the Rome Statute and the Elements of Crimes do not contemplate a different mental element for the war crimes that can be committed by LAWS, but the different modes of criminal responsibility might require a lower mental element.

8.3.1.2 Modes of Criminal Responsibility

If we consider their autonomous nature, only those modes of liability in which a person is indirectly involved are suitable to allocate responsibility on its operator, programmer, or commander for war crimes committed by LAWS. In this context, only the modes of liability of indirect perpetration; ordering, soliciting, or inducing; and aiding and abetting, enshrined in Article 25(3)(a)(b) and (c) of the Rome Statute, may be suitable.

Nevertheless, these modes of liability do not lower the mental element requirements or are not suitable for the unpredictability of LAWS. Indeed, under indirect perpetration, the actor has to have full control of the crime,[71] therefore, in order to commit a crime under this mode of liability a person must comply with the requirements of intent and knowledge.[72] Furthermore, when ordering, inducing, soliciting, aiding, abetting, or in any way assisting with a crime, a person is only required to know

---

[66] Werle and Jeßberger 2014, p. 179.

[67] There is controversy on whether this phrase includes only situations otherwise provided in the Statute itself, the Elements of Crimes, or also treaties and the principles and rules of international law. There is little evidence in support of the idea that this phrase refers exclusively to the Rome Statute since Article 21 of the Statute expressly lists the Elements of Crime as one of the applicable sources of law, and the ICC has already conceded that they may provide for a different mental element than Article 30. Furthermore, there are no other treaties that detail with the same precision as the Rome Statute what is the required mental element for war crimes, and there is no uniform State practice that could support the emergence of a different rule of customary international law.

[68] Article 28 of the Rome Statute is an example of a provision that lowers the general standard of intent by allowing reckless commission. See Finnin 2012, p. 177; Schabas 2016, p. 628; Werle and Jeßberger 2014, pp. 187–188, and 191–192; Van der Vyver 2004, p. 67; Ambos 2013, p. 300.

[69] The standard can be increased when a specific crime does not allow for *dolus directus* in the second degree, but only *dolus directus* in the first degree. See Van der Vyver 2004, p. 66.

[70] E.g., the crime of genocide requires a specific "intent to destroy, in whole or in part, a national, ethnical, racial or religious group"; crimes against humanity require knowledge of "a widespread or systematic attack directed against any civilian population"; and the war crime of using, conscripting or enlisting children requires that the perpetrator "knew or should have known that such person or persons were under the age of 15 years".

[71] *Prosecutor v. Lubanga*, Case No. ICC-01/04-01/06, Decision on the Confirmation of Charges, para 329 (29 January 2007). See also Werle and Jeßberger 2014, pp. 205–206.

[72] Werle and Jeßberger 2014, p. 199; Gil 2014, p. 96; Halajová 2020, p. 141.

of the perpetrator's specific intent, without the need of sharing it.[73] The exclusion of intent constitutes a lower mental element, however, because of the unpredictable nature of LAWS, an operator, programmer or commander will never be able to know, with the level of certainty required by Article 30 of the Rome Statute, that a war crime will be committed.

Accordingly, these modes of individual criminal liability are not sufficient to hold operators, programmers, and commanders criminally responsible for deploying LAWS when there is a high risk of a crime being committed. However, as will be analysed in the following subsection, this does not mean that no one can be held responsible.

8.3.2 Commander Responsibility

Another mode of criminal liability is superior responsibility, under which a commander can be held criminally liable for an international crime in two different ways. First, for its individual responsibility in ordering an international crime,[74] as addressed in Sect. 8.3.1; and second, for its command responsibility.[75] The latter is not a war crime itself, rather a method "to hold the commander accountable for his or her subordinates war crimes",[76] in which the superior is held responsible for his own culpable omission.[77]

Pursuant to customary international law,[78] a commander may be liable if (i) he or she exercises effective control over its subordinates, (ii) knows of or has reason to know of the subordinate's actual or intended criminal acts, and (iii) fails to take necessary and reasonable measures to prevent or punish them.[79] Since LAWS are not subject to punishment for their breaches of international humanitarian law,[80] this type of responsibility could only arise when a commander knows, or should know,

---

[73] Werle and Jeßberger 2014, pp. 215, 218–219.

[74] Henckaerts and Doswald-Beck 2009, p. 556.

[75] Henckaerts and Doswald-Beck 2009, Rule 153. See also Cass 2015, p. 1064.

[76] Cass 2015, pp. 1017, 1064–1065.

[77] Yokohama 2018, p. 302.

[78] See Additional Protocol I, art. 86(2); Rome Statute, art. 28; Statute of the International Criminal Tribunal for the Former Yugoslavia (as amended on 17 May 2002) arts. 73, 25 May 1993, available at https://www.icty.org/x/file/Legal%20Library/Statute/statute_sept09_en.pdf (accessed on 31 August 2021); and Henckaerts and Doswald-Beck 2009, p. 558.

[79] Crootof 2016, p. 1378. See also Cass 2015, p. 1065; Williamson 2008, pp. 306–307; Dungel and Ghadiri 2010, p. 6; Martinez 2007, p. 642.

[80] This hypothesis only arises in cases where LAWS have been used by the operator in a manner contrary to international humanitarian law that was not directly ordered by the commander, in which case, the commander is liable for his or her omission to punish the operator in question. In this situation holding the commander accountable poses no other difficulty than it does in any other case where an operator uses a non-autonomous weapon in an illegal manner. Thus, it will not be addressed in this chapter.

that the LAWS could violate the law of war,[81] and fails to take reasonable steps to prevent it.[82]

8.3.2.1 Effective Control

The first element of commander's responsibility is the existence of a superior-subordinate relationship between the commander and an individual. That is to say, the commander has "effective control" over another.[83] Effective control in this context entails "the material ability to prevent and punish criminal conduct".[84]

In relation to this requirement, it has been argued that since LAWS may operate at high speeds that impede commanders from being able to call off an attack, preventing them would be difficult.[85] This means that commanders will not be able to exercise effective control over them, and that, accordingly, no responsibility would arise.[86]

Nevertheless, such conclusions are somewhat misled by the false premise in which they are founded. As explained in the previous section, unforeseen actions by LAWS are considered within the range of human mistakes that exist in the deployment of any type of weapon; and, as long as they are accidental and within the range of mistakes of a standard human being operator,[87] they cannot be the source of any type of individual criminal liability.

As will be explained later when discussing necessary and reasonable measures, this does not mean that illegal conduct of LAWS cannot be prevented, and as such, these actions do fall within the scope of the effective control of the commander in charge of its deployment.

8.3.2.2 Mental Element

The second requirement of commander responsibility is the state of mind of the commander, which prevents this type of responsibility from becoming one of strict liability.[88] Namely, knowledge or constructive knowledge.[89]

International criminal jurisprudence has not been completely clear as to whether the commander has a general duty to collect information,[90] in which case, his failure

---

[81] Bills 2014, p. 197.

[82] API, at arts. 86(2), 87(3). See also Margulies 2012, p. 413; Williamson 2008, p. 307.

[83] Dungel and Ghadiri 2010, p. 6. See also Human Rights Watch and IHRC 2015, p. 25.

[84] Dungel and Ghadiri 2010, p. 6 (citing the Čelebići case before the ICTY and the Kajelijeli case before the ICTR). See also Krupiy 2018, p. 65.

[85] Human Rights Watch and IHRC 2015, p. 24; and Halajová 2020, p. 144.

[86] Human Rights Watch and IHRC 2015, p. 24.

[87] Henderson et al. 2017, p. 343.

[88] Dungel and Ghadiri 2010, p. 7.

[89] Dungel and Ghadiri 2010, p. 7. See also Henckaerts and Doswald-Beck 2009, p. 561.

[90] Martinez 2007, pp. 650–652.

to seek this information would imply a breach of his duty to prevent; or whether the commander needs to come into specific information relating to the possible commission of a particular crime, that would necessarily require him to conduct an investigation.[91]

This chapter does not attempt to resolve this issue. However, in either case, because LAWS will adapt their performance according to the environmental data they collect while operating, it is foreseeable that at least constant monitoring and updating of the data bases is necessary to prevent any unwanted and irregular conduct. Thus, every commander in charge of the deployment of a particular LAWS has, or should have, sufficient information to warrant the measures detailed below.[92]

8.3.2.3 Necessary and Reasonable Measures

Article 86(2) of Protocol I Additional to the Geneva Conventions instructs commanders to take all feasible measures within their power to prevent or repress grave breaches of international humanitarian law committed by a subordinate. In the case of the deployment of LAWS there is real risk that they would behave in unforeseeable ways, which will require the employment of several precautions to minimize this risk.

As with many modern complex weapons, a dedicated command structure, specialized in their operation and maintenance, would be required for the deployment of LAWS.[93] It should entail a support staff who has the technical expertise[94] to perform an ongoing evaluation of the LAWS compliance with international humanitarian law.[95]

The first step in this assessment would be to conduct a thorough weapons review stage, that allows the commander and its team to become familiar with the *modus operandi* of the weapon systems.[96] Like for any other means and methods of warfare, a commander in charge of its deployment must properly understand how the weapon functions.[97] It will then require periodic assessment of the LAWS performance in the field to ensure that its software is functioning in compliance with international humanitarian law,[98] and continued updates and adjustments to the LAWS databases

---

[91] Williamson 2008, p. 307 (citing the Bagilishema Judgement by the ICTR). See also Martinez 2007, p. 656 (citing the Čelebići case before the ICTY).

[92] Contra Halajová 2020, p. 145.

[93] Margulies 2012, p. 433.

[94] Margulies 2012, p. 433.

[95] Margulies 2012, p. 407.

[96] Margulies 2012, p. 407, 411. See also Sassóli 2014, p. 324; Davison 2017, p. 13; Dunlap 2016, p. 70.

[97] Sassóli 2014, p. 324. See also Dunlap 2016, p. 71.

[98] Margulies 2012, p. 407.

and interface.[99] The guidelines and parameters that should be applied to achieve this purpose should be determined by each State.[100]

In this sense, if the commander cannot confirm that the database is updated or that recent testing demonstrates that the LAWS is still observing international humanitarian law targeting parameters, the commander is under an obligation to pause the LAWS.[101]

Consequently, if a State deploys LAWS with such a dedicated command structure,[102] many illegal situations would be prevented, reducing the accidental situations to a minimum that complies with the human standard of reliability.

8.3.2.4 Commander Responsibility for a Subordinate's War Crime

The only problem that seems to arise with the employment of commander responsibility for the breaches caused by LAWS, is that the doctrine of command responsibility can only be invoked when a war crime has been committed by a subordinate.[103] Yet, as explained above, war crimes require the existence of a mental element that LAWS are incapable of having.[104] While this is true, the punishable omission under commander's responsibility is not the war crime itself, but the failure to prevent serious breaches of international humanitarian law.

In the case of Article 86 of Protocol I Additional to the Geneva Conventions, during its preparatory work, experts and government officials were looking to introduce an international rule on omission.[105] Furthermore, under the light of its object and purpose[106] we find that its purpose is to punish the failure to act[107] and to promote compliance with the rules of international humanitarian law,[108] particularly reaffirming the protection to persons[109] and reducing the number of crimes committed.[110] Hence, under customary rules of treaty interpretation[111]—even if

---

[99] Margulies 2012, pp. 407, 431.

[100] Sassóli 2014, p. 325.

[101] Sassóli 2014, p. 436.

[102] See Margulies 2012, p. 433.

[103] Dungel and Ghadiri 2010, p. 5.

[104] See Cass 2015, pp. 1017, 1064–1065; Crootof 2016, p. 1378.

[105] Pilloud et al. 1977, commentary to art. 86, para 3526.

[106] Vienna Convention on the Law of Treaties, art. 31(1), 23 May 1969, 1155 U.N.T.S 331. See also *Prosecutor v. Delalić et. al.*, Case No. IT-96-21-A, Appeals Chamber Judgement, para 73 (Int'l Crim. Trib. for the Former Yugoslavia, 20 February 2001).

[107] Pilloud et al. 1977, at commentary to art. 86, para 3529.

[108] Dungel and Ghadir 2010, p. 12.

[109] Dungel and Ghadiri 2010, p. 17.

[110] Dungel and Ghadiri 2010, p. 12.

[111] The International Court of Justice has repeatedly stated that Articles 31 and 32 of the Vienna Convention on the Law of Treaties reflect customary rules of treaty interpretation (i.e., Immunities and Criminal Proceedings (Equatorial Guinea v. France), Judgment, I.C.J., para 61; Jadhav (India v.

LAWS cannot comply with the mental element of war crimes[112]—the duty to prevent serious breaches of international humanitarian law should apply to the action of LAWS.[113] To the contrary, the unenforceability of this type of liability completely defeats the purpose of its existence.

Furthermore, the implementation of the other three requirements ensure that its application is fair for the commander,[114] who would not be held accountable for events that are truly unforeseeable after the implementation of all the aforesaid precautionary measures. The application of this standard of responsibility would guarantee that the people deploying the LAWS are constantly reviewing and adjusting the parameters of the weapon to ensure that any foreseeable mistake is avoided; and it allows for criminal responsibility to be placed accordingly based on the level or degree of guilt.[115]

8.4 Conclusion

The question of accountability for grave breaches of international humanitarian law is one of the many concerns that arise with the development and deployment of Lethal Autonomous Weapon Systems. This concern stems from their capability to select their targets without the confirmation of a human operator, which renders their actions highly unpredictable.

Even though there are several modes of accountability under our current legal framework that are available to allocate responsibility for serious breaches of international humanitarian law caused by LAWS,[116] this chapter's focus was the criminal responsibility that arises from these types of violations.

Criminal responsibility can only be assigned when there is some degree of culpability, which varies depending on the mode of liability. Thus, the fact that no criminal responsibility can be assigned in truly accidental and unforeseeable cases, does not constitute an accountability gap, since they do not constitute a breach of international humanitarian law.

Individual criminal liability, that requires perpetrators to have certainty about the commission of a crime, is not suitable to address these concerns. The mere likelihood of a breach taking place is not enough to comply with the mental element that is required under the more modern rules of criminal international law. This means that if an operator or commander orders the continued use of a LAWS that has already

---

Pakistan), Judgment, I.C.J. Reports 2019 (II), pp. 437–438, para 71; and Avena and Other Mexican Nationals (Mexico v. United States of America), Judgment, I.C.J. Reports 2004 (I), p. 48, para 83)).

[112] Ohlin 2016, p. 21.

[113] See Halajová 2020, p. 143.

[114] Contra Bills 2014, p. 197.

[115] Badar 2009, p. 467.

[116] State responsibility, criminal responsibility, manufacturer's liability, and administrative responsibility.

shown signs of malfunction, he or she cannot be held individually responsible for any deaths of protected persons or damage to protected property.

However, this does not mean that the unpredictability factor of LAWS may render their continued use under risky circumstances unpunished. Several precautions can and should be taken to prevent any erratic behaviour of these types of weapon systems. First, the deployment of any LAWS requires a dedicated command structure and support team with the requisite technical expertise in the operation and maintenance of the weapon systems. Second, before its deployment a thorough weapons review stage must be conducted to allow the commander and its team to become familiar with the LAWS *modus operandi*. Lastly, a frequent and periodic evaluation of the LAWS performance in the field must be undertaken to allow for the necessary updates and adjustments to the LAWS databases and interface.

In this sense, it appears that command responsibility allows for the maximum prevention of the malfunction of LAWS. As explained throughout this chapter, command responsibility has a lesser mental element requirement that would cover this type of situation.

Furthermore, of all the possibly responsible persons and entities for any malfunction of LAWS, commanders are in the best position to control the way and environment in which the weapon systems are deployed and to monitor their everyday operation. However, for this supervision to be possible, there needs to be a specialized command structure that includes a team of people with the technical expertise to constantly test and monitor the functioning of the weapon systems.

References

Books, (Online) Articles and Chapters in Books

Ambos K (2013) Treatise on International Criminal Law: Volume 1: Foundations and General Part. Oxford University Press, Oxford

Badar M (2009) Dolus Eventualis and the Rome Statute Without It? New Crim. L. Rev. Int'l & Interdisc. J. 12:433–467

Badar M, Porro S (2015) Rethinking the Mental Elements in the Jurisprudence of the ICC. In: Stahn C (ed) The Law and Practice of the International Criminal Court. Oxford University Press, Oxford, pp 649–668

Bills G (2014) LAWS unto Themselves: Controlling the Development and Use of Lethal Autonomous Weapons Systems. Geo. Wash. L. Rev. 83:176–208

Bo M (2021) Autonomous Weapons and the Responsibility Gap in light of the Mens Rea of the War Crime of Attacking Civilians in the ICC Statute. J. of Int'l Crim. Just. mqab005, https://doi.org/10.1093/jicj/mqab005 Accessed 31 August 2021

Cass K (2015) Autonomous Weapons and Accountability: Seeking Solutions in the Law of War. Loy. L.A. L. Rev. 48:1017–1067

Clark R (2008) Drafting a General Part to a Penal Code: Some Thoughts Inspired by the Negotiations on the Rome Statute of the International Criminal Court and by the Court's First Substantive Law Discussion in the Lubanga Dyilo Confirmation Proceedings. Crim. Law Forum 19:519–552

Crootof R (2015) War, Responsibility, and Killer Robots. N.C. J. Int'l L. & Com. Reg. 40:909–932

Crootof R (2016) War Torts: Accountability for Autonomous Weapons. U. Pa. L. Rev. 164:1347–1402

Davison N (2017) A legal perspective: Autonomous weapon systems under international humanitarian law. UNODA Occasional Papers 30:5–18

Dungel J, Ghadiri S (2010) The Temporal Scope of Command Responsibility Revisited: Why Commanders Have a Duty to Prevent Crimes Committed after the Cessation of Effective Control. U.C. Davis J. Int'l L. & Pol'y 17:1–40

Dunlap C (2016) Accountability and Autonomous Weapons: Much Ado About Nothing? Temple Int'l & Comp. L.J. 30:63-76

Egeland K (2016) Lethal Autonomous Weapon Systems under International Humanitarian Law. Nordic J. Int'l L. 85:89–118

Finnin S (2012) Elements of accessorial modes of liability: Article 25 (3)(b) and (c) of the Rome Statute of the International Criminal Court. Brill-Nijhoff Publishers, Leiden

Geiß R, Lahmann H (2017) Autonomous weapons systems: a paradigm shift for the law of armed conflict? In: Ohlin J (ed) Research Handbook on Remote Warfare. Edward Elgar Publishing Limited, Cheltenham, pp 371–404

Gil A (2014) Mens Rea in Co-Perpetration and Indirect Perpetration according to art. 30 of the Rome Statute: Arguments against Punishment for Excesses Committed by the Agent or the Co-Perpetrator. Int'l Crim. L. Rev. 14:82–114

Halajová L (2020) Individual Criminal Responsibility for War Crimes Resulting from the Use of Autonomous Weapons Systems. The Law. Q. 10:130–152

Hammond D (2015) Autonomous Weapons and the Problem of State Accountability. Chicago J. Int'l L. 15:652–687

Henckaerts J, Doswald-Beck L (2009) Customary International Humanitarian Law, Volume I, Rules. Cambridge University Press, Cambridge

Henderson I, Keane P, Liddy J (2017) Remote and autonomous warfare systems: precautions in attack and individual accountability. In: Ohlin J (ed) Research Handbook on Remote Warfare. Edward Elgar Publishing Limited, Cheltenham, pp 335–370

Human Rights Council (2013) Report of the Special Rapporteur on extrajudicial, summary or arbitrary executions, Christof Heyns. U.N. Doc. A/HRC/23/47

Human Rights Watch & International Human Rights Clinic at Harvard Law School (2012) Losing Humanity - the Case Against Killer Robots. https://www.hrw.org/report/2012/11/19/losing-hum anity/case-against-killer-robots Accessed 31 August 2021

Human Rights Watch & International Human Rights Clinic at Harvard Law School (2015) Mind the Gap: The Lack of Accountability for Killer Robots. https://www.hrw.org/report/2015/04/09/mind-gap/lack-accountability-killer-robots Accessed 31 August 2021

ICRC (2016) Views of the International Committee of the Red Cross (ICRC) on Autonomous Weapon Systems. https://www.icrc.org/en/document/views-icrc-autonomous-weapon-system Accessed 31 August 2021

Krupiy T (2018) Regulating a Game Changer: Using a Distributed Approach to Develop an Accountability Framework for Lethal Autonomous Weapon Systems. Geo. J. Int'l L. 50:45–112

Margulies P (2012) Making autonomous weapons accountable: Command responsibility for computer-guided lethal force in armed conflicts. In: Ohlin J (ed) Research Handbook on Remote Warfare. Edward Elgar Publishing Limited, Cheltenham, pp 405–442

Martinez J (2007) Understanding Mens Rea in Command Responsibility. J. Int'l Crim. Just. 5:638–664

Mull N (2018) The Roboticization of Warfare with Lethal Autonomous Weapons Systems (LAWS): Mandate of Humanity or Threat to It? Houst. J. Int. Law 40:461–530

Ohlin J (2013) Targeting and the Concept of Intent. Mich. J. of Int'l L. 35:79–130

Ohlin J (2016) The Combatant's Stance: Autonomous Weapons on the Battlefield. Int'l L. Stud. 92:1–30

Pilloud C et al. (1977) Commentary on the Additional Protocols. Martinus Nijhoff Publishers, Leiden

Russel S (1996) Machine Learning. In: Boden M (ed) Artificial Intelligence. Academic Press, San Diego, pp 89–133

Sassóli M (2014) Autonomous Weapons and International Humanitarian Law: Advantages, Open Technical Questions and Legal Issues to be Clarified. Int'l L. Stud. 90:308–340

Schabas W (2016) The International Criminal Court: A Commentary on the Rome Statute. Oxford University Press, Oxford

Schmitt M, Thurnher J (2013) Out of the Loop: Autonomous Weapon Systems and the Law of Armed Conflict. Harv. Nat'l Sec. J. 4:231–281

Sparrow R (2016) Robots and Respect: Assessing the Case Against Autonomous Weapon Systems. Ethics & Int'l Aff. 30:93–116

Van der Vyver J (2004) The International Criminal Court and the Concept of Mens Rea in International Criminal Law. U. Miami Int'l & Comp. L. Rev. 12:57–149

Wagner M (2014) The Dehumanization of International Humanitarian Law: Legal, Ethical, and Political Implications of Autonomous Weapon Systems. Vand. J. Transnat'l L. 47:1371–1424

Werle G, Jeßberger F (2005) Unless Otherwise Provided: Article 30 of the ICC Statute and the Mental Element of Crimes under International Criminal Law. J. Int'l Crim. Just. 3:35–55

Werle and Jeßberger, 2014.Werle G, Jeßberger F (2014) Principles of International Criminal Law. Oxford University Press, Oxford

Williamson J (2008) Some Considerations on Command Responsibility and Criminal Liability. Int'l Rev. of the Red Cross 90:303–317

Yokohama K (2018) The Failure to Control and the Failure to Prevent, Repress and Submit: The Structure of Superior Responsibility under Article 28 ICC Statute. Int'l Crim. L. Rev. 18:275–303

Table of Cases

Prosecutor v. Delalić et. al, Case No. IT-96-21-T, Trial Chamber Judgement, (Int'l Crim. Trib. for the Former Yugoslavia, 16 November 1998) (Čelebići case)

Prosecutor v. Kvočka et al., Case No. IT-98-30/1-T, Trial Chamber Judgement (Int'l Crim. Trib. for the Former Yugoslavia, 2 November 2001)

Prosecutor v. Milomir Stakić, Case No. IT-97-24-T, Trial Judgement (Int'l Crim. Trib. for the Former Yugoslavia, 31 July 2003)

Prosecutor v. Blaškić, Case No. IT-95-14-A, Appeals Chamber Judgement, (Int'l Crim. Trib. for the Former Yugoslavia, 29 July 2004)

Prosecutor v. Kordić and Čerkez, Case No. IT-95-14/2-A, Appeals Chamber Judgement, (Int'l Crim. Trib. for the Former Yugoslavia, 17 December 2004)

Prosecutor v. Galić, Case No. IT-98-29-A, Appeals Chamber Judgement, (Int'l Crim. Trib. for the Former Yugoslavia, 30 November 2006)

Prosecutor v. Kayishema and Ruzindana, Case No. ICTR-05-1-T, Trial Chamber Judgement (21 May 1999)

Prosecutor v. Bemba, Case No. ICC-01/05-01/08, Decision Pursuant to Article 61(7)(a) and (b) of the Rome Statute on the Charges of the Prosecutor Against Jean-Pierre Bemba Gombo (15 June 2009)

Prosecutor v. Lubanga, Case No. ICC-01/04-01/06, Decision on the Confirmation of Charges (29 January 2007)

Prosecutor v. Lubanga, Case No. ICC-01/04-01/06, Judgment pursuant to Article 74 of the Statute (14 March 2012)

Valeria Chiappini Koscina is a Chilean lawyer who works at the National Department of Boundaries and Border Areas of the Chilean Ministry of Foreign Affairs. She studied law at Universidad Adolfo Ibáñez (2012), and later obtained her Master of Laws (LL.M.) at Cornell University (2020) with a focus in public international law. Her previous work includes complex litigation on criminal, civil and commercial matters. She has been a teaching assistant of Public International Law, Litigation in Public International Law, and International Humanitarian Law courses at Universidad Adolfo Ibáñez, and is currently a teaching assistant for the International Criminal Law course at Pontificia Universidad Católica de Chile. She has been coaching teams for the Philip C. Jessup International Law Moot Court Competition since 2015.

Chapter 9
The Risks of Social Media Platforms for Democracy: A Call for a New Regulation

Erik Longo

Contents

Abstract This chapter critically discusses how the democratic arena is changing and deteriorating due to the impact of the power of social media platforms. The focus is on the consequences that personalized forms of information and digital affordances can produce, leading to online information cocoons or filter bubbles that limit the range of political ideas that people can encounter. Then, the threats to democracy and liberty produced by closed online spaces in which people of similar opinions can congregate are discussed. Finally, the chapter analyses an approach to the regulation of social media based on assessing the nature of digital capitalism and how we pay for the digital services offered by social media platforms.

Keywords Democracy · Digital affordances · Regulation · Filter bubbles · Fundamental rights

E. Longo (✉)
University of Florence, Florence, Italy
e-mail: erik.longo@unifi.it

© T.M.C. ASSER PRESS and the authors 2022
B. Custers and E. Fosch-Villaronga (eds.), *Law and Artificial Intelligence*,
Information Technology and Law Series 35,
https://doi.org/10.1007/978-94-6265-523-2_9

169

9.1 Introduction

At the beginning of this new millennium, many scholars and commentators dreamed that the internet would render an excellent service to the development of democracy,[1] transforming people from passive receivers of information, as readers of newspapers or television viewers, into content producers.[2] The internet would have guaranteed more participation,[3] greater transparency in decision-making processes and reducing the gap of representation between elected representatives and voters.[4] At that time, many began to assert that technology could be an intrinsic democratic force by facilitating power from below.[5]

After twenty years, we can confirm that the internet has undoubtedly changed the panorama of politics yielding to an era of "internet democracy" or cross-media democracy combining broadcasting and interactive media.[6] This situation is more evident in a historical period of continuous electoral rounds, reduced government stability worldwide, and intense political communication on social media platforms.[7] The expansion of digital communication has triggered some significant political processes (such as during the "Arab Spring" or the protests of the "Umbrella Movement" in Hong Kong),[8] allowed the development of numerous political and social movements (such as the "Movimento Cinque Stelle" in Italy),[9] and, generally speaking, "made elected officials and candidates more accountable and accessible to voters."[10]

Alongside the promises and some positive results, the internet and the web have also developed a negative side, allowing the rise of numerous risks and threats for the free formation of public opinion and democratic representation, as was first experienced during the US presidential elections of 2016 and the referendum for Brexit in the same year.[11]

---

[1] Morris 2000; Davis et al. 2002; Browning 2002. Only a few authors declared that accessible, reliable and valid information is not sufficient for democracy (Hacker and van Dijk 2000).

[2] This effect has been called "disintermediation of information". See Gellman 1996. In general *disintermediation* describes a general situation in which citizens, thanks to the lower cost of producing content generated by the internet, are regularly equipped to compete with traditional mediating organizations. Castells 2010; Robles-Morales and Córdoba-Hernández 2019.

[3] Grossman 1995.

[4] Cohen and Fung 2021, pp. 23–26.

[5] Ferdinand 2000; Margetts et al. 2015.

[6] Dommett et al. 2020; Van Dijk and Hacker 2018, p. 2.

[7] Dommett and Temple 2017.

[8] As Willems 2020, p. 2 affirms, "the 2011 uprising in North Africa and the middle East provoked much hope about the ability of social media to function as a 'technology of freedom' and bring about political change". See also Eltantawy and Wiest 2011; Wolfsfeld et al. 2013.

[9] Bassini 2019; Gerbaudo 2018; Lanzone and Woods 2015; Manucci and Amsler 2018.

[10] As recognized by Murse 2018 who regarded the "direct contact with voters" as the first dramatic change in politics since the advent of social media.

[11] Kaiser 2019; Wylie 2019. If we want to describe another event consider the use of Facebook for the Rohingya genocide, as reported by the New York Times (Stevenson 2018).

Thus, the reality is much more complicated than most people imagined. It is not by chance that today we hear more and more about the "death"[12] of democratic discourse at the hands of the massive manipulation and disinformation produced on the web.[13] Every day we are inundated with entirely or partially false news.[14] Even the word "fake news" has become so inflated that it no longer causes a scandal. The neologism "post-truth" has been coined to indicate the widespread tendency to welcome and defend everything that excites and amuses people, even if it is blatantly false.[15]

Governments and supranational institutions have raised several concerns about the harmful effects of online viral disinformation.[16] Hence, they propose greater legal control over tech companies' power in areas covered by constitutional liberties.[17]

Our societies are becoming increasingly polarised, divided and unequal under the effect of online life.[18] Indeed, one of the biggest threats to democracy comes from the fact that, despite the old media, new online media like Facebook, YouTube, Twitter, Tik Tok, rely on an abundance of data never seen before, produced—yet not owned—by users. This economic system gives these firms undisputed advantages in terms of political resources and leads to the onerous responsibility of preventing the public discourse from being "polluted". Social media had a determinant role in the riots occurred the 6 January 2021 which saw Donald Trump's supporters storm US Congress.

Against this background, this chapter critically discusses how "democratic arenas" are changing and deteriorating due to the impact of the power of platforms. Sections 9.2 and 9.3 analyse from a social science point of view the disruption made by big data and social network algorithms. Sections 9.4 and 9.5 discuss the threats to democracy and liberty produced by closed online spaces in which people of similar opinions can congregate. In the conclusions (Sect. 9.6) a legal framework is proposed based on assessing the digital affordances of platforms and their capacity to reinforce the logic behind both representation and participation.

---

[12] Kurlantzick 2013; Runciman 2018.

[13] Bloom and Sancino 2019; Runciman 2018; Levitsky and Ziblatt 2018; Hindman 2018; Keller 2017.

[14] Pew 2019; House 2018; ISD Global 2019.

[15] According to the Oxford English Dictionary the expression is "relating to or denoting circumstances in which objective facts are less influential in shaping public opinion than appeals to emotion and personal belief". See also Sawyer 2018.

[16] Today governments are worried about disinformation campaigns that target public health measures and institutions, and, particularly give rise of global antivaccination campaigns. See Bernard et al. 2021, pp. 3–10.

[17] See: the statute law approved by the German Bundestag "Netzicerkdurchsetzungsgesetz—NetzDG". Giannone Codiglione 2017; the Report of the High Level Group on Fake News and Online Disinformation of the European Commission Disinformation 2018; the European Commission 2018 of the European Commission.

[18] Ansell and Samuels 2014.

9.2 A Destabilising Technological Change: Big Data and Algorithms

Some may remember the example of the "Daily me" imagined by Negroponte:[19] the idea that one day everyone would be able to take advantage of information selected personally, without relying on newspapers or television networks to choose this information. This mechanism would entrust the responsibility of an "architecture of control" of information to every user.[20] It would make it possible to overcome many of those problems that the press and television have always produced in terms of manipulation, lack of pluralism, abuse of their position in the market.

Whereas the idea at that time seemed like science fiction, it took only a few years for the "Daily me" to happen without us even realising it. With the rise of computational sciences and algorithmic power, private companies have developed the ability to create multiple forms of a personal newspaper without our knowledge and automatically—with a level of precision that makes even the original project seem old-fashioned.

The importance of platforms and internet search engines for seeking information and public communication is now undisputed and so crucial that some scholars have coined the word "platformization of information" to name this process.[21] Others have stressed the new "narrative" of media platform capitalism.[22]

For a company like Google operating in an era of massively abundant data, it is unnecessary to use theoretical models because new forms of data processing produce better results.[23] The success of this shift relies on the idea of "correlation" and the abandonment of "causation" as the old way of understanding the cause-effect relationship.[24] Authors suggest to forget "taxonomies, ontology and psychology" and not to ask ourselves why "people do what they do", but to look at "what they do", so it will be easier to follow and measure human action "with unprecedented fidelity".[25] In short, having data in abundance, the numbers speak "for themselves".[26]

The perspective shows a total trust in algorithms and statistical correlations, not only in terms of efficiency and speed but in "decision-making", as it relies on the machines for objective analysis capabilities. We can ask the algorithms to tell us what and where to eat, what music to listen to, what to read, what movie to see. Thanks to the measurability of everything, the primary production of vast amounts of data (datafication) and the ability of automatic processes to create correlations, algorithms

---

[19] Negroponte 1996, p. 53.

[20] Sunstein 2017.

[21] Van Dijck et al. 2018, p. I, pinpoints the "promise" of platforms: "they offer personalized services and contribute to innovation and economic growth, while efficiently bypassing incumbent organizations, cumbersome regulations, and unnecessary expenses".

[22] Pasquale 2016.

[23] Saetnan Rudinow et al. 2018.

[24] Pearl and Mackenzie 2018.

[25] Helbing 2018, p. 50.

[26] Anderson 2008.

replace the critic, the expert and ultimately our ability to judge. It is, therefore, not just a technology that has brought us into the future but a socio-cultural transformation generated by a new epistemic paradigm—a new form of bio-politics that is much stronger than that envisioned by Bentham in his Panopticon.[27]

9.3 The Datafication

In the early days, social networks like Facebook and Twitter were created to allow users to generate public profiles and maintain connections with other people. When the ability to collect, interpret and analyse large amounts of data emerged, thanks to the development of "Big Data" and "Data Mining",[28] it became clear that it was not just a matter of "social networks". They were tools capable of disseminating information and acting as real social media platforms with the ability to spread news and collect commercial advertisements. Although they are not categorised as publishers or advertising companies, Facebook and Twitter have become—thanks to conveying content—large scale managers of information and advertising companies.

The secret weapon of this operation was the technology behind the process of data collection itself, the use of recommendation and relevance algorithms, i.e. the algorithms behind social media, which select information for users through a much larger pool of information than of the individual user.[29] Based on a particular set of rules, the algorithm decides that the selected data are the most important (or adequate) for a specific user. This functionality is present in the scenario of social networks acting as "mediators", with algorithms that make automated decisions about the content to be provided.

At the heart of this mechanism is "Machine Learning", a set of AI techniques and tools that allow computers to learn AI based on accumulated data.[30] In the practical process of learning from data, platforms use Machine Learning to predict our behaviour by elaborating data that symbolises our preferences, movements, actions, or reactions. The method—when applied to individuals—is called "automatic profiling" because algorithms automatically process personal data to evaluate certain aspects relating to an individual, namely to analyse or predict unimaginable facets of our behaviour.[31] Section 9.3.1 focuses on the economic incentive and Sect. 9.3.2 examines attention and distraction.

---

[27] Han 2017, pp. 76–77.
[28] Calders and Custers 2013; Battaglini and Rasmussen 2019.
[29] Gillespie 2014, pp. 167–169.
[30] Robins 2020; Jordan and Mitchell 2015.
[31] Hildebrandt 2018.

9.3.1 The Economic Incentive

Social media platforms and search engines make money essentially from advertising.[32] Therefore, the greater the possibility of grabbing the users' attention by encouraging them to choose certain (targeted) goods or services, the greater the economic return for the platforms.[33] To identify preferences and needs of users, the use profiling and nudging.[34]

The mechanism works by collecting data on people and yielding the enormous capacity of some services to persuade and distract. Indeed, platforms influence people by tricking them into believing that their services are desperately needed. Facebook, Google, Amazon, Tik Tok work as authentic "nets" in which users are manipulatively entangled. Of course, they operate not through the power of brute force but the weight of numbers.[35]

The conditioning power of the social networks translates into a considerable political force. Thanks to the continuous algorithmic optimisation underlying search engines and social networks, it has become not only impossible to escape their "surveillance", but it is increasingly impossible to distinguish between it and the search for information. It has been pointed out that paradoxically it is our curiosity that betrays us.[36] It is the desire to improve our position as consumers that leads to us to being more supervised. Besides, if search engines earn from advertisements and the ranking of information, the more data we provide, the greater the possibility we have of receiving targeted information. Thus, paradoxically, "to seek" becomes more and more synonymous with "to be sought".[37]

At a quick glance, we could say that we pay for information with our data, yet to a more profound and informed understanding, we should take note that the currency is another: our "attention". In a market where information is abundant, and attention remains a "scarce resource", social media fight dirty to catch and harvest our attention.[38] This process exploits another economic leap. Smartphones have substantially expanded the number of internet users all over the world. The growing popularity of social media platforms has taken place alongside a spatial shift in internet access from fixed desktop computers to mobile smartphones.[39]

---

[32] Hendricks and Vestergaard 2019, pp. 1–17.

[33] Following the prophecy of Simon 1971, pp. 40–41.

[34] Crawford 2015; Shaffer 2019, p. 10; Yeung 2017, p. 123.

[35] As Cohen 2017, p. 143 affirms platforms are not just networks since they "exploit the affordances of network organization and supply infrastructures that facilitate particular types of interactions, but they also represent strategies for bounding networks and privatizing and controlling infrastructures".

[36] Pariser 2011.

[37] Zuboff 2019.

[38] Hendricks and Vestergaard 2019, p. 6.

[39] Goggin 2014.

9.3.2 Attention and Distraction

The new data economy is based on an equivocal mechanism that tries to influence our behaviour even in an unconscious and subliminal way,[40] often using our cognitive errors and "heuristics".[41] It is also for these purposes that algorithms of Machine Learning and Data Mining are used. The phenomenon has also been called "hypernudging" to indicate the fact that

(B)y highlighting the correlations between data that would otherwise not be observable, these techniques are used to model the context of informed choice in which individual decision-making occurs, to direct attention and decision-making in the directions preferred by the architect of choice.[42]

Suppose an online platform needs to maximise our attention and acquire as much data as possible. In that case, their attachment to our activities must be as broad as possible, and their way of operating must be as pleasant as possible and, above all, free. This is why Amazon, Facebook, Google, Twitter, Tik Tok tend to function according to one-stop-shop systems: they give us and ask us for information on several fronts. But when their contents catalyse attention, their algorithms classify and target the audience and, thanks also to the exploitation of cognitive biases, direct users' behaviour towards specific results.[43]

Some authors stigmatise the phenomenon by highlighting that a new form of propaganda can be generated by developing the data economy.[44] Other scholars even use the expression "information laundering"[45] to reveal the undetectable operation whereby originally corrupt information can be easily "cleaned up". The mechanism is as easy as it is mighty. The circulation of biased and opaque messages creates the perfect environment for disinformation by exploiting the inattentiveness of users.

The phenomenon affects privacy and usually produces discrimination because it is often based on acquiring data that are not entirely lawful or that deceive the consumer, user or voter.[46] Besides, these practices limit the freedom of expression, freedom of information and even, until now, the otherwise impalpable—on a legal level—"freedom of thought", which is the basis of democratic coexistence and the freedoms themselves.[47]

---

[40] As Han 2017 reminds us: "This new medium is reprogramming us, yet we fail to grasp the radical paradigm shift that is underway. We are hobbling along after the very medium that, below our threshold of conscious decision, is definitively changing the ways that we act, perceive, feel, think, and live together".

[41] Tversky and Kahneman 1974.

[42] Yeung 2017, p. 122.

[43] Although this phenomenon has been known for a long time among cognitive psychology scholars (see Rose 2010) it is in recent years that we talk about it with regard to the platform economy (Hendricks and Vestergaard 2019).

[44] These mechanisms, while trying to make people subordinate, greatly reduce the cost of power, as pointed out in Ellul 1973.

[45] Shaffer 2019, p. 45.

[46] On the effects of the creation of groups profiles, see Custers 2018, pp. 277–9.

[47] As pointed out wittily by Richards 2015, p. 95 speaking of "intellectual privacy".

Therefore, as scholars have pointed out, the ongoing debate on the regulation and control of algorithms implies a crucial challenge for the survival of liberal regimes.[48] On the one hand, it regards managing the strong push of Big Data to create conformity and polarisation while safeguarding the possibility of dissent as an excellent common and vital thrust of democratic systems. On the other hand, it ensures that marginal and minority opinions are not submerged under the deluge of large numbers and prevailing tendencies that impede freedom for all and generate inequalities.[49]

9.4 Filter Bubbles, Polarisation and Misinformation

The way algorithms help predict and determine our behaviour is called "collaborative filtering", which is a set of automated systems that ultimately serve to infer the tastes of specific users from the preferences of others.[50]

The idea behind *collaborative filtering* is as simple as it is effective. If platforms need to make recommendations on what we want or what we might buy, they need a lot of data—certainly more data than they can glean from any user.[51] The solution to this is statistical computation and correlation.[52] It is necessary to compare users who, thanks to profiling, express characteristics or simply data similar to ours to determine if we will be interested in a particular thing.[53] This is why social platforms can predict our future behaviour accurately or merely offer us music that we might enjoy by using relatively incomplete information about us. Platforms, indeed, consider us in association with others and deceptively make us collaborate them so that our profiles become in a while "mega-profiles" while maintaining individual characteristics. Thus, automated profiling, which uses Machine Learning and Data Mining to attract us and extract data from our behaviour, works both individually and collectively.[54]

However, *collaborative filters* cause some problems. If we consider the results of our Google searches or the content of threads on Facebook or Twitter newsfeed, they are based on data generated by us and similar profiles. It follows therefore that people "collaborating" will see mainly data decided by the filter with minimal exposure to

---

[48] Balkin 2017.

[49] Simoncini and Suweis 2019, pp. 91–93.

[50] "Collaborative filtering" is the most widely used technique in recommender systems for predicting the interests of a user on particular items. The idea is to learn hidden features of the user's past activities so as to build an accurate model for recommendation. Konstan and Riedl 2012; Shin 2020.

[51] It is also for this reason that data has become a real market where the marketing of data aims to monetize its value through their circulation, rather than through their in-house analysis.

[52] For example, this is how the Netflix algorithm works. See Hindman 2018, pp. 43–44.

[53] As Chen et al. 2017, p. 197 argue "Successful pricing strategies, marketing campaigns, and political campaigns depend on the ability to optimally target consumers and voters". See also Büchi et al. 2019, pp. 5–10.

[54] On this issue, see Pearl and Mackenzie 2018; Büchi et al. 2019; Hildebrandt 2008; Bosco et al. 2015.

divergent information. This phenomenon is called "filter bubble"[55] because it creates an environment where similar profiles are stored. *Filter bubbles* have a clear purpose: to classify us, to control us as well as direct our present and future preferences. In short, watch over us.[56]

One of the most critical issues generated by filter bubbles touches the heart of the dialectical mechanism by which opinions are formed. In the filter bubbles, the cognitive errors that lead many people to behave in a certain way and the information laundering—as a phenomenon closely linked to disinformation—tend to amplify.[57] Not only will it be easier to come across (dis)information, but it will also be very likely that it is fed in by *disseminators*. We will be much more superficial since that information comes to us from people who are part of our "bubble" or, worse, from a newsfeed built for us by the search engine or the social platform. The bubbles also affect trust, so that content can be considered authentic not by being based on a critical analysis of the sources but on the online reputation of the person sharing that information.[58]

Furthermore, in the bubble, people are scarcely aware that divergent opinions exist.[59] They generate "echo chambers", which are environments for meeting beliefs or opinions that coincide with their own and do not admit alternative ideas.[60]

We should remember that everything arises from the need to achieve an asymmetrical optimisation of information circulation through an environment in which whoever offers a product can reach the consumer as quickly and efficiently as possible. The consequence is that we find ourselves at the mercy of the lack of informative pluralism, false news, and forces capable of persuading and manipulating.[61]

Perhaps the worst characteristic of filter bubbles is the lack of transparency, harm for media pluralism, and impartiality they help generate.[62] This happens because the data analysis made upstream through predictive algorithms takes place through codes that, despite being written by humans, are difficult to control by the creators themselves once put into operation.[63] No one beyond the developers themselves knows how Facebook or Google's algorithms are programmed.[64] Users may not be able to understand why any individual newsfeed has those particular characteristics,

---

[55] Pariser 2011.

[56] Zuboff 2019; Richards 2012; Büchi et al. 2019.

[57] This was very evident in the Cambridge Analytica scandal.

[58] Shaffer 2019.

[59] Noble 2018.

[60] Burbach et al. 2019.

[61] Susser et al. 2019.

[62] This concerns have been raised by the Council of Europe in 2018 with an important "Recommendation on media pluralism and transparency of media ownership".

[63] Scholars affirmed that these complex and uninterpretable predictive models function like "black boxes". See Pasquale 2015; Burrell 2016.

[64] In the past Facebook has come under severe criticism with regard to how information is distributed on the platform. See Griffin 2018; Hern 2018.

except that its effect is to give us information with a specific hierarchy on things that the platform itself has decided.[65]

We do not choose to enter the bubbles, they are looking for us, and above all, they make us imagine that the information provided is objective, neutral and created to guarantee us comfort. Inside the bubbles, it is almost impossible to know how much data addressed to individuals is targeted and responsive to the will of the "architects" in order to customise input and output.[66]

This phenomenon explains another problem generated by filter bubbles. Within them, we live in "solitude". We are neither a mass nor a crowd, because we are "isolated individuals".[67] Technically speaking, filter bubbles operate as "invisible"[68] mechanisms that, based on the operation of "centrifugal" forces, "polarise" us.[69] The illusion generated by polarisation fragments society into watertight compartments, and it is more difficult for people of different convictions to interact or even find common ground. Therefore, it is not surprising that those studying politics and digital media observe a growing lack of communication when it comes to political issues (strong emotions, reduced nuances, grouped ideological positions).[70]

Although their destructive force is known and opposed, the phenomena described appear almost unstoppable. Since Facebook experimented with the "Voter's megaphone" in 2010, politics has no longer been the same—at least in the United States and perhaps soon also in Europe.[71] Recent surveys show that search engine results are subject to constant manipulation for consumer purposes and consensus.[72]

The adverse effects on the fronts of equality, freedom of speech, political participation are undisputed.[73] This type of activity is not fully restricted even by the heavy European Union legislation currently in force.[74]

The EU Commission, taking note of the need for a common European regulation that overcomes the existing regulatory fragmentation, especially with regard to the obligations and responsibilities of digital platforms, and after extensive consultation with the main stakeholders, has thus prepared two proposals for regulation: the "Digital Services Act" and "Digital Markets Act".[75] They are devoted explicitly to governing the rise of large technological platforms. The proposals aims at surpassing the by now old "e-Commerce Directive" (Directive 2000/31/EC). Inside the broad

---

[65] Schwartz and Mahnke 2020.

[66] Büchi et al. 2019.

[67] Han 2017, p. 10.

[68] Vilella 2019, p. 16.

[69] Pariser 2011, p. 10.

[70] Bennett and Gordon 2020.

[71] O'Neil 2017; Bond et al. 2012, p. 1.

[72] Grind et al. 2019. See also the interesting report of the European Parliamentary Research Service (STOA) 2019.

[73] Balkin 2017.

[74] Even the strict rules of the GDPR do not manage to limit many of the paradoxical effects on personal data produced by automated decision-making. See Mendoza and Bygrave 2017.

[75] European Commission 2020a, b.

frame of "2030 Digital Compass: the European way for the Digital Decade", the Commission has undertaken to update the rules defining the responsibilities and obligations of digital service providers. A specific target of the whole strategy regards the respect of fundamental rights, starting with data protection and freedom of speech.

9.5 Approaches to the Regulation of Social Media

The regulation of social media implies a careful examination of the nature of digital capitalism and how we pay for the digital services we have.[76] We have seen that digital platforms, such as Facebook, Twitter, YouTube, Tik Tok, rely on far more advanced and individualised targeted advertising than was available to twentieth-century broadcasting media.[77] The more interactive method of communication exploits data collection and analysis, allowing targeted advertising and producing more significant revenues.

Several strategies can be followed to stop this situation. Since only a small number of companies dominate the market of social media platforms, probably the most important and feasible way of addressing this transformation is to appeal to antitrust and competition law and raise a question about the condition of the media and information ecosystem.[78] Indeed, their activity can have a stranglehold on the advertising market and be an impediment to creating competition.

As the recent Australian Act No. 21/2021 (News Media and Digital Platforms Mandatory Bargaining Code) shows, another way to address the disruptions associated with digital technologies is to compensate news outlets for original news production content.[79] This statute aims at addressing the fundamental imbalance in bargaining power between traditional news media and online media platforms identified in the "Final Report of the Australian Competition and Consumer Commission's Digital Platforms Inquiry".[80]

The Australian example clarifies that reliance upon platform self-governance has failed to see significant public concerns adequately addressed. It is true that their qualification as "public services" is far from portraying the real setting.

The strategy based on self-governance is by no means sufficient to guarantee adequate user protection, mainly because it does not distinguish between the various automated treatments.[81] The platforms themselves are well aware of this as they move towards new forms of legal tools to protect users from misinformation.[82]

---

[76] Balkin 2018, p. 1.

[77] Balkin 2018, p. 2.

[78] Gillespie 2018. On this side see the recent decision of the German Bundesgerichtshof, Beschluss vom 23 Juni 2020, Kvr 69/19, *Facebook*.

[79] Flew and Wilding 2021.

[80] A. C. C. Commission 2019. See also Dearman and Pyburne 2021.

[81] See Council of Europe 2019, pp. 1–3.

[82] See Facebook 2019.

However, the uncertainty about the rules no longer appears sustainable.[83] Despite being based on statistical correlations derived from vast amounts of data extrapolated from the use of digital technologies, the algorithms underlying social media and search engines do express inferential mechanisms and opinions on what is right to disseminate, its form, and, possibly, its limits.[84] Therefore, when these effects are produced, online behaviour should be treated and protected in a different way, considering that today most of the development of individual autonomy and self-determination increasingly depend on algorithms.

Thus, new forms of legislation must consider the "attention economy" that social media exploits and how this happens, mainly through the use of "digital affordances".[85] Social media have their distinctive *affordances*, which have significant feedback on users and their actions. They facilitate the transmission of certain types of content and, at the same time, hinder forms of expression due to the fundamental logic that informs the functioning of the platform itself.

Affordance is not, in reality, a concept limited only to the forms of expression on the internet. Indeed, from a factual point of view, any context affects a person's ability to act freely. However, two distinct circumstances need to be emphasised in the case of social media.

Firstly, their ability to use feedback is much more powerful and structured than any other tool. Social media, indeed, allow users to express themselves in multiple ways and reach a worldwide audience. This is why scholars have put forward a systematic categorisation of the relationship between social media and democratic participation.[86]

Secondly, despite the appearance, users cannot know and master these tools because they do not understand precisely how and to what degree the information infrastructure affects their expression. Typical of "digital affordances" is that they intuitively show the purposes and uses of platforms. Still, they do not make intelligible and clear the exact extent to which social media retroacts users' goals and changes their behaviour.[87]

9.6 Conclusions

This chapter started with the assumption that the new means of communication enabled through the internet do not bring about new ways of curing democracy

---

[83] As pointed out in Lee 2019, pp. 789–790.

[84] Koltay 2019, 146 ss.

[85] In the digital milieu, the term *affordances* can be utilized as the "mutuality of actor intentions and technology capabilities that provide the potential for a particular action". See Majchrzak et al. 2013, p. 39. For the literature on *affordances*, see also Hopkins 2020.

[86] Dahlberg 2011.

[87] Defaults, framing of choices and dark patterns can substantially influence user choices, likely contributing to the privacy paradox and limiting opportunities to discover new perspectives. See the report of the UK CMA, CMA 2020 and Hayes et al. 2018.

issues or producing more political participation *per se*. No technology can fix a lack of political motivation, time, efforts and skills required to participate in the democratic arena fully.

However, social networks have created a new media ecology that yields new problems, such as massive disinformation and polarisation of ideas. This chapter examined the processes that lead to the creation of "filter bubbles" and micro-targeting political marketing for citizens who follow the same views. We have shown how algorithms designed to capture user attention produce self-segregating and social-political fragmentation. To address these issues, we called for new regulation of these phenomena at the EU level. Such regulation should treat and protect online behaviour differently, better taking into account the "attention economy" that social media exploits.

A legal framework based on assessing the digital affordances of platforms would reinforce the logic behind both representation and participation.[88] This perspective might help the potential of digital technologies and support a public sphere in which free, autonomous and equal persons are more fully enabled to use their common reason in public, political engagement.[89]

References

Anderson C (2008) The End Of Theory: The Data Deluge Makes The Scientific Method Obsolete. Wired, 23/06/2008. Retrieved from https://www.wired.com/2008/06/pb-theory/.

Ansell B W, Samuels D J (2014) Inequality and democratization: an elite-competition approach. Cambridge University Press, Cambridge.

Australian Competition & Consumer Commission (2019) Digital platforms inquiry - final report. Sydney. https://www.accc.gov.au/publications/digital-platforms-inquiry-final-report Accessed 21 March 2021.

Balkin J M (2017) Free Speech in the Algorithmic Society: Big Data, Private Governance, and New School Speech Regulation. UCDL Rev. 51:1149–1210.

Balkin J (2018) Fixing Social Media's Grand Bargain. Aegis Series Paper No. 1814. https://www.lawfareblog.com/advanced-persistent-manipulators-and-social-media-nationalism-national-security-world-audiences.

Bassini M (2019) Rise of Populism and the Five Star Movement Model: An Italian Case Study. Italian Journal of Public Law 11:302–333.

Battaglini M, Rasmussen S (2019) Transparency, automated decision-making processes and personal profiling. Journal of Data Protection & Privacy 2:331–349.

Bennett C, Gordon J (2020) Understanding the "Micro" in Micro-Targeting: An Analysis of Facebook Digital Advertising in the 2019 Federal Canadian Election. Available at SSRN 3589687.

Bernard R, Bowsher G, Sullivan R, Gibson-Fall F (2021) Disinformation and Epidemics: Anticipating the Next Phase of Biowarfare. Health Security 19:3–12.

Bloom P, Sancino A (2019) Disruptive Democracy: The Clash Between Techno-Populism and Techno-Democracy. SAGE, London.

Bond R M, Fariss C J, Jones J J, Kramer A D, Marlow C, Settle J E, Fowler J H (2012) A 61-million-person experiment in social influence and political mobilization. Nature 489:295.

---

[88] Cardone 2021.

[89] See generally Habermas 1996.

Bosco F, Creemers N, Ferraris V, Guagnin D, Koops B-J (2015) Profiling technologies and funda-
mental rights and values: regulatory challenges and perspectives from European Data Protection
Authorities. In: Gutwirth S, Leenes R, De Hert P (eds) Reforming European Data Protection Law.
Springer, Cham, pp. 3–33.

Browning G (2002). Electronic democracy: Using the Internet to transform American politics.
Information Today, Medford, NJ.

Büchi M, Fosch Villaronga E, Lutz C, Tamò-Larrieux A, Velidi S, Viljoen S (2019) Chilling Effects
of Profiling Activities: Mapping the Issues. Available at SSRN 3379275.

Burbach L, Halbach P, Ziefle M, Calero Valdez A (2019) Bubble Trouble: Strategies Against Filter
Bubbles in Online Social Networks. Springer International Publishing, pp. 441–456.

Burrell J (2016) How the machine 'thinks': Understanding opacity in machine learning algorithms.
Big Data & Society 3:2053951715622512.

Calders T, Custers B (2013) What is data mining and how does it work? In: Custers B, Toon C,
Schermer B, Zarsky T Z (Eds.), Discrimination and Privacy in the Information Society. Springer,
Cham, pp. 27–42.

Cardone A (2021) "Decisione algoritmica" vs decisione politica? A.I. Legge Democrazia. Editoriale
Scientifica, Naples

Castells M (2010) The network society. Wiley-Blackwell, Oxford.

Chen D, Fraiberger S P, Moakler R, Provost F (2017) Enhancing transparency and control when
drawing data-driven inferences about individuals. Big Data 5:197–212.

Cohen J E (2017) Law for the platform economy. UCDL Rev. 51:133.

Cohen J, Fung A (2021) Democracy and the Digital Public Sphere. In: Bernholz L, Landemore
H, Reich R (eds) Digital Technology and Democratic Theory. University of Chicago Press,
Chicago/London, pp. 23–61.

Council of Europe (2018) Recommendation CM/Rec(2018)11 of the Committee of Ministers to
member States on media pluralism and transparency of media ownership. Strasbourg. Accessed.

Council of Europe (2019) Declaration by the Committee of Ministers on the manipulative capabilities of algorithmic processes. Strasbourg. https://www.coe.int/en/web/data-protection/-/declar
ation-by-the-committee-of-ministers-on-the-manipulative-capabilities-of-algorithmic-processes
Accessed 21 March 2021.

Crawford M B (2015) The world beyond your head: On becoming an individual in an age of
distraction. Farrar, Straus and Giroux, New York.

Custers B (2018) Data Mining and Profiling in Big Data. In: Arrigo B (ed) The SAGE Encyclopedia
of Surveillance, Security, and Privacy. Sage, London, pp. 277–279.

Dahlberg L (2011) Re-constructing digital democracy: An outline of four 'positions'. New Media &
Society 13:855–872.

Davis S, Elin L, Reeher G (2002) Click on democracy: The Internet's power to change political
apathy into civic action. Westview Press.

Dearman P, Pyburne P (2021) Treasury Laws Amendment (News Media and Digital Platforms
Mandatory Bargaining Code) Bill 2020. Bills Digest 48.

Dommett K, Fitzpatrick J, Mosca L, Gerbaudo P (2020) Are Digital Parties the Future of Party
Organization? A Symposium on The Digital Party: Political Organisation and Online Democracy
by Paolo Gerbaudo. Italian Political Science Review/Rivista Italiana di Scienza Politica 51:136–
149.

Dommett K, Temple L (2017) Digital Campaigning: The Rise of Facebook and Satellite Campaigns.
Parliamentary Affairs 71.

European Parliamentary Research Service (STOA) (2019) Polarisation and the use of technology
in political campaigns and communication. Brussels. https://www.europarl.europa.eu/RegData/
etudes/STUD/2019/634414/EPRS_STU(2019)634414_EN.pdf Accessed 21 March 2021.

Ellul J (1973) Propaganda. The Formation of Men's Attitude. Vintage Books, New York.

Eltantawy N, Wiest J B (2011) Social Media in the Egyptian Revolution: Reconsidering Resource
Mobilization Theory. International Journal of Communication 5:18.

European Commission (2018) EU Code of Practice on Disinformation. Brussels. https://ec.europa.eu/digital-single-market/en/news/code-practice-disinformation Accessed 10 March 2021.

European Commission (2020a) Proposal for a Regulation of the European Parliament and of the Council on a Single Market For Digital Services (Digital Services Act) and amending Directive 2000/31/EC. Brussels. https://eur-lex.europa.eu/legal-content/en/TXT/?uri=COM:2020:825:FIN Accessed 15 December 2020.

European Commission (2020b) Proposal for a Regulation of the European Parliament and of the Council on contestable and fair markets in the digital sector (Digital Markets Act). Accessed 21 March 2021.

Facebook (2019) Oversight Board Charter. https://about.fb.com/wp-content/uploads/2019/09/oversight_board_charter.pdf Accessed 21 March 2021.

Ferdinand P (2000) The Internet, democracy and democratization. Democratization 7:1–17.

Flew T, Wilding D (2021) The turn to regulation in digital communication: the ACCC's digital platforms inquiry and Australian media policy. Media, culture & society 43:48–65.

Freedom House (2018) The Rise of Digital Authoritarianism. Freedom on the Net 2018. Retrieved from: https://freedomhouse.org/report/freedom-net/2018/rise-digital-authoritarianism Accessed 19 March 2021.

Gellman R (1996) Disintermediation and the internet. Government information quarterly 13:1–8.

Gerbaudo P (2018). The Digital Party: Political Organisation in the Era of Social Media. Pluto Press, London.

Giannone Codiglione G (2017) La nuova legge tedesca per l'"enforcement" dei diritti sui "social media". Dir. inf. 27:728–735.

Gillespie T (2014) The relevance of algorithms. In: Gillespie T, Boczkowski P J, Foot K A (eds) Media technologies: Essays on communication, materiality, and society. MIT Press, Cambridge, pp. 167–194.

Gillespie T (2018) Custodians of the Internet: Platforms, content moderation, and the hidden decisions that shape social media. Yale University Press, New Haven.

Goggin G (2014) Facebook's mobile career. New Media & Society 16:1068–1086.

Griffin A (2018) Facebook news feed: Why it is changing and what it actually means for users. The Independent, 12 January 2018. Retrieved from https://www.independent.co.uk/life-style/gadgetsand-tech/features/facebook-news-feed-latest-why-change-users-fake-news-media-markzuckerberg-a8156491.html.

Grind K, Schechner S, McMillan R, West J (2019) How Google Interferes With Its Search Algorithms and Changes Your Results. The Wall Street Journal, 15 November 2019.

Grossman L K (1995) The Electronic Republic: Reshaping Democracy in the Information Age. Viking, New York.

Habermas J (1996) Between Facts and Norms: Contributions to a Discourse Theory of Law and Democracy. MIT Press, Cambridge.

Hacker K L, van Dijk J (eds) (2000) Digital democracy: Issues of theory and practice. Sage, London.

Han B-C (2017) In the swarm: Digital prospects. MIT Press, Boston.

Hayes R A, Wesselmann E D, Carr C T (2018) When Nobody "Likes" You: Perceived Ostracism Through Paralinguistic Digital Affordances Within Social Media. Social Media + Society 4:2056305118800030.

Helbing D (2018) Towards Digital Enlightenment: Essays on the Dark and Light Sides of the Digital Revolution. Springer, Cham.

Hendricks V F, Vestergaard M (2019) Reality Lost: Markets of Attention, Misinformation and Manipulation. Springer, Cham.

Hern A (2018) Why Facebook's news feed is changing – and how it will affect you. The Guardian, 12 January 2018. Retrieved from https://www.theguardian.com/technology/2018/jan/12/why-facebooks-news-feed-changing-how-will-affect-you.

High Level Group on Fake News and Online Disinformation (2018) A multi-dimensional approach to disinformation. Brussels. https://ec.europa.eu/digital-single-market/en/news/final-report-high-level-expert-group-fake-news-and-online-disinformation Accessed 15 March 2021.

Hildebrandt M (2008) Defining Profiling: A New Type of Knowledge? In: Hildebrandt M, Gutwirth S (eds) Profiling the European citizen. Springer.

Hildebrandt M (2018) Algorithmic regulation and the rule of law. Phil. Trans. R. Soc. A 376:20170355.

Hindman M (2018) The Internet trap: How the digital economy builds monopolies and undermines democracy. Princeton University Press, Princeton.

Hopkins J (2020) The concept of affordances in digital media. In: Friese H, Nolden M, Rebane G, Schreiter M (eds) Handbuch Soziale Praktiken und Digitale Alltagswelten. Springer, Cham, pp. 47–54.

ISD Global (2019) Hate Speech and Radicalisation Online. The OCCI Research Report. Retrieved from https://www.isdglobal.org/isd-publications/hate-speech-and-radicalisation-onl ine-the-occi-research-report/ Accessed 19 March 2021.

Jordan M I, Mitchell T M (2015) Machine learning: Trends, perspectives, and prospects. Science 349:255–260.

Kaiser B (2019) Targeted: The Cambridge Analytica Whistleblower's Inside Story of How Big Data, Trump, and Facebook Broke Democracy and How It Can Happen Again. HarperCollins, New York.

Keller W W (2017) Democracy betrayed: The rise of the surveillance security state. Counterpoint, Berkeley.

Koltay A (2019) New Media and Freedom of Expression: Rethinking the Constitutional Foundations of the Public Sphere. Bloomsbury Publishing.

Konstan J A, Riedl J (2012) Recommender systems: from algorithms to user experience. User modeling and user-adapted interaction 22:101–123.

Kurlantzick J (2013) Democracy in retreat: The revolt of the middle class and the worldwide decline of representative government. Yale University Press, New Haven/London.

Lanzone L, Woods D (2015) Riding the Populist Web: Contextualizing the Five Star Movement (M5S) in Italy. Cogitatio 3:54–64.

Lee K (2019) Your Honor, on Social Media: The Judicial Ethics of Bots and Bubbles. Nevada Law Journal 19:4.

Levitsky S, Ziblatt D (2018) How democracies die. Broadway Books, New York.

Majchrzak A, Faraj S, Kane G C, Azad B (2013) The contradictory influence of social media affor- dances on online communal knowledge sharing. Journal of Computer-Mediated Communication 19:38–55.

Manucci L, Amsler M (2018) Where the wind blows: Five Star Movement's populism, direct democracy and ideological flexibility. Rivista italiana di scienza politica 48:109–132.

Margetts H, John P, Hale S, Yasseri T (2015) Political Turbulence: How Social Media Shape Collective Action. Princeton University Press, Princeton.

Mendoza I, Bygrave L A (2017) The Right not to be Subject to Automated Decisions based on Profiling. In: Synodinou T-E, Jougleux P, Markou C, Prastitou T (eds) EU Internet Law. Regulation and Enforcement. Springer, Cham, pp. 77–98.

Morris D (2000) Direct democracy and the Internet. Loy. LAL Rev. 34:1033–1054.

Murse T (2018) How Social Media Has Changed Politics. 10 Ways Twitter and Facebook Have Altered Campaigns. https://www.thoughtco.com/how-social-media-has-changed-politics-3367534 Accessed 29 August 2019.

Negroponte N (1996). Being digital. Hodder and Stoughton, London.

Noble S U (2018) Algorithms of oppression: How search engines reinforce racism. NYU Press, New York.

O'Neil C (2017) Armi di distruzione matematica. Bompiani, Milan.

Pariser E (2011) The Filter Bubble: What the Internet Is Hiding from You. Penguin, London.

Pasquale F (2015) The black box society: The secret algorithms that control money and information. Harvard University Press, Cambridge/London.

Pasquale F (2016) Two narratives of platform capitalism. Yale L. & Pol'y Rev. 35:309.

Pearl J, Mackenzie D (2018) The book of why. Basic Books, New York.

Pew (2019) Publics in Emerging Economies Worry Social Media Sow Division, Even as They Offer New Chances for Political Engagement. Retrieved from https://www.pewinternet.org/2019/05/13/publics-in-emerging-economies-worry-social-media-sow-division-even-as-they-offer-new-chances-for-political-engagement/ Accessed 10 March 2021.

Richards N (2015) Intellectual privacy: Rethinking civil liberties in the digital age. Oxford University Press, New York.

Richards N M (2012) The dangers of surveillance. Harv. L. Rev. 126:1934.

Robins M (2020) The Difference Between Artificial Intelligence, Machine Learning and Deep Learning. https://www.intel.com/content/www/us/en/artificial-intelligence/posts/difference-between-ai-machine-learning-deep-learning.html Accessed 27 May 2020.

Robles-Morales J M, Córdoba-Hernández A M (2019) Digital Political Participation, Social Networks and Big Data. Disintermediation in the Era of Web 2.0. Palgrave Macmillan, Cham.

Rose E (2010) Continuous partial attention: Reconsidering the role of online learning in the age of interruption. Educational Technology 50:41–46.

Runciman D (2018) How democracy ends. Profile Books, London.

Saetnan Rudinow A, Schneider I, Green N (2018) The politics of Big Data. Principles, policies, practices. In: Saetnan Rudinow A, Schneider I, Green N (eds) The politics of big data: big data, big brother? Routledge, New York.

Sawyer M S (2018) Post-Truth, Social Media, and the "Real" as Phantasm. In: Stenmark M, Fuller S, Zackariasson U (eds) Relativism and Post-Truth in Contemporary Society. Springer.

Schwartz S A, Mahnke M S (2020) Facebook use as a communicative relation: exploring the relation between Facebook users and the algorithmic news feed. Information, Communication & Society 1–16.

Shaffer K (2019) Data versus Democracy: How Big Data Algorithms Shape Opinions and Alter the Course of History. Apress, Colorado.

Shin D (2020) How do users interact with algorithm recommender systems? The interaction of users, algorithms, and performance. Computers in Human Behavior 109:106344.

Simon H A (1971) Designing Organizations for an Information-Rich World. In: Greenberger M (ed) Computers, Communication, and the Public Interest. Johns Hopkins Press, Baltimore, MD.

Simoncini A, Suweis S (2019) Il cambio di paradigma nell'intelligenza artificiale e il suo impatto sul diritto costituzionale. Rivista di filosofia del diritto 8:87–106.

Stevenson A (2018) Facebook Admits It Was Used to Incite Violence in Myanmar. https://www.nytimes.com/2018/11/06/technology/myanmar-facebook.html Accessed 6 November 2018.

Sunstein C R (2017) #Republic: Divided democracy in the age of social media. Princeton University Press, Princeton.

Susser D, Roessler B, Nissenbaum H (2019) Online Manipulation: Hidden Influences in a Digital World. Georgetown Law Technology Review.

Tversky A, Kahneman D (1974) Judgment Under Uncertainty: Heuristics and Biases. Science 185:1124–1131.

UK CMA (2020) Online platforms and digital advertising Market study final report. Retrieved from https://assets.publishing.service.gov.uk/media/5efc57ed3a6f4023d242ed56/Final_report_1_July_2020_.pdf Accessed 28 June 2021.

Van Dijck J, Poell T, De Waal M (2018) The Platform Society: Public Values in a Connective World. Oxford University Press, Oxford.

Van Dijk J A, Hacker K L (2018) Internet and Democracy in the Network Society: Theory and Practice Continued. Routledge.

Vilella G (2019) E-Democracy: On Participation in the Digital Age. Nomos Verlag, Baden-Baden.

Willems W (2020) Beyond platform-centrism and digital universalism: the relational affordances of mobile social media publics. Information, Communication & Society 1–17.

Wolfsfeld G, Segev E, Sheafer T (2013) Social media and the Arab Spring: Politics comes first. The International Journal of Press/Politics 18:115–137.

Wylie C (2019) Mindf*ck: Cambridge Analytica and the Plot to Break America. Random House, New York.

Yeung K (2017) 'Hypernudge': Big Data as a mode of regulation by design. Information, Communication & Society 20:118–136.

Zuboff S (2019) The Age of Surveillance Capitalism: The Fight for a Human Future at the New Frontier of Power. PublicAffairs, New York.

Professor Erik Longo (PhD) is currently associate professor of Constitutional Law at University of Florence (Italy). He visited the Center for Civil and Human Rights of the Notre Dame University-Program for Law in 2012, attended the University of Sussex–School of Global Studies in 2014, and Queen's University (Belfast, Ireland) in 2018. From 2007 to 2019 he was adjunct professor of Constitutional Law at the University of Macerata (Italy). Areas of Expertise: Italian and European constitutional law, fundamental rights, law and technology, regulation.

Chapter 10
Biased Algorithms and the Discrimination upon Immigration Policy

Clarisse Laupman, Laurianne-Marie Schippers and
Marilia Papaléo Gagliardi

Contents

Abstract Artificial intelligence has been used in decisions concerning the admissibility, reception, and even deportation of migrants and refugees into a territory. Since decisions involving migration can change the course of people's lives, it is imperative to verify the neutrality of the algorithms used. This chapter analyses how AI has been applied to the decision-making process regarding migration, mainly evaluating whether AI violates international pacts related to the protection of human rights. This chapter considers the case studies of Canada, New Zealand, the United Kingdom, and a pilot project that might be implemented in Europe. It is concluded that automated decisions regarding immigration have the potential to discriminate against migrants, and likely have been doing so since their creation, due to intrinsic biases

C. Laupman
Pontifical Catholic University of São Paulo (PUC-SP), São Paulo, SP, Brazil
e-mail: clflima@pucsp.br

L.-M. Schippers · M. Papaléo Gagliardi (✉)
Center for Education and Research on Innovation (CEPI), FGV São Paulo Law School, São
Paulo, SP, Brazil

© T.M.C. ASSER PRESS and the authors 2022   187
B. Custers and E. Fosch-Villaronga (eds.), *Law and Artificial Intelligence*,
Information Technology and Law Series 35,
https://doi.org/10.1007/978-94-6265-523-2_10

present in the current application methods and the systems themselves. Possible solutions that might help these systems provide equal treatment to migrants consist of greater transparency regarding the variables used in training. Consistent evaluations of methods and performance, to detect and remove biases emerging from historical data or structural inequity might also be a solution.

Keywords Immigration policy · Refugee policy · Algorithmic discrimination · Immigration automated decision-making · Artificial intelligence · Algorithms and migration

10.1 Introduction

Global human mobility is an international issue that cannot be ignored in the 21st century. According to the International Organization for Migration (IOM),[1] it is estimated that 272 million people were classified as international migrants in 2020, which corresponds to 3.5% of the world's population. It is important to highlight that a large percentage of those migrations did not occur voluntarily. They were a response to extreme situations: natural or environmental disasters, chemical or nuclear disasters, famine, civil or international wars, persecution, and others. Indeed, according to the United Nations High Commissioner for Refugees (UNHCR), there were at least 80 million forcibly displaced people worldwide,[2] a number that might have been surpassed by mid-2020.

Aiming to meet the existing migratory demand, some countries have not only adopted their own migratory policies, but also started relying on technologies, including artificial intelligence (AI), used to assist the decision-making process regarding migration. Therefore, it is possible to say that automated systems and algorithms are assisting or making decisions about the arrival of migrants, displaced persons, or refugees, as well as about their permanence or expulsion. This is the case for New Zealand, the UK, Canada, and a few European countries,[3] for instance.

Even though it is allowed for both the countries of departure and of destination to establish rules for their migratory process and implement the resources suiting their domestic policy, there are some limitations on how these technologies shall operate. That is because all countries, despite their sovereignty, must comply with international treaties concerning the protection of human rights.

When addressing technologies that might handle the decision-making process concerning the future of a migrant, whether in part or in full, it is important to consider the challenges present. Algorithms, and therefore, AI, might produce discriminatory output in several situations. This conclusion comes with no surprise, since those technologies are programmed and developed by human agents that might be biased in matters of gender, race, nationality, and so forth.

---

[1] International Organization for Migration 2019.

[2] See UNHCR 2020a

[3] This chapter studies the examples of Hungary, Latvia and Greece.

Although there is no international binding treaty on migration and the use of technology, there are some general principles that should be regarded in this context. For instance, the principle of non-discrimination imposed by the 1948 UN Declaration of Human Rights, establishes that everyone must be treated equally. The same principle appears in other human rights instruments, even though not targeted exclusively to migrants. The 1951 Refugee Convention, the "Global Compact for Safe, Orderly and Regular Migration" and "The Global Compact on Refugees", which applies specifically to migrants, also emphasizes the non-discrimination principle. All those conventions, binding or not, lead to the understanding that there are limitations to the use of AI in the context of the migratory process, which consists of the equal treatment and non-discrimination of migrants.

Thus, when using an automated decision-making system, it is imperative to know if the decisions made are also influenced by biases and prejudices, and/or if it is possible to manage them to reach the neutrality that allows for a fair decision.

The chapter is divided into different sections to address issues related to AI and migration. Section 10.2 will discuss some aspects related to the definition of migrants and refugees as subjects of rights from an international perspective. Section 10.3 analyses international treaties that are relevant as a framework for a non-discriminatory environment for these subjects. Section 10.4 brings case studies of AI systems' application in migration control and what were the problems that arose in their use. Section 10.5 focuses on how AI systems and algorithms can generate biased outcomes and at what stages of its construction the biases might be inserted in the migratory process. Section 10.6 debates the consequences that migrants, refugees, and asylum seekers may suffer in the event of a wrong decision regarding their entry, stay or deportation. Finally, the conclusion is that the use of AI in the migration decision-making context can generate harmful results, and some solutions that might help avoid biased outcomes are listed (Sect. 10.7).

10.2 Migrants as Subjects of Human Rights

All human beings are born free and equal in dignity and rights. That is what the first article of the 1948 UN's Universal Declaration of Human Rights establishes.[4] It is safe to say that this principle is not only the pillar of human rights but also represents the way human rights are perceived on an international level in modern days. Although the declaration is not binding, and hence, not mandatory to the States that have signed it, it shows the spirit of international human rights.

The idea that every person is entitled to dignity, respect, and to be treated as equals in a non-discriminatory way, despite their origin, sex, gender, sexual orientation, colour, race, and religion, is essential to understand the rights that apply to migrants and refugees. Indeed, this idea implies that no matter the domestic laws of each

---

[4] See United Nations 1948.

country, they must respect and guarantee the minimum rights of every single human being, including those other than their nationals.

In that sense, even though some countries might not have signed a specific treaty regarding migration, refuge, or asylum, they might protect the individuals who fall into these categories. This is a consequence of the concept of international human rights and the intrinsic rights of equal treatment and dignity.

Therefore, to understand the rights of migrants in the face of new technologies, it is important to mention not only the conventions about the migratory and refugee process but also the documents that oblige the countries to treat every single person equally and fairly—migrants and refugees included.

10.3 International Commitments to End the Discrimination that Applies to Migratory Policies

The 1951 Convention Relating to the Status of Refugees,[5] along with its 1967 Protocol, specifically states that refugees shall not be discriminated against. The UNHCR also issued guidelines to counter discrimination against refugees.[6] These provisions are the closest there is to an internationally binding treaty on migrants. Although those documents have as their object only refugees and asylum seekers, it is evident the existing concern to ensure that all individuals are treated equally, regardless of their origin.

The problem, of course, is that not every State is part of these treaties, and also that not all migrants are refugees. There are, however, many different international treaties that predict equality rights and non-discrimination obligations. Among them, it is worth mentioning: the International Covenant on Economic, Social and Cultural Rights (ICESCR),[7] the International Covenant on Civil and Political Rights (ICCPR),[8] the International Convention on the Elimination of All Forms of Racial Discrimination (ICERD),[9] the Convention on the Elimination of All Forms of Discrimination Against Women (CEDAW),[10] the Convention on the Rights of Persons with Disabilities (CRPD),[11] and the Convention on the Rights of the Child (CRC).[12]

---

[5] See UNHCR 1951. According to article 3 of the Convention, "The Contracting States shall apply the provisions of this Convention to refugees without discrimination as to race, religion or country of origin".

[6] See UNHCR 2020b.

[7] See Article 2.2 ICESCR. United Nations 1966.

[8] See Article 4.1 ICCPR. United Nations 1966.

[9] See Article 1.1 ICERD. United Nations 1965.

[10] See Article 1 CEDAW. United Nations 1979.

[11] See Article 5 CRPD. United Nations 2006.

[12] See Article 2.1 CRC. United Nations 1989.

Those treaties follow the path established by the 1948 UN's Declaration regarding non-discrimination and equal rights,[13] which shows how non-binding instruments might influence other international human rights treaties, and therefore affect the lives of many people, including migrants.

In this regard, it is noteworthy that, although not binding, the "Global Compact for Safe, Orderly and Regular Migration"[14] and "The Global Compact on Refugees"[15] (both from 2019), also predict the right to be treated without discrimination in the migratory process. The existence of those compacts shows that the international community is aware that there are risks and suppression of rights regarding migration. It also shows that the community is concerned about how to make these travels safer, in a way that preserves human dignity and, as consequence, the human rights of the migrants and refugees.

One can conclude that migrants are subjects of human rights around the world, and shall not suffer from any kind of discrimination. Those rights are protected in the international sphere, whether predicted in domestic law or not. Thus, migratory policies are not allowed to impose any kind of discrimination, nor use a biased or discriminatory AI device. Hence, it remains to be seen whether, despite legal provisions, governments make discriminatory decisions in migratory processes, induced by biased AI decisions.

10.4 Application of Algorithms in the Decision-Making Process of Migratory Policies

Different countries have already incorporated automated systems to develop their migration policies. In this section, we aim to demonstrate how the UK, Canada, New Zealand and a pilot project that might be implemented in Europe use AI in their systems. The selected countries are examples of different phases of the migratory process. This broad view is necessary since depending on the type of migration (voluntary or forced),[16] there are different stages in which migrants can have their entry assessed and, consequently, suffer some type of discrimination.

When migration is voluntary, the migratory process begins before the arrival of the migrant. It entails a visa grant from the destination country; the effective arrival in a new country; and the procedure to stay there. Finally, there are specific processes for deportation in the event of a violation of the domestic laws of the destination countries. In other words, there are at least four decisive moments in the life of a migrant that can be decided through AI when there is an organized plan to migrate.

---

[13] See Article 7 Universal Declaration Of Human Rights. United Nations 1948.

[14] See objective n. 17 of the Intergovernmentally Negotiated and Agreed Outcome 2018.

[15] See topic III, "Program Of Action", Section B "Areas in need of support", 2.10. of The Global Compact on Refugees. United Nations 2018.

[16] The concepts of voluntary and forced migration will be further explored in Sect. 10.6.

In the case of involuntary migration (forced migration), the procedure regarding the granting of asylum is different. It is done after the arrival in the country of destination. This specific situation needs more attention, considering the vulnerability of these migrants—and that the use of a biased system can have great consequences.

In that sense, the listed cases show how AI can be used (i) in the decision-making processes to grant a visa, explored in the UK case; (ii) policing the migrant's arrival in the new country, explored in the EU case; (iii) in determining whether he or she will remain, explored in the New Zealand case and even (iv) their deportation, explored in the Canadian case. The Canadian case will also explore entry applications.

10.4.1   United Kingdom—Granting Visas

The first step in the regular migration process is receiving a visa to migrate. For this, the UK's classificatory procedure for visa concession is analysed. It is necessary to understand how the UK migration system works, then to understand the application of artificial intelligence.

The department responsible for migration control in the UK is the Home Office. It is up to this department, among other things, to issue passports and visas.[17] To implement the decision-making process, the British government decided to use an AI system. This AI was responsible for the decisions concerning the results of the visa application for all persons who have applied for entry into the UK for almost five years. The Home Office described this AI as a digital "streaming tool".[18]

The algorithm used a traffic-light system (red, amber, or green) to grade every entry visa application. This "visa streaming" algorithm supposedly used nationality information to decide how to rate the risk of the applications and which colour they would be assigned. Migrants who were nationals from some specific places received a higher risk score. It was even reported by JCWI (Joint Council for Welfare of Immigrants)[19] that the Home Office held a "secret list of suspect nationalities".

Although the UK government agency has not indicated which countries belonged to this list, JCWI indicates that migrants from these locations had their applications examined with more attention, took longer, and were more likely to be refused. Even worse, the system used its previous decisions to reinforce its future classifications. This resulted in a feedback loop: biased past decisions reinforced future biased classifications.

---

[17] Home Office (undated) About us. https://www.gov.uk/government/organisations/home-office/about Accessed 23 January 2021.

[18] The Joint Council for the Welfare of Immigrants 2020.

[19] See n. 18.

This system was denounced as racist by the JCWI,[20] which would violate the Equality Act 2010.[21] In august of 2020, the Home Office's independent review verified that the AI used decades of institutionally racist practices in the building up of their software. This led to biased practices, such as targeting particular nationalities for immigration raids. As a result, the department understood that the immigration system should be rebuilt and that an Equality Impact Assessment and Data Protection Impact Assessments were needed to guarantee a non-discriminatory approach to the new immigration AI system.

The next step in the migration process is the arrival of the migrant in the new country, where their documents will be verified, as well as their conditions for regular migration. In this case, it is worth analyzing measures for the reception of migrants on the European continent.

10.4.2   EU—Arrival

European countries have different tools for migratory control. Every country might use their own technology, as long as they do not violate the principles of protection of human dignity and non-discrimination. However, for reasons of internal relations, sometimes the same technology is implemented in different countries. In this sense, it is worth mentioning the pilot project developed by the consortium called iBorderCtrl.[22] This project developed an AI system that conducts interrogations and collects video footage to be used to detect lies and project risk, as well as risk scoring. This system is programmed to be implemented at points at the borders of the countries, to check whether passengers are lying during their arrival. If the system verifies any case of irregularity, it will become more "sceptic", change the tone, and will ask more difficult and more complex questions, in addition to having the migrant later selected to speak with a responsible officer.

This system, which is already being considered for implementation, was tested at the airports in Hungary, Latvia and Greece.[23] It is still unclear, however, how it would be possible to identify whether someone is experiencing a moment of stress, which could make the person more likely to be confused in questions or demonstrate greater facial tension. Still, it is not explained how this system would identify and cope with the cultural differences of each region.

Although there is still no final decision on the use of this technology, it is important to demonstrate how a plan for AI to assume a leading role in the migration process already exists. Even though this tool is programmed to direct the migrant that was "unsuccessful" in their analyses to a human officer, it is still up to the AI to identify

---

[20] See n. 18.

[21] The Equality Act 2010 is an internal UK legislation, see https://www.legislation.gov.uk/ukpga/2010/15/contents Accessed 23 January 2021.

[22] See iBorderCtrl undated; Molnar 2019a, p.2.

[23] See n. 22.

some inconsistencies at the border checkpoint. It is also noteworthy that if cultural differences are not considered by this technology, decisions may always end up doubting a group of people from a specific culture.

10.4.3 New Zealand—(Over) Staying

The next step regarding the arrival in a new country concerns staying in the country. In that case, the events reported[24] in 2018 by the media in New Zealand help to demonstrate how AI tools may also impact decisions regarding the permanence or even deportation of migrants. The reports indicate that Immigration New Zealand was conducting a pilot to profile migrants (especially overstayers) to identify possible "troublemakers" that could impose burdens for the country.

Some of the data used as a basis for this profiling were: age, gender, ethnicity, hospital debt information, information on criminal convictions, failed immigration applications, and visa type. Based on this profile, it would be possible to identify people who would offer risks to the country and then proceed with their deportation.

Once again, it can be observed the problem of seeking to predict people's future behaviour based on a profile built through past data. It is not possible to guarantee that an individual will take the same actions according to their said profile—and thus important decisions regarding their future in the country would be anchored in mere probabilities.

Although the initial target of this profiling is illegal immigrants (overstayers)— which in no way legitimizes the practice—there are suspicions that this mechanism may also be used in cases of visa application from other migrants in general. In addition, attention has also been drawn to concerns related to racism, since the profiling takes ethnic data into account.[25]

10.4.4 Canada—Entry Application

In the Canadian scenario, concerns have also been raised about the use of AI systems in the context of migrants and refugees, with experimentations with the use of these technologies being done since 2014.[26] The following are some stages in the country's immigration process that already have or may have in the future automated systems assisting in the decision-making and its related challenges.

The first moment would be precisely the entry applications (such as by means of visa applications), i.e., before the arrival on Canadian soil. These systems are already being used in the country's immigration programs (such as the Express Entry

---

[24] Bonnett 2018; Tan 2018.

[25] Bashir 2018; Robson 2018.

[26] Molnar and Gill 2018.

Comprehensive Ranking System), but there is a lack of transparency regarding which criteria are used and how the system works as a whole.[27]

When in the country—at the border, more precisely—it is possible for the individual to apply for refugee or protected person status, in addition to other types of permanent or temporary status. At this stage, there is an assessment of whether the individual represents a security risk, for example, which may even result in deportation from the country.[28] The use of AI for decision making, at this point, may offer several concerns, for instance,[29] whether and how the AI can define if a person poses a high risk to national security or should go through an interrogation and whether it is possible to question the system's decision in any way.

10.4.5   *Canada—Deportation*

Lastly, and once the border is crossed, it is also possible to make requests for refugee status, visa extensions, citizenship requests, among others. In the refuge's specific case, there is also the intention of using algorithms and AI to verify risks and frauds.[30] The concerns that may arise in this context are, for instance,[31] which aspects the algorithm should consider to determine whether an application offers a risk or is fraudulent, and how this analysis of the algorithm can perhaps harm the applicant.

A noteworthy Canadian case is the 2017 usage of a questionnaire for asylum seekers.[32] It performed ethnic and religious profiling, with questions about political beliefs, values, and religion with an Islamophobic bias. In this sense, there is a concern about the kind of data entering the AI system and the government database, which can serve as a framework for relevant decisions regarding a person's life and future in the country they are trying to enter.

The following topic then presents a technical explanation about how these biases can be inserted into the AI systems which operate in the migratory process.

10.5   The Incorporation of Biases in Algorithms

Some of their aspects might lead the algorithms, which are at the basis of AI, to reach biased results. In general, the focus relies mainly on the composition of the dataset created to promote the algorithm training, since the data used for it is produced by

---

[27] See n. 26.

[28] See n. 26

[29] See n. 26.

[30] See n. 26.

[31] See n. 26.

[32] See n. 26.

an already biased and discriminatory society. In this sense, by learning from such data, algorithms would autonomously reinforce these historic biases.[33]

However, the sourcing and conditioning of the training database is not the only possible source of discriminatory function—the algorithm design, training adjustments, and deployment can also yield such results.[34] These factors will be better explored below.

Therefore, it is important to emphasize that the algorithms which compose the AI are not discriminatory or biased *per se*.[35] They will only reflect the decisions made by the human agents both during its creation and its subsequent use: "Algorithms do not build themselves. The Achilles' heel of all algorithms is the humans who build them and the choices they make about outcomes, candidate predictors for the algorithm to consider, and the training sample".[36] Algorithms do what they are programmed to do, and artificial intelligence develops from the algorithmic base embedded in it. The outcomes, therefore, only have a meaning when used by a person or a company (or any other agent that has a human factor involved) in a specific context.[37]

To illustrate that argument and how biases can be inserted into the algorithm's functioning, two examples will be considered: one regarding an algorithm for data mining, and the other, an algorithm used for prediction. As both systems share similar stages of development, they will be presented simultaneously. These types of automated systems may not correspond to those of the cases presented in Sect. 10.4, but the warnings raised may be of great value and should be taken into account in the development of new automated systems to be used in the migration field or during the improvement of the existing ones. Therefore, the following considerations will be linked to the examples mentioned above where relevant.

There are some points and moments during the algorithm development (and, therefore, of the AI development) at which it is possible, to a greater or lesser degree, to insert biases or discriminatory intentions by human agents, intentionally or unintentionally.[38] These are, for instance: (i) the definition of the outcome and class labels; (ii) the definition of the training data and data collection; (iii) the feature selection and the decision of which to make available to the algorithm; (iv) the proxies; and (v) the masking.[39]

The first important decision regarding the operation of an algorithm is to establish which are its target variables, or the desired outcome, and its possible classifications

---

[33] Beduschi 2020, p. 10.; Molnar 2019a, p. 2.

[34] It is argued that "As such, bias can be introduced into every stage of the development and deployment of systems: as from the intention that initially governs the algorithm's development, during the creation of the computer code, the executable code, during execution, in the context of execution and maintenance". Défenseur des droits and Commission Nationale Informatique & Libertés 2020.

[35] See Kearns and Roth 2020, p. 61 and p. 87.

[36] Kleinberg et al. 2019, p. 4.

[37] See Borgesius 2018.

[38] See n. 37.

[39] Barocas and Selbst 2016, pp. 677 to 693; Kleinberg et al. 2019, pp. 17 and 18.

and values, by means of the class labels.[40] For instance, describing abilities, features, level of productivity that a company is looking for, etc.[41] Considering that this process of definition takes place through human action, and since it is necessary to translate a concrete problem into a language accessible to the computers, it is possible that programmers do it in a somehow biased manner, intentionally or not, depending on the criteria chosen.[42]

The second concern regards the database built for the algorithm training. It can be summarized as the definition of the data, features, predictors, and other factors that will form the training database to be applied to the algorithm. Since the algorithm learns and enhances its operation based on the data it is presented to, if the dataset is discriminatory, then the algorithm will offer the same tendencies.[43] The training data might be biased in distinct ways: (i) it is possible for the agent to intentionally select a feature that benefits one group of people over another; (ii) by the erroneous labelling and classification of the data, which is done by human agents; (iii) by the statistical misrepresentation of some groups in the data collection, which affects the accurate representation of reality by the algorithm; (iv) use of subjective variables over objective variables, which might represent a human judgment.[44]

The concern with the database used by the algorithm arises in some of the cases discussed above. For instance, it was pointed out by the UK's Home Office that decades of institutionally discriminatory practices were used for software development—which could likely represent a database formation issue.

A similar analysis could be applied to the automated systems that could be used in Canada and the hypothesis of the implementation of iBorderCtrl. In Canada, the case of the Islamophobic biased questionnaire has raised concerns about the types of data that now compose the government database and may be used as parameters for future decisions regarding migrants. At the same time, in the case of iBorderCtrl, it may be relevant to build a diversified database capable of satisfactorily representing the cultural differences of all people who cross borders to avoid discriminatory outcomes during the arrival process. The developers may also not be able to create such a rich database and, because the AI will not be formed considering different scenarios, it can be discriminatory.

The next concern regards the feature selection, i.e., what elements, aspects, abilities, and so forth will be taken into consideration for the algorithm analyses.[45] As in the previous stage, a potential issue is that the features chosen to be considered might be very general, failing to represent an individual in their entirety.[46] It is also possible that some characteristics may be chosen to achieve a discriminatory effect.[47]

---

[40] Barocas and Selbst 2016, p. 678.

[41] Kleinberg et al. 2019, p. 18.

[42] Barocas and Selbst 2016, pp. 678 and 680; Kleinberg et al. 2019, pp. 21 and 22.

[43] Barocas and Selbst 2016, pp. 681, 683 and 684.

[44] Barocas and Selbst 2016, p. 681; Kleinberg et al. 2019, p. 22.

[45] Barocas and Selbst 2016, p. 688; Kleinberg et al. 2019, p. 18.

[46] Barocas and Selbst 2016, p. 688.

[47] Kleinberg et al. 2019, p. 22.

This may have been another issue in the case of the system used in the UK, given the allegations that the system would use nationality data as one of the factors to hamper the visa application process. This could also be the case for the pilot project to profile migrants in New Zealand in search of "troublemakers", considering that ethnicity data would be used by the system for this purpose.

Another issue that arises is that algorithms might identify patterns that can cause biased decisions even if there is no intention through development or explicit mention regarding belonging to a specific group of people in the selected features.[48] This information may be indirectly contained in other data and features chosen, serving "as reliable proxies for class membership".[49]

Lastly, all the aforementioned manners of inserting bias in an algorithm can be purposefully applied by the human agent.[50] This is what is called "masking", that is, when the agent knows the potential problems that the algorithm could cause in discriminatory terms and takes advantage of these possibilities.[51]

Based on the descriptions above presented, it is safe to argue that the process of building a decision-making algorithm for any purpose is intrinsically permeated with risks of insertion of biases by human agents, whether it is intentional or not. The examples point out risks related to the definition of outcomes, to the construction of the training dataset, to the decision regarding which features will be taken into consideration in the algorithm's analysis, among others. Even the very moment of training can be a factor, considering that human agents may intentionally or not create a procedure that makes the algorithm learn in a way as to benefit one group over another (for instance when it is decided to use an already biased dataset for the algorithm training).[52]

Although there is no specific mechanism to prevent algorithms from being biased, there are two possible ways of dealing with this fact. The first is to accept that the algorithm will reflect a bias, and in that sense, choose to shape its operation on a certain definition of fairness. It should be considered that the notion of fairness itself does not have a single meaning.[53] For instance, in an algorithmic context, fairness can mean statistical parity, "equality of false negatives",[54] among other definitions.[55] Depending on the adopted notion, the systems can come out with different results. Therefore, the decisions related to the concepts of fairness are up to the human agents themselves and the choices of what is considered fair as a society.[56]

---

[48] Barocas and Selbst 2016, pp. 691 and 692.

[49] Barocas and Selbst 2016, p. 691.

[50] Barocas and Selbst 2016, p. 692.

[51] See n. 50.

[52] Kleinberg et al. 2019, p. 23.

[53] Kearns and Roth 2020, p. 68.

[54] Kearns and Roth 2020, p. 73.

[55] Kearns and Roth 2020, pp. 68 and 69.

[56] Kearns and Roth 2020, p. 63.

Furthermore, it is worth mentioning that the quest for fairness may involve a trade-off between reaching fairer results and the accuracy of the algorithm's decisions, and vice versa. As an example, if the notion of fairness adopted prevents the use of sensitive information in the decision-making process (such as ethnicity), the achieved result could be more biased than if this data were considered in the system by means of affirmative action.[57] Considering also that there are often strong correlations between the predictors and features used, letting information aside may also impair the accuracy of the decision.[58]

Based on that, it is clear that there are no simple choices to be made. However, applying the principles of human rights protection to the decision-making process in the migration context might be a good starting point.

The second alternative is to try to apply measures to mitigate biased decisions. One of them, for example, may consist of establishing policies and practices that enable responsible algorithm development.[59] This can be done by documenting the AI development and providing documents describing the treatment of data, leaving the processes more transparent. It can also be suggested that the bases used do not reflect old decisions—which may be discriminatory. Finally, you can program the algorithm so that it assigns certain aspects as a "random component", in a way that a discriminatory factor is no longer designed to interfere—for example, if the category of "country of origin" has no impact on the final decision, a person's origin can no longer represent a factor of discrimination.

Despite those possible solutions to mitigate the discriminatory process, it is certain that, when using automated decision-making tools, all the presented issues must be taken into consideration. In the context of migration, many people are in a delicate life situation, and wrong or biased decisions can mean drastic consequences in one's social, economic, and even life safety aspects, which will be further discussed in Sect. 10.6. To deal with all these topics in the elaboration of an automated system to be used in the migration environment may not be easy and the decisions to be taken when translating the concrete context to the computer are not trivial. "The complexity of human migration is not easily reducible to an algorithm".[60] The following topic will address concrete examples that justify these concerns.

10.6 Consequences of Biased/Wrong Decisions

To fully understand the consequences of biased and wrong decisions made by AI, it is important first to understand some of the vulnerabilities inherent to the migration itself.

---

[57] Kearns and Roth 2020, pp. 67 and 77.
[58] Kearns and Roth 2020, p. 67.
[59] Smith and Rustagi 2020.
[60] Molnar 2019b, p. 321.

Although there is a wide range of motivations for migration, they can be classified as "voluntary" or "forced", as mentioned above. While a "voluntary migration" derives from the will of the migrant, who wants to travel to obtain advances of a social or economic nature, such as employment or education; a "forced migration" occurs when the migrant must leave his or her country to preserve his or her own life and the minimum conditions of human dignity.

Sometimes these migratory flows are mixed, as people may be leaving situations of extreme vulnerability and, at the same time, looking for better economic conditions. This differentiation, however, is not relevant to the present study, as all migrants take risks in rebuilding life in a new nation, even if some are more vulnerable for not having a safe option of return.

Within forced migration, some people manage to be classified as refugees. According to the 1951 Geneva Convention and its protocol, refugees are only those who suffer specific persecution from their countries of origin, whether due to race, religion, nationality, social group, or political opinions. In some cases, this status can also be granted to people fleeing from serious and widespread human rights violations.

Not all forced migration, however, implies refugee status. For instance, there are 80 million forcibly displaced people but only 26.3 million are identified as refugees and 4.2 million are classified as asylum seekers.[61] The granting of refugee status, however, depends on the will of the State that receives the migrant, as well as on a case-by-case analysis—a classification that may or may not have the intervention of AI.

The difference to be considered which generates a high risk is that, from the moment a person is considered a refugee, he or she cannot be forced to return to the country of origin, under penalty of violating Article 33 of the Geneva Convention.

However, if there is bias in the technology applied to assess if a person fits the profile of a refugee, there is the risk of an erroneous classification—intentional or not. Consequently, it is possible to send the person back to a place where life, freedom, and physical integrity are at risk. This is magnified in deployments without any case-by-case consideration before a rejection, as errors could not be identified before harm.

Imagine that a person is in a life-threatening situation, but is from a country considered as "suspect" by an AI system. This person has a higher chance of having a visa denied largely by nationality and, therefore, of suffering the consequences of a historic prejudice reproduced as bias in decision-making by a supposedly neutral tool.

Finally, it is worth considering that, even if the migration is voluntary, a wrong AI decision can cause serious damage to individuals. Migration itself often involves new life projects. And its interruption by a mistake of a technology that uses some prejudiced precedent can unfairly hamper and even end an individual's life.

Notably, it was in a case of voluntary migration that it was publicly recognized by a government that the results from an AI system used in a process that dealt with

---

[61] See n. 2.

migrants were not accurate. In this case, several students in the UK were accused of cheating or defrauding on their English exams. This was concluded by an algorithm observing response patterns in exams and led to more than 36,000 deportations by the end of 2016. Subsequently, however, it was identified that the technology failed in 20% of the cases. Therefore, an average of 7,000 students may have been deported due to a technological misunderstanding.[62]

This means that 7,000 immigrants, after great sacrifice and expense, had their studies and their lives interrupted, with no possibility of appealing, due to this technological failure. Furthermore, only foreigners were subject to an imprecise evaluation system and, in addition to the affected schooling were removed from the country they were established in. Worse still is that it is not possible to identify which ones were wrongly classified. Therefore, due to their migrant status, 20% of these students suffered undue deportation. Such conduct and error are inexcusable by the standard of a non-discriminatory society.

Thus, regardless of the migratory classification, both forced and voluntary migrants can have the course and development of their lives hindered, and even interrupted, in cases of application of wrong decisions made in the course of the migration process. In the hypothesis of biased decisions taken by artificial intelligence, this risk is systematized and applied on a large scale.

10.7   Conclusion

The use of automated decision-making tools in the migration field has the potential for harm. Algorithms can present discriminatory outcomes as a consequence of their programming, training, and/or database selection, which are done by humans. And humans can discriminate, whether consciously or not. Therefore, when used to assist in decisions regarding migrants, refugees, and asylum seekers, algorithms, as human creations, can disrespect the human rights of those already vulnerable—especially the right to be treated without discrimination.

The case studies addressed in Sects. 10.4 and 10.6 demonstrate that this concern with the harmful potential of AI use in the migration context is not mere speculation, but a real problem. The systems employed at the borders (figuratively speaking) can help to discriminate against people based on their nationality, ethnicity, and religion, for instance, reproducing the same value judgment that human agents have, making it difficult to analyse their documents, their entry, and permanence in the country, and even causing their deportation. Nowadays, many of these decisions still go through human revision, but considering that there is a belief in the neutrality of machines, there is a great chance that these agents will trust the results that the algorithm finds, or conveniently mask human and institutional prejudice with autonomous bias from a seemingly neutral algorithm: "Recommendations by computers may have an air of

---

[62] Baynes 2019; Molnar 2019a, p. 2.

rationality or infallibility, and people might blindly follow them. (...) The tendency to believe computers or to follow their advice is sometimes called 'automation bias'."[63]

As shown in Sects. 10.2 and 10.3, although there is no specific legislation protecting migrants from discrimination, there is a large legal repertoire that prohibits any type of discrimination, especially if the target of such violation is part of a vulnerable group. The current legislation is, therefore, sufficient to indicate that discrimination against migrants, even if done by AI, represents a violation of international law. In other words, there is no need for the advent of a new legal framework focusing on the prohibition of discrimination when applying technologies in the migratory context. Biased decisions about migrants can already be considered a violation of human rights.

That does not mean, however, that the use of these technologies in the migration field should be stopped or prohibited. As previously stated, the great migration flow may require that more efficient solutions be employed to benefit both migrants and States. Nevertheless, attention must be paid to the programming, the criteria chosen for analysis, the database built, and the training of systems to prevent them from becoming tools for reinforcing discrimination and stereotypes.

In this sense, as possible methods for avoiding bad results and the misuse of algorithms, it is important to (i) constantly verify its outcomes regarding biases;[64] (ii) make sure that the set of data that form the database is updated so that the algorithm can constantly enhance its learning and portray reality accurately; (iii) carry out audits/impact and risk assessments to verify potential biases and harms to the people's rights and freedoms in its operation[65] and proceed to its correction. Finally, both the entities that use the tools and their direct operators must be informed of the risks related to the use of AI systems "so that they are able to understand the tool's general operation, increase their vigilance as regards the risk of bias and ensure that they have effective control over the processing".[66] This awareness could also help avoid overconfidence in the results obtained by the machines (the automation bias).[67]

Artificial intelligence can be an important tool to assist human agents in migratory processes, make it more dynamic and less time-consuming. For this, however, it must be ensured that the technology is not being used to undermine human rights, nor is it being used under the discriminatory biases already present in our society.

---

[63] See n. 37.

[64] Défenseur des droits and Commission Nationale Informatique & Libertés 2020.

[65] See n. 64.

[66] See n. 64.

[67] See n. 37.

References

Barocas S, Selbst AD (2016) Big Data's Disparate Impact. California Law Review 104:671–732.

Bashir S (2018) Immigration NZ: profiling by race is racial profiling. https://www.rnz.co.nz/news/on-the-inside/354298/immigration-nz-profiling-by-race-is-racial-profiling Accessed 30 January 2021.

Baynes C (2019) Government 'deported 7,000 foreign students after falsely accusing them of cheating in English language tests'. https://www.independent.co.uk/news/uk/politics/home-office-mistakenly-deported-thousands-foreign-students-cheating-language-tests-theresa-may-win drusha8331906. html Accessed 16 January 2021.

Beduschi A (2020) International migration management in the age of artificial intelligence. Migration Studies 0:1–21.

Bonnett G (2018) Immigration NZ using data system to predict likely troublemakers. https://www.rnz.co.nz/news/national/354135/immigration-nz-using-data-system-to-predict-likely-troublemakers Accessed 30 January 2021.

Borgesius FZ (2018) Discrimination, artificial intelligence, and algorithmic decision-making. https://rm.coe.int/discrimination-artificial-intelligence-and-algorithmic-decision-making/168 0925d73 Accessed 19 June 2021.

Défenseur des droits and Commission Nationale Informatique & Libertés (2020) Algorithms: preventing automated discrimination. Accessed 5 January 2021.

iBorderCtrl (undated) The project. https://www.iborderctrl.eu/The-project Accessed 23 January 2021.

Intergovernmentally Negotiated and Agreed Outcome (2018) Global Compact for Safe, Orderly and Regular Migration. https://refugeesmigrants.un.org/sites/default/files/180713_agreed_out come_global_compact_for_migration.pdf Accessed 8 January 2021.

International Organization for Migration (2019) World Migration Report 2020. https://publications.iom.int/system/files/pdf/wmr_2020.pdf Accessed 20 February 2021.

Kearns M, Roth A (2020) The Ethical Algorithm: The Science of Socially Aware Algorithm Design. Oxford University Press, Oxford.

Kleinberg J, Ludwig J, Mullainathan S, Sunstein CR (2019) Discrimination in the age of algorithms. https://papers.ssrn.com/sol3/papers.cfm?abstract_id=3329669 Accessed 29 December 2020.

Molnar P (2019a) New technologies in migration: human rights impacts. https://www.fmreview.org/ethics/molnar Accessed 13 June 2021.

Molnar P (2019b) Technology on the margins: AI and global migration management from a human rights perspective. Cambridge International Law Journal 8:305–330.

Molnar P, Gill L (2018) Bots at the Gate: a human rights analysis of automated decision-making in Canada's Immigration and Refugee System. https://citizenlab.ca/wp-content/uploads/2018/09/IHRP-Automated-Systems-Report-Web-V2.pdf Accessed 31 January 2021.

Robson S (2018) Deportation modeling 'bringing back the dawn raids'. https://www.rnz.co.nz/news/national/354217/deportation-modelling-bringing-back-the-dawn-raids Accessed 30 January 2021.

Smith G, Rustagi I (2020) Mitigating Bias in Artificial Intelligence: An Equity Fluent Leadership Playbook. https://haas.berkeley.edu/wp-content/uploads/UCB_Playbook_R10_V2_spreads2.pdf Accessed 14 February 2021.

Tan L (2018) Immigration NZ's data profiling 'illegal' critics say https://www.nzherald.co.nz/nz/immigration-nzs-data-profiling-illegal-critics-say/P5QDBGVDGFSI6I3NV4UHPOSBRA/ Accessed 30 January 2021.

The Joint Council for the Welfare of Immigrants (2020) We won! Home Office to stop using racist visa algorithm. https://www.jcwi.org.uk/news/we-won-home-office-to-stop-using-racist-visa-algorithm Accessed 23 January 2021.

United Nations (1948) Universal Declaration of Human Rights.https://www.un.org/en/about-us/universal-declaration-of-human-rights Accessed 8 January 2021.

United Nations (1965) International Convention on the Elimination of All Forms of Racial Discrimination. https://www.ohchr.org/en/professionalinterest/pages/cerd.aspx Accessed 8 January 2021.

United Nations (1966) International Covenant on Economic, Social and Cultural Rights. https://www.ohchr.org/EN/ProfessionalInterest/Pages/CESCR.aspx Accessed 8 January 2021.

United Nations (1979) Convention on the Elimination of All Forms of Discrimination against Women. https://www.ohchr.org/en/professionalinterest/pages/cedaw.aspx Accessed 8 January 2021.

United Nations (1989) Convention on the Rights of the Child. https://www.ohchr.org/en/professionalinterest/pages/crc.aspx Accessed 8 January 2021.

United Nations (2006) Convention on the Rights of Persons with Disabilities. https://www.un.org/disabilities/documents/convention/convoptprot-e.pdf Accessed 8 January 2021.

United Nations (2018) Report of the United Nations High Commissioner for Refugees Part II: global compact on refugees. https://www.unhcr.org/gcr/GCR_English.pdf Accessed 8 January 2021.

United Nations High Commissioner for Refugees (UNHCR) (1951) Convention and Protocol Relating to the Status of Refugees. https://www.unhcr.org/3b66c2aa10 Accessed 8 January 2021.

United Nations High Commissioner for Refugees (UNHCR) (2020a) Refugee Data Finder. https://www.unhcr.org/refugee-statistics/ Accessed 8 January 2021.

United Nations High Commissioner for Refugees (UNHCR) (2020b) Guidance on Racism and Xenophobia. https://www.unhcr.org/5f7c860f4.pdf Accessed 8 January 2021.

Prof. Dr. Clarisse Laupman Ferraz Lima is a lawyer and Doctor in International Law from the Pontifical Catholic University of São Paulo (2016). Master in Law from the Pontifical Catholic University of São Paulo (2011). Graduated in Law from the Pontifical Catholic University of São Paulo (1999). Professor at the Faculty of Law at the Pontifical Catholic University of São Paulo. Concentration on International Law and Human Rights. Voluntary researcher at Mackenzie Presbyterian University.

Lauriane-Marie Schippers is a lawyer and Researcher at the Center for Education and Research on Innovation at FGV São Paulo Law School, having worked on the compliance project of Fundação Getulio Vargas regarding personal data protection laws, and currently works on the project concerning the Brazilian general data protection law (LGPD) and innovation in the healthcare startup market. Graduated in Law from FGV São Paulo Law School (2019). Coordinator of the Study Group in Law and Technology at FGV São Paulo Law School.

Marília Papaléo Gagliardi is an immigration and personal data protection lawyer. Researcher in Human Rights and Technology. Former Researcher at the Center for Education and Research on Innovation at FGV São Paulo Law School, having worked on the compliance project of Fundação Getulio Vargas regarding personal data protection laws. Volunteer Researcher at RESAMA (South American Network for Environmental Migrations). Volunteer Lawyer at the Federal Public Defender. Member of the Study Group on Comparative Law at USP (GEDC). Special Student in International Relations at USP (Emotions and International Relations). Graduated in Law from the Pontifical University of São Paulo - PUC/SP (2018).

Chapter 11
AI in Criminal Law: An Overview of AI Applications in Substantive and Procedural Criminal Law

Bart Custers

Contents

Abstract Both criminals and law enforcement are increasingly making use of the opportunities that AI may offer, opening a whole new chapter in the cat-and-mouse game of committing versus addressing crime. This chapter maps the major developments of AI use in both substantive criminal law and procedural criminal law. In substantive criminal law, A/B optimisation, deepfake technologies, and algorithmic profiling are examined, particularly the way in which these technologies contribute to existing and new types of crime. Also the role of AI in assessing the effectiveness of sanctions and other justice-related programs and practices is examined, particularly risk taxation instruments and evidence-based sanctioning. In procedural criminal law, AI can be used as a law enforcement technology, for instance, for predictive policing or as a cyber agent technology. Also the role of AI in evidence (data analytics after search and seizure, Bayesian statistics, developing scenarios) is examined. Finally, focus areas for further legal research are proposed.

B. Custers (✉)
eLaw–Center for Law and Digital Technologies at Leiden University, Leiden, The Netherlands
e-mail: b.h.m.custers@law.leidenuniv.nl

© T.M.C. ASSER PRESS and the authors 2022
B. Custers and E. Fosch-Villaronga (eds.), *Law and Artificial Intelligence*,
Information Technology and Law Series 35,
https://doi.org/10.1007/978-94-6265-523-2_11

Keywords cyber agent technology · deepfake technologies · evidence-based sanctioning · law enforcement technology · predictive policing · risk taxation instruments

11.1 Introduction

Artificial Intelligence (AI) is the new hype. In many countries, large amounts of funding are available for further research on AI.[1] It may be expected that AI will bring significant changes in several sectors of society, including transport (e.g., self-driving cars), healthcare (e.g., automated drug discovery), education (e.g., adaptive virtual tutors catering to personalized individual needs), and language (e.g., real-time translations of conversations). Also in the legal domain AI is expected to bring change. On the one hand, developments in AI may call for new, different or further regulation and, on the other hand, AI may offer more and more applications for legal research and legal practice.[2] This chapter aims to provide an overview of AI developments in the area of criminal law, both in substantive criminal law and procedural criminal law. When discussing substantive criminal law, this chapter focuses on the use of AI by criminals and the use of AI when imposing sanctions or other justice-related programs. When discussing procedural criminal law, the focus of this chapter is on the use of AI in criminal investigation and prosecution and the role of AI in criminal evidence. In both parts it is investigated which new (types of) legal questions these developments raise.

All examples used and described in this chapter are real, existing examples, not future or hypothetical examples. Furthermore, this chapter does not include a section defining what AI is and which technologies can be considered AI. No clear definition of AI exists in literature and at points there is even a lack of convergence on what AI exactly is.[3] To steer clear of this debate on what counts as AI and what not, this chapter only discusses AI technologies that are self-learning and autonomous. Most of the AI discussed in this chapter is technology based on machine learning.[4]

This chapter is structured as follows. Section 11.2 discusses developments in substantive criminal law and Sect. 11.3 discusses developments in procedural criminal law. Section 11.4 provides conclusions and identifies focus areas for further legal research.

---

[1] Rosemain and Rose 2018. In the US: Harper 2021. In the Netherlands: https://nlaic.com and https://www.universiteitleiden.nl/en/sails. Many countries worldwide are thinking about developing policies for AI, see Jobin et al. 2019, pp. 389–399.

[2] Custers 2018, pp. 355–377.

[3] Calo 2017.

[4] Calders and Custers 2013.

11.2   AI and Substantive Criminal Law

11.2.1   Crimes

Developments in AI technologies such as data mining and machine learning enable several new opportunities for criminals to commit new types of crimes and new ways of committing well-known crimes. This section describes several examples of new types of crime enabled by AI and types of crime that have are rapidly becoming more prevalent due to the use of AI. Most of the technologies used for the applications discussed in this section, such as A/B optimisation, are based on data mining and machine learning and focus on the discovery of patterns. Deepfake technologies are not necessarily focused on pattern discovery, but also are a form of deep learning, usually based on artificial neural networks.

11.2.1.1   A/B Optimisation

Many websites, such as online stores, websites for booking hotel rooms, and news websites, use so-called *A/B testing*[5] (also referred to as A/B optimisation). A/B testing means that some visitors to the website are offered screen A (or version A) and other visitors get screen B (or version B). Version A and B only have one difference, sometimes very subtle. For instance, the difference can be black versus dark blue text colours, or the background colour is pale yellow instead of pale blue, or the headers in the text are underlined in one version, but not in the other version. Both versions are then monitored in terms of how long visitors stay on the website, click on advertisements, or order something. If version A turns out to yield better results than version B, the latter version is rejected and the former is continued with. By repeating this many times and offering different versions to large numbers of visitors, an optimized result can be achieved. In fact, all internet users are used as guinea pigs to find out what works best.[6]

Obviously, this A/B testing is not a manual procedure—it is automated and usually self-learning, which makes it a form of AI. Usually it is algorithms (based on technologies like data mining and machine learning) that discover particular patterns. Self-learning software can also create on its own these variations in the lay-out of a website or the text in a message. Via algorithmic decision-making, the information is then offered to the users in a specific way. It is important to stress that A/B testing does not require any personal data. It can also be applied to anonymous visitors of a website and it is not a form of personalisation. It is about general preferences, not about personal preferences.

Companies can use A/B testing to retain people longer on their websites, supporting the attention economics, and even to increase the number of product

---

[5] Kohavi and Thomke 2017, pp. 74–82.

[6] Gallo 2017.

sales. Also criminals use this approach. When criminals start using phishing (i.e., trying to obtain bank account details of their victims), ransomware (i.e., trying to lock computers or files of their victims and order a ransom), or WhatsApp fraud (i.e., trying to convince their victims to transfer money to a friend in need), the challenge for the criminals is always the same: convincing a victim to click on a link or an attachment that will install malware or, even more directly, to transfer money.[7] In other words, criminals are always looking for the most convincing screens. The use of A/B testing and many guinea pigs can help achieve this. The spam used in all these types of cybercrime is not simply a free trial (like the term phishing suggest), it also offers criminals to watch and see what works (i.e., when victims take the bait) and optimise their methods (like the term spear phishing expresses).[8]

As a result of these developments, the fake screens we see look increasingly real. Distinguishing what is real and what is fake becomes more and more difficult, for instance, for messages from a bank or employer. In WhatsApp fraud, for instance, often profile pictures of friends or family members are used to increase the trustworthiness of messages. It is not surprising that unsuspecting victims fall into these traps in increasingly large numbers. Europol reports a rise in these types of cybercrime year after year for several years now.[9]

11.2.1.2   Deepfake Technology

Related to this, there is another AI technology that deserves attention. Deepfake technology offers the possibility of merging images and videos. It is also possible to generate completely new footage, for instance, of non-existing people through AI.[10] This technology is cheap and little technological knowledge is required. Deepfake technology can make someone look better or worse, or even completely different, as is shown in Fig. 11.1. In some cases, deepfake technology can merge pictures or videos of people's faces, rendering the identity of the personal unrecognizable,[11] and this can be misleading.

If deepfake technology is used to portray a person favourably or unfavourably, this can obviously affect the perception that other people may have of this person. Potentially, this could threaten democratic elections, if people are portrayed saying things that significantly differ from their actual viewpoints.[12] Misleading messages can also be used to incite people to criminal behaviour or even acts of terrorism.

Another type of deception using deepfakes is the possibility to create pornographic images of celebrities (Fig. 11.2).[13] This technology 'undresses' people,

---

[7] Custers et al. 2019, pp. 728–745.

[8] Jingguo et al. 2012, pp. 345–362.

[9] Europol 2020.

[10] See, for instance, www.thispersondoesnotexist.com.

[11] Source: Facebook.

[12] See https://www.youtube.com/watch?v=T76bK2t2r8g.

[13] Popova 2020.

Fig. 11.1 Original and deepfake image of a woman [*Source* Facebook][14]

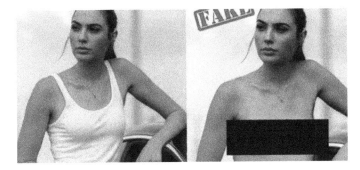

Fig. 11.2 Deepfake technology can be used for creating pornographic images of celebrities [*Source* https://www.ethicsforge.cc/deepfake-the-age-of-disinformation/][15]

by merging footage of celebrities with pornographic images. Actresses like Emma Watson, Natalie Portman and Gal Gadot were victims of this practice.[16] Also people who are not famous are increasingly victimised by pornographic deepfakes. This kind of footage can severely ruin people's reputations, (usually a tort, but potentially also constituting criminal acts like insult, libel or slander) deeply affecting their lives, particularly if the images become widely disseminated online.[17]

Another highly controversial type of deepfakes is the creation of virtual child pornography. Although it could be argued that this does not involve child abuse, it could lead to this. It is for this reason that virtual child pornography is a criminal

---

[14] Source: Facebook.

[15] Source: https://www.ethicsforge.cc/deepfake-the-age-of-disinformation/.

[16] Lee 2018.

[17] See https://www.elle.com/uk/life-and-culture/a30748079/deepfake-porn/.

offence in many countries, via the implementation of the Convention on Cybercrime[18] and EU Directive 2011/92/EU combating the sexual abuse and sexual exploitation of children and child pornography.[19]

Yet another type of deepfakes is the creation of (images of) new or different persons. The current technology allows for generating highly realistic footage of existing and non-existing persons. In the former category, deceased people can be brought back to life and incorporated in present-day images. This can go well beyond entertainment,[20] as was clearly shown in 2019, when the president of Gabon addressed his country in a deepfake video.[21] This was after months without public appearance due to hospitalisation abroad. The video led to all kinds of speculations and, shortly after, a coup attempt. Footage of non-existing persons can, in the long term, raise even more confusion. Persons only known from the screens, may very well not exist at all. When deepfakes are applied as actors, the risk may be unemployment of human actors, but when deepfakes are applied as politicians, it may become untraceable who really has the power in a country.

11.2.1.3 *Algorithmic Profiling*

Next to these mostly visual applications of AI technology, also types of AI using other types of data exist. Like in other sectors of society, also criminals make use of *profiling*,[22] a technique that can help identify characteristics and preferences of people. Criminals can use this to convince victims, as described above, but also to select which individuals and groups of people may be easy or wealthy targets.

One thing that differentiates profiling from A/B testing is that profiling requires the processing of personal data, for instance, via cookies and other online trackers. Criminals can select potential victims on the basis of preferences that internet users reveal, either explicitly or implicitly, for instance, through reading and clicking behaviour. Also money mules for the laundering of criminal profits can be recruited in this way.[23]

Other types of cybercrime that make use of these approaches are CEO fraud and WhatsApp fraud. Both exist in different varieties, but CEO fraud usually boils down to sending an order to a company's financial department, on behalf of the CEO (or perhaps the CFO), to transfer money. WhatsApp fraud usually boils down to a criminal imposing a friend or family member in urgent need of money. For both types

---

[18] Convention on Cybercrime, Budapest, 23 November 2001, https://www.coe.int/en/web/conven tions/full-list/-/conventions/rms/0900001680081561.

[19] https://eur-lex.europa.eu/legal-content/EN/TXT/HTML/?uri=CELEX:32011L0093&from=NL.

[20] Like the painter Dali who is brought to life by the use of deepfake technology in the Dali Museum, see Lee 2019.

[21] Cahlan 2020.

[22] Custers 2013.

[23] Custers et al. 2020, pp. 121–152.

of cybercrime, criminals first need to collect personal data on their victims and on the person whom they like to impose.

11.2.2 Sanctions and Justice-Related Programmes

11.2.2.1 Evidence-Based Sanctioning

One of the most important goals of sanctions and other justice-related programs is specific prevention (or specific deterrence), i.e., preventing the perpetrator from committing another crime in the future.[24] On the basis of large amounts of data and with the use of automated analyses, empirical research can be done on which interventions yield the best results in terms of reducing recidivism. This research problem can be modelled in the same way as a doctor treating a patient: on the basis of the disease or condition (and increasingly also the characteristics of the patient),[25] the doctor determines the best medication, therapy or treatment. Similarly, courts, judges and mediators can 'administer' interventions depending on the characteristics of perpetrators (such as the crime and the situation in which the crime was committed, but also personality traits of the perpetrator and the victim).[26] All this can be included in assessing which intervention is the most effective in terms of reducing recidivism (i.e., recidivism as classifier in the models). Potential 'treatments' and 'therapies' include the type of sanction (imprisonment, community service, or a fine), conditional or unconditional sentences, probation, parole, and the eligibility and expected effectiveness of justice-related programs (such as training and education programs, for instance, focused on improving cognitive or social skills, or dealing with aggressive behaviour or addictions).

This evidence-based algorithmic profiling approach in sanctioning can be applied on a group level (what works best for specific categories of people) or at an individual level (what works best in a specific case). At both levels applications already exist in several countries. In the United States, the National Institute of Justice publishes evaluation research on its website Crime Solutions.[27] For each justice-related program it is indicated whether it is effective or not. In the Netherlands, the government publishes data on recidivism at an aggregated level via a system called REPRIS.[28] On the basis of these and other evaluation research results, an expert committee examines the programs on their quality and effectiveness and then decides on officially recognizing them.[29] A lot of research in this field is still traditional empirical

---

[24] As opposed to general prevention (or general deterrence), which aims to deter others than the perpetrator, mostly by setting an example to others when imposing a sanction in a specific case.

[25] This is referred to as personalized medicine.

[26] Cf. Weijer and Leukfeldt 2017, pp. 407–412.

[27] https://crimesolutions.ojp.gov.

[28] https://data.overheid.nl/dataset/repris.

[29] https://www.justitieinterventies.nl.

research, but analyses are increasingly automated to include larger amounts of data in these evaluations. Obviously, this may entail some risks, which will be discussed below.

11.2.2.2 Instruments for Risk Assessments

Also at an individual level, this approach has added value, particularly for instruments for risk assessments. Instruments for risk assessments are commonly used in criminal law, for instance, when courts and judges are considering probation or parole. In several of the United States, the system COMPAS is used to assess recidivism risks.[30] Courts heavily weigh these models (or rather the results they spit out) in their decisions. In the Netherlands, the probation services use a system called RISC. Part of that is OXREC, an actuarial risk assessment tool that can be used to predict statistical risks.[31] These models increasingly play a role in the work of probation services and the decisions of courts.

The use of such models offers several benefits: assessments can be done in more structured and objective ways. Subjective assessors can be prone to human failure or can be influenced by bias and prejudice. If the models are self-learning, they can also recognize and incorporate new trends and developments. This obviously can also increase efficiency and reduce costs. However, there is also criticism with regard to this way of working, because the instruments do not seem to outperform assessments by human experts and there are risks involved, such as bias that can lead to discrimination.[32] In the United States, COMPAS seemed to systematically assign higher recidivism risks to Afro-Americans.[33] It is often argued that these models do not process any ethnicity data and, therefore, cannot be discriminating.[34] However, characteristics like ethnicity can easily be predicted and are therefore often reconstructed by self-learning technologies, without being visible for users.[35] Caution is advised.

11.2.3 Legal Questions

From the above subsections, it becomes clear that AI entails a substantial change in the criminal law domain. In three categories of legal questions can be distilled for

---

[30] https://assets.documentcloud.org/documents/2840784/Practitioner-s-Guide-to-COMPAS-Core.pdf.

[31] https://oxrisk.com/oxrec-nl-2-backup/.

[32] Van Dijck 2020.

[33] Angwin et al. 2016.

[34] Maas et al. 2020, pp. 2055–2059.

[35] Cf. Kamiran et al. 2013.

substantive criminal law. The first category concerns questions regarding the interpretation of existing law and legislation. This concerns questions on whether particular actions are covered by specific provisions in criminal codes. For instance, it can be investigated which technologies qualify as a 'computer system' in the Convention on Cybercrime. The second category concerns questions regarding which actions or behaviour should be considered criminal, even though it may not (yet) be criminal according to the provisions in criminal codes. For instance, it may be argued that several types of deepfake technology should perhaps be prohibited by criminal law. The third category concerns questions regarding the use of data. These are questions regarding the extent to which data can be collected and processed, for instance, in the risk assessments discussed above, or questions regarding proportionality, to protect the interests of others involved, such as intellectual property of profiles and other knowledge, privacy, and equal treatment (not only of suspects, but also of non-suspects in control groups).

11.3 AI and Procedural Criminal Law

11.3.1 Criminal Investigation

Law enforcement agencies and public prosecution services can also use AI in different ways. In criminal investigation and prosecution, AI can support or even replace some parts of the work. This section will provide examples of both developments. In this section, predictive policing and cyber agent technology are discussed as examples of AI in criminal investigation and prosecution.

11.3.1.1 Predictive Policing

With the use of large amounts of data and sophisticated data analytics, trends and developments in crime can be disclosed. These technologies can also be used to predict crime, including the locations where crime is likely to take place, who perhaps will be a criminal or a victim of crime, and how criminal networks and criminal careers may develop. This is referred to as *predictive policing*.[36]

A typical example here are so-called *crime heat maps* (Fig. 11.3), in which crime rates are visualised on maps of metropolitan areas. On such maps, neighbourhoods with high crime rates ('hot spots') can easily be recognized. With the help of AI, not only static maps with snapshots can be created, but also dynamic, real-time maps can be generated. Looking back in time then becomes possible, but also looking

---

[36] Ferguson 2019; Schuilenburg 2016, pp. 931–936.

Fig. 11.3 *Crime heat maps* show crime rates for each neighbourhood. With the use of AI, real-time and prospective maps can be generated [*Source* https://spo tcrime.wordpress.com/2009/ 07/20/houston-crime-map-new-data-and-shooting-heat-map/][37]

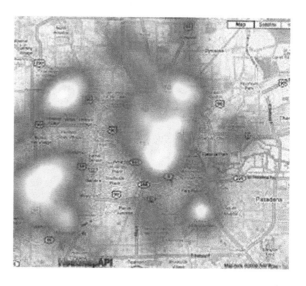

forward in time, by incorporating prediction models in the maps. This makes such maps useful when planning surveillance and developing policing strategies.[38]

Predictive policing can be based on location, but also on persons. With the use of profiling strategies described above, predictions can be made regarding who may commit a crime. This may be relevant for recidivism, but also for first offenders. On the basis of personal and situational characteristics, it can be predicted who constitutes a high risk to become a criminal.[39] AI related technologies can discover novel, unexpected patterns in this area and provide real time information, for instance, by also including social media data in the models. Real time information allows law enforcement to intervene on the spot, when the probability of catching a criminal is the highest. Although this approach may offer benefits in terms of efficiency and effectiveness, it should be used with caution, though: there may be crime displacement,[40] there may be disparate impact,[41] and there may be tunnel vision, with false positive and false negative rates resulting from limited reliability.[42]

---

[37] Source: https://spotcrime.wordpress.com/2009/07/20/houston-crime-map-new-data-and-sho oting-heat-map/.

[38] Weisburd and Telep 2014, pp. 200–220.

[39] Kleemans and De Poot 2008, pp. 69–98.

[40] Weisburd et al. 2006, pp. 549–592.

[41] Barocas and Selbst 2016.

[42] Custers 2003, pp. 290–295.

11.3.1.2 *Cyber Agent Technology*

Crime rates have been steadily decreasing for many years in Western countries, but this does not seem to apply to cybercrime. In fact, for cybercrime, there seems to be an increase. That may not be surprising, since for cybercriminals the chances of being caught are low and the profits can be very high compared to offline crime. Also traditional types of crime, such as organised crime groups trafficking and trading drugs, have gone online, via online marketplaces on the darkweb (the part of the internet that has not been indexed by search engines and is only accessible with special software). One of the first illegal market places was Silk Road, established in 2011 and taken down by the FBI in 2013, where illegal substances and weapons were traded and even the services of hitmen could be purchased. After Silk Road was taken down, other websites followed, including Silk Road 2.0 (in 2014), Evolution (in 2015), AlphaBay (in 2015), Hansa (in 2017), Outlaw (in 2017), Digital Shadows (in 2018), Dream Market (in 2019), DeepDotWeb (in 2019) and Darkmarket (in 2021).[43]

It can be complicated and time-consuming for law enforcement agencies to monitor activities on these online marketplaces. For instance, access to these marketplaces requires carefully building a reputation, as the criminals on the platforms are very reluctant to allow access to new people. For law enforcement agencies it may also be required to use extensive criminal investigation competences, including the use of systemic surveillance, working undercover, secretly recording private conversations, and infiltrating in criminal organisation. Obviously, such police competences may differ per jurisdiction. Usually these competences can only be applied after a court has approved this. When applied, law enforcement agencies should be very careful not to use these competences in ways that may be seen as entrapment, as this may render any evidence collected useless in courts.

Due to the invasive and precarious nature of criminal investigations on darkweb marketplaces, it may be helpful to deploy AI. This can be done with cyber agent technology, i.e., technology that supports cyber agents (online actors). This technology can have a certain degree of autonomy and act according to the circumstances.[44] This is intelligent software that can interact with others and act without human intervention.[45] With the use of this technology, many more interactions with actors on darkweb forums can be maintained than human law enforcement officers could take care of.

One of the most concrete applications in this area is a chatbot (an automated interlocutor) called Sweetie (Fig. 11.4).[46] The chatbot is designed to look like a 10-year-old girl from the Philippines and can have conversations online with people that show sexual interests in children. The goal obviously is to track and identify

---

[43] For more background, see also Mirea et al. 2019, pp. 102–118.

[44] Schermer 2007.

[45] Nwana 1996, 205–244; Luck et al. 2004, 203–252.

[46] https://www.terredeshommes.nl/programmas/sweetie-20-webcamseks-met-kinderen-de-wer eld-uit. See also van der Wal 2016.

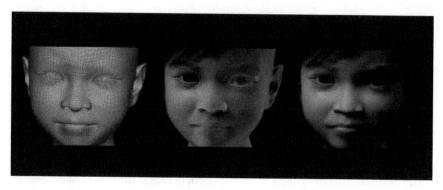

Fig. 11.4 Sweetie 2.0 is cyber agent technology that can contribute to online criminal investigation [*Source* https://www.universiteitleiden.nl/en/news/2019/07/sweetie-2.0-using-artificial-int elligence-to-fight-webcam-child-sex-tourism][47]

paedophiles and to prosecute or rebuke them. This technology can also be used by secret services and intelligence agencies in the interest of national security.[48]

The AI technology can only be used if it is sufficiently advanced, i.e., if it can pass the Turing test,[49] in which people do not realise that they are communicating with AI. In the case of Sweetie 2.0, the Turing test was not an issue: approximately 20.000 men from 71 countries reached out to her, believing she was a real child.[50] Furthermore, the technology cannot provoke illegal behaviour and should not learn and adopt criminal behaviour itself.[51] That criterion is significantly more complicated to meet: in many jurisdictions, the technology can be qualified as entrapment under criminal procedure codes.[52] Another issue was that convictions for child abuse proved to be difficult in several jurisdictions, as there was no real abuse (it is impossible to sexually abuse software).[53] And even if intentions to commit child abuse constituted a criminal act, it could be hard to prove, since Sweetie is no real child. Nevertheless, the technologies led to convictions in Australia, Belgium and the UK.[54]

---

[47] Source: https://www.universiteitleiden.nl/en/news/2019/07/sweetie-2.0-using-artificial-intellige nce-to-fight-webcam-child-sex-tourism.

[48] Custers 2017.

[49] Turing 1950, pp. 433–460.

[50] http://www.dawn.com/news/1054244.

[51] Like Microsoft's chatbot Tay, which started using racist language a few hours after it was released, see: Mason 2016.

[52] van der Hof et al. 2019.

[53] Schermer et al. 2019, pp. 1–94.

[54] https://nl.wikipedia.org/wiki/Sweetie_%28virtueel_personage%29.

11.3.2   Evidence

When collecting and assessing forensic evidence, AI can play a role in different ways. This section discusses searching large amounts of data that are collected during seizures, assessing evidence, and building scenarios for reconstructing crimes.

11.3.2.1   Searching Large Amounts of Data after Seizure

In specific situations and under certain conditions (usually including a court warrant), law enforcement officers can seize digital storage devices for further searching.[55] Law enforcement can let forensics experts search the devices, including smartphones, tablets, laptops, and USB keys, for evidence. Apart from issues with damaged devices or encryption, a major problem in digital forensics often is the tremendous volume of the data on these devices. Oftentimes, only small pieces of information turn out to be relevant as evidence, for instance, to complete parts of an irrefutable narrative. In fact, these are needle-in-the-haystack kind of problems and AI can be useful in addressing these problems.[56]

In the Netherlands, the National Forensics Institute developed a tool for this, called Hansken.[57] This system, an example of big data analytics, can process large amounts of data from different sources and in different formats (such as text, video, audio, etc.), including storage, indexation and making the data searchable. The labelling of data is automated. The searchability of the seized data increases the effectiveness of criminal investigations, since relevant data is overlooked less often.[58] Also, Hansken delivers very fast results, which is a major benefit in criminal investigations, in which the first 48 hours are often the most crucial and decisive, both with regard to identifying, tracing, and finding suspects and with regard to collecting forensic evidence.

11.3.2.2   Assessing Evidence

Criminal evidence exists in different types and sizes. Technical evidence, such as DNA, fingerprints, ballistics reports, always come with margins or error. In turn, this can lead to false positives and false negatives, for instance, when matching DNA found at a crime scene with DNA profiles in databases. Also, the DNA secured by forensic experts at a crime scene is a mixture of traces of DNA. With the help of AI,

---

[55] Or data can be intercepted, see Custers 2008, pp. 94–100.

[56] Hoelz et al. 2009, pp. 883–888.

[57] https://www.forensischinstituut.nl/forensisch-onderzoek/hansken. See also van Beek et al. 2015, pp. 20–38.

[58] Sunde and Dror 2021.

so-called *probabilistic genotyping* is possible, which can be used to assess whether someone's DNA really is in these mixed traces of DNA found at the crime scene.[59]

When assessing the reliability, the focus is often on the probability of a match (for instance, a 95% likelihood), but also the reliability of this probability is important (for instance, with an error margin of 3%, a likelihood in the range of 92–98%). In case of an error margin of 2%, the probability of a match was determined much more precisely than in case of an error margin of 12%. With the help of very large numbers of data and self-learning systems, the reliability of the matches can be assessed more precisely, reducing the error margins. In this way, the reliability of the evidence can be quantified much more precisely, with smaller error margins, resulting in increased reliability of the forensic evidence.[60]

The use of AI in forensics does entail some risks. Obviously, the data may contain errors and humans are not so great at understanding risks, which may result in errors in judgements. Also, the focus may shift from narratives to numbers, and from legal experts to technological experts, which a defendant in court may find harder to challenge. A potential problem with highly specialised expertises in forensics is that there may be only a very limited number of experts (which often know each other), entailing risks of tunnel vision. In court cases in which different kinds of highly sophisticated forensics are introduced, an issue may be that no expert is able to oversee all aspects of the case. Obviously, this oversight is the responsibility of the judges in the court, but as legal experts they may not be familiar with all intricacies of the forensic technologies used. These are well-known challenges, which may further increase with the use of AI in evidence.

11.3.2.3   Building Scenarios When Reconstructing Crimes

In behavioural psychology it is well-known that humans perform poorly when assessing probabilities and risks: often a narrative is more convincing than statistics, mostly because trough evolution humans have learned to quickly pick up any causal relationships.[61] Humans apparently are much better in assessing probabilities when presented with different scenarios. AI can contribute to constructing various scenarios that can be compared and weighed in courts.[62] This can be done by attaching different weight to the available evidence per scenario. The different scenarios can also be visualised, including the extent to which they are supported by the available evidence (see Fig. 11.5). In this way, it becomes clear which parts of a particular scenario need further substantiation and additional or more detailed evidence.

Bayesian statistics play an important role in this, to express conditional probabilities. A conditional probability is a probability that includes other evidence or, more precisely, the probability of the extent to which other evidence supports a

---

[59] Kwong 2017, pp. 275–301.

[60] Kwan et al. 2008.

[61] Kahnemann 2012.

[62] Bex et al. 2016, pp. 22–29; Schraagen et al. 2018.

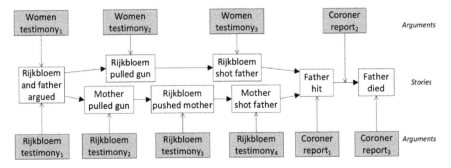

Fig. 11.5 AI technology can help construct different scenarios by varying the weight of different pieces of evidence [*Source* Bex 2015].[63]

proposition. This can be helpful in reducing the numbers of potential suspects or scenarios in a case. With the help of AI, conditional probabilities can be calculated automatically for different combinations of conditions. In other words, the AI cannot only contribute to comparing and weighing scenarios, but also to developing novel, perhaps unexpected scenarios.

11.3.3   Legal Questions

The examples in the area of procedural criminal law presented in this section may raise several ethical and legal questions. Incorrect and incomplete data, the choice of instruments for data analysis, and the interpretation of discovered profile scan all lead to limited reliability of the conclusions that are drawn. As a result of this, prejudice and discrimination may sneak into the process of criminal investigation, prosecution and sentencing. This raises ethical and legal questions with regard to substantive justice (for instance, what are suitable sentences for new types of AI enabled crime) and procedural justice (for instance, with regard to the right to a fair trial). Since AI is complex and its workings can be non-transparent or hard to explain, it may be difficult for suspects to defend themselves against this. If decisions in criminal law procedures increasingly rely on the results of AI, this could lead to situations similar to those in Kafka's novel The Trial,[64] in which suspects do not know what they are accused of, where the accusations come from, and on which information (data, analysis, conclusions) these accusations are based.

More traditional, legal positivist questions relate to the scope of the competences of law enforcement agencies. Questions include how far police powers extend in this new context of AI, how entrapment can be prevented, and how it can be guaranteed that self-learning AI will not show criminal behaviour itself after operating for some

---

[63] Source: Bex 2015.
[64] Kafka 2015.

time in a criminal context. Apart from interpreting the extent of existing criminal investigation competences, an important question is whether these competences are actually sufficient for criminal investigations in this rapidly developing context. This is not to argue in favour of creating more police competences, but to argue research is needed on what is perhaps missing or where existing competences can be amended to fill any gaps.

Another issue is the regulation of data analyses in criminal law. It is striking that collecting data is strictly regulated in criminal law (including data protection law), but the use of data analyses is hardly regulated.[65] In other words, once data has been collected and aggregated, law enforcement agencies and public prosecution services have a large degree for freedom to subject the data to all kinds of analyses. Regulating this could contribute to better legal protection of all actors in criminal procedures (not only suspects), for instance, via more transparency and participation. This could also increase legal certainty.

11.4 Conclusions

The goal of this chapter was to provide a concise overview of different AI developments in criminal law. The examples in this chapter illustrate that AI is increasingly used by criminals, but also by law enforcement agencies and public prosecutions services. It can be argued that the cat-and-mouse game between them has moved on to a new stage with the introduction of AI.[66] In order to keep up with developments, law enforcement agencies, public prosecution services and courts will need to invest heavily in knowledge and expertise during the next coming years.

With regard to substantive criminal law, further research is needed on the interpretation and scope of provisions in criminal codes and on whether new provisions need to be included in criminal codes in the near future to ensure that particular undesirable behaviour enabled by AI becomes punishable. With regard to procedural criminal law, further research is needed on the scope of existing criminal investigation competences, on potential modifications in these competences, and on how to properly balance criminal investigation competences and fundamental rights. The use of AI can offer many benefits in criminal investigation, but only if prejudice, discrimination, and other risks are avoided or mitigated. Regulating data analysis in criminal investigations, which is currently virtually absent, could contribute to this.

---

[65] Custers and Stevens 2021.

[66] Cf. similarities of other technologies introduced previously in the security domain: Teeuw et al. 2008.

References

Angwin J, Larson J, Mattu S, Kirchner L (2016) Machine Bias. ProPublica, 23 May 2016. https://www.propublica.org/article/machine-bias-risk-assessments-in-criminal-sentencing.

Barocas S, Selbst AD (2016) Big Data's Disparate Impact. 104 California Law Review 671.

Bex FJ (2015) An integrated theory of causal scenarios and evidential arguments. In: Proceedings of the 15th International Conference on Artificial Intelligence and Law (ICAIL 2015), 13–22, ACM Press, New York.

Bex FJ, Testerink B, Peters J (2016) AI for Online Criminal Complaints: From Natural Dialogues to Structured Scenarios. ECAI 2016 workshop on Artificial Intelligence for Justice (AI4J), The Hague, August 2016, pp. 22–29.

Cahlan S (2020) How misinformation helped spark an attempted coup in Gabon. The Washington Post, 13 February 2020, https://www.washingtonpost.com/politics/2020/02/13/how-sick-president-suspect-video-helped-sparked-an-attempted-coup-gabon/.

Calders T, Custers BHM (2013) What is data mining and how does it work? In: Custers BHM, Calders T, Schermer B, Zarsky T (eds) Discrimination and Privacy in the Information Society. nr.3. Springer, Heidelberg

Calo R (2017) Artificial Intelligence Policy: A Primer and Roadmap: https://ssrn.com/abstract=3015350.

Custers BHM (2003) Effects of Unreliable Group Profiling by Means of Data Mining. In: Grieser G, Tanaka Y, Yamamoto A (eds) Lecture Notes in Artificial Intelligence. Proceedings of the 6th International Conference on Discovery Science (DS 2003) Sapporo, Japan. Springer-Verlag, Berlin/Heidelberg/New York, Vol. 2843, pp. 290–295.

Custers BHM (2008) Tapping and Data Retention in Ultrafast Communication Networks. Journal of International Commercial Law and Technology, Vol. 3, Issue 2, 2008, pp. 94–100.

Custers BHM (2013) Data Dilemmas in the Information Society. In: Custers BHM, Calders T, Schermer B, Zarsky T (eds) Discrimination and Privacy in the Information Society. Springer, Heidelberg.

Custers BHM (2017) Cyber agent technology en de Wet op de Inlichtingen- en Veiligheidsdiensten (WIV). Universiteit Leiden, Leiden, 30 September 2017.

Custers BHM (2018) Methods of data research for law. In: Mak V, Tjong Tjin Tai E, Berlee A (eds) Research Handbook in Data Science and Law. Edward Elgar, Cheltenham, pp. 355–377

Custers BHM, Pool, R, Cornelisse R (2019) Banking Malware and the Laundering of its Profits. European Journal of Criminology, Vol. 16, nr. 6, pp. 728–745. https://doi.org/10.1177/1477370818788007.

Custers BHM, Oerlemans JJ, Pool R (2020) Laundering the Profits of Ransomware: Money Laundering Methods for Vouchers and Cryptocurrencies. European Journal of Crime, Criminal Law and Criminal Justice, 28 (2020), pp. 121–152.

Custers BHM, Stevens L (2021) The Use of Data as Evidence in Dutch Criminal Courts. European Journal of Crime, Criminal Law and Criminal Justice, Vol. 29, No, 1.

Europol (2020) The Internet Organised Crime Threat Assessment (IOCTA) 2021. Europol, The Hague. https://www.europol.europa.eu/activities-services/main-reports/internet-organised-crime-threat-assessment-iocta-2020.

Ferguson AG (2019) Predictive Policing Theory. In: Rice Lave T, Miller EJ (eds) The Cambridge Handbook of Policing in the United States. Cambridge University Press.

Gallo A (2017) A Refresher on A/B Testing. Harvard Business Review, 28 June 2017, https://hbr.org/2017/06/a-refresher-on-ab-testing.

Harper J (2021) Federal AI Spending to Top $6 Billion. National Defense Magazine, 10 February 2021, https://www.nationaldefensemagazine.org/articles/2021/2/10/federal-ai-spending-to-top-$6-billion.

Hoelz B, Ralha C, Geeverghese R (2009) Artificial intelligence applied to computer forensics. Proceedings of the ACM Symposium on Applied Computing. Honolulu, 9-12 March 2009, pp. 883–888.

Jingguo W, Herath T, Rui C, Vishwanath A, Rao HR (2012) Phishing susceptibility: An investigation into the processing of a targeted spear phishing email. IEEE Trans. Prof. Commun., vol. 55, no. 4, pp. 345–362.

Jobin A, Ienca M, Vayena E (2019) The global landscape of AI ethics guidelines. Nature Machine Intelligence, 1(9), pp. 389–399.

Kafka F (2015) The Trial. Penguin Books, London.

Kahnemann D (2012) Thinking, fast and slow. Penguin Books, New York.

Kamiran F, Calders T, Pechenizkiy M (2013) Techniques for discrimination-free predictive models. In: Custers BHM et al. (eds) Discrimination and Privacy in the Information Society. Springer, Heidelberg.

Kleemans ER, De Poot CJ (2008) Criminal Careers in Organized Crime and Social Opportunity Structure. European Journal of Criminology. Vol. 5 Nr. 1, pp. 69–98.

Kohavi R, Thomke S (2017) The Surprising Power of Online Experiments. Harvard Business Review, September 2017, pp. 74–82.

Kwan M, Chow KP, Law F, Lai P (2008) Reasoning About Evidence Using Bayesian Networks. In: Ray I, Shenoi S (eds) Advances in Digital Forensics IV, IFIP — The International Federation for Information Processing. Springer, Heidelberg.

Kwong K (2017) The Algorithm Says You Did it: The Use of Black Box Algorithms to Analyse Complex DNA Evidence. Harvard Journal of Law & Technology, Vol., 31, Nr. 1, pp. 275–301.

Lee D (2018) Deepfakes porn has serious consequences. BBC News, 3 February 2018. https://www.bbc.com/news/technology-42912529.

Lee D (2019) Deepfake Salvador Dali takes selfies with museum visitors: it's surreal, all right. The Verge, 10 May 2019. https://www.theverge.com/2019/5/10/18540953/salvador-dali-lives-deepfake-museum.

Luck M, McBurney P, Preist C (2004) A Manifesto for Agent Technology: Towards Next Generation Computing, Autonomous Agents and Multi-Agent Systems, 9, 203–252.

Maas M, Legters E, Fazel S (2020) Professional en risicotaxatie-instrument hand in hand: hoe de reclassering risico's inschat. NJB afl. 28, pp. 2055–2059.

Mason P (2016) Racist hijacking of Microsoft's chatbot shows how the internet teems with hate. The Guardian, 29 March 2016.

Mirea M, Wang V, Jung J (2019) The not so dark side of the darknet: a qualitative study. Security Journal, 32, pp. 102–118.

Nwana HS (1996) Software Agents: An Overview. Knowledge Engineering Review. 21 (3): 205–244.

Popova M (2020) Reading out of context: pornographic deepfakes, celebrity and intimacy. Porn Studies, 7:4, 367–381, DOI: https://doi.org/10.1080/23268743.2019.1675090.

Rosemain M, Rose M (2018) France to spend $1.8 billion on AI to compete with US, China, 29 March 2018. Reuters, https://www.reuters.com/article/us-france-tech/france-to-spend-1-8-billion-on-ai-to-compete-with-u-s-china-idUKKBN1H51XP.

Schermer BW (2007) Software agents, surveillance, and the right to privacy: a legislative framework for agent-enabled surveillance. Leiden University Press, Leiden.

Schermer BW, Georgieva I, van der Hof S, Koops BJ (2019) Legal aspects of Sweetie 2.0. In: van der Hof S, Georgieva I, Schermer BW, Koops BJ (eds) Sweetie 2.0. Using artificial intelligence to fight webcam child sex tourism. Information Technology & Law Series nr. 31. T.M.C. Asser Press, The Hague, pp. 1–94.

Schraagen M, Testerink B, Odekerken D, Bex F (2018) Argumentation-driven information extraction for online crime reports. CKIM 2018 International Workshop on Legal Data Analysis and Mining (LeDAM 2018), CEUR Workshop Proceedings.

Schuilenburg M (2016) Predictive policing: de opkomst van gedachtepolitie? Ars Aequi, December 2016, pp. 931–936.

Sunde N, Dror I (2021) A Hierarchy of Expert Performance (HEP) applied to Digital Forensics: Reliability and Biasability in Digital Forensics Decision Making. Forensic Science International: Digital Investigation, Vol. 37. https://doi.org/10.1016/j.fsidi.2021.301175.

Teeuw WB, Vedder AH, Custers BHM, Dorbeck-Jung BR, Faber ECC, Iacob SM, Koops B-J, Leenes RE, de Poot HJG, Rip A, Vudisa JN (2008) Security Applications for Converging Technologies: Impact on the constitutional state and the legal order. O&B 269. WODC, The Hague.

Turing A (1950) Computing machinery and intelligence. Mind 59, pp. 433–460.

van Beek HMA, van Eijk EJ, van Baar RB, Ugen M, Bodde JNC, Siemelink AJ (2015) Digital Forensics as a Service: Game On. Digital Investigation, Vol. 15, pp. 20–38.

van der Hof S, Georgieva I, Schermer BW, Koops BJ (2019) Sweetie 2.0. Using artificial intelligence to fight webcam child sex tourism. Information Technology & Law Series nr. 31. T.M.C. Asser Press, The Hague.

Van Dijck G (2020) Algoritmische risicotaxatie van recidive: over de Oxford Risk of Recidivism tool (OXREC), ongelijke behandeling en discriminatie in strafzaken. NJB 2020/1558.

van der Wal C (2016) Sweetie 2.0: nieuw virtueel meisje gaat op pedojacht, Algemeen Dagblad, 13 February 2016. https://www.ad.nl/binnenland/sweetie-2-0-nieuw-virtueel-meisje-gaat-op-pedojacht~ad3739ca/.

Weijer SGA, Leukfeldt ER (2017) Big Five Personality Traits of Cybercrime Victims. Cyberpsychology, Behavior, and Social Networking, 20(7), pp. 407–412.

Weisburd D, Telep CW (2014) Hot Spots Policing. Journal of Contemporary Criminal Justice, 30(2), pp. 200–220.

Weisburd D, Wyckoff LA, Ready J, Eck JE, Hinkle JC, Gajewski F (2006) Does Crime Just Move Around the Corner? A Controlled Study of Spatial Displacement and Diffusion of Crime Control Benefits. Criminology 44 (3), pp. 549–592.

Bart Custers PhD MSc LLM is (full) professor of Law and Data Science and director of *eLaw, Center for Law and Digital Technologies* at Leiden University, the Netherlands. He has a background in both law and physics and is an expert in the area of law and digital technologies, including topics like profiling, big data, privacy, discrimination, cybercrime, technology in policing and artificial intelligence. As a researcher and project manager, he acquired and executed research for the European Commission, NWO (the National Research Council in the Netherlands), the Dutch national government, local government agencies, large corporations and SMEs. Until 2016 he was the head of the research department on Crime, Law enforcement and Sanctions of the scientific research center (WODC) of the Ministry of Security and Justice in the Netherlands. Before that, he worked for the national government as a senior policy advisor for consecutive Ministers of Justice (2009–2013) and for a large consultancy firm as a senior management consultant on information strategies (2005–2009). On behalf of the Faculty of Law, he is the coordinator of the SAILS project. This project, funded by the Executive Board of Leiden University, deals with the societal and legal implications of Artificial Intelligence. Bart Custers published three books on profiling, privacy, discrimination and big data, two books on the use of drones and one book on the use of bitcoins for money laundering cybercrime profits. On a regular basis he gives lectures on profiling, privacy and big data and related topics. He has presented his work at international conferences in the United States, Canada, China, Japan, Korea, Malaysia, Thailand, the Middle East and throughout Europe. He has published his work, over a hundred publications, in scientific and professional journals and in newspapers.

Chapter 12
Black-Box Models as a Tool to Fight VAT Fraud

Aleksandra Bal

Contents

Abstract More and more tax administrations are using algorithms and automated decision-making systems for taxpayer profiling and risk assessment. While both provide benefits in terms of better resource allocation and cost-efficiency, their use is not free from legal concerns from the perspective of EU data protection and human rights legislation. Since 2017 the Polish National Revenue Administration has been using STIR—a data analytics tool to detect VAT fraud in nearly real-time. STIR calculates a risk indicator for every entrepreneur on the basis of his financial data. If an entrepreneur is considered at high risk of being involved in VAT fraud, the National Revenue Administration may impose severe administrative measures. From the taxpayer perspective, STIR operates in a black-box manner as the way in which the risk indicators are calculated is not disclosed to the general public. Although STIR's effectiveness in fighting VAT fraud would be reduced if the algorithms that it uses were publicly known, it is questionable whether STIR complies with the principle of proportionality and the right to explanation, both of which are mandated under the EU data protection regulation and human rights legislation.

Keywords value added tax · data protection · general data protection regulation · human rights · European Union · black-box model · artificial intelligence

A shorter version of this chapter was first published by Tax Analysts in *Tax Notes International*, volume 95, number 12 (16 September 2019).

A. Bal (✉)
Indirect Tax Technology & Operations Lead, Stripe, Amsterdam, Netherlands
e-mail: aleksandrabal@stripe.com

12.1   Introduction

The use of automated decision-making systems is on the rise. Algorithms already control, or at least affect, large parts of our lives. They make decisions about recruitment, credit scoring or job promotion. In the foreseeable future, they will be driving our cars. And we are fine with it as long as we more or less understand what the algorithms are doing. If their decisions depart significantly from our perception of what is right and proper,[1] we immediately become concerned about ceding so much control to artificial intelligence (AI).

AI provides massive opportunities to do things better, more efficiently and more cheaply for both tax departments and tax administrations. Predictive analytics allows tax administrations to identify taxpayers that are most likely to be non-compliant. Tax administrators can allocate their resources more efficiently by focusing on the high-risk cases, which leads to fewer and better targeted audits. Through the use of analytics, they can also deliver better-targeted services based on a deep understanding of taxpayers' needs and circumstances. AI tools can help communicate differently with different groups of taxpayers for maximum impact. They can also be used to explain tax consequences of certain situations in simple language (tax chatbots). In the business sector, AI is commonly used to scan invoices to identify opportunities for VAT recovery or to detect anomalies in transaction data.

A number of AI algorithms operate in a black-box manner, meaning that it is difficult to understand how the system has arrived at a decision. A black-box model will not explain itself and give the logic used to produce certain results. The increasing use of black-box models has sparked a debate about algorithmic accountability and led to calls for increased transparency in algorithmic decision-making, including both transparency in the form of explanation towards individuals and transparency in the form of audits that enable expert third-party oversight.

The aim of this chapter is to investigate the acceptability and legality of the use of black-box models in tax law. Is it lawful to cede decision-making powers about taxpayers to such models? Shall explicability and transparency be paramount criteria in designing a model or is accuracy the overriding consideration? Following a brief introduction to the general concepts of AI and machine learning in Sect. 12.2, this chapter focuses on STIR—a new Polish algorithm-supported system to detect VAT fraud. As the logic used by STIR algorithms is kept secret, STIR is an example of a black-box model, at least from the taxpayer's perspective. Section 12.3 provides a description of the STIR system. Sections 12.4 and 12.5 examine whether the use of black-box models, such as STIR, is compatible with data protection law and fundamental human rights.

---

[1] Algorithmic decisions may produce discriminatory results. As algorithms learn from observation data, if this data is biased, this will be picked up by the algorithm. For example, a recruiting tool developed by one large company tended to discriminate against women for technical jobs. The company's hiring tool used artificial intelligence to give job candidates scores ranging from one to five. As most resumes came from men, the system taught itself that male candidates were preferable. It penalized resumes that included the word "women's". The discussion of biased algorithmic decisions is outside the scope of this chapter.

12.2 Artificial Intelligence: Brief Introduction

AI is the replication of human analytical and decision-making capabilities by machines. Almost every AI model in use today heavily relies on machine learning (i.e. the use of algorithms and statistical models to analyze data).

The most common output produced by machine learning algorithms are predictive models. These models are constructed on the basis of development samples consisting of observation and outcome data. The algorithms capture relationships (correlations) between the observation and outcome data sets in the form of a model that can be used to predict future, yet unknown, events. In other words, they learn from data to respond intelligently to new data.

The most popular types of predictive models are linear models, decision trees, neural networks, and ensembles. Linear models[2] and decision trees[3] are relatively easy to understand as they make predictions in a transparent way. They are "white box" in nature as it is very easy to see which data items contributed most significantly to the outcome and which were less important. Neural networks[4] and ensembles[5] tend to be more complex and "black box" in nature. They tend to deliver more accurate predictions, but it is difficult to understand why and how they produced a particular result. The outcomes they generate are not intuitive.[6]

No type of predictive models can be said to be generally better than others. Data scientists frequently build various models, compare them against each other to determine which proves to be the most optimal to solve a particular problem.

Predictive models tend to be more accurate than humans, do not display deliberate bias, and are fast and cost-efficient as they can evaluate a large number of cases within seconds. However, they can get things wrong as well. The quality of a model is as good as that of the data that was used to construct the model. If this data is biased or incomplete, the results produced by the model will be flawed as well. The same applies if the model developers make incorrect assumptions about how the model will operate. A common mistake in building a predictive model is to include every piece of information that is available into the machine learning process. Data that is outdated, unstable (i.e. it will not be available when the model is applied), or not representative

---

[2] In linear models, the outcome is calculated by multiplying the value of each factor by its relevant weight and then summing up all the results. Examples of linear models are logistic and linear regressions.

[3] Decision tree is created by recursively segmenting a population into smaller and smaller groups.

[4] Neural networks are a set of algorithms, modeled loosely after the human brain, that are designed to recognize patterns in data. Deep learning involves feeding a lot of data through multi-layered neural networks that classify the data based on the outputs from each successive layer.

[5] Ensemble models are large collections of individual models, each of which has been developed using a different set of data or algorithm. Each model makes predictions in a slightly different way. The ensemble combines all the individual predictions to arrive at one final prediction.

[6] Google has developed AlphaGo, a computer system powered by deep learning, to play the board game Go. Although AlphaGo made several moves that were evidently successful, its reasoning for making certain moves has been described as "inhuman" since no human could comprehend the decision-making rationale.

of the target population should be excluded. It is important to remember that a model is built based on past data, but it will be deployed in the future. Therefore, if certain data is not available going forward, it should be excluded from the development sample. Another common problem with AI solutions is the possibility of overfitting: it occurs when parameters of a model are tuned for very high accuracy on the training data set, but do poorly on the unseen examples. Overfitting[7] could be a problem if, for example, the administration developed an anti-fraud VAT algorithm on the basis of data on fraud on intra-Community supplies and tried to deploy it to detect e-commerce VAT fraud. Although some cases of e-commerce VAT fraud would be immediately identified by a tax inspector, an algorithm would not recognize them as they would be significantly different from the ones observed in the training data set. Finally, AI models do get old over time. It is possible that the relationships between data will change in the future and this may lead to a decrease in predictive accuracy. If the model monitoring shows that accuracy tends to fall, it is time for a new model to be developed.

There are two main types of machine learning. Machine learning that applies to development samples where each observation has an associated outcome that one wants to predict is referred to as supervised learning. The algorithms learn how to map from input (observation data) to output (outcome data) by the provision of data with "correct" values already assigned to them. The initial phase of supervised learning creates a predictive model that can subsequently be used for making predictions

If outcome data is not available, unsupervised learning can be applied. The aim of unsupervised learning is to discover interesting patterns in the data or identify groups of objects based on similarities between them. Unsupervised learning does not generate predictions. The most common type of unsupervised learning in use is clustering (i.e. grouping similar cases together). Clustering can be used by tax administrations to identify outliers or unusual cases: taxpayers are grouped into clusters and if their return data deviate from that of their peers in a particular sector, they are flagged for further investigations.

12.3   STIR: A Tool to Detect VAT Fraud in Poland

VAT is the biggest source of revenue for the Polish state budget. Unfortunately, Poland was losing a lot of revenue due to VAT fraud. According to reports by the European Commission, the Polish VAT gap[8] grew sharply between 2006 and 2011, rising from 0.4 to 1.5% of the GDP. In 2012, its size reached PLN 43.1 billion (approximately EUR 9.5 billion). Because of the prevalence of VAT fraud and its impact on the

---

[7] Overfitting refers to a modeling error that occurs when a function corresponds too closely to a particular set of training data and does not generalize well on new unseen data.

[8] VAT Gap is the difference between expected VAT revenues and VAT actually collected. It provides an estimate of revenue loss due to tax fraud, tax evasion and tax avoidance, but also due to bankruptcies, financial insolvencies or miscalculations.

country's financial stability, Poland started implementing a comprehensive plan to strengthen its VAT system. The plan included broadening the catalogue of goods and services subject to the reverse charge mechanism, criminal sanctions, the introduction of split payment and the SAF-T reporting obligation.[9]

In 2017, Poland adopted STIR—an innovative anti-fraud measure aimed at reducing the VAT gap and detecting carousel fraud.[10,11] The abbreviation STIR stands for *System Teleinformatyczny Izby Rozliczeniowej*, which is the Polish name for the IT System of the Clearing House (*Izba Rozliczeniowa*).[12] In simple terms, STIR is a system allowing risk analysis and the exchange of information between the financial sector, the National Revenue Administration (*Krajowa Administracja Skarbowa*) and the Central Register of Tax Data (*Centralny Rejestr Danych Podatkowych*).

Under the STIR system, banks and credit unions must report information on bank accounts and all transactions carried out by entrepreneurs (including the identities of parties to these transactions) to the Clearing House on a daily basis. The Clearing House establishes a risk indicator for each entrepreneur. The risk indicator is calculated by algorithms developed by the Clearing House on the basis of certain criteria used by the financial sector to combat tax fraud. These criteria include *inter alia* customer residence, complex ownership structure and unusual circumstances of transactions. The algorithms used to calculate the risk indicator are kept secret. Taxpayers are not allowed to find out how the risk indicators are determined.

The Clearing House transmits the information received from the banks and the risk indicator to the National Revenue Administration on a daily basis. If the Head of the National Revenue Administration concludes that an entrepreneur is at high risk of being involved in VAT fraud, he may impose administrative measures.[13] These measures include the blocking of a bank account for up to 72 h and cancelling the entrepreneur's VAT registration. Within the period of 72 h, the Head of the National Revenue Administration is expected to examine the case to determine whether there

---

[9] SAF-T (Standard Audit File for Tax) is a standardized electronic file that the OECD developed in 2005 to facilitate the electronic exchange of tax and accounting information between taxpayers and tax authorities. As the trend toward digitalizing tax compliance progressed, the OECD's SAF-T idea began to receive increasing attention across the globe. Many EU countries implemented their own version of the SAF-T file that significantly deviates from the OECD standard.

[10] Carousel fraud is a common form of missing trader fraud where fraudsters exploit the VAT rules providing that the movement of goods between Member States is VAT-free. In carousel fraud, VAT and goods are passed around between companies and jurisdictions, similar to how a carousel revolves.

[11] Act of 24 November 2017 on Preventing the Use of the Financial Sector for VAT fraud (*Ustawa z dnia 24 listopada 2017 r. o zmianie niektórych ustaw w celu przeciwdziałania wykorzystywaniu sektora finansowego do wyłudzeń skarbowych*).

[12] The Clearing House is an entity of the Polish payment system infrastructure. It is responsible for ensuring complete and reliable interbank clearing in PLN and EUR, providing services supporting cashless payments, providing common services and R&D for the Polish banking sector, and providing services supporting participation of the banking sector in the programs for public administration.

[13] In 2019, the authorization to impose administrative measures was extended to the heads of tax and customs offices and directors of the regional chambers of the revenue administration.

is a probability that it concerns tax fraud. The period of 72 h can be extended up to three months if there is a justified suspicion that the entrepreneur will fail to settle his tax liability which exceeds EUR 10,000. As long as the bank account is blocked, the entrepreneur cannot make bank transfers, and no funds can be withdrawn. The Head of the National Revenue Administration may authorize certain payments to be made from a blocked bank account (e.g. tax liabilities, maintenance payments, employee remuneration).

Another administrative measure that may be imposed upon entrepreneurs that are at risk of carrying out fraudulent activities is the refusal or cancellation of their VAT registration. The purpose of this measure is to protect honest taxpayers from entering into transactions with potential fraudsters as a register of persons whose registration has been cancelled or refused is publicly available. The law does not specify what procedural rules apply to the decision to refuse or cancel a VAT registration. Moreover, the Head of the National Revenue Administration does not need to inform the entrepreneur that his VAT registration has been cancelled or refused.

STIR proves to be a useful tool in the fight against VAT fraud as it allows the National Revenue Administration to monitor bank accounts and transactions in nearly real time. The tax administration is immediately informed if a fraudster opens a new bank account to carry out a large transaction or to transfer the funds abroad. In today's fast-paced business environment, speed is a key consideration in preventing carousel fraud. Prior to the STIR implementation, the tax administration was able to detect VAT fraudulent schemes (VAT carousels) after two months of their activity.

According to the information published by the Polish Finance Ministry, in 2018, the STIR system was used to monitor 11.56 million bank accounts of 3.44 million entrepreneurs on the basis of information provided by 619 banks. In 2018, 29,000 entrepreneurs received a high-risk indicator; however, only 23 had their bank accounts blocked (41 bank accounts were blocked in total). In all cases, the blockage was extended beyond the 72-h period. The total amount of funds accumulated in the blocked accounts was PLN 10.3 million (EUR 2.2 million).[14]

In 2019, the number of blocked bank accounts increased by more than five times (from 41 to 566). The STIR system monitored 15.74 million bank accounts of 3.95 million entrepreneurs on the basis of information provided by 614 banks. A high-risk indicator was given to 58,000 entrepreneurs and 120 entrepreneurs had their accounts blocked for 72 h. In almost all cases, the blockage was extended beyond the 72-h period. The total amount of funds accumulated in the blocked accounts was PLN 69.7 million (EUR 15.4 million).[15]

From the taxpayer's perspective, the STIR is clearly a black-box model. The algorithms used to determine the risk indicator are not disclosed. A high-risk indicator plays a fundamental role in the risk assessment by the National Revenue Administration and in deciding whether to apply measures, such as the blockage of a bank account or cancellation of VAT registration. Wrongly getting a high-risk indicator may have disastrous consequences for entrepreneurs. A blocked bank account may

---

[14] National Revenue Administration 2019.

[15] National Revenue Administration 2020.

lead to insolvency and bankruptcy. The cancellation of a VAT registration and the publication of this fact in a special register may cause serious disruptions of business activity. Additionally, the unclarity about procedures applicable to measures taken as a result of a high-risk indicator makes it difficult for entrepreneurs to challenge these decisions.

12.4 Data Protection Legislation

The most compressive data protection legislation ever enacted came into force on 25 May 2018 in the European Union. The General Data Protection Regulation (GDPR) imposes numerous obligations upon organizations regarding how they manage, collect and process individuals' personal data (i.e. any information relating to an identified or identifiable natural person).

Under the GDPR, the individual may determine who can collect his data and how it will be used. To store and process an individual's data without his permission is illegal.[16] The individual must give his consent and he has the right to withdraw his consent at any time, requiring the company to erase all his data (the right to be forgotten).

An important characteristic of the GDPR is its extraterritorial application: the GDPR applies to all organizations processing personal data of individuals residing in the European Union, regardless of their location. The regulation is binding on non-EU businesses that offer goods or services to, or monitor the behavior of, EU individuals. Companies that are found in breach of the GDPR can be fined up to 4% of annual global turnover or EUR 20 million (whichever is greater). This is the maximum fine that can be imposed for the most serious infringements.

The GDPR contains four articles that explicitly address algorithmic decision-making. As they impose strict obligations on the developers of AI models, there have been numerous articles in the media suggesting that the GDPR will slow down the development and use of AI in Europe by holding developers to a standard that is often infeasible.[17]

Article 22 of the GDPR addresses "automated individual decision-making, including profiling." It gives an individual the right to opt out from automatic processing by stating that "The data subject shall have the right not to be subject to a decision based solely on automated processing, including profiling, which produces legal effects concerning him or her or similarly significantly affects him or her." This means that it is not permitted to make decisions about people using an auto-mated process unless they give their consent that automated decision-making can be

---

[16] Other circumstances in which personal data processing is lawful without an individual's consent include, for example, (1) processing that is necessary for the performance of a contract to which the individual is party or in order to take steps at the request of the individual prior to entering into a contract; or (2) processing that is necessary for the performance of a task carried out in the public interest.

[17] Wallace 2017.

used. A company applying automated decision-making tools must implement "suitable measures to safeguard the data subject's rights and freedoms and legitimate interests". Suitable safeguards must include "at least the right to obtain human intervention on the part of the controller, to express his or her point of view and to contest the decision." In other words, individuals who are affected by decisions based on automated processing have the right to have this decision reviewed by a person and to challenge this decision.

Articles 13, 14, and 15 of the GDPR establish the "right to explanation" by requiring organizations handling personal data of EU citizens to provide them with an explanation as to how an automated decision has been arrived at ("meaningful information about the logic involved") and the consequences of that decision.

The Guidelines on Automated Decision-Making note that "complexity is no excuse for failing to provide information."[18] The organization must mention "factors taken into account for the decision-making process" and "their respective 'weight' at an aggregate level." The Guidelines list examples of information that should be provided to individuals: (1) the categories of data that have been or will be used in the profiling or decision-making process, (2) why these categories are considered pertinent, (3) how any profile used in the automated decision-making process is built, including any statistics used in the analysis, (3) why this profile is relevant to the automated decision-making process, and (4) how it is used for a decision concerning the individual. The organization does need to provide a complex mathematical explanation about how algorithms work or disclose the algorithm itself, but the information provided must be comprehensive enough for the individual to act upon it—to contest a decision, or to correct inaccuracies or to request erasure.

The GDPR creates a barrier to using black-box models to make decisions about individuals if a suitable explanatory mechanism does not exist. Whereas the white-box models (i.e. linear models and decision trees) can explain themselves, it is often not practical or even possible, to explain decisions made by more complex machine learning algorithms. Ensemble methods or neural networks pose the biggest challenge as predictions result from an aggregation or averaging procedure. The requirements for explicability and manual intervention that are mandated by the GDPR can have significant impact on the costs of developing and maintaining automated decision-making systems. These costs need to be included into the cost-benefit analysis undertaken before the project begins.

When evaluating the STIR system from the GDPR perspective, it must be noted that it does not subject individuals to purely automated decisions. Although the risk indicator is determined by secret algorithms, it is reviewed by a person (the Head of the National Revenue Administration and other authorized officials). The statistics (58,000 entrepreneurs with a high-risk indicator but only 120 had their accounts blocked in 2019) indicate that the human review is not a mere formality.

However, it may be questionable whether the STIR system is in line with the right to explanation laid down by the GDPR. An individual against whom sanctions (72-h blockage of the bank account) are imposed does not have an opportunity to quickly

---

[18] Article 29 Data Protection Working Party 2018.

contest this decision or to provide an explanation for a high-risk indicator. He is just informed about the decision to block his bank account after the measure has taken effect. On the one hand, an anti-fraud tool would not be efficient if fraudsters were informed about potential sanctions beforehand. Also, if the underlying logic of the algorithm became public, fraudsters could structure their activities so as to avoid detection. On the other hand, a person subject to sanctions is entitled to receive an explanation on which grounds these measures are taken. To make the STIR system entirely "GDPR-proof", the affected entrepreneurs should be provided with reasons for which they are suspect of VAT fraud.

12.5 Fundamental Human Rights

In Europe, the legal framework for the protection of human rights consists of many sources. They include the European Convention for the Protection of Human Rights and Fundamental Freedoms (ECHR), general principles of EU law, the EU Treaties, the Charter of Fundamental Rights of the European Union (EU Charter) and various national fundamental rights guarantees (e.g. constitutional principles).

As there is a significant overlap among the fundamental rights protected by all these sources, the reminder of this section will focus on the ECHR. Signed in 1950, this international convention has 47 signatory countries, including all EU Member States. The ECHR guarantees lie behind many of the general principles of EU law and its provisions were used as a basis for the EU Charter. Article 52(3) of the EU Charter mentions that the meaning and scope of the fundamental rights it seeks to protect shall be the same as those laid down by the ECHR. However, the ECHR should operate as a minimum standard, not preventing the European Union from providing more extensive human rights protections.

One of the fundamental guarantees established by the ECHR is the right to fair trial (article 6 of the ECHR), which guarantees the right of an accused to participate effectively in a criminal trial. This includes not only the right to be present, but also the right to hear and follow the proceedings. Although article 6 of the ECHR refers to "criminal charges", it can also be invoked in the context of taxation if a measure is imposed on the basis of a legal rule with both a deterrent and a punitive purpose of exerting pressure on taxpayers to comply with their obligations.[19] The right to fair trial applies not only to the trial stage but throughout the entire process: from the investigation to the final decision. The right to fair trial includes the following two minimum guarantees: the equality of arms and the right of defence.

Equality of arms is an inherent feature of a fair trial. It requires each party be given a reasonable opportunity to present his case under conditions that do not place him at a disadvantage vis-à-vis his opponent. The European Count for Human Rights (ECtHR) ruled that equality of arms may be breached when the accused has limited

---

[19] ECHR 2019.

access to his case file or other documents on public-interest grounds.[20] In other words, unrestricted access to the case file is an important element of a fair trial. In another case, the ECtHR held that the failure to lay down procedural rules in legislation may breach equality of arms since the purpose of such rules is to protect the defendant against any abuse of authority and it is therefore the defense which is the most likely to suffer from omissions and lack of clarity in such rules.[21]

Another key element in determining whether the proceedings as a whole were fair is the right of defence. The right of defence includes the right to be promptly informed of the nature and cause of the accusation. The accused must be provided with sufficient information to understand fully the extent of the charges against him.[22] He must be given an opportunity to challenge the authenticity of the evidence and to oppose its use. In addition, the quality of the evidence must be taken into consideration, as must the circumstances in which it was obtained and whether these circumstances cast doubt on its reliability or accuracy. The Court of Justice of the European Union (CJEU) held that the observance of the right of defence is a general principle of EU law and applies if the tax authorities adopt a measure which will adversely affect an individual. This principle requires the addressees of decisions which significantly affect their interests be placed in a position in which they can effectively make known their views as regards the information on which the authorities intend to base their decision.[23]

The right of defence and equality of arms mean that taxpayers must be placed in a position in which they can effectively make known their views about information on which the authorities base their decisions. This indicates that the tax administration must give reasons for its decision. The affected individual must have proper access to his case file. A decision that is made solely on the basis of a black-box model will likely be in conflict with the right of defence and equality of arms. If the taxpayer is not aware how the decision was reached, there is no fair balance between the parties. The taxpayer is hindered in his ability to provide evidence as he does not understand which objective factors were taken into account by the algorithm making the decision. Therefore, the use of black-box models may be questioned from the perspective of the right to fair trial.

As the Polish STIR system allows the Head of the National Revenue Administration to impose measures of punitive and deterrent character (blockage of the bank account or cancellation of VAT registration) and is targeted at preventing a criminal offence (VAT fraud), it falls within the scope of the right to fair trial. The fact that the algorithms used to determine the risk score are kept secret means that the addressee of these punitive measures does not know the objective facts that triggered the application of the sanctions. The entrepreneur is not provided with sufficient information

---

[20] ECHR, 24 April 2007, *Matyjek v. Poland* [2007] ECHR 317; ECHR, 9 October 2008, *Moiseyev v. Russia*, [2008] ECHR 1031.

[21] ECHR, 22 June 2000, *Coëme and Others v. Belgium*, [2000] ECHR 250.

[22] ECHR, 25 July 2000, *Mattoccia v. Italy*, [2000] ECHR 383.

[23] CJEU, 17 December 2015, *WebMindLicenses Kft. v. Nemzeti Adó- és Vámhivatal Kiemelt Adó- és Vám Főigazgatóság*, C-419/14.

to understand fully the extent of the charges against him, and this puts him at a disadvantage as opposed to the tax administration and creates imbalance between the parties. Moreover, the entrepreneur is deprived of a possibility to challenge the 72-h bank account blockage.

Although the STIR system puts significant restrictions on the right to fair trial, the ECtHR held on numerous occasions that the fundamental rights may be limited if it is strictly necessary to safeguard public interests and the measures employed are reasonably proportionate to the legitimate aim they seek to achieve. The STIR system pursues a legitimate objective in the public interest as it seeks to combat VAT fraud and prevent revenue losses. Disclosing the algorithms would reduce the STIR's effectiveness in fighting VAT fraud as fraudsters would structure their transactions so as to avoid detection. However, it is questionable whether the STIR system complies with the principle of proportionality. The non-disclosure of reasons for which the punitive measures were applied and the lack of possibility to challenge these measures impose serious limitations of the right to fair trial. A less restrictive and more proportional solution would be to provide the taxpayer with the grounds for the decision at the time the sanction is imposed upon him and establish procedural rules to challenge the punitive measures. On the other hand, the Polish law ensures that STIR sanctions are imposed only where there is a strong suspicion of VAT fraud. STIR sanctions cannot be applied by ordinary tax inspectors: the only person that can use them is the Head of the National Revenue Administration. This could be interpreted as limiting punitive measures to what is strictly necessary for an effective tax collection.

12.6   Conclusions

AI-powered algorithms can be used to make more accurate, cheaper and faster decisions than those made by humans in the area of taxation. However, just like humans, algorithms may make mistakes or may be biased. Therefore, appropriate checks and balances need to be put in place to prevent misuse of decision-making systems that rely on machine learning.

In developing new models for the tax administration, accuracy should not be the overriding consideration. Having an explicable model is far more important than having a model that is slightly more accurate but much less understood by regulators and business users. When building a model, the transparency and explicability of the resulting solution should be considered in light of the applicable legal framework. Black-box models that produce very accurate but inexplicable outcomes may not be a good option as they may conflict with legislation protecting personal data or fundamental human rights.

The GDPR has established the "right to explanation" in the case where automated decision-making systems are used, and the ECHR requires an individual to be promptly provided with sufficient information of the nature and cause of penalizing measures. Both legal frameworks have significant legal implications for the design and deployment of automated data processing systems. It can be predicted that algorithmic auditing and transparency will become key considerations for enterprises deploying machine learning systems both inside and outside of the European Union.

To achieve a proper level of transparency in algorithmic decision-making, it should be ensured that any decisions produced by an automated system can be explained to people affected by them. These explanations must be understandable by the target audience. Also, it should be clear who has the authority to review and potentially reverse algorithmic decisions. Finally, algorithms should be monitored and regularly checked to ensure their societal relevance and up-to-dateness.

References

Article 29 Data Protection Working Party (2018) Guidelines on Automated Individual Decision-Making and Profiling for the Purposes of Regulation 2016/679. Adopted on 3 October 2017. As last Revised and Adopted on 6 February 2018. https://ec.europa.eu/newsroom/article29/items/612053 Accessed 28 June 2021.

ECHR (2019) Guide on Article 6 of the European Convention on Human Rights, Right to a fair trial (criminal limb). https://www.echr.coe.int/documents/guide_art_6_criminal_eng.pdf Accessed 28 June 2021.

National Revenue Administration (2019) 2018 Annual Report on Preventing the Use of Banks and Credit Unions for VAT fraud purposes (*Sprawozdanie za 2018 rok w zakresie przeciwdziałania wykorzystywaniu działalności banków i spółdzielczych kas oszczędnościowo-kredytowych do celów mających związek z wyłudzeniami*).

National Revenue Administration (2020) 2019 Annual Report on Preventing the Use of Banks and Credit Unions for VAT fraud purposes (*Sprawozdanie za 2019 rok w zakresie przeciwdziałania wykorzystywaniu działalności banków i spółdzielczych kas oszczędnościowo-kredytowych do celów mających związek z wyłudzeniami*).

Wallace N (2017) EU's Right to Explanation: A Harmful Restriction on Artificial Intelligence. https://www.techzone360.com/topics/techzone/articles/2017/01/25/429101-eus-right-explanation-harmful-restriction-artificial-intelligence.htm Accessed 28 June 2021.

Aleksandra Bal is a tax and technology specialist. She has worked for companies in the software and information services industry, leading the development of digital solutions and software for tax professionals. She holds a PhD in International Taxation (Leiden University), Executive MBA (Rotterdam School of Management), LLM International Tax Law (Maastricht University), MSc Tax Management (Maastricht University) as well as other degrees. She has published over 70 articles in tax journals and is a frequent speaker at tax events. Aleksandra is the author of *Taxation, virtual currency and blockchain* (Wolters Kluwer, 2018)—the first book to examine the taxation of virtual currency from a comparative perspective.

This chapter was written in a personal capacity and does not reflect the views of the organisation the author is affiliated to.

Part III
Private Law

Chapter 13
Bridging the Liability Gaps: Why AI Challenges the Existing Rules on Liability and How to Design Human-empowering Solutions

Silvia De Conca

Contents

Abstract This chapter explores the so-called 'liability gaps' that occurs when, in applying existing contractual, extra-contractual, or strict liability rules to harms caused by AI, the inherent characteristics of AI may result in unsatisfying outcomes, in particular for the damaged party. The chapter explains the liability gaps, investigating which features of AI challenge the application of traditional legal solutions and why. Subsequently, this chapter explores the challenges connected to the different possible solutions, including contract law, extra-contractual law, product liability, mandatory insurance, company law, and the idea of granting legal personhood to AI and robots. The analysis is carried out using hypothetical scenarios, to highlight both the abstract and practical implications of AI, based on the roles and interactions of the various parties involved. As a conclusion, this chapter offers an overview of the fundamental principles and guidelines that should be followed to elaborate a comprehensive and effective strategy to bridge the liability gaps. The argument made

S. De Conca (✉)
Transnational Legal Studies Department, Vrije Universiteit Amsterdam, Amsterdam,
The Netherlands
e-mail: s.deconca@vu.nl

© T.M.C. ASSER PRESS and the authors 2022
B. Custers and E. Fosch-Villaronga (eds.), *Law and Artificial Intelligence*,
Information Technology and Law Series 35,
https://doi.org/10.1007/978-94-6265-523-2_13

is that the guiding principle in designing legal solutions to the liability gaps must be the protection of individuals, particularly their dignity, rights and interests.

Keywords Artificial Intelligence · Contract law · Damages · European law · Liability · Tort

13.1 Introduction

In the autumn of 2019, software developer David Heinemeier Hansson and his wife applied for Apple Card, a brand-new credit card service offered by Apple Inc. and issued by Goldman Sachs. Much to their surprise, when their Apple Cards were issued, they discovered that Mr. Hansson's credit limit was 20 times that of his wife. Some factual circumstances made this difference particularly troubling: the couple had been married for a long time in a community-property regime, filed joint tax returns, and Mr. Hansson even had a lower credit score than his wife![1] The couple suspected that the algorithm had learned to discriminate against women. They contacted Apple's customer support, which re-directed them to Goldman Sachs. The latter affirmed they were certain that there was no discrimination of Mrs. Hansson and that some other factors had probably influenced the decision. Which factors, however, they could not tell, because neither they nor Apple knew exactly how the complex algorithm tasked with screening the customers had reached its decision.[2] The couple took it to Twitter to voice their terrible suspicion and discovered they were not alone: several other cases emerged—including the one of Steve Wozniak, Apple's co-founder, whose wife had also been discriminated against by Apple Card.[3] Eventually, the Apple Card service was put under investigation by the New York State Department of Financial Services.[4]

The case of Apple Card's involuntary algorithmic discrimination against women is paradigmatic: it shows that when an AI system[5] damages a person, uncertainties arise regarding which subject should be liable for the damage and its redress. These uncertainties, as will be explained below, derive from technological and organizational factors that challenge the traditional balances and solutions provided by private

---

[1] Vincent (2019) Apple's credit card is being investigated for discriminating against women https://www.theverge.com/2019/11/11/20958953/apple-credit-card-gender-discrimination-algorithms-black-box-investigation. Accessed 19 February 2021.

[2] Ibid.

[3] Ibid.

[4] Vigdor (2019) Apple Card Investigated After Gender Discrimination Complaints https://www.nytimes.com/2019/11/10/business/Apple-credit-card-investigation.html. Accessed 19 February 2021. Please note that as of February 2021 no additional information on the investigation or its outcomes appears to have been made available.

[5] In this chapter, AI system indicates a product, device, service, or machine deploying a form of AI. AI should be intended in this chapter as any Machine Learning or other data analytics techniques presenting the capability to achieve a certain objective with a significant degree of autonomy, following supervised or unsupervised learning or other forms of software learning capability.

law regarding damages and liability. As a result, gaps are created in the existing legal regimes that jeopardize the possibility for damaged parties to obtain redress. It is to these gaps, referred to as the liability gaps, that this chapter is dedicated. The analysis focuses on the issues connected to the liability gaps for damages caused by AI from a European perspective, leveraging the efforts and initiatives of European policymakers, as well as the lively debate happening among experts and scholars.

Section 13.2 offers a definition of the liability gaps, with an overview of the main features of AI systems that challenge the traditional allocation of legal liability among the relevant parties. Subsequently, Sect. 13.3 explores the main doctrinal solutions suggested so far to bridge the liability gaps, spanning from contract and extra-contractual law to corporate law, insurance, and even to the idea of granting a form of legal agency to AI. The analysis is developed using hypothetical scenarios describing various AI systems deployed in different settings: financial services, autonomous vehicles, and smart consumer products. Finally, Sect. 13.4 concludes the chapter, offering principles and guidelines that should be taken into consideration in elaborating a solution to the liability gaps. In doing so, Sect. 13.4 stresses the importance of maintaining a human-centred perspective while designing a combined approach to intervene at different levels, adjusting existing regulations and introducing new ones, where necessary.

13.2 Mind the Gap: The Disruption to the Liability Rules Caused by AI

The term 'liability gaps' refers to a situation in which, in the presence of damages, the allocation of legal liability to the parties involved is disrupted by certain circumstances. Due to the disruption, the existing legal institutes do not provide satisfactory tools to remedy the harms suffered, and the damaged parties might be unable to obtain redress.[6]

Typically, whenever damages occur, the allocation of liability would depend on some or all of the following elements: the existence of the damage, any relationship existing among the parties involved, possible conducts that the parties were supposed to adhere to according to the law, the actual conduct of the parties, the existence of defects if the damage derives from a product, the causal link between the conduct and the damage, the nature of the damage.

As an example, consider the case of a driver that, while backing out of a parking spot, hits and damages a neighbour's letterbox. Temporarily leaving aside the fact that most European countries provide for a special liability regime for car accidents, it is nevertheless possible to identify the main elements based on which the liability is ascribed. As represented in Fig. 13.1, the two main parties involved are the driver (indicated by way of Alice in the figure) and the neighbour (indicated by way of

---

[6] The phenomenon is often referred to as responsibility gaps or liability gaps, cfr, among many, Johnson 2015, p. 2, Bertolini 2013, p. 231, European Commission 2019, p. 17.

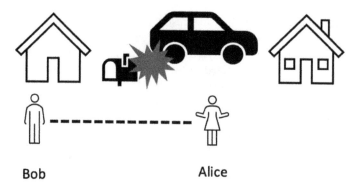

Fig. 13.1. Alice accidentally crashes into her neighbour Bob's letterbox [*Source* The author]

Bob). The dotted line between them represents the relation between the two: they are connected by the event itself, which is accidental, random, and not persistent over time (hopefully). Their personal spheres came into contact because of the damage to the letterbox and are not connected by any form of pre-existing contract or agreement. With regard to Alice's conduct, the law imposes certain duties on drivers, due to the potential dangers connected with cars. By behaving in a more careful way, for instance looking into the car's mirror, Alice could have prevented the accident. Alice's behaviour (driving without checking the mirrors) is the source of the damage (the broken letterbox), which can be easily quantified in the cost of a new letterbox (or of the repairs to the damaged one).[7]

Emerging technologies can disrupt the allocation of liability, interfering with the elements listed above. The arrival of new technologies, as well as the novel application of existing technologies, can often give life to an initial period of regulatory uncertainty,[8] during which liability gaps might become evident, until a proper liability solution is established by the legislator. This was, for instance, the case of industrial machines in the 19th century United States. At the time, the country suffered a staggering increase of accidents involving steam-powered heavy machinery.[9] The numbers and circumstances being unprecedented, it was not clear initially who was liable and how the damaged individuals could obtain redress. Throughout the second half of the 19th and the beginning of the 20th century, attempts were made at deploying existing legal and institutional mechanisms to solve this novel problem, until a branch of tort law prevailed, becoming the main framework for the regulation

---

[7] The example is a simplification. In real life, special liability regimes would create a presumption of fault of Alice. Alice would have a mandatory civil responsibility insurance to cover possible damages occurred while driving. Furthermore, additional parties might be involved, such as the manufacturer of the car or of any of its components, that might exempt Alice from any liability or to which she could demand to be indemnified, in case of defects or malfunctioning.

[8] Pagallo et al. 2018, p. 19.

[9] Witt 2001, p. 694.

of damages caused by heavy machinery and other kinds of machines (sometimes referred to as accident law).[10]

In the case of AI, several factors contribute to the emergence of liability gaps and, in particular, the fact that AI systems are composed of several hardware and software parts interacting with each other, sometimes in unpredictable manners; the many actors involved, such as the various manufacturers and providers of the different components, as well as possible intermediaries and developers of connected applications or products; the capability of the algorithm to learn from data sets, changing over time; the changes that updates might induce to the software component sometimes triggering new or unexpected vulnerabilities or problems.[11]

AI systems are particularly complex, because they are composed of several hardware and software parts, and often developed at the crossroads of different industries besides computer science (such as robotics, healthcare, automotive, cloud computing, Internet of Things or IoT, telecommunications, and so on). From this complexity, two disruptive factors emerge: the presence of several actors, potentially responsible for the various components, the programming, the data sets based on which the algorithm elaborates its models; and the additional layer of unpredictability deriving from the ways in which the AI element might interact with the various components, with interconnected technologies (for instance, the IoT, where several 'smart' devices interact with each other), or even with the humans around it.[12]

AI-based products are not as static as their traditional counterparts but change over time. First and foremost, they change because the AI keeps learning and evolving based on the data collected from sensors and other sources. AI is inherently dynamic and designed to learn, respond to external stimuli, and elaborate new solutions to reach a goal. AI systems also change over time because, like many other digital technologies, they require periodical updates to fix vulnerabilities and/or errors in their functioning (the infamous bugs).[13]

Some of these factors are not new (like the presence of several components and parties, or the updates), and merely enhance problems that have already emerged in the past with other technologies. The capability to learn over time, instead, is specific to Artificial Intelligence and represents a new challenge for the law.

Each of the abovementioned factors can have a disruptive effect on the essential elements of the allocation of liability. The presence of several different components, and the possibility of unexpected effects deriving from their interaction, can affect the causal link between the conduct of the parties and the damage.[14] Consider, for instance, a smart thermostat, composed of temperature and humidity sensors distributed around the house and a central thermostat unit: possible errors in the temperature-setting of the thermostat might be the consequence of an erroneous data collection in the sensor, of a defect in the physical components of the sensors, or

---

[10] Witt 2001, p. 745.

[11] European Commission 2019, p. 21.

[12] Leenes et al. 2017, p. 9.

[13] European Commission 2019, p. 21.

[14] Scherer 2016, p. 363.

of the software optimizing and analysing all the data collected. If the thermostat is also connected to other IoT devices around the house, errors in the collection and analysis of the data collected by these other devices, or defects in their components, might also affect the smart thermostat. The interaction of several components and devices can give unexpected results, which makes it difficult to identify the origin of the damage. It also multiplies the actors involved. For the smart thermostat, the parties involved might include not only the manufacturer of the thermostat itself, but also the manufacturers of the sensors, other components (like processors or motherboards), or other devices (and of their components). The presence of several actors affects the identification of the conduct that the parties should have adhered to: each party involved is bound by a certain duty of care and professional standards, based on each field and the relative state of the art.

The same disruptive effect on the causal link can derive from the learning capability of AI. The autonomy of AI can challenge the traditional human-centred perspective of liability.[15] If the above-mentioned thermostat has 'learned' autonomously (by elaborating a certain model based on the data collected) how to regulate humidity and temperature in the house, is the manufacturer responsible for possible damages? Is it a defect or a design error if an AI autonomously learns a certain behaviour? If an AI system learns from the data derived from the behaviour of its users, are these users responsible for training the algorithm?[16] These elements appear difficult to reconcile with the traditional approach of the law, which is based on products that do not react to external input in an autonomous (or semi-autonomous) way, but whose behaviour is entirely anticipated and pre-programmed by their manufacturers. The learning capability of AI also increases the possibilities that a machine might cause not only damages that are patrimonial in nature, but also pure economic loss or even psychological and existential (as is the case with the discrimination of women carried out by the algorithm of Apple Card). The nature of the damages can affect the possibility to obtain redress, because not all legal systems regulate psychological, existential, or pure economic loss.[17]

13.3 State of the Art: Proposed Legal Solutions to the Liability Gaps

Several possible solutions to the liability gaps created by AI systems have been explored by experts and European policy makers. Overall, there is consensus on the

---

[15] In most legal systems only humans that are capable and of age are liable, even if the damage has been caused by a machine, an animal, or an underage or incapable person (with few exceptions). Cfr. Asaro et al. 2011, p. 176, Pagallo 2012, p. 55.

[16] Pagallo 2013b, p. 504, Asaro 2011, p. 174.

[17] There is no universal definition of pure economic loss, and the rules concerning it vary widely among European countries. As a general definition, pure economic loss entails the suffering of an economic loss not connected to a pre-existing harm. Cfr. Bussani and Palmer 2003.

fact that currently the law offers tools to address damages caused by AI systems, but the existing tools might present shortcomings that lead to undesirable or less optimal results.[18] The application of the main existing legal tools to the liability gaps for damages caused by AI systems is illustrated below, using hypothetical scenarios.

13.3.1 Contractual and Extra-contractual Liability (Fault or Negligence)

In all European legal systems, civil liability (as opposed to criminal liability) derives from the breach of an obligation. The source of the obligation determines the kind of liability. The two main sources of obligations are contracts and delicts.[19]

By entering into a contract, the parties agree to comply with certain obligations, such as providing a product or service and, in return, paying the price. The breach of contractual obligations gives life, therefore, to the contractual liability of the party that did not comply with the obligation (unless certain excusatory circumstances occur).[20]

Extra-contractual liability (tort in common law jurisdictions) occurs when two or more parties are not in a contract or in any other form of sanctioned relationship but, due to the behaviour of one party, the other suffers a damage.[21] In this case, the behaviour of the damaging party breaches a general duty of not causing harm (*neminem laedere*) either intentionally (fault) or because of negligence. In general, extra-contractual liability applies when two strangers come into contact and one of the two is damaged by the actions of the other: this is, for instance, the case of a passer-by hit by a vase falling from a window. The person living in the house from which the vase fell is liable to pay the damages, because of negligent behaviour resulting in the breach of the general duty of care (i.e., not harming anyone). Extra-contractual liability can also be applied regardless of fault or negligence, in the form of the so-called strict liability for special categories of activities or products.

Most 'grey area' cases should be traced back to either contractual or extra-contractual liability, based on the origin of the obligation: if a contract cannot be identified in the relationship between the parties, then the obligation (and the liability deriving from it) would be put under the extra-contractual umbrella. This distinction has concrete consequences, in particular with regard to the burden of proof and prescription. Contractual liability usually puts the burden of proof on the party that has breached the contract (and not on the damaged party), with longer prescription times (up to 10 years in some European countries). Within extra-contractual liability the burden of proof is on the subject who brings the action (the damaged party)

---

[18] Johnson 2014, p. 2, European Commission 2019, p. 16.

[19] von Bar and Drobnig 2009.

[20] Fauvarque-Cosson and Mazeaud 2009.

[21] Ibid.

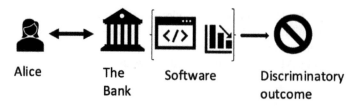

Fig. 13.2 A simplified representation relationship between Alice and The Bank. Alice has a contractual relationship with The Bank, whose software produces a discriminatory outcome [*Source* The author]

and prescription is usually of maximum 5 years.[22] The burden of proof is important with regard to AI systems, because their opacity, the fact that they are proprietary knowledge of a party, and the necessity to hire expensive experts to analyse them, represent factual barriers to the access to justice for damaged parties.[23]

Both contractual and extra-contractual liability can apply to cases of damages caused by an AI system, depending on the underlying obligations and relationships existing among the parties involved. Currently, however, applying any of these two types of liability to AI systems might give unsatisfactory results, as will be illustrated by the scenarios below and in the next subsection, respectively.

13.3.2 Scenario A: Alice and The Bank

The first hypothetical scenario starts with a "simple" two-actor situation: an individual and a company. In a situation similar to the case of Apple Card, Alice applies with a bank (The Bank) for a credit (see Fig. 13.2). The Bank uses predictive analytics software to select which applicants can obtain the credit. The software rejects Alice's application. It appears that the reason for the rejection can be traced back to a bias accidentally incorporated by the software in the models created from training data sets. The Bank, however, claims that it does not know the reasons behind the software's decision, denies the existence of biases, and affirms that it cannot be held accountable for the algorithmic outcome. From the perspective of liability, it can be difficult to identify the obligations of The Bank and, consequently, whether The Bank is in breach: The Bank is not obliged to grant Alice the credit.[24] Due to the opacity of the AI technology involved, it is also not easy to identify possible involuntary discrimination or whether The Bank wilfully instructed the algorithm. If the

---

[22] Marsh 1994, Farnsworth 2006.

[23] Pagallo 2013a, p. 135, European Commission 2019, p. 51.

[24] Please note that the relationship between Alice and The Bank might be either contractual or precontractual, depending on the kind of documents exchanged and the rules existing in a certain jurisdiction. The existence of a contractual or pre-contractual relationship does not automatically imply the existence of contractual liability in this case, because the damage derives from discrimination, which is an action prohibited by the law.

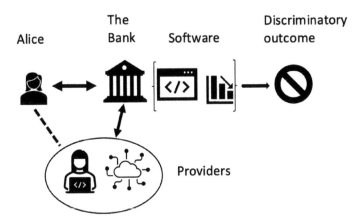

Fig. 13.3 The relationship between Alice and The Bank is complicated by the presence of the Providers, who provided The Bank with the AI software and the datasets to train it [*Source* The author]

discrimination is identified and traced back to the algorithm learning a bias from the input data, the causal connection between the damage (the discrimination) and the conduct of The Bank is particularly weak.

This scenario is complicated by two additional factors. The first one is that other parties, for instance, the company developing the algorithm or a third-party company providing the dataset to train the AI (called Providers in Fig. 13.3), might also play a role. The discrimination might be connected to the actions of the Providers, who do not have a contract with Alice (the dotted line in Fig. 13.3).

The position of Alice vis-à-vis the Providers can be traced back to extra-contractual liability. If they provided The Bank with a component or software that results in harm to a third party, they breach a general principle of not harming. The extra-contractual liability regime is less favourable to Alice under several perspectives. It affects the burden of proof, the prescription, and in general the kind of compensation Alice might be entitled to. With regard to the burden of proof, for instance, should this case be considered as extra-contractual liability, in many jurisdictions Alice would have to prove the damage, its economic value, the causal connection with the behaviour of one of the additional parties, as well as their fault or even intent to damage her.[25] This is a significant burden of proof, especially because Alice would hardly have access to the AI and would most likely need to hire an expert to support her claim, which would be expensive. These circumstances would affect the access to justice and the possibility to obtain redress.

The complexity of this scenario is worsened by the fact that the kind of prejudice suffered by Alice can fall into the pure economic loss (Alice might not be able to purchase a house, or start a company, and so on) and/or into moral damage (discrimination). The possibility to obtain redress for any of these types of prejudice have

---

[25] Pagallo 2012, p. 55, Pagallo 2013a, p. 115, Karnow 2016, p. 51.

been and often still are debated in many legal systems and is often excluded in case of extra-contractual liability.[26]

It is important to consider that Alice has suffered a prejudice in her rights (economic means, potential lack of chances and the right not to be discriminated against). Furthermore, Alice trusted The Bank, assuming that in assessing her application it would have acted diligently and used professional care, not following biases and discriminatory behaviour. In this scenario, the law offers tools for the damaged party in the form of contractual or extra-contractual liability rules. These tools appear, however, insufficient to ensure that the damages or losses suffered by a party are moved back into the sphere of those parties that had control over the cause of the damage and/or that benefited from it.

13.3.3 Another Form of Extra-contractual Liability: Strict Liability

European legal systems generally provide for special forms of extra-contractual/tort liability, with limited application. This is the case for strict liability and its derivatives, namely product liability, liability from driving automobiles (or other forms of registered movable property like airplanes or ships), as well as sector-specific regimes (special provisions exist for doctors, stock market brokers and financial institutions, teachers, and so on).[27]

In the context of these special forms of liability, usually the requisite of negligence or fault is withdrawn, and the burden of proof is often simplified or reversed: it is the damaging party that must prove that its conduct did not cause the damage or that all reasonable efforts have been made to avoid the damage, while the damaged party only needs to prove that the damage occurred, the defect, and the connection between the two.[28] The configuration of these forms of special liability makes them particularly appropriate to deal with dangerous activities (driving) or situations of asymmetry of information or power (consumer products).

Forms of special or strict liability could be applied to situations in which AI systems cause damages, to correct some of the shortcomings highlighted in the previous section. However, strict liability, product liability, liability from traffic accidents, and the other special regimes are exceptions to the norm. They cannot be used as a general rule, and their applicability is limited to certain circumstances, activities, or industries. Their deployment with damages caused by AI systems could only be possible for certain applications. For instance, the liability regime for automobiles could apply to autonomous vehicles[29] (the so called self-driving cars), while

---

[26] European Commission 2019, p. 51.

[27] Buyuksagis and van Boom 2013, p. 609.

[28] Ibid.

[29] Royakkers and van Est 2016, p. 185.

product liability could apply to smart consumer products.[30] The application of special liability regimes to AI is not without uncertainties and grey areas: it might not solve the liability gaps but reiterate them, as shown in the scenarios below.

Alternatively, a solution could be to create a special liability *ad hoc* for AI, to deal specifically with the liability gaps it creates.[31] While the idea appears tempting, it would most likely be unfeasible: AI presents a wide range of applications and uses, in almost every industry and sector. A unique regime applicable to all of this would likely be impossible. For this reason, the idea has been put forward to create special liability regimes for certain applications of AI that are high risk.[32] This would likely offer a solution at least for some liability gaps that emerge in connection with the use of AI. However, in determining what applications pose high-risks, legislators need to consider that, besides the most prominent examples (such as autonomous weapons and autonomous vehicles, due to their potential to injure or kill individuals),[33] trivial and daily AI products might still be prejudicial to the fundamental rights of individuals (as the Apple Card case shows). The more individuals carry out their lives immerged into digital and 'smart' environments, the higher the risks that even minor AI applications present important negative consequences.[34] The proposal for an AI Regulation made public by the European Commission in 2021 seems to acknowledge this, as it lists among the high-risk AI systems not only life-threatening applications, but also systems used to determine the access to education, to welfare and benefits, or AI software for recruitment.[35]

13.3.4   Scenario B: Alice and Autonomous Vehicles

The beginning of Sect. 13.2 shows the allocation of liability when a driving accident results in damages to property (Fig. 13.1). What happens if Alice, instead of driving a traditional car, "drives" an autonomous vehicle?

It has been highlighted that the introduction of AI systems can increase the complexity of a situation, because of the opacity of the algorithm and the presence of multiple actors due to interoperable technologies. This is also the case with regard to autonomous vehicles. In a traditional, 'dumb' car, the driver is assumed to be liable, under a special liability regime. In some cases, if the driver can prove that

---

[30] Asaro et al. 2011, p. 170, Bertolini 2013.

[31] Bertolini 2013, p. 219.

[32] European Commission 2018, 2019.

[33] UNESCO 2017, p. 19.

[34] This idea has been brought forward at the Sixth T.M.C. Asser Annual Lecture, given by Prof. Andrew Murray and entitled 'Almost Human: Law and Human Agency in the Time of Artificial Intelligence' that took place online on 26 November 2020. See also Murray 2021.

[35] Proposal for a Regulation of the European Parliament and of the Council laying down harmonised rules on Artificial Intelligence (Artificial Intelligence Act) and amending certain Union legislative acts, of 21 April 2021 [2021/0106(COD)], Annex III.

the damage is the result of a defect or manufacturing of the car, the manufacturer will be liable, either alone or together with the driver.[36]

In this scenario, even though Alice is sitting in the driver's seat, the car is backing out of the parking spot by itself, based on the analysis of the data collected by its multiple sensors. Technically, Alice is not driving the car and does not have control over the decisions taken by the car itself. When the car hits the neighbour's letterbox, different hypotheses can be advanced about who is liable for the damage.

Initially, when the Sci-Fi dream of a car driving itself started to become a reality, the circumstance that the driver was not in control of the driving created some doubts about whether or not the driver could be considered liable.[37] It should, however, be taken into consideration that the driver of the autonomous vehicle, the individual that is being transported by the autonomous vehicle, can be assumed to be liable for the mere fact of owning and/or operating it without driving.[38] This solution is based on the fact that Alice is not in control of the decisions taken by the autonomous vehicle, but benefits from using it. This solution is currently already in use in those jurisdictions that allow for autonomous and semi-autonomous vehicles to circulate on the road. Usually, the driver is also obliged to have an additional insurance, or a traditional civil responsibility insurance that also covers damages deriving from autonomous vehicles.[39]

Other parties might also be involved. The accident might be due to a defect in one of the car's components (e.g., the sensors failed and did not inform the system driving the car of the presence of an obstacle), or to an error of the car's software (e.g., the sensors detected the obstacle, but the AI software did not understand the data correctly). If, as it is currently prospected, autonomous vehicles in the future will circulate in a smart infrastructure, communicating at all times with the road, other autonomous vehicles, and traffic lights, the accidents might also result from an error or defect of the infrastructure. In case of a system failure of the autonomous vehicle or of the infrastructure, the car manufacturer, as well as the entities in charge of the infrastructure or its components might also be liable, either alone or with the driver. It is important to consider that with AI systems it can be difficult to identify defects, malfunctioning, or errors. These systems are complex and opaque, and often even the manufacturers and programmers cannot be certain of the reasons why a particular decision was taken. The following scenario shows how AI systems challenge the way in which errors or defects are defined.

---

[36] Royakkers and van Est 2016, p. 185.

[37] Marchant and Lindor 2012, p. 1326.

[38] European Commission 2019, p. 39.

[39] Hevelke and Nida-Rümelin 2015, Marchant and Lindor 2012, p. 1339.

Fig. 13.4 Alice's coffee maker pours coffee on the countertop based on its own elaboration of Alice's habits [*Source* The author]

AI-coffee maker   Alice

13.3.5 Scenario C: Alice and the Smart Home

Many AI systems are marketed to consumers, that is, their target buyers are individuals that will use them for personal use and not commercial or work-related purposes.[40] These include an array of IoT devices (smart speakers, fridges, coffee makers, mattresses, light bulbs, children's toys, even toothbrushes and sex toys). If traditional, 'dumb' products are prejudicial to a consumer or his/her patrimony, the European regime for consumer protection applies. Under this regime, the producers and resellers of a product are liable for the damages. The burden of proof is simplified for the damaged consumer, who must prove the damage, the defect, and the causal link between the two. It is up to the producer then to prove the existence of circumstances that exclude the liability (for instance that the defect came to be after it was put into circulation, or that the state of the art did not allow the producer to identify or foresee the defect),[41] and a favourable prescription term applies. This regime reinforces the protection of the consumer on the basis that he is in an unfavourable position vis-à-vis the manufacturers and resellers, due to the asymmetry of information on the products, their design, features, and manufacturing processes.[42]

What happens if the consumer protection regime is applied to an AI system? Assume that, as shown in Fig. 13.4, individual consumer Alice purchases an AI-powered coffee maker. The coffee maker uses sensors and data collected to deduce the presence of a mug, analyse Alice's habits and preferences, and have her favourite coffee ready in time for breakfast. One morning, however, the coffee maker's algorithm pours the boiling coffee on the kitchen countertop while Alice is sleeping, severely damaging it. There appear to be no broken parts, no faulty components: the algorithm has made an evaluation based on the data collected and has established that it was the time to brew and pour the coffee.

---

[40] Weatherill 2013.

[41] Council Directive 85/374/EEC of 25 July 1985 on the approximation of the laws, regulations and administrative provisions of the Member States concerning liability for defective products [OJ L 210, 7.8.1985, pp. 29–33], article 7.

[42] Weatherill 2013.

The application of the consumer protection regime to this scenario is not without doubts.[43] Two elements are particularly challenged by AI: the definition of product, and what constitutes a defect.

It is not clear whether the existing European provisions concerning consumer products include software.[44] For the purposes of product safety, for instance, software is only considered when they represent an integrated and necessary component of hardware, while stand-alone software is not regulated.[45] Furthermore, many digital goods offered via the Internet can be categorized as services, depending on national provisions regulating contracts.[46] The applicability of the product liability regime to AI is rendered uncertain by the fact that software is not univocally considered a product.[47]

In addition, product liability applies when a product is defective either by design or due to errors in the assemblage and manufacturing processes, or because of transportation.[48] As the scenario shows, however, AI systems might result in damages even when there is no defect.[49] The algorithm might learn something wrong, or even something in itself not wrong, but something that does not apply to the context in which the AI system operates. Algorithms operate opaquely through correlation, not causation, and therefore might identify patterns in the data that do not match with how humans interpret reality. Whether or not this behaviour of AI systems is a defect is not yet established by the law. As a result, applying product liability to AI systems might still result in liability gaps.

13.3.6 Beyond Liability: Other Legal Tools

Contractual or extra-contractual liability have not been the only legal tools proposed to mitigate the uncertainty in the allocation of liability or to redistribute the economic damages, with regard to AI. The most notable other solutions proposed are mandatory insurance schemes, using limited liability companies or other company types, and creating an *ad hoc* type of legal personality for AI systems and/or robots.

Regardless of the allocation of liability, insurance schemes are already in use to make sure that individuals carrying out certain activities can keep possible victims indemnified in case of damages, as is the case for cars. It has, therefore, been proposed

---

[43] Bertolini 2013, Asaro et al. 2011.

[44] Council Directive 85/374/EEC of 25 July 1985 on the approximation of the laws, regulations and administrative provisions of the Member States concerning liability for defective products [OJ L 210, 7.8.1985, pp. 29–33], article 2.

[45] European Commission 2020, p. 10.

[46] Jaquemin 2017.

[47] European Commission 2020, p. 4.

[48] Weatherill 2013; see also the definition of defect provided by article 6 of the Council Directive 85/374/EEC.

[49] European Commission 2020a.

that owners or operators of AI systems could be obliged to take up insurance, especially for certain sectors or activities considered at high risk.[50] While, however, this could help maintain victims indemnified, insurance schemes do not substitute a liability regime. They can only complement it. Even in the presence of insurance it would still be necessary to identify one or more liable parties.[51]

The idea has also been considered of incorporating a limited liability company (or another form of company) 'around' the AI, having the AI system as its shareholder, so that damaged parties could avail themselves of the patrimony of the company to compensate damages.[52] While it is believed that this solution could be already feasible in some legal systems, it is difficult to see how it can bridge the liability gaps concretely. The company would need to acquire a patrimony: this can only be done if shareholders with legal personality (natural or legal persons) contribute it. The company would still necessitate human intervention, and its incorporation would only add intermediate passages to the possibility of damaged parties to obtain redress.[53]

Finally, a daring solution has recently gained some momentum: creating a special form of legal personality for AI systems and robots. The idea was already put forward in 1992[54] and has now been revived, becoming the centre of a heated debate. The European Parliament seemed to have embraced it in 2017 when, under the term Electronic Personality, it was proposed as a possible option to be considered by the European Commission to regulate liability issues connected to robotics and AI.[55] The underlying concept is that just like companies have a form of legal personality, different from that recognized to natural persons (that is, human beings), so could artefacts, by virtue of their autonomy and potential societal relevance.[56] The idea is not *per se* impossible or wrong, as the law can identify which entities are entitled to rights and subject to duties.[57] It could provide for a solution to the liability gaps, provided that together with (some form of) legal personhood AI systems are also granted the agency necessary to acquire patrimony, enter into contracts, or stand in court. The recognition of legal personhood would open the way to the liability of AI systems, possibly together with other parties, such as their manufacturers or users (a solution necessary to incentivize the latter to ensure high quality and appropriate care in the creation and use of AI systems). To compensate the damaged parties for their losses, AI systems would also need to have a 'wallet', funds and assets. The proposal of the European Parliament has, in any case, been criticized in an open

---

[50] Turner 2019, p. 112.

[51] European Commission 2019, p. 61.

[52] Bayern 2015.

[53] Scherer 2019.

[54] Solum 1992.

[55] European Parliament 2017, p. 61.

[56] Teubner 2006, van den Hoven van Genderen 2019.

[57] Hage 2017, Teubner 2018.

letter signed by over one hundred experts.[58] It has been considered to undermine
the dignity of human beings, unethical, and not really based on reality, especially
because completely autonomous and intelligent robots do not exist yet, as the ones
currently on the market have very limited capabilities. The idea of granting legal
personhood to AI systems or robots remains, for the moment, only hypothetical and
the Parliament proposal has been disregarded by the Commission.[59]

13.4 Reflections: Putting Humans Back at the Centre

Any intervention to tackle liability gaps created by AI systems should take into
consideration that the applications of AI are endless, and AI is used in almost every
sector and industry. Consequently, one-size-fits-all solutions are unlikely to be satisfactory while the risk of fragmenting the protection of those who suffered damage is
high. The transborder nature of many transactions involving AI systems (with multinational corporations offering products and services to individuals and companies
located in several different countries) also implies that a harmonized and holistic
approach—at least at a European level—could be necessary to prevent damaged
parties from suffering further undesired consequences due to, for instance, forum
shopping.

This does not mean that liability gaps for damages created by AI systems cannot
be solved in a satisfactory fashion, providing effective redress to damaged parties.
The phenomenon of liability gaps should be observed from the perspective of European policymaking, that at its core has the protection of the dignity and freedom of
individuals, democracy, and equality.[60] Any legal solution to it should put humans at
the centre, focusing on the damaged individuals, their rights and interests. To bridge
the liability gaps, the starting point should be to acknowledge that the law operates
now in a socio-technological ecosystem, in which individuals, companies, and institutions interact both online and offline with a plethora of devices and services that
are digital, responsive, (semi)autonomous. A holistic, systemic approach is necessary to predict how the law interacts with this ecosystem, its actors and dynamics.
The design of legal solutions to the liability gaps should make sure that "No one
is left behind in the digital transformation".[61] To draw order from chaos, attention
should be given to human-centred values,[62] to empower the individuals harmed by

---

[58] Open Letter to the European Commission: Artificial Intelligence and Robotics 2017, https://www.
politico.eu/wp-content/uploads/2018/04/RoboticsOpenLetter.pdf. Accessed 19 February 2021.

[59] The European Commission, in the context of its AI strategy for Europe, has not embraced the
view of the European Parliament concerning a special legal personality for artificial agents. Cfr.
European Commission 2018 and European Commission's High-Level Expert Group on Artificial
Intelligence 2019.

[60] These values are expressly protected by the main tools constituting and regulating the EU, such
as the Treaty on European Union and the Charter of Fundamental Rights.

[61] European Commission 2018, p. 2.

[62] European Commission 2020b.

AI systems, compensating the effects of detrimental factors, such as the asymmetry of information and power, the lack of expertise, or the fragmentation generated by the presence of several parties.

In the light of the above, it is necessary to intervene on multiple fronts, combining existing solutions with special regimes created *ad hoc* for AI systems.[63]

This combined approach implies clarifying the scope and modalities of implementation of existing regimes, such as insurances, product liability or liability for driving accidents, with regard to AI systems. The modalities to apply contractual and extra-contractual liability regimes to AI must also be clarified. These two forms of liability represent the baseline of protection, the safety net covering the spaces left empty in-between special regimes or application-specific regulations and can help mitigate the risk of fragmentation of the liability regime. Complementarily, it is also necessary to establish solutions tailored to the reality of AI. *Ad hoc* solutions can focus on specific uses or applications (for instance, regulating the liability for damages deriving from AI software operating in the stock market, or liability and chain of command in the case of autonomous weapons).

Underlying this combined intervention, there needs to be a strong set of values, to guarantee uniformity and maintain internal systemic coherence. Some of these values have been identified at a European level and include: distributing the loss connected to the damages in a fair and efficient way; granting access to justice to the damaged party; addressing in a similar way situations which present comparable risks; the duty of producers to ensure transparency of the technology and its functioning/use; introducing, besides insurances, compensation funds to support victims even in situations in which insurances are absent.[64]

At a practical level, some of these principles can be declined into more detailed guidelines. Allocating the loss in a fair and efficient way, for instance, includes identifying as liable all those parties that benefited from the AI system, were in control of the AI system, and/or operated the AI system.[65] This, for instance, mitigates the risk of a party invoking the autonomy of the AI system to exclude liability, if that party benefited from the use of the AI in the first place. Granting access to justice to a damaged party translates into making sure that the burden of proof is allocated with the party that can actually comply with it (for instance, the company that owns or manufactured the AI system) and not automatically with the damaged party acting as plaintiff in a judicial procedure.[66] Similarly, prescription times are important to ensure the effective access to justice of a damaged party and need to take into consideration elements such as the changes occurring after an update or the self-learning capability of AI. Currently, applying contractual and extra-contractual liability might lead to solutions that do not reflect the above-mentioned principles. Implementing these principles in the context of both liability regimes might imply distancing from a rigid interpretation of the boundaries between contract and delicts. As an example,

---

[63] European Commission 2019, p. 32.

[64] Ibid.

[65] Ibid., p. 39.

[66] European Commission 2020b.

holding liable the many parties involved (producers, users that benefited from the AI system, operators) implies that less importance is attributed to the existence of contractual obligations among the parties involved. Normally, the lack of a contract would exclude the application of contractual liability. At the same time, moving the burden of proof away from the damaged party would not be always possible based on extra-contractual liability. A more human-centred solution to the liability gaps should contain a mix of contractual and extra-contractual elements, to compensate for the asymmetry of information and power created by the technical and business features of AI systems.[67]

Based on the nature and application of specific AI systems, it is also reasonable to intervene on the opacity of AI systems, establishing a duty of transparency for producers, for example through mandatory logs in which important passages and events are included, that can be revised in case of damages to assess what went wrong, when, where, and, possibly, why.[68]

13.5 Conclusions

In the past, legal solutions—contractual and extra-contractual liability, special liability regimes, insurances, company law—have been developed having in mind 'dumb' machines and products. Artefacts that are non-autonomous, not interconnected, and not self-learning. The solutions analysed throughout this chapter revolve around more traditional relationships between two or more parties, that can be traced back to a contract or a delict, at least in most cases.[69]

The abovementioned solutions are challenged by AI's features: autonomy, self-learning capability, opaqueness, complexity, interoperability. In applying the existing legal tools to ascribe liability, such as contractual, extra-contractual, or strict liability, the inherent features of AI systems create uncertainty and unsatisfactory results (liability gaps). Elements such as the absence of a contractual relationship between the damage party and producers, providers, or users of an AI system, or the allocation of the burden of proof might lead to the undesired result of precluding an effective remedy to those damaged by an AI system.

Bridging the liability gaps requires the reintroduction and reaffirmation of those rationales and values that already informed the existing legal tools but were affected by the uncertainty deriving from the characteristics of AI. Any intervention to ascribe liability for damages caused by AI must be based on one, fundamental value: putting humans at the centre.

---

[67] De Conca 2020.

[68] European Commission 2019, p. 49.

[69] The application of contractual and extra-contractual liability in the past has been challenged by complex situations, such as the case of pre-contractual liability, or the duty of care vis-à-vis third parties. Cfr. for instance Michoński 2015.

References

Asaro P M (2011) A Body to Kick, but Still No Soul to Damn: Legal Perspectives on Robotics. In: Lin P et al (ed) Robot Ethics: The Ethical and Social Implications of Robotics. MIT Press, pp 169–186.

Bayern S (2015) The Implications of Modern Business-Entity Law for the Regulation of Autonomous Systems. Stan. Tech. L. Rev. 19:93–112.

Bertolini A (2013) Robots as Products: The Case for a Realistic Analysis of Robotic Applications and Liability Rules. LIT 5(2):214–247.

Buyuksagis E, van Boom W H (2013) Strict liability in contemporary European codification: Torn between objects, activities, and their risks. Georgetown Journal of International Law 44(2):609–640.

Bussani M, Palmer V V (eds) (2003) Pure economic loss in Europe. Cambridge University Press.

De Conca S (2020) Bridging the liability gap using human-centered legal design: three scenarios to apply the liability from social contact. WeRobot 2020, Ottawa 22-25 September 2020. https://techlaw.uottawa.ca/werobot/papers Accessed on 20 July 2021.

European Commission (2018) Artificial Intelligence for Europe: Communication from the Commission to the European Parliament, the European Council, the Council, the European Economic and Social Committee and the Committee of the Regions [COM(2018) 237].

European Commission (2019) Liability for Artificial Intelligence and other emerging digital technologies – Report from the Expert Group on Liability and New Technologies.

European Commission (2020a) Report from the commission to the European Parliament, the Council and the European Economic and Social Committee on the safety and liability implications of Artificial Intelligence, the Internet of Things and robotics [COM(2020) 64].

European Commission (2020b) White Paper on Artificial Intelligence - A European approach to excellence and trust [COM(2020) 65].

European Commission's High-Level Expert Group on Artificial Intelligence (2019) Ethics Guidelines for Trustworthy AI.

European Parliament (2017) Draft Report of the Committee on Legal Affairs with recommendations to the Commission on Civil Law Rules on Robotics [2015/2103(INL)].

Farnsworth E A (2006) Comparative Contract Law. In: Reimann M, Zimmermann R (eds) The Oxford Handbook of Comparative Law. Oxford University Press.

Fauvarque-Cosson B, Mazeaud D (eds) (2009) European Contract Law, Materials for a Common Frame of Reference: Terminology, Guiding Principles, Model Rules. Sellier European Law Publishers.

Hage J (2017) Theoretical foundations for the responsibility of autonomous agents. Artif Intell Law 25:255–271.

Hevelke A, Nida-Rümelin J (2015) Responsibility for Crashes of Autonomous Vehicles: An Ethical Analysis. Sci Eng Ethics 21:619–630.

Jacquemin H (2017) Digital content and sales or service contracts under EU law and Belgian/French law. Journal of Intellectual Property, Information Technology and Electronic Commerce Law 8(1):27–38.

Johnson D G (2015) Technology with No Human Responsibility? Journal of Business Ethics 127(4):707–715.

Karnow C E A (2016) The application of traditional tort theory to embodied machine intelligence. In: Calo R, Froomkin M A, Kerr I (eds) Robot Law. Edward Elgar Publishing, pp 51–77.

Leenes R, Palmerini E, Koops B J, Bertolini A, Salvini P, Lucivero F (2017) Regulatory challenges of robotics: some guidelines for addressing legal and ethical issues. Law, Innovation and Technology, 9:1, pp 1–44.

Marchant G E, Lindor R A (2012) The coming collision between autonomous vehicles and the liability system. Santa Clara Law Review 52(4):1321–1340.

Marsh P D V (1994) Comparative Contract Law: England, France, Germany. Gower

Michoński D (2015) Contractual or Delictual? On the Character of Pre-contractual Liability in Selected European Legal Systems. Comparative Law Review 20:151–175.

Murray A (2021) Almost Human: Law and Human Agency in the Time of Artificial Intelligence - Sixth Annual T.M.C. Asser Lecture. Annual T.M.C. Asser Lecture Series. T.M.C. Asser Press, The Hague.

Pagallo U (2012) Three Roads to Complexity, AI and the Law of Robots: On Crimes, Contracts, and Torts. In: Palmirani M et al (eds) AICOL Workshops 2011, LNAI 7639. Springer, pp 48–60.

Pagallo U (2013a) The Laws of Robots: Crimes, Contracts, and Torts. Springer.

Pagallo U (2013b) Robots in the cloud with privacy: A new threat to data protection? CLSR 29(5):501–508.

Pagallo U, Corrales M, Fenwick M, Forgó N (2018) The Rise of Robotics & AI: Technological Advances & Normative Dilemmas. In: Corrales M et al (eds) Robotics, AI and the Future of Law. Springer, pp 1–14.

Royakkers L, van Est R (2016) Just Ordinary Robots: Automation from Love to War. CRC Press.

Scherer M (2016) Regulating Artificial Intelligence Systems: Risks, Challenges, Competence, and Strategies. Harvard Journal of Law & Technology 29(2):354–400.

Scherer M (2019) Of Wild Beasts and Digital Analogues: The Legal Status of Autonomous Systems. NEV. L.J. 19:259–291.

Solum L B (1992) Legal Personhood for Artificial Intelligences. N.C. L. Rev. 70(4):1231–1287.

Teubner G (2006) Rights of Non-humans? Electronic Agents and Animals as New Actors in Politics and Law. Journal of Law and Society 33(4):497–521.

Teubner G (2018) Digital Personhood? The Status of Autonomous Software Agents in Private Law. Ancilla Iuris 106–149.

Turner J (2019) Robot Rules: Regulating Artificial Intelligence. Palgrave Macmillan.

UNESCO (2017) Report of the World Commission on the Ethics of Scientific Knowledge and Technology (COMEST) on Robotics Ethics [SHS/YES/COMEST-10/17/2 REV].

van den Hoven van Genderen R (2019) Does Future Society Need Legal Personhood for Robots and AI? In: Ranschaert E et al (eds) Artificial Intelligence in Medical Imaging. Springer, pp 257–290.

von Bar C, Drobnig U (eds) (2009) The Interaction of Contract Law and Tort and Property Law in Europe, A Comparative Study. Sellier European Law Publishers.

Weatherill S (2013) EU Consumer Law and Policy. Edward Elgar Law.

Witt J (2001) Toward a New History of American Accident Law: Classical Tort Law and the Cooperative First-Party Insurance Movement. Harvard Law Review 114(3):690–841.

Dr. Silvia De Conca is Assistant Professor in Law & Technology at the Transnational Legal Studies department and researcher in Law of AI and robotics at the Amsterdam Law & Technology Institute (ALTI), both part of the Faculty of Law of the Vrije Universiteit Amsterdam. Silvia is the co-chair of the Human Rights in the Digital Age working group within the Netherlands Network for Human Rights Research (NNHRR), and part of the management team of the Demonstrator Lab of VU Amsterdam. Her research interests include, besides AI and robotics, regulation of manipulation through technology, privacy and data protection, regulation of emerging technologies. Silvia combines traditional and empirical legal research with insights from STS, sociology, behavioral sciences, philosophy, and computer science. Silvia holds a PhD in law and technology from Tilburg University, an LL.M. in IT Law from the London School of Economics and Political Science, and master's and bachelor degrees in law from Roma Tre University, and has practiced in International law firms in Milan and Rome.

Chapter 14
Contractual Liability for the Use of AI under Dutch Law and EU Legislative Proposals

Tycho J. de Graaf and Iris S. Wuisman

Contents

Abstract In this chapter, the contractual liability of a company (the 'user') using an AI system to perform its contractual obligations is analysed from a Dutch law and EU law perspective. In particular, we discuss three defences which, in the event of a breach, the user can put forward against the attribution of that breach to such user and which relate to the characteristics of AI systems, especially their capacity for autonomous activity and self-learning: (1) the AI system was *state-of-the-art* when deployed, (2) the user had no control over the AI system, and (3) an AI system is not a tangible object and its use in the performance of contractual obligations can thus not give rise to strict liability under Article 6:77 of the Dutch Civil Code. Following a classical legal analysis of these defences under Dutch law and in light of EU legislative proposals, the following conclusions are reached. Firstly, the user is strictly liable, subject to an exception based on unreasonableness, if the AI system was unsuitable for the purpose for which it was deployed as at the time of deployment. Advancements in scientific knowledge play no role in determining suitability. Secondly, a legislative proposal by the European Parliament allows the user to escape

T. J. de Graaf (✉) · I. S. Wuisman
Leiden Law School, Leiden University, Leiden, The Netherlands
e-mail: t.j.degraaf@law.leidenuniv.nl

I. S. Wuisman
e-mail: i.s.wuisman@law.leidenuniv.nl

© T.M.C. ASSER PRESS and the authors 2022
B. Custers and E. Fosch-Villaronga (eds.), *Law and Artificial Intelligence*,
Information Technology and Law Series 35,
https://doi.org/10.1007/978-94-6265-523-2_14

liability for damage caused by a non-high-risk AI system if the user took due care
with respect to the selection, monitoring and maintenance of that system. Thirdly,
the defence that the user is not liable because an AI system is not a tangible object
is unlikely to hold.

Keywords Artificial intelligence · Autonomous systems · Self-learning systems ·
Contractual liability · Force majeure · Strict liability · Damages

14.1 Introduction

Artificial intelligence (AI)[1] is now an integral part of our lives and is expected to take
an increasingly prominent place in society.[2] We can distinguish two forms in which
AI is interwoven in the decision-making activities of companies. The first form is
where it is used to support decision-making and the execution of activities by people
within the organisation. In such cases, the AI serves as a source of knowledge or
information on the basis of which a natural person acts and is used to support that
person's own actions. Think, for example, of a company's decision as to whether or
not to increase production based on AI-generated expectations regarding turnover
and prices for the procurement of products and services. The second form is where an
AI system acts autonomously, without human intervention, such as via an AI-driven
device (e.g. a robot). Autonomous action is also possible without software being
embedded in 'hardware', such as in the case of algorithmic-based high-frequency
securities trading systems.[3] In both forms, the system is often trained by the operator
or trains itself.

In all of the above situations, damage may occur for which recovery is sought
contractually or extra-contractually. Claims of this nature raise various questions,
including the suitability of the current liability regime in AI-related cases.[4] Reports
and legal literature emphasise that clarity on the applicable legal framework is
important with regard to consumer protection and legal certainty for companies.[5]

---

[1] High-Level Expert Group on Artificial Intelligence 2019, p. 6: 'Artificial intelligence (AI) systems
are software (and possibly also hardware) systems designed by humans that, given a complex goal,
act in the physical or digital dimension by perceiving their environment through data acquisition,
interpreting the collected structured or unstructured data, reasoning on the knowledge, or processing
the information, derived from this data and deciding the best action(s) to take to achieve the given
goal. AI systems can either use symbolic rules or learn a numeric model, and they can also adapt
their behaviour by analysing how the environment is affected by their previous actions.'

[2] Zhang et al. 2021.

[3] A description of the legal aspects of high-frequency securities trading systems and the relationships
between the parties involved can be found in Verwilst 2014, pp. 351–359. See also: Busch 2019,
pp. 253–277 and De Vey Mestdagh 2019, pp. 230–236.

[4] Expert Group on Liability and New Technologies—New Technologies Formation 2019, European
Parliament 2020a, and European Commission 2020.

[5] European Parliament 2020a, p. 1, Prins 2020, p. 2804 and, in general, Tjittes 2018, pp. 27–29 and
36–37.

In this chapter, we analyse the contractual liability of a 'user' under Dutch law in the scenario in which: (i) the user acquires an AI system from a third party (usually the producer/developer) and deploys that system to fulfil an agreement concluded with a customer, and (ii) the AI system, acting autonomously and in a self-learning manner, causes damage to the customer. We therefore focus on the liability of the middleman, the user, and not the producer/developer. This chapter focuses on Dutch law, but we also discuss developments in EU legislation.[6]

In order to hold the user liable for such damage under Dutch contract law, the customer must allege (and, in the event of a sufficiently substantiated rebuttal, prove) (1) that the user has failed to perform its contractual obligations (commonly known as breach of contract), (2) that the customer has suffered damage, and (3) that a causal connection (*condicio sine qua non*) exists between the breach and damage.[7] The user can then, in defence, allege (and, in the event of a sufficiently substantiated rebuttal, prove) that (4) the breach of contract cannot be attributed to it (e.g., because it was not at fault).[8] For the sake of clarity and brevity, we focus on three grounds for non-attribution that the user can raise as a defence in the above scenario and that are related to the autonomous and self-learning character of the AI system used in that scenario. In Sect. 14.2 we discuss the defence that the AI system was *state-of-the-art*. In Sect. 14.3 we discuss the defence that the user had no control over the autonomous action and self-learning of the AI system that caused the damage. In Sect. 14.4 we discuss the defence that strict liability on the grounds of having used an unsuitable object in the performance of the contract (set out in Article 6:77 of the Dutch Civil Code and to be explained further below) applies only where the object is tangible and susceptible to human control. In Sect. 14.5 we provide conclusions.

14.2 Breach of Contract

A contract is breached if the debtor's[9] performance falls short of the performance that is due.[10] The term breach of contract (*tekortkoming*) is a neutral concept and does

---

[6] See for an analysis of the user's contractual liability for the use of AI pursuant to Belgian law: Appelmans et al. 2021, pp. 342–344. And see for such an analysis pursuant to German law: Eichelberger 2020, pp. 192–197 and Kaulartz and Braegelmann 2020, pp. 262–269.

[7] Article 6:74(1) Dutch Civil Code (DCC).

[8] Article 6:74(1) jo. 75 DCC. For the sake of completeness, it should be noted that there is a requirement (5): either the debtor is in default (e.g. because a notice of default has been sent and the reasonable period set therein for rectifying the breach has lapsed without proper rectification, Article 6:82 DCC) or the performance is permanently impossible (e.g. because the damage suffered cannot be reversed by rectification, in which case sending a notice of default and requiring rectification does not make sense, see HR 4 February 2000, ECLI:NL:HR:2000:AA4732, *NJ* 2000/258 (*Kinheim/Pelders*), see Article 6:74(2) DCC.

[9] Throughout this chapter, we have used the terms 'creditor' and 'debtor' even though reference is made to both monetary and non-monetary obligations because we find 'obligee' and 'obligor' more difficult to read.

[10] Sieburgh 2020, no. 317.

not imply culpability.[11] In order to determine whether a contract has been breached it is important to understand the parties' respective obligations to each other under the contract. Obligations can be divided into result obligations (*obligations de resultat*) and effort obligations (*obligations de moyen*).[12] The former are obligations to achieve a specific result while effort obligations are obligations to perform to the best of one's ability to achieve a specific result. A debtor can make use of an object (such as a crane or, for the purposes of this chapter, an AI system) in the performance of both result and effort obligations.

In two recent judgments, the Dutch Supreme Court emphasised that in cases involving the use of an object in the performance of medical treatment contracts, the court must first ascertain whether the contract has been breached before considering the debtor's defence that the breach cannot be attributed to it.[13] The Supreme Court ruled in the PIP case that such an object must be suitable for the purpose for which it was used as at the time of use,[14] and in the Miragel case that if the object was *state-of-the-art* at the time of the treatment, the mere fact that it is subsequently found to be unsuitable based on advancements in scientific knowledge does not give rise to a breach of contract.[15]

Although these cases specifically concern the use of objects in the performance of medical treatment contracts—which usually involve effort obligations—some legal writers defend the application of the Miragel rule in cases involving result obligations, for example where products are sold that only later turn out to be defective as a result of advancements in scientific knowledge.[16] This is not as strange as may seem at first sight. We are used to this from product liability law, namely Article 6(2) of the EU Product Liability Directive 1985/374: 'A product shall not be considered defective for the sole reason that a better product is subsequently put into circulation.'[17] Here too, advancements in scientific knowledge *ex nunc* do not lead to a defect *ex tunc*. What is new, at least for the Netherlands, is that this interpretation of the concept of defect now plays a role not only in extra-contractual (i.e. tort) but also in contractual settings. It is applied in any event to contractual liability arising from the use of objects in the performance of medical treatment contracts, perhaps also to contractual liability arising from the use of objects in the performance of effort obligations in general and

---

[11] See in the parliamentary history of the DCC: Van Zeben et al. 1981, pp. 252 and 257.

[12] Sieburgh 2020, nr. 192, Sieburgh 2017, no. 205 and Tjong Tjin Tai 2006, p. 107.

[13] Dutch Supreme Court (HR) 19 June 2020, ECLI:NL:HR:2020:1090, *NJ* 2021/16 with annotation by Lindenbergh SD (*PIP*) and HR 19 June 2020, ECLI:NL:HR:2020:1082, *NJ* 2021/15 with annotation by Lindenbergh SD after *NJ* 2021/16 (*Miragel*).

[14] HR 19 June 2020, ECLI:NL:HR:2020:1090, *NJ* 2021/16 with annotation by Lindenbergh SD (*PIP*), para 2.8.2.

[15] HR 19 June 2020, ECLI:NL:HR:2020:1082, *NJ* 2021/15 with annotation by Lindenbergh SD after *NJ* 2021/16 (*Miragel*), para 3.2.2.

[16] Van Boom 2021, pp. 268–278. On development risk defences in relation to innovation, see inter alia De Jong 2020, pp. 203–205.

[17] Council Directive 85/374/EEC of 25 July 1985 on the approximation of the laws, regulations and administrative provisions of the Member States concerning liability for defective products, Official Journal L 210, 07/08/1985, pp. 0029–0033.

perhaps even, and more broadly, to contractual liability arising from the use of objects in the performance of result obligations. If we accept the broadest application of this interpretation, the change is more revolutionary than may first appear. In product liability law, the consequences of a limited interpretation of 'defect' are less than in contract liability law. In a product liability case, the consequence is 'only' that a particular type of damage (i.e. 'damage caused by death or by bodily injury' and 'damage to or destruction of, any item or property other than the defective product itself … for private use or consumption') suffered by the consumer is not eligible for compensation. (See Article 9, Product Liability Directive). In contractual liability law the consequences are more extreme, because the injured party (consumer or business) is suddenly denied the right to several other remedies and types of damages as well, namely: specific performance, and termination for breach of contract, as well as transaction damages (damages to the product itself) and pure economic loss. In other words, this application of the *state-of-the-art* concept to contract liability law entails an all-or-nothing approach with far-reaching consequences.

The consequences of extrapolating from this line of reasoning to damage caused by the use of AI are as follows. Regardless of whether the user has entered into an effort or a result obligation, it is in breach of contract if, when performing the obligation, it uses an AI system that was unsuitable as at the time of its use. Imagine a security company that undertakes, as an effort obligation, to analyse security images using AI, and the AI system fails to detect an intruder, resulting in damage to its customer. Or consider a website where a company commits, pursuant to a result obligation, to purchase a second-hand machine for another company (agreeing on type, price and delivery date) and to use AI for that purpose, and the AI system subsequently purchases the wrong machine, causing damage to the purchaser. If the damage was caused by an AI system that was unsuitable according to the *state-of-the-art* at the time it was used, the user is in breach of contract and liable for the resulting damage unless it can show that attribution of the breach to it would be unreasonable on certain specific grounds (see Sect. 14.3). The mere fact that subsequent advancements in scientific knowledge render the AI system unsuitable does not mean that there was a breach of contract. The *state-of-the-art* at the time of use remains decisive.

User liability is also being considered in proposed EU legislation. For example, on 20 October 2020, the European Parliament launched a proposal for a regulation on liability for the operation of artificial intelligence systems.[18] At the time of writing this chapter, the European Commission has not yet published a legislative proposal on this subject. The European Commission's legislative proposal of 21 April 2021 for a regulation laying down harmonised rules on AI relates to product safety (combined with public law enforcement mechanisms) but not to civil law liability.[19] A legislative proposal for a regulation on civil law liability is expected by mid-2022. According to the European Parliament's proposal, the person using the AI system is liable if he/she can be considered an operator (recital 11). This term covers both back-end and

---

[18] European Parliament 2020b, on which Prins 2020, p. 3141.

[19] European Commission 2021.

front-end operators (Article 3(d), (f) and (e)). The former is usually the AI developer or the party who provides maintenance and support, and the latter is the user who has a certain degree of control[20] over the operation and benefits from it. Both are jointly and severally liable (Article 11) to the injured party 'for any harm or damage that was caused by a physical or virtual activity, device or process driven by that AI-system' (Article 4(1) and Article 8(1)). This liability can be broken down into two mandatory[21] liabilities of the operator to the injured party: strict liability for high-risk AI (Article 4(1)) up to a certain amount (Article 5) and (ii) fault-based liability for other forms of AI (Article 8(1)).

If we compare Dutch contractual liability for the use of objects with the European Parliament's proposal on AI liability, the following can be observed. In the Netherlands, due to the general nature of contractual liability, the focus is understandably on the breach of the contractual obligation. In the case of damage caused by an AI system, such damage is borne by the user of that system if it was unsuitable, to be determined according to the *state-of-the-art* at the time of its use. In contrast, the European Parliament's proposal focuses on AI and considers liability to have been established if damage is caused by an AI system over which the user has control and from whose operation it benefits (i.e. a front-end operator). The proposal does not affect the availability of additional contractual liability, product liability and consumer protection claims (Article 2(3)). Furthermore, there are of course ways to avoid liability for damages, both under the Dutch Civil Code (DCC) and the proposal of the European Parliament. These will be dealt with in Sect. 14.3.

14.3 Attribution

A user can avoid liability for a breach of contract if the breach cannot be attributed to it (Article 6:74(1) DCC). Attribution can take place on the basis of (1) fault, (2) the law, (3) a juridical act[22] (*rechtshandeling*) or (4) common opinion (*verkeersopvatting*) (Article 6:75(1) DCC). Attribution can thus be based on fault or on a kind of strict liability: even if the user is without fault, a breach can still be attributed to it if the

---

[20] For the concept that the degree of control determines liability, see Wagner 2019, pp. 37–40, Wendehorst and Grinzinger 2020, pp. 166–170, Navas 2020, pp. 165–166 and Appelmans et al. 2021, pp. 342–344.

[21] Mandatory in the sense that 'Any agreement between an operator of an AI-system and a natural or legal person who suffers harm or damage because of the AI-system, which circumvents or limits the rights and obligations set out in this Regulation, concluded before or after the harm or damage occurred, shall be deemed null and void as regards the rights and obligations laid down in this Regulation.' (Article 2(2)).

[22] A 'juridical act' is an act intended to have legal consequences. Here it refers to the act from which the obligation in question emanates, usually a clause in the contract itself. But a juridical act can also take the form of, for example, a unilateral declaration by one of the contracting parties.

breach is for its account pursuant to the law, a juridical act or common opinion.[23] From a procedural law perspective, it is up to the user to invoke a defence based on non-attributability, also known as force majeure. Invoking such a defence is not without difficulties. The user will have to allege (and, in the event of a sufficiently substantiated rebuttal, prove) not only that it was not at fault for the breach of contract, but also that the abovementioned other attribution grounds do not apply.[24] We will start by discussing the concept of fault and then turn to attribution based on the law and common opinion. We will assume that the parties have not entered into an agreement or undertaken any other juridical act pursuant to which the breach can be attributed to the user (e.g. because the user has guaranteed that it will be liable even in the event of force majeure) or cannot be attributed to the user (e.g. because the parties have agreed that the user will not be liable for damage caused by the use of a certain object in the performance of its contractual obligations), and will therefore disregard this ground.

14.3.1 Fault

'Fault' refers to the failure to perform with respect to the behaviour required.[25] The user is not at fault for such a failure if it neither could nor should have prevented the impediment which led to the failure and neither could nor should have prevented the consequences thereof.[26] Only then is the impediment deemed to be beyond the user's control and the user not at fault. Unfortunately, this rule is not included in the Dutch Civil Code in so many words. Article 79(1) of the UN Sale of Goods Convention does, however, state something similar: '*A party is not liable for a failure to perform any of his obligations if he proves that the failure was due to an impediment beyond his control and that he could not reasonably be expected to have taken the impediment into account at the time of the conclusion of the contract or to have avoided or overcome it, or its consequences.*'[27] In a case in which the failure to perform involved the use of a crane to move an airplane wing (the Airplane Wing case), the Dutch Supreme Court ruled that the user was not at fault if 'this failure could not have been foreseen by it, was not the result of a lack of care in the acquisition, maintenance and inspection of the equipment and moreover was not otherwise due to its fault …'.[28]

---

[23] Sieburgh 2020, no. 337, De Jong 2017, p. 17, Abas 1998, pp. 85–87 and Tjong Tjin Tai 2006, p. 93.

[24] Boonekamp and Valk 2021, comment on Article 6:75 DCC.

[25] Tjong Tjin Tai 2006, p. 101.

[26] Cauffman and Croes 2020, Article 6:75 DCC, comment 4.1.

[27] United Nations Convention on Contracts for the International Sale of Goods (Vienna 1980) (CISG), 11 April 1980.

[28] HR 5 January 1968, ECLI:NL:HR:1968:AB6963, *NJ* 1968/102, with annotation by Scholten GJ (*Airplane Wing or Fokker/Zentveld*).

There are not yet any specific legal rules with which a company using an AI system in the performance of its contractual obligations must comply with when acquiring, maintaining and monitoring the system. However, inspiration can be drawn from the previously discussed proposal of the European Parliament for a regulation on liability for the operation of artificial intelligence systems. Under that proposal, in the case of strict liability for high-risk AI the operator is liable (Article 4(1)) unless the damage was caused by force majeure (Article 4(3)). Unfortunately, the concept of force majeure is not further defined, but the provision also states that operators of high-risk AI systems cannot escape liability 'by arguing that they acted with due diligence or that the harm or damage was caused by an autonomous activity, device or process driven by their AI-system.' (Article 4(3)).[29] In the case of liability for damage caused by other (i.e. non high-risk) AI systems, the rules on force majeure and autonomous activity are repeated (Article 8(2)). More interesting is the possibility offered to escape liability if the damage occurred without the operator's fault in the following situations: '(a) the AI-system was activated without his or her knowledge while all reasonable and necessary measures to avoid such activation outside of the operator's control were taken, or (b) due diligence was observed by performing all the following actions: selecting a suitable AI-system for the right task and skills, putting the AI-system duly into operation, monitoring the activities and maintaining the operational reliability by regularly installing all available updates' (Article 8(2)).

The difficulty with requiring the operator to take the measures and actions outlined above is that this presupposes that it is in a position to do so. A back-end operator (the AI developer or person who provides maintenance and support) is more likely to be in such a position than a front-end operator (the user). Since back-end and front-end operators are jointly and severally liable to the injured party, the determination of what specific measures and actions are reasonable and necessary and what specific diligence is required will be made as if there is one operator, and not on the basis of the extent to which each operator has the necessary control. The operators' relative degree of control is only relevant for assessing their indemnification claims against each other (Article 12(2)).

The division of responsibilities between front-end and back-end operators is more evident in the European Commission's proposal of 21 April 2021 for an AI regulation. As mentioned previously, that proposal does not cover the civil liability of front-end and back-end operators to the injured party, or the division of liabilities between them. For other reasons too, it is unwise to compare the Commission's proposal to that of the European Parliament: terminology and definitions differ and the concretisation of the division of responsibilities in the Commission's proposal relates only to high-risk AI systems. That said, it is useful to draw some inspiration from it. The provider of a high-risk AI system (in short, the developer who brings it to the market) must, pursuant to Article 16 in conjunction with Article 8, among other things, ensure that:

---

[29] To that extent, the European Parliament does not accept that the 'responsibility gap' (between the pre-programmed actions and the actual autonomous actions after self-learning) should be borne by the party suffering damage. On the responsibility gap, see Fosch-Villaronga 2020, pp. 151–155 and the references to other literature included therein.

1. users can control the output (Article 13(1)),
2. users are informed of the operation and risks by means of user documentation and know what kind of maintenance and human supervision is required (Article 13(2) and (3)),
3. human supervision can be carried out with a view to preventing or minimising risks (Article 14),
4. requirements relating to robustness, accuracy and cybersecurity are met consistently throughout their lifecycle (Article 15),
5. all relevant events are logged by the provider in such a way that they can be traced (Article 12 in conjunction with Article 16(d)),
6. the technical documentation contains (and continues to contain) all information relating to the technical solutions used by the provider to make the AI system comply with the requirements of the Regulation (Article 11); and
7. the AI-system has a quality management system in place (Article 16(b) in conjunction with Article 17) and must take the necessary corrective actions or withdraw or recall the system if the provider knows or has reason to believe that it no longer complies with the requirements of the regulation (Article 21).

The user (in short, the person under whose authority or responsibility the AI system is used[30]) has far fewer obligations, including:

A. to use the system in accordance with the instructions (Article 29(1)),
B. to ensure that input data over which the user exercises control is relevant in view of the intended purpose of the high-risk AI system (Article 29(3))
C. to monitor the operation of the system on the basis of the instruction of use and, if the user has reasons to consider that the use in accordance with the instructions may result in the AI system presenting a risk (within the meaning of Article 65(1)), to inform the provider and suspend the use of the system (Article 29(4)),
D. to keep the logs automatically generated by the high-risk AI system (Article 29(5)) and
E. to carry out a data protection impact assessment under European law (Regulation (EU) 2016/679 and Directive (EU) 2016/680), where applicable (article 29(6)).

---

[30] A user is, however, considered a provider for the purposes of the proposed regulation when the user (a) places a high-risk AI system on the market or into service under its name or trademark, (b) modifies the intended purpose of a high-risk AI system already placed on the market or put into service and/or (c) makes substantial modifications to the high-risk AI system (Article 28(1)). In those circumstances the obligations of the provider under Article 16 apply to the user and the provider that initially placed the AI system on the market or put into service under (b) and (c) is no longer considered a provider for the purposes of the proposed regulation (Article 28(2)).

14.3.2 The Law

If the user is not at fault for a breach, the breach can still be attributed to it on the basis of the law (more specifically, Article 6:77 DCC) where the breach arose through the use of an unsuitable object. Under Article 6:77 DCC, the breach is attributed to the user (main rule) unless it alleges (and, in the event of a sufficiently substantiated rebuttal, proves) that this would be unreasonable 'in view of the content and purpose of the juridical act giving rise to the obligation, common opinion and the other circumstances of the case ...' (exceptions to the main rule). The main rule in essence imposes strict liability on the user for a breach of contract caused by the use of an unsuitable object to perform the contract. We will now discuss the exceptions to this main rule.

The first exception—the content and purpose of the underlying juridical act—has its origin in one of the arguments justifying the abovementioned main rule: the user's freedom to choose the object used and even to not use an object at all.[31] Where this freedom is non-existent or extremely limited, it may well be unreasonable to attribute the breach of contract to the user, for example, if the customer provides the user with the object[32] or orders the user to use a specific object[33] or if for some other reason the user does not in fact choose the object itself.[34] If, as will usually be the case, the contract between the user and customer requires the user to choose the object used, the juridical act exception will generally not apply.

The second exception, common opinion, is more interesting. Common opinions are extra-legal sources that form a starting point for judicial law-making.[35] They are shared views or convictions in society, which do not necessarily have to be shared by everyone. They may also be the views of a limited circle of (natural or legal) persons.[36] Views are changeable and that is exactly why the legislature has included this open concept in certain legal provisions. It gives the law room to develop.[37] Changes in common opinion lead to changes in the standards applied by the courts, because those standards are drawn in part from common opinion. The input of common opinion adds a moral element[38] to the law of obligations, requiring courts to seek out the views in society on the nature of a particular legal relationship and

---

[31] Hiemstra 2018, p. 126 refers to this as the hazard theory.

[32] District Court of Den Bosch 15 June 2005, ECLI:NL:RBSHE:2005:AT7353 and ECLI:NL:RBSHE:2005:AT7382 (*Implanon*), paras 3.27 and 4.27; see comment by Van 2011, pp. 44–49.

[33] HR 25 March 1966, ECLI:NL:HR:1966:AC4642, *NJ* 1966/279 with annotation by Scholten GJ (*Moffenkit*).

[34] HR 13 December 1968, ECLI:NL:HR:1968:AC3302, *NJ* 1969/174 with annotation by G.J. Scholten (*Cadix/AEH, Polyclens*).

[35] Jansen 2020, pp. 26–41 and Tjong Tjin Tai 2010, pp. 101–106.

[36] Memelink 2009, p. 226 and Wolters 2013, p. 70.

[37] See in the parliamentary history of the DCC: Van Zeben et al. 1981, p. 268.

[38] Rossel draws a distinction between: (1) common opinions that are purely factual in nature and without any moral connotation, i.e. the assessment of a fact complex as it is and not as it should be and (2) common opinions or 'generally accepted views' which do have a moral connotation, i.e.

the appropriate legal consequences of a certain specific situation.[39] This creates an intertwined relationship with the concept of reasonableness and fairness,[40] a concept which permeates Dutch civil law. The issue of whether a breach of contract can be attributed to the breaching party then becomes a question of the view that exists in society regarding the distribution of risk.[41]

Circumstances which, on the basis of common opinion, are generally considered to be for the breaching party's account (and therefore do not justify an exception to the strict liability rule under Article 6:77 DCC) are circumstances which were foreseeable at the time the contract was concluded or which relate specifically to that party, such as lack of ability, illness or financial incapacity.[42] Other relevant circumstances in determining whether the exception applies are the nature and content of the contract and related insurance aspects. Who benefits from the situation is also important.[43] An assessment of these and other factors in a particular situation yields a common opinion on the reasonableness of the Article 6:77 DCC risk allocation in that situation. It is unlikely that, at least where the user is free to choose the object used and, in an extreme case, even decide not to use the object at all, common opinion will be held to require a reversal of that risk allocation in the sense that there is no strict liability.

In light of the user's freedom of choice and because the user is usually more knowledgeable than the customer about the quality of the object and is in a better position to obtain information about it, the three reasonableness exceptions should be interpreted restrictively and applied sparingly. This means that it is more likely that the user will be held liable for damage caused by the materialisation of unknown risks than that the customer will be required to bear this damage itself,[44] despite the user having exercised sufficient care in acquiring, monitoring and maintaining the object.

---

views on the consequences that should be given to a certain fact complex: Rossel 1994, pp. 335–344. See also: Jansen 2020, pp. 26–41.

[39] Memelink et al. 2008, pp. 31–51 and Memelink 2009, p. 140.

[40] Katan 2017, pp. 103–104 and Parket bij de Hoge Raad 13 September 2013, ECLI:NL:2013:1111, point 2.11. There are different opinions about the role of reasonableness and fairness in common opinion. See Cauffman and Croes 2020, Article 6:75 DCC, comment 8.12.

[41] Hiemstra 2018, p. 99. See with respect to the imputation of knowledge from a person to a company (on the basis of the views of the market and on how organisations should function) and the resulting risk allocation: Katan 2017, p. 102.

[42] Hijma and Olthof 2020, para 370 and Sieburgh 2020, nos. 353–361.

[43] Schutgens 2018, pp. 95–121.

[44] Broekema-Engelen 2020, Article 6:77 DCC, comment 3.7a.

14.4   AI and Property Law

14.4.1   The Concept of Object in the Dutch Civil Code

As explained above, Article 6:77 DCC only applies where an unsuitable object is used in connection with the performance of a contract. The term 'object' (*zaak*) appears in various provisions of the Dutch Civil Code.[45] When drafting the Code, the legislature intended that term to have the same meaning in all those provisions. Book 3 DCC contains the property law provisions and Article 2 of that book defines 'objects' as 'tangible property susceptible to human control'. Whenever 'object' is used in Book 6 DCC (which contains the law of obligations) reference is made to the Book 3 definition. The question therefore arises whether an AI system is an object under the Book 3 definition and, if not, whether a different interpretation of the concept of object can be applied in Book 6 of the Civil Code—which contains the law of obligations—and more specifically in Article 6:77 DCC.

Because of the opacity of AI, an AI system may fail to meet the 'susceptibility to human control' requirement,[46] but a more serious obstacle is the requirement that an object be tangible.[47] AI systems, however, are essentially algorithms implemented in software; software is not tangible, and the fact that it may be stored on a tangible hard disk does not change this.[48] This strict approach is perhaps understandable from a property law perspective, considering the need for individualisation and third-party notice. Third parties must, for example, be able to assume that the owner of registered property (or a right to such property) is the person who is entered as such in the relevant register[49] and, to a lesser extent, that the person who physically possesses non-registered property does so for himself/herself and is also the owner.[50]

For the sake of coherence and consistency it would be better if the term 'object' had the same meaning throughout the Civil Code and accordingly that the Book 3 definition—'tangible property susceptible to human control'—also applied in Article 6:77 DCC. However, as a result of new technological developments which the legislature was unable to take into account when drafting the Civil Code, strict adherence to this approach is no longer desirable. Two examples from sales law illustrate this. In both examples, it must be borne in mind that a sales contract is defined in Book 7 of the Dutch Civil Code (containing the law applicable to specific types of contracts) as a contract for the sale of an 'object' (*zaak*) (Article 7:1 DCC) or of a property

---

[45] See the following articles in Book 6 DCC: 27, 28, 41, 42, 66, 67, 70, 77, 90, 101, 173, 175, 176, 180, 187, 190, 191, 193, 230l, 230m, 230o, 230s, 230t, 230z and 236.

[46] Hildebrandt 2016, pp. 241–306.

[47] Physical objects are objects that can be perceived by the senses, see: Van der Steur 2003, pp. 110, 113 and 116.

[48] Van Erp and Loof 2016, pp. 30–31, Tweehuysen 2019, pp. 133–148. Of a different opinion with respect to software are: Kleve and De Mulder 1989, pp. 1342–1345 and Kleve 2004, especially Chapters 5 and 6.

[49] Article 3:24-26 DCC.

[50] Article 3:109 jo. 3:107(1) jo. 3:119(1) DCC.

right (*vermogensrecht*), such as an intellectual property right (Article 7:47 DCC). The first example is that when implementing EU Directive 97/7/EC on the protection of consumers in respect of distance contracts[51] in Dutch law in 2001, the legislature chose to classify a contract to acquire software at a distance (e.g. via a web shop) as a purchase agreement rather than a service agreement.[52] This was at odds with the legislative intent to use the same definition of 'object' throughout the Civil Code because software is not 'tangible property' and the licensing of software from a software company to a customer does not amount to a transfer of a property right within the meaning of Book 3. A second example is the 2012 Dutch Supreme Court judgment in *De Beeldbrigade/Hulskamp*. In that judgment, the Court ruled that a contract to acquire standard computer software for an unlimited period upon payment of a fixed amount falls within the scope of sales law, regardless of whether the software is supplied on a data carrier or via a download. However, the Court went on to say that its judgment did not pertain to the nature of software or license rights under property law.[53] The Supreme Court thereby clearly implied that whenever the word 'object' (*zaak*) is used in contract law (including sales law and, in our case, Article 6:77 DCC), it can be interpreted differently than when it is used in property law.

14.4.2 The Doctrine of Functional Equivalence

Relieved of the necessity to interpret the concept of 'object' as used in the law of obligations under the Dutch Civil Code in the same way as in property law, the next question is how to determine the interpretation that should be used in its place. An obvious solution is to apply the doctrine of functional equivalence. This doctrine entails, in short and stated abstractly, an examination of the function and effect of an existing rule in order to determine whether it will serve the same function and/or have the same effect in a new situation and, if not, whether and how it can be adapted to

---

[51] Article 6(3), 4th bullet point Directive 97/7/EC of the European Parliament and of the Council of 20 May 1997 on the protection of consumers in respect of distance contracts, OJ L 144, 4.6.1997, pp. 19–27, since replaced by Directive 2011/83/EU of the European Parliament and of the Council of 25 October 2011 on consumer rights, amending Council Directive 93/13/EEC and Directive 1999/44/EC of the European Parliament and of the Council and repealing Council Directive 85/577/EEC and Directive 97/7/EC of the European Parliament and of the Council, OJ L 304, 22.11.2011, pp. 64–88.

[52] See the former Article 7:46d(4) under c (excluding the right of withdrawal for "sale at a distance … of … computer software, if the purchaser has broken its seal" jo. the former Article 7:46a under b (definition of a distance sale as "the distance which is not a consumer purchase" and Article 7:5(1) DCC definition consumer purchase as the B2C "purchase with respect to a tangible good"), see Stb. 2001, 25.

[53] HR 27 April 2012, ECLI:NL:HR:2012:BV1301, *NJ* 2012/293 (*De Beeldbrigade/Hulskamp*), paras 3.5 and 3.4 respectively. See also Article 7:5(5) DCC in which the provisions on consumer purchase are declared applicable to the B2C 'supply of digital content which is not supplied on a tangible carrier, but which is individualised and over which actual power can be exercised…'.

serve that function and/or have that effect in the new situation.[54] Think, for example, of the early days of e-commerce when a recurring question was whether the legal requirement that a contract be entered into and signed in writing could also be met electronically. When devising new rules in this context, the EU and UNCITRAL examined the function (e.g. to ensure that the parties have read and considered the contract before signing, that they can be identified and that the document cannot be altered) and/or effect of that requirement (e.g. provide a certain degree of evidentiary protection) in order to determine whether electronic contracts could and should be equated with their paper counterparts in light of that function and effect and, if not, what further criteria had to be met.[55] Think also of liability situations. The High Level Expert Group on AI has proposed to expand the notion of vicarious liability (either directly or by means of analogous application) to functionally equivalent situations where AI systems are used instead of human auxiliaries.[56] According to the Group, the use of an AI system can serve the same function and have the same effect as the use of a human auxiliary and differential treatment of these two situations would be undesirable.

However, application of the functional equivalence doctrine does not automatically mean that the same rule should apply. It may be that the characteristics of the new situation require that the existing rule be modified in order to serve the same function and have the same effect.[57]

14.4.3 Application of the Functional Equivalence Doctrine

To apply the functional equivalence doctrine within the framework of Article 6:77 DCC, the functions and effect of that article must be determined. The article applies to situations in which the unsuitability of an object used in the performance of a contract has caused a breach. In the parliamentary history of Article 6:77 DCC, the object's form plays no role; its supportive function in the performance of the contract by the breaching party is decisive.

---

[54] UNICITRAL Model Law on Electronic Commerce with Guide to Enactment 1996 with additional article 5 bis as adopted in 1998, p. 20. https://uncitral.un.org/sites/uncitral.un.org/files/media-doc uments/uncitral/en/19-04970_ebook.pdf. Accessed 1 August 2021.

[55] See in a general sense the UNICITRAL Model Law on Electronic Commerce, p. 20 with respect to agreements concluded electronically Article 9 Directive 2000/31/EC of the European Parliament and of the Council of 8 June 2000 on certain legal aspects of information society services, in particular electronic commerce, in the Internal Market, OJ L 178, 17.7.2000, pp. 1–16 and with respect to electronic signatures (nowadays) Regulation (EU) No 910/2014 of the European Parliament and of the Council of 23 July 2014 on electronic identification and trust services for electronic transactions in the internal market and repealing Directive 1999/93/EC, OJ L 257, 28.8.2014, pp. 73–114 (in the Netherlands supplemented by Article 3:15a DCC). See for the electronic private deed Article 156a Dutch Code of Civil Procedure.

[56] Expert Group on Liability and New Technologies—New Technologies Formation 2019, inter alia on pp. 7, 11, 25 and 45/46.

[57] Koops 2006, pp. 77–108.

Neither Article 6:77 DCC nor its parliamentary history explicitly addresses the requirements that an object be tangible and susceptible to human control. Even without fulfilling these requirements, an AI system can be used to support the performance of a contract and, if it is unsuitable, can cause damage to the other party. One of the reasons for the introduction of Article 6:77 DCC was to prevent the party using the object from avoiding liability by hiding behind, *inter alia,* the producers, while at the same time profiting from its use.[58] The 'unless'-clause in the article then ensures that the risk is not imposed on the user where this would be unreasonable. Similarly, in the context of AI, it would be undesirable to allow the user—at least where it has made the decision to use an AI system and has selected that system—to hide behind the system's developer in order to avoid the strict liability envisaged by that article. There is no reason why the protection afforded to the injured party by the main rule in Article 6:77 DCC and to the breaching party by the 'unless' clause should not also apply to the situation in which AI is used in the performance of obligations. The two situations are functionally equivalent.

If we apply the attribution rule in Article 6:77 DCC to AI, this means that a party using an unsuitable AI system to perform a contract will be strictly liable to the injured party for any resulting damage unless this would be unreasonable on one of the stated grounds. The first ground—the content and purpose of the underlying juridical act (in this case the contract between the user and the customer)—will generally not apply if, under that contract, the user is responsible for selecting the AI system itself (but will apply if, for example, the contract requires the use of a specific system). The second ground—common opinion—will generally not help the user either, at least where the user has in fact selected the AI system used. Since the user's main purpose in deploying the AI system is probably to save costs and improve efficiency and the user thereby benefits from its deployment, and since the user can be expected to have more expertise with regard to the AI system than the customer and could have chosen not to use it at all, it is unlikely that under common opinion it will be considered unreasonable for the user to bear the risk. The third ground—other circumstances of the case—cannot be assessed outside a specific factual context.

14.5 Conclusion

Under Dutch law, a party who breaches an effort and/or result obligation is contractually liable for the other party's damage caused by that breach. The breaching party can under Article 6:74 and 6:75 DCC avoid liability by alleging and, if necessary, proving that the breach cannot be attributed to it because (1) it was not at fault and (2) based on a juridical act, common opinion or the law, the breach was not for its account. Where the breaching party (the user) uses an unsuitable object to perform its contractual obligations, the breach will be attributed to the user under Article 6:77 DCC unless such attribution would be unreasonable based on a juridical act, common

---

[58] See in the parliamentary history of the DCC: Van Zeben et al. 1981, p. 268.

opinion or other circumstances of the case. In effect, Article 6:77 DCC imposes strict liability on a party using an object to perform its contractual obligations, with exceptions based on unreasonableness. Pursuant to the functional equivalence doctrine, the defence that Article 6:77 DCC does not apply to the user of an AI system because that system is not a tangible object is unlikely to hold. The European Parliament's proposal for an AI civil liability regime also provides for strict liability, but only in relation to high-risk AI systems. Here too, a force majeure exception applies but what it entails is not clear. For non-high-risk AI systems, fault-based liability applies. According to the proposal, the fact that an AI system acts autonomously does not mean that the user or operator cannot be at fault. Circumstances that may give rise to such fault include a lack of diligence in selecting a suitable AI system, in monitoring its activities and in maintaining its operational reliability. These circumstances are very similar to the circumstances under Dutch case law that can make it possible to successfully invoke the defence of absence of fault: exercising sufficient care in the acquisition, maintenance and inspection of the object. However, in determining whether sufficient care has been exercised, the feasibility of the possible measures must be taken into account. The involvement of multiple parties in the operation of an AI system is a complicating factor. The European Commission's legislative proposal on product safety and its announced but not yet released civil liability proposal will have to be aligned with each other with respect to the required measures.

References

Abas P (1998) Wat komt – in de zin van art. 6:75 BW – naar de in het verkeer geldende opvattingen voor rekening van de schuldenaar? [What is for the account of the debtor within the meaning of Art. 6:75 Dutch Civil Code - according to common opinion?] NTBR 3:85–87.

Appelmans A, Herbosch M, Verheye B (2021) AI in Belgian Contract Law: Disruptive Challenge or Business as Usual. In: De Bruyne J, Vanleenhove C (eds) Artificial Intelligence and the Law. Intersentia, Brussels, pp 342–344.

Boonekamp RJB, Valk WL (eds) (2021) Stelplicht & Bewijslast [Burdens of allegation & proof]. Wolters Kluwer, Deventer.

Broekema-Engelen BJ (2020) Art. 6:77 Dutch Civil Code, comment 3.7a. In: Klomp RJQ, Schelhaas HN (eds) Groene Serie Verbintenissenrecht [Green Series Law of Obligations]. Wolters Kluwer, Deventer.

Busch D (2019) Flitshandel, andere vormen van algoritmische handel en directe elektronische markttoegang [Flash trading, other forms of algorithmic trade and direct electronic access to markets]. In: Jansen CJH, Schuijling BA, Aronstein IV (eds) Onderneming en digitalisering [Business and digitalisation]. Wolters Kluwer, Deventer, pp 253–277.

Cauffman C, Croes P (2020) Art. 6:75 DCC. In: Klomp RJQ, Schelhaas HN (eds) Groene Serie Verbintenissenrecht [Green Series Law of Obligations]. Wolters Kluwer, Deventer.

De Jong ER (2020) Een kroniek van ontwikkelingen op het snijvlak van aansprakelijkheid en innovatie op drie niveaus. Over innovatiebeleid, systemen van aansprakelijkheid en ontwikkelingsrisicoverweren [A chronicle of developments at the intersection of liability and innovation on three levels. Concerning innovation policy, systems of liability and development risk defences]. NTBR 28:202–206.

De Jong GT (2017) Niet-nakoming van verbintenissen. Monografieën BW B33 [Non-performance of obligations. Monograph Dutch Civil Code B33]. Wolters Kluwer, Deventer.

De Vey Mestdagh CNJ (2019) Calculo Ergo Sum (2): Over het recht en de ethiek van autonome systemen in computernetwerken [Calculo Ergo Sum (2): Concerning the law and ethics of autonomous systems in computer networks]. Tijdschrift voor Internetrecht 6:230–236.

Eichelberger J (2020) Zivilrechtliche Haftung für KI und smarte Robotik [Civil law liability for AI and smart robotics]. In: Ebers M, Heinze C, Krügel T, Steinrötter B (eds) Künstliche Intelligenz und Robotik. Rechtshandbuch [Artificial Intelligence and Robotics. Legal handbook]. C.H. Beck, Munich, pp 262–269.

European Commission (2020) WHITE PAPER: On Artificial Intelligence - A European approach to excellence and trust, 19 February 2020, COM (2020) 65 final. https://ec.europa.eu/info/publicati ons/white-paper-artificial-intelligence-european-approach-excellence-and-trust_en Accessed 1 August 2021.

European Commission (2021) Proposal for a Regulation of the European Parliament and of the Council laying down Harmonised Rules on Artificial Intelligence (Artificial Intelligence Act) and amending certain Union legislative acts', 21 April 2021, COM(2021) 206 final, 2021/0106 (COD). https://digital-strategy.ec.europa.eu/en/library/proposal-regulation-european-approach-artificial-intelligence.

European Parliament (2020a) Artificial Intelligence and Civil Liability. Study requested by the JURI committee, July 2020, PE 621.926. https://www.europarl.europa.eu/RegData/etudes/STUD/2020/621926/IPOL_STU(2020)621926_EN.pdf Accessed 1 August 2021

European Parliament (2020b) Resolution of 20 October 2020 with recommendations to the Commission on a civil liability regime for artificial intelligence (2020/2014(INL)), P9_TA(2020)0276. https://www.europarl.europa.eu/doceo/document/TA-9-2020-0276_EN.html Accessed 1 August 2021.

Expert Group on Liability and New Technologies – New Technologies Formation (2019) Liability for Artificial Intelligence and other emerging digital technologies, 27 November 2019. https://op.europa.eu/en/publication-detail/-/publication/1c5e30be-1197-11ea-8c1f-01aa75ed71a1/language-en/format-PDF Accessed 1 August 2021.

Fosch-Villaronga E (2020) Robots, Healthcare, and the Law. Regulating Automation in Personal Care. Routledge, Abingdon.

Hiemstra JT (2018) De aansprakelijkheid voor ongeschikte medische hulpzaken. Een rechtsvergelijkende en rechtseconomische analyse van de aansprakelijkheid van de hulpverlener jegens de patiënt. Recht en Praktijk nr. CA19 [Liability for unsuitable medical devices. A comparative law and law and economics analysis of the liability of a healthcare provider to the patient]. Wolters Kluwer, Deventer.

High-Level Expert Group on Artificial Intelligence set up by the European Commission (2019) A Definition of AI: Main Capabilities and Disciplines, 8 April 2019. https://digital-strategy.ec.europa.eu/en/library/definition-artificial-intelligence-main-capabilities-and-scientific-discip lines Accessed 1 August 2021.

Hijma J, Olthof MM (2020) Compendium van het Nederlandse Vermogensrecht [Compendium of Dutch property law]. Wolters Kluwer, Deventer.

Hildebrandt M (2016) Homo digitalis in het strafrecht [Homo digitalis in criminal law]. In: Moerel EML et al (eds) Homo digitalis. NJV Preadviezen. Wolters Kluwer, Deventer, pp 241–306.

Jansen KJO (2020) Verkeersopvattingen en private regelgeving: Over maatschappelijke opvattingen als bron van ongeschreven privaatrecht [Common opinions and private law legislation. Concerning societal opinions as a source of unwritten private law]. NTBR 5:26–41.

Katan BM (2017) Toerekening van kennis aan rechtspersonen. Serie Onderneming en Recht Deel 98 [Attribution of knowledge to legal persons]. Wolters Kluwer, Deventer.

Kaulartz M, Braegelmann T (2020) Rechtshandbuch Artificial Intelligence und Machine Learning [Handbook Artificial Intelligence and Machine Learning]. C.H. Beck, Munich.

Kleve P (2004) Juridische iconen in het informatietijdperk [Legal icons in the information era]. Kluwer, Deventer.

Kleve P, De Mulder RV (1989) De juridische status van software [The legal status of software]. NJB 37:1342–1345.

Koops BJ (2006) Should ICT Regulation be Technology-Neutral? In: Koops BJ et al (eds) Starting Points for ICT Regulation. Deconstructing Prevalent Policy One-Liners. IT&Law Series Vol. 9. T.M.C. Asser Press, The Hague, pp 77–108.

Memelink P (2008) De maatman en de verkeersopvatting [The reference person and the common opinion]. In: Castermans AG et al (eds) De maatman in het burgerlijk recht [The reference person in civil law]. Kluwer, Deventer, pp 31–51.

Memelink P (2009) De verkeersopvatting [Common opinion]. Boom Juridische Uitgevers, The Hague.

Navas S (2020) Robot Machines and Civil Liability. In: Ebers M, Navas S (eds) Algorithms and Law. Cambridge University Press, Cambridge.

Prins C (2020) Aansprakelijkheid voor AI-systemen [Liability for AI systems]. NJB 41:2804.

Rossel HJ (1994) De verkeersopvatting [Common opinion]. In: Hartlief T, Heisterkamp AHT, Reehuis WHM (eds) CJHB (Brunner-Bundel). Kluwer, Deventer, pp 335–344.

Schutgens RJB (2018) Automatische toerekening revisited. Een pleidooi voor herwaardering van het schuldvereiste bij rechtsvorming door de rechter [Automatics attribution revisited. A plea for reevaluation of the fault requirement in judicial lawmaking]. In: Jansen CJH, Van de Moosdijk MMC, Van Leuken R (eds) Nijmeegs Europees Privaatrecht. Serie Onderneming en Recht Deel 102 [Nijmegen European Private Law. Series Business and Law Volume 102]. Wolters Kluwer, Deventer, pp 95–121.

Sieburgh CH (2017) Mr. C. Assers Handleiding tot de beoefening van het Nederlands Burgerlijk Recht. 6. Verbintenissenrecht. Deel II. De verbintenis in het algemeen, tweede gedeelte (Asser/Sieburgh 6-II (2017)) [Mr. C. Assers Practical guide for the practice of Dutch Civil Law. 6. Law of obligations. Part II. The obligation in general, second part]. Wolters Kluwer, Deventer.

Sieburgh CH (2020) Mr. C. Assers Handleiding tot de beoefening van het Nederlands Burgerlijk Recht. 6. Verbintenissenrecht. Deel I. De verbintenis in het algemeen, eerste gedeelte (Asser/Sieburgh 6-I (2020)) [Mr. C. Assers Practical guide for the practice of Dutch Civil Law. 6. Law of obligations. Part I. The obligation in general, first part]. Wolters Kluwer, Deventer.

Tjittes RJPL (2018) Commercieel Contracteren [Commercial Contracting]. Boom Juridisch, The Hague.

Tjong Tjin Tai TFE (2006) Zorgplichten en zorgethiek [Duties of care and medical ethics]. Wolters Kluwer, Deventer.

Tjong Tjin Tai TFE (2010) De verkeersopvatting [Common opinion] (review of Memelink 2009). MvV 1:101–106.

Tweehuysen V (2019) Digitaal Goederenrecht – Een introductie [Digital property law - An introduction]. In: Jansen CJH, Schuijling BA, Aronstein IV (2019) Onderneming en digitalisering [Business and digitalisation]. Wolters Kluwer, Deventer, pp 133–148.

Van AJ (2011) De aansprakelijkheid voor gebrekkige medische hulpmiddelen – Implanon revisited [The liability for defective medical devices]. TVP 2:44–49.

Van Boom WH (2021) Gebrekkige hulpzaak bij medische behandeling [Defective auxillary objects in medical treatments]. Ars Aequi March:268–278.

Van Erp JHM, Loof W (2016) Eigendom in het algemeen; eigendom van digitale inhoud (titel 1) [Ownership in general; ownership of digital content (title 1)]. In: Verstappen LCA (ed) Boek 5 BW van de toekomst. KNB Preadviezen 2016. SDu, The Hague, pp 23–63.

Van der Steur JC (2003) Grenzen van rechtsobjecten. Een onderzoek naar de grenzen van objecten van eigendomsrechten en intellectuele eigendomsrechten [The boundaries of 'legal objects'. An exploration of the boundaries defining the types of the property that can be the subject of ownership rights and intellectual property rights]. Kluwer, Deventer.

Van Zeben CJ, Du Pon JW, Olthof MM (eds) (1981) Parlementaire Geschiedenis van het nieuwe Burgerlijk Wetboek. Boek 6, Algemeen gedeelte van het verbintenissenrecht [Legislative History of the new Civil Code. Book 6. General part of the law of obligations]. Parl. Gesch. Boek 6 BW. Kluwer, Deventer.

Verwilst GAM (2014) Geautomatiseerde handel in Europa onder MiFID II [Automated trade in Europe under MiFID II]. Tijdschrift voor Financieel Recht, 9:351–359.

Wagner G (2019) Robot Liability. In: Lohsse S, Schulze R, Staudenmayer D (eds) Liability for Artificial Intelligence and the Internet of Things. Münster Colloquia on EU Law and the Digital Economy IV. Nomos Verlagsgesellschaft, Baden-Baden, pp 37–40.

Wendehorst C, Grinzinger J (2020) Vertragsrechtliche Fragestellungen beim Einsatz intelligenter Agenten [Contract law questions when employing intelligent agents]. In: Ebers M, Heinze C, Krügel T, Steinrötter B (eds) Künstliche Intelligenz und Robotik. Rechtshandbuch [Artificial Intelligence and Robotics. Legal handbook]. C.H. Beck, Munich, pp 166–170.

Wolters PTJ (2013) Alle omstandigheden van het geval: Een onderzoek naar de omstandigheden die de werking van de redelijkheid en billijkheid beïnvloeden. Serie Onderneming en Recht Deel 77 ['All the circumstances of the case': An exploration of the circumstances which influence the operation of reasonableness and fairness]. Wolters Kluwer, Deventer.

Zhang D et al (2021) The AI Index 2021 Annual Report, AI Index Steering Committee, Human-Centered AI Institute, Stanford University, Stanford, CA. https://aiindex.stanford.edu/wp-content/uploads/2021/03/2021-AI-Index-Report_Master.pdf Accessed 1 August 2021.

Tycho J. de Graaf is an associate professor in civil law at Leiden University. His research and teaching covers civil law and focuses on technology and law. He researches, amongst other things, the civil law aspects of artificial intelligence in Leiden University's interdisciplinary programme SAILS (Society, Artificial Intelligence and Life Sciences). He is also a deputy judge at the district court in The Hague and an arbitrator at the SGOA (a foundation for the resolution of ICT disputes). Before becoming a fulltime academic, he worked as a lawyer at NautaDutilh N.V. for twenty years.

Iris S. Wuisman is Professor of Company Law at Leiden University since 2011 and was formerly an entrepreneur and lawyer. She is interested in the broad area of company law and more specifically the implications of artificial intelligence and blockchain technologies with regard to company law aspects. Her research on those topics is part of Leiden University's interdisciplinary programme SAILS (Society, Artificial Intelligence and Life Sciences). Iris established the Business & Liability Research Network (BLRN) together with her colleagues from the Company Law department and the department of Business Studies in January 2018. Furthermore, she is a board member of the Law Firm School and the Harry Honée foundation. She is also editor of the Yearbook Corporate Governance and the Dutch Journal of Company Law.

Chapter 15
Digging into the Accountability Gap: Operator's Civil Liability in Healthcare AI-systems

Kostina Prifti, Evert Stamhuis and Klaus Heine

Contents

Abstract The increasing autonomy of artificial intelligence systems (AI-systems) has put the debate about a possible 'accountability gap' in liability law center stage. The debate is about a possible failure of incumbent liability regimes to pinpoint the accountable agent, if in the wrongdoing an AI-system is involved. A recent attempt to address this 'accountability gap' is a proposal of the European Parliament, which advances laws on civil liability for the entities that control AI-systems. These newly created entities, which have no blueprint yet in liability law, are called 'Operators'. By branching out on the healthcare applications of AI-systems, this chapter analyzes the concept of operator's civil liability. It starts with a description of the liability

K. Prifti (✉) · E. Stamhuis · K. Heine
Erasmus School of Law, Erasmus University Rotterdam, Burgemeester Oudlaan 50, 3062 PA
Rotterdam, The Netherlands
e-mail: prifti@law.eur.nl

E. Stamhuis
e-mail: stamhuis@law.eur.nl

K. Heine
e-mail: heine@law.eur.nl

E. Stamhuis
Court of Appeal's Hertogenbosch, Den Bosch, The Netherlands

University of Aruba, Oranjestad, Aruba

© T.M.C. ASSER PRESS and the authors 2022
B. Custers and E. Fosch-Villaronga (eds.), *Law and Artificial Intelligence*,
Information Technology and Law Series 35,
https://doi.org/10.1007/978-94-6265-523-2_15

concepts presented in the proposed legislation, and how they fit doctrinally with the laws and regulations of the current medical liability regime. Complementing the doctrinal analysis, this chapter employs a law and economics analysis, which showcases that the accountability gap is a serious challenge also from a consequentialist point of view. Lastly, this chapter proposes a few legal alternatives that depart from the incumbent concept of strict liability.

Keywords Accountability gap · Liability · AI-systems · European Parliament · Operator · Law and economics

15.1 Introduction

In October 2020, the European Parliament (EP) accepted a resolution containing a proposal to the European Commission (EC), for the civil liability of operators of AI-systems ('the proposal'),[1] with operators being defined as the actors who are in control of, and benefit from AI-systems.[2] The proposal introduces this concept in the regulatory system of liability in the EU, along with specific rules of strict or negligence liability for this new actor. These changes are proposed because of a perceived shift in context factors that AI-systems raise in relation to the incumbent liability regime. Moreover, a timely adaptation of the EU liability regime shall support transactions in the single market and promote the development and deployment of AI in the EU.

There are three ways how AI-systems pose a shift in context factors in relation to the liability regime: The autonomy risk, the association risk, and the network risk.[3] Firstly, the increasing autonomy of AI-systems implies a learning process that enables those systems to change their own program and become unpredictable. Secondly, the interaction between humans and AI-systems becomes complex and perplexes the possibility to understand the exact separation of roles and tasks between humans and AI-systems. And thirdly, the network risk considers the complex interactions between AI-systems among each other, creating "an ensemble of concurrently active polymorphic intelligent agents".[4]

These disruptions relate to the liability regime through key concepts like causation, fault, and deterrence. The inability of operating actors to predict the actions and decisions of AI-systems risks breaking the chain of causation, as foreseeability is a

---

[1] European Parliament Resolution 2020b. This proposal can be seen as a continuation and manifestation of other related documents issued by expert bodies of EU institutions, such as the "Liability for artificial intelligence and other emerging digital technologies" by the Expert Group on Liability and New Technologies—New Technologies Formation and the "Ethics Guidelines for Trustworthy Artificial Intelligence" by the High-Level Expert Group on AI. This chapter was basically concluded before publication of the draft AI Act by the European Commission, COM (2021) 206 final, but we could conclude that this latter proposal does not relate to civil liability.

[2] Article 3 of the proposal.

[3] Teubner 2018, p. 107.

[4] Karnow 1996, p. 191.

central tenet of causation.[5] Lack of foreseeability also makes deterrence ineffective, because the actors involved cannot be incentivized to avoid a damage they reasonably cannot foresee. Moreover, the inability to understand what the wrongful actions of each actor are in the complex network makes it difficult to assign responsibility. Such disabilities are also referred to as the 'responsibility gap 'or 'liability gap'.[6] Perhaps a terminology clarification is in order. Firstly, denoting a liability gap expresses a function of location, rather than nature. The term responsibility gap may be more appropriate, however, responsibility has a higher threshold than accountability, due to the cognitive requirements that it implies (e.g., intentionality).[7] Accountability ensures a proper functioning of the liability regime, even when there is a gap in responsibility, so the nature of the problem is better perceived as an accountability gap, i.e., the inability to pinpoint an accountable agent who needs to compensate the harm, in situations where an AI system is involved.

A full assessment of the proposal comprises both the doctrinal quality as well as its economic efficiency. While there is considerable convergence, as well as some divergence, between the proposal and the various documents mentioned in footnote, 1 the proposal adopts and develops the concepts that are present in a more or less systematic framework. As such, it presents itself as a meaningful legislative step on the idea and mechanisms for strict liability of operators, which in turn calls for— *inter alia*—a doctrinal and economic analysis. Consequently, Sect. 15.2 provides a description of the proposal, its main concepts, and relevant mechanisms. In Sect. 15.3 the chapter offers an analysis of the proposal in the dimension of legal criteria as conceptual clarity, systematic consistency and matching the subject matter. Then, in Sect. 15.4, the discussion will be expanded into the economics dimension and it will be asked to what extent the proposal can meet the ambition to allocate liability in a socially optimal way. Thereby the focus will be on a specific sector: The medical application of AI-systems. Medical use of AI-systems will very likely be listed as high risk and fall under the proposal. Moreover, the medical sector provides an excellent context for discussing the intricacies of the proposal as such, because AI-systems become specifically developed and deployed there. Finally, the newly proposed law will—upon acceptance—interact with the incumbent liability laws, that have shown a tendency to diversity, of which medical liability law is one quite specific branch.

15.2   The Proposal

The proposal on civil liability for operators of AI-systems takes as its starting point a shift in context factors that are identified in the literature as the 'accountability gap'. The proposal refers specifically to the opacity of AI-systems (black-box problem),

---

[5] Ibid.

[6] Matthias 2004, p. 175.

[7] Floridi and Sanders 2004, p. 364.

the multitude of actors, and the increasing autonomy of AI-systems.[8] It then seeks to overcome the liability issues created by AI-systems by introducing four categories of actors: front-end operators, back-end operators, users, and producers. The first two categories are a novelty in EU liability law. The proposal defines the front-end operator broadly as the entity that has control over the AI-system and that benefits from operating the AI-system.[9] The back-end operator is defined along the same lines; it is the entity that offers continuous back-end services, such as defining the features of the technology and providing data.[10] Both categories of operators are considered to exercise a certain level of control over the AI-systems.

When the same actor is both the front-end and back-end operator, also the legal regime is the same. It is also possible that the operator is the producer of the AI-system, in which case the Directive on Product Liability (PLD)[11] becomes relevant. In case that the front-end operator is also the producer of the AI-system, the EP proposes that the liability regime of operators should prevail. If the back-end operator is also the producer, the proposal gives way to the PLD as the prevailing applicable law. When there is only one operator, it is proposed that civil liability of operators should prevail as applicable law. It is important to note that the proposal counts on the inclusion of software as a product under the scope of PLD, along with inclusion of software 'makers' as producers.[12]

With this regime the EP expects to guide the liability allocation clearly and predictably to the relevant actors, so that courts will be able to resolve conflicts over it, when they arise. In practice, the exercise to allocate roles can be more complicated than it appears. Two examples taken from health care may showcase this lack of clarity. Consider the Smart Tissue Autonomous Robot (STAR), used for intestinal laparoscopic surgery.[13] It is able to develop the suturing plan in an automated way, with the surgeon supervising and having the ability to make positional adjustments that in turn impact the suturing plan. The hospital may be considered an operator, as it is in control of and benefits from the use of STAR, but the doctor also has an important supervisory role. It is unclear if the doctor would be an operator, a user, or simply irrelevant, especially considering that the doctor might not be employed by the hospital. In another example, we consider Sweet Home, a home automation system typically used to monitor a patient's wellbeing.[14] The daily operation of Sweet Home may be handled by the producer, which the hospital or another care institution contracts for its patients. It is not clear if the hospital would be considered a user or an operator in this case. And what is the patient? The distinction between users and

---

[8] Recital 3 of the proposal.

[9] Article 3 of the proposal.

[10] Ibid.

[11] Council Directive 85/374/EEC of 25 July 1985 on the approximation of the laws, regulations and administrative provisions of the Member States concerning liability for defective products OJ L 210, 7.8.1985, pp. 29–33.

[12] See Point 8 of the Introduction to the proposal.

[13] Shademan et al. 2016, p. 341.

[14] Shishhegar et al. 2018, p. 1.

Table 15.1 Liability regimes according to the proposal [*Source* The authors]

Actor/risk level	High-risk	Low-risk
User	Negligence liability	Negligence liability
Front-end operator	Strict liability	Negligence liability
Back-end operator	Strict liability	Negligence liability
Producer	Strict liability	Strict liability

end-users becomes more relevant through these examples, however this is missing in the proposal.[15] By qualifying the actors involved, the various positions for liability of any harm are supposed to be defined. While the doctor is distinguished from the operator based on the level of control over the AI-system,[16] it is yet not clear what one may use as a threshold to separate the user from the operator in each context. As soon as the doctor has a level of control, she may fall into the operators' category, with a shift in liability. As said, this distinction is important in order to understand which liability regime is applicable. However, the proposal clarifies in article 2(3) that the victim is not refrained from seeking compensation based on other liability regimes, such as medical malpractice.

Beside the distinction of actors and introducing the new category of operator, the proposal makes a distinction between high-risk and low-risk sectors and uses. This adds another level of sophistication to the liability regime. The outcome of this is a matrix with eight cells of liability regimes (Table 15.1).

It is important to note that under negligence liability the operator must be found in default of a certain action or omission before being held liable, whereas under strict liability the operator is liable merely because the harm or damage has occurred. It is also worth noting that Article 8 of the proposal shifts the burden of proof for negligence liability to the operator, for the latter to prove that one of the circumstances described there applies. Shifting the burden of proof from the victim to the operator facilitates the allocation of liability and eventual compensation for the victim, since the latter may not always be able to prove the negligence of the operator, due to lack of insight, even when there is negligence in the case.

The proposal does not list the high-risk areas and uses of AI-systems; the list is left to be drawn and updated by the EC.[17] However, in a related proposal of the EP on an ethical framework for artificial intelligence,[18] healthcare as an area, and medicine as a use, are listed as high risk. Similar categorizations follow in other legal acts, such as in the GDPR.[19] Therefore, this chapter treats healthcare AI-systems as belonging

---

[15] It is however found in the "Ethics Guidelines for Trustworthy Artificial Intelligence" by the High-Level Expert Group on AI.

[16] Recital 11 of the proposal.

[17] Recital 14 of the proposal.

[18] European Parliament Resolution 2020a and European Commission 2020.

[19] Regulation (EU) 2016/679 of the European Parliament and of the Council of 27 April 2016 on the protection of natural persons with regard to the processing of personal data and on the free movement of such data, and repealing Directive 95/46/EC, OJ L 119, 4.5.2016, pp. 1–88, Article 9.

to the high-risk category, and as a result assumes that operators of healthcare AI-systems would face strict liability whenever a harm or damage arises from these AI-systems.

15.3 The Doctrinal Instability

15.3.1 The Product/Service Dichotomy

In this section the doctrinal inconsistencies and deficiencies are highlighted, arising from the proposal. They result from the combination of strict liability with the new category of operator. Those inconsistencies are also the drivers against closing the accountability gap and attaining the behavioral economic objectives of the liability regime, as elaborated in Sect. 15.4.

The actual medical liability framework in the EU is based on two pillars: the PLD and national laws regulating medical malpractice. The former is harmonized, while the latter are not.[20]

The PLD induces a strict liability regime for damages caused by defective products, which includes medical devices. While the victim is required to prove the defect, the damage, and the causal link between defect and damage, the victim is not required to prove fault or negligence of the producer. Simultaneously, the producer is not shielded from liability by proving lack of fault or negligence. Hence, the producer must compensate whenever a defective product causes a damage, save for some exceptions.[21]

Medical malpractice is not harmonized by EU law. In fact, the EU attempted to harmonize liability of services through a Directive, albeit unsuccessfully.[22] As a result, medical malpractice is regulated under the national laws of Member States.[23] Although variations exist, medical malpractice, similarly to liability of other services, is based on negligence liability.[24] The potentially wrongful behavior of the medical professional is tested under an objective standard of care.[25] Oftentimes, the negligence-based liability is fine-tuned in national law by shifting the burden of proof to the defender, and by variations of vicarious liability or enterprise liability of the hospital.[26] The latter is also referred to as "negligence liability with an extra debtor",[27] the result of which, in practice, is that the employer or contractor is strictly liable to

---

[20] Koch 2011, pp. 1–39.

[21] Article 7 of the PLD.

[22] Proposal for a Council Directive on the liability of suppliers of services, COM (90) 482 final—SYN 308 of 20 December 1990.

[23] For a systematic analysis of member state laws on medical liability, see Koch 2011.

[24] Koch 2011, pp. 10–21.

[25] Koch 2011, pp. 8–10.

[26] Koch 2011, pp. 10–21.

[27] Van Dam 2013, p. 300.

compensate the damage caused by its employee or contracted party, but only when negligence is proven on the side of the acting professional.

The co-existence of these two regimes in the medical liability framework is a manifestation of the product/service dichotomy, maintained in case law even in hybrid cases, such as when the service provider supplies both a product and a service. The European Court of Justice (ECJ) has sharply distinguished that the service provider would be strictly liable if the product was defective, while if the service was defective there would be liability based on negligence.[28] Such distinctions are much harder to identify in cases where AI-systems are involved, as, for example, microsurgical robots that work under the supervision of a surgeon.[29] The hospital would firstly purchase the robot as a product, but may also purchase the service of maintaining and feeding the robot with datasets and learning techniques from the same AI company. As one can easily see, the complexity of robots in the medical context makes it difficult to maintain the distinction of the ECJ, leading to very difficult exercises to allocate liability. What failure led to the harm and to what degree? Was it the failing robot or the absence of proper oversight of the doctors and nurses? The tight man-machine cooperation in AI-systems makes it challenging to dissect all components with regard to causal inference.

It boils down to the question: are AI-systems products, services, or both? The proposal is not explicit about the issue, although the terms used to refer to the nature of AI-systems are 'activities, devices, and processes',[30] which can be interpreted in a way that we have an interplay between a product and a service. This brings forth a major deficiency of the proposal. It presupposes that the distinction between products and services is irrelevant for liability. However, on closer inspection, this stance would lead to infractions on the PLD regime to the detriment of the victim. For example, when the producer of an AI-system also provides updates and maintenance under a comprehensive maintenance (service) contract, the PLD regime would be undermined because negligence liability would be applicable,[31] with possibly less protection for the victim.[32] This is also true when the PLD regime would be extended to software.

---

[28] Ibid.

[29] Ficuciello et al. 2019, p. 30.

[30] Recital 17 of the proposal.

[31] See Article 8 of the proposal for negligence-based liability rules.

[32] Besides defect, harm, and causal link, the negligence-based regime requires a higher threshold for liability, specifically a breach of duty of care, which in turn offers less protection for the victim compared to the PLD regime which would allocate liability regardless of any specified breach in the duty of care.

15.3.2   The Causation Turbulence

The element of causation is indispensable for a proper understanding of the concept of liability. It is the ability to distinguish an injury from a misfortune and to isolate the accountable actor(s) from the multitude of events/actions leading to the injury/harm.[33] In the medical context many professionals and devices play an important part in the treatment and care of patients. Causation is therefore an important instrument with which to find the accountable actor(s). If causation cannot be proven, then the accountability gap widens, and the liability framework produces legal as well as economic failure.

The literature explains the likelihood for failure by using two concurring elements: Control and foreseeability.[34] For example, the producer of a medical device is assumed to be in control of the manufacturing process, as well as to be able to reasonably foresee all the uses of the device and the expectations of the users (doctor, nurse, laboratory analyst etc.). When the producer can prove that a defect was not reasonably foreseeable,[35] or that the defect occurred due to circumstances out of his control,[36] the producer may escape liability, because there is no causal link between the harm and the product defect. Therefore, any liability regime must keep a keen eye on control and foreseeability of damages.

The concept of control plays an important role in the proposal. It is one of the elements used to define the operator.[37] Recital 10 explains that the rationale of the proposal is based on the fact that the operator exercises a degree of control over the AI-system, comparable to the control that an owner has over its car. However, there appears to be a contradiction between Recital 10 and Article 3, as the latter defines control as *any* action that influences the operation of an AI-system. Perceiving control as *any* action of influence is a lower standard than the control normally required under strict liability. Therefore, it is unclear which version of control the proposal assumes to exist with operators over AI-systems. Is it 'any influence' or the standard level of control?

Both versions of control are problematic. Firstly, if we consider that the standard of control can be lowered to equate influence, then we can support the conclusion that operators are in control over the performance of the AI-systems. They can substantially influence the learning process, the data sets that are fed, and the environment where the AI-system will be deployed.[38] However, such an interpretation of control is incompatible with the concept of control that currently justifies the strict liability rationale. Producers are not able to merely "influence" the manufacturing process, but they must control it to such a degree that they get the desired output. The driver

---

[33] Karnow 1996, p. 191.

[34] Matthias 2004 and Karnow 1996. The role of control and foreseeability is also evident in the PLD, respectively Article 7(e).

[35] O'Quin 2000, p. 287 and Karnow 1996, p. 191.

[36] Matthias 2004, p. 175.

[37] Article 3 of the proposal.

[38] Ibid.

of a (non-autonomous) vehicle is not "influencing" but controls every move of the vehicle. To put it briefly, if one accepts that the operator's degree of control over an AI-system is on a level of influencing the system, and not being in control of its performance, the rationale for strict liability of such operators fails its doctrinal requirements. A compromised level of control is insufficient to support causation in all variety of circumstances.

Similarly, if one was to assume that operators have a high degree of control over AI-systems in healthcare, comparable to the driver of a vehicle or the producer of a product, it would fulfil the causation requirements. However, the ability of operators to have such a degree of control is unsubstantiated by research.[39] The machine learning rationale, supervised or unsupervised, is based on unpredictability of the learning process as one of its main benefits.[40] While methods to audit what the algorithm has learned exist, these methods are yet not perfect and often it is not even possible for the programmer to know how the algorithm made the decision, specifically in cases of deep learning.[41] This problem is also known as the 'black-box' problem, which the proposal also recognizes.[42] Based on this understanding, the assumption that operators have such a degree of control over the AI-systems that they are able to foresee and predict the damage that AI-systems may cause is not mirrored by reality.

To summarize, it is evident that AI-systems cause a turbulence of the elements of causation, leading to a lack of control and foreseeability. The proposal largely overlooks the turbulence in causation by introducing strict liability for operators. An adoption of the proposal would therefore lead to two unwelcomed consequences: Either operators would still be able to escape liability, because the causal link fails, or an overstretch of the liability framework is accepted, according to which causation is no longer conditioned on control and foreseeability of the damage. Both options have the potential to disrupt the intention of the liability regime and the objectives behind it. The former would leave the victim with less recourse vis-à-vis the operator, while the latter makes the actual use of the technology unattractive. Moreover, the economic rationale associated with liability regimes becomes thwarted as will be shown in the next section.

---

[39] See Matthias 2004 and the discussion on the accountability gap in Sect. 15.1.

[40] Alpaydin 2016, pp. 1–28.

[41] Annany and Crawford 2018.

[42] Recital 3 of the proposal.

15.4   Economic Analysis

In this section we reflect on the operator's liability more conceptually, supplementing the doctrinal analysis by an economic analysis that sheds more light on the requirements that a modern liability regime must fulfil. To that end it is necessary to distinguish between three analytical steps: (1) the basic function of liability law; (2) the situational context factors for attributing liability; (3) the expected effect of the liability regime and its social desirability.

15.4.1   The Two Basic Functions of Liability Law

Liability law has two functions: Compensation of victims and deterrence of wrongdoing.[43] Providing a fair compensation for victims in case of a mischief is largely with which liability law scholars are concerned. There exists a plethora of legal doctrinal literature that tries to find out what fair compensation is, and under which circumstances a specific rule applies.[44]

Any compensation must come from some funds, and becoming sentenced to pay compensation has repercussions on the behavior of agents. Thereby it obviously makes a difference whether one operates under unlimited personal liability or if one is exempted from liability, has limited liability, or is insured. That means that there is, beyond the question of what is seen as a morally fair compensation, another question which asks how the likelihood of a wrongdoing leads to an obligation to pay compensation and how this affects the activity and care level of selling products and services. This question covers the second function of liability law, in which the economic analysis is mostly interested. Which design of liability law drives decision making over risky activities towards the socially optimal amount of damages?[45]

In this chapter it cannot be discussed how liability law affects the activity and care level of (risky) activities in detail. For the purposes of this chapter, it is more important to recollect why, next to individual liability the doctrine of enterprise liability is in place, putting liability not only on individuals but also on companies, for example, hospitals.[46]

The generic logic for enterprise liability follows from a simple syllogism: (a) The majority of products and services are delivered by manufacturers organized in enterprises (that is not different in health care); (b) holding enterprises liable is setting optimal incentives; (c) therefore, holding enterprises liable is socially beneficial.[47]

For the future it can be expected that most AI-systems will be active in enterprises; for example, surgery robots will be around in hospitals or nursery robots in elderly

---

[43] Posner 1972 and Shavell 2007.

[44] See, e.g., van Dam 2013.

[45] Shavell 2007. For an overview, see Cooter and Ulen 2012 and Posner 2011.

[46] Heine and Grabovets 2015, p. 44. For a discussion see also Arlen 1994.

[47] Engstrom 2013.

homes. Hence, condition (a) of the syllogism is applicable. But one may wonder whether condition b) is still fulfilled. Condition (b) assumes that letting enterprises pay compensation sets incentives for the enterprise to control the risk and to do the necessary research and development for improving the product quality. Besides that, it is assumed that considerable profits accrue to enterprises and that, therefore, enterprises have the capacity to pay compensation. But what if this intuition would no longer be true? What if the nexus between liability and incentivizing firms to manage developmental risks is no longer given? What if a surgeon can neither control nor improve a surgery-robot, not even in conjunction with the technicians of a hospital? Then the enterprise—the hospital—might still be able to pay compensations to victims, thereby fulfilling the first function of liability law, but it would no longer fulfil the second function, which is optimal deterrence and bringing damages down to the optimal social level.

This creates three challenges for the legislator: (1) identifying a target for liability law that is better suited than the enterprise, while maintaining the two functions of liability and its doctrinal requirements; (2) adapting the doctrines of liability law and thereby embracing AI-systems within a new perimeter of liability law (3) or stepping out of liability law and regulate damages caused by AI by other legal means.

15.4.2 A Change in Context Factors

Whether there is a serious problem for the application of incumbent liability law for cases in which AI-systems are involved depends on whether AI-systems create a change in the context factors in which incumbent liability law usually operates. As already mentioned in the introduction, there exist three risks. [48] (1) The autonomy risk: if an AI learns, decides, and acts in a non-predictable way, then it comes closer to an autonomous agent that might be treated as an entity with a separate legal personhood. This understanding raises new questions with regard to incentivizing the optimal behavior in AI-systems. (2) The association risk: it is not necessarily clear who the master and who the servant is in each possible situation, for instance a surgeon and a robot learning from each other. (3) The network risk: This risk emerges when, e.g., algorithmic platforms interconnect local AI-systems in hospitals, in order to accelerate machine-learning and to maintain the robots' performance. This risk raises questions on the possibility to design a 'network liability'. [49]

AI-systems change the landscape in which incumbent liability law is used to operate. One may compare that with a situation in which a Formula 1 racing car would be supposed to drive off-road. The importance of the fit between context factors and advanced technology was already highlighted by Nobel laureate Herbert Simon in 1960 when he was asked to sketch out the challenges of automation 25 years ahead in

---

[48] Teubner 2018, pp. 129–149.
[49] Ibid.

1985.[50] Again, this is not an issue of 1 or 0, but a question of overstretching incumbent liability law. This is similarly to a car (liability law) with not enough horsepower (inappropriate doctrinal law) and a weak clutch (not well-prepared courts) cruising through the Alps (a world of digitalization). Then it is only a matter of a few kilometers climbing the hills before the car overheats and the machine collapses.

15.4.3 The Expected Effect of the Liability Regime

The foregoing analysis did not highlight all intricacies with which liability law is confronted in a world of AI and Big Data. However, it became clear that the two functions of liability law—compensation and deterrence—are no longer easily fulfilled by incumbent liability law doctrines. They neither set an accurate incentive for doctors in health care, nor for the health care institutions to maintain an optimal level of damages when AI-systems are at play. That has largely to do with the fact that AI-systems cannot fully be controlled by the doctor or the hospital and—that seems even more important—cannot technically be improved by them. That means the deterrence effect of liability law has no effect or may lead to unintended consequences. For example, health care providers might largely abandon advanced AI-systems or marginalizing it to a degree which does not overstretch the incumbent legal doctrines. Or, similarly as in US hospitals, where doctors are not employees of the hospital in order to avoid vicarious liability, strange contractual relations between hospitals, doctors and AI-system operators would be created to somehow fit in the new technologies in the incumbent legal framework.[51] It is apparent that those individual avoidance strategies are not collectively rational and are diminishing potential social welfare gains through the new technology.

What also becomes clear is that the manufacturer or the intermediate providers of AI services must get a more prominent role in the liability regime than it is the case today. It is the manufacturer or provider who has primary control and can monitor the developmental risks of AI-systems.[52] This becomes prominently apparent in the network risk of AI, but it is also prevalent in the autonomy and association risk. For that background it is intuitively clear to put forward a concept like in the proposal that aims at allocating the liability to the entity that can control and foresee potential harms. But shifting strict liability without any further reflections to a so-called operator or the producers of AI-systems is inherently an overstretch of the incumbent system. This approach makes the same mistake as leaving the current system unchanged, because it is only broadening the incumbent doctrines of liability law without making any substantial changes to it. Operators will find ways to contract around, avoiding a position of being held strictly liable; similar to US hospitals avoiding vicarious liability for the malpractice of their doctors. Or,

---

[50] Simon 1960, pp. 17–55.

[51] See, e.g., Abraham and Weiler 1994, and Cebul et al. 2008.

[52] Galasso and Luo 2019, pp. 493–504.

operators and producers will simply not provide advanced AI-system solutions if they must fear strict liability. A chilling effect on innovation is then the result.

A more comprehensive approach to liability law reform is advisable, which is more likely to bring damages caused by AI-systems on a social optimal level. It comprises changes within liability law as well as regulatory measures outside the classical perimeter of liability law.[53] A *first* line of reform would include a debate about introducing legal personhood for AI-systems.[54] That way a more tailored attribution of responsibility for autonomous decision making would become possible as well as a better alignment with contract and property law. More technically, AI-systems would be integrated into the "nexus of contracts" that a firm basically is.[55] Thereby it is not meant to create legal personality in analogy to a human, but according to the functions and purposes AI-systems fulfill in a specific context. That is like the invention of company law that has evolved over the last 200 years into a highly differentiated legal tool to facilitate innovation and productivity in modern societies.[56]

A *second* line of reform would have to focus on so-called *design regulations*. Those regulations would prescribe *ex ante* for AI-systems a specific technical design, as for example a robot arm must not be longer than 1 meter for a specific application, or the software must not include a specific sort of algorithm. But a design regulation may also prescribe that a surgeon co-working with a robot needs a specific training and license to work with the robot. In that sense design regulations contain a whole spectrum of regulations ranging from hardware requirements[57] to the law of professions.

A *third* line of reform would have to consider the social relevance of AI-systems vis-à-vis the risk that it may bear for the single individual.[58] Individuals may realize the enormous benefit of AI for society as such, but may fear at the same time becoming an uncompensated victim of the new technology. In order to avoid that individual rationality inhibits collective rationality, compensation of harm must be guaranteed. There is the possibility of mandating liability insurance for AI-systems (as already indicated in the proposal), whenever it is economically feasible. But that might not be applicable in all cases, and mandating compensation from liability law indifferently

---

[53] A collection of alternative regulations added to liability law can be found in Rachum-Twaig 2020. Similarly, Galasso and Luo 2019, pp. 493–504.

[54] In 2017 the European Parliament was open to this attribute of electronic entities; Res. P8_TA(2017)0051. The sometimes-furious responses (e.g. Robotics, *Open letter to the European Commission Artificial Intelligence and robotics,* http://www.robotics-openletter.eu/) appear to have wiped the whole idea off the table. The Commission's White Paper of February 2020 remains silent; EC White Paper of 19 February 2020, COM (2020) 65 final.

[55] The basic idea of conceiving the firm as a "nexus of contracts" has been put forward by Jensen and Meckling 1976. For a legal discussion, see also Easterbrook and Fischel 1989.

[56] For the facilitative effect of corporate law for industrialization in a comprehensive political setting see, for example, Pistor et al. 2002.

[57] Design regulations are also discussed for 3D-printing, which is another disruptive digital technology. See Heine and Li 2019.

[58] See Fosch-Villaronga 2019 for a risk-based approach to regulation of healthcare robots.

may thwart the technology as such.[59] Thus, as it is already the case with new vaccines, new aircrafts or nuclear technology, a partial and temporary liability exemption for AI-systems might be in order.[60] This exemption must then be accompanied by a compensation scheme paid out by the government as the most potent insurer of a socially desired innovation that otherwise would not be provided.[61]

In summary, the debate about operator's liability in healthcare is part of a larger debate about the applicability of incumbent liability law to cases in which AI-systems are involved. Whether granting legal personhood to AI-systems is the key to avoid a "doctrinal overstretch" of incumbent liability law on the one hand and to avoid an accountability gap on the other hand, will only become clear in future decennia, similarly to the introduction of the limited liability company, in a reaction to the socio-economic and technological disruptions of the colonial trade boost and consec-utively, the industrial revolution.[62] For the time being it is advisable to have a mix of legal reforms that consider very specific design regulations to avoid non-acceptable harm, as well as insurance schemes for compensation—including the government as guarantor of last resort—to facilitate and disseminate the application of AI-systems in society.

15.5 Conclusion and Further Research

This chapter undertakes a critical analysis of the idea to put strict liability on operators of AI-systems in healthcare, as has been recently proposed by the EP. An important finding is that the legislative proposal does not address the product/service dichotomy in relation to AI-systems. This leads to uncertainties and disruptions in the product liability framework of the EU. Moreover, the analysis highlights a doctrinal incon-sistency in the level of control needed for operators of AI-systems to fall under strict liability. Either operators would be able to escape liability because the causal link for wrongdoing is missing, or an overstretch of the liability framework is accepted, according to which causation is no longer conditioned on control and foreseeability of the damage.

The economic analysis points out that the deterrence effect, as one of the two rationales behind a liability framework, does not work in cases when the enterprise is not in control of the harm or damage that may occur from the use of AI-systems. That means that as a necessary condition the doctrinal law must be consistent to make

---

[59] The economic effects of granting limited liability are yet not fully understood and are dependent on specific contexts. A recent study by Koudijs and Salisbury 2020 on the effect of limited liability in marital property law sheds more light on the "social innovation" of limited liability.

[60] For a similar argument, see Galasso and Luo 2019, pp. 97–98.

[61] Here it might be interesting to learn from the literature on catastrophe insurance by smart public-private insurance schemes. This literature puts less the deterrence aspect into focus (a catastrophe is to a large degree an unavoidable random shock), but the compensation of victims. See, e.g., Bruggeman et al. 2010.

[62] For a recent discussion on AI and legal personality, see Chesterman 2020.

the economics work towards a welfare improvement. Moreover, the shift in context factors, namely the autonomy risk, the association risk, and the network risk, implies the need to introduce a new actor in the liability framework, such as the operator of AI-systems, to whom harm and damage can be rightly attributed. However, affording strict liability to the operator of the AI-system as foreseen in the proposal would lead either to attempts of bypassing liability as such by complex contractual arrangements between the operators and users of AI-systems, or a chilling effect for the use of the AI-systems can be expected. Both cases are detrimental to social welfare.

It has not been the aim of this contribution to make normative suggestions how to develop the liability framework in the wake of technological disruption. One line of thought is to further consider legal personality for AI-systems and to create with that a clear target for responsibility. However, this avenue for reform of liability law needs more detailed studies, including an elaborated ethical discourse about how much risk society is ready to bear in order to make advanced AI-systems available. Focus has also to be put on the man-machine interaction in health care. More empirical and practice research will yield valuable insights into the workability of specific medical regulations, but also in the challenges that stem from the product/service dichotomy. Finally, regulatory ex-ante approaches of AI-systems, such as design regulations, also merit further attention.

References

Abraham K S, Weiler P C (1994) Enterprise Medical Liability and the Evolution of the American Health Care System. Harvard Law Review 108:381–436.

Alpaydin E (2016) Machine Learning. MIT Press, Cambridge MA.

Annany M, Crawford K (2018) Seeing without knowing: Limitations of the transparency ideal and its application to algorithmic accountability. New Media & Society 20: 973–989.

Arlen J (1994) The Potentially Perverse Effects of Corporate Criminal Liability. Journal of Legal Studies 23:832–867.

Bruggeman V et al (2010) The Government as Reinsurer of Catastrophic Risks? Geneva Papers on Risk and Insurance Theory 35:369–390.

Cebul R D et al (2008) Organizational Fragmentation and Care Quality in the U.S. Health Care System. Journal of Economic Perspectives 22:93–113.

Chesterman S (2020) Artificial intelligence and the limits of legal personality. International and Comparative Law Quarterly 69:819–844.

Cooter R, Ulen Th (2012) Law and Economics, 6th edn. Addison-Wesley, Boston.

Easterbrook F H, Fischel D R (1989) The Corporate Contract. Columbia Law Review 89:1416–1448.

Engstrom N F (2013) 3-D Printing and Product Liability: Identifying the Obstacles. University of Pennsylvania Law Review Online 162:35–42.

European Commission (1990) Proposal for a Council Directive on the liability of suppliers of services COM/90/482FINAL - SYN 308. https://eur-lex.europa.eu/legal-content/EN/TXT/PDF/?uri=CELEX:51990PC0482&from=EN Accessed 16 August 2021.

European Commission (2020) White Paper 'On Artificial Intelligence - A European approach to excellence and trust' COM(2020) 65 final. https://ec.europa.eu/info/publications/white-paper-art ificial-intelligence-european-approach-excellence-and-trust_en 25 February 2021 Accessed 16 August 2021.

European Parliament Resolution (2020a) A framework of ethical aspects of artificial intelligence, robotics and related technologies. https://oeil.secure.europarl.europa.eu/oeil/popups/ficheproc edure.do?lang=en&reference=2020/2012(INL) Accessed 16 August 2021.

European Parliament Resolution (2020b) Civil liability regime for artificial intelligence. https:// oeil.secure.europarl.europa.eu/oeil/popups/ficheprocedure.do?lang=en&reference=2020/201 4(INL) Accessed 16 August 2021.

Ficuciello F et al (2019) Autonomy in surgical robots and its meaningful human control. https:// doi.org/10.1515/pjbr-2019-0002.

Floridi L, Sanders J (2004) On the morality of artificial agents. Minds and Machines 14.3:349–379.

Fosch-Villaronga E (2019) Robots, Healthcare and the Law: Regulating Automation in Personal Care. Routledge, New York.

Galasso A, Luo H (2019) Punishing Robots: Issues in the Economics of Tort Liability and Innovation in Artificial Intelligence. In: Ajay A et al (eds) The Economics of Artificial Intelligence: An Agenda. University of Chicago Press, Chicago, pp. 493–504.

Heine K, Grabovets K (2015) From individuals to organizations: The puzzle of organizational liability in tort law. Dovenschmidt Quarterly 2:44–53.

Heine K, Li S (2019) What Shall we do with the Drunken Sailor? Product Safety in the Aftermath of 3D Printing. European Journal of Risk Regulation 10:23–40.

Jensen M C, Meckling W H (1976) Theory of the firm: Managerial behavior, agency costs and ownership structure. Journal of Financial Economics 3:305–360.

Karnow C EA (1996) Liability for distributed artificial intelligences. Berkeley Technology Law Journal 11:147–204.

Koch B (2011) Medical Liability in Europe: A Comparison of Selected Jurisdictions. De Gruyter, Berlin.

Koudijs P, Salisbury L (2020) Limited liability and investment: Evidence from changes in marital property laws in the US South, 1840–1850. Journal of Financial Economics 138:1–26.

Matthias A (2004) The responsibility gap: Ascribing responsibility for the actions of learning automata. Ethics and Information Technology 6:175–183.

O'Quinn J C (2000) Not-So-Strict Liability: A Foreseeability Test for Rylands v. Fletcher and Other Lessons from Cambridge Water Co. v. Eastern Counties Leather PLC. Harvard Environmental Law Review 24:287–314.

Pistor K et al (2002) Evolution of Corporate Law: A Cross-Country Comparison. University of Pennsylvania Journal of International Economic Law 23:791–872.

Posner R A (1972) A Theory of Negligence. Journal of Legal Studies 1:29–96.

Posner R A (2011) Economic Analysis of Law, 8th edn. Wolters-Kluwer, New York.

Rachum-Twaig O (2020) Whose Robot Is It Anyway?: Liability for Artificial-Intelligence-Based Robots. University of Illinois Law Review 4:1141–1175.

Shademan A et al (2016) Supervised autonomous robotic soft tissue surgery. Science Translational Medicine 8:337–364.

Shavell S (2007) Economic Analysis of Accident Law. Harvard University Press, Cambridge MA.

Shishehgar M et al (2018) A systematic review of research into how robotic technology can help older people. Smart Health 7:1–18.

Simon H (1960) The Corporation: Will it be Managed by Machines? In: Ansehn M, Bach G L (eds) Management and Corporations. McGraw Hill, New York, pp. 17–55.

Teubner G (2018) Digital Personhood? The Status of Autonomous Software Agents in Private Law. Ancilla Iuris 106:107–149.

van Dam C (2013) European Tort Law. Oxford University Press, Oxford.

Kostina Prifti is a PhD student at Erasmus School of Law, Erasmus University, and a Junior Fellow at the Jean Monnet Centre of Excellence on Digital Governance. His research interests lie on regulation of new technologies, with a special focus on regulation by design for autonomous robots used in specific healthcare contexts. He is also a Member of the Albanian Bar Association.

Prof. Dr. Evert Stamhuis holds a chair for Law and Innovation at Erasmus School of Law since 2017 and is Senior Fellow of the Jean Monnet Centre of Excellence on Digital Governance. His research is on the interaction between law, governance and new technologies, with a special focus on the public domain, health care and regulated markets. See for more affiliations https://www.lin kedin.com/today/author/evertstamhuis?trk=author-info__article-link

Prof. Dr. Klaus Heine is Professor of Law and Economics at Erasmus School of Law, Erasmus University Rotterdam. He also holds a Jean Monnet Chair and is a Director of the Jean Monnet Centre of Excellence on Digital Governance. He is a member of Platform Learning Systems that advises the German government on policy questions concerning Artificial Intelligence. He has published in leading journals and presents his research at international conferences. His main interests are questions about the legal personality of AI systems and new modes of data ownership.

Chapter 16
Automated Care-Taking and the Constitutional Rights of the Patient in an Aging Population

Andrea Bertolini and Shabahang Arian

Contents

Abstract Social Robots represent a broad spectrum of AI-based robotic applications that could be largely deployed in the care of elderly and frail individuals, primarily to reduce associated welfare costs. Indeed, they could provide assistive (feeding, cleaning, moving), monitoring (health parameters and overall well-being of the user), and companionship (entertaining and interacting with the user) services. This chapter questions whether all these uses are to be deemed licit, and pursuant to which criteria. To do so, it first describes the different kinds of robotic applications divided into categories pursuant to the functions they serve. Then it defines the right to care within the existing legal framework, in light of international conventions, constitutional

A. Bertolini (✉)
Scuola Superiore Sant' Anna, Piazza Martiri della Libertà, 33, 56127 Pisa, Italy
e-mail: andrea.bertolini@santannapisa.it
URL: https://www.eura.santannapisa.it

S. Arian
Scuola Superiore Sant' Anna, Pisa, Italy
e-mail: shabahang.arian@santannapisa.it

© T.M.C. ASSER PRESS and the authors 2022
B. Custers and E. Fosch-Villaronga (eds.), *Law and Artificial Intelligence*,
Information Technology and Law Series 35,
https://doi.org/10.1007/978-94-6265-523-2_16

principles, and national provisions. In so doing it shows how care is kept distinct from mere cure, and entails addressing the overall well-being of patients, including their socialization, personal independence and dignity. The different technologies are then assessed. To do so, alternative ethical paradigms are considered, typically recalled in the bioethical debate revolving around the use and acceptability of advanced technologies. The analysis shows how a deontological approach is the only one that conforms to the current constitutional framework. Reference is made to the ethical and legal notion of human dignity as an external and objective criterion that limits freedom of self-determination, and prevents humans from being manipulated (in their emotions), instrumentalized and isolated. Technologies that could be deemed deceptive—inducing the delusional perception that the machine cares for the user— and whose primary purpose is to replace human relations and contact, should be deemed violating the fundamental rights to care and the dignity of the individuals being cared for. Instead, those technologies that favour physical and psychological independence should be not just welcomed but eventually supported through ad-hoc policy initiatives.

Keywords AI-based technologies · Social robots · Constitutional frameworks · Fundamental rights · Right to care · Human dignity

16.1 Introduction

Policymakers facing a progressively aging population[1] look at advanced robotics as a potential tool to address the rising welfare costs associated with elderly care.[2] Social robots could be programmed to replace human caregivers in providing a range of services and assistance to frail individuals in the near future. This, in turn, could eventually reduce costs and possibly provide a better and economically sustainable service to society.[3] The only concern could then appear to be mere technological

---

[1] Medical advancements and improvements in health care increase life expectancy. In 1990, the average life expectancy at birth for the world was about 64 years, while in 2019, it exceeds 73 (see United Nations Economic and Social Affairs 2017). Today, there are 125 million people aged 80 years or older, and according to the World Health Organization, by 2050, it will reach to 2 billion people (see World Health Organization 2018).

[2] Although an increase of life span reflects the success of human development, it challenges the existing welfare system, requiring budget adjustments to accommodate long-term care services and facilities. If such fashion continues, countries may face a "demographic time bomb" phenomenon and as a result, the old-age dependency ratio (OADR) will rapidly increase (see Pekarek 2018, p. 69). For example, in the EU, the OADR will increase from 29.6% in 2016 to 51.2% in 2070 (see European Commission 2018).

[3] Japan being the first super-aging society has introduced a system of robotic technologies for aged care and intensifies its investment in the field (see OECD 2018. See also Ministry of Internal Affairs and Communication. Similarly, the European Union has increased its financing on researches in the field of robotics through its funding actions (see European Commission 2019)). The United States justifies subsidizing on the development of robotic assistive technologies because it is assumed that

feasibility, dependent upon the state of advancement of engineering research and prototypes.

However, if we were to maintain a human-centric approach—as clearly stated by the European Commission in its Strategy for AI,[4] or in its recent proposal for an AI regulation[5] (henceforth AIA)—the legitimacy of such specific technology uses needs to be discussed. Indeed, it is necessary to determine (i) whether the replacement of human caregivers with machines would affect the fundamental rights of the individual, and in what way, and (ii) whether such a replacement could be deemed licit, and eventually pursuant to which paradigm—legal and ethical—and under which conditions.

To do so, it is necessary to briefly discuss the fundamental rights of the elderly *vis-à-vis* their national welfare systems, focusing on the right to care. Due to evident constraints, this chapter performs such an assessment with respect to three legal systems that could be deemed representative of correspondingly different approaches at the European level. The British, Swedish and Italian legal systems represent a more liberal option, a welfare state option, and an intermediate solution respectively. All three, however, converge in identifying a separate right to care, distinct from the right to cure, which extends to include the right to meaningful human-human interactions and socialization.

We then briefly discuss the different kinds of AI-based technologies that fall within the domain of care robots, and their typical use cases, by reference to some existing models and devices currently deployed, at least for experimental purposes. This allows us to identify specific applications whose primary purpose is to provide care services and interact with and entertain the human user, eventually replacing human caregivers in such tasks.

Finally, we then consider three different ethical paradigms, typically proposed in this domain to address the research question posed here, namely a utilitarian, a capability-based, as well as a deontological or neo-Kantian approach. We conclude that the deontological approach converges most clearly with the fundamental-rights-based analysis performed in light of the European legal system. The latter, in particular, allows us to identify the principle of human dignity as the essential criterion to discern all advanced technologies, and their uses, including care robots. As elaborated in case law and jurisprudence, the principle is indeed to be intended as an external and objective limit to freedom of self-determination, whenever the human condition may be affected by the use of a specific application. This in turn appears to be the case when potentially manipulative care-robot applications are considered that could contribute to the isolation of the frail individual, by replacing a human relationship with an artificial human-machine interaction.

This chapter is structured as follows. Section 16.2 presents different kinds of social robots distinguishing the function these machines serve in the caring of the

---

its innovative potential is comparable to that of the internet and modern media. (See University of California San Diego and others 2020).

[4] European Commission 2018.

[5] European Commission 2021.

elderly, namely Sect. 16.2.1 assistance, Sect. 16.2.2 monitoring, and Sect. 16.2.3 companionship. Section 16.3 discusses the right to care as a fundamental right and in its implementation at national level, by reference to three different legal systems: Sect. 16.3.1, and displays how different kinds of social robots could be used to provide such services: Sect. 16.3.2. Finally, Sect. 16.4 discusses whether it is lawful and admissible to offer care services through technologies. To do so, it takes into account three different ethical approaches (Sects. 16.4.1, 16.4.2 and 16.4.3), and identifies human dignity as the primary legal criterion to address such an assessment (Sect. 16.4.4). The conclusions in Sect. 16.5 apply those criteria to determine what kind of uses of technology ought to be welcomed, and which ought to be dismissed.

16.2 The Role and Functions of Social Robots in the Care of the Elderly

The kind of applications considered in this chapter are differentiated according to the purpose they serve, distinguishing merely assistive robots from those used for monitoring or companionship. The latter, in particular, are those that raise the more relevant concerns, being primarily intended to replace human relationships with interactions with the machine itself.

16.2.1 Robots for Assisting the Elderly

Assistive care robots are designed to address the physiological and vital needs of the user, such as feeding, cleaning, bathing, lifting and the like.[6] Different kinds of such applications are already today present in the market, displaying different levels of autonomy and complexity. Among these is 'Bestic',[7] an assistive eating and drinking aid bot, designed to support elderly and disabled individuals with feeding. The robot is equipped with a robotic arm and attached spoon, which enables it to pick up the food from the plate while the user is still in control. The user gives command to the robot by pressing a button to indicate to pick up the food that he prefers.[8]

Riba is a humanoid robot, with a teddy bear-like appearance and strong human-like arms designed to assist users as well as caregivers with body movements and carrying patients in and out of bed, and/or wheelchair. The robot is equipped with two cameras and microphones facilitating the interaction with the operator.[9] Other

---

[6] Sharkey and Sharkey 2012, p. 28, Coeckelbergh 2012, p. 282, Van Wynsberghe 2013, p. 426, Vallor 2016, p. 218, Fosch-Villaronga and Drukarch 2021, pp. 32–43.

[7] See, for instance, Camanio undated.

[8] Nylande et al. 2012, p. 799.

[9] See, for instance, https://newatlas.com/riba-robot-nurse/12693/.

application in this category include El-E[10] that performs a broad range of tasks, including grasping many different objects and delivering it by resorting to a laser point interface which provides communication with the robot and allows the user to indicate where it must go.

Such robots are mainly designed to provide additional support and help to care givers, rather than replacing them, and ultimately increase the individual's autonomy. Indeed, these robots are not fully autonomous and still require some forms of human intervention (such as chopping foods, putting food on a plate, controlling the direction, using laser to command the robot) in order to ensure the intended objective is achieved.

16.2.2   Robots for Monitoring and Supervision

Some robots are intended to supervise and monitor the elderly. Pearl is a nurse robot, programmed to remind seniors about routine activities (e.g., eating, drinking, taking medicine and doctor appointments). Enabled with voice recognition, the robot is also able to communicate through a computer-generated human voice. Besides, the robot can navigate and guide elderly through the environment.[11] Additionally, the bot can monitor various health parameters like the user's heart rate and blood pressure.[12]

RP-7 is, instead, a tele-operated mobile robot, used to facilitate doctor-patient interactions and deliver medical consultation by sending and receiving audio and video information in real time.[13] It is remotely controlled by a doctor using a joystick to easily be manoeuvred around the environment.

16.2.3   Robots for Companionship

Companion robots are instead mainly designed to entertain the user and compensate for their loneliness. To this end, they are typically capable of natural language communication, and of simulating human-like (or animal like) emotions and reactions, to better engage the user.

For instance, Pepper is a humanoid robot, developed to facilitate active communication and engage in conversation. It can display emotions and use verbal language to interact. Cameras and microphones are used to recognize human emotions (e.g.,

---

[10] See, for instance, http://pwp.gatech.edu/hrl/el-e-an-assistive-robot/.

[11] Pollack et al. 2002, p. 3.

[12] See, for instance, https://www.telegraph.co.uk/news/worldnews/northamerica/usa/1457427/Meet-Pearl-shes-the-robo-nurse-designed-to-look-after-the-elderly.html.

[13] See, for instance, https://www.assistedlivingconsult.com/issues/03-04/alc78-BeamMeUp-719a.pdf.

hostility and joy) and respond appropriately with a smile or indications of sadness.[14] In a similar way, Paro,[15] a baby harp seal-like robot, was designed for therapeutic uses for people with dementia. The bot can simulate emotions and respond to external stimuli such as temperature, once it is petted or reacts to sounds when it is being called. Also, by means of its light sensors, it becomes active in daylight time and prefers to "sleep" during night time. As studies indicate, it has proved to induce a positive psychological effect on patients making regular use.[16]

However, the interactions through such devices are very limited, and they hardly replace human interactions. Indeed, the reason why a seal-pup—rather than any other animal—is chosen by developers is due to the limited direct experience of the average person with such kind of wild animal that, in turn, reduces user's expectations about its behaviour. The overall perceived experience is thus more satisfactory. Limited knowledge and understanding of what a seal-pup does simplifies the technological challenge of replicating it in an adequate way, causing its functioning to become plausible. However, the true challenge companion robots are facing is that of replicating more complex, skilled, and articulate social interactions, of the kind that could be perceived as radically replacing human interactions. An example in that sense is provided by Jibo, an application developed by MIT intended to become someone's "new best friend".[17] The primary goal of designing Jibo was to interact with family members through natural voice commands. However, Jibo failed to meet consumers' needs and expectations, and ultimately stopped to be marketed further.

Such problems, however, primarily depend upon current technological constraints that future advancements could reasonably overcome. What, instead, is relevant for the analysis in this chapter is the intention of developers to produce a machine whose primary—if not sole—function is to engage users emotionally, and ultimately replace human relationships.

16.3   The Right to Care in its Moral and Legal Dimensions

The robotic applications described in Sect. 16.2 are intended to offer services that fall under the notion of care as defined by the international, European and national legal system. It is therefore necessary to briefly define the legal dimension of the right to care and its specific implementation in three different states, representing alternative welfare models in Europe.

---

[14] See, for instance, http://doc.aldebaran.com/download/Pepper_B2BD_guidelines_Sept_V1.5.pdf.

[15] See, for instance, http://www.parorobots.com.

[16] Birks et al. 2016, p. 5, Sheba et al. 2018, p. 408, Hamada et al. 2008, p. 174.

[17] See, for instance, Youtube undated.

Current philosophical research considers human beings to be vulnerable[18] and dependent on one another,[19] as a very consequence of their human condition.[20] Frailty is considered a natural status, that does not diminish the value of human life, no matter the condition. At the same time, inspired by the principle of solidarity, an individual's well-being and the common good are deemed to be tightly intertwined in modern societies,[21] and that clearly encompasses the needs and interests of vulnerable and frail human beings.

Within this theoretical framework, the right to care is nowadays defined as a primary and fundamental social right, rooted in the principle of solidarity,[22] to be distinguished from the right to cure. Indeed, while cure entails the physical or psychological improvement of the specific condition afflicting the patient, care encompasses the full human and relational dimension.[23] Care therefore includes the full respect for individual dignity and independence, as well as the possibility to actively participate in society, and not be isolated.

Already in 1946, the World Health Organization's (WHO) provided a definition of "health" that included both "the absence of disease or infirmity", and a "state of complete physical, mental, and social well-being".[24] (WHO 1946). Not much later, the Universal Declaration of Human Rights (UDHR)[25] paid special attention to the concept of "care", and stipulated the entitlement of individuals with special disabilities or impairments, to "necessary social services" (article 25).[26]

At the European level, the right to care is also affirmed by article 13 of the European Social Charter (ESC), calling on Member States to ensure that the "right to adequate assistance" for individuals who are in need of care due to their "condition or sickness" is guaranteed.[27] Furthermore, the right to live independently and be included in the community was expressly recognized by the Convention on the Rights of Persons with Disabilities.[28] The elderly right to "dignity" and "independence" are articulated as fundamental rights in article 25 of the Charter of Fundamental Rights of the European Union (CFR)[29] and, specifically recalled in The European Charter of Rights and Responsibilities of Older People in Need of Long-Term Care and Assistance.[30]

---

[18] Coeckelbergh 2013, p. 7.

[19] Macintyre 1999, pp. 119–128.

[20] Arendt 1958, pp. 7–17.

[21] Kelly 2004, p. 285.

[22] Spicker 2000, p. 40.

[23] Noddings 2015, p. 1, Tronto 2015, p. 12, Bertolini and Arian 2020, p. 36.

[24] WHO 1947.

[25] United Nations 1948.

[26] The UDHR makes additional accommodations for security in case of physical debilitation or disability, and makes special mention of care given to those in motherhood or childhood.

[27] Council of Europe (18 October 1961) European Social Charter, ETS 35. Available at: https://rm. coe.int/168006b642. Accessed 3 June 2021.

[28] United Nations 2006.

[29] European Union 2007.

[30] European Union 2010.

The most important characteristic of social rights is that they are generally considered to be "goals" rather than "immediate rights".[31] However, States cannot overlook them and are instead required to progressively implement them by adopting specific legal provisions and measures,[32] whenever necessary, as well as by providing adequate economic resources to meet corresponding needs.[33]

The European Social Charter asks Member States to ensure "the effective exercise of the right to protection of health" (Article 11), and pursuant to Article 168 TFEU[34] health care policies are an area of Member State competence and the EU shall complement national policies. From this perspective, it is useful to provide a brief account of how three different European states—not all current European Member States—concretely enact the right to care. Sweden, the United Kingdom and Italy were chosen as representing three alternative welfare models.[35] Sweden is, in fact, deemed the archetype of a social democrat welfare system,[36] while the United Kingdom[37] represents a liberal model, and Italy somewhat of an intermediate solution.[38]

16.3.1   Comparing the Functioning of Different Welfare Systems in Europe

Despite divergences, clear common trends emerge, in particular in the field of medical assistance and care services. To exemplify, it shall suffice to recall how in the UK, the Care Act 2014 (Care Act)[39] and its supporting guidance[40] set new arrangements, duties and responsibilities about care and support of adults.[41] By emphasizing the importance of "well-being", the Care Act establishes criteria by which care services

---

[31] Rodríguez-Pinzon and Martin 2003, p. 919.

[32] Hendriks 1998, p. 392.

[33] Rodríguez-Pinzon and Martin 2003, p. 921.

[34] European Union (Consolidated version 2016), Treaty on the Functioning of the European Union. Available at: https://eur-lex.europa.eu/resource.html?uri=cellar:9e8d52e1-2c70-11e6-b497-01aa75ed71a1.0006.01/DOC_3&format=PDF. Accessed 3 June 2021.

[35] Esping-Andersen 1990, p. 20.

[36] Sweden, in Andersen's welfare typology, is categorized as a "social-democrat" country. Sweden adopted a universalist approach and life-time welfare benefits for all. In other words, high quality services are provided to all citizens, in all social groups according to their needs rather than their ability to pay. Care assistance is funded by general taxation, correspondingly, high standards of services offered, intended to reduce class and income differences. See Isakjee 2017, p. 6. See also Szebehely and Trydegård 2011, p. 300.

[37] Esping-Andersen 1990, p. 20.

[38] Id.

[39] Care Act 2014.

[40] Guidance for Providers on Meeting the Regulations (Social Care Act 2008 & Care Quality Commission 2009) 2015.

[41] Department of Health and Social Care 2016.

must be delivered, including but are not limited to the (1) respect to individual dignity, the (2) provision of emotional and social care, the (3) fostering of family and personal relationships, the (4) guarantee of the individuals' right to participate in society, and the (5) protection of care receivers from abuse and neglect.[42] This clearly exhibits a broad approach to the notion of care, more associated with the individuals overall "well-being" than mere medical improvement.

Care services encompass helping recipients with bathing, washing, preparing meals, monitoring diet, placing and adjusting equipment like wheelchairs, getting patients in and out of bed, getting them dressed, giving companionship and walking them outside the home.[43] Depending on the type of schemes, a patient can receive other forms of care assistance such as fitness classes or yoga, holiday tours or other extracurricular activities.[44] Since social care is seen as a kind of commodity, the UK has formulated a care allowance system so that family members of older people may be paid for the amount of care they have provided to their beloved ones.[45] Care allowance depends on the financial status of the caregivers, but may be taxed. Similarly, older people in need of substantial personal care or supervision may be eligible to receive the additional economic support in the form of attendance allowance. This entitlement is not means tested and is tax free, being governmental financial aid to help the older or disabled people with extra costs. Recently, the UK's new green paper to deal with long term care and elderly care sets out new numbers of reforms into British health care policies that might lead to a sustainable and fully funded social care system in the future.[46] Special attention is given to innovation and new technologies for providing better quality of care to the elderly.

With respect to the right to care, Sweden has adopted a similar stance. The Health and Medical Service Act (HMSA)[47] has clearly regulated the content and scope of that specific right. Dignity, need, and solidarity[48] are the governing principles of the HMSA and must be applied to everyone.[49] Thus, the Swedish universal approach is not merely embodied as a protection of the right to treatment but recognizes the importance of the right to care and assistance to all for the respect to the equal dignity of all human beings and for the dignity of the individual. "Need" is then the main criterion to determine priority in accessing care services.

When it comes to frail individuals' rights, Sweden displays a well-structured system. Elderly care is then specifically regulated in Chapter 5, Sections 4–6 of the Social Service Act,[50] in which the social welfare committee must guarantee the

---

[42] Article 1(2) Care Act 2014.

[43] See, for example, Age UK, Care and Support for the Elderly undated-a.

[44] See, e.g., Age UK, Care and Support for the Elderly undated-b.

[45] See, for example, Government of UK Carers' Allowance. https://www.gov.uk/carers-allowance.

[46] Jarrett 2019.

[47] The Health and Medical Services Act (HMSA) 1982.

[48] Section 2 (a) HMSA 1982.

[49] Lind 2014, pp. 51–78.

[50] Social Services Act 2001.

elderly "independent lives", "meaningful lives in the company of the others" and "good living conditions".

The available formal care in Sweden shall be delivered in three models: home help in regular housing (home care), special housing (institutional care), day activities and home medical services (home nursing home). [51] Home-care services include assistance with performing household tasks, such as cleaning, shopping, laundry and cooking (or the delivery of readymade food), and personal care, such as bathing, getting dressed and moving around. The basic medical assistance services provided include insulin injections and treatment of wounds. Emotional and social support is also regarded as an important aspect of the service.

The amount of home care can vary, from once a month to six or more visits per day. On average, a home-care user receives around seven hours of help per week; the average is the same for younger and older age groups.[52] Day activities, home medical services, meals services, personal safety alarms, home adaptation, and transportation services for elderly and functionally impaired people who cannot ride regular public transport are additional services supplied by the municipalities and are also forms of social care services regulated by law.[53]

In Esping-Andersen's[54] archetypes classification of welfare systems, Italy falls into the social democrat's model. However, Ferrera[55] later claimed that the new categorization of the Italian welfare system is a combination of occupationalism in income maintenance, and universalism with respect to health care.[56] In Italy, the right to health is identified as a fundamental right according to the Italian constitution (article 32). Alongside this, the right to care has acquired constitutional value. Indeed, Article 38 of the Italian Constitution affirms the right to "welfare support" for "every citizen unable to work and without the necessary means of subsistence". The second paragraph of this provision specifically recognizes the right of elderly and people with disability to government welfare assistance in case of disability or old age. Furthermore, the right to care of persons with disabilities is indirectly elaborated starting from article 3 of the Italian constitution when jointly interpreted with the principle of "dignity" and "social solidarity" put forth by article 2, whereby it demands the State "to remove the economic and social obstacles" which limit the equality of all citizens and their development as human beings.[57]

More specifically, in 2016, new legislation on Assisting Persons with Disability[58] was enacted with the aim to support and protect their well-being, full inclusion and best interest.[59] This legislation granted a statutory right in favour of this category

---

[51] Fukushima et al. 2010, p. 5.

[52] Aldre [Care and Services to Older Persons Act] 2008.

[53] Fukushima et al. 2010, p. 3.

[54] Esping-Andersen 1990, p. 20.

[55] Ferrera 1998, p. 86.

[56] Blackman et al. 2001, pp. 96–106.

[57] Violini 2006, p. 5.

[58] Law 22 2016, n. 112.

[59] Vivaldi 2019, pp. 19–25.

of frail individuals, irrespective of whether inability is caused by natural aging, pathologies, or medical condition, and in the absence of family support they can receive essential benefits and services free of charge (article 1, para 2, Law 112/2016). This has created mechanisms to facilitate financial aids through private individuals, insurance policies, trusts, and other funds so that it provides services to disabled persons (article 1, para 3, Law 112/2016).

The long-term care (LTC) system in Italy operates in a fragmented institutional environment. The main actors involved are municipalities and local health agencies, nursing homes and the Istituto Nazionale Previdenza Sociale, INPS (National Institute of Social Security) while other institutions have a role of planning and financing such services.[60] In Italy, LTC for older persons includes three main kinds of formal assistance: community care, residential care and cash benefits.[61] Some regions provide household services at home; for instance, assisting elderly with preparation of meals, shopping, transportation and laundry services. Some other regions provide personal assistance; services such as elder personal hygiene, occupational therapy, assistive devices and home transformations (Table 16.1).[62]

16.3.2 Technology-Based Care Services, and the Problem of Human-Machine Interaction

Both merely assistive and monitoring services may be provided via technological applications that could be deemed to satisfy those primary needs identified by both the Care Act, section 1(2) and the Swedish HMSA, section 2a. Such applications, despite being more or less effective, are primarily aimed at automating menial and material tasks. They are typically not intended to radically replace human caregivers, but rather assist them, freeing more time in potentially more meaningful human interaction. If the caregiver is not occupied with feeding the user he might enjoy the meal together with him and indulge in a normal conversation, as he would with any other dining companion. If the robotic application ensures the possibility for the person with reduced mobility to dress autonomously, the overall experience will be empowering, fostering independence, as required by the Care Act, section 1(2)(g) and the Swedish HMSA, section 2a.

The overall effect is potential normalization of the living conditions of frail individuals, by tackling the need for assistance in performing everyday tasks that have become increasingly complex for the individual, in light of his condition. From this perspective, all those applications are to be favoured, possibly above and beyond less technological solutions, as they ensure increased independence and autonomy of their users.

---

[60] See https://www.loc.gov/law/foreign-news/article/italy-legislation-on-support-for-the-disabled/.

[61] Tediosi and Gabriele 2010, p. 3.

[62] See   https://www.alzheimer-europe.org/Policy/Country-comparisons/2007-Social-support-systems/Italy.

Table 16.1 Comparative case study analysis of social service programs in UK, Sweden and Italy [*Source* The authors]

	Assistance with Household Tasks (preparing meals/shoppi ng/laundry services)	Assistance in the Caring of the Person (personal hygiene/lifting and moving/dressing)	Social Interaction (provide companionship and other dedicated services)
The United Kingdom	Yes, free in case of need Care Allowance system for family members providing such services	Yes, means tested. additional economic support in the form of Attendance Allowance may be provided	Yes, including fitness or yoga courses, arranging holiday tours and other activities. These services are often taxed depending on the type of schemes that a person is enrolled in
Sweden	Yes, the care assistance is free for all	Yes. It is a universal service, and free of charge	Yes, it provides emotional and social support for seniors such as companionship and empathic communication. Not taxed
Italy	Yes, differences at regional level, generally means tested and free for low income individuals. Care Allowance is also available for family members who provide care services	Yes, means tested	Yes, including occupational therapy (e.g. engaging elderly in memory-enhancing activities, social activities such as dancing, playing sport, yoga, etc.)

Incentivizing the development, diffusion and implementation in care services provided through national welfare systems could also include adopting alternative regulatory frameworks, which could be deemed more favourable, eventually with respect to the applicable liability model.[63]

At the same time, however, companion robots are clearly conceived to provide companionship and interactions considered to be part of care services, as described by the Care Act, section 1(2)(f) and (g) and the Swedish HMSA, section 2a(4). Indeed, ensuring the individual's dignity and preventing social isolation are requirements put forth by those norms, as much as the completion of more menial and practically assistive tasks. While there are no doubts that such tasks may be effectively replaced by automation, companionship is not as easily replicated. On the one hand, there is no doubt that machines—of any sort, existing and reasonably foreseeable—do not possess any emotion, are not aware of their own existence, and of the alterity of the

---

[63] Bertolini 2015, pp. 126–130.

human being they are interacting with. Machines are not agents, or subjects, neither in an ethical nor legal point of view.[64] Machines are things, objects, and artefacts conceived by human intellect.[65] On the other hand, they may simulate those mental and emotional states, and elicit empathic reactions,[66] due to the specific ways in which they are designed and programmed to operate, eventually deceiving human users.[67] Indeed, the Turing test itself defines artificial intelligence as the ability of the machine to induce human judges into thinking they are interacting with a fellow human being, while instead they are not.[68] To some extent the manipulative component is intrinsic to AI-based technologies designed to entertain human beings. Those, indeed, induce the perception of an apparent reality that is instead radically detached from the ontology of the device itself. Because of this, we might define them as manipulative and deceptive.

16.4 Ethical Frameworks for the Assessing the Impact on the Rights of Users and Patients

From an objective viewpoint, robotic applications do not care, and therefore cannot substitute those activities that appear to be essentially rooted in the humanity of the caregiver and justified by the dignity of the patient.[69]

Nonetheless, their operation might be perceived as beneficial—eventually improving the health, condition, and wellbeing of the user[70]—and desirable, in a comparative perspective. It might ensure a greater degree of interaction, absent other alternatives that involve resorting to human caregivers, but might be too expensive for existing national budgets. T, the manipulation of the user by leveraging human biases and cognitive weaknesses can provide what is perceived as a pleasant experience, eventually causing the user to feel cared for, even if this is objectively not the case.

From this perspective, we should question the legitimacy of the use of technology in providing assistance that is to be considered the expression of the fundamental rights of the individual and that is primarily intended to promote his social integration and prevent isolation. To answer such a complex question, different philosophical stances—often recalled in the bioethical debate—need to be considered. These, in fact, feed into the legal debate offering alternative models to balance opposing legally relevant interests and models to interpret and substantiate fundamental rights. This,

---

[64] Bryson 2011, pp. 63–74, Coeckelbergh 2011, p. 57, Decker and Gutmann 2012, p. 64.

[65] Bertolini 2013, p. 225.

[66] Choi et al. 2021, p. 6.

[67] Bertolini 2018, pp. 645–659.

[68] Turing 1950, p. 433.

[69] Bertolini and Arian 2020, p. 46, Scheutz 2009, p. 205.

[70] Hamada et al. 2008, pp. 174–179.

in turn, provides basis for both court decisions and policy considerations, including new legislation.[71] In this section, we discuss four different ethical approaches.

16.4.1 A Utilitarian Approach

One possible approach to the ethical assessment of social robots is the utilitarian approach, pursuant to which a given application is desirable when it improves on the prior human condition. However, determining those parameters that need to be measured and weighted to conclude on the desirability of a specific technology is anything but obvious.

To exemplify, if by resorting to social robots—such as Paro—the overall condition of the patient affected with dementia is improved and a measurement of that change is possible, then the ethicality of the technology and of the treatment is logically and unequivocally necessitated.

However, there are at least two possible criticisms to such a stance that challenge its application. Firstly, it is not always possible to identify and discern which criteria need to be considered when conducting such an assessment. The well-being of the patient is of the utmost importance, yet it cannot be reduced to the improvement of one specific parameter to be observed through diagnosis. On the one hand, any treatment might have side effects that might only be observed in a longer run or that are overlooked, either because they are still unknown or not yet fully described at the moment the observation takes place. On the other hand, the fact that a value improves through a specific treatment does not immediately imply that the overall quality of life and conditions also do.

Indeed, a successful treatment—or one that theoretically increases the life expectancy of the patient—might still cause other physical and psychological suffering that, from the perspective of the individual, outweighs those objective benefits. For this reason, legal systems typically allow the patient to choose not to undergo life-saving procedures.

Also other interests than those of the individual undergoing treatment ought to be taken into account. There might be relevant societal implications for other human beings that depend on the choice to provide a treatment, that ought also to be considered when assessing the overall effect of the cure. An otherwise beneficial treatment could give rise to relevant ethical concerns for it might directly and indirectly affect the fundamental rights of others. A methodology that isolates a subject completely, depriving him of meaningful human relations might be deemed in conflict with human dignity. The comparative assessment of the performance of two alternative treatments shall not be so restricted as to not take into account such concerns. Typically, defining which other interests are of relevance is not obvious and requires a complex value-based judgment that is not neutral, and closely resembles that which

---

[71] A relevant case in point is represented by the recent AI Act. See European Commission 2021.

a deontological approach to ethics presupposes, ultimately compromising a purely utilitarian reasoning.

Finally, there is a relevant problem of performance measurement and assessment in robotics. Robotics has many problems in benchmarking. The core issue is the reproducibility or replicability of experimental results which is, indeed, essential to assess the overall effect of a given application and compare it to available— technologically less sophisticated—alternatives.[72] Even from a purely materialistic perspective that neglects all other considerations, intrinsic to the legal system (such as the impact on fundamental rights and human dignity), a utilitarian approach encounters relevant constraints, preventing an objective, value neutral, and reliable (i.e., reproducible) measurement of the comparative benefits of a specific application.

16.4.2 A Capability Approach

Alternatively, a capability approach[73] might be considered[74] that assesses the effect of the solution with respect to the way it influences existing capabilities, eventually enabling the acquisition of new ones. In this theory, there are general goals[75] that must be achieved in order to have a life worthy of human dignity. Indeed, both "the ends" and all capabilities matter, and we need to enjoy all of them to live a life with dignity. The underlying rationale is not radically different from the utilitarian one, as the assessment is grounded on the balancing of conflicting criteria that are deemed objectively relevant. These, however, are not limited to the observation of material consequences (the improvement in a function and/or parameter of the user), but include a broader set of elements derived from the cultural, political, religious, and legal discourse, with an all-encompassing and at times holistic approach. Its attractiveness is derived from the apparent value-neutrality that emerges from the algebraic sum of all possible different components of the social debate. Indeed, it promises to provide the most inclusive and theoretically diversity-tolerant perspective, as it is tightly rooted in a cultural rather than natural[76] understanding of the human condition.[77]

---

[72] Bonsignorio 2017, pp. 178–182.

[73] Nussbaum 2011, p. 17.

[74] Sharkey 2014, pp. 63–75.

[75] Nussbaum 2009, pp. 76 and 77. The criteria addressed by Nussbaum as a central requirement for life with dignity include, among others, being able to have good health, being able to move freely from place to place and being protected against any violence, being able to use senses, imagination, thinking and reasoning. Being able to have attachments to things and people outside ourselves. Being able to form a conception of good and to engage in critical reflection about the planning of one's life. Being able to live with and toward others, to engage in various forms of social interaction and also having the social bases of self, of self-respect, and non-humiliation.

[76] Hull 1986, pp. 3–13.

[77] Arendt 1958, pp. 7–17.

However, there are two different criticisms, of a theoretical and practical nature respectively. Firstly, this approach relies on the notion of human rights that is as vaguely defined and presents as relevant variations in its very definition, interpretation and application as that of capabilities. Reference to it does not increase precision and objectiveness to the analysis. Secondly, the identified parameters against which different approaches to the care of the elderly ought to be tested and assessed appear to a large extent arbitrary and capable of contradictory interpretation. The notion of a "life worth living" is extremely problematic and might be used as an argument to support euthanasia practices that are instead prohibited in many countries worldwide. The selection of the criteria may not be all-inclusive, representing different social and cultural stances present in society. Selection as well as the determination of how the balancing is operationalized is then arbitrary. Ultimately, it would merely displace the debate from what use of technology in the care of fragile individuals is ethical, to which criteria ought to be selected to operate such a choice.

16.4.3   A Deontological Perspective

Thirdly, a deontological approach may be pursued, in which a human is by definition an end-in-itself,[78] possessing an intrinsic value that shall not be compromised due to social, economic, or policy constraints.

From this perspective, all treatment of frail individuals ought to be assessed for its ability to preserve this value, before and beyond any other consideration, that might only occur subsequently to an ascertainment of that kind. To further characterize in an objective way that immutable element, reference should be made to those principles that our legal system poses at its roots, primarily at a constitutional level. Those, by definition, represent the minimum ethical denominator of a society and are conceived as immutable, deeply rooted in its cultural and social fabric.

Selecting such criteria would prevent any criticism about the arbitrary nature of the choice, as it can be deemed a logical and juridical requirement, mandated by the legal system itself within which the evaluation needs to occur. Criteria so conceived and defined in the applicable normative framework would allow for effective discrimination among possible uses of technology. Despite not being universal in nature—for different legal orderings might possess different guiding principles or radically different interpretations of the same principles—the conclusions can be deemed objective[79] within the given system.

Neo-Kantianism sheds light on the set of values that society as whole agreed upon. Broader sets of relevant interests, beyond mere performance, play a central role in

---

[78] Kant 1785. GR 429. Kant's formula of the categorical imperative states: "Act in such a way as to treat humanity, whether in your own person or in that of anyone else, always as an end and never merely as a means".

[79] *Rectius* that might be objectively discussed, as logically and technically derived from well-defined principles, as any other legal reasoning, requiring the application of an abstract norm to a specific and concrete case.

the selection of facts in scientific observation. Since every human is an end in itself, the theory would try to ensure that both elderly and people with disability are treated equal to any other person.

From a legal perspective, not all ethical models are equally admissible. Constitutional values are non-negotiable and quite clearly defined, with substantive and not purely procedural content. Hence, when discussing admissible policies, legal interpretation and possible normative intervention, only those ethical frameworks may be considered that are fully compatible with extant binding legal principles. This entails that merely comparative considerations—typical of a utilitarian approach—in which a given technological solution appears to be more efficient and/or cost effective over a traditional one (e.g. involving a human carer), would not per se justify the adoption of the new methodology. If care robots can assist the elderly and protect their independency, they should not impinge upon other individuals' values and interests, for instance, by isolating them or reducing their human contact.

This requires acknowledging a specificity and pre-eminence of law—primarily in the form of constitutional law and fundamental rights—over ethics in the policy and regulatory debate, even when both deal with elastic and broad notions, such as those considered here. At the same time, following such considerations, a neo-Kantian perspective appears preferable to other competing ethical models, as it is coherent with the relevant constitutional framework.

16.4.4 Dignity as an Ethical and Legal Concept

From this perspective, we shall acknowledge that all humans are ends in themselves[80] and possess intrinsic and insuppressible values that we may call dignity. This notion, widely debated both in the philosophical and legal discourse, is also expressly proclaimed in most constitutional charters, including the European Charter of Human Rights (henceforth ECHR) and national constitutions.[81]

These considerations ground two fundamental corollaries, that possess theoretical and practical bearing in the analysis here conducted, providing that objective ground of analysis that approaches described above lack.

Firstly, dignity may not be overlooked, dismissed, or replaced by other concepts for it is a legal principle and one of the highest values and binding forces. As a constitutional principle, it is one of those criteria every other law or act adopted within the corresponding legal system needs to conform to. Any ethical framework that suggests its overcoming or replacement would be radically inapplicable at least within the European legal tradition. The legal value of dignity constrains any philosophical

---

[80] Kantian categorical imperative, "Act in such a way as to treat humanity, whether in your own person or in that of anyone else, always as an end and never merely as a means".

[81] Article 1 ECHR states "Human dignity is inviolable. It must be respected and protected"; similarly art. 1 of the German Constitution, whereby "The dignity of man is inviolable. To respect and protect it is the duty of all state authority".

speculation and at the same time provides an objective ground to further pursue this analysis.

Secondly, the very notion of human dignity is up for debate. It is often deemed to be vague, insufficiently defined, and inconsistent.[82] Indeed, some authors deem human dignity as a merely relational concept in the sense that individual dignity only prevents unwanted interference by others,[83] which is subjective and therefore mostly an expression of individual autonomy and self-determination.

However, the notion of human dignity, framed within the European Union's legal system and rooted in the tradition of its Member States, may vary over time, but is currently defined according to fundamental criteria. Therefore, even if the notion is indeed not narrowly nor sufficiently defined and would benefit from further clarification through both a philosophical and legal debate, it is no vaguer than many other legal concepts. Examples of equally vague concepts include the notion of good faith, typical of continental legal systems, the notion of legitimate interest in common law,[84] and effectiveness under EU law.

Relevant guidance on the concept of human dignity can be derived from fundamental examples, and cases that were already addressed and solved by national courts. Prototypical cases are *le lancer du nain*, addressed by the French *Conseil d'État*[85] in 1995[86] and the peep-show, decided by the German Federal Administrative Court (BVerwG).[87] In both cases the circumstance that the directly involved parties had openly agreed—and were remunerated—to participate in the activities whose legality was being questioned, did not appear relevant to the courts.[88] They instead found those activities to be violating the dignity of the individual and of any other human, and therefore to be contrary to public order. Dignity was interpreted as an external and objective criterion—neither relational, nor measurable—that no one might violate with his own decisions, no matter how informed, therefore also limiting freedom of self-determination.

So conceived, human dignity grounds a fundamental-right-based approach that might lead an assessment of advanced technologies of the kind here considered. Dignity could provide an objective and legally relevant criterion to limit individual choices when selecting certain kinds of technological applications to provide or even receive care services.

---

[82] Sharkey 2014, p. 63.

[83] Bostrom et al. 2008, p. 180.

[84] Resta 2002, p. 801, Fabre 2007, p. 1.

[85] Judgments of the Conseil d'Etat 1995, Cases no. 136727 and 143578.

[86] A mayor of a small French town exercised the police power to ban any spectacle of dwarf-tossing in local clubs in order to secure respect for human dignity and public order.

[87] Decision of 15 December 1981, 64 Entscheidungen des Bundesverwaltungsgerichts, [BVerwG] 274.

[88] On the French case, see Beyleveled and Brownsword 2001, p. 26; on the German, see Foster and Sule 2010, p. 41.

16.5   Conclusion

If all humans are ends in themselves and possess human dignity, they might not be instrumentalized. Decisions on the care of the elderly thus should not be primarily based on budget constraints, or considerations about the structure of current and future populations. Although those elements should not be denied, the perspective ought to be reversed. All measures and solutions adopted should maximize the overall well-being of the user, including personal, psychological, and relational elements, enacting his proclaimed right to care, defined in light of those elements.

The analysis conducted identifies two clear constraints. First, the illegitimacy of any practice that is deceptive, including care robots simulating emotions and attachment to the user. The described application of human dignity in the case law allows us to infer that even when freely accepted by a consenting adult, intentional user's deception would still be deemed illicit. No one possesses the right to choose to be deceived because deception, by leading to delusional emotions and attachment, directly affects the dignity of the human being deceived, as well as that of all other human beings.[89]

Second, care is necessarily relational and, given that machines merely interact with humans rather than really relate to them, no machine can be used to replace humans in caring for any individual, particularly frail individuals. All applications need to be assessed to exclude that they are used to replace or anyway reduce human interaction. Major concerns arising from the use of robotic applications in the care of the elderly arise from the fear that such applications could further limit the amount of human contact individuals receive, giving rise to feelings of loneliness, leading to dementia,[90] inducing feelings of objectification,[91] causing the development of delusional emotional bonds,[92] or manipulating behaviour in consumption-related decisions.[93] In all other instances, cure, and eventually care, is more efficiently provided by a human agent (such as medical doctors, operators, caregivers), it should be favoured.

Finally, such a conclusion, as well as its framing within a fundamental-rights-based approach, as here described, acknowledging the pre-eminence of human dignity, appears to be adopted by the European Commission in its recent proposal for an AI regulation.[94] Indeed, art. 5, lett. (a) and (b) of this proposal precisely define as prohibited those AI practices that appear to be manipulative in nature, in particular those that may exploit the frailties of specific classes of human users deserving special attention, such as the elderly, and children. The proposed norm, short of being

---

[89] On such a matter, please allow reference to Bertolini 2018, 645 ff; similarly Zardiashvili and Fosch-Villaronga 2020, pp. 138–139.

[90] Cacioppo and Hawkley 2009, pp. 1464–1504.

[91] Vandemeulebroucke et al. 2018, pp. 15–25.

[92] Bertolini 2018, p. 647.

[93] Itoh et al. 2006, p. 260.

[94] European Commission 2021 Proposal on Artificial Intelligence (AIA).

perfect, clearly demonstrates that the current European legal framework is incompatible with applications that manipulate human emotions and perceptions of the kind here considered. The threshold the norm advances for the practice to be deemed illicit is indeed too high, yet the underlying rationale is commendable, and closely corresponds to the one here proposed.

References

Age UK, Care and Support for the Elderly (undated-a) Homecare: How to find the care you need at home https://www.ageuk.org.uk/information-advice/care/arranging-care/homecare/ Accessed 3 June 2021.

Age UK, Care and Support for the Elderly (undated-b) Finding and arranging social care. https://www.ageuk.org.uk/information-advice/care/arranging-care/ Accessed 3 June 2021.

Arendt H (1958) The Human Condition. The University of Chicago Press, Chicago.

Bertolini A (2013) Robots as Products: The Case for a Realistic Analysis of Robotic Applications and Liability Rules Law, Innovation and Technology, 5(2): 214–247.

Bertolini A (2015) Robotic Prostheses as Products Enhancing the Rights of People with Disabilities. Reconsidering the Structure of Liability Rules. International Review of Law, Computers & Technology 29: 116–136.

Bertolini A (2018) Human-Robot Interaction and Deception. Osservatorio Del Diritto Civile e Commerciale 1: 645–659.

Bertolini A, Aiello G (2017) Social Robots: A legal and ethical analysis. The Information Society 34: 130–140.

Bertolini A, Arian S (2020) Do Robots Care? Towards an Anthropocentric Framework in the Caring of Frail Individuals Through Assistive Technology. In: Haltaufderheide J et al (eds) Aging Between Participation and Simulation: Ethical Dimensions of Socially Assistive Technologies in Elderly Care. De Gruyter, Berlin, Germany, 35–52.

Beyleveld E, Brownsword R (2001) Human dignity in Bioethics and Biolaw. Oxford University Press, Oxford.

Bilir M K, Açikgöz O (2017) The Southern European Model in Welfare Regime Types and a Comparison Among the Health Care Provisions in Italy and Turkey. Hacettepe Journal of Health Administration 20(4): 503–516.

Birks M et al (2016) Robotic Seals as Therapeutic Tools in an Aged Care Facility: A Qualitative Study. Journal of Aging Research 2016: 1–7.

Black's Law Dictionary (2009) What is a Demographic Time Bomb. https://thelawdictionary.org/demographic-time-bomb/ Accessed 3 June 2021.

Blackman T et al (2001) Social Care and Social Inclusion: A Comparative Study of Older People's Care in Europe. Palgrave, Hampshire.

Bonsignorio F (2017) A New Kind of Article for Reproducible Research in Intelligent Robotics [From the Field]. IEEE Robotics & Automation Magazine, 24(3): 178–182.

Borzaga C, Fazzi L (2004) Civil Society, Third Sector, and Healthcare: The Case of Social Cooperatives in Italy. Social Science & Medicine, 123: 234–241.

Bostrom N (2008) Dignity and enhancement. In: Schulman A, Daniel Davis F, Dennett DC et al. (eds) Human dignity and bioethics: Essays commissioned by the President's Council on Bioethics. Washington, DC, USA, 173–207.

Bryson J, Kime P (2011) Just an artifact: why machines are perceived as moral agents. In: Walsh T (ed) Proceedings of the Twenty-Second International Joint Conference on Artificial Intelligence. AAAI Press. Barcelona, Spain, 1641–1646.

Caccioppo J T, Hawkley L C (2009) Perceived Social Isolation and Cognition. Trends Cognitive Sci, doi: https://doi.org/10.1016/j.tics.2009.06.00.

Cacioppo S, Capitanio JP, Cacioppo JT (2014) Toward a neurology of loneliness. Psychol. Bull. 140:6:1464–1504.

Camanio (undated) Bestic - Increase Your Mealtime Independence. Available at: https://www.camanio.com/us/products/bestic/ Accessed 3 June 2021.

Care Quality Commission (2015) Guidance for providers on Meeting the Regulations: Health and Social Care Act 2008 (Regulated Activities) Regulations 2014 & Care Quality Commission (Registration) Regulations 2009. Available at:https://www.cqc.org.uk/sites/default/files/20150210_guidance_for_providers_on_meeting_the_regulations_final_01.pdf Accessed 3 June 2021.

Choi H et al (2021) On the Use of Simulation in Robotics: Opportunities, Challenges, and Suggestions for Moving Forward. PNAS, https://doi.org/https://doi.org/10.1073/pnas.1907856118.

Coeckelbergh M (2011) Can We Trust Robots? Ethics and Information Technology 14(1): 53–60.

Coeckelbergh M (2012) Care robots, virtual virtue, and the best possible life. In: Brey PAE, Briggle AR, Spence EH (eds) The good life in a technological age. Routledge, pp. 281-293. http://www.routledge.com/books/details/9780415891264/.

Coeckelbergh M (2013) Human Being (at) Risk: Enhancement, Technology, and the Evaluation of Vulnerability Transformations. Springer, Dordrecht.

Comandè G (2014) Medical Law in Italy. In International Encyclopedia for Medical Law. Kluwer Law Intl, Netherlands, 1–293.

Decker M, Gutmann M (2012) Robo- and Informationethics Some Fundamentals. LIT-Verlag.

Department of Health and Social Care (2016) Guidance the Care Act Fact sheets. https://www.gov.uk/government/publications/care-act-2014-part-1-factsheets/care-act-factsheets. Accessed 3 June 2021.

Esping-Andersen G (1990) The Three Worlds of Capitalism. Princeton University Press, New Jersey.

European Commission (2018) EU Aging Report: Policy Challenges for Aging Societies. https://ec.europa.eu/info/news/economy-finance/policy-implications-ageing-examined-new-report-2018-may-25_en Accessed 3 June 2021.

European Commission (2019) EU Budget for 2021-2027: Commission Welcomes Provisional Agreement on Horizon Europe, the Future EU Research and Innovation Programme. https://ec.europa.eu/programmes/horizon2020/en/news/eu-budget-2021-2027-commission-welcomes-provisional-agreement-horizon-europe-future-eu-research Accessed 3 June 2021.

European Commission (2021) Proposal for a Regulation of the European Parliament and of the Council laying down harmonised rules on Artificial Intelligence (Artificial Intelligence Act) and amending certain union legislative acts. COM/2021/206 final. European Commission, Brussels.

Fabre-Magnan M (2007) La Dignité en Droit: Un Axiome. Revue Interdisciplinaire d'études Juridiques 58(1): 1–30.

Ferrera M (1998) The Four 'Social Europes': Between Universalism and Selectivity. In: Rhodes M, Meny Y (eds) The Future of European Welfare, A New Social Contract. Palgrave Macmillan, UK, 81–96.

Figueroa D (2016) Italy: Legislation on Support for the Disabled. Available at: https://www.loc.gov/law/foreign-news/article/italy-legislation-on-support-for-the-disabled/ Accessed 3 June 2021.

Fosch-Villaronga E, Drukarch H (2021) On Health Care Robots: Concepts, definitions, and considerations for healthcare robot governance. eLaw Center for Law and Technologies, The Netherlands.

Foster NG, Sule S (2010) German Legal System and laws. Oxford University Press, Oxford.

Fukushima N et al (2010) The Swedish Long _Term Care System. Enepri Research Report n. 89: 1–24.

Georgia Tech Healthcare Robotics Lab (2016) EL-E: An Assistive Robot. http://pwp.gatech.edu/hrl/el-e-an-assistive-robot/ Accessed 3 June 2021.

Gutman M et al (2012) Action and Autonomy: A Hidden Dilemma in Artificial Autonomous Systems. In: Decker M, Gutman M (eds) Robo- and Informationethics Some Fundamentals. Lit Verlag.

Hamada T et al (2008) Robot Therapy as for Recreation for Elderly People with Dementia – Game Recreation Using a Pet-type Robot. Proceedings of the 17th IEEE International Symposium on Robot and Human Interactive Communication 174–179.

Hendriks A (1998) The Right to Health in National and International Jurisprudence. European Journal of Health Law, 5(4), 389–408.

Hull D L (1986) On Human Nature. In PSA: Proceedings of the Biennial Meeting of the Philosophy of Science Association. JSTOR 3–13.

Isakjee A (2017) Welfare State Regimes: A Literature Review IRiS Working Paper Series, No. 18/2017(UPWEB Working Paper Series, No. 5/2017) Institute for Research into Superdiversity, Birmingham, 1–16.

Italy Social Support System (2007) Organisation and financing of social support to people with dementia and carers. Available at: https://www.alzheimer-europe.org/Policy/Country-compar isons/2007-Social-support-systems/Italy Accessed 3 June 2021.

Itoh K et al (2006) Mechanical Design of Emotion Expression Humanoid Robot WE-4RII. CISM Courses and Lectures Romansy 16,255-262. doi:https://doi.org/10.1007/3-211-38927-x_33.

Jarrett T (2019) Social Care: Adult Social Care: The Government's Ongoing Policy Review and Anticipated Green Paper. UK House of Commons Library. Available at: https://commonslibrary. parliament.uk/research-briefings/cbp-8002/ Accessed 3 June 2021.

Kant E (1785) The Groundwork of The Metaphysics of Moral.

Kelly J E (2004) Solidarity and Subsidiarity: "Organizing PRINCIPLES" for Corporate Moral Leadership in the New Global Economy. Journal of Business Ethics 52(3): 283–295.

Lind A (2014) The Right to Health in Sweden. In: Flood C, Gross A (eds) The Right to Health at the Public/Private Divide: A Global Comparative Study. Cambridge University Press, Cambridge, UK, 51–78.

Macintyre A (1999) Dependent Rational Animals: Why Human Beings Need the Virtues. Duckworth & Co, London.

Meagher G, Szebehely M (2013) Long Term Care in Sweden Trends Actors and Consequences. Doi:https://doi.org/10.1007/978-1-4614-4502-9_3.

Mickelburgh R (2004) Meet Pearl -She's the Robo-Nurse Designed to Look After the Elderly https://www.telegraph.co.uk/news/worldnews/northamerica/usa/1457427/Meet-Pearl-shes-the-robo-nurse-designed-to-look-after-the-elderly.html Accessed 3 June 2021.

Ministry of Internal Affairs and Communication (MIC) (2017) AI Strategy and Related Activities in Japan http://events.science-japon.org/dlai17/doc/MIC%20-%20France-Japan%20Symposium% 2020171025.pdf Accessed 3 June 2021.

Noddings N (2015) Starting at home: Caring and social policy. Braille Jymico, Charlesbourg, Quebec.

Nussbaum M (2009) Frontiers of Justice: Disability, Nationality, Species Membership. CNIB, Toronto

Nussbaum M (2011) Creating Capabilities: The Human Development Approach. Harvard University Press, Boston.

Nylande S et al (2012) A Complementing Approach for Identifying Ethical Issues in Care Robotics – Grounding Ethics in Practical Use. IEEE RO-MAN: The 21st IEEE International Symposium on Robot and Human Interactive Communication 2012: 797–802.

OECD (2018) Japan: Promoting Inclusive Growth for An Aging Society. OECD Better Policies for Better Lives. https://www.oecdilibrary.org/docserver/9789264299207en.pdf?expires= 1622599748&id=id&accname=guest&checksum=6A7453C3C6092E63750E16EC1965E98B Accessed 3 June 2021.

Parorobotics (2003) Paro Therapeutic Robot. http://www.parorobots.com Accessed 3 June 2021.

Pekarek S (2018) Population Aging and Economic Dependency Ratio. Comparative study of The Czech Republic and Slovakia 104 :1–7.

Pollack M et al (2002) Pearl: A Mobile Robotic Assistant for Elderly. Workshop on Automation as Caregiver: The Role of Intelligent Technology in Elder Care 2002: 85–92.

Resta G (2002) La Disponibilita Dei Diritti Fondamentali e i Limiti Della Dignita (note a margine della carta dei diritti). Rivista di Diritto Civile 801–848.

Rodríguez-Pinzón D, Martin C (2003) The International Human Rights Status of Elderly Persons. American University International Law Review 18(4): 915–1008.

Salton J (2009) RIBA the Friendly Robot Nurse. https://newatlas.com/riba-robot-nurse/12693/ Accessed 3 June 2021.

Scheutz M (2009) The Inherent Dangers of Unidirectional Emotional Bonds between Humans and Social Robots. In: Lin P et al (eds) Robot Ethics: The Ethical and Social Implications of Robotics. MIT Press, 205-222, Cambridge, MA.

Sharkey A (2014) Robots and Human Dignity: A Consideration of The Effects of Robot Care on the Dignity of Older People. Ethics and Information Technology 16(1): 63–75.

Sharkey A, Sharkey J (2012) Granny and the Robots: Ethical Issues in Robot Care for the Elderly. Ethics and Information Technology 14(1):27–40.

Sharkey A, Sharkey N (2010) Granny and the robots: Ethical issues in robot care for the elderly. Ethics and Information Technology, 14(1), 27–40. doi:https://doi.org/10.1007/s10676-010-9234-6.

Sheba JK et al (2018) Development of Rehabilitative Multimodal Interactive Pet Robot for Elderly Residents. Procedia Computer Science 133: 401–408.

SoftBank Robotics (2017) How to Create a Great Experience with Pepper. http://doc.aldebaran.com/download/Pepper_B2BD_guidelines_Sept_V1.5.pdf Accessed 3 June 2021.

Spicker P (2000) The Welfare State: A General Theory. Sage Publications Ltd, London.

Szebehely M, Trydegård GB (2011) Home Care for Older People in Sweden: a Universal Model in Transition. Health & Social Care in the Community 20(3): 300–309.

Tediosi F, Gabriele S (2010) The Long-Term Care System for The Elderly in Italy. Enerpi Research Report N0. 80. European Network of Economic Policy Research Institutes 1–24.

Tronto J (2015) Moral boundaries: A political argument for an ethic of care. Routledge. Oxford, UK.

Turing A (1950) Computing Machinery and Intelligence. Mind 59 (236): 433–460.

United Nations Economic and Social Affairs (2017) World Mortality. https://www.un.org/en/development/desa/population/publications/pdf/mortality/WMR2019/WorldMortality2019DataBooklet.pdf Accessed 3 June 2021.

United Nations, Department of Economic and Social Affairs, Population Division (2015) World Population Ageing 2015 https://www.un.org/en/development/desa/population/publications/pdf/ageing/WPA2015_Report.pdf Accessed 3 June 2021.

University of California San Diego and others (2020) A Roadmap for US Robotics – From Internet to Robotics. http://www.hichristensen.com/pdf/roadmap-2020.pdf Accessed 3 June 2021.

Vallor S (2016) Technology and the virtues. Oxford University Press, New York.

Van Wynsberghe A (2013) Designing Robots for Care: Care Centered Value-Sensitive Design. Sci Eng Ethics 19, 407–433 (2013). https://doi.org/10.1007/s11948-011-9343-6.

Vandemeulebroucke T et al (2018) The Use of Care Robots in Aged Care: A Systematic Review of Argument-based Ethics Literature. Archives of Gerontology and Geriatrics 74: 15–25.

Vìolini L (2006) Articolo 38. In: Bifulco R, Celotto A, Olivetti M (eds) Commentario alla Costituzione. Utet, Turin, p. 775.

Vivaldi E (2019) Disabilità, Autonomia, Diritti. Alcune Riflessioni a Tre Anni Dall'approvazione Della Legge n. 112/2016. Dritti Fondamentali. http://dirittifondamentali.it/wp-content/uploads/2019/06/E.-Vivaldi-Disabilit%C3%A0-autonomia-diritti.pdf Accessed 3 June 2021.

Winner S (2007) Beam Me Inside, Scotty! Assisted Living Consult. https://www.assistedlivingconsult.com/issues/03-04/alc78-BeamMeUp-719a.pdf Accessed 3 June 2021.

World Health Organization (2018) Aging and Health. https://www.who.int/news-room/fact-sheets/detail/ageing-and-health Accessed 3 June 2021.

YouTube (undated) JIBO: The World's First Social Robot for the Home. https://www.youtube.com/watch?v=H0h20jRA5M0 Accessed 3 June 2021.

Zardiashvili L, Fosch-Villaronga E (2020) "Oh, Dignity Too?" Said the Robot: Human Dignity as The Basis for the Governance of Robotics. https://doi.org/10.1007/s11023-019-09514-6.

Legislation and Other Documents

Aldre – va °rd och omsorg a °r 2007 [Care and Services to Older Persons Act], 2008, Available at: https://www.socialstyrelsen.se/globalassets/sharepoint-dokument/artikelkatalog/statistik/2008-44-7_rev2.pdf Accessed 3 June 2021.

Basic Law for Federal Republic of Germany, 23 May 1949, available at: https://www.btg-bestellservice.de/pdf/80201000.pdf Accessed 3 June 2021.

Charter of Fundamental Rights of the European Union (CFR), 14 December 2007, available at: https://eur-lex.europa.eu/legal-content/EN/TXT/PDF/?uri=OJ:C:2007:303:FULL&from=EN Accessed 3 June 2021.

Decision of 15 December 1981, 64 Entscheidungen des Bundesverwaltungsgerichts, [BVerwG] 274.

Government of UK Career's Allowance. https://www.gov.uk/carers-allowance Accessed 3 June 2021.

Ha¨ lso- Och Sjukva ° rdslag [The Health and Medical Services Act (HMSA)], 1982, Available at: http://www.riksdagen.se/sv/Dokument-Lagar/Lagar/Svenskforfattningssamling/Halso--och-sjukvardslag-1982_sfs-1982-763/ Accessed 3 June 2021.

International Convention on the Elimination of All Forms of Racial Discrimination, 21 December 1965, available at : https://www.ohchr.org/en/professionalinterest/pages/cerd.aspx Accessed 3 June 2021.

International Covenant on Economic, Social and Cultural Rights (ICESCR), 16 December 1966. Available at: https://www.ohchr.org/en/professionalinterest/pages/cescr.aspx Accessed 3 June 2021.

Judgments of the Conseil d'État (Assemblée), 27 October 1995, Cases no. 136727 and 143578, Revue française de droit administratif 1 l(6) nov.46c. 1995.

Law 22 giugno 2016, n.112. "Disposizioni in materia di assistenza in favore delle persone con disabilità grave prive del sostegno familiar" (Provisions on Assistance Benefitting Persons with Serious Disabilities Who Are Deprived of Family Support). Available at: https://www.gazzettaufficiale.it/eli/id/2016/06/24/16G00125/sg Accessed 3 June 2021.

Social Services Act 2001:453, 7 June 2001, available at: https://ec.europa.eu/antitrafficking/sites/default/files/social_services_act_sweden_en_1.pdf Accessed 3 June 2021.

The Constitution of the World Health Organization (WHO), 17 November 1947, available at: https://www.who.int/governance/eb/who_constitution_en.pdf Accessed 3 June 2021.

The European Charter of Rights and Responsibilities of Older People in Need of Long-Term Care and Assistance, 9 September 2010, available at: https://eur-lex.europa.eu/legal-content/EN/TXT/PDF/?uri=CELEX:52010IP0313&from=EN. Accessed 3 June 2021.

The European Social Charter (ESC), 18 October 1961, available at: https://rm.coe.int/168006b642 Accessed 3 June 2021.

The National Health Service (NHS) Constitution for England, 25 July 2015, available at: https://www.ghc.nhs.uk/wp-content/uploads/nhs-constitution-handbook-acc.pdf Accessed 3 June 2021.

The United Nations Convention on the Rights of Persons with Disabilities and Optional Protocol (CRPD), 13 December 2006, available at: https://www.un.org/disabilities/documents/convention/convoptprot-e.pdf Accessed 3 June 2021.

The United Nations Universal Declaration of Human Rights(UN UDHR), 10 December 1948, available at: https://www.ohchr.org/en/udhr/documents/udhr_translations/eng.pdf Accessed 3 June 2021.

Treaty on the Functioning of the EU, in the consolidated version of 7 June 2016, available at: https://eur-lex.europa.eu/legal-content/EN/TXT/PDF/?uri=OJ:C:2016:202:FULL&from=EN.

UK Care Act, 2014. Available at: http://www.legislation.gov.uk/ukpga/2014/23/contents/enacted Accessed 3 June 2021.

Andrea Bertolini Ph.D., LL.M. (Yale), is an assistant professor of private law at the Scuola Superiore Sant'Anna in Pisa (SSSA). His research ranges from private law to technology regulation (robotics and AI) with a comparative and functional approach. He coordinated a number of national and European projects on issues of regulation of robotics and AI. Since October 2018, he directs the European Centre of Excellence on the Regulation of Robotics and AI (EURA), funded by the European Commission under the Jean Monnet Action. On such matters, he is often heard as an expert by policy makers and international organizations, and has written studies and expert opinions, for the European Parliament and Commission. He is responsible for Sects. 16.1, 16.3.2, 16.4 and its subsections and Sect. 16.5.

Shabahang Arian holds a LL.B. degree from the University of Isfahan and a Masters of Law (LLM) in Business Law and Comparative Law from Dale E. Fowler, School of Law, Chapman University, California. She also qualified as a practicing attorney in Iran. Since 2018, Shabahang is a PhD candidate at the Dirpolis Institute, Scuola Superiore Sant'Anna in Pisa, Italy. Her research focuses on artificial intelligence and robotics, bio-ethics, care-ethics, medical law, technology law, safety and liability. In addition, she is an active researcher on European research projects such as INBOTS H2020 and H2020-FETPROACT. She is also a member of the EURA Centre of Excellence on the Regulation of Robotics and AI. She is responsible for Sect. 16.2 and its subsections and Sects. 16.3, 16.3.1 and 16.5. All online documents were last accessed 3 June 2021. The usual disclaimer applies.

Chapter 17
Generative AI and Intellectual Property Rights

Jan Smits and Tijn Borghuis

Contents

Abstract Since the inception of AI, researchers have tried to generate novel works in media ranging from music through text to images. The quality of works produced by generative AI-systems is starting to reach levels that make them usable in contexts where until now human creations are employed. In addition, new contexts are emerging in which humans unskilled in a creative domain can generate works by cooperating with generative AI-tools. Generative AI could lead to an abundance of individually customized content, where works are generated for a particular user in a specific situation and presented once, perhaps never to be repeated again. These developments challenge core concepts of Intellectual Property Rights: "authorship"

J. Smits (✉) · T. Borghuis
Eindhoven University of Technology, P.O. Box 513, 5600 MB Eindhoven, The Netherlands
e-mail: j.m.smits@tue.nl

T. Borghuis
e-mail: v.a.j.borghuis@tue.nl

© T.M.C. ASSER PRESS and the authors 2022
B. Custers and E. Fosch-Villaronga (eds.), *Law and Artificial Intelligence*,
Information Technology and Law Series 35,
https://doi.org/10.1007/978-94-6265-523-2_17

obviously, but also "work". Although the content produced by generative systems is new, these systems are often trained on a corpus of (parts of) existing works produced by humans. Hence, practices of (un)authorised imitation need to be considered. In this chapter we want to study these questions, which are emerging in all creative domains, with generative AI for music as the central example.

Keywords Generative AI · Authorship · Work · Unauthorized Imitation · Human-Al Cooperation · Era of Abundance · Public Domain

17.1 Introduction

With the advent of practical deep learning techniques, around 2012, new powerful machine learning models for content generation were invented.[1] These models were first deployed in music,[2] but rapidly found applications in other creative domains such as drawing,[3] painting,[4] cartoons,[5] poetry[6] and rap lyrics.[7] The quality of works produced by generative AI-systems is starting to reach levels that make them usable in contexts where until now human creations are employed.

Historically, generative AI-systems where used as tools assisting and inspiring artists in their creative practice[8]. Operating them required a great deal of knowledge of the creative domain. But as technology develops, there is a trend towards more and more autonomous systems, to the point where only a push of a button is required to create a work. Generative AI opens the door to personalization and customization of creative works on a massive scale. Venture capitalist Vinod Khosla famously predicted that, thanks to AI, we will be listening to "custom made song equivalents that are built around our mood" in a decade.[9]

Clearly the rise of generative AI raises new questions related to Intellectual Property Rights, which are increasingly addressed in academic and policy debates:[10] Can an AI-system be the author of a work it generates? Is a work generated by an AI original? Is it feasible to attach rights to separate works in an era of abundance? In this chapter we want to study these questions, which are emerging in all creative

---

[1] Most notably Autoencoders and Generative Adversarial Networks (GANs).

[2] Boulanger-Lewandowski et al. 2012.

[3] Gregor et al. 2015.

[4] Elgammal 2017.

[5] Liu et al. 2017.

[6] Yu et al. 2016.

[7] Karsdorp et al. 2018.

[8] The first experiments in this field date back to the 1950s, see Hiller and Isaacson 1958.

[9] Hanbury M (2019) A billionaire venture capitalist thinks music as we know it will be dead in 10 years, https://www.businessinsider.nl/venture-capitalist-vinod-khosla-talks-future-of-music-2019-6/?international=true&r=US, accessed 10 June 2021.

[10] Last December, Allan et al. 2020 was published, an EU commission study containing a legal assessment of these matters with literature overview and case law.

domains, with generative AI for music as the central example, as we are active in this field ourselves. Section 17.2 introduces the relevant technical concepts and methods in generative AI. With this background in place, we turn to the question of authorship for works generated by AI-systems in Sect. 17.3. Finding a disconnect between the new generation methods and existing copyright law, we discuss the various ways in which legal scholars are trying to reconstruct authorship rights on AI-generated works in Sect. 17.4. Before drawing conclusions in Sect. 17.6, we examine the assumptions underlying these reconstructions and explore the alternative to let AI-generated works fall in the public domain in Sect. 17.5.

17.2 AI: The Generative Form

In legal discussions on generative AI, the AI is often treated as a black box. We think that opening the box, at least partially and with care, can help inform these discussions. Section 17.2.1 introduces the two main approaches to music generation with AI and Sect. 17.2.2 describes the entire workflow that goes into the generation of a song.

17.2.1 Main Approaches

In AI for music generation (and other creative domains) we can distinguish two main approaches: *rule-based* and *learning-based*.

In the rule-based approach, generation is based on the formalization of musical knowledge. By analysing regularities in the harmonic, melodic, rhythmic and timbric structure of compositions in a certain genre of music, the "unwritten rules" by which humans compose this kind of music can be approximated. Where such rules can be made formal enough, they can be translated into computer code. A program implementing the body of rules for a genre can then be used to generate new music. This body of rules can be quite complex, allowing for many different possible executions of the program that implements it.[11] Each of these possible executions results in a different composition. Although historically this approach has long been dominant and produced notable results,[12] it is now superseded by a rapidly expanding family of so-called deep learning methods.[13]

In the learning-based approach, there is no basis in musical knowledge. Instead, a collection of examples of the kind of music one would like to generate is compiled,

---

[11] Execution is often 'primed' with random numbers or incoming data from outside the system, examples of which will be discussed in Sect. 17.5.1.

[12] For instance, David Cope's *Experiments in Musical Intelligence software*, which was able to write pieces in the style of several composers.

[13] See Briot et al. 2019 for a systematic overview of generative machine learning methods for music.

the *dataset*. These pieces of music are treated as samples drawn from an unknown statistical distribution (describing all possible pieces of the required kind), and the objective of machine learning is to extract enough information about this distribution to create new samples (pieces of music) from it. The machine learning *model*, the computer program that is able to create the new samples, is produced by optimising a predefined mathematical structure in a process of *training*. Such structures consist of a network of many nodes linked by connections through which numerical values can be exchanged, and are called Artificial Neural Networks as their functioning is (loosely) inspired by electrochemical activity in networks of neurons in the human brain.

To build a model, machine learning specialists create a network in software by specifying the lay-out of the nodes and connections. Nodes in the network take the values they receive on incoming connections, sum them and pass them on to other nodes through outgoing connections. In summing they give more importance ("weight") to some incoming connections than to others. The weights in the network are optimised by passing the dataset compositions (rendered as patterns of numerical values) through the network and tuning the weights until the network is able to reproduce them with a reasonable degree of accuracy. Although the process of training is automated, it is not guaranteed to work. Many choices have to be made regarding the structure of the network and the organization of the training. In absence of a mathematical criterion for the musical quality of the generated output, human judgment is needed to determine the success. This currently makes the development of a model for a certain genre of music an experimental process, requiring iteration and cooperation between machine learning specialists and musicians. When the training is successful, the model will be able to generate new pieces of music of the kind of the examples in the dataset. Through the trained network a mathematical space is created in which each point represents a piece of music. By traversing this space and inspecting different points, new compositions can be created.[14]

An interesting feature of deep learning methods is that they can be applied to both representations of music that are protected under copyright. In principle, one could learn directly from music recordings, generating both new compositions and their performances ("impersonating" human artists). Although there is some work in this direction,[15, 16] it is currently technically very difficult and too computation-intensive to be widely applicable. The more common approach is to use the representation of music as notated in scores, in particular MIDI files, a machine-readable format for music notation. AI-systems trained on a dataset of scores are able to generate novel scores, that can be performed by humans (reading them as sheet music) or electronic instruments (reading them as MIDI files).

---

[14] It is important to point out is that the compositions from the dataset are *not* present in the model. During training they are processed to change the weights internal to the model, but the compositions are *not* stored in or retained by the system. Once trained, it generates new compositions without consulting the dataset.

[15] Carr and Zukowski 2018.

[16] Dieleman et al. 2016.

17.2.2 *Walk in the Park*

To make the abstract description of generative methods more tangible, we will briefly describe the entire workflow that went in to the generation of a single composition: the track "Walk in the Park'", which can be listened to on the Musi-co website.[17] The main ingredients are a novel machine learning model for music generation, developed with a team of researchers from the University of Florence,[18] and a dataset of musical examples, produced specifically for the purpose.[19]

To create the dataset, we selected three related genres of music, acid jazz, soul and funk, and briefed a human composer by pointing out specific artists and recordings that we deemed representative for these genres. Inspired by these examples, the composer wrote a total of 910 original short pieces (4 bars) in these genres, all for a simple electro-acoustic quartet: drums, bass, electric piano and rock organ. The scores for these pieces were delivered in the form of MIDI-files and used by the machine learning researchers to train the model.

Once the model was trained, it was able to generate new short pieces across the three genres. By traversing the mathematical space between random combinations of given start and end points, a collection of new scores in the form of MIDI-files was generated. Among those was the MIDI-file for Walk in the Park. To turn this score into something audible, a musician selected synthesizers and samplers to play the parts of the four instruments using standard music software, and balanced the volume levels of the instrument tracks before exporting the sound file for Walk in the Park.[20]

The entire workflow leading up to the song clearly requires the contributions of (highly) specialized humans, but once the trained model is in place this is no longer the case. To demonstrate this, we built a webpage where anyone can access the trained model to create a new song.[21] On this page, an end-user only has to choose the genre for the start of the song, the genre of the end of the song and the desired length of the song. After submitting these choices, the model generates a new score according to this specification without any human intervention. It returns the score as a MIDI file, which the user can play back using synthesizers and samplers embedded in the webpage. Alternatively the user can choose to download the MIDI-file and import it in any common music software for use as raw material in her own music productions. The few choices made by the end-user could easily be delegated to the system itself (using randomization), reducing the human effort in creating a song to a single push of a button.

---

[17] https://www.musi-co.com/listen/track/walk-in-the-park, accessed 10 June 2021.

[18] Angioloni et al. 2020.

[19] Published as 'ASF-4', additional material to the paper, https://paolo-f.github.io/CONLON/dat asets.html, accessed 10 June 2021.

[20] Mixing is in itself a domain of important creative choices in music production, but in this case the objective was to present the composition generated by the deep learning model as faithfully as possible.

[21] Musi-co Live AI, https://www.musi-co.com/listen/live, accessed 10 June 2021.

In terms of the phases of the creative process in machine-aided production proposed by Allan et al.[22] human creativity plays a role in the conception phase ("creating and elaborating the design or plan of a work"). Although we cannot expect the effects of choices made in the design and training of the deep learning model and the curation of input data to be traceable in any single generated work, this phase clearly involves creative choices. The execution phase ("converting the design or plan into what could be considered (rough) draft versions of the final work") is fully automated, and a redaction phase ("processing and reworking the draft versions produced in the execution phase into a finalised cultural product or output ready to be delivered to a publisher or other intermediary, or directly to the market") is absent in the generation services envisioned in this chapter (see Sect. 17.5.1). The user directly experiences the generation result without selection or other forms of post-production by humans.

17.3 AI-Generated Works in IPR

We now return to the issues the advent of generative AI raises for IPR, starting from a simple question: "Does the AI that generated Walk in the Park hold the copyrights to that song?". European legislation does not provide for a general definition as to who can be considered an author. The Software Directive[23] and the Database Directive[24] give no clear picture. But we already have some indications where the European Court of Justice (ECJ) will go. On the question: Who can be an author? The ECJ, decided in the Painer case that an original work should be the "author's own intellectual creation". And decided that two elements are important: (1) who is the author and (2) originality. We will discuss the second point shortly, but AI could certainly not pass the human being test. In the words of the Court: "an intellectual creation is an author's own if it reflects the author's personality. That is the case if the author was able to express his creative abilities in the production of the work by making free and creative choices. (…) By making those various choices, the author of a portrait photograph can stamp the work created with his 'personal touch'."[25] So, under EU law only a human being can be the originator and hence rights holder according to the court. Whereas the song Walk in the Park came out of an AI system

---

[22] Allan et al. 2020, pp. 79–80.

[23] DIRECTIVE 2009/24/EC OF THE EUROPEAN PARLIAMENT AND OF THE COUNCIL of 23 April 2009 on the legal protection of computer programs, Official Journal of the European Communities, No L111/16.
https://eur-lex.europa.eu/legal-content/EN/TXT/PDF/?uri=CELEX:32009L0024&from=EN

[24] DIRECTIVE 96191EC OF THE EUROPEAN PARLIAMENT AND OF THE COUNCIL of 11 March 1996, on the legal protection of databases, Official Journal of the European Communities, No L77/20 https://eur-lex.europa.eu/legal-content/EN/TXT/PDF/?uri=CELEX:31996L0009&from=EN

[25] Case C-145/10 Eva-Maria Painer v Standard Verlag GmbH and others, Luxembourg, 1 December 2011.

that "wrote" the song, and applying the verdict of the ECJ the answer whether the AI system is a person is simple to answer: No. Therefore, the AI system cannot become a rights holder. AI cannot be vested with the copyright on the song Walk in the Park.

Would Walk in the Park be legally protected under US copyright law? The US Copyright Office states in its Compendium in §306: "The U.S. Copyright Office will register an original work of authorship, provided that the work was created by a human being."[26] US copyright law does not differentiate between humans and non-humans, but when asked whether a monkey could hold a copyright on a photo the monkey took,[27] the court decided that a monkey, and more generally an animal, could not hold a copyright.[28] Whereas AI clearly is not a human, it cannot therefore hold a copyright under US law. AI as an author is therefore considered not possible under either US or EU copyright laws. Mutatis mutandis, the resulting outcome of AI technology (Walk in the Park) is currently not eligible for IPR protection.

Setting this conclusion aside for a moment, we look at the second aspect: would Walk in the Park satisfy the conditions for something to be classified as a 'work'? Under the InfoSoc Directive[29] there are two conditions, according to the CJEU: "First, the subject matter concerned must be original in the sense that it is the author's own intellectual creation (…) Secondly, only something which is the expression of the author's own intellectual creation may be classified as a 'work' ".[30] The test for originality was set out by the CJEU in the context of photographs in Painer v. Standard Verlag,[31] namely: the work must be the author's own intellectual creation (AOIC), it must reflect the author's personality. This is the case if the author was able to express his/her creative abilities by making free and creative choices the author stamps the work with his/her 'personal touch'.

In the workflow described above, there are free and creative choices made by humans in the development of the AI-system that affect the music generation. The compilation of the dataset and the choices made in constructing and tuning the machine learning model require musical (and mathematical) creativity. However, while these choices affect all compositions the AI-system generates, they cannot be meaningfully linked to an individual composition, let alone said to stamp it with the personal touch of the humans that made them. If the originality test is to be applied to an individual work and the AI-system that generated it, we end up with

---

[26] U.S. Copyright Office, Compendium of U.S. copyright office practices (3d ed. 2014), §306. p. 8. "To qualify as a work of 'authorship' a work must be created by a human being.... Works that do not satisfy this requirement are not copyrightable. The Office will not register works produced by nature, animals, or plants."

[27] The fight between the photographer and animal rights activists is well described in Guadamuz 2018.

[28] Naruto v. Slater, no. 16-15469 (9th Cir. 25 May 2018) concluded the case.

[29] DIRECTIVE 2001/29/EC OF THE EUROPEAN PARLIAMENT AND OF THE COUNCIL of 22 May 2001 on the harmonisation of certain aspects of copyright and related rights in the information society, https://eur-lex.europa.eu/legal-content/EN/TXT/PDF/?uri=CELEX:32001L0029&from=EN.

[30] Levola Hengelo v Smilde Foods (Case C-310/17; 13 November 2018).

[31] Case C-145/10.

the question whether an AI can make free and creative choices, or have a personal touch. Whether this is possible in principle is an open philosophical question,[32] but for current systems and those of the foreseeable future this threshold is too high.

US law is very clear: protection will not be given "for works produced by a machine or mere mechanical process".[33] "Similarly, the [US Copyright] Office will not register works produced by a machine or mere mechanical process that operates randomly or automatically without any creative input or intervention from a human author".[34] Or in the words of Hristov: "Randomness, just like autonomously learned behavior is something that cannot be attributed to the human programmer of an AI machine. As such, the resulting autonomous works are not eligible for copyright protection (…)".[35] Although we can discuss to what extent the behaviour of machine learning models is autonomously learned, it seems clear that under US law as well as EU law, Walk in the Park would not qualify as a work.

To avoid confusion between the different senses of "work" in the following discussion, we will henceforth refer to an AI-generated work as a "qwrk".[36]

17.4 Constructing Authorship Rights for AI-Generated Works

When no author for a qwrk can be established, it falls into the public domain. In policy documents and in literature, this is assumed to be problematic. As Hristov puts it "There is a considerable disadvantage to the release of independently generated AI creative works into the public domain. Without an established period of protection, there is no tangible incentive for developers of AI machines to continue creating, using, and improving their capabilities".[37] We will address this assumption in the next section, but first look at the directions in which solutions to this problem are sought: the made for hire doctrine (Sect. 17.4.1), legal personhood for AI-systems (Sect. 17.4.2), a separate status for Computer Generated Works (Sect. 17.4.3), and Sui Generis rights (Sect. 17.4.4). If it were possible to vest authorship of qwrks in natural or legal persons through one of these approaches, there is still the issue of subsistence, which is discussed in Sect. 17.4.5. Indirect protection through related rights is discussed in Sect. 17.4.6.

---

[32] See for instance the discussion of Artificial Moral Agents in Müller 2020, Section 2.9.

[33] Supra note 14.

[34] Ibid., p. 22.

[35] Hristov 2017, p. 436.

[36] Abbreviation of "quasi-work", pronounced "quirk".

[37] Hristov 2017, pp. 436–437.

17.4.1 Made for Hire

Under the 'made for hire' doctrine of the U.S. Copyright Act, copyright can be awarded to a party other than the original creator of a work. Two types of copyrightable creations are distinguished: "a work prepared by an employee during the scope of his or her employment" and "a work specifically ordered or commissioned for use (…) if the parties expressly agree in a written instrument signed by them that the work shall be considered a work made for hire." Viewing qwrks as being of the first type, owners and programmers of AI systems could enter the frame as copyright holders, viewing them as being of the second type, end-users could come into the picture.

Hristov proposes to allow a relative interpretation of the terms "employer" and "employee" within the doctrine. By considering an employer as "someone who employs the services of another entity to achieve a goal or complete a task", owners or programmers of AI-systems can be seen as employing the services of the AI-system (an entity) in generating creative works. This would allow transfer of authorship of the generated works from the AI-system to its owners or programmers. As Hristov points out, the relative interpretation that allows AI-systems to be considered as "employee" within the doctrine is at odds with the way this term must be viewed in terms of agency law in other contexts. It is questionable whether creating such a local incongruity is desirable. Also, it is not clear how the transfer of rights could be implemented as the usual mechanisms of consent such as written contracts between employer and employee are not available. In any case, the solution is not suitable for European law.[38]

In his proposal Hristov makes a clear choice not to allow for the transfer of rights to end-users, for which the second type of copyrightable creation specified above could be a basis. He argues that since the goals of assigning copyrights on qwrks is to provide financial incentives for the development of the AI industry, these incentives should go to the programmers and owners of AI-systems since they are "the greatest contributors to the development and dissemination of AI" (…) "By losing copyright claims to end users, owners and programmers may restrict the use of AI by third parties. These protective measures would allow developers to maintain copyright over the works generated by AI but would also limit the applications of AI and the numerous benefits associated with them. As a result, society would likely see a significant decline in AI generated works and a decline in the overall development of the AI industry." Putting aside the economic magnitude of the respective contributions, this argument seems to ignore scenarios in which the end-user has a role in the creation of the AI-system that generates the works, which we will discuss below (Sect. 17.4.3).

---

[38] Rognstad 2018.

17.4.2 The Attribution of Legal Personhood to AI-Systems

Rather than giving "authorship in name only" of qwrks to humans, a more principled idea is to consider AI-systems authors in their own right. This could be achieved by attributing legal personhood to AI-systems: as legal persons they could be authors of copyrighted works and own them.

Current copyright regimes in the EU leave no room for such a move, as "it seems unlikely that attribution of rights to machines will be considered within copyright domain shortly",[39] and the European Economic and Social Committee has taken a stand against the idea of attributing legal personhood to robots because of the effects it would have on liability law and the possibility of creating a "risk of moral hazard (...) and opportunities for abuse".[40] However, the European Parliament has explored the possibility for granting rights and obligations (regarding civil liability) to robots, and their report leaves open the possibility of "creating a specific legal status for robots in the long run, so that at least the most sophisticated autonomous robots could be established as having the status of electronic persons responsible for making good any damage they may cause, and possibly applying electronic personality to cases where robots make autonomous decisions or otherwise interact with third parties independently".[41] Being an author of copyrighted works could be such a case.

The proposal to create a special legal status has proven to be highly controversial and sparked a wider societal debate on what have been dubbed "Robot Rights".[42] In this far-ranging and far from settled debate, issues regarding IP on generated works are but a small strand amidst more consequential considerations.

17.4.3 Computer-Generated Works

Rather than changing the legal status of the generative AI-system, a solution can also be sought in changing the status of the generated work. One possible point of departure is the notion of "Computer-Generated Work" (CGW) in UK copyright legislation: "In the case of a literary, dramatic, musical or artistic work which is computer-generated, the author shall be taken to be the person by whom the arrangements necessary for the creation of the work are undertaken".[43] Computer-generated is taken to mean that "the work is generated by computer in circumstances that there is no human author of the work".[44] Irish law[45] defines a CGW as meaning "that the work is generated by computer in circumstances where the author of the

[39] De Cock Buning 2018, pp. 511–535.

[40] European Economic and Social Committee 2017, para 1.12.

[41] EU Parliament Committee on Legal Affairs 2015, Section 59(f).

[42] Gunkel 2018.

[43] UK Copyright, Designs and Patents Act 1988, Section 12(7).

[44] Ibid., Section 178.

[45] Section 2(1) of the Irish Copyright and related Rights Act 2000.

work is not an individual", and equally designates the author as "the person by whom the arrangements necessary for the creation of the work are undertaken". It defines a computer program as "a program which is original in that it is the author's own intellectual creation and includes any design materials used for the preparation of the program".

Qwrks were not foreseen by these laws, but they could be categorised as a kind of CWG. As Lambert points out,[46] the emergence of new forms of CWG will necessitate detailed discussions on what "arrangements" and "arrangements necessary" actually mean for these forms. Where the intention is to grant the authorship of the generated works to the company owning the AI-system or the technical staff that enabled the computer to generate the work,[47] the use of machine learning in AI-systems complicates the picture. Before such a system can autonomously generate a work, it has to be trained on a dataset of examples. It is not far-fetched to imagine scenarios in which the end-user provides the dataset or parts thereof (e.g., by curating a collection of pieces of music) on which the AI-system is trained before it generates a qwrk. If we consider the training of the AI-system as belonging to the "preparation of the program" and the dataset as being among the "design materials" used therein, the end-user would be undertaking part of the "arrangements necessary". Another example of such involvement is the further training of the AI-system after deployment, where in a setting of reinforcement learning the feedback of end-users on generated works is used to improve the quality of the generation.

Hence, adopting this solution for qwrks would require a further clarification of "arrangements necessary" and the roles of owners, programmers and end-users in the creation of AI-systems.[48] Another obstacle to a wider adoption is that the concept of CGW is not compatible with the body of copyright law accumulated by the European Union.

17.4.4 Sui Generis *Rights*

A final direction for solving the problem could be to create a new category of protection not resulting from any general copyright laws, specifically for qwrks. There are precedents for such "sui generis" rights, such as the protection for original designs of vessel hulls[49] and mask works for semiconductor chips[50] in the United States

---

[46] Lambert 2017.

[47] Clark and Smyth 1997, p. 252.

[48] For an analysis of different possible configurations of co-authorship of these parties, see Maunder-Cockram 2019, chapter 4.

[49] The Vessel Hull Design Protection Act, published as chapter 13 of Title 17 of the United States Code, was signed into law on 28 October 1998.

[50] The Semiconductor Chip Protection Act (SCPA) of 1984 established a new type of intellectual property protection for mask works that are fixed in semiconductor chips. It did so by amending title 17 of the United States Code, adding chapter 9.1.

Code. Another example is the European database directive that attributes the authorship over databases to "the natural person or group of natural persons who created the base or, where the legislation of the Member States so permits, the legal person designated as the rights holder by that legislation".[51]

Although the database directive could be used to protect the datasets (curated collections of materials) used to train AI-systems employing machine learning, it cannot be used to protect the works generated by AI-systems. The assumption is that the contents of the database are known, and the works generated by the AI-system are unknown beforehand, i.e. they cannot be anticipated. The directive does not cover the creation of data, only "any investment in obtaining, verifying or presenting the contents of a database for the limited duration of the right; whereas such investment may consist in the deployment of financial resources and/or the expension of time, effort and energy".[52] However, the database directive could be used as a model in designing a specific sui generis regime for qwrks. As in the directive, the authorship of qwrks could be attributed to either natural or legal person(s), such as owners, programmers and end-users of AI-systems.[53] Alternatively, rights and protections could be awarded without recognising an author.[54] The terms of protection could be tailored to fit the rapid pace of technological development in the field, and to balance the interests of human creators and persons using generative AI-systems. Through specific rules regarding the use of qwrks and the use of AI-systems, risks related to liabilities and anti-competitive actions could be mitigated.

17.4.5 Originality: The Elephant in the Room

Each of the directions for a solution comes with its own set of problems. Assuming for the sake of argument that they would somehow suffice to vest authorship of qwrks in a natural or legal person, this leaves the question of subsistence: is there a work to protect in the first place?

As we have seen in Sect. 17.3, qwrks cannot pass the intellectual creation test of EU copyright law or the "works produced by a machine or mere mechanical process"-barrier of US copyright law. The CGW approach does not have such impediments attached to it, but is unlikely to be widely adopted. Here, the sui generis approach seems to hold the best promise, since the freedom available in designing a new space could be used to remove the originality criterion. As Hubert puts it: "It would be much easier to transpose an exception regarding AI-generated works, if this (originality) criterion were to be erased within a new sui generis rule and not the general copyright

---

[51] Directive 96/9/EC (n48) art 4(1).

[52] Noto La Diega 2019.

[53] Hubert 2020, Section 7.3.

[54] Ihalainen 2018.

legislation".[55] We are not aware of a concrete proposal for sui generis rights for qwrks that would allow us to analyse this point in more detail.

17.4.6 Related Rights

Although qwrks do not qualify for IPR protection, a qwrk used in another by IP rights protected output could be indirectly protected through a neighbouring or related right, such as a broadcasting right or phonogram producer's right. In view of what was discussed above, it is interesting to note that "(...) related rights do not require originality or authorship".[56]

EU member states have implemented related rights in all kinds of deviating forms and due to these national differences the EU harmonised these related rights in the Rental and Lending Rights Directive.[57]

Apart from the related rights discussion we need to consider the effect of the usage of (through IP rights protected) small parts in making products or the sampling of music. The courts decided in the Metall auf Metall case [58] that such taken fragments cannot be regarded as 'copies' as no substantial part of the phonogram has been copied. Use of a sound fragment cannot be regarded as a 'quote' if it is unrecognisable. The use can only be regarded as a quotation if the sound clip is recognisable, the use is intended to enter into a dialogue with that work and the other conditions for the right to quote are met.[59]

Recently a new phase in dealing with the usage of other people's works without paying for the usage was the fine that Google got in France[60] through the application

---

[55] Hubert 2020, p. 65.

[56] Allan et al. 2020, p. 88.

[57] Examples of related rights that might qualify for the so-called related (neighbouring rights) protection are: rights of performing artists, phonogram producers, broadcasting organisations and film producers, as of 7 June 2021 press publishers were added as falling under the Rental and Lending Rights Directive. Directive 2006/115/EC of the European Parliament and of the Council of 12 December 2006 on rental right and lending right and on certain rights related to copyright in the field of intellectual property (codified version).

[58] See for an extensive analysis of the usage of samples Bernd Justin Jütte & Giulia Priora, The end of a legal franchise—The German BGH concludes the sampling saga in Metall auf Metall IV, http://copyrightblog.kluweriplaw.com/2020/08/05/the-end-of-a-legal-franchise-the-german-bgh-concludes-the-sampling-saga-in-metall-auf-metall-iv/.

[59] Article 2 Copyright Directive and article 9(1)(b) Rental Right and Lending Right Directive: ECJ 29 July 2019, http://curia.europa.eu/juris/liste.jsf?num=C-476/17"C-476/17, ECLI:EU:C:2019:624, Pelham c.s.\ Hütter c.s. (Metall auf Metall).

[60] See the website of the French competition authority for an in-detail basing of the fine: https://www.autoritedelaconcurrence.fr/fr/communiques-de-presse/remuneration-des-droits-voisins-lautorite-sanctionne-google-hauteur-de-500.

of Article L 218-4 Code de la propriété intellectuelle.[61] The application of the article is a direct consequence of Copyright in the Digital Single Market Directive.[62]

17.5 Should AI-Generated Works Be Protected?

The discussion up to this point clearly shows that concepts of author and work in current IPR do not fit generative AI-systems and their output, but the question whether this is a problem has not yet been addressed: should IPR be extended to cover qwrks, or should they be left to the public domain?

Most accounts in favour of protecting qwrks start from the tenet that it would be economically detrimental not to do so. In Sect. 17.5.1, we examine the arguments commonly used to support this view. Section 17.5.2 discusses how protecting qwrks would stretch the original myth of copyright by putting generative AI systems and human musicians on equal footing. Finally, in Sect. 17.5.3, we consider the societal benefits of extension vs. non-extension of IPR to qwrks.

17.5.1 The Utilitarian Argument for Protection

All attempts to construct authorship rights on qwrks start from the statement that it would be detrimental to society to let these works fall outside of the protection of IPR. Where arguments for this position are provided, they are usually of a utilitarian nature surmising that without protection for qwrks there is no incentive for developers of AI-systems to continue creating and improving their capabilities, or for the AI-industry to grow and develop. This line of argumentation ignores the possibility that with the advent of new technologies also new business models arise, which is widely held to apply for AI in particular.[63]

An instructive musical case in point is the cooperation between Endel, a company that uses AI to generate soundscapes that are fitting for a user's current environment, state, and mood, with the record label Warner. Citing from a Rolling Stone article: "Endel's co-founder and sound designer Dmitry Evgrafov tells Rolling Stone. "Our whole idea is making soundscapes that are real-time and adaptive. But they were like, 'Yeah, but can you still make albums?' So we did it as an experiment. When a label like Warner approaches you, you have to say 'Why not'." The other 15 records on the contract are themed around focus, relaxation and "on-the-go" modes and will roll out over the course of the year. All 20 albums will come out of Endel's core algorithm,

---

[61] https://www.legifrance.gouv.fr/codes/article_lc/LEGIARTI000038826736.

[62] DIRECTIVE (EU) 2019/790 OF THE EUROPEAN PARLIAMENT AND OF THE COUNCIL of 17 April 2019 on copyright and related rights in the Digital Single Market and amending Directives 96/9/EC and 2001/29/EC.

[63] See for instance Lee et al. 2019.

so they were technically, as Evgrafov says, "all made just by pressing one button." Is it now because you say we act as if we are humans but meanwhile the machine composes music, and because Warner Bros signed us we have become economically relevant (we got paid) and therefore we (the machine) exists?".[64] Where Endel's new business model is based on users paying for access to the generator (in the form of an app or an API for integration), Warner tries to apply its traditional model of making users pay for specific pieces of generated content.

In the evolving competition landscape for AI music generation, companies are moving towards contexts for functional and non-authorial uses of music such as in relaxation, sports and gaming where the interaction and adaptation that AI allows is advantageous, or the generation of soundtracks (for social media, videos and presentations) where the personalisation or mass-customisation that AI enables is valuable. Although it is too early to predict economic success, it is already clear that these companies do not bet their future on the possibility of claiming copyright on the music their AI-systems generate. Rather, their services will be based on providing access to the generative AI-system in one form or another. These systems can be protected under existing IPR. Kop discusses in detail which types of protection that are applicable to the different elements of AI-systems,[65] and characterises the situation as follows: "The software, the way in which the AI is trained, the algorithm and the neural network may each contain IP rights. Even though the objectives of the patent system and the copyright system differ in part, patents and copyrights could be substitutes for each other in providing incentives for AI development. Maximisation of intellectual property on AI can be realised using a mixture of rights".

A survey carried out by Allen et al supports these observations: "There was consensus among experts that there is no clear economic rationale for granting copyright or related rights protection to AI outputs. There is no obvious market failure in relation to the development of AI systems or resulting outputs. In the absence of such market failure, additional recognition of protection beyond what would result from the regular application of copyright law rules appears unjustified".[66]

17.5.2 Stretching the Original Myth

Copyright in music has come a long way from its origins in the printing and publication of musical scores in the 18th century. Along the way it has adapted to many innovations in the production, performance and distribution of music, but at its core lies the idea that copyright should protect the work of composers and musicians and reward them for it, as it serves a societal interest to have more creative works produced. Although this original myth is already stretched substantially by

---

[64] Wang 2019.

[65] Kop 2020, Section VI.

[66] Allan et al. 2020, p. 152.

current copyright practices,[67] considering generative AI-systems and their output for protection stretches it even further.

A human composer (like an author in any creative domain) is inherently limited in the number of works she can create, as it takes substantial effort to compose a piece of music. To bridge the time between subsequent publication of compositions she depends on some form of repetition, selling multiple copies of the same work. These limitations do not hold for a generative AI-system: once fully developed and deployed the generation of a new composition does not take significant effort. Such a system could generate the volume of a human composer's lifetime worth of works in a couple of days. The AI-system would not have to depend on repeated sales of particular pieces of output. It could compose a different piece of music for every listener in any context, and it is this potential for personalisation and customisation that is put to use in the business models described above. The prediction of Vinod Khosla mentioned in the introduction that in a decade we will be listening to "custom made song equivalents that are built around our mood", conjures up an image of personalised music streams, adaptively composed by AI-systems taking personal data of the listener as input. A piece of music composed for a specific listener in a specific context may very well be listened to once, never to be repeated again. In such an era of abundance these uses of music no longer fit the conception of "work" as a separately recognisable and repeatable unit.

The comparison between composers and generative AI-systems makes clear that competing on an equal footing in the traditional music business models could be hard for composers if the quality of AI-generated music keeps improving. Hence, it is not surprising to see calls appearing from the side of musicians to place all AI-generated music in the public domain.[68] The worst-case scenario for musicians would be to have their work used without compensation for training the neural networks that subsequently become their competitors in creating copyrighted works. The first part of this scenario need not become reality, as 'feeding' copyrighted works to a machine learning system qualifies as a reproduction and requires permission of the owners of those works.[69] The music industry already has such a process of clearance for the use of audio samples of other artists' recordings in a new work,[70] which could be adapted for this purpose. The second part, direct competition, may also not become reality as AI-generative systems combined with a more and more automatable downstream

---

[67] See for an account and its legal consequences of the extension as implemented through the Sonny Bono Copyright Term Extension Act of 1998 (CTEA) in het US https://arstechnica.com/tech-pol icy/2019/01/a-whole-years-worth-of-works-just-fell-into-the-public-domain/commonly referred to as the Mickey Mouse Extension. In Europe almost the same happened, not due to Disney but to The Beatles and The Rolling Stones (concerning the song "I wanna be your man" written by Lennon/McCartney and performed by The Rolling Stones), see Bernt Hugenholtz, O No, Not Again: Term Extension, 6 April 2011 http://copyrightblog.kluweriplaw.com/2011/04/06/o-no-not-again-term-extension/.

[68] Carlisle 2019.

[69] Kop 2020, Section VII.

[70] McLeod and DiCola 2011, chapter 5.

music production process[71] enable new instant and adaptive uses of music that could not be supported by human composers.

17.5.3 Carving Out Spaces

If we consider copyright a tool, it is a ploughshare in the original myth: creating a fertile ground on which artists can grow their works. In present day reality it is also considered a weapon: a sword used to "suppress speech, frustrate competition, punish third parties and silence criticism and erase facts", as Cathay Smith puts it.[72] As with the introduction of any new technology, algorithms are neither good, nor bad, nor neutral in this context.

In January 2020, lawyer and musician Damien Riehl and programmer and musician Noah Rubin used a rule-based algorithmic method to generate a catalogue of about 68 billion 8-note melodies, all the possible melodies of that length. These melodies were then copyrighted and released into the public domain in the hope of saving musicians from frivolous copyright infringement lawsuits based on melodic similarity alone.[73] Here algorithms are used to try to preserve creative space for composers, but their effect can also be to limit creative possibilities.

Article 17 of the DSM Directive[74] makes platforms hosting user content liable for copyright infringements, but not flat out liable.[75] They should try to obtain authorisation and "(…) if no authorisation is granted, online content-sharing service providers shall be liable for unauthorised acts of communication to the public, including making available to the public, of copyright-protected works and other subject matter, unless the service providers demonstrate that they have:

(a) made best efforts to obtain an authorisation, and
(b) made, in accordance with high industry standards of professional diligence, best efforts to ensure the unavailability of specific works and other subject matter for which the right holders have provided the service providers with the relevant and necessary information; and in any event
(c) acted expeditiously, upon receiving a sufficiently substantiated notice from the right holders, to disable access to, or to remove from their websites, the notified works or other subject matter, and made best efforts to prevent their future uploads in accordance with point (b).[76]

---

[71] Performance, recording, mixing, mastering, in all of which AI is increasingly applied as well.

[72] Smith 2021, p. 71.

[73] Riehl 2020.

[74] DIRECTIVE (EU) 2019/790 OF THE EUROPEAN PARLIAMENT AND OF THE COUNCIL of 17 April 2019 on copyright and related rights in the Digital Single Market and amending Directives 96/9/EC and 2001/29/EC, https://eur-lex.europa.eu/legal-content/EN/TXT/PDF/?uri=CELEX:320 19L0790&from=EN.

[75] See supra Sect. 17.4.6 the fine Google was given in France.

[76] See supra note 75, Article 17.4.

Barrett in a recent master thesis concluded: "The implementation of the DSM-directive will probably lead--as intended--to a fairer distribution of profit between right holders and online content-sharing service providers (OCSSPs)".[77] Article 17 in the making proved to be highly controversial and sparked an intense debate[78] that was informed by experiences with the YouTube platform, which has been evolving a digital fingerprinting system "Content ID" able to identify and manage copyrighted content uploaded by users since 2007. The application of this automated system has led to a lot of disputes between YouTube users and rights holders, mostly regarding fair use,[79] as there are many YouTube channels dedicated to memes, parody, commentary and so on.

The fact that possible infringements are detected and acted upon proactively by algorithms, rather than by humans after the fact, significantly increases the possibilities for using copyright as a sword, even across legal domains. A remarkable example of this is the practice developed by some American police officers to play copyrighted music on their phones while they are lawfully being filmed by citizens they are interacting with, with the aim of causing algorithmic takedown of the recorded video (stream).[80] Hence, in considering the societal benefits of generative AI, we should look at the combined effects of algorithmic generation and algorithmic detection of infringement.

Considered by itself, it is clear that generative AI offers great prospects for new ways of exploring and processing our musical heritage. It extends the existing analogue and digital methods for remixing music history in the form of sound recordings with the possibility to 'remix' music history at the symbolic level (in the form of scores). With qwrks falling in the public domain, they can themselves become input to a next generative process (being recombined with other compositions into new datasets), setting up the conditions for a virtuous cycle of creation. Granting copyrights on qwrks breaks these conditions, as for every reuse of a qwrk as input approval of the rights holder would be required.

Copyrighted qwrks in the context of automated infringement detection would allow for strategies creating "thickets" to obstruct legitimate use of works. For instance, works of a certain composer that are about to fall into the public domain, could be used by the rights holder to train a machine learning model and generate an abundance of new copyrighted qwrks very close to the originals. Users trying to upload the original works after they have fallen into the public domain could then face being flagged for infringing on the qwrks. With the kind of imagination displayed by the police officers mentioned above, it is very likely that new sword-like uses of

---

[77] Barrett 2019, p. 49.

[78] At that time centred around the precursor Article 13.

[79] Alexander J (2018) 'Internet is under threat': what you need to know about the EU's copyright directive, https://www.polygon.com/2018/9/11/17843664/copyright-directive-europian-union-parliament-explained-internet-article-13-youtube-fair-use, accessed 10 June 2021.

[80] Thomas D (2021) Is This Beverly Hills Cop Playing Sublime's 'Santeria' to Avoid Being Live-Streamed?, https://www.vice.com/en/article/bvxb94/is-this-beverly-hills-cop-playing-sublimes-santeria-to-avoid-being-livestreamed, accessed 10 June 2021.

copyright employing generative AI would be developed, also spilling over into other legal domains.

The fight for creative space is inextricably linked to a fight for economic space. In Sect. 17.5.1 we argued that the fact that qwrks cannot be copyrighted creates the space for new business models for the generative uses of music that would not have been feasible otherwise. In the more general debate on how to strike a balance between regulation and innovation, others have also taken the position that qwrks should not be copyrightable. One of the most outspoken proponents of this view is Maurits Kop, who holds that "extending copyrights hinders innovation, cultural diversity and even fundamental freedoms. Adding extra layers to the existing rainbow of IP rights is not a good solution to balance the societal impact of technological progress". He proposes the creation of a "Res Publica ex Machina" (Public Property from the Machine) for both physical and intangible AI creations and inventions,[81] accompanied by a world-wide formal AI public domain mark by a government institution.

17.6   Conclusion

The use of AI-systems in creative domains is not new, but traditionally their role was to inspire and assist human creators. With the advent of generative machine learning models, both the autonomy of AI-systems and the quality of qwrks have grown strongly over the past decade. Under current copyright law, autonomous AI-systems cannot be considered authors and the content they generate cannot be considered a work. Different ideas are being developed to extend IPR to cover AI-generated works, but this has not yet resulted in a widely acceptable and applicable solution. In the absence of an extension, AI-generated works fall in the public domain.

We consider this a fortunate outcome. The utilitarian argument underlying the push for extension of copyright is flawed. Moreover, generative AI systems, even those with a high degree of autonomy, can be considered instruments. Just like piano manufacturers do not own the rights to the tunes customers play on their pianos, the owners and developers of generative AI-systems should not own the rights to the output of their systems. In creative domains such as music, more societal benefits are to be expected from letting generated works fall in the public domain than making them copyrightable. Generalising this conclusion to other areas of IPR requires a more extensive and rigorous argumentation than this chapter can provide, but we hope our discussion of generative AI has clearly brought the legal questions and issues it raises to the fore.

---

[81] Kop 2020, Section VIII.

References

Allan J, Gervais D J, Hartmann C, Hugenholtz P, Quintais J (2020) Trends and Developments in Artificial Intelligence: Challenges to the Intellectual Property Rights Framework: Final Report 2020. https://op.europa.eu/en/publication-detail/-/publication/394345a1-2ecf-11eb-b27b-01aa75ed71a1/language-en Accessed 10 August 2021.

Angioloni L, Borghuis T, Brusci L, Frasconi P (2020) CONLON: A Pseudo-song Generator Based on a New Pianoroll, Wasserstein Autoencoders, and Optimal Interpolations. In: Cummings J et al (eds) Proceedings of the 21st Int. Society for Music Information Retrieval Conf. ISMIR, Montreal, pp. 876–883.

Barrett S A J (2019) Article 17 of the DSM-directive: Striking a Fair Balance? An assessment of the compatibility of article 17 with the fundamental right to freedom of expression of users. http://arno.uvt.nl/show.cgi?fid=148248 Accessed 10 August 2021.

Boulanger-Lewandowski N, Bengio Y, Vincent P (2012) Modeling Temporal Dependencies in High-Dimensional Sequences: Application to Polyphonic Music Generation and Transcription. In: Langford J, Pineau J (eds) Proceedings of the 29th International Conference on Machine Learning. Omnipress, Edinburgh, pp. 1881–1888.

Briot P, Hadjeres G, Pachet F (2019) Deep Learning Techniques for Music Generation, Computational Synthesis and Creative Systems. Springer Nature, Switzerland.

Carlisle S (2019), Should Music Created by Artificial Intelligence Be Protected by Copyright? http://copyright.nova.edu/ai/ Accessed 10 June 2021.

Carr C J, Zukowski Z (2018) Generating Albums with SampleRNN to Imitate Metal, Rock, and Punk Bands. https://arxiv.org/abs/1811.06633v1 Accessed 10 June 2021.

Clark R, Smyth S (1997) Intellectual Property Law in Ireland. Butterworths, Dublin.

De Cock Buning M (2018) Artificial Intelligence and the creative industry: new challenges for the EU paradigm for art and technology by autonomous creations. In: Barfield W, Pagalio U (eds) Research Handbook On The Law Of Artificial Intelligence Edward Elgar Publishing Cheltenham, pp. 511–535.

Elgammal A, Liu B, Elhoseiny M, Mazzone M (2017) CAN: Creative Adversarial Networks, Generating "Art" by Learning About Styles and Deviating from Style Norms. http://arxiv.org/abs/1706.07068 Accessed 10 June 2021.

EU Parliament Committee on Legal Affairs (2015) Draft Report with Recommendations to the Commission on Civil Law Rules on Robotics. https://www.europarl.europa.eu/doceo/document/JURI-PR-582443_EN.pdf Accessed 1 August 2021.

European Economic and Social Committee (2017) Opinion on 'Artificial intelligence - The consequences of artificial intelligence on the (digital) single market, production, consumption, employment and society'. https://eur-lex.europa.eu/legal-content/EN/TXT/PDF/?uri=CELEX:52016IE5369&from=EN.

Gregor K, Danihelka I, Graves A, Jimenez Rezende D, Wierstra D (2015) DRAW: A recurrent neural network for image generation. https://arxiv.org/abs/1502.04623 Accessed 10 June 2021.

Guadamuz A (2018) Can the monkey selfie case teach us anything about copyright law? https://www.wipo.int/wipo_magazine/en/2018/01/article_0007.html Accessed 10 June 2021.

Gunkel D J (2018) Robot Rights. MIT Press, Cambridge MA.

Hiller Jr L A, Isaacson L M (1958) Musical Composition with a High-Speed Digital Computer. Journal of the Audio Engineering Society 6(3):154–160.

Hristov K (2017) AI and the Copyright Dilemma. IDEA-The Journal of the Franklin Pierce Center for Intellectual Property 57(3):431–453.

Hubert E (2020) Artificial Intelligence and Copyright Law in a European context, A study on the protection of works produced by AI-systems. https://lup.lub.lu.se/luur/download?func=downloadFile&recordOId=9020263&fileOId=9020290 Accessed 10 June 2021.

Ihalainen J (2018) Computer creativity: artificial intelligence and copyright. Journal of Intellectual Property Law & Practice, 13(9):724–728.

Karsdorp F, Manajavacas E, Kestemont M, Stokhuysen B (2018) Deepflow. https://deep-flow.nl/ (link no longer active).

Kop M (2020) AI & Intellectual Property: Towards an Articulated Public Domain. Texas Intellectual Property Law Journal 28(1):1–39.

Lambert P (2017), Computer Generated Works and Copyright: Selfies, Traps, Robots, AI and Machine Learning. European Intellectual Property Review 39(1):12–20.

Lee J, Suh T, Roy D, Baucus M (2019) Emerging Technology and Business Model Innovation: The Case of Artificial Intelligence. Journal of Open Innovation: Technology, Market, and Complexity, 5(3):44.

Liu Y, Qin Z, Luo Z, Wang H (2017) Auto-painter: Cartoon Image Generation from Sketch by Using Conditional Generative Adversarial Networks. http://arxiv.org/abs/1705.01908 Accessed 10 June 2021.

Maunder-Cockram K (2019) Authorship in AI Made Works. Vrije Universiteit Amsterdam, Amsterdam.

Mcleod K, DiCola P (2011) Creative License The Law and Culture of Digital Sampling. Duke University Press, New York.

Müller V C (2020) Ethics of Artificial Intelligence and Robotics. https://plato.stanford.edu/entries/ethics-ai/ Accessed 10 June 2021.

Noto La Diega G (2019) Artificial Intelligence and databases in the age of big machine data. In: Conference Artificial Intelligence (AI), Data Protection, and Intellectual Property Law in a European context, held 13 December 2019 at Lund University, Lund, Sweden.

Riehl D (2020) Copyrighting all the melodies to avoid accidental infringement. https://www.youtube.com/watch?v=sJtm0MoOgiUt=255s Accessed 10 June 2021.

Rognstad O-A (2018) EU copyright, quo vadis? In: Conference Artificial Intelligence and Copyright-Ownership, held 25 May 2018 at Université Saint-Louis, Brussels, Belgium.

Smith C Y N (2021) Copyright Silencing. Cornell Law Review Online 71: 71–86.

Van den Oord Aaron, Dieleman S, Zen H, Simonyan K, Vinyals O, Graves A, Kalchbrenner N, Senior A, Kavukcuoglu K (2016) Wavenet, A Generative Model for Raw Audio. https://arxiv.org/abs/1609.03499 Accessed 10 June 2021.

Wang A X (2019) Warner Music Group Signs an Algorithm to a Record Deal. https://www.rollingstone.com/pro/news/warner-music-group-endel-algorithm-record-deal-811327 Accessed 10 June 2021.

Yu L, Zhang W, Wang J, Yu Y (2016) SeqGAN: Sequence Generative Adversarial Nets with Policy Gradient. http://arxiv.org/abs/1609.05473 Accessed 10 June 2021.

Prof. em. dr. J.M. Smits LL.M. (Jan, 1953) started his law studies in 1972 at University of Tilburg. He took his degree in law in 1982. After having worked for three years as a assistant professor at the Legal Faculty of the University of Nijmegen, he joined the Legal Informatics group at the Utrecht University as a lecturer, where he defended his PhD in December 1990. This group published extensively on AI and law. From 1992–2019 he held the chair Law and Technology at the University of Technology in Eindhoven. From 2003–2013, he was member of the Scientific Technical Council (WTR) for the SURF Foundation (the higher education and research partnership organisation for network services and information and communications technology). As a project member for a EU-China WTO project transferring know-how from the EU about the relationship of IPR and standards he was responsible for the legal chapter. He has been a Member of the Editorial Review Board for The International Journal of IT Standards & Standardization Research, JITSR since its inception. Between 2016–2020 he published five Massive MOOCs on Privacy and international legal developments on Coursera.

Dr V.A.J. Borghuis (Tijn, 1963) studied philosophy in Groningen and Amsterdam (MSc University of Amsterdam 1989). He came to Eindhoven University of Technology to work on a big AI project (DenK) aiming at constructing a generic cooperative interface combining linguistic and visual interaction, first as PhD student (graduated 1994), later as postdoc and research coordinator at the Department of Computing Science and Mathematics. In 1999 he became assistant director of the Institute for Programming research and Algorithmics, a national research school in the field of computer science. Following his interest in education, he joined and later led the project ACQA (Academic Criteria for Quality Assurance), which developed instruments for measuring and designing curricula in terms of competences. Since 2009, Tijn works as a project manager and teacher in the Philosophy & Ethics group at the Department of Industrial Engineering & Innovation Sciences. He is currently managing director of the 4TU.Centre for Ethics and Technology. Outside of academia, he is co-founder of the company Musica Combinatoria (Musi-co), that develops technologies for real-time adaptive music generation.

Chapter 18
The Role and Legal Implications of Autonomy in AI-Driven Boardrooms

Hadassah Drukarch and Eduard Fosch-Villaronga

Contents

Abstract The rapid emergence of increasingly autonomous AI systems within corporate governance and decision-making is unprecedented. AI-driven boardrooms bring about legal challenges within the field of corporate law, mainly due to the expanding autonomy and capabilities AI has to support corporate decisions. Recurrent legal questions revolve around the attribution of legal personhood to autonomous systems and who is responsible if something goes wrong due to a decision taken thanks to the power of AI. This chapter introduces autonomy levels for AI in the boardroom and discusses potential legal and regulatory challenges expected from a corporate law frame of reference. Building on existing literature and other related examples from the automotive and medical sectors, this chapter presents a six-layered model depicting the changing roles and responsibilities among human directors and AI systems as the latter become increasingly autonomous. This research shows that although boardrooms appear to move towards autonomous corporate governance and decision-making without human responsibility, this is not true in practice. What this does indicate, however, is that the more autonomous and powerful AI systems become, the more decision-making processes shift from human-based to AI-powered. This shift raises a number of concerns from a corporate law perspective tied to the role of autonomy in the boardroom, especially with respect to responsibility and liability.

H. Drukarch (✉) · E. Fosch-Villaronga
eLaw Center for Law and Digital Technologies, Leiden University, Leiden, The Netherlands
e-mail: h.g.drukarch@law.leidenuniv.nl

E. Fosch-Villaronga
e-mail: e.fosch.villaronga@law.leidenuniv.nl

© T.M.C. ASSER PRESS and the authors 2022
B. Custers and E. Fosch-Villaronga (eds.), *Law and Artificial Intelligence*,
Information Technology and Law Series 35,
https://doi.org/10.1007/978-94-6265-523-2_18

345

This chapter alerts corporations about the potential consequences of using increasingly autonomous AI systems in the boardroom, helps policymakers understand and address the potential responsibility gap that may arise from this development, and lays a basis for further research and regulatory initiatives in this regard.

Keywords Artificial Intelligence · Corporate law · Autonomy · Responsibility · Corporate governance · Corporate management · Board of Directors · Electronic personhood · Responsibility gap · Liability

18.1 Introduction

In 2014, the venture capital firm Deep Knowledge Ventures appointed an algorithm to its Board of Directors (BoD). They named it Validating Investment Tool for Advancing Life Sciences - Vital. Vital was a robo-director that was given the right to vote on business investment decisions, just like the other (human) board members. More specifically, VITAL was appointed due to its ability to "automate due diligence and use historical datasets to uncover trends that are not immediately obvious to humans surveying top-line data".[1] As such, Vital was attributed the role of co-creation/co-direction and control/supervision by assisting Deep Knowledge Ventures in approving investment decisions and crediting it with preventing the fund from going under due to excessive investments in overvalued projects.

Due to increases in the quality of data available and further diversification of data sources, the algorithm was later replaced by a much more intelligent Vital 2.0, which integrated data from scientific literature, grants, patent applications, clinical trials, and even the biographies of individual team members of companies in which the company was interested.[2] Despite its impressive track record, however, Vital was not granted an equal vote on the board, and legally speaking, it did not acquire the status of a corporate director under the corporate laws of, in this case, Hong Kong. Although its human fellow board members treated Vital as a board member with merely an observer status, Vital has widely been acknowledged as the world's first AI company director.

Although the scale of development of autonomous AI-driven directors has so far remained relatively limited and so-called *Roboboards* do not yet exist, AI-based technologies are playing an increasingly important role within corporations and their boards, significantly impacting the corporate governance process and its outcomes.[3] This is because business decisions increasingly require the weighing of numerous and complex sets of data and AI technologies—which are rapidly becoming superior to humans in this regard—can play a central role in management decisions based on such data across many business sectors.[4] Examples already exist in the financial

---

[1] Möslein 2018.

[2] Burridge 2017.

[3] Mosco 2020.

[4] Nikishova 2018; Ashour 2020; Möslein 2018.

industry.[5] As such, computational progress and digitalization will increasingly lead to corporate directors being supported—if not replaced—by AI.[6]

However, inserting AI into the BoD is not straightforward from a legal perspective. That is because the legal strategies to regulate, steer and control corporate governance as envisioned within corporate laws are tailored to human decision-makers, not to artificial agents.[7] Moreover, AI's increased autonomy levels and complex interaction with humans blur the roles and responsibilities within the boardroom context. As such, advances in this area will increasingly affect our understanding of the concepts of corporate directorship—and within that, legal personhood—and responsibility. However, while the pace of technology dramatically accelerates, understanding the implications of technology does not follow suit.[8] The deployment of AI within the boardroom context challenges existing legal frameworks that regulate corporations and corporate conduct and calls for lawyers, regulators, and legal scholars to clarify whether and how existing legal rules apply to these fundamentally new technological phenomena or whether new regulations will have to be developed. Therefore, as we head towards the future, there will be a growing necessity for current legal frameworks to be thoroughly re-examined, clarified, and, where necessary, amended to prevent any potential adverse implications of the introduction of increasingly autonomous AI on the BoD.

This chapter explores the role and legal implications of autonomy in challenging responsibility in highly-automated boardrooms. Section 18.2 maps the capabilities and applications of AI in corporate governance and decision-making. Section 18.3 introduces autonomy levels for AI in the BoD and explains what these entail for the division of roles and responsibilities of human directors and AI systems in the BoD. Section 18.4 reflects on some of the concerns from a corporate law perspective tied to these autonomy levels and the deployment of increasingly autonomous AI in the BoD, which is becoming more pressing due to the rapid advancements in the field of AI. Section 18.5 provides conclusions. This chapter alerts corporations about the potential consequences of using increasingly autonomous AI systems in the BoD, helps policymakers understand and address the potential responsibility gap that may arise from this development, and lays a basis for further research and regulatory initiatives in this regard.

---

[5] Agarwal et al. 2021; Brynjolfsson and McAfee 2017.
[6] Möslein 2018.
[7] Möslein 2018.
[8] Fosch-Villaronga and Heldeweg 2018.

18.2 Integrating Artificial Intelligence into the BoD

Lately, AI has made particular progress in the areas of perception, cognition, and problem-solving, gradually transcending the boundaries of merely human decision-makers.[9] Although the field of AI has been rapidly progressing for more than half a century, its impact on the concept of the corporation and its governance has largely been disregarded until only recently.[10] Given the velocity and (often claimed) effectiveness of AI in automating business processes and with the knowledge that AI can assist in problem-solving, it is unsurprising to see corporations across the globe increasingly deploying AI for more than merely automating specific tasks and processes. Nowadays, AI also supports the BoD in corporate governance activities and facilitates strategic decision-making processes, thereby encouraging profitable interaction between smart machines and people.[11]

Moreover, as AI becomes increasingly autonomous, it has been argued that this technology will soon not merely offer the possibility to support directors in corporate governance and decision-making activities but may perhaps even replace them.[12] Consequently, research in the field of AI places the technology used within this context on an ascending scale of autonomy levels, thereby defining it as either assistive, augmentative, amplifying, autonomous, or autopoietic based on the role it plays within the decision-making process.[13] This section defines the corporate anatomy and its functioning to clarify AI's position within the corporate anatomy. It also maps the capabilities and applications of AI in the boardroom context and establishes the levels of autonomy of these AI technologies.

18.2.1 Defining the BoD Anatomy and Functioning

Although national laws differ widely in terms of the roles and responsibilities assigned to the BoD, directors are generally assigned (a combination of) three key functions which are similar across all jurisdictions, namely: supervisor, co-creator, and supporter, or co-director, controller and coach, and which are accompanied by varying decision types (see Table 18.1).[14]

In clarifying the specific role or combination of roles that directors ought to play, the BoD must understand what the corporation needs, what its capabilities are, and how that affects the nature of its involvement in strategic questions, allowing it to

---

[9] Schwab and Davis 2018; Mosco 2020.

[10] Bhattacharya 2018; Libert et al 2017.

[11] Burridge 2017.

[12] Möslein 2018.

[13] Mosco 2020; Hilb 2020.

[14] Cossin and Metayer 2014; Hilb 2020.

Table 18.1 BoD key functions and decision types (Adapted from Hilb 2020)

BoD role	Key functions	Decision types
Supervisor/controller	Controls and monitors corporate performance and executive team behavior to ensure full compliance with the law, accounting codes, and the company's statutory rules, and to ensure the performance of the organization and its executives in developing, designing, selecting and implementing a course of action	Decisions on target achievements, meeting accounting standards, legal compliance, and ethical compliance
Co-creator/co-director	Responsible for strategic leadership, developing the corporate strategy together with the executive team, and ensuring proper strategy implementation by setting objectives, thereby contributing directly to company performance	Decisions on innovation, collaboration, optimization, transformation, diversification/concentration, and internationalization
Supporter/coach	Responsible for appointing and coaching the executive team, thereby lending the executive team its credibility, objectivity, and authority to ensure effective leadership	Decisions on executive appointments, executive development, executive compensation, and board composition

address better how it will support the company's strategy and organize its communication and contacts with internal and external stakeholders.[15] This involves the collecting and processing of vast amounts of information about the organization's state of affairs and projection in time to ulteriorly support the decision-making process.

Decision-making inherently revolves around consciously choosing between two or more options that can be either binary or multifaceted and always depends on the chosen criteria. Such an informed decision generally covers three phases—conceptualization, information, and prediction[16]—which can again be subcategorized into the processes of decision sensing, decision framing, information collection, information selection, option identification, and option assessment.[17] Although these processes seem rather straightforward, organizations generate a remarkable volume of information that the BoD may deem essential to support decisions at any given level. The BoD may also be interested in knowing the company's estimated projects, supporting strategic decision-making, avoiding losses, and remaining competitive in a global market. As one can imagine, such decisions may involve different degrees of complexity depending on various factors.[18] These include:

---

[15] Hilb 2020.

[16] Still et al. 1958.

[17] Hilb 2020.

[18] Cossin and Metayer 2014; Hilb 2020.

- common (or simple) decisions: the decision outcomes are certain, making them relatively straightforward and agreeable to all,
- complicated decisions: the decision is placed in a multi-optional context, requiring varying points of view,
- complex decisions: decisions made in a context characterised by total uncertainty or disagreement,
- chaotic decisions: decisions are made in completely fluid contexts, naturally leading to different points of view.

Table 18.2 clarifies how each of the above discussed board roles, decision types, and levels of complexity relate to one another (based on the work of Hilb 2020).

These different levels of complexity, coupled with the need to avoid the paradox of "being data-rich but information-poor simultaneously",[19] drive organizations towards using tools and technology that can help them make sense of the vast volume of information they generate, including future projections. In this respect, AI involves machine learning and natural language processing that serves exceptionally well in revolutionizing any knowledge-intensive sectors, including organizations.[20] However, to better understand how AI fits into the basic structure of corporations and how it affects corporate governance from the BoD's perspective, it is first necessary to understand the nature, capabilities, and shortcomings of AI.

18.2.2   The Applications and Capabilities of AI on the BoD

Artificial Intelligence was officially coined in 1956 after some pioneers described it as "programming computers to solve problems which require a high degree of intelligence in humans".[21] More recently, the European Commission defined AI as "systems that display intelligent behaviour by analysing their environment and taking actions—with some degree of autonomy—to achieve specific goals".[22] AI covers many techniques and tools, including, for instance, symbolic logic, artificial neural networks, fuzzy systems, evolutionary computing, intelligent agents, and probabilistic reasoning models.[23] In recent times, AI has made considerable progress in perception, cognition, and problem-solving, mainly due to the advancements in rule-based systems, machine learning (ML), and—within that—deep learning. Here, rule-based systems refer to systems that require humans to fully understand a given context and define the rules that the machine should execute. ML covers systems that can learn and derive conclusions based on a set of data and learning algorithms without understanding context. Finally, deep learning, which can be divided into

---

[19] Wang 2021.

[20] Garbuio and Lin 2019.

[21] McCarthy et al. 1955.

[22] European Commission 2018.

[23] Jain and de Wilde 2001; Jain and Martin 1999.

Table 18.2 Corporate governance decisions by decision type (Adapted from Hilb 2020)

	Conceptualization		Information		Prediction	
	Decision sensing	Decision framing	Information collection	Information selection	Option identification	Option assessment
Co-direction						
Innovation	Chaotic	Complex	Complex	Complicated	Complicated	Complicated
Collaboration	Complex	Complex	Complex	Complex	Complicated	Complex
Optimization	Complicated	Complicated	Complicated	Common	Complicated	Common
Transformation	Complex	Complex	Complicated	Complex	Complex	Complicated
Diversification	Complex	Complex	Complicated	Complex	Complex	Complicated
Internationalization	Complex	Complicated	Complicated	Complex	Complex	Complicated
Control						
Target achievement	Common	Common	Complicated	Common	Common	Common
Accounting standards	Common	Common	Complicated	Common	Common	Common
Legal compliance	Complicated	Complicated	Complicated	Common	Complicated	Common
Ethical Compliance	Complex	Complicated	Complex	Complex	Complex	Complicated
Coaching						
Executive appointments	Complex	Complicated	Complex	Complex	Complex	Complicated
Executive development	Complex	Complex	Complex	Complex	Complicated	Complicated
Executive compensation	Complicated	Complicated	Complicated	Common	Complicated	Common
Board compensation	Complicated	Complicated	Complicated	Common	Complicated	Common

supervised learning (SL), reinforcement learning (RL), and unsupervised learning (UL), relates to an AI function that imitates the workings of the human brain in processing data and creating patterns for decision-making, enabling systems to cluster data and make predictions with incredible accuracy.

Currently, AI has already mastered common (or simple) decisions (through SL for target achievement, e.g., image classification or house price determination), complicated decisions (through RL for legal compliance, for instance), and complex decisions (through UL to predict how fruitful a partnership will be) (see Table 18.2).[24] Moreover, recent advancements are overcoming the current separation between the machine and the mind, which Hilb 2020 refers to as Mind Machine Learning (MML). MML would allow machines to also succeed in mastering chaotic decisions that currently only humans are capable of.[25] Taking into account the fact that the levels of complexity of board roles and decision types can for the large majority be characterised as either common, complicated, or complex (see Table 18.2), the concept of intelligence indicates that AI could theoretically support or even replace humans in many processes, including those related to corporate governance.[26]

The thoroughly developed and sophisticated techniques and functionalities covered by AI, including retrieving relevant information, providing improved financial, sales, or other forecasts, optimizing logistics flows, and many more, are among the most popular AI uses in corporate governance and decision-making.[27] Indeed, AI is very attractive to organizations because it provides real-time coordination of data delivery, the analysis of data trends, the provision of forecasts, the development of data consistency, the quantification of uncertainty, the anticipation of users' data needs, the provision of information to users in the most appropriate form and the suggestion of courses of action.[28]

AI's place within the corporate anatomy arguably lies in its support for or even replacement of human decision-making particularly under conditions of uncertainty and where strategic business decisions need to be taken within corporations.[29] AI technologies are already widely used within corporations to recruit personnel, evaluate profitability, manage information, develop investment strategies, pricing, accounting auditing, and monitor product quality and labour productivity.[30] In this sense, AI complements the capabilities of human directors and can give recommendations based on the analysis of large amounts of data that allow the BoD to make quick decisions under challenging circumstances. Additionally, the ability of AI technologies to process vast amounts of data simplifies the BoD's work, as the BoD may not have continuous access to the necessary information. Such support

---

[24] Wilson and Daugherty 2018.

[25] Hilb 2020.

[26] Frey and Osborne 2017.

[27] Bhattacharya 2018.

[28] Möslein 2018.

[29] Phillips-Wren and Jain 2006; Möslein 2018; Bhattacharya 2018.

[30] Tokmakov 2020.

allows the BoD to focus on those decisions that still require a particular perspective and the empathy that, until now, only humans can provide.

However, although the appointment of 'robo-directors' on the executive board certainly may be beneficial to the functioning of a corporation, when it comes down to the actual governance of the corporation, AI nevertheless seems to have limitations in certain respects. Economists argue, for instance, that even though artificial intelligence may well be superior at making predictions, humans are relied on to make judgments. Human directors are still relied on to estimate the benefits and costs of different decisions in different contexts, and this requires "an understanding of what the corporation cares about most, what it benefits from, and what could go wrong".[31] Moreover, AI systems still lack the necessary empathy, which makes them acceptable in a corporate context. From an organizational standpoint, AI systems have proved to be advantageous due to their ability to perform specific tasks quicker and more accurately in comparison to humans while at the same time being more cost-efficient. However, to maintain the high standards of a brand, they have to be accepted by consumers and deliver socially adequate performance.[32] While its 'self-learning' capabilities often characterize AI, AI cannot exercise the necessary judgment and empathy. It also seems to be lacking the necessary creativity and innovation to do so, though paradoxically, it is precisely these abilities that play a pivotal role within the context of corporate governance where the subject and outcome of decision-making activities could potentially have a far-reaching impact on the lives and wellbeing of individuals across the globe.

18.3 Autonomy Levels of AI in the Boardroom Context

There is an increasing interest in having (embodied) autonomous, artificially intelligent systems, commonly named robo-directors, that act as board directors and are actively involved in corporate governance and decision-making. This interest is fuelled by the increased resource efficiency and ease of using AI systems to process very complex information, including cognitive information.[33] As the capabilities of AI increase, the use of AI within the corporate governance and decision-making context is expected to shift from being merely assistive, to serving as an augmentative decision-support tool, and finally to conforming to the stage of a fully autonomous BoD.[34] The latter refers to the stage at which machines ultimately take over all human decision rights, either because humans increasingly trust the machines' abilities to decide or because the complexity of corporate decision-making requires unprecedented levels of speed and quantities of data as a result of which this process

---

[31] Möslein 2018; Agrawal et al. 2018; Agrawal et al. 2017.

[32] Pelau et al. 2021.

[33] Frey and Osborne 2017.

[34] Wilson and Daughtery 2018.

becomes unbearable to human directors.[35] This has also been concluded by Petrin (2019), who argued that BoDs will merely decrease in size as AI provides more opportunities and knowledge. Petrin (2019) predicts there may be in the future a merger of BoDs (fused boards) into a single AI director. A final stage could be a "fused management" of companies in which BoDs and executive management merge and the two-tier corporate governance structure (i.e. the corporate structure system that consists of two separate Boards of Directors—the Supervisory Board and the Management Board, that govern a corporation), if applicable, is abolished.

As AI becomes more sophisticated, its capabilities to act autonomously—even replace human directors, in this case—increase. Here, the term autonomy refers to 'the quality or state of self-governing'.[36] In this sense, the term 'AI autonomy' refers to an AI's capability to execute specific tasks based on its current functions without human intervention. Different levels of autonomy can be distinguished, which define the system's progressive ability to perform particular functions independently. These ascending levels of autonomy constitute a fundamental aspect of contemporary machine intelligence, as until not long ago, automated processes were not possible, and play a determinant role in allocating responsibility if something goes wrong.[37] More importantly, understanding the role autonomy plays within highly complex processes becomes essential the closer it gets to making vital decisions that may ulteriorly affect an organization and its people.

While the Society of Automotive Engineers (SAE) has established automation levels for automobiles by the standard SAE J3016, there are no universal standards that define the levels of autonomy for AI used within corporate governance. A similar finding was made within the domain of healthcare, where Yang et al. (2017) proposed a generic six-layered model for medical robots' autonomy levels depicting a spectrum ranging from no autonomy (level 0) to full autonomy (level 5) to bridge this gap. Although this is a significant step in investigating the different levels of automation outside the automotive industry, Fosch-Villaronga and colleagues (2021) argued that this model needed more detailing on how it applies to specific types of medical robots, thereby introducing a revised model explicitly tailored to the autonomy levels for surgery robots. Similarly, to address the potential responsibility gap that may arise following the deployment of AI systems on the board and inform the global regulatory landscape in this regard, a fundamental understanding of autonomy levels and the resulting interplay between human board directors and AI is of fundamental importance.

The discussion on the capabilities and applications of AI in corporate governance indicates that deploying and integrating AI into the BoD's functioning is complex and dynamic.[38] Consequently, when framing responsibility in AI-driven boardrooms, the discussion should consider multiple scenarios and not merely a single point at a time and should be looked at from a perspective of duality—machines, and

---

[35] Möslein 2018.

[36] Definition retrieved from the Merriam-Webster Online Dictionary, see Merriam-Webster 2020.

[37] Fosch-Villaronga et al. 2021.

[38] Hilb 2020.

humans can be considered as either competing or complementary.[39] Within this context, earlier research has referred to five levels of so-called synergic intelligence: assisted intelligence, augmented intelligence, amplified intelligence, autonomous intelligence, and autopoietic intelligence.[40]

Here, we use these levels of synergic intelligence as a basis to establish a six-layered model depicting the levels of autonomy for AI deployed within corporate governance and decision-making, namely: no autonomy (level 0) (which is added to the 5 levels of synergic intelligence to provide a starting point for the determination of autonomy), assistance (level 1), augmentation (level 2), amplification (level 3), high autonomy (level 4), and full autonomy (level 5), which differ based on the allocation of decision rights between human and machine and which have implications along with the three essential functions (control/supervision, co-creation/co-direction and support/coaching) and decisions types of the board.[41]

- Autonomy level 0: no autonomy, human directors are the sole decision-makers supported by simple digital devices/equipment. Here, the technology merely has a task-specific and practical application driven by human commands and actions and, thus, lacks any form of (intellectual) autonomy.
- Autonomy level 1: assistance, human directors are the sole decision-makers, although they may now also rely on selective support from task-specific AI-driven applications (e.g., translation or speech recognition) within this context.
- Autonomy level 2: augmentation, human directors and AI systems share decision rights and learn from each other. Here, the AI-based solutions relied upon for selective support are now more sophisticated, allowing the decision-maker to use the technology in a way that surpasses human intelligence (e.g., by identifying oddities in stacks of data or automated reporting).
- Autonomy level 3: amplification, human directors and AI systems are required to perform decision-making tasks jointly. In practice, an AI tool might make a recommendation that must be approved by a human board director and provided with any additional input and feedback.
- Autonomy level 4: high autonomy, AI systems can make decisions independently and operate within a predefined range without constant decision inputs from human directors. AI systems take over a vast portion of decision rights previously held by human directors because human directors increasingly trust these systems as decision-makers or because they are no longer effectively capable of performing decision-making tasks in practice due to increased complexity and speed. Examples of AI systems that have reached this level of autonomy include self-regulating control mechanisms or highly developed robots—robo-directors.
- Autonomy level 5: full autonomy, AI systems are capable of making independent decisions for a particular scenario, and develop and expand this scenario over time, thereby marginalizing the necessity and influence of human decision-making

---

[39] Hilb 2020.

[40] Hilb 2020; Mosco 2020; Möslein 2018; Nalder 2017; Armour and Eidenmueller 2019.

[41] Möslein 2018.

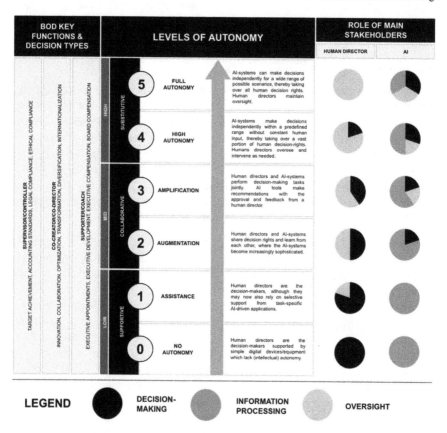

Fig. 18.1 Autonomy levels and the role of humans in AI-driven boardrooms (Adapted from Fosch-Villaronga et al. 2021)

capacities and capabilities, and ultimately taking over all decision rights of human directors. These AI systems are not found in practice yet and merely form a representation of science fiction for the foreseeable future.

Based on this six-layered model, the transitioning levels of autonomy for AI used within corporate governance and decision-making can be categorized as either supportive, collaborative, or substitutive. The difference between these categories essentially revolves around the AI's autonomy level, the degree of support provided by AI systems during the execution of decision-making tasks, and the control exercised by the human director.[42]

Figure 18.1 considers the categories and autonomy levels of AI used within corporate governance and the board's essential functions and decision types and illustrates how these relate to and impact one another and the transitioning role of humans within this context.

---

[42] Fosch-Villaronga et al. 2021.

18.4   Discussion

While most AI systems used within corporate governance and decision-making are augmentative in nature, AI systems encompassing higher levels of autonomy have already found their way into the BoD, albeit at a slow pace. Moreover, the slow yet steady emergence of increasingly autonomous AI systems, such as robo-directors, into the boardroom context indicates that although fully autonomous AI directors seem distant, they are already being conceptualized. Like cruise control and park assistance have made their way into cars progressively before realizing fully autonomous driving, and fully autonomous surgical devices are believed to enter clinical practice gradually,[43] fully autonomous AI directors may become part of the BoD in the same way, albeit in the distant future.

While the shift towards more autonomous boardrooms may seem to indicate that we are gearing towards corporate governance and decision-making free from any human intervention, this is not at all the case. On the contrary, until AI reaches levels of intelligence and empathy equal to that of humans, humans will remain in the loop and maintain an integral and crucial role within the boardroom environment, in the form of either performance or oversight. In practice, with the increased levels of autonomy of AI in the BoD, the human role in the decision-making process is moving progressively to tasks which are more foremost overseeing in nature. On the contrary, with increased levels of autonomy, AI increasingly has other capacities—mainly oversight and decision-making powers—that grow in parallel to the original information processing capabilities typically attributed to AI systems.

In theory, it thus seems that human directors will maintain a position of oversight until the most autonomous and sophisticated AI systems have reached the boardroom. However, when AI systems reach the level of MML (i.e., the stage within AI at which the current separation between the machine and the mind has been overcome), it will become increasingly hard to argue that it is necessary to keep humans in the loop. Turning to the above example of VITAL, while the AI system deployed by Deep Knowledge Ventures was highly autonomous in nature, this did not mean that the human board directors were eliminated from the corporate governance and decision-making process. On the contrary, the BoD of Deep Knowledge Ventures agreed not to make any positive investment decisions without corroboration by VITAL,[44] indicating that increasingly autonomous AI is relied upon to make independent decisions, but until AI reaches or surpasses human levels of cognitive and emotional intelligence this will not be without human oversight to ensure such decisions are in line with the corporation's goals and objectives.

From a corporate law frame of reference, the law grants corporations unique privileges to harness their capacities and serve their needs. However, as corporations' objectives shift towards mere financial value generation to maximize profits for shareholders, the legal focus shifts to endow corporations with an extended and stricter responsibility towards serving the needs and protecting the rights of the wider

---

[43] Svoboda 2019; Fosch-Villaronga et al. 2021.

[44] Burridge 2017.

community of stakeholders affected by the corporations' functioning. An example of this can be found in a corporations' responsibility to protect human rights. Although states are usually the recipients of human rights treaties, the United Nations Human Rights Council has shown growing attention to the responsibility that corporations, sectors, and industries worldwide have for respecting human rights.[45] The integration of increasingly autonomous AI into the boardroom will only complicate the relationship between corporations and the broader community of stakeholders that are affected by its decisions and resulting operations, making it increasingly complex for affected parties to understand who is responsible for what and how to seek redress in the case of harm and disproportionality.

Corporate laws generally stipulate specific requirements which directors ought to satisfy in the performance of their duties, while some sector-specific laws add further preconditions. The European Capital Requirements Directive, for instance, provides that "members of the management body shall at all times be of sufficiently good repute and possess sufficient knowledge, skills, and experience to perform their duties." As current corporate laws are often tailored to human directors, it is highly questionable whether increasingly autonomous AI systems tasked with corporate governance and decision-making powers would qualify as directors under existing corporate laws at all. For instance, only natural and legal persons can be appointed as board directors under Dutch corporate law. AI systems do not qualify as either, although in January 2017, the EU Parliament's Legal Affairs Committee published a report regarding 'electronic personalities' for AI agents and self-learning robots. While this report was met by much dissent both from a legal and ethical perspective from the different EU Member States, 'electronic personalities' nevertheless remains a topic of debate within the EU,[46] and–if so–whether they would be capable of fulfilling all requirements. Bearing this in mind, the biggest issue—from a corporate law perspective—that should be addressed within this context revolves around determining who ought to be held liable when something goes wrong.

Accordingly, understanding the role of both humans and AI in highly automated boardrooms is essential to understand who is responsible when harm results from decisions and actions by corporations' BoDs. While autonomy levels 0 and 1 are generally accepted and appreciated within society and have already been subjected to regulation, the more autonomous AI systems become, the less societal acceptance and legal response they receive.[47] Currently, the regulation of augmentative AI systems is at the top of the regulatory agenda as these systems become more common in practice.

For instance, in October 2020, the European Parliament[48] put forward a detailed resolution proposing a civil liability regime for artificial intelligence, which sets out

---

[45] OHCHR 2012.

[46] EP Committee on Legal Affairs 2016; European Commission 2018; Robotics Open Letter 2018.

[47] Hilb 2020.

[48] European Parliament resolution of 20 October 2020 with recommendations to the Commission on a civil liability regime for artificial intelligence. Available at https://www.europarl.europa.eu/doceo/document/TA-9-2020-0276_EN.html.

rules for the civil liability claims of natural and legal persons against operators. These operators can be any natural or legal person who exercises a degree of control over a risk connected with the operation and functioning of the AI system, either at the front-end or back-end of AI systems. The proposal establishes a two-fold liability regime consisting of "high-risk" AI systems and "other" AI systems. The common principles for operators of both high-risk and other AI systems establish that operators cannot exonerate themselves from liability because an autonomous activity, device, or process driven by their AI system caused harm or damage unless such harm or damage was caused by force majeure (Art. 4(3) of the EU Parliament Resolution on Civil Liability for AI).

Also, an autonomously operating AI system is considered high-risk when it has significant potential to cause harm or damage to one or more persons in a random manner and goes beyond what can reasonably be expected (Art. 3(c) of the EU Parliament Resolution on Civil Liability for AI). Within the context of AI used in the boardroom, this would cover AI systems that have reached levels 4 and 5 in terms of autonomy (see Fig. 18.1). This depends on the interplay between the severity of possible harm or damage, the degree of autonomy of decision-making, the likelihood that the risk materializes, and the manner and the context in which the AI system is used. Moreover, operators of high-risk AI systems shall be strictly liable for any harm or damage caused by a physical or virtual activity, device, or process, driven by that AI system. (art. 4(1) of the EU Parliament Resolution on Civil Liability for AI). For other AI systems, the resolution brings forward a fault-based liability regime. Here, the operator may be able to establish that he was not liable for any harm caused by an AI system if he can establish that the AI system was activated without his knowledge.

Moreover, to illustrate the difficulties related to liability attribution in the context of increasingly automated BoDs, consider Dutch corporate law. Under Dutch corporate law, directors are generally required to fulfil their tasks in a manner that is in line with how a reasonably competent and reasonably acting director would do so given the circumstances. It is precisely this test of reasonableness, in which the director in question in the performance of his duties ought to be compared to "a reasonably competent and reasonably acting board director acting under the given circumstances" that seems to be problematic when it comes down to the determination of liability for AI-driven board directors. After all, such directors are not the same as human directors, and therefore the applied testing measure cannot be identical. The difficulty in using such a testing measure and, therefore, the complexity that accompanies allocating liability in this context revolves around the difference in nature between the directors and the contrasting incentives according to which they act. After all, AI systems, regardless of their capability to mimic human intelligence and empathy, do not suffer financial losses or benefit from so-called 'pay-for-performance regimes,' as they can neither earn money nor work towards the objective of doing so. Furthermore, they will be less tempted to divert corporate assets, opportunities, or information for their benefit, nor is a breach of their fiduciary loyalty very likely because AI does not make decisions based on personal interests. As a result, existing liability regimes could turn out to be largely ineffective in this regard and leave the possibly far-reaching implications of integrating increasingly autonomous AI systems into the BoD without adequate regulatory attention.

Having more clarity about the status of autonomous AI systems in the context of the BoD would increase legal certainty, which the EU is mainly concerned with. However, what seems to be disregarded is precisely the role that autonomy plays in using AI in boardrooms. This open question will inevitably have to be addressed in the transition period in which AI acts as a mere support system until it eventually becomes fully autonomous. Having a layered approach as presented in this chapter could help the legislator, AI developers, and BoDs that employ these systems make some compromises concerning the boundaries and each level's implications with respect to the changing roles and responsibilities for both the AI developers and the deployers of such systems.

18.5   Conclusion

The field of AI has advanced tremendously over the past two decades, and there is good reason to believe that AI technologies will become even smarter and more autonomous over time. Nevertheless, it is impossible to predict the future with complete accuracy and it, therefore, remains questionable whether we will one day encounter a boardroom filled with only robo-directors. A survey conducted by the World Economic Forum 2015 predicted that the first robo-director might be serving as a full and autonomous board-member as soon as 2025.[49] Moreover, the global economic crisis caused by the COVID-19 pandemic will undoubtedly continue to drive this technological process within corporations.[50]

Given the increasing levels of autonomy AI has in different applications, in this chapter, we presented the autonomy levels for AI in the boardroom and reasoned about their potential legal and regulatory implications from a corporate law perspective. We presented a six-layered model depicting the roles of human directors and AI systems, building on existing literature and other related examples from the automotive and medical sectors. Although more autonomous boardrooms appear to indicate autonomous corporate governance and decision-making without human responsibility, this does not seem to be the case in practice. At least, not just yet. What it indicates, though, is that the more autonomous and powerful AI systems become, the more the decision-making process will shift from human-based to AI-powered. For the highest levels of autonomy, humans will mostly have an overseeing role in favour of AI having a more prominent role in terms of decision-making.

This nuance is essential to avoid ascribing responsibility to the AI system or extending this, which literature has repeatedly highlighted as a legitimate course of

---

[49] World Economic Forum 2015.
[50] Tokmakov 2020.

action in complex technological ecosystems, to ensure we do not end up having technology in place without human responsibility.[51] Especially as corporations become more powerful and their decisions and actions continue to affect the lives of many people across the globe significantly, it is necessary to establish a sound regulatory framework for the use of increasingly autonomous AI in the boardroom with clear responsibilities.

References

Agrawal A, Gans J, Goldfarb A (2017) How AI Will Change the Way We Make Decisions. Harvard Business Review. https://hbr.org/2017/07/how-ai-will-change-the-way-we-make-decisions.

Agrawal A, Gans J, Goldfarb A (2018) Exploring the Impact of Artificial Intelligence: Prediction versus Judgment. Working Paper. http://www.nber.org/papers/w24626.pdf.

Agrawal A, Singhal C, Thomas R (2021) AI-powered decision making for the bank of the future. McKinsey & Company. https://www.mckinsey.com/~/media/mckinsey/industries/financial%20services/our%20insights/ai%20powered%20decision%20making%20for%20the%20bank%20of%20the%20future/ai-powered-decision-making-for-the-bank-of-the-future.pdf.

Armour J, Eidenmueller HGM (2019) Self-Driving Corporations? Harvard Business Law Review, Forthcoming, European Corporate Governance Institute-Law Working Paper No. 475/2019, Oxford Legal Studies Research Paper No. 5/2020. https://doi.org/10.2139/ssrn.3442447.

Ashour S (2020) Artificial Intelligence in the Boardroom: An Outright Exposure to Directorial Liability? Oxford Business Law Blog. https://www.law.ox.ac.uk/business-law-blog/blog/2020/10/artificial-intelligence-boardroom-outright-exposure-directorial.

Bhattacharya P (2018) Artificial Intelligence in the Boardroom: Enabling 'Machines' to 'Learn' to Make Strategic Business Decisions. In: 2018 Fifth HCT Information Technology Trends (ITT), 170–174.

Brynjolfsson E, McAfee A (2017) The Business of Artificial Intelligence. Harvard Business Review. https://hbr.org/2017/07/the-business-of-artificial-intelligence.

Bryson JJ, Diamantis ME, Grant TD (2017) Of, for, and by the people: the legal lacuna of synthetic persons. Artif Intell Law 25, 273–291 (2017). https://doi.org/10.1007/s10506-017-9214-9.

Burridge N (2017) Artificial intelligence gets a seat in the boardroom. NIKKEI Asia. https://asia.nikkei.com/Business/Artificial-intelligence-gets-a-seat-in-the-boardroom.

Cossin D, Metayer E (2014) How strategic is your board? Cambridge: MIT Sloan Business Review. https://sloanreview.mit.edu/article/how-strategic-is-your-board/.

European Commission (2018) Artificial Intelligence: Commission outlines a European approach to boost investment and set ethical guidelines. https://ec.europa.eu/commission/presscorner/detail/en/IP_18_3362.

European Parliament Committee on Legal Affairs (2016) Draft Report with recommendations to the Commission on Civil Law Rules on Robotics (2015/2103 (INL)) committee on Legal Affairs Rapporteur (Initiative - Rule 46 of the Rules of Procedure). https://www.europarl.europa.eu/doceo/document/JURI-PR-582443_EN.pdf?redirect.

Fosch-Villaronga E (2019) Robots, healthcare, and the law: Regulating automation in personal care. Routledge.

Fosch-Villaronga E, Heldeweg M (2018) "Regulation, I presume?" said the robot–Towards an iterative regulatory process for robot governance. Computer law & security review, 34(6), 1258–1277.

---

[51] Johnson 2015; Bryson and Diamantis 2017; Fosch-Villaronga 2019.

Fosch-Villaronga E, Khanna P, Drukarch H et al (2021) A human in the loop in surgery automation. Nat Mach Intell 3, 368–369 (2021). https://doi.org/10.1038/s42256-021-00349-4.

Frey CB, Osborne MA (2017) The future of employment: How susceptible are jobs to computerisation? Technological forecasting and social change, 114, 254–280.

Garbuio M, Lin N (2019) Artificial intelligence as a growth engine for healthcare startups: Emerging business models. California Management Review, 61(2), 59–83.

Hilb M (2020) Toward artificial governance? The role of artificial intelligence in shaping the future of corporate governance. J Manag Gov 24, 851–870. https://doi.org/10.1007/s10997-020-095 19-9.

Jain L, De Wilde P (eds) (2001) Practical applications of computational intelligence techniques (Vol. 16). Springer Science & Business Media.

Jain LC, Martain NM (1999) Fusion of Neural Networks, Fuzzy Sets, and Genetic Algorithms: Industrial Applications (pp. 3–12). In: Martin NM, Jain LC (eds) CRC Press, Boca Raton.

Johnson DG (2015) Technology with no human responsibility? Journal of Business Ethics, 127(4), 707–715.

Libert B, Beck M, Bonchek M (2017) AI in the boardroom: the next realm of corporate governance. MIT Sloan Management Review Blog.

McCarthy J, Minsky M, Rochester N, Shannon C (1955) A Proposal for the Dartmouth Summer Research Project on Artificial Intelligence. http://www-formal.stanford.edu/jmc/history/dartmo uth/dartmouth.html.

Merriam-Webster (2020) Definition Of AUTONOMY. Merriam-Webster.Com. https://www.mer riam-webster.com/dictionary/autonomy.

Mosco GD (2020) AI and Board Within Italian Corporate Law: Preliminary Notes. European Company Law, 17(3), 87.

Möslein F (2018) Robots in the boardroom: artificial intelligence and corporate law. In: Barfield W, Pagallo U (eds) (2018) Research handbook on the law of artificial intelligence. Edward Elgar Publishing, 649–669.

Nalder J (2017) Future-U A3 Model: how to understand the impact of tech on work, society and education. Future-U. https://www.nmc.org/blog/are-we-there-yet-artificial-intelligence-in-education.

Nikishova MI (2018) Prospects of digital technologies application in corporate governance. In: 8th International Conference Social Science and Humanity, 86–95.

Pelau C, Dabija DC, Ene I (2021) What makes an AI device human-like? The role of interaction quality, empathy and perceived psychological anthropomorphic characteristics in the acceptance of artificial intelligence in the service industry. Computers in Human Behavior, 122, 106855. https://doi.org/10.1016/j.chb.2021.106855.

Petrin M (2019) Corporate Management in the Age of AI. Colum, Bus. L. Rev., 965.

Phillips-Wren G, Jain L (2006). Artificial intelligence for decision making. In: International Conference on Knowledge-Based and Intelligent Information and Engineering Systems. Springer, Berlin/Heidelberg, (pp. 531–536).

Robotics Open Letter (2018) Open letter to the European Commission—artificial intelligence and robotics. Retrieved from http://www.robotics-openletter.eu/.

Schwab K, Davis N (2018) Shaping the future of the fourth industrial revolution. Currency.

Still RR, Cundiff EW, Govoni NA (1958) Sales management: decisions, policies, and cases. Prentice-Hall, Englewood Cliffs.

Svoboda E (2019) Your robot surgeon will see you now. Nature, 573(7775), S110–S111. https://doi.org/10.1038/d41586-019-02874-0.

Tokmakov MA (2020) Artificial Intelligence in Corporate Governance. In: International Online Forum named after A. Ya. Kibanov: " Innovative Personnel Management". Springer, Cham, pp. 667–674.

United Nations Human Rights Office of the High Commissioner (OHCHR) (2012) The corporate responsibility to respect human rights - an interpretative guide. United Nations, New York. https://www.ohchr.org/Documents/publications/hr.puB.12.2_en.pdf.

Wang Y (2021) When artificial intelligence meets educational leaders' data-informed decision-making: A cautionary tale. Studies in Educational Evaluation, 69, 100872.

Wilson J, Daugherty PR (2018) Collaborative Intelligence: Humans and AI Are Joining Forces. Harvard Business Review. https://hbr.org/2018/07/collaborative-intelligence-humans-and-ai-are-joining-forces.

World Economic Forum (WEF) (2015) Global Agenda Council on the Future of Software & Society (2015), p. 7. http://www3.weforum.org/docs/WEF_GAC15_Technological_Tipping_Points_report_2015.pdf.

Yang GZ, Cambias J, Cleary K, Daimler E, Drake J, Dupont PE, Hata N, Kazanzides P, Martel S, Patel RV, Santos VJ, Taylor RH (2017) Medical robotics - Regulatory, ethical, and legal considerations for increasing levels of autonomy. Science Robotics, 2(4), eaam8638.

Legislation and Other Documents

Communication from the Commission to the European Parliament, the European Council, the Council, the European Economic and Social Committee and the Committee of the Regions, Artificial Intelligence for Europe COM/2018/237 final. https://ec.europa.eu/transparency/regdoc/rep/1/2018/EN/COM-2018-237-F1-EN-MAIN-PART-1.PDF.

European Parliament resolution of 20 October 2020 with recommendations to the Commission on a civil liability regime for artificial intelligence. https://www.europarl.europa.eu/doceo/document/TA-9-2020-0276_EN.html.

HR 8 April 2005, NJ 2006/443; ECLI:NL:HR:2005:AS5010 (Laurus). https://uitspraken.rechtspraak.nl/inziendocument?id=ECLI:NL:HR:2005:AS5010.

HR 10 January 1997, LJN ZC2243, NJ 1997/360 (Staleman/Van de Ven). https://uitspraken.rechtspraak.nl/inziendocument?id=ECLI:NL:HR:1997:ZC2243.

Hadassah Drukarch is currently a student at the Advanced LL.M. in Law and Digital Technologies at Leiden University, The Netherlands. Additionally, she is the founder and host of The Law of Tech Podcast which aims to provide insights into how new technologies are impacting upon the law and legal industry. Previously, she worked as a Research Assistant at the *eLaw Center for Law and Digital Technologies* at Leiden University where she worked on LIAISON, an FSTP from the H2020 COVR project that aimed to link robot development and policymaking to reduce the complexity in robot legal compliance under the EU's H2020 Research and Innovation Program Grant Agreement No 779966. Moreover, she was a research trainee at the *eLaw Center for Law and Digital Technologies* in 2020, working on Healthcare Robotics, including Robotic Assisted Surgery regulatory and liability aspects. Hadassah's work navigates between law, digital technologies, governance, business & entrepreneurship, diversity & inclusion, and human rights. She holds an LL.B. in International Business Law and an Honours College Law Program certificate from Leiden University.

Eduard Fosch-Villaronga is an Assistant Professor at the *eLaw Center for Law and Digital Technologies* at Leiden University (The Netherlands), where he investigates legal and regulatory aspects of robot and AI technologies, with a special focus on healthcare, diversity, governance, and transparency. Currently, he is the PI of PROPELLING, an FSTP from the H2020 Eurobench project, a project using robot testing zones to support evidence-based robot policies. Previously, Eduard served the European Commission in the Sub-Group on Artificial Intelligence (AI), connected products and other new challenges in product safety to the Consumer Safety Network (CSN) and was the PI of LIAISON, an FSTP from the H2020 COVR project that aimed to link robot development and policymaking to reduce the complexity in robot legal compliance.

In 2019, Eduard was awarded a Marie Skłodowska-Curie Postdoctoral Fellowship and published the book *Robots, Healthcare, and the Law* (Routledge). Eduard holds an Erasmus Mundus Joint Doctorate in Law, Science, & Technology, coordinated by the University of Bologna (Italy, 2017), an LL.M. from University of Toulouse (France, 2012), an M.A. from the Autonomous University of Madrid (Spain), and an LL.B. from the Autonomous University of Barcelona (Catalonia, Spain, 2011). Eduard is also a qualified lawyer in Spain.

Chapter 19
Artificial Intelligence and European Competition Law: Identifying Principles for a Fair Market

Gera van Duijvenvoorde

Contents

Abstract Creating a fair and competitive economy is one of the pillars of the programme for Shaping Europe's Digital Future. Artificial Intelligence could contribute to a more innovative, efficient, sustainable, and competitive economy, as well as a wide array of societal benefits. European Competition law is an important regulatory instrument to safeguard competition in markets, promote innovation and protect consumer interests. The concepts of 'markets' and 'competition' are broad, which means that digital markets are automatically in scope. Nevertheless, there is a discussion about the fitness of competition law to safeguard fair and contestable digital markets due to the role of online platforms, data, and algorithms on the markets. Harmonisation regulations emerge with detailed provisions for digital services and online platforms aiming to shape fair digital markets, without conducting a prior assessment of relevant markets and the impact on markets when

G. van Duijvenvoorde (✉)
eLaw Center for Law and Digital Technologies, Leiden University, Leiden, The Netherlands
e-mail: g.p.van.duijvenvoorde@law.leidenuniv.nl

© T.M.C. ASSER PRESS and the authors 2022
B. Custers and E. Fosch-Villaronga (eds.), *Law and Artificial Intelligence*,
Information Technology and Law Series 35,
https://doi.org/10.1007/978-94-6265-523-2_19

defining unfair, restrictive practices, as is common practice under European Competition law. Both approaches should serve the goal of fair competition. This chapter identifies principles for a fair market in European Competition law, describes their limitations, and discusses how they could be applied in the context of algorithms and data while taking into account the harmonisation regulations.

Keywords Digital economy · Fair markets · EU Competition law · Data · Online platforms

19.1   Background and Structure

The framework for European Competition law ("competition law") aims to prevent restrictions of competition in markets. Since the entry into force of the first treaty on establishing the European Economic Community in 1958, competition law principles have been included to ensure 'fair competition' as is reflected in its preamble.[1] The first Commissioner on Competition Policy elaborated on the concept in the early days of the European Economic Community: "Freedom and fairness in competition are mutually dependent. Any competition policy aimed at establishing a system in which competition is protected against distortion must therefore try to ensure that the law on unfair competition is made uniform by conventions or by approximating legislation in the various countries."[2] The meaning of fairness is not clear as it is related to competition in markets instead of protecting the specific interests of individual companies or consumers.[3] The European Union (EU) has exclusive competence in establishing competition rules necessary for the functioning of the internal market.[4] As of the introduction of the EU, competition policy is no longer mentioned as a

---

[1] See the fourth preamble to the Treaty on the Functioning of the European Union ("TFEU"), "RECOGNISING that the removal of existing obstacles calls for concerted action in order to guarantee steady expansion, balanced trade and fair competition", Consolidated Version of the TFEU, [2012] OJ C 326/49. In 1966 the Court of Justice (ECJ) Case 32/65 [1966] ECR 389 at 405, confirmed that Article 85 (now Article 101 TFEU) should be read in conjunction with the provisions of the preamble to the Treaty.

[2] Speech by the first commissioner Hans von der Groeben, Competition in the Common Market, made during the debate on the draft regulation pursuant to Articles 85 and 86 of the EEC Treaty in the European Parliament, 19 October 1961, p. 11, http://aei.pitt.edu/14786/1/S49-50.pdf (Accessed on 31 August 2021).

[3] See, for instance, Korah 1990, p. 7: "Should small firms be helped to compete against supermarkets, even if they are less efficient in producing what consumers want to buy. Where one firm has invested in promotion for the benefit of a brand as a whole, is it fair to let other firms take advantage of this investment for free? If they are permitted to do so, would this remove the incentive for providing services that consumers want?"

[4] Article 3(b) TFEU. Council Regulation 1/2003 is giving effect to the enforcement of the Articles 101 and 102 TFEU by the European Commission, Council Regulation (EC) No. 1/2003 of 16 December 2002 on the implementation of the rules on competition laid down in Articles 81 and 82 of the Treaty, [2003] OJ L 1, and amendments (latest amendment [2009] OJ L 148/1) (Regulation 1/2003).

specific measure to pursue the goals of the EU,[5] but as one of the internal market measures to ensure that competition is not distorted.[6] Articles 101 and 102 TFEU list types of behaviour that may restrict competition and be incompatible with the internal market.[7] They have remained unchanged since their introduction.[8] The provisions are formulated negatively, meaning that they do not describe the desirable level of competition but indicate what is not allowed. An elaborated framework on the principles of competition law is developed by the European Commission ("Commission") in decisions, regulations, and guidelines[9] as well as by European courts in case law.[10] The concept of fairness is often not specifically mentioned but is reflected in the application of the competition principles, for example, by substantiating the restrictive behaviour in case of infringement.[11]

Artificial Intelligence (AI) could contribute to a more innovative, efficient, sustainable, and competitive economy, and offer a wide array of societal benefits.[12] Although digital markets, including data, algorithms, and platforms, are in the scope of competition law, the Commission explored ways to make competition policy fit for the digital age.[13] At the same time, a revival of the concept of fairness in competition law can be noticed.[14] One of the pillars of the EU programme for 'Shaping Europe's Digital Future' is to create a fair and competitive economy.[15] As underlined in the early days of competition law, the revival of the concept of fairness goes hand in hand with

---

[5] See Article 3(*f*) Treaty of Rome.

[6] Protocol (No 27) to the TEU and TFEU on the internal market and competition.

[7] See Article 3(3) Treaty on the European Union (TEU). The Articles on public undertakings (Article 106) and state aid (Articles 107-109) are also part of the competition rules in the TFEU. The scope of this chapter is restricted to Articles 101 and 102.

[8] Except as to their reference to the internal market.

[9] All decisions, regulations and guidelines of the Commission can be accessed through the website ec.europa.eu/competition/antitrust (Accessed on 31 August 2021).

[10] National courts may also apply Articles 101 and 102; the competences of national competition authorities to apply Articles 101 and 102 are restricted, see Regulation 1/2003, Articles 5 and 6.

[11] See for instance, *Google Search (Shopping),* Case AT.39740, 27 June 2017 and the press release of the Commission opening an investigation into possible anti-competitive conduct by Google in the online advertising technology sector, IP/21/3143, 22 June 2021, "Fair competition is important–both for advertisers to reach consumers on publishers' sites and for publishers to sell their space to advertisers, to generate revenues and funding for content. We will also be looking at Google's policies on user tracking to make sure that they are in line with fair competition."

[12] Counsel conclusions on shaping Europe's digital future, [2020] OJ C 202/1, recital 19.

[13] See Mandate of Commissioner Vestager, https://ec.europa.eu/commission/commissioners/sites/comm-cwt2019/files/commissioner_mission_letters/mission-letter-margrethe-vestager_2019_en.pdf (Accessed on 31 August 2021).

[14] See as examples Speech 2 March 2020, https://ec.europa.eu/commission/commissioners/2019-2024/vestager/announcements/keeping-eu-competitive-green-and-digital-world_en (Accessed on 31 August 2021) and Speech 25 February 2021 Industry as a motor for Digital, Digital as a motor for Industry, https://ec.europa.eu/commission/commissioners/2019-2024/vestager/announcements/industry-motor-digital-digital-motor-industry_en (Accessed on 31 August 2021).

[15] Communication from the Commission to the European Parliament, the Council, the European Economic and Social Committee and the Committee of the Regions, Shaping Europe's digital future, 19 February 2020, COM(2020) 67 final.

the enactment of harmonisation regulations. In 2019, an expert report discussed how competition policy should evolve to promote pro-consumer innovation in the digital age.[16] The report addresses the role of platforms, data and mergers in the digital markets. It stressed that competition law and other legal regimes complement each other.[17]

The Commission started a review of the general competition law principles in 2018. This broad review resulted in draft amendments of the Vertical Block Exemption Regulation[18] and the Guidelines for Vertical Restraints in July 2021.[19] The Commission Regulations on Research & Development,[20] and Specialisation Agreements[21] as well as the Guidelines for Horizontal Cooperation are under consultation.[22] The notice on the definition of relevant markets[23] and the Merger Control Regulation[24] are also under review. The developments in digital markets are taken

---

[16] Crémer et al. 2019.

[17] Ibid. p. 126.

[18] Commission Regulation (EU) No 330/2010 of 20 April 2010 on the application of Article 101(3) of the Treaty on the Functioning of the European Union to categories of vertical agreements and concerted practices ("Vertical Block Exemption Regulation" or "VBER"), [2010] OJ L 102/1. On 9 July 2021, a draft amendment was published as Annex to the Communication from the Commission, C(2021) 5026 final.

[19] Guidelines on Vertical Restraints, [2010] OJ C 130/1 ("Guidelines Vertical Restraints"). On 9 July 2021, a draft amendment was published as Annex to the Communication from the Commission, C(2021 5038 final ("draft Vertical Guidelines").

[20] Commission Regulation (EU) No 1217/2010 of 14 December 2010 on the application of Article 101(3) of the Treaty on the Functioning of the European Union to certain categories of research and development, OJ [2010] L 335/36 ("R&D Regulation").

[21] Commission Regulation (EU) No 1218/2010 of 14 December 2010 on the application of Article 101(3) of the Treaty on the Functioning of the European Union to certain categories of specialisation agreements, [2010] OJ L [2010] 335/43 ("Specialisation Regulation").

[22] Guidelines on the applicability of Article 101 of the Treaty on the Functioning of the European Union to horizontal co-operation agreements ("Horizontal Guidelines"), [2011] OJ C 11/1. See the Commission Staff Working Document Evaluation of the Horizontal Block Exemption Regulation, SWD(2021) 103 final of 6 May 2021.

[23] Commission Notice on the definition of relevant market for the purposes of Community competition law [1997] OJ C 372/5. The evaluation of the notice is published in the Commission Staff Working Document, SWD(2021) 199 final and the Executive Summary, SWD(2021) 200 final of 12 July 2021.

[24] Council Regulation (EC) No. 139/2004 of 20 January 2004 on the control of concentrations between undertakings ("Merger Control Regulation"), [2004] OJ 2004 L 24/14; the review of the Merger Control Regulation can be found in Commission Staff Working Documents Evaluation of procedural and jurisdictional aspects of EU merger control, SWD(2021) 66 final of 26 March 2021 and SWD(2021) 67 final of 26 March 2021. On 26 March 2021, the Commission issued a Guidance on the application of the referral mechanism set out in Article 22 of the Merger Control Regulation to certain categories of cases, C(2021) 1959 final. The Guidance is meant to promote referrals of Member States of transactions that do not have a European dimension because they generate little or no turnover but that could have a significant impact on competition, for example, by building up a significant user base and/or commercially valuable data inventories. These transactions could, therefore, be considered 'killer acquisitions'. An example of a referral case is the Facebook/WhatsApp decision, COMP/M.7217 of 3 October 2014, see Bagnoli 2019.

into account as one of the factors that may lead to adaptations of the framework. In 2019 the Commission used its power under competition law to carry out a Sector Inquiry on E-commerce to get insights into restrictive practices in online trading.[25] These insights have been used as input for the review of Vertical Agreements. In addition to the review, the Commission consulted a novel measure in competition law in 2020: a New Competition Tool to regulate digital markets based on competition law.[26] The status of this proposal is uncertain, also given the proposals for harmonisation regulation in digital markets,[27] digital services,[28] data[29] and AI[30] published shortly after the consultation on the tool.

On a national level, policy documents were published with a call to reform competition law so that it can be applied in an adequate way to prevent distortions on digital markets.[31] Academic publications emerge reflecting on the developments in digital

---

[25] Final report on E-commerce Sector Inquiry COM (2017) 229 final ("Final Report on E-commerce") and Commission Staff Working Document SWD (2017) 154 final of 10 May 2017 ("E-commerce Staff Working Document").

[26] Inception Impact Assessment, "New Competition Tool (NCT)", https://ec.europa.eu/info/law/better-regulation/have-your-say/initiatives/12416-Single-Market-new-complementary-tool-to-strengthen-competition-enforcement_en (Accessed on 31 August 2021).

[27] Proposal for a Regulation of the European Parliament and of the Council on contestable and fair markets in the digital sector (Digital Markets Act), 15 December 2020, COM(2020) 842 final, ("DMA-proposal") https://ec.europa.eu/info/strategy/priorities-2019-2024/europe-fit-digital-age/digital-markets-act-ensuring-fair-and-open-digital-markets_en (Accessed on 31 August 2021).

[28] Proposal for a Regulation of the European Parliament and of the Council on a Single Market For Digital Services (Digital Services Act) and amending Directive 2000/31/EC, 15 December 2020 COM(2020) 825 final, https://ec.europa.eu/info/sites/info/files/proposal_for_a_regulation_on_a_single_market_for_digital_services.pdf (Accessed on 31 August 2021).

[29] Proposal for a Regulation of the European Parliament and of the Council on European data governance (Data Governance Act), 25 November 2020, COM(2020) 767 final, and Staff Working Document, 25 November 2020, SWD (2020) 295 final and Communication from the Commission to the European Parliament, the Council, the European Economic and Social Committee and the Committee of the Regions, A European strategy for data, 19 February 2020, COM(2020) 66 final.

[30] Proposal for Regulation of the European Parliament and of the Council laying down harmonised rules on artificial intelligence (Artificial Intelligence Act) and amending certain union legislative acts, 21 April 2021, COM(2021) 206 final ("Proposal Artificial Intelligence Act").

[31] See the joint reports of the Bundeskartellamt and Autorité de la concurrence on Competition Law and Data (2016) and on Algorithms and Competition (2019), https://www.bundeskartellamt.de/EN/AboutUs/Publications/Reports/reports_node.html (Accessed on 31 August 2021); A report by the by the Commission 'Competition Law 4.0 for the German Ministry for Economic Affairs and Energy, A new competition framework for the digital economy" (2019), https://www.bmwi.de/Redaktion/EN/Publikationen/Wirtschaft/a-new-competition-framework-for-the-digital-economy.pdf?__blob=publicationFile&v=3 (Accessed on 31 August 2021); the UK Furman Report Unlocking digital competition (2019), https://assets.publishing.service.gov.uk/government/uploads/system/uploads/attachment_data/file/785547/unlocking_digital_competition_furman_review_web.pdf (Accessed on 31 August 2021); https://www.belgiancompetition.be/en/about-us/publications/joint-memorandum-belgian-dutch-and-luxembourg-competition-authorities (Accessed on 31 August 2021); Batchelor & Janssens 2020 provide an overview of the different policy recommendations for the digital economy, p. 222.

markets, online platforms,[32] data[33] and algorithms,[34] understanding their impact and exploring the question of whether the existing competition law principles can be applied satisfactorily. The outcome of this exploration roughly differs from a reserve to change the principles of competition law,[35] to preferences to use harmonisation regulation,[36] and to pleas to adapt competition law to fill in the gaps of enforcement in digital markets or parts thereof.[37] The explorations illustrate the need for a rethinking of competition law[38] and the notion of fairness.[39]

This chapter elaborates on the application of competition law on AI and aims to identify principles for fair markets. The main question is: Which principles can be identified under EU competition law to secure a fair market given the role of AI? The chapter focuses on the application of Articles 101 and 102 TFEU on the use of algorithms and data.[40] The scope is further refined to two specific elements in the assessment of these articles: the relationship between companies and the position of the company on the market. First, it discusses the use of algorithms and how this may affect the relationship between companies. Second, it elaborates on data cooperation as well as the position of companies using data. Based on this analysis, it highlights what the principles in competition law would mean for companies using algorithms, data and online platforms by assessing the way they contribute to fair markets, and their relationship to the proposals for harmonisation regulation.

This chapter consists of five sections. Section 19.2 elaborates on Articles 101 and 102 TFEU and their relationship to the concept of fairness. Section 19.3 focuses on the use of algorithms in the context of the relations between companies and their interaction. Section 19.4 discusses the use of data and the framework for assessing cooperations, like data pooling, and the position of companies and online platforms. Section 19.5 highlights the main principles and evaluates what they mean for the concept of fair competition in markets using algorithms and data. Section 19.6 provides a conclusion.

---

[32] E.g. Devine 2008; Lundqvist 2019; Evans and Schmalensee 2014; Khan 2017.

[33] E.g. Kupčík and Mikeš 2018; Hayashi et al. 2018; Batchelor and Janssens 2020; Schawe 2020.

[34] E.g. Ezrachi and Stucke 2017; Picht and Loderer 2018; Roman 2018; Beneke and Mackenrodt 2018; Calvano et al. 2019; Sonderegger 2021; OECD 2017 (non-academic).

[35] E.g. Lindsay and McCarthy 2017; Schmidt 2019; Hayashi and Arai 2019.

[36] E.g. Picht and Loderer 2018; Vessozo 2019.

[37] E.g. Crawford et al. 2020; Sonderegger 2021.

[38] E.g. Claassen and Gerbrandy 2016.

[39] E.g. Graef et al. 2018; Clutterbuck 2020.

[40] The focus is on substantive law. Procedural aspects and enforcement questions are not discussed.

19.2 Basic Concepts of Competition Law

The two main articles on the prohibition of cartels and abuse of a dominant position are concise.[41] The cartel provision provides the basic requirements for behaviour of all companies (Sect. 19.2.1). The abuse of dominance provision is only applicable to companies with a dominant position (Sect. 19.2.2.). Competition law provides the boundaries for behaviour, but choices made in the system have their consequences for fair markets (Sect. 19.2.3).

19.2.1 Basics for All Companies

Article 101(1) TFEU forbids all agreements between undertakings, decisions by associations of undertakings and concerted practices between one or more undertakings that affect trade between the Member States and have as their object or effect the prevention, restriction, or distortion of competition within the internal market. The concept of an undertaking is understood to mean every entity engaged in an economic activity, regardless of the legal status of the entity and the way it is financed.[42] The cartel provision mentions certain examples of restrictions like directly or indirectly fixing purchase or selling prices or any other trading conditions and limiting or controlling production, markets, technological development, or investment. Although agreements or decisions infringing the article are automatically void (Article 101(2)), exemptions may exist under certain conditions (Article 101(3)).

The agreement or decision by an association or 'concerted practice' must affect trade between Member States and have as its object or effect the prevention, restriction or distortion of competition within the internal market. Restrictions 'by object' or hardcore restrictions are assumed to have a high potential for adverse effects on the competition so that they are forbidden 'per se' without demonstrating any actual or likely anti-competitive effects on the market. Three classical types of hardcore restrictions in agreements between competitors are price-fixing, output or sales limitation, and market sharing by the allocation of markets or customers.[43] Other examples concern bid-rigging, collective boycott systems, and the information sharing on

---

[41] The chapter only highlights some key notions of competition law. See for a full understanding of Competition law handbooks like Whish and Bailey 2018 and specifically on case law Verloren van Themaat and Reuder 2014. Van Duijvenvoorde 2018 provides an overview of the application of Competition law to the ICT sector.

[42] ECJ Case C-41/90 Höfner [1991] ECR 1991, p. I–1979, para 21. In this chapter undertakings are referred to as companies.

[43] In its 2014 Guidance on restrictions of competition 'by object', the European Commission describes case law and provides examples of restrictions of competition 'by object' for the purpose of defining which agreements may benefit from the De Minimis Notice, 25 June 2014, SWD(2014) 198 final; para 2.1–2.3 refer to price fixing, market sharing and output restriction.

strategic data like future prices and quantities.[44] Such practices reduce or remove the degree of uncertainty as to the operation of the market in question, resulting in competition between companies being restricted.[45] Hardcore restrictions in agreements between non-competitors, for example, between a supplier and a distributor, may consist of allocations of markets by territory and/or customer groups or limitations on the buyer's ability to determine its resale price (resale price maintenance). If agreements or decisions do not have the *object* of restricting competitions, they may fall under Article 101(1) if their *effect* is an appreciable restriction of competition in the relevant market. Markets can be defined on the basis of their product and geographical dimension. A relevant product market comprises all products and services regarded as interchangeable or substitutable by the consumer given their characteristics, prices, and intended use. The relevant geographical market is the area in which the conditions of competition are sufficiently homogenous.[46]

To non-hardcore restrictions, an exemption may apply if justified under Article 101(3).[47] The assessment weighs the pro-competitive aspects and anti-competitive aspects. This provides room for taking into account aspects of innovation and consumer interests. For example, when agreements contribute to the production or distribution of goods or the promotion of technical or economic progress while allowing consumers a fair share of the resulting benefit.[48] It is not necessary, in principle, for each consumer individually to derive a benefit as the overall effect on consumers in the relevant markets must be favourable.[49] The Commission issued block exemptions for some specific agreements indicating under which conditions they benefit from the exemption. The Vertical Block Exemption Regulation [50] relates to the agreements between companies on a different level in the distribution chain, like a supplier and a distributor. Three general[51] block exemption regulations exist for agreements on research & development,[52] specialisation[53] and technology transfer,[54] providing room for innovative cooperation and optimalisation of production. The

---

[44] Ibid. para 2.3–2.6.

[45] ECJ Case C-8/08 T-Mobile [2009] ECR I-04529, para 35.

[46] Notion on the definition of the relevant market [1997], OJ C 372/5, II.

[47] Guidelines on the application of Article 81(3) of the Treaty, [2004] OJ C 101/97.

[48] But this may not impose on the undertakings concerned restrictions which are not indispensable to the attainment of the objectives and afford such undertakings the possibility of eliminating competition in respect of a substantial part of the products in question, as is reflected in Article 1013(a) and (b).

[49] ECJ Case-238/05 Asnef-Equifax [2006] ECR I-11125, as regards agreements between financial institutions for the exchange of information on customer solvency.

[50] See footnote 18.

[51] Sector specific regulations apply to agriculture, motor vehicles, transport.

[52] See footnote 20.

[53] See footnote 21.

[54] Commission Regulation (EU) No. 316/2014 on the application of Article 101(3) of the Treaty on the Functioning of the European Union to categories of technology transfer agreements, [2014] L 93/17 ("Technology Transfer Agreements Regulation").

Horizontal Guidelines[55] provide principles for the assessment of pro-competitive and anti-competitive aspects in agreements between companies at the same level of a distribution chain. The block exemptions and guidelines are important for companies as they enable them to carry out a self-assessment of their activities as regards their compliance with competition law.

19.2.2 Basics for Dominant Companies

Article 102 TFEU forbids any abuse by one or more undertakings of a dominant position within the internal market or in a substantial part in so far as it may affect trade between Member States. A dominant position relates to a position of economic strength enjoyed by a company which enables it to prevent effective competition from being maintained in the relevant market by giving the power to behave to an appreciable extent independently of its competitors, customers and ultimately of its consumers.[56] Some examples of abuses are mentioned in the text of Article 102, although the list of examples is not exhaustive. They may consist in (a) directly or indirectly unfair purchase or selling prices or other unfair trading conditions[57] or (b) limiting production, markets or technical development to the prejudice of consumers. Unfair pricing may exist when considering the price itself or when compared to competing products.[58] A price may be excessive because it has no reasonable relation to the economic value of the product supplied.[59] Excessive pricing, but also predatory pricing, may be abusive. Other forms of abuse are tying,[60] discrimination,[61] refusals to supply, or denying access to indispensable essential facilities.

In a 2009 Communication, the Commission published its priorities for enforcing Article 102 in case of alleged abuse leading to restriction of competition.[62] The enforcement guidelines introduced a more economic and effects-based approach of

---

[55] See footnote 22.

[56] ECJ Case 27/76 United Brands [1978] ECR 1978, p 207.

[57] For example, in the Amazon e-book case by imposing a price parity clause on e-book suppliers to notify and offer to Amazon the same or equivalent terms for the distribution of e-books as any e-book retailer other than Amazon, IP/17/137 of 24 January 2017 and IP/17/1223 of 4 May 2017, and the Commitments offered by Amazon: Case COMP/AT.40.153 E-Book MFNs and related matters.

[58] ECJ Case 27/76 United Brands [1978] ECR 1978, p 207, para 252.

[59] Ibid. para 250.

[60] See for example the Microsoft Tying Cases, on tying of the Internet Explorer to the Windows system, CFI Case T-201/04 Microsoft v EC Commission [2007] ECR II-03601 and Commission Decision of 6 March 2013, AT.39530–Microsoft (Tying). On the pre-instalment of Google's Chrome browser and tying to Google's Play Store or Search, Commission infringement decision, Case AT.40099 Google Android, 18 July 2018.

[61] Such as price discrimination, see ECJ Case C-525/16 MEO [2018] ECLI:EU:C:2018:270 with respect to copyrights and pay tv.

[62] Communication from the Commission, Guidance on the Commission's Enforcement Priorities in Applying Article 82 EC Treaty to Abusive Exclusionary Conduct by Dominant Undertakings, [2009] C 45/7.

the assessment of exclusionary conduct and the application of Article 102, although case law prevails.

19.2.3 Fair Competition

Articles 101 and 102 have a broad scope and are not specifically designed for a particular sector or market, nor one type of conduct or agreement. As such, they ensure the fairness of competition in the markets, including digital markets. Competition law is designed to protect not only the immediate interests of individual competitors or consumers, but also the structure of the market and, thus, competition as such.[63] The assumption is that a competitive market leads to the best outcome for companies and customers. It is difficult to generally qualify what is fair competition. Or, to say it differently, to argue when competition is not fair.[64]

But competition law has its limitations due to choices made in the system that influence the way it addresses fairness.

First, competition law must be seen in the context of the market. Only hardcore restrictions, such as price-fixing, market sharing, or exchange of information on future prices[65] may be considered unfair without in-depth assessment of the impact of the market as the restrictions take out the uncertainty that normally exists in a situation of competition. Other restrictions must be evaluated regarding their effects on the competition in the markets, which means that often no simple answer can be given to whether competition law is infringed. Interests of competitors or consumers may play a role in the evaluation, although a direct relationship between the infringement and the harm to the interests of competitors or consumers is not required.[66] This is a difference with unfair competition regulation, aimed at the protection of competitors or consumers against specific behaviour harming their interests.[67]

Second, choices have been made regarding the assessment of the impact of the position of the companies on the market and the application of the competition rules by using market shares as important indicators. Only in the case of very low joint

---

[63] ECJ Case C-8/08 T-Mobile [2009] ECR I-04529, para 38.

[64] Csurgai-Horváth 2020 notices that the concept of fairness are far from clear and debated. The concept is connected to the term "competing on the merits", but also goes along with "level playing field" in the digital society. The protection of the competitive process, the structure of the market and the long-term interests of consumers are associated with fairness and level playing field. Clutterbuck 2020 elaborates on the concept of fairness and distributive fairness to satisfy consumers (price fairness) in the short run; as this can only be achieved to the detriment of competition and long-run consumer outcomes it is questioned which should be prioritised, see p. 326.

[65] See Sect. 19.2.1.

[66] ECJ Case C-8/08 T-Mobile [2009] ECR I-04529, para 39, in which the Court stated that there does not need to be a direct link between an anti-competitive practice and consumer prices to find that a concerted practice has an anti-competitive object.

[67] See, for example, consumer protection rules against unfair commercial practices, like misleading, in Directive (EU) 2019 of 27 November 2019 amending different directives as regards the better enforcement and modernisation of consumer protection rules, [2019] L 328/7.

market shares, competition law may not apply (*de minimis*).[68] Market shares are also relevant for benefitting from the block exemptions under Article 101(3), which means that, generally, the market shares must be below a range of 20 to 30%. Article 102 is only applicable to companies with a dominant position in the market.[69] Although this means that the company has the power to behave independently in the relevant market, market shares play a role in deciding whether such a position exists. Generally, a market share above 40% may lead to such a position, depending on other criteria like the strength and number of competitors.[70] The result is that only the unilateral conduct of companies that can, individually or jointly, be qualified as dominant fall under the prohibitions of Article 102. Without dominance, such unilateral behaviour is assumed not to restrict competition as customers or consumers may switch to other companies for alternative options.

Third, any monitoring of the development in the position of companies and whether they attempt to become dominant is absent. Not only do companies without a dominant position fall under Article 101, also Article 102 applies as soon as the dominant position has been reached. It does not cover companies that are close to such position or autonomously grow from, for example, a 35% to a 50% market share.[71] The Merger Control Regulation[72] applies to transactions with a European dimension requiring a clearance before getting control in another company. Such non-autonomous growth is monitored and can be blocked if this leads to a significant impediment of competition, particularly due to the creation or strengthening of a dominant position.[73] As the thresholds are based on turnover, transactions with a value that is not expressed in turnover but in, for example, data or knowledge could escape from the *ex-ante* clearance.[74]

---

[68] See Notice on agreements of minor importance which do not appreciably restrict competition under Article 101(1) of the Treaty on the Functioning of the European Union (De Minimis Notice), [2014] OJ C291/1-4, below a joint market share of 10% (competitors) or 15% (non-competitors).

[69] Schmidt 2019, pp. 50–70 describes the different criteria for assessing market power and concludes that the legal assessment of market power is in itself a flexible tool, that could also be applied to the digital economy.

[70] ECJ Case 27/76 United Brands [1978] ECR 1978, p. 207, para 107–110 (dominance with market shares between 40 and 50%). In the Amazon e-book case the market shares on the e-book markets were between 40 and 60% but there were a number of barriers to entry and a lack of counter-vailing buying power while Amazon appeared to be the unavoiding trading partner, according to the Commission, Case AT.40153 E-book MFNs and related matters (Amazon), para 61–67.

[71] As is emphasised in the Joint memorandum of the Belgian, Dutch and Luxembourg competition authorities on challenges faced by competition authorities in a digital world (2019) the strategies and economic dynamics to become dominant do not necessarily create competition problems as consumers and other companies benefit from strong growth, innovation and new services.

[72] See footnote 24.

[73] Article 2(3) Merger Control Regulation.

[74] This is one of the reasons for the review of the Merger Control Regulation and the publication of the guidance on referring cases, see footnote 24.

Fourth, the application of Articles 101 and 102 is *ex post*, and not *ex ante*.[75] It is related to the current behaviour in the market or over a certain period of time in the past. Any forward-looking assessment of the markets, position of companies and regulation of behaviour for the future is missing.[76]

Fifth, Articles 101 and 102 aim to protect economic interests, like competition in the markets. If agreements or decisions are made to serve societal, non-economic goals, the assessment will concentrate on the impact on the competition in the market.[77]

The choices made in the system have their effect on the application of the concept of fairness. Although hardcore restrictions, like fixing prices or sharing markets, are considered unfair, most practices require an assessment of the impact on the market, taking into account technological and economic progress as well as the impact for consumers. Fair competition is the outcome of such an assessment, which may differ on a case-by-case basis.[78] Choices have been made on the scope of competition law. As positions of companies are not monitored, and no forward-looking assessment takes place, any emergence of a dominant position or 'tipping of the market' cannot be prevented. Purely unilateral behaviour without dominance is not regulated.

As a result, expectations on fair competition or fair markets may not be met when applying the system to digital markets. The next two sections elaborate on the application of competition law to algorithms and data, and the challenges related to this.

19.3 The Use of Algorithms

Algorithms can be used for many purposes. If companies use them for their economic activities they may fall under the scope of competition law. As algorithms may vary from simple instructions to 'deep learning algorithms' that can make their own decisions, questions arise regarding the interaction of algorithms and the notices of

---

[75] An exception is the ex-ante assessment of transactions with a European dimension under the Merger Control Regulation.

[76] For example, potential competition is not taking into account when defining markets, see Notice Relevant Market, footnote 23, para 24. Commitments made by companies after the start of an investigation by the Commission may include behaviour for the future in the specific case. For example, the commitments of Amazon were provided for a five-year period in the e-book case (Case AT.40153 E-book MFNs and related matters). However, the commitments are given as a result of the investigation of behaviour in the past.

[77] The point of departure that the non-economic values are not taken into account in competition law is under discussion, see Claassen and Gerbrandy 2016 proposing a framework for assessing these values by means of a capability approach looking into the capabilities companies or consumers need.

[78] Graef et al. 2018, pp. 204–205 describe that there is no single way of defining fairness as it is interpreted differently in different contexts and there are no straightforward criteria to assess the fairness of conduct under competition law; the role of fairness in competition law is less explicit than in the regimes of data protection and consumer law.

agreement and 'concerted practice' (Sect. 19.3.1). The position of a company using algorithms is relevant (Sect. 19.3.2.). Harmonisation legislation aims to increase the transparency of algorithms to contribute to fairness (Sect. 19.3.3).

19.3.1 Relations and Interaction of Algorithms

A company may use an algorithm to do its business like it uses hardware, software and systems.[79] It may use price monitoring software and pricing algorithms. In the report on the E-commerce Sector Inquiry,[80] the Commission indicates that 53% of the respondents track the online prices of competitors, out of which 67% use automatic software programmes for that purpose. The majority (78%) adjust their own prices to those of their competitors. Nearly 30% of the suppliers indicated that they systematically track the online retail prices of products sold via independent distributors.[81] Given these developments, the use of algorithms has led to an increased attention by the Commission in the context of the compliance to the framework on vertical agreements and relations in Article 101.[82]

In general, the monitoring and increased pricing transparency by algorithms are allowed under Article 101(1) unless a supplier uses the monitoring to 'punish' the distributor for his behaviour so that distributors are forced to apply the recommended prices to their customers. Due to the transparency of algorithms, the results might also be picked up by other companies using algorithms as they will notice that the end user price will be in accordance with the recommended price. Price monitoring and adjustment software programmes multiply the impact of price interventions.[83] If this results in price-fixing (resale price maintenance), a hardcore violation may occur.[84] In four cases the Commission concluded that the pressure on webshops to adhere to follow the prices, *e.g.*, sanctioning them by blocking the supply, resulted in resale price maintenance and forbidden price-fixing.[85]

---

[79] Ezrachi and Stucke 2017, pp. 1784–1787 describe three categories of algorithms: the computer as messenger, hub-and-spoke and predictable agent. See also Picht and Loderer 2018, pp. 15–20. Calvano et al. 2019, pp. 158–165 distinguish adaptive and learning algorithms as well as Q-learning algorithms that learn the optimal policy by experimenting.

[80] E-commerce Staff Working Document, para 149.

[81] E-commerce Staff Working Document, para 576. Reasons for this behaviour are the protection of brand image and the quality standard of distribution, see para 538.

[82] See the draft Vertical Guidelines, para 176 on tracking of resale prices.

[83] See Decision of the Commission of 24 July 2018, AT.40182 (Pioneer), para 155. Dealers used so-called spiders that are software programmes that track the prices online and automatically adjust to match the lowest price available online, often even without the dealer being aware of that price adjustment, para 136.

[84] In Commission Decision of 17 December 2018, C(2018) 8455 final, Case AT.40428 Guess the Commission fined Guess for different restrictions on its selective distributors, *e.g.* for restricting the ability to determine their resale price independently.

[85] Decisions of the Commission of 24 July 2018, AT.40181 (Philips), AT.40182 (Pioneer), AT.40465 (Asus) and AT.40469 Denon & Marantz.

Article 101(1) refers to the existence of an agreement. The concept of agreement centres around the existence of a concurrence of wills between at least two parties, the form in which it is manifested being irrelevant as long as it constitutes the faithful expression of the parties' intention.[86] The interaction between algorithms may qualify as an agreement, if there is a 'concurrence of the wills'. A purely unilateral interaction by an algorithm might be more difficult to qualify as 'concurrence of the wills'.[87] Without the express or implied participation of another undertaking, a genuine unilateral measure does not fall under Article 101(1). If the unilateral character of the measure is merely apparent, it must be regarded as revealing an agreement between undertakings and may therefore fall within the scope of an agreement. This is, for example, the case with "practices and measures in restraint of competition which, though apparently adopted unilaterally by the manufacturer in the context of its contractual relations with its dealers, nevertheless receive at least the tacit acquiescence of those dealers".[88] Such acquiescence can, however, not be assumed on the basis of the mere fact that it falls within the context of continuous business relations.[89] Depending on the circumstances, a unilateral action of an algorithm may be considered as an agreement if it is used in the context of existing contractual relations of the company using the algorithm, such as the relationship between supplier and dealer.

An association developing an algorithm for its members or the decision of the members of the association to share commercially sensitive information and use a certain algorithm may fall in the scope of Article 101.[90] A forbidden alignment may also occur when companies decide to use an algorithm developed by a third party. If that third party receives price information from different companies, and uses the algorithm to align the prices, such alignment may be considered as 'hub-and-spoke' alignment. Even if each company has its own relationship with the third party, the third party may act as a 'hub' to dissolve price information to other companies by means of the algorithm.[91] Exchange of commercially sensitive information, like

---

[86] CFI Case T-41/96 Bayer v. Commission [2000] ECR II-3383, para 69.

[87] OECD 2017, p. 38 found it very hard to draw firm conclusions as to whether algorithmic interactions (or a "meeting of algorithms") should be treated similar to a "meeting of the minds" under the definition of agreement covered by competition rules. Lindsay and McCarthy 2017, p. 537 caution against extending the boundaries of the law on anti-competitive agreements to catch conduct that is lawful as the law currently stands.

[88] Ibid. para 71.

[89] Ibid. para 173, and ECJ Joined cases C-2/01 P and C-3/01 P Bundesverband der Arzneimittel-Importeure e.a. v. Bayer [2004] ECR, p I-000023, para 141.

[90] These types of decisions are likely to be taken in the usual way of decision taking within an association. Should an association use algorithms to come to a decision, the outcome, *i.e.* the decision, will be in scope of Article 101(1).

[91] For example, a coordination of setting prices by means of an algorithm in platforms like Uber may qualify as 'hub-and-spoke' if this leads to an alignment of the prices of independent service providers using the platform.

future prices, by using such third party, is considered to be a hardcore infringement of Article 101.[92]

Should the behaviour not qualify as an agreement nor a decision by an association, the notion of 'concerted practice' might apply. It refers to a stage where no agreement has been concluded but where coordination exists, which becomes apparent from the behaviour of the participants.[93] Although similar behaviour may not in itself be identified as a concerted practice, it may, however, amount to strong evidence of such practice if it leads to conditions of competition that do not correspond with the normal conditions of the market, having regard to the nature of the products, the size and number of the undertakings, and the volume of the market.[94] The exchange of information might result in a parallel behaviour and may remove uncertainties concerning the intended conduct of the participating companies.[95] Exchange of information could already happen in one meeting, so it does not require several meetings.[96]

Self-learning algorithms may take decisions on the basis of the data without a connection to a decision by a company.[97] A company is responsible for developing the algorithm but may lose control over an algorithm that learns from the data and takes independent decisions.[98] One may argue that as long as the self-learning algorithms conduct economic activities, like setting prices, the company using the outcome of these self-learning algorithms for the pricing of its products will be responsible and may fall in the scope of Article 101.[99] However, if such companies do not know how the algorithms came to the price setting, it might be difficult to make them responsible only because, for instance, their products were priced in line with the outcome of the self-learning process.[100] It is questionable whether a company can be held responsible for the tacit coordination or 'concerted practice' of the self-learning algorithms.

Even if the interaction by algorithms falls under the broad notion of agreement and 'concerted practice,' it should prevent, restrict or distort competition in the markets unless it results in hardcore restrictions, like price-fixing. The risk of algorithms is

---

[92] Horizontal Guidelines, para 55.

[93] Ibid. para 64-65. See also ECJ Case 74/14 Eturas [2016] ECLI:C:2016:42, para 41-46 on a message sent by an administrator of an information system concerning a common anti-competitive action (maximum discounts) to the travel agencies participating in that system. A travel agency may be presumed to have participated in the concertation if it was aware of the content of the message, unless it has rebutted the presumption, for example, by means of publicly distancing or reporting to the administrator.

[94] ECJ Case 48/69 ICI v. Commission [1972] ECR 619, para 66. Also indicated as "parallelism plus" approach, see Sonderegger 2021, p. 215.

[95] ECJ Case C-8/08 T-Mobile [2009] ECR I-04529, para 71.

[96] Ibid. para 62; Horizontal Guidelines, para. 62.

[97] Ezrachi and Stucke 2017, pp. 1801–1803, the 'Digital Eye' scenario.

[98] Ezrachi and Stucke 2017, p. 1803.

[99] Roman 2018, argues that an agency law approach in which undertakings are to be kept liable for the actions of algorithms does not relieve the need to prove a 'concurrence of wills', see pp. 43–44.

[100] Sonderegger 2021 supports a broader liability and suggests to extend the concept of 'meeting of minds' with 'meeting of the codes', see pp. 213–214, 225.

that they allow firms to sustain profits above the competitive level more easily without necessarily having to enter into an agreement.[101] In case algorithms are not designed to align prices, but the effect is that prices are aligned in a market as all market players use the same algorithm, a restriction or distortion of competition may occur as the algorithms may remove the uncertainty in the markets. Without an exchange of competitively sensitive information, a distortion of competition by a 'concerted practice' is less likely. Monitoring competitors and reacting to the behaviour of competitors by using algorithms, even when this results in a continuous adaptation of prices matching the prices of other companies, is not prohibited. Increased transparency of prices as a result of the use of algorithms cannot be forbidden. Consumers may also benefit from better insight into the prices, for example, if they can use price comparison tools by websites or apps to search for products and compare their prices across several retailers. However, restrictions on companies using price comparison tools, such as prohibition of distributors to promote their product in these tools, needs to be assessed under the Vertical Block Exemption Regulation and Guidelines.[102] The extent of transparency on the supply or demand side of a market and its effects on competition may lead to a delicate balance considering the potentially pro-competitive and anti-competitive effects on the market.

19.3.2 Position of Users of Algorithms

Companies use business algorithms to find out the preferences of customers and provide them with individually tailored offers. They may also be able to continuously monitor the behaviour of their customers as well as of their competitors. But this does not necessarily lead to an infringement of Article 101, even in the case of pricing algorithms.[103] The existing (contractual) relationships, like between supplier and distributor, may bring the interaction by algorithms in the scope of Article 101. Companies offering online platforms may use algorithms, so the contractual relationship and dual role will also be relevant in assessing these algorithms. If an online platform is provided by a company that also competes with the services and products offered by third parties using the online platform, possible restrictions in competition may occur due to this dual role.[104] The assessment of a dual position is not new. It has been done for airline reservation systems resulting in a code of conduct.[105] An online platform may infringe Article 101 if it prioritises its products and services

---

[101] OECD 2017, p. 24.

[102] See the draft Vertical Guidelines, para 192 listing online restrictions, such as on the use of price comparison tools and search engines, as examples of hardcore restrictions.

[103] See Beneke and Mackenrodt 2018, pp. 118–125 on interdependent pricing.

[104] An in-depth analysis of Amazon's platform, the dual role of Amazon and anti-competitive restraints can be found in Khan 2017.

[105] Regulation (EC) No 80/2009 of the European Parliament and of the Council of 14 January 2009 on a Code of Conduct for computerised reservation systems and repealing Council Regulation (EEC) No. 2299/89, [2009] OJ L 35/47 and the Evaluation, SWD(2020) 9 final, 23 January 2020.

when presenting, for example, the result of a search of a customer on the platform.[106] This preferencing might lead to discrimination of other parties using the platform. An online platform imposing unreasonable conditions that have no connection with the subject of the contract could also fall under Article 101(1) if such behaviour leads to a restriction of competition in the market. Algorithms may support self-preferencing and the monitoring of the behaviour of third parties on the platform.[107] As a result, the competition by third parties using the online platform is hindered, but it is not obvious that the competition in the market is restricted.[108] Given the two-sided character of online platforms and the variety in online platforms it is complicated to define the affected markets and demonstrate a restriction in the markets.[109] The existence of competing platforms and possibilities for companies and end-users to switch to other platforms or use them in combination with other platforms (multihoming) are factors to be taken into account when assessing the impact.

The requirements of defining markets and assessing the impact are also obstacles when applying Article 102 to dominant online platforms. Online platforms unilaterally using an algorithm that, for example, sets unfair pricing, applies unfair conditions, or discriminates, will only be considered abusive if the dominant position in the market can be substantiated. An example of unfair conditions is the Google case on abusive behaviour of its dominant position by offering the search engine and giving an advantage to another product, the Google comparison shopping service.[110] Google's conduct was considered abusive because it diverted traffic from competing comparison-shopping services to Google's own comparison-shopping service. It decreased traffic from Google's general results pages to competing comparison-shopping services and increased traffic from Google's general search results pages to Google's own comparison-shopping service. According to the Commission, this conduct can have anti-competitive effects in the national markets for comparison shopping services and general search services. The case illustrates that if dominance can be determined, the use of algorithms facilitating unfair behavior may be in the scope of Article 102.

See also Press Release European Commission of 25 November 2018, IP/18/6538 announcing an investigation in airline ticket distribution services.

[106] See the initiations of proceedings against Google for the alleged preferencing of its own online display advertising technology services (ad tech), IP/21/3143, 22 June 2021.

[107] Csurgai-Horváth 2020 describes that self-preferencing is a new form of abuse, related to the problem of leveraging market power by vertically integrated digital platforms, pp. 68–70.

[108] See also Csurgai-Horváth 2020, p. 74 supporting the economic approach in case of self-preferencing and opposing the qualification of self-preferencing as a *per se* violation by shifting the burden of proof on dominant platforms.

[109] See Devine 2008; Evans and Schmalensee 2014.

[110] AT.39740–Google Search (Shopping) of 27 June 2017. See on obligations for manufactures who wish to pre-install Google's Play Store or Search, also to pre-install Google's Chrome browser, Commission infringement decision, Case AT.40099 Google Android, 18 July 2018.

19.3.3 Evaluation

Algorithms may lead to more transparency on price and trade conditions on the supply side. The use of algorithms will be assessed like any other way of inter-action between companies. Article 101 does not apply to all exchanges by algo-rithms, especially if these are self-learning algorithms and the unilateral use does not take place in an existing contractual relationship. In the first situation, the attri-bution to a company may fail, and in the second situation, the 'concerted practice' concept may not cover the interactions failing the existence of an agreement or deci-sion.[111] As a result, restrictions, like price-fixing, including hardcore restrictions, could escape from the scope of Article 101. It is questionable whether such gap can be filled in by, for example, amending the Guidelines on Horizontal and Vertical Restraints as the 'concurrence of the wills' is an essential requirement for the concept of 'concerted practice' in Article 101. Changing this concept needs an amendment of Article 101 and will considerably change the scope of Article 101. This gap cannot be filled in either by, for example, adapting the Horizontal Guidelines. In other situ-ations, amending guidelines or block exemptions clarify the concept of fairness in the context of the use of algorithms. A clarification on algorithms facilitating a 'hub-and-spoke' alignment could be included in Guidelines on Horizontal Agreements.[112] First steps for including a clarification of the concept of fairness with respect to the use of algorithms in vertical relationships between suppliers and distributors and by online platforms are taken in the proposals for an amendment of the Vertical Block Exemption Regulation and the Vertical Restraints Guidelines.[113]

Pure unilateral behaviour may be caught under Article 102, but this requires a dominant position in a relevant market.[114] This would take some forms of alignment by algorithms out of the scope of competition law.[115] Adapting competition law by, for example, deleting the definition of relevant markets or lowering the thresholds of market shares determining a dominant position when applying Article 102 risks to stifle innovation. It has been argued that competition law should stand back if another set of regulatory tools exists or evolves.[116] Others explore the possibility

---

[111] A New Competition Tool, as discussed in Sect. 19.4.3, might be used to cover the harms arising from tacit collusion by algorithms, *e.g.* if they lead to higher prices, as recommended by Crawford et al. 2020.

[112] See the evaluation document on the Horizontal Block Exemption Regulations, SWD(2021) 103 final, 6 May 2021, consisting of feedback stating that there is a lack of guidance on data pooling/data sharing, the use of algorithms and data exchanges in ecosystems, p. 57.

[113] See footnote 19.

[114] See also the 2019 Report of Algorithms and Competition November 2019 by the Bundeskartel-lamt and Autorité de la concurrence, https://www.bundeskartellamt.de/SharedDocs/Meldung/EN/Pressemitteilungen/2019/06_11_2019_Algorithms_and_Competition.html (Accessed on 31 August 2021).

[115] See Chauhan 2019, p. 139.

[116] See Picht and Loderer 2018, pp. 33–35.

of 'competition-by-design' so that the compliance of companies with core competition provisions and principles is not exclusively ensured *ex post* but built into algorithms.[117]

The importance of developing another set of rules is felt to increase the transparency and accountability of algorithms.[118] At first sight, these rules are not in scope with competition law unless they relate to cooperation like a standardisation agreement on algorithms, in which case transparency may be a requirement to provide third parties access to the standardised algorithms. Transparency obligations in standardisation agreements relate to the process of designing a standard as well as the access to the standard.[119] An obligation to be transparent on the content of the standard and access to the standard might be imposed in case of a dominant position.[120] Outside these specific situations no transparency obligation on the basis of competition law exists.[121]

Transparency is one of the purposes of enacting harmonisation regulation. A regulation on promoting fairness and transparency for business users of online intermediation services entered into force in 2019 (P2B Regulation).[122] The regulation aims to establish a fair, predictable, sustainable, and trusted online business environment. To this end, it contains transparency rules, such as a ranking resulting from the use of algorithmic sequencing.[123] These rules even apply in the absence of a contractual relationship with users or providers and to unilaterally unfair behaviour.[124] Business practices covered by the P2B Regulation do not necessarily have an anti-competitive object or effect.[125] The P2B Regulation leaves open the application of competition law.[126]

---

[117] Vezzoso 2019, pp. 116–117. Although there are difficulties to integrate into the already complex competition policy regime (p. 116), per se prohibitions (hardcore restrictions) might be suitable for hardcoding in firms' algorithms (p. 119).

[118] OECD 2017, 46–48, referring to the Statement of the Association for Computing Machinery US Public Policy Council (USACM) https://www.acm.org/binaries/content/assets/public-policy/2017_usacm_statement_algorithms.pdf (Accessed on 31 August 2021).

[119] Horizontal Guidelines, para 7.

[120] See, for example, the Microsoft-cases on abuse of a dominant position due to refusals to provide specifications and service interoperability information, CFI Case T-201/04 Microsoft v. Commission [2007] ECR II-03601 and GC Case T-167/08 Microsoft Corp. v. Commission [2012] ECLI:EU:T:2012:323.

[121] And the question is whether regulation is desirable, see Hayashi and Arai 2019, pp 455-456 for a plea for an international non-regulated governance of AI.

[122] Regulation (EU) 2019/1150 of the European Parliament and of the Council of 20 June 2019 on promoting fairness and transparency for business users of online intermediation services ("P2B Regulation"), [2019] OJ L 186/57.

[123] Ibid. recital 24, Article 5 on ranking and Article 7 on differentiated treatment.

[124] See P2B Regulation, recital 4.

[125] Lundqvist 2019, p. 25 doubts whether legislation like P2B that require fair terms for business users and to some extent require access to data or to devices/platforms will be pro-competitive; as no competition harm is analysed, the possibility is invited that an anti-competitive decision will be granted.

[126] Article 1(5) P2B Regulation.

In order to meet the strategic objectives in the Communication 'Shaping Europe's digital future,' the DMA-proposal[127] aims to ensure that the digital markets across the EU are contestable and fair independently from the actual, likely or presumed effects of the conduct of the online gatekeeper platform.[128] The regulation is complementary to competition law. As online gatekeepers are not necessarily dominant in competition law terms[129] they are defined on the basis of turnover and active users instead of market shares. The proposal aims to increase the transparency of these online gatekeeper platforms and provide the Commission with powers to request information regarding the algorithms used.[130]

A proposal for an Artificial Intelligence Act[131] contains harmonised transparency rules for artificial intelligence systems. It has a broad scope, for instance, to classify AI systems as regards their risks for safety or health and algorithmic discrimination. The proposal contains an obligation of national supervisory authorities to report to the Commission and relevant competition authorities any information in the course of surveillance activities that may be of potential interest for the application of competition law.[132] This example illustrates that although harmonisation legislation leaves the application of competition law open, it may influence the application of competition law, especially if the insights provided on the basis of the transparency obligations may reveal anti-competitive behaviour that might qualify as infringement of competition law.

19.4 Data

Algorithms need data. They may also continuously generate new data. The use of "big data" may allow companies to become more efficient and provide a better and more targeted, individualised offer to customers. Competition concerns may arise, for example, in case of the exchange of competitively sensitive data between competitors (Sect. 19.4.1). The use of data by dominant platforms is subject to a constant concern (Sect. 19.4.2), which increases the need to regulate data to safeguard fairness (Sect. 19.4.3).

---

[127] See footnote 27.

[128] DMA-proposal, recitals 8 and 10.

[129] DMA-proposal, recital 5.

[130] DMA-proposal, Article 19 providing a basis to request information on algorithms and Article 21 on on-site inspection and the access to algorithms.

[131] See footnote 30, Article 1(c).

[132] Proposal Artificial Intelligence Act, Article 63(2).

19.4.1 Cooperation on Data

In a data economy, sharing data is important,[133] for example to provide companies with data needed to develop new services, like machine-to-machine applications.[134] Sharing agreements will be reviewed under Article 101. If the data does not contain sensitive commercial information and no hardcore restriction on the use of data exists, then the impact of a restriction on the competition on the market will be assessed. Innovation may benefit from data sharing, implying that these pro-competitive effects must be weighed against potential anti-competitive effects, such as a limitation of access to the data or tying the use of data sets to sales. Cooperation between multiple companies, all providing and using data, should also be considered as to the potential effects of companies not participating. This may result in an obligation to provide access to the cooperation and/or data to third parties under objective, non-discriminatory and transparent conditions to mitigate the anti-competitive effects.[135]

The market for data, however, has some peculiarities as to the working of the market. Data cannot only be the object of a data pooling agreement but may also serve as a 'price' paid for the offering of a certain product or service. As data is important for many economic sectors, this impact will be felt broader. As a result, traditional economic theories on perfect competition, market definitions and obtaining the optimal price in a market, cannot apply.[136] Economic tests to define markets are dependent on models on (hypothetical) prices.[137] This results in a different way of assessing the traditional concept of markets.[138] The assumptions underlying the 1997 notice on the definition of relevant markets are considered not fully adequate for the definition of the relevant market in the digital economy[139] due to the lack of clarification on which type of metrics should be used for services provided at a zero monetary price, and data markets.[140]

---

[133] Custers and Bachlechner 2017.

[134] Commission Staff Working Document, Preliminary Report–Sector Inquiry into Consumer Internet of Things, SWD(2021) 144 final, 9 June 2021, para 8.4 listing data related concerns.

[135] This approach might be comparable to standardisation agreements or the cooperation by companies through trade associations, see Horizontal Guidelines, para 263–335.

[136] See Ferro 2019, pp. 261–263, Newman 2015.

[137] Like the test of a small but significant and non-transitory increase in price (SSNIP) to define markets. See on the definition of gratuitous markets, Ferro 2019, p. 264.

[138] See Hayashi et al. 2018, pp. 168–169, Newman 2015.

[139] Shaping Europe's digital future, 19 February 2020, COM(2020) 67 final, section B.

[140] See Evaluation of the notice in the Commission Staff Working Document, SWD(2021) 199 final, 12 July 2021, pp. 50, 55–56 on zero-monetary prices.

19.4.2 Position of Owners of Data

The unilateral use of data does not fall under Article 101 but may be considered abusive in the case of the use by dominant companies. Online platforms collect many data. Independent resellers use the platform to offer their products and services, and consumers using the platform generate data. The practices of online platforms may be assessed under Articles 101 and 102.[141] Given their immense data sets, the platforms may be considered as gatekeepers to other companies and end-users. A risk of 'tipping of the market' exists, which means that online platforms by gathering enormous amounts of data may become so large that the market is no longer contestable, with the effect that competitors can no longer compete or enter the market. Hence, an online platform may become dominant. Although Article 102 is meant to prevent abuses of a dominant position, the application of Article 102 is dependent on the substantiation of the market, the value of data and restrictions in the market.[142] Data can lead to dominance if the data is not available for other companies. Such dominance by having data may extend to adjacent markets (leveraging) and provide competitive advantages.[143] A platform owner using business data from independent sellers that use its platform may lead to a leverage of its dominance to competing markets.[144]

19.4.3 Evaluation

Cooperation on sharing or pooling data is assessed under Article 101 and is most likely to require a balancing act to assess the pro-competitive and anti-competitive effects. The framework is in principle adequate, although some guidance is needed to assess the effects of such agreements in markets.[145]

---

[141] See investigation of Amazon by the Commission in which the Commission focuses on the dual role and on whether and how the use of accumulated marketplace seller data by Amazon as a retailer affects competition, Antitrust: Commission opens investigation into possible anti-competitive Conduct of Amazon, IP/19/4291, 17 July 2019.

[142] Kupčík and Mikeš 2018 distinguish big data as barrier to entry, big data as input product and big data as a factor for assessing market power, pp. 368–369. Given the problems to identify relevant product markets in case of big data an investigation of how big data is used as input for creating and offering products and services may be required.

[143] See Crémer et al. 2019, p. 49.

[144] See Commission Press release Statement of Objections to Amazon for the use of non-public independent seller data, IP/20/2077, 10 November 2020 and Press release on opening of an investigation into possible anti-competitive conduct of Facebook by leveraging its position on social networks and online advertising to neighbouring markets, like online classified ads, IP/21/2848, 4 June 2021.

[145] See for example Crémer et al. 2019, pp. 92–98. They suggest that the Commission may need to contemplate the adoption of a block exemption, p. 98. This is also supported by the Commission in its communication on A European strategy for data, see footnote 29, para 5A. More guidance on forms of cooperation on data pooling, data sharing and data access agreements is suggested in

The immense amounts of data gathered and used by online platforms provide them with a high degree of market power, enabling them to set the rules of the platform and unilaterally impose conditions for access and use of data. They may also leverage this power in new markets.[146] Online platforms may act as regulators of interactions with an impact beyond "pure" market power.[147] Data access may not always be possible[148] and transparency may be lacking.[149] Fair competition mainly means transparency but also recognition of the different roles of platform owners.

The DMA-proposal provides for online gatekeeper platform regulation and rules for the use of data. The proposal contains a list of practices that limit contestability or are unfair. They include limitations on combining personal data and discriminatory practices towards business users.[150] Platforms must also refrain from using, in competition with business users, any data not publicly available, which is generated through activities by these business users (including by the end users of the business user).[151] They also need to provide for the portability of data.[152] The regulation is meant to fill in the enforcement gap for online gatekeeper platforms that may exist if Article 102 may not apply or if dominance cannot be proven.[153] The harmonisation regulation is not based on competition law although it includes obligations that are a lookalike of competition law principles for dominant companies. Competition law remains fully applicable, even when online gatekeeper platforms comply with the regulation.

In addition to this, the Commission proposed a New Competition Tool based on competition law to impose *ex ante* regulation in digital or other markets.[154] The tool could be a dominance-dominated tool or market-structure-based tool. A dominance-dominated tool addresses concerns arising from unilateral conduct by dominant companies without any prior finding of an infringement of Article 102. The market structure-based tool aims to identify and remedy structural competition problems that cannot be addressed (at all or effectively) under competition law. The tool may be applied to all sectors of the economy or only to certain digital or digitally enabled markets.[155] It might fill in the gap for online platforms and companies in digital markets owning or generating data that may not be considered gatekeepers

---

the consultation on the review of the Horizontal Guidelines, SWD(2021) 103 final, 6 May 2021, p. 115.

[146] See European strategy for data, para 4, see footnote 29.

[147] Crémer et al. 2019, p. 71.

[148] Schawe 2020, pp. 189–191.

[149] Crémer et al. 2019, pp. 71–72.

[150] Article 5(a) and 5(b) DMA-proposal.

[151] Article 6(a) DMA-proposal.

[152] Article 6(h) DMA-proposal.

[153] This is reflected in the articles on enforcement, Chapter V DMA-proposal.

[154] Inception Impact Assessment, New Competition Tool ('NCT'), https://ec.europa.eu/info/law/better-regulation/have-your-say/initiatives/12416-New-competition-tool (Accessed on 31 August 2021).

[155] Ibid. under B, options 1 up to 4.

under the DMA-proposal. The tool does not seem to require a market definition and dominance. Therefore, it is different from existing forms of *ex ante* regulation, like in telecommunications, based on regulating companies with market power in defined relevant markets.[156] At the moment it is not clear whether the tool will actually be introduced in addition to the DMA-proposal and, if so, which impact it could have on the competition law framework.

19.5 A Fair Market

Competition law has clear principles regarding conduct that may restrict competition in the market. The principles have been formulated in a negative way. Article 101 deals with (contractual) relations and contains some 'no go' areas regarding the hardcore restrictions. At the same time, a detailed framework has been developed to weigh the anti-competitive and pro-competitive effects of agreements as to whether they restrict competition in the market appreciably. Article 102 only applies to companies dominant in a market and contains clear principles on abusive conduct. Fairness in the context of these articles is linked to the prohibition of certain clear examples of unfair behaviour of joint conduct by competitors, a detailed framework to assess the effects of agreements in the markets and an additional set of unfair unilateral prohibitions for dominant companies. The system, however, has its limitations as has been set forth in Sect. 19.2.3. Applying the framework to the use of algorithms and data in competition law, as done in Sects. 19.3 and 19.4, leads to the following seven observations regarding how competition law contributes to the fairness principles.

First, unilateral alignment is considered fair. The assessment of the use of algorithms is linked to the restrictions in the market as a result of an agreement, decisions or 'concerted practice'. The unilateral use of algorithms may evade the application of Article 101 as this may not qualify as an agreement of 'concerted practice'. This means that the use of pricing algorithms is allowed, unless they are used to enforce certain behaviour in the context of existing relationships, like on distributors to follow recommended prices or in the context of an online marketplace or leading to a 'hub-and-spoke' alignment by using a third party (platform). Self-learning algorithms reacting to each other and adapting prices as a result of their interaction are not caught by Article 101. It has been considered fair that companies notice prices of other companies, giving them the possibility to decide on their pricing. Changing this principle would mean a fundamental change of the scope of Article 101 with a broad impact as to which alignment will be considered as inherent to competition and which alignment will be considered as 'concerted practice' and unfair.

Second, fairness means balancing. Cooperation as to the use of data may benefit from the balanced approach of Article 101. Weighing the pro-competitive effects

---

[156] See for a comparison of the *ex ante* regulation in telecommunications and the NCT proposal, Van Duijvenvoorde 2020.

and the anti-competitive effects is necessary to promote competition and innovation. It also provides room for an assessment of the value of data, although this may need an adaptation of the traditional way of assessing products and services and their substitutability. Examples of these balancing acts developed in the field of cooperation on standardisation and technology transfer may serve as a framework for assessing cooperation, like a data pool, and its impact on market competition. The enormous amount of data in the data economy might raise concerns, also as regards the non-economic effects. Although the balancing under Article 101 is limited to the economic effects, there is some room to take into account aspects as impact on technology and consumer interests in the assessment of the conditions of exemptions on the basis of Article 101(3).

Third, the position matters. If the user of algorithms is dominant in a market, restrictions apply to the unilateral use of pricing algorithms if they lead to abuses like imposing unfair prices or conditions. Also, companies using enormous amounts of data with the ability to act independently, must behave in a fair way and may not, for example, use the data to leverage their power to other markets.

The choice to apply Article 102 only to companies dominant in certain markets is deemed insufficient to ensure fairness, especially for companies operating online platforms and the considerable market position they may have, given the enormous amounts of data and users, even if they are not dominant. The definition of relevant markets and the substantiation of dominance in the relevant markets is considered problematic due to the two-sided character of platforms and changing market dynamics resulting from the role of data.

Harmonisation regulation like the P2B Regulation regulates platforms irrespective of the definition of markets and market power. A new dominance or online gatekeeper platform criterion dependent on concrete figures (like turnover and users) instead of a market-related assessment is proposed in the DMA proposal. The obligations imposed on online (gatekeeper) platforms sometimes mirror competition law principles, like the principle to refrain from applying unfair conditions and discrimination; sometimes, they reflect principles that go beyond the scope of competition law when focussing on the unfair behaviour of platforms towards businesses and end-users. This means that the position will matter even more in the future. Not only do the online platform gatekeepers need to consider the detailed framework to safeguard fair behaviour but they also need to be aware of competition rules even if they fulfil the obligations of the specific regulations. Recent case law in telecommunications law shows that the fact that a company has complied with sector-specific regulation, like the provision to provide access to its telecommunications networks, may influence the assessment of abuse of a dominant position by such a company.[157] Compliance by online gatekeepers with the specific regulations may lead to greater responsibility as regards compliance with Article 102. This means that the position of online platform

---

[157] See ECJ Case C-857/19 Slovak Telekom v. European Commission [2021] ECLI:EU:C:2021:139 and ECJ Case C-152/19 Deutsche Telekom AG [2021] ECLI:EU:C:2021:238, para 57 "it should be considered that a regulatory obligation can be relevant for the assessment of abusive conduct, for the purposes of Article 102 TFEU, on the part of a dominant undertaking that is subject to sectoral rules".

matters, not only as regards Article 102, which may always be applied in addition to the harmonisations regulations but also as regards the fact that regulations may be applicable and influence the assessment of Article 102.

Fourth, freedom to acquire market shares exists. Competition law does not prevent companies from growing and gaining market shares autonomously. This means that a company increasing its market share by generating data will not be monitored, implying that it will not be clear when the market tends to be no longer contestable and the company will become dominant. Monitoring will require regular market investigations. Such inquiries, like the E-commerce Sector Inquiry, are existing instruments the Commission may use on the basis of competition law to get insight into the dynamics of specific markets.[158]

Fifth, fair acquisition of control is monitored. Pursuant to the Merger Control Regulation, the Commission can monitor acquisitions by companies with a European dimension by prior assessment of the possibility of the transaction to impede competition. Each transaction meeting the European thresholds related to the turnover of the relevant companies needs to get prior approval. In the digital economy, the value of companies and services offered in markets is not only determined by turnover but also by the value of data; the value of a company may not be addressed sufficiently in the thresholds of the Merger Control Regulation. 'Killer acquisitions,' meaning acquisitions of smaller, innovative companies owning data, could fall outside the scope of the Merger Control Regulation. An evaluation of the Merger Control Regulation and the guidance for referrals might bring these transactions in the scope of an *ex ante* review.[159] By adding an obligation in the DMA-proposal to inform the Commission on mergers by gatekeepers in digital markets, an additional means might be introduced to investigate transactions by online gatekeeper platforms, even if they do not fall under the scope of the Merger Control Regulations, for example in case of acquisitions of start-ups having important data or algorithms.[160] As a result, an assessment of the fairness of an acquisition and the effect on the competition in the market will no longer depend on turnover data. This will enable the Commission to monitor disruptive acquisitions that can turn online platforms into gatekeepers. If necessary to prevent an impediment of competition, the Commission may block the transaction or impose remedies to safeguard competition.

Sixth, fairness is assessed *ex post*. The current or past behaviour is investigated with respect to its compliance with competition law. Although the block exemption regulations, guidelines, and case law guide a company regarding compliance, also in the future, the application of competition law itself is not forward-looking, taking into account possible restrictions in the near future. This is different from *ex ante* regulation, like in the telecommunications sector, which is based on market-based concepts in competition law and on a forward-looking assessment of markets with

---

[158] The DMA-proposal includes market investigation powers for the Commission to investigate the position of companies in view of the criteria for online gatekeeper platforms, Article 15.

[159] See footnote 24 on the review of the Merger Control Regulation and the publication of the Guidance on referring cases.

[160] See Article 12 DMA-proposal.

the power to impose *ex ante* obligations that are necessary and proportional to remedy potential restrictions in competition by a dominant company. Markets are continuously monitored and obligations are adapted to the competition in the markets. The P2B Regulation and the DMA-proposal deviate from this system. They refrain from considering the market definition and market position but focus on companies that carry out certain platform activities and fulfil the turnover and user criteria in the definition of online gatekeeper platforms.[161] They risk being less flexible to adjust to changes in the markets or technologies as is possible on the basis of *ex ante* market regulation.

Seventh, fairness is economic-oriented. Competition law regards economic activities and markets. Consequently, the position of online gatekeeper platforms as regulators of the content is only taken into account if this regards the economic behaviour. It may cover the commercial relations with advertisers but may not cover the content itself, like disinformation. Although possibilities exist and are explored to include non-economic factors, like data protection,[162] in the competition law assessment, the focus is still economical, and therefore, limits the scope of fairness that can be pursued by applying competition law. Regulation may consider the non-economic aspects of, for example, the behaviour of platforms or the transparency of algorithms and contribute this way to a broader approach of fairness. An increase in transparency might give insights into both the economic and non-economic aspects of the behaviour of platforms or the use of algorithms. As such, these insights might be used when investigating potential anti-competitive effects in markets under competition law.

Competition law may support the goal to create a fair and competitive economy by setting the boundaries for the behaviour of companies. The seven observations reflect on the fairness principles inherent to the system of competition law and its applications to digital markets, algorithms, and data. Both competition law and harmonisation regulation, like the P2B Regulation and the DMA proposal, may be instruments to contribute to fairness from different perspectives. Although harmonisation regulation leaves room for the application of competition law, it is unclear how they are aligned. This may lead to new questions as to whether the online gatekeepers can trust that they comply with competition law if they comply with the specific obligations in the harmonisation regulation and to what extent the existence of harmonisation regulation may influence the application of competition law. The fairness principles in harmonisation regulations leave it open to what would be a fair market under competition law. As harmonisation regulation has less flexibility of assessing the pro-competitive aspects regarding innovation than competition law, it could have risks for the development of digital markets and potentially for fairness in the long term.

---

[161] The New Competition Tool also seems to keep the market definition out of the analyses.

[162] See the German Court in the Facebook case, 23 June 2020, alleging that the infringement of data protection regulation in the GDPR by Facebook results in an abuse of a dominant position, https://www.bundeskartellamt.de/SharedDocs/Publikation/EN/Pressemitteilungen/2020/23_06_2020_BGH_Facebook.pdf?__blob=publicationFile&v=2 (Accessed on 31 August 2021).

19.6   Conclusion

Freedom and fairness in competition are mutually dependent. Competition and harmonisation may both contribute to a fair economy. They go hand-in-hand. The review of the fitness of competition law has led to a discussion on the effectiveness of applying the principles to digital markets and a revival of the concept of fairness. New harmonisation regulation has been enacted and proposed aiming to create fair digital markets. This results in a less market and competition-based approach for online platforms using algorithms and data.

Qualifying a fair market under competition law requires weighing the pro-competitive and anti-competitive effects on the markets. The value and impact of data and algorithms on market mechanisms and the dynamics of markets, competition, innovation, and consumer interests are all considered. The interactions between algorithms, the huge amount of available data, and the online platforms challenge competition law and the underlying principles. Although competition law applies in these situations, it has its limitations as a consequence of choices made in the system. This influences the way it addresses fairness. Principles may be identified as regards the use of algorithms and data as well as the position of online platforms.

A fair and competitive digital market requires the alignment of harmonisation proposals and competition law. Although the market-oriented fairness principles in competition law may be less clear and have limitations, the framework is equipped to assess digital markets, the use of AI and restraints in competition. Only if both competition law and harmonisation legislation are aligned and go hand-in-hand, may they contribute to fair markets providing opportunities for innovation and growth.

References

Bagnoli V (2019) Questions that Have Arisen since the EU Decision on the Whatsapp Acquisition by Facebook, Market and Competition Law Review / Volume iii / No. 1 / April 2019 pp. 15–51. Available at SSRN: https://ssrn.com/abstract=3576051.
Batchelor B, Janssens C (2020) Big data: understanding and analysing its competitive effects. E.C.L.R. 2020, 41(5), pp. 217–224.
Beneke F, Mackenrodt M-O (2018) Artificial Intelligence and Collusion. IIC (2018) 50: 109–134, DOI https://doi.org/10.1007/s40319-018-007773-x.
Calvano E, Calzolari G, Denicolò V, Pastorello S (2019) Algorithmic Pricing What Implications for Competition Policy? Review of Industrial Organization (2019) 55: 155–171.
Chauhan S (2019) Artificial Intelligence–a Competition Law Perspective. E.C.L.R. 2019, 40(3), 139–140.
Claassen R, Gerbrandy A (2016) Rethinking European competition law: From consumer welfare to capability approach. Utrecht Law Review, 12(1), 1–15.
Clutterbuck E (2020) Competition policy and the issue of fairness. E.C.L.R. 2020, 41(7), 323–326.
Crawford G S, Rey P, Schnitzer M (2020) An Economic Evaluation of the EC's Proposed "New Competition Tool", Luxembourg, Publications Office of the European Union, 2020, https://doi.org/10.2763/329087.

Crémer J, De Montjoye Y-A, Schweitzer H (2019) Competition policy for the digital area. Final Report. European Commission. Directorate-General for Competition. https://ec.europa.eu/com petition/publications/reports/kd0419345enn.pdf.

Custers B H M, Bachlechner D (2017) Advancing the EU Data Economy; Conditions for Realizing the Full Potential of Data Reuse. Information Polity, SSRN: https://ssrn.com/abstract=309 1038 or https://doi.org/10.2139/ssrn.3091038.

Csurgai-Horváth G (2020) An old concept for an old-new type of abuse of dominance in the digital sector: self-preferencing. E.C.L.R 2020, 41(2) 68–74.

Devine K L (2008) Preserving Competition in Multi-Sided Innovative Markets: How Do You Solve a Problem Like Google? North Carolina Journal of Law & Technology, Volume 10, Issue 1: Fall 2008, 59–118.

Evans D S, Schmalensee R (2014) The Antitrust Analysis of Multisided Platform Businesses. In: Blair RD, Sokol DD (eds) The Oxford Handbook of International Antitrust Economics, Volume 1, 2014, Chapter 18. DOI:https://doi.org/10.1093/oxfordhb/9780199859191.013.0018

Ezrachi A, Stucke M E (2017) Artificial Intelligence & Collusion: When Computers Inhibit Competition. University of Illinois Law Review, no. 5 (2017): 1775–1810.

Ferro M S (2019) Market Definition in EU Competition Law. Edward Elgar Publishing, Cheltenham, UK. doi: https://doi.org/10.4337/9781788118392.

Graef I, Clifford D, Valcke P (2018) Fairness and enforcement: bridging competition, data protection, and consumer law. International Data Privacy Law, 2018, Vol. 8, No. 3, 200–223. doi:https://doi.org/10.1093/idpl/ipy013.

Hayashi S, Arai K (2019) How Competition law Should React in the Age of Big Data and Artificial Intelligence. The Antitrust Bulletin 2019, Vol. 64(3) 447–456.

Hayashi S, Wu K, Tangsatapornpan B (2018) Competition policy and the development of big data and artificial intelligence. In: Nihoul P, Van Cleynenbreugel P (eds) The Roles of Innovation in Competition Law Analysis. Edward Elgar Publishing, Cheltenham, UK. doi: https://doi.org/10. 4337/9781788972444.00016, pp. 162–177.

Khan L M (2017) Amazon's Antitrust Paradox. The Yale Law Journal, 126:710–805.

Korah V (1990) An Introductory Guide to EEC Competition Law and Practice. ESC Publishing Limited, Oxford.

Kupčík J, Mikeš S (2018) Discussion on big data, online advertising and competition policy. E.C.L.R. 2018, 39(9), 393–402.

Lindsay A, McCarthy E (2017) Do we need to prevent pricing algorithms cooking up markets? E.C.L.R. 2017, 38(12), 533–537.

Lundqvist B (2019) Regulating competition in the digital economy. In: Lundqvist B, Gal M S (eds) Competition Law for the Digital Economy. Edward Elgar Publishing, Cheltenham, UK, pp 2–28. doi: https://doi.org/10.4337/9781788971836.00010.

Newman J M (2015) Antitrust in Zero-Price Markets: Foundations. University of Pennsylvania Law Review Vol. 164: pp. 149–206.

OECD (2017) Algorithms and Collusion–Background Note by the Secretariat. DAF/COMP (2017) 4.

Picht P G, Loderer G T (2018) Framing Algorithms–Competition law and (Other) Regulatory Tools. Max Planck Institute for Innovation and Competition Research Paper No 18–24.

Roman V D (2018) Digital markets and pricing algorithms-a dynamic approach towards horizontal competition. E.C.L.R. 2018, 39(1), 36–45.

Sonderegger G (2021) Algorithms and collusion. E.C.L.R. 2021, 42(4), 213–225.

Schawe N (2020) It's all about data: Time for a data access regime for the sharing economy? Information Polity Vol. 25 No 2, pp 177–195, DOI https://doi.org/10.3233/IP-190206.

Schmidt H K (2019) Taming the shrew: is there a need for a new market power definition for the digital economy? In: Lundqvist B, Gal M S (eds) Competition Law for the Digital Economy. Edward Elgar Publishing, Cheltenham, UK, pp 29–70. doi: https://doi.org/10.4337/978178897 1836.00010.

Van Duijvenvoorde G P (2018), Articles 101, 102 and 106-109 TFEU–Competition law in the IT and E-Commerce Sectors. In: Gijrath S et al (eds) Concise European Data Protection, E-Commerce and IT Law. Kluwer Law International B.V., The Netherlands, pp. 899–935.
Van Duijvenvoorde G P (2020) Towards Implementation of the European Union Telecom Code: Ex Ante Reflections. Computer and Telecommunications Law Review, 26(7), pp 205–215.
Verloren van Themaat W, Reuder B (2014) European Competition law. A Case Commentary, Edward Elgar, Cheltenham, UK/Northampton, MA, USA.
Vessozo S (2019) Competition by design. In: Lundqvist B, Gal M S (eds) Competition Law for the Digital Economy. Edward Elgar Publishing, Cheltenham, UK, pp 93–124. doi: https://doi.org/10.4337/9781788971836.00010.
Whish R, Bailey D (2018) Competition law, 9th edn. Oxford University Press, Oxford.

Prof. Dr G. P. (Gera) van Duijvenvoorde is a Professor by special appointment in Telecommunications Law at Leiden University, eLaw Center for Law and Digital Technologies, the Netherlands, g.p.van.duijvenvoorde@law.leidenuniv.nl. Gera combines her part-time appointment with a function as Competition Counsel and in-house attorney-at-law admitted to the Dutch Bar at KPN, a telecommunications company in Rotterdam. In 1996 she obtained her doctorate, her dissertation being "Information Technology and European Competition Law". In her academic research and education activities she focuses on aspects of regulation, markets and society. One of the specific themes is the interaction between sector regulation of telecommunications markets and competition law, both from a national and European perspective. Gera is a member of the editorial board of Mediaforum, Journal for Media and Communications Law, and a contributor to the Dutch Journal on European Law (Nederlands Tijdschrift voor Europees Recht), Section on Telecommunications Law. She is a member of the Board of the Dutch Association on Competition Law. This chapter is based on independent research and reflects the objective findings and personal opinions of the author.

Chapter 20
Personalised Shopping and Algorithmic Pricing: How EU Competition Law Can Protect Consumers in the Digital World

Rebecca Owens

Contents

Abstract Commercial transactions in the online world are increasingly dependent on machine learning algorithms. Independently, they automate transactions, reduce labour costs, and react to microscopic fluctuations within the marketplace. The use of personalised algorithms is fundamental to the online shopping experience which is increasingly tailored to the consumer. Whilst price discrimination already affects consumers through loyalty and status discounts, the use of advanced algorithms can enable e-commerce to precisely target consumers with personalised prices in a dynamic form that was not previously possible. This chapter critically examines this new phenomenon and applies the case law of *Art 102(c) TFEU* to determine if EU competition law can protect the end consumer from exploitative cases of personalised pricing. Through references to the normative values of welfare and fairness this chapter employs an economic perspective that assesses the efficiency of personalised prices. Concluding thoughts are offered as to whether competition law has the necessary flexibilities to deal with this new form of online price discrimination and protect end consumers.

Keywords algorithmic pricing · personalised pricing · competition law · *Article 102 TFEU* · welfare · fairness

R. Owens (✉)
School of Law and Social Justice, University of Liverpool, Liverpool, UK
e-mail: hsrowens@liverpool.ac.uk

© T.M.C. ASSER PRESS and the authors 2022
B. Custers and E. Fosch-Villaronga (eds.), *Law and Artificial Intelligence*,
Information Technology and Law Series 35,
https://doi.org/10.1007/978-94-6265-523-2_20

20.1 Background and Structure of the Chapter

The relationship between algorithmic pricing and consumer welfare has received increasing attention from academics and policy makers alike.[1] Concerns have been raised about the proliferation of 'big data' and its implications for user's privacy and digital competition as the information asymmetry caused by 'big data' can be used to distort competition and potentially harm consumer welfare.[2] Rather than relying on personal data such as gender, age and location, algorithms[3] can now utilise 'big data' and accumulate behavioural information such as browsing history or previous purchases to target consumers with personalised adverts and prices.[4] In many cases, such personalisation is beneficial to the consumer. Indeed, many of us are happy to trade our information for a better song choice or a more relevant movie suggestion. Yet, this digital trade may have a darker side for the consumer as advances in artificial intelligence now allow companies to predict and manipulate market demand.[5] Through an amalgamation of consumer information a detailed user's profile is compiled. This information informs algorithmic decisions on price through the determination of a consumer's willingness to pay. For instance, Uber's algorithm categorises users with a low smartphone battery as more likely to accept a surcharge.[6]

Whilst evidence for personalised pricing does exist,[7] researchers point out that the unethical nature of the practice means that many instances are hidden from public view.[8] Indeed, as algorithms continue to develop, there is an expectation amongst policy makers that personalised pricing may be the future of online shopping and there may be need for regulation.[9] With these preliminary considerations in mind, this chapter aims to critically examine personalised pricing through reference to normative values of welfare and fairness. Through these concepts the normative desirability of personalised pricing can be assessed and its application under EU competition law can be evaluated. This is an important study to undertake as the underenforcement of competition law in the online sphere has become a pervasive

---

[1] E.g., CMA 2018 and OECD 2018a. It is important to note that this attention has not always been positive. Yeoman 2016 states that "many in the public policy community are aligned with consumerist lobbies in being at least suspicious of (if not directly hostile to) personalised pricing".

[2] E.g., Robertson 2020; Zuiderveen Borgesius and Poort 2017; Townley et al. 2017 and Colangelo and Maggiolino 2017.

[3] At its most basic an algorithm is "a sequence of computational steps that transform the input into the output", Cormen et al. 2001, p. 5.

[4] Baker et al. 2001 states "just as it's easy for customers to compare prices on the Internet, so is it easy for companies to track customers' behaviour and adjust prices accordingly."

[5] This is primarily through the creation of Artificial Neural Networks.

[6] CMA 2021, para 2.17.

[7] In a study examining the adoption of algorithms on the Amazon Marketplace researchers found that over 500 sellers had adopted algorithmic pricing; see Le Chen et al. 2016.

[8] Steele et al. 2019.

[9] For instance, in the UK the CMA have issued consultations on algorithmic harm and have established a Digital Markets Unit to promote online competition: see CMA 2021.

problem.[10] As such, the growth of personalised pricing represents an opportunity to re-examine the scope of *Art 102(c)* considering new exploitative pricing practices.

The study outlined in this chapter begins by conceptualising online price discrimination in Sect. 20.2. Here, the rationale underpinning price discrimination is delineated, and the various forms of price discrimination found within economic literature are discussed. After that, Sects. 20.3 and 20.4 examine price discrimination in terms of the normative values of fairness and welfare respectively. The application of abuse of dominance provisions under *Article 102 TFEU* to algorithmic price discrimination is then discussed in Sect. 20.5, continuing with a targeted analysis of *Article 102(c) TFEU* in Sect. 20.6. The chapter is concluded in Sect. 20.7, acknowledging that whilst significant challenges remain in the application of *Article 102(c) TFEU*, competition law does have the necessary flexibilities to accommodate new forms of abusive practices such as algorithmic price discrimination.

Before beginning this study, it is important to note that economic theory regarding price discrimination draws a distinction between 'primary line' and 'secondary line' injury. This chapter situates its focus exclusively upon secondary line injury as it explores whether abuse of dominance provisions can be applied in situations where the price discrimination effects the end consumer. It contributes to the emerging scholarship around algorithmic personalised pricing by examining EU competition law to see if it can protect the end consumer from exploitative cases of personalised pricing.

20.2 Conceptualising Online Price Discrimination

In a competitive market, there is a predisposition for a producer to sell the same product or service at different prices.[11] This dispersion of prices gives companies an incentive to engage in price discrimination to obtain maximum profit based upon a consumer's willingness to pay.[12] The practice of price discrimination is not new, as loyalty, multibuy and status discounts are a commonly accepted feature of today's retail landscape. As such, there is a useful taxonomy of three conceptualisations of price discrimination that can be found within economic literature.[13]

Beginning with first-degree price discrimination, this occurs in a market when a company can perfectly discriminate between their customers and can price each

---

[10] Andrea Coscelli (2021) Ahead of the curve - Bannerman Competition Lecture. https://www.gov.uk/government/speeches/andrea-coscelli-ahead-of-the-curve-bannerman-competition-lecture Accessed 30 June 2021.

[11] The practice of price discrimination has been defined in Case C-209/10 *Post Danmark A/S v Konkurrencerådet* [2012] ECR I-172, as "charging different customers or different classes of customers different prices for goods or services whose costs are the same or, conversely, charging a single price to customers for whom supply costs differ", para 30.

[12] According to Odlyzko 2004 the motivation to profit through price-discrimination has been a central reason for the adoption of information practices that track consumers.

[13] Pigou 1920.

unit based upon the consumer's willingness to pay. True algorithmic personalised pricing would fall under this category as the retailer is able to personalise prices on an individual level. Given that historically it has often been very difficult for companies to precisely calculate an individual customer's willingness to pay, a more practical form of pricing discrimination that is often utilised is second degree price discrimination. This is characterised by a retailer having no information about a consumer's willingness to pay. Instead, retailers utilise strategies such as "product line pricing" or "market segmentation" to create a situation where they use their knowledge of consumer tastes to ensure the customer has a menu of prices for related products.[14] An example of this is airline tickets. When selling tickets an airline has no information to distinguish between budget and business travellers. To accommodate this, they offer a selection of seats, some with extra features that may appeal to business travellers, and other basic seats to appeal to budget travellers.[15] The final category is third-degree price discrimination. This is a demographic discrimination and involves selling products at different prices to different groups.[16] For instance, many retailers offer status related discounts accessible only to pensioners or students.[17] Alternatively, some retailers can increase prices based on whether you are a Mac or PC user. In 2012, travel website Orbitz was observed to increased prices for Mac users by up to 30%.[18]

Historically, literature has regarded first degree price discrimination as impossible.[19] As previously, the retailer had no way of gathering precise information on consumer's willingness to pay. However, increased capabilities within artificial intelligence and big data analytics have resulted in algorithms which can support retailers by determining a consumer's willingness to pay and personalising consumer prices to optimise output.[20] Indeed, a detailed consumer profile can shift price discrimination from the socially acceptable third-degree price discrimination to an imperfect form of first-degree price discrimination[21] in which algorithms can set a personal price for each user.

Whilst the technology is ready to be applied to online shopping, policy makers have acknowledged that the extent of the application of online personalised pricing remains largely unknown.[22] As early as the year 2000, shoppers were surprised to discover that Amazon had sold identical DVDs at different prices to different users. Following the scandal, Amazon apologised for the "random prices" and called it a

---

[14] Varian 1985.

[15] Graef 2018.

[16] Varian 1985.

[17] Jones et al. 2019, p. 313.

[18] Mattioli D (2012) The Wall Street Journal. On Orbitz, Mac Users Steered to Pricier Hotels. https://www.wsj.com/articles/SB10001424052702304458604577488822667325882 Accessed 30 June 2021.

[19] Geradin and Petit 2006.

[20] Ettl et al. 2019 and Miklós-Thal and Tucker 2019.

[21] Ezrachi and Stucke 2016.

[22] OECD 2018b, para 1.1.6.

"price test" swiftly refunding affected consumers.[23] The resulting public outcry and potential reputational impact might explain why the practice has not been openly adopted by companies.[24] However, given the advances in artificial intelligence and the ease and availability of accessing personal data online, many researchers and policy makers expect personalised prices to become more widespread in the future.[25]

20.3 Welfare Analysis of Personalised Pricing

To examine the suitability of competition law enforcement, a consideration of the welfare challenges posed by personalised pricing is a necessary starting point.[26] It is generally presumed that price discrimination is beneficial to societal welfare if economic output is increased.[27] In fact, classic economic models have determined that if first degree price discrimination is permitted and the retailer has complete information about a customer's willingness to pay, all consumer surplus is captured and an efficient outcome is reached.[28] However, as the retailer appropriates the entire trade, consumers are left with nothing as they are at their maximum willingness to pay. This can leave them unable to buy further products and can lead to different producers competing for a limited market.[29] As such, it becomes up to policy makers to decide which standard of welfare is more important to protect: either a total welfare standard where personalised pricing can help reach an efficient economic outcome, or a consumer welfare standard which can help protect the vulnerable from the effects of personalised pricing.[30]

When considering whether to intervene in cases of personalised pricing, competition authorities must consider that any welfare effects of personalised pricing are highly ambiguous and dependent on factors such as market structures, demand conditions and the trade-off between the market appropriation and the market expansion

---

[23] Townley et al. 2017.

[24] CMA 2021 argues that retailers may "employ other techniques to personalise prices that are harder for consumers to detect." Para 2.2.

[25] E.g., Botta and Wiedemann 2020; Townley et al. 2017; van der Rest et al. 2020.

[26] Consumer welfare is a key principle of Competition Law. Indeed, the General Court has held that "The ultimate purpose of the rules that seek to ensure that competition is not distorted in the internal market is to increase the wellbeing of consumers" Cases T-213/01 and T-214/01 *Österreichische Postsparkasse und Bank für Arbeit und Wirtschaft v. Commission* [2006] ECR II-1601, para 115. See also Case C-209/10, *Post Danmark A/S v. Konkurrencerådet,* [2012] E.C.R. I-172, 22-24.

[27] E.g., Varian 1985.

[28] For an example of this, see Rayna et al. 2015.

[29] Armstrong and Vickers 2001.

[30] Townley et al. 2017 states that "vulnerable groups of consumers who lack the digital literacy and sophistication required to search for the best deal and fail to switch providers in circumstances where it would otherwise be economically rational for them to do so, pay more. In some circumstances, the failure of consumers of this kind to shop around or switch providers may be misinterpreted by online suppliers as an indication of brand preference and willingness to pay, and so they may be charged higher prices than those offered to more informed, savvy consumers." See p. 31.

effect.[31] The market appropriation effect is the capture of consumer surplus through the utilisation of a consumer's maximum willingness to pay and this can have negative effects on consumer welfare. However, the market expansion effect allows the capture of consumers with a low willingness to pay through targeted pricing and can increase consumer welfare.[32] For example, a discriminatory price scheme can allow a monopolist to expand output and charge a lower price to consumers who would be excluded from the market with a uniform price. This could increase welfare distribution amongst consumers as it allows them access to products they would not have been able to afford.[33] Furthermore, in oligopolies price discrimination may be beneficial to consumer welfare as it could increase competition. In these situations, each company will try to attract customers by offering price cuts to consumers that it knows would not ordinarily purchase their products.[34]

The ambiguity as to the welfare effects of personalised pricing indicates that a total prohibition may be counterintuitive. Instead, a case-by-case analysis of the welfare effects and normative desirability of personalised pricing may be more appropriate. As such, the individual remedies available within competition law may provide policy makers with the opportunity to encourage the welfare enhancing aspects of personalised pricing.

20.4   Fairness Considerations of Personalised Pricing

The intervention of competition law may also be motivated by fairness considerations. Whilst the concept of fairness is contextualised within the framework of competition law[35] its application can often conflict with efficiency considerations since efficiency is concerned with total societal welfare and not the equability of a particular outcome.[36] Therefore, personalised pricing may be desirable on an economic level, but on a personal level such practices may seem unfair to the consumer. In such situations, the courts have added additional constraints to the application of competition law by considering the equity of the outcome[37] and whether the practices are in

---

[31] OECD 2018c, p. 5.

[32] Ibid.

[33] However, some academics argue that personalised prices can increase consumer's search costs and soften competition see, e.g., Ellison and Ellison 2009.

[34] Woodcock 2019.

[35] See Margrethe Vestager (2017) Address at the 10th Annual Global Antitrust Enforcement Symposium: Competition for a Fairer Society, https://wayback.archive-it.org/12090/201911292 10739/, https://ec.europa.eu/commission/commissioners/2014-2019/vestager/announcements/com petition-fairer-society_en accessed 30 June 2021, and Zimmer et al. 2007.

[36] Ducci and Trebilcock 2019.

[37] Competition Commission Report (2003) Vodafone, O2, Orange and T-Mobile: Reports on References under section 13 of the Telecommunications Act 1984 on the charges made by Vodafone, O2, Orange and T-Mobile for terminating calls from fixed and mobile networks, as cited in Akman 2012 at 260.

the public interest.[38] Unfortunately, this has led to situations in which the European Commission found that price discrimination which enabled consumers from low-income areas to be charged less is against the public interest even though uniform prices would leave them paying more.[39] However, much of the precedent is at a national level and concerns offline personalised pricing. Therefore, it is unclear what the European approach may be when it comes to algorithmic personalised pricing.

A starting point may be to assess how a personalised price is conceptualised by the consumer. Research has demonstrated that a consumer's fairness perception is a key factor in determining the fairness of personalised prices.[40] This can be shaped by the consumers perception of the seller's costs,[41] competitors prices[42] and the process utilized to set prices.[43] As such, academics argue that price discrimination can be perceived by consumers as fair if they can recognise a "substantive explanation" for the price difference or if the process regarding the calculation of prices is considered fair.[44] How a personalised price is 'framed' may also impact upon a consumer's perception of its fairness.[45] In situations where personalised pricing happens surreptitiously, and consumers realise that they are paying more than their peers then personalised pricing can be perceived as unfair. However, if the personalised prices are framed as an exclusive deal and prices offered to other customers are obfuscated then they are more likely to be perceived as fair and accepted by the consumer.[46]

The transient nature of the fairness related to personalised pricing means that it is difficult for policy makers to proactively legislate against the practice. For instance, if online personalised prices were to become normalised the unfairness aspect would be marginalised. However, as competition law has the flexibility to consider fairness then issues such as the transparency of personalised prices and the extensive customer data that is utilised within algorithmic personalised pricing may make it a useful policy tool to protect consumers. This can be demonstrated by the flexibilities offered by the courts when it assesses fairness considerations on an individual level in cases that focus on issues such as price discrimination.[47]

---

[38] Competition Commission Report (2000) Supermarkets: A Report on the supply of groceries from multiple stores in the United Kingdom, as cited in Akman 2012 at 260.

[39] Ibid.

[40] Elegido 2011.

[41] E.g., Bolton and Alba 2006 and Darke and Dahl 2003.

[42] Bolton and Alba 2006.

[43] Xia et al. 2004.

[44] Townley et al. 2017, see also Richards et al. 2016.

[45] E.g. Weisstein et al. 2013 and Priester et al. 2020.

[46] Zuiderveen Borgesius and Poort 2017.

[47] E.g., Case C-179/90 *Merci convenzionali porto di Genova SpA v Siderurgica Gabrielli SpA* [1991] ECR I5889 at 19.

20.5 Application of Abuse of Dominance Provisions to Personalised Pricing

To put it simply, *Article 102 TFEU* prohibits undertakings in a dominant position from pursuing abusive practices within a defined market.[48] The treaty provides a non-exhaustive list of examples of abusive practices[49] that distinguish between two types of abuses: (a) exclusionary abuses which refer to a dominant undertaking seeking to harm a competitor through excluding them from the market[50] and (b) exploitative abuses where a dominant undertaking's practice harms the final consumer.[51] The courts have stated that price discrimination is not in itself indicative of an exclusionary abuse and must be accompanied by other harmful practices.[52] As such, a more appropriate categorisation of algorithmic personalised pricing could be exploitative abuse due to its effects on the end customer. This is reflected in its status as a secondary line injury due to the distortion of downstream competition between consumers.[53] However, the extent of competition liability for a dominant undertaking that engages in exploitative abuses has yet to be settled by the courts. Furthermore, the treaty is unclear whether the abuse must harm competitors or end consumers.

From a historical perspective, an examination of the *travaux préparatoires* of the Rome Treaty indicates a desire for *Article 102* to prohibit only exploitative abuses that harmed the end consumer.[54] However, the European Commission has rarely investigated exploitative abuses such as price discrimination[55] due to possible overlaps with sector-regulation and consumer protection law. Instead, the courts in the case of *Continental Can*[56] expanded the scope of *Article 102* and allowed exploitative practices by a dominant undertaking to be considered abuse.[57] This policy shift can be seen in the Commission's *Guidance on Article 102 Enforcement Priorities* which

---

[48] It provides that "any abuse by one or more undertakings of a dominant position within the internal market or in any substantial part of it shall be prohibited as incompatible with the internal market in so far as it affects trade between member states."

[49] Case C-333/94 P, *Tetra Pak International SA v Commission of the European Communities*, [1996] ECR I-5951, OCL 170.

[50] Akman 2008.

[51] Ibid.

[52] Case C-209/10, *Post Danmark A/S v. Konkurrencerådet (Post Danmark I)*, [2012] ECLI:EU:C:2012:172 para 30.

[53] Graef 2018.

[54] Akman 2012 at 94. It should be noted that finding the drafters intention in the *travaux préparatoires* has been criticised as "unrealistic".

[55] According to the OECD, between 2000 and 2017 exploitative abuses represented 7% of the abuse of dominance cases enforced by the European Commission, see OECD 2018b at 27.

[56] Case 6-72 *Europemballage Corporation and Continental Can Company Inc. v Commission of the European Communities* [1973] ECR 1973–00215 In this way, Akman 2008 argues that the case is an example of the courts "making law' rather than interpreting law.

[57] Literature also identifies a shift to more economic based assessment of *Article 102* as a reason for the focus on exploitative abuse.

has limited itself to an effects-based discussion on exclusionary abuses between competitors which indirectly harm consumers.[58]

However, there is indirect precedent to apply competition law to cases of price discrimination between end consumers. For instance, in the *Football World Cup*[59] decision the Commission found that the French Football Association had abused its dominant position by discriminating against foreign supporters in imposing arbitrary and unfair conditions in relation to sale of tickets for the 1998 World Cup. A further illustration can also be found in the *Deutsche Post*[60] case. Here, the Commission stated that *Article 102* may also be applied in situations where a dominant undertaking's behaviour causes damage directly to consumers.[61] However, as these cases were Commission decisions it is unclear the extent to which the courts would find that *Article 102* can be applied to exploitative abuses to the end customer.

Whilst the courts have contended that cases of secondary line injury are rare[62] advances in technology mean that end consumers are at a greater risk of exploitative practices in today's digital economy. Yet, competition authorities have not remained stagnant and new forms of exploitative abuse continue to be sanctioned under *Article 102*. For instance, in the German *Facebook* case[63] the exploitation of consumers for personal information was found to be an abuse of dominance as consumers were forced to supply huge amounts of personal information to have an account. Therefore, it is not unlikely to assume that policy makers can adapt competition law's enforcement priorities to cover cases of exploitative abuses of end consumers due to algorithmic personalised pricing.

20.6   Price Discrimination under *Article 102(C) TFEU*

Arguably, the most appropriate provision to apply to personalised pricing is *Article 102(c)* which, when applied, prohibits a dominant undertaking from utilising "dissimilar conditions to equivalent transactions with other trading parties, thereby placing them at a competitive disadvantage." This indicates the applicability of the article in prohibiting secondary line injury and ensuring protection for the end consumers. As of now, no competition authority has issued proceedings in relation to algorithmic

---

[58] Guidance on the Commission's Enforcement Priorities in Applying Article 82 of the EC treaty to Abusive Exclusionary Conduct by Dominant Undertakings [2009] OJ C45/3 For a critical discussion of the Guidance, see Akman 2010 and Geradin 2010.

[59] Case IV/36.888-1998 *Football World Cup*, [2000] OJ L 5/55.

[60] COMP/C-1/36.915 *Deutsche Post AG—Interception of cross-border mail* [2001] OJ L 331/40.

[61] Para 133.

[62] Case C-525/16.MEO—Serviços de Comunicações e Multimédia SA v. Autoridade da Concorrência.[2018] ECLI:EU:C:2018:270.

[63] B6-22/16 available in English at https://www.bundeskartellamt.de/SharedDocs/Entscheidung/EN/Fallberichte/Missbrauchsaufsicht/2019/B6-22-16.pdf?__blob=publicationFile&v=3 Accessed 30 June 2021.

personalised pricing. Therefore, some assumptions need to be made for this theoretical application of competition law to proceed. The first concern is whether the accused company has a dominant position. To determine this, the courts must define the relevant market in which the company operates. However, as literature has already explored the various issues around defining online markets and outlined the barriers of entry in online markets,[64] this chapter will assume that the online retailer has a significant amount of market power and can be considered dominant under *Article 102* provisions.[65]

The next stage in the application of *Article 102(c)* is to determine if the company has entered equivalent transactions with other trading parties. The key factors to be considered when determining the constitution of an equivalent transaction were outlined by the courts in the case of *United Brands*.[66] The case concerned price discrimination of the supply of bananas between member states. It was held that the court should consider "differences in transport costs, taxation, customs duties, the wages of the labour force, the conditions of marketing, the differences in the parity of currencies, the density of competition"[67] when coming to their assessment. Whilst identical products such as bananas can be clearly considered as equivalent transactions, further clarification is needed to understand the extent to which this equivalence applies.[68] In terms of the digital economy, this requirement for equivalent transactions could pose a significant problem to the application of competition law to personalised pricing. For instance, if the product was tangible, such as a book from Amazon, then it would be relatively straightforward for competition authorities to determine an equivalent transaction. They could simply compare the discriminatory transaction to one concerning a different customer who ordered the same book at a similar time. The competition authority could consider additional and easily comparable factors, such as the costs of delivery when making their assessment. However, if the discrimination concerned personalised prices relating to a service such as an Uber taxi ride, then these factors become more difficult to assess as the service itself is tailored to the consumer's needs since no two rides are the same. As such, difficulties are created for competition authorities seeking to determine an equivalent transaction and apply the abuse of dominant provisions to personalised pricing.

The area of *Article 102(c)* that is the most problematic is that of 'competitive disadvantage.' Academics acknowledge that the case law regarding competitive disadvantage has been largely inconsistent and the subject of much revision by the courts.[69]

---

[64] E.g. Graef 2015 and Rubinfeld and Gal 2017.

[65] In cases of personalised pricing this assumption can be made as the service offered by the retailer becomes more personalised though consumer data and the associated effects may impact competition.

[66] Case 27/76 *United Brands Company and United Brands Continentaal BV v. Commission,* [1978] ECLI:EU:C:1978:22.

[67] Ibid. at 228.

[68] Townley et al. 2017.

[69] See Graef 2018 and Townley et al. 2017.

Traditionally, a presumption has existed that price discrimination is a distortion of competition and an abuse of dominance, as it places the customer who pays a higher price for the same product at a competitive disadvantage in comparison to other customers.[70] Research suggests that *Article 102(c)* only applies to unequal treatment between intermediate customers.[71] Therefore, this presumption of a competitive disadvantage is logical as more transactions occur before the product reaches the end consumer.

Case law regarding the competitive disadvantage continued to develop in the case of *British Airways*.[72] Here, the courts moved away from the presumption of a competitive advantage, stating that there must be a competitive disadvantage present but setting a low threshold for the Commission to prove such abuse.[73] However, the courts in *Clearsteam* added confusion when it was concluded that discriminating against a trading partner for a long period of time could "not fail" to result in a competitive disadvantage for the trading partner.[74] As such, this may give rise to the presumption that price discrimination is likely to result into a competitive disadvantage.[75] A possible explanation for the confusion regarding the term 'competitive disadvantage' may stem from the fact that *Article 102(c)* has been interpreted broadly by the courts to encompass a range of discriminatory pricing behaviour including geographical price discrimination. For instance, in the case of *United Brands,* member states were not competitors and as such no competitive disadvantage could be found.

Some clarification came in the case of *Meo*[76] where the notion of any presumption of a competitive advantage was overruled[77] and instead, the court confirmed that it was not necessary for the European Commission to estimate the competitive disadvantage experienced by the consumer.[78] The courts created a stricter effects-based approach that considered all relevant circumstances allowing the court to determine if a competitive disadvantage had occurred due to price discrimination. In many ways,

---

[70] Botta and Wiedemann 2020 This is reflected in the *Corsica Ferries* decision in which AG Van Gerven stated that the provision should be interpreted broadly, and it was unnecessary to demonstrate that the trading partners suffered a competitive disadvantage, see Opinion of Advocate General Van Gerven in Case C-18/93 *Corsica Ferries Italia Srl v. Corporazione dei Piloti del Porto di Genova*, [1994] ECLI:EU:C:1994 at 34.

[71] Ibid. at 538.

[72] Case C-95/04 P *British Airways plc v. Commission*, [2007] ECLI:EU:C:2007:166.

[73] The Commission only had to demonstrate that the price discrimination typically distorts competition, and it was not essential to prove that the price discrimination caused "an actual quantifiable deterioration in the competitive. position" of the consumer. See also Case C-52/07, *Kanal 5 Ltd and TV 4 AB v Föreningen Svenska Tonsättares Internationella Musikbyrå (STIM) upa*, [2008] ECLI:EU:C:2008:703.

[74] Case T-301/04, *Clearstream Banking AG and Clearstream International SA v. Commission*, [2009] ECLI:EU:T:2009:317 at 194.

[75] Graef 2018.

[76] Case C-525/16 *MEO v. Serviços de Comunicações Multimédia* SA ,[2008] ECLI:EU:C:2018:270.

[77] Indeed, Ag Wahl stated that the decision was out of date. Opinion of Advocate General Wahl in Case C-525/16, *MEO v. Serviços de Comunicações Multimédia* SA, [2008] ECLI:EU:C:2017:102.

[78] Ibid. at 27.

the court's decision was similar to the approach in the case of *Intel*[79] and clarified that its effects-based assessment was applicable to all forms of pricing abuses.

However, applying such a narrow effects-based approach to conduct such as personalised pricing presents several issues. The first issue is that it increases the burden of proof on a competition authority to sanction abuses of discriminatory personalised pricing.[80] The court has stated that a finding of a competitive disadvantage "does not require proof of actual quantifiable deterioration in the competitive situation, but must be based on an analysis of all the relevant circumstances of the case leading to the conclusion that that behaviour has an effect on the costs, profits or any other relevant interest of one or more of those partners, so that that conduct is such as to affect that situation".[81] This has increased the burden on competition authorities to consider the impact discriminatory prices have on competition and the disfavoured parties' costs and profits.[82] As such, it is harder to prove exploitative practices such as personalised pricing are an abuse of dominance as the competition authority must show repeated examples of this abusive conduct and analyse the dominant companies algorithm to determine whether it systematically discriminates between different categories of consumers in a pro or anti-competitive way.[83]

Unfortunately, the determination of repetitive behaviour places a huge evidential burden upon competition authorities as any assessment would have to consist of a dynamic analysis of the algorithm's code and the establishment of tangible criteria for determining equivalent transactions.[84] One emerging approach to assessing the algorithmic impact of systematically discriminating between consumers is the proposed New Competition Tool. This would allow competition authorities to identify structural risks within a market and impose behavioural or structural remedies on all companies within the sector. This could include limits on the collection of personal data or algorithmic transparency requirements that let users know that online platforms are utilising algorithmic personalised pricing. Yet, any assessment by competition authorities needs to be carefully measured against the pro- and the anti-competitive market effects of pricing algorithms to minimise impact upon the market.

The other key element of the *Meo* decision is the court's recognition that the application of *Article 102 (c)* "requires different prices or terms which 'tend to distort that competitive relationship, in other words, to hinder the competitive position of some of the *business partners* of that undertaking in relation to the others."[85] Whilst this may seem uncontroversial, it must be interpreted alongside the court's other statement that "the undertaking in a dominant position, in principle, has *no*

---

[79] See Case C-413/14 P. *Intel Corp. V. European Commission.* [2017] ECLI:EU:C:2017:632. para. 139–140 and *Meo* para 31.

[80] Botta and Wiedemann 2020 and *Meo* para. 37.

[81] Summary *Meo.*

[82] O'Donoghue 2018.

[83] Botta and Wiedemann 2020.

[84] Townley et al. 2017 at 726.

[85] *Meo* at 25, emphases added.

interest in excluding one of its trade partners from the downstream market."[86] Both these statements read in conjunction indirectly indicate that the primary purpose of *Article 102 (c)* is now the resolution of primary line discrimination. However, as this discussion of case law has demonstrated, the scope of *Article 102(c)* has varied considerably and whilst there are hurdles to the categorisation of personalised pricing as an abuse of dominance under *Article 102 (c),* its flexibility can incorporate this new form of price discrimination.

For completeness, it is important to note that if the courts found that personalised pricing cannot be categorised as an abuse under *Article 102 (c)* then it may still attract liability under the general prohibition of abuse of dominant position or under *Article 102(a)* which prohibits unfair prices. However, as *Article 102(c)* is the leading provision on abusive discriminatory pricing practice it necessitates this close examination of its case law when considering personalised pricing.

20.7 Conclusion

Advances in big data collection and artificial intelligence have the potential to enable personalised pricing to become more prevalent within today's digital economy. As such, the economic analysis provided in this chapter has illustrated the potential of personalised pricing algorithms to enable first degree price discrimination and the ambiguous welfare effects this may have. The case-by-case enforcement offered by competition law may allow personalised pricing to be considered on an individual basis. This would allow an in-depth consideration of welfare and fairness issues around personalised prices enabling competition authorities to make an informed decision around their enforcement.

However, significant challenges remain in the application of *Article 102(c) TFEU to* personalised pricing. A key issue is that it is unclear whether the abuse must harm competitors or the end consumers. Whilst this chapter has argued that the courts could utilise the flexibilities within competition law to apply to the end consumers in situations such as personalised pricing, it remains a policy issue that has yet to be clarified by the courts. More issues arise following the *Meo* judgement as the lack of tangible criteria for determining equivalent transactions makes it difficult for competition authorities to meet the increased burden of proof to sanction instances of personalised pricing. As such, further guidance is needed from the European Commission to establish a combined legal and technological approach which may facilitate a fairer and more efficient use of pricing algorithms potentially allowing policy considerations to be integrated within the algorithm. This could eventually negate the need for competition enforcement within the sector.

Following the analysis presented in this chapter, it is clear that through utilising instruments such as the proposed New Competition Tool, competition law is equipped with the necessary flexibilities to deal with this new form of price discrimination.

---

[86] *Meo* at 35.

However, the present discussion is limited to competition law. Given the unique nature of personalised pricing liability, concerns may arise in relation to data protection[87] and consumer protection law,[88] whereby the concept of fairness has been suggested as a mechanism to enhance collaboration between these areas.[89] As such, this cooperation can allow competition authorities to fill in the legislative gaps within artificial intelligence policies and ultimately ensure that consumers are protected from personalised prices.

References

Akman P (2008) Exploitative Abuse in Article 82EC: Back to Basics? CCP Working Paper 9:1–37.

Akman P (2009) Searching for the Long-Lost Soul of Article 82ec. Oxford Journal of Legal Studies 29:267–303.

Akman P (2010) The European Commission's Guidance on Article 102tfeu: From Inferno to Paradiso. The Modern Law Review 73:605–360.

Akman P (2012) The Concept of Abuse in EU Competition Law: Law and Economic Approaches. Bloomsbury Publishing, London.

Armstrong M, Vickers J (2001) Competitive Price Discrimination. The RAND Journal of Economics 32:579–605.

Baker W, Marn M, Zawada C (2001) Price Smarter on the Net. Harvard Business Review 79:122–127.

Bolton L, Alba J (2006) Price Fairness: Good and Service Differences and the Role of Vendor Costs. Journal of Consumer Research 33:258–265.

Botta M, Wiedemann K (2020) To Discriminate or Not to Discriminate? Personalised Pricing in Online Markets as Exploitative Abuse of Dominance. European Journal of Law and Economics 50:381–404.

Chen L, Mislove A, Wilson C (2016) An Empirical Analysis of Algorithmic Pricing on Amazon Marketplace. Proceedings of the 25th International Conference on World Wide Web 1339–1349.

CMA (2018) Pricing Algorithms, Economic Working Paper on the Use of Algorithms to Facilitate Collusion and Personalised Pricing. https://assets.publishing.service.gov.uk/government/uploads/system/uploads/attachment_data/file/746353/Algorithms_econ_report.pdf Accessed 30 June 2021.

CMA (2021) Consultation Outcome, Algorithms: How They Can Reduce Competition and Harm Consumers. https://www.gov.uk/government/publications/algorithms-how-they-can-reduce-competition-and-harm-consumers/algorithms-how-they-can-reduce-competition-and-harm-consumers: How they can reduce competition and harm consumers-GOV.UK (www.gov.uk) Accessed 30 June 2021.

Colangelo G, Maggiolino M (2017) Data Protection in Attention Markets: Protecting Privacy through Competition? Journal of European Competition Law & Practice 8:363–369.

Cormen TH, Leiserson CE, Riverst RL, Stein C (2001) Introduction to Algorithms. MIT Press, MA.

Darke PR, Dahl DW (2003) Fairness and Discounts: The Subjective Value of a Bargain. Journal of Consumer Psychology 13:328–338.

Ducci F, Trebilcock M (2019) The Revival of Fairness Discourse in Competition Policy. The Antitrust Bulletin 64:79–104.

Elegido J M (2011) The Ethics of Price Discrimination. Business Ethics Quarterly 21:633–660.

---

[87] Zuiderveen Borgesius and Poort 2017.

[88] Sartor 2020.

[89] Graef 2018.

Ellison G, Fisher Ellison S (2009) Search, Obfuscation, and Price Elasticities on the Internet. Econometrica 77:427–452.

Ettl M, Harsha P, Papush A, Perakis G (2019) A Data-Driven Approach to Personalized Bundle Pricing and Recommendation. Manufacturing & Service Operations Management 22:461–480.

Ezrachi A, Stucke ME (2016) The Rise of Behavioural Discrimination. European Competition Law Review 37:485–492.

Geradin DAAG (2010) Is the guidance paper on the commission's enforcement priorities in applying article 102 TFEU to abusive exclusionary conduct useful? In Etro F, Kokkoris I (eds) Competition law and the enforcement of article 102. OUP, Oxford

Geradin D, Petit N (2006) Price Discrimination under EC Competition Law: Another Antitrust Doctrine in Search of Limiting Principles? Journal of Competition Law & Economics 2:479–531.

Graef I (2015) Market Definition and Market Power in Data: The Case of Online Platforms. World Competition 38:473–505.

Graef I (2018) Algorithms and Fairness: What Role for Competition Law in Targeting Price Discrimination Towards Ends Consumers. Columbia Journal of European Law 24:541–559.

Graef I, Clifford D, Valcke P (2018) Fairness and Enforcement: Bridging Competition, Data Protection, and Consumer Law. International Data Privacy Law 8:200–223.

Jones A, Dunne N, Sufrin BE (2019) Jones & Sufrin's EU Competition Law: Text, Cases, and Materials. OUP, Oxford.

Miklós-Thal J, Tucker C (2019) Collusion by Algorithm: Does Better Demand Prediction Facilitate Coordination between Sellers? Management Science 65:1552–1561.

O'Donoghue R (2018) The Quiet Death of Secondary-Line Discrimination as an Abuse of Dominance: Case C-525/16 Meo. Journal of European Competition Law & Practice 9:443–445.

Odlyzko A (2004) Privacy, Economics, and Price Discrimination on the Internet. In: Camp LJ et al (eds) Economics of Information Security. Springer US, pp. 187–211.

OECD (2018a) Algorithms and Collusion: Competition Policy in the Digital Age. https://www.oecd.org/daf/competition/Algorithms-and-colllusion-competition-policy-in-the-digital-age.pdf Accessed 30 June 2021.

OECD (2018b) Personalised Pricing in a Digital Era. https://www.oecd.org/competition/personalised-pricing-in-the-digital-era.htm Accessed 30 June 2021.

OECD (2018c) The Regulation of Personalised Pricing in the Digital Era - Note by Marc Bourreau and Alexandre De Streel. https://www.oecd.org/officialdocuments/publicdisplaydocumentpdf/?cote=DAF/COMP/WD(2018)150&docLanguage=En Accessed 30 June 2021.

Pigou AC (1920) The Economics of Welfare. Macmillan, London.

Priester A, Robbert T, Roth S (2020) A special price just for you: effects of personalized dynamic pricing on consumer fairness perceptions. Journal of Revenue and Pricing Management 19:99–112.

Rayna T, Darlington J, Striukova L (2015) Pricing Music Using Personal Data: Mutually Advantageous First-Degree Price Discrimination. Electronic Markets 25:139–154.

Richards TJ, Liaukonyte J, Streletskaya NA (2016) Personalized Pricing and Price Fairness. International Journal of Industrial Organization 44:138–153.

Robertson VHSE (2020) Excessive Data Collection: Privacy Considerations and Abuse of Dominance in the Era of Big Data. Common Market Law Review 57:161–190.

Rubinfeld DL, Gal MS (2017) Access Barriers to Big Data. Ariz. L. Rev 59:339–381.

Sartor G (2020) New Aspects and Challenges in Consumer Protection: Digital Services and Artificial Intelligence. https://www.europarl.europa.eu/RegData/etudes/STUD/2020/648790/IPOL_STU(2020)648790_EN.pdf Accessed 30 June 2021.

Seele P, Dierksmeier C, Hofstetter R, Schultz MD (2019) Mapping the Ethicality of Algorithmic Pricing: A Review of Dynamic and Personalized Pricing. Journal of Business Ethics 170:697–719.

Townley C, Morrison E, Yeung K (2017) Big Data and Personalized Price Discrimination in EU Competition Law. Yearbook of European Law 36:683–748.

van der Rest JPI, Sears AM, Miao L, Wang L (2020) A Note on the Future of Personalized Pricing: Cause for Concern. Journal of Revenue and Pricing Management 19:113–118.

Varian HR (1985) Price Discrimination and Social Welfare. The American Economic Review 75:870–875.

Weisstein FL, Monroe KB, Kukar-Kinney M (2013) Effects of Price Framing on Consumers' Perceptions of Online Dynamic Pricing Practices. Journal of the Academy of Marketing Science 41501–514.

Woodcock RA (2019) Personalized Pricing as Monopolization. Connecticut Law Review 51:311–373.

Xia L, Monroe KB, Cox JL (2004) The Price Is Unfair! A Conceptual Framework of Price Fairness Perceptions. Journal of Marketing 68:1–15.

Yeoman I (2016) Personalised Price. Journal of Revenue and Pricing Management 15:1–1.

Zimmer D (2007) On Fairness and Welfare: The Objectives of Competition Policy Comment on David J. Gerber, Christian Ahlborn and A. Jorge Padilla. In: Ehlermann CD et al (eds) European Competition Law Annual 2007–A Reformed Approach to Article 82 EC. Hart Publishing, Oxford, pp. 103–107.

Zuiderveen Borgesius F, Poort J (2017) Online Price Discrimination and EU Data Privacy Law. Journal of Consumer Policy 40:347–366.

Rebecca Owens is a Ph.D. candidate in law at the University of Liverpool. Her interdisciplinary research explores the interaction of law with pioneering technology such as Artificial Intelligence and CRISPR focusing on aspects of Intellectual Property and Competition Law. She holds an LLM degree (Distinction) and an LLB (Hons) degree from the University of Liverpool. Her exceptional research has been recognised by the University of Liverpool as she has been awarded both the John Lennon Memorial Scholarship for her master's project and the Sir Joseph Rotblat Alumni Scholarship for her Ph.D. research.

Part IV
Legal Practice

Chapter 21
Lawyers' Perceptions on the Use of AI

Stuart Weinstein

Contents

Abstract This chapter examines lawyers' perceptions on the use of artificial intelligence (AI) in their legal work. A meta-synthesis of published large-scale surveys of the legal profession completed in 2019 and 2020 in several leading jurisdictions, e.g., the UK, US, and EU, reveals some dissonance between hype and reality. While some lawyers see the potential contribution that AI and machine-learning (ML) driven legal tech innovation can make to transform aspects of legal practice, others have little awareness of the existence of the same. While there appears to be first mover advantage for some legal practitioners to incorporate innovative AI and ML based legal tech tools into their developing business model, there are few metrics that exist that can help legal teams evaluate whether such legal tech tools provide a sustainable competitive advantage to their legal work. A non-representative expert sampling of UK-based non-lawyer legal tech professionals whose work focuses on the utilisation of AI and ML based legal tech tools in different legal practice environments confirms the findings derived from the meta-synthesis. This expert sampling was

S. Weinstein (✉)
Aston Law School, College of Business and Social Science, Aston University, Birmingham B4 7ET, United Kingdom
e-mail: s.weinstein@aston.ac.uk

© T.M.C. ASSER PRESS and the authors 2022
B. Custers and E. Fosch-Villaronga (eds.), *Law and Artificial Intelligence*,
Information Technology and Law Series 35,
https://doi.org/10.1007/978-94-6265-523-2_21

413

also evaluated against published peer-reviewed research featuring semi-structured interviews of UK lawyer and non-lawyer legal tech professionals on the challenges and opportunities presented by AI and ML for the legal profession. Further research in the form of undertaking a qualitative survey of non-lawyer legal tech professionals with follow-on semi-structured interviews is proposed.

Keywords Artificial Intelligence · Legal Tech · Machine Learning · Meta-synthesis · Sustainable Competitive Advantage · Expert Sampling

21.1 Introduction

This chapter examines lawyers' perceptions on the use of artificial intelligence (AI) in their legal work. Some lawyers see the potential contribution that AI and machine-learning (ML) driven legal tech innovation can make to transform aspects of legal practice, but others have little awareness of the existence of any of this. While general media articles appear apace with lurid headlines such as 'Will AI Replace Lawyers?',[1] '23-year-old British entrepreneur's 'robot lawyer' raises $12m from top Silicon Valley investors'[2] and 'The Robot Lawyers are here–and they're winning',[3] some legal scholars have been warning for some time that the technological acceleration in computational power "makes it the single most important phenomenon with which the legal profession will need to grapple in the coming decades."[4] A more nuanced view from academia is that "at the risk of oversimplifying....much of the current debate regarding legal technologies [is seen] as existing at the extremes."[5]

The research questions this chapter explores are the following:

- What is the awareness of lawyers of AI and machine learning (ML) based legal tech tools available to them?
- Do lawyers see new practice opportunities with AI and ML based legal tech tools that did not exist before?
- How can lawyers judge the effectiveness of these new tools when they may not fully understand how they work?
- Do lawyers believe that using these AI and ML based legal tech tools in legal practice can create competitive advantages that over time might become sustainable?

This chapter attempts to generate theory from data systematically obtained by quantitative survey evidence of the perceptions of lawyers on the usefulness of AI in

[1] Watkins and Mew 2019.
[2] Rudgard 2020.
[3] Cellan-Jones 2017.
[4] McGinnis and Pearce 2014, p. 3042.
[5] Remus and Levy 2017, p. 556

their own present legal work. It creates three results: (a) first, it frames an on-going tension point or challenge regarding the use of AI in current legal practice, (b) second, it highlights a few unifying themes that weave through the different surveys and the commentaries they have generated, and (c) it proposes follow-on work from theoretical research to practise-informed research by undertaking qualitative survey work with non-lawyer legal tech professionals to gain their perspectives on these findings.[6]

The research questions are answered on the basis of a meta-synthesis of published large-scale surveys of the legal profession completed in 2019 and 2020 in several leading jurisdictions, e.g., the UK, US, and EU, which reveals a striking polarity between hype and reality. Even if sustainable leadership in legal tech can create a first mover advantage[7] for some innovators, there are few metrics developed that can assist to evaluate whether the use of such AI and ML based legal tech tools can bring a lasting sustainable competitive advantage[8] to the legal teams that use them. The findings from the meta-synthesis were tested against a non-representative expert sampling of UK-based non-lawyer legal tech professionals whose work involves using AI and ML based legal tech tools in different legal practice environments. This expert sampling was also evaluated against published peer-reviewed research featuring semi-structured interviews of UK (lawyer and non-lawyer) legal tech professionals on the challenges and opportunities presented by AI and ML for the legal profession.

This chapter is structured as follows. Section 21.2 explores the relevant substantive literature that defines the critical concepts that form the scope of this enquiry. Section 21.3 sets out the meta-synthesis analysis detailing the key findings made. Section 21.4 makes use of a non-representative expert sampling to confirm the findings derived from the meta-synthesis. Section 21.5 draws conclusions and makes suggestions for further questions to be considered.

21.2   Review of the Substantive Literature

In this section, a review of selected elements of the substantive literature relevant to this inquiry is made. Section 21.2.1 explores the definition of legal tech, AI and ML. After this discussion, Sect. 21.2.2 examines the concept of achieving a sustainable competitive advantage which is seen as the driving force behind legal teams adapting legal tech which makes use of AI and/or ML elements.

---

[6] See Tannenbaum et al. 2012, p. 56, for guidance on defining research outputs.

[7] Lieberman and Montgomery 1988, pp. 41–42.

[8] Coyne 1986, p. 54.

21.2.1 Defining Legal Tech, AI and ML

The Stanford Law School CodeX Techindex hosts a curated list of 1742 legal tech (short for "legal technology") companies "changing the way legal is done".[9] Legal tech means digital systems that have been specifically designed to help lawyers carry out legal work, but it has developed in recent years to include applications that perform legal tasks, such as contract creation, negotiation, review and analysis.[10] Any discussion of legal tech must start with an acknowledgment that it has become 'all too common to use' ML and AI as catch-all phrases for an ever-changing family of things.[11] For starters, AI systems are software (and possibly also hardware) systems designed by humans that, given a complex goal, act in the physical or digital dimension by perceiving their environment through data acquisition, interpreting the collected structured or unstructured data, reasoning on the knowledge, or processing the information, derived from this data and deciding the best action(s) to take to achieve the given goal.[12]

A 2018 qualitative study of UK legal firms at different stages in their technology adoption journey involving a total of 15 in-depth semi-structured interviews with participants selected by purposive sampling (2018 UK Interviews) has shown that there is 'fuzziness' around what represents AI in the legal tech sphere.[13] One must differentiate between automation, which underpins the majority of new legal technologies and which in the view of participants in the 2018 UK Interviews should not be labelled as AI, and 'true AI' involving largely ML, natural-language processing (NLP), and vast amounts of data to perform more advanced 'cognitive' functions such as interpretation.[14] While AI may be able to automate a legal task where there is some underlying structure or pattern that it can harness, those lawyering tasks that involve abstract thinking, problem-solving, advocacy, counselling of clients, human emotional intelligence, policy analysis or 'big picture' strategy which cannot be so easily automated are not within the reach of available AI technology today.[15]

ML refers to an automated process of discovering correlations (sometimes alternatively referred to as relationships or patterns) between variables in a dataset, often to make predictions or estimates of some outcome.[16] NLP enables computers to effectively communicate in the same language as their users, advancing the ability of the machines to understand written and spoken human language and more closely approximate human cognitive patterns. ML can be applied to 'a plethora of legal

---

[9] Stanford Law School, CodeX Techindex.

[10] Practical Law UK Practice Note 2021.

[11] Lehr and Ohm 2017, p. 669.

[12] AI HLEG 2019, p. 8.

[13] Brooks et al. 2019, p. 142.

[14] Brooks et al. 2019, p. 142.

[15] Surden 2019, p. 1332

[16] Murphy 2012, p. 1.

services' including e-disclosure, predictive forensics, assessment of evidence, case law analysis, argumentation mining, analysis of applicable law and quantitative legal prediction.[17] These ML techniques perform NLP by seeking to develop statistically accurate relationships between an input (documents that are potentially relevant for evidence, case law, legal briefs or memos, doctrinal text, legislation and other types of regulation) and a desired output (relevant documents, relevant lines of argument, precedent, doctrine, applicable legislation or regulation).[18] A simplified example of ML in use in legal practice is document review where ML can be used to identify "like for like" documents alongside deviating documents derived from a standard setting original batch of documents identified in advance of the search. The very same search can also use ML to pull up equally useful "wild card" documents based on previously unknown anomalies or variables that were not envisioned before the ML search was done.

21.2.2   Sustainable Competitive Advantage

Competitive advantage exists when a firm creates value for its buyers that exceeds the firm's cost of creating it; superior value stems from offering lower prices than competitors for equivalent benefits or providing unique benefits that more than offset a higher price.[19] The competitive advantage must also be sustainable so that rivals are unable to adopt the same strategy.[20] In a world where law touches every aspect of business operations and decision making, high quality legal resources such as AI and ML based legal tech tools when employed appropriately can help a legal team seize competitive advantage.[21]

Competitive advantage will be found working in the six areas where AI is currently used in the legal arena,[22] namely, (1) e-discovery (software that allows for large scale review of documents to be surveyed and identified through defined search criteria reducing the time necessary for human eyes to do the same, e.g., Disco or Everlaw); (2) expertise automation (allows users to create intelligent web-based applications that replicate the advice a subject matter expert would provide, e.g., Neota); (3) legal research (legal publishing companies offer software packages that enable lawyers to do online research with greater and speed than ever before, e.g., LexisNexis, Westlaw, etc.); (4) document management (law firms and legal departments make use of document management software to manage paperwork and create e-files to store internally

---

[17] Hildebrandt 2018, p. 27.
[18] Hildebrandt 2018, p. 27.
[19] Porter 1985, p. 3.
[20] Porter 1985, p. 11.
[21] Siedel and Haapio 2010, p. 643.
[22] Davis 2020 (Introduction).

and share externally, e.g., Clio); (5) contract and litigation document analytics and generation (these tools review contracts and other case materials extracting information, identifying problematic clauses and assisting in contract review and due diligence, e.g., Kira, Leverton or Luminance); and (6) predictive analytics (this is software that examines the case record of judges, opposing counsel and parties to predict litigation behaviour for strategic purposes, e.g., LexMachina).

Moving beyond simple competitive advantage to achieving truly sustainable competitive advantage will come from reinventing processes and procedures, externally, through the development of and delivery of complex AI solutions to clients' problems and, internally, in transforming the composition, structure, and economics of legal teams when these new AI-driven tools become pervasive in the delivery of legal services.[23] While some organisations may invest in AI and ML based legal tech tools to gain a first-mover status, first-mover status, in and of itself, may or may not produce a sustainable competitive advantage because of a multiplicity of controllable and uncontrollable forces.[24] One such factor is the ability of an organisation to attract and retain lawyers of an entrepreneurial mindset who can recognise and take advantage of opportunities in the law created by information inadequacies, inefficient allocation of resources, uneven technological capacity across the sector and a lack of transparent pricing structures.[25]

One of the problems with evaluating the value of legal tech is that the legal services industry lacks standard metrics to evaluate data and any applications developed with it. For instance, one of the surveys studied in this chapter reveals that only 7% of respondents have formal legal tech metrics in place in their organisation and that 21% report that they have not even informal methods of measuring the value of their legal tech either.[26] The importance of "the extraction of objective, measurable characteristics of legal work that helps facilitate automation, quality control, and continued improvement of the field" cannot be underestimated.[27] Future research from a technological viewpoint needs to be directed toward developing such metrics and then validating it through appropriate case studies.[28]

21.3   Meta-Synthesis Analysis

The goal of this section is to explain the variables considered in completing the systemic review of the various large-scale surveys of the legal profession's attitude towards the use of AI. Section 21.3.1 details the meta-synthesis undertaken and the interpretative research. Section 21.3.2 explains the criteria used to search

---

[23] Davis 2020 (Introduction).

[24] Kerin et al. 1992, p. 33.

[25] Evans and Gabel 2014, p. 406.

[26] Palmer 2020; Survey 4.

[27] Dolin 2017, p. 1.

[28] Ganguly et al. 2010, p. 43.

for relevant surveys. Section 21.3.3 evaluates the quality of the surveys examined. Section 21.3.4 delineates the analysis made and integrates the survey outcomes obtained. Section 21.3.5 relates the findings from the meta-synthesis.

21.3.1 Meta-Synthesis and Interpretative Research

A meta-synthesis is an exploratory, inductive research designed to synthesise primary qualitative case studies for the purpose of making contributions beyond those achieved in the original studies.[29] Meta-synthesis occurs at the level at which the original researchers of the primary studies have constructed their insights in accordance with their own understanding and interpretation of the data and seeks to empirically consolidate primary studies to build refined, extended or even new theory.[30] Going beyond the findings of any one individual study to make the whole into something 'more than the parts alone imply' is at the heart of meta-synthesis.[31]

Interpretive research describes how different meanings held by different persons or groups produce and sustain a sense of truth, particularly in the face of competing definitions of reality.[32] Here we examine the views held by lawyers on the use of AI and ML based legal tech tools in their day-to-day practice gleaned from several jurisdiction-wide surveys incorporating different methodologies taken in 2019 and 2020 and draw universal values from such survey results. The goal is to uncover unknown linkages or dynamics across the survey results that cannot be obtained from a review of just one or two of the surveys involved to reveal unknown phenomena of a qualitative nature. When meta-synthesising qualitative surveys using different techniques and studying different groups attention must be paid to both analysing evidence across surveys to build theory as well as to ensuring sensitivity toward the contextual considerations of the primary surveys;[33] as such, a rigorous research design approach is needed "to avoid nonreconcilable islands of knowledge that do not contribute significantly to our full understanding of a phenomenon of interest".[34]

Working with the research questions defined in Sect. 21.1, the inclusion criteria is drawn to include recent professionally-formulated surveys employing a variety of techniques ranging from online questionnaires, structured phone interviews and face-to-face focus groups. A clear preference is for surveys that record the views of a large cohort of participants, e.g., more than 300 individuals at a minimum, across one or more jurisdictions and soliciting responses from lawyers in a variety of professional settings, e.g., in-house, law firms and multi-disciplinary practice groups. All surveys used are evaluated for hallmarks of quality on two fronts: first, in how the

[29] Hoon 2013, p. 527.
[30] Hoon 2013, p. 527.
[31] Noblit and Hare 1988, p. 28.
[32] Gerhart 2004, p. 457.
[33] Hoon 2013, p. 528.
[34] Hoon 2013, p. 523.

survey was conducted and, second, in how the results were reported. Transparency of reporting results is as critical as survey methodology in evaluating the usefulness of a particular survey. Once the kernels from these surveys can be extracted and compared side-by-side, unifying themes emerge which constitute the synthesis offered here.

Our ontological approach[35] involves uncovering causal linkages and interpreting related strands to explain phenomena as existing in the legal tech sector and its use by legal practitioners. The epistemological approach[36] is designed to build a new theory from interpreting knowledge across different surveys to find a few unifying themes across the different jurisdictions. If the ontological and epistemological approaches suggest that further inquiry is needed into the personal experiences of lawyers with legal tech, a narrative approach directed at obtaining data through semi-structured interviews may be warranted. The research approach to be followed is post-positivist: it is broad rather than specialised. Moreover, we should not ignore the motivations that shape the research enquiry or fail to acknowledge that the end result produced here must be seen as more significant than whether the research we have undertaken demonstrated appropriate techniques of collecting and categorising information.[37]

21.3.2 Searching for Relevant Surveys

Figure 21.1 sets forth the proposed large-scale surveys examined for purposes of this meta-synthesis. In excluding surveys published before 1 January 2019, the decision was made to ensure that the views examined were current.[38] Surveys published after 1 March 2021 were not included in the meta-analysis. Equally important is who had commissioned the survey. Either it had to be a leading representative body of the legal profession as in Surveys 1 and 8 below or a leading multinational provider of legal research solutions for the profession as in all the other surveys listed. While admittedly surveys in this latter category may have a self-serving element to them, it became evident upon closer examination that these recurring annual surveys are done in a meticulous and dispassionate manner so as to manifest themselves as critical to review to ensure a (mostly) exhaustive list of relevant surveys to consider.

Except for Survey 1 where survey data remained behind a "paywall" and could not be examined, each of the remaining Surveys 2 to 10 offered a sound critical analysis of their respective results which was helpful for the meta-synthesis exercise. Surveys 2, 3, and 4 (Bloomberg Law) were introduced with journalistic analysis offered by Bloomberg Law's own data analysis team that gave insights across the three different

---

[35] Ontology is the study of the nature and properties of reality, see Epstein 2018.

[36] Epistemology is a study of how people or systems of people know things and how they think they know things, see Ryan 2006, p. 15.

[37] Ryan 2006, pp. 12–13.

[38] Such a randomised "cut-off" date might raise methodological issues in a quantitative meta-analysis; however, "qualitative research is characterised by flexibility, openness and responsivity to context, the steps of data collection and analysis are not as separate and consecutive as they tend to be in quantitative research." Busetto et al. 2020, p. 2.

Survey	Author	Name of Survey	Published Date	Survey Dates	Number of Survey Participants
1	American Bar Ass'n (ABA)	2020 Legal Technology Survey Report	6 October 2020	Unknown	Survey of over 50,000 US lawyers regarding the technology and software utilised and available in their firms.
2	Bloomberg Law	Legal Ops & Technology	14 May 2019	April 2019	Features responses from nearly 500 US law practitioners representing a mix of law firms and corporate legal departments across the US
3	Bloomberg Law	Legal Operations Survey	6 March 2020	Online survey done during 1st quarter of 2020.	Bloomberg Law surveyed nearly 600 US legal and operations professionals (98 in-house and 490 law firms). Wide range of organisations surveyed in terms of size, revenue, number of employees and a good spread between in-house and law firms.
4	Bloomberg Law	Legal Technology Survey 2020	27 August 2020	July 2020	Bloomberg Law surveyed 331 US practicing lawyers (in house and law firms) about legal tech – including the use, adoption, and procurement of legal tech at their organization, as well as their thoughts on efficiencies, ethics, and spend.
5	Lexis Nexis	2020 Legal Analytics Study Bringing Value Into Focus	4 February 2020	December 2019	The study gathers insights from 163 large US law firm (50 or more attorneys) professionals parsed into two major categories: those whose firms offer/utilise legal analytics and those who do not.
6	Thomson Reuters Institute	Legal Department Operations Index, Fifth Edition	December 2020	June 2020	The report analyses the survey responses of more than 200 legal departments—more than 80 of which are in the Fortune 1000. This study incorporates responses gathered from more than 2,000 telephone interviews, each lasting approximately 30 minutes, including more than 600 in the US. It also assessed Legal Tracker benchmarking data comprised of more than $90 billion in legal spending from more than 1,450 legal departments. This is a fully global survey with those surveyed in all regions of the world.
7	Thomson Reuters Institute	2021 State of Corporate Law Departments	February 2021	Same as in .6 above.	Same survey done for .6 used again with additional qualitative focus on Covid-19 and its impact on corporate law departments.
8	Oxford University/ The Law Society of England & Wales	Lawtech Adoption and Training Findings - Survey of Solicitors	March 2020	Online survey: November 2019 to January 2020	Survey examines current usages of, training in, and attitudes towards, law tech by qualified solicitors in England and Wales. Survey yielded a total of 353 valid responses who are not representative.
9	Wolters Kluwer	The 2019 Future Ready Lawyer	29 March 2019	December 10, 2018 to January 13, 2019	Quantitative interviews with 700 lawyers in law firms, legal departments and business services firms across the US and 10 European countries – UK, Germany, Netherlands, Italy, France, Spain, Poland, Belgium, Hungary and the Czech Republic – to examine how technology and other factors are affecting the future of law across core areas and how legal organisations are prepared to address these.

Fig. 21.1 Proposed large-scale surveys to be examined for purposes of this meta-synthesis *Source* The author[39]

surveys done over the past year and a half and offered some future trendspotting as

---

[39] Survey 1 above is available only by purchase from ABA at a price of US $2000.

well. Survey 8 (Oxford University-Law Society)[40] had excellent secondary coverage in the Law Society Gazette, the weekly magazine of the Law Society, with an eye-catching quote, namely, that the survey reveals that "despite much hype—and many millions of pounds in investments—AI has yet to take over even the most mundane of legal professionals' work."[41] All of the surveys except Survey 8 are done annually so previous years' surveys were used in each of them as a benchmark to measure progress or the lack of progress over time which was helpful.

21.3.3 Evaluating the Quality of Surveys

The three Bloomberg Law Surveys [Surveys 2, 3, and 4] provided survey reports that would have benefited from greater coverage of survey design and an explanation as to whether those individuals who were successfully surveyed were representative either the US legal profession, Bloomberg Law clientele or neither. Sponsorship bias issues need further consideration[42] as Bloomberg Law offers a suite of AI based commercial products.[43]

The Lexis-Nexis survey [Survey 5] was exceptional in its granularity with an appendix reproducing the full survey results in whole. However, the survey was limited to professionals working at a diverse group of US law firms and did not cover individuals working in-house or in multi-disciplinary practices. Sponsorship bias needed further evaluation here as the survey was done by Lexis Nexis Legal & Professional and ALM Intelligence which offer data analytics products and consultancy.

Thomson Reuters Institute prepared survey data for use in the 2020 Legal Department Operations Index, 5th edition [Survey 6]. This survey data was also incorporated into Thomson Reuters Institute the 2021 State of Corporate Law Departments Survey [Survey 7] as well which did not have new survey work done in conjunction with this latter study but has a specific Covid-19 focus to it. Both Surveys 6 and 7 are extensive in their incorporation of a vast survey pool of in-house legal departments for which these surveys are the definitive resource. Moreover, the use of Legal Tracker benchmarking data which is identified as comprising of more than US \$90B in legal spending from more than 1,450 legal departments adds a costing component to these surveys that the others lacked. The same sponsorship bias issues must be addressed here as identified in the other surveys.

Survey 8 [Oxford University—Law Society] because of its academic research focus "ticks the right boxes" in terms of explaining its research methodology, survey design and for being the only survey to explicitly identify how many potential survey respondents were solicited (more than 10,000 solicitors) to obtain 427 responses

---

[40] Sako et al. 2020 [Survey 8].

[41] Cross 2020.

[42] See Reutlinger 2020 generally for a discussion of this theme.

[43] Bloomberg Law 2021 AI-Analytics Website.

of which only 353 were usable. The research methodology section identifies with excellent detail the age and career intentions of respondents, e.g., that a significant minority (15%), were amenable to working for, or establishing either an alternative legal service provider or a law tech solutions provider.[44] The Law Society, the independent professional body for solicitors in England and Wales, does not offer commercial services in the legal tech sector so sponsorship bias concerns need not be considered here.[45]

21.3.4 Analysis and Integration of Survey Outcomes

The Bloomberg Law 2019 Legal Operations & Technology Survey [Survey 2] revealed a surprising result in that although many lawyers probably use AI technology in their daily work, they are often not aware of this fact. This paradox is captured by the team lead for the three Bloomberg Law Surveys [Surveys 2, 3, and 4] who writes:

> "Are you using AI? Probably, but how knowledgeable are you about the AI that backs the technology you are using and how aware are you of the regulatory landscape and the potential ethical concerns? In our survey, 23% of law firm and in house counsel reported using legal technology with AI. However, does that mean the other 77% aren't? Maybe, but more likely, they're unaware that the natural language searches inherent in most legal technologies are powered by AI."[46]

This issue was highlighted again in the Bloomberg Legal Technology Survey 2020 [Survey 4] which was completed in July 2020. While in-house legal departments and law firms frequently use technologies that likely employ AI or ML driven legal tech tools such as legal research, e-discovery and document review, only one-third of respondents said they are aware of this fact with the other two-thirds being either unsure whether AI or ML is being used in the tools they are relying upon or believe that AI is not being used at all. This lack of awareness of where AI or ML driven legal tech can be found in daily work flows is confirmed by the response to a question asking how well is your understanding of the algorithms that underlie legal tech to which the response was mixed with 44%–somewhat or very well, 39%–not very well or not at all, and 17%–neutral.[47]

Oxford University-Law Society [Survey 8] noted a difference in who uses AI driven legal tools in law firms with an interesting age-gap emerging. In comparing responses of junior solicitors to those of senior solicitors in law firms, "e-discovery/e-disclosure/technology assisted review" was more likely to be used by assistants/associates (17%) than by partners (9%), while AI use cases in "regulatory

---

[44] Sako et al. 2020, p. 20 [Survey 8].
[45] Law Society Website 2021.
[46] Huie 2020.
[47] Bloomberg Law 2020b Legal Technology, p. 4 [Survey 4].

compliance", "fee earner utilisation analytics", and "contract analytics" were more prevalent among partners than among assistants/associates.[48]

This observation was confirmed in the Wolters Kluwer 2019 Future Ready Lawyer Survey [Survey 9] which notes that a driving force for change is generational— for lawyers and their clients—as by 2025, 75% of the global workforce will be Millennials who see the impact technology transformation will have and understand better how these technologies apply to their work over the next three years.[49] In comparison with more longstanding law tech solutions, such as document/knowledge management and accounts/time recording, usage of AI-assisted law tech by respondents was typically lower. This technology was used most prevalently in relation to legal research" (27% of respondents), "due diligence" (16%), and "e-discovery/e-disclosure/technology assisted review" (13%).[50] One may surmise that the lack of familiarity on the part of solicitors at law firms may have some basis in the fact that these AI-driven tools may be used less in law firm practice in the UK than in the US.

While Oxford University-Law Society [Survey 8] confirms an AI-driven knowledge gap in law firms, the opposite is true in the case of solicitors who work in multidisciplinary teams (MDTs) where solicitors work on a day-to-day basis with nonlegal professionals in data science, project management, and other areas. Respondents working in MDTs were more likely to use AI-assisted law tech than those not working in MDTs and the adoption of AI-assisted law tech were most likely to be in the following use-cases: "legal research" (33.8% of MDT respondents compared to 27.2% of non-MDT respondents), "due diligence" (36.8% compared to 16.4%) and "contract analytics" (27.9% compared to 9.6%).[51]

The Lexis Nexis 2020 Legal Analytics Study [Survey 5] makes the best case for the use of AI and ML driven legal tech tools to achieve a sustainable competitive advantage when it comes to competing against other law firms for winning new business or cases. Legal analytics harnesses technologies, such as ML, AI, and searching, to clean up, structure, and analyse raw data from dockets and other legal documents.[52] The Lexis Nexis 2020 Legal Analytics [Survey 5] concludes that law firm lawyers find the greatest use of legal analytics in gathering strategic insights for legal matters, showcasing the value of their firm to existing clients and winning new business; that value extends beyond the users themselves to clients who also recognise its importance: 98% of those surveyed said that legal analytics helps them to improve their firm's performance; 81% are encouraged by clients to use legal analytics; and 91% believe legal analytics is useful for the practice of law.[53] More than half of those surveyed agree that the adoption of legal analytics is driven by competitive pressures—the need to win (57%), but also by client expectation (56%).[54] The two

---

[48] Sako et al. 2020, p. 5 [Survey 8].

[49] Wolters Kluwer 2019 Future Ready Lawyer, p. 11 [Survey 9].

[50] Sako et al. 2020, p. 5.

[51] Sako et al. 2020, p. 17.

[52] Cincinnati University Library Website 2021.

[53] Lexis Nexis 2020 Legal Analytics Study, pp. 5–7 [Survey 5].

[54] Lexis Nexis 2020 Legal Analytics Study, pp. 5–7 [Survey 5].

Thomson Reuters Institute Studies [Surveys 6 and 7] confirm this trend identified in the Lexis Nexis 2020 Legal Analytics Study [Survey 5] that legal departments as well as law firm lawyers believe there is competitive advantage in acquiring new AI and ML based legal tech tools to help address a growing workload with 61%.[55]

The 2019 Wolters Kluwer Future Ready Lawyer [Survey 9] confirms that AI and ML tools when part of a well-designed and implemented legal tech strategy at a technology leading organisation may help such an organisation achieve a sustainable competitive advantage over competitors who are currently in the process of transitioning to such technology leading status or are currently trailing in their use of technology.[56] More than one-half of lawyers surveyed in Survey 9 expect to see some impact from transformational technologies (TT) already here today, such as AI, big data, predictive analytics and ML—but fewer than 24% say they understand them.[57] This confirms the point made in Bloomberg Legal Technology Survey 2020 [Survey 4].[58] When it comes to TT, adoption rates are still in the early stages although significant growth is expected with usage rates approximately doubling by 2022 when more than two-thirds of technology leading legal teams will be using AI and ML driven legal tech tools.[59]

The 2020 Wolters Kluwer Future Ready Lawyer [Survey 10] found that the increasing importance of legal tech is the top trend for 76% of respondents across Europe and the US, and across law firms, corporate legal departments and business services firms.[60] This same survey found performance blockers, however, and revealed a number of gaps in understanding, expectations, experience and capabilities—within, as well as between, law firms and corporate legal departments—that inhibit top performance; only 28% of respondents said they were very prepared to incorporate legal tech into practice and operations.[61] Legal departments, ranked both AI and ML at 58% as the most important TT that will have a significant impact over the next three years, although only 23% of respondents understand AI well at 23% with ML lagging behind AI at 17%.[62] The 2020 Wolters Kluwer Future Ready Lawyer [Survey 10] pinpoints that 59% of law firms surveyed recognise AI as the most important TT that will have a significant impact over the next three years, although only 22% of respondents understand it very well; ML learning came in in the same question at 57% however, only 19% of law firms feel they understand ML very well.[63]

---

[55] Thomson Reuters Institute 2020 LDO Index, pp. 21–22 [Survey 6].

[56] Wolters Kluwer 2019 Future Ready Lawyer, pp. 3–4 [Survey 9].

[57] Wolters Kluwer 2019 Future Ready Lawyer, pp. 10–12 [Survey 9].

[58] Bloomberg Law 2020a, b Legal Technology, p 4 [Survey 4].

[59] Wolters Kluwer 2019 Future Ready Lawyer, p. 12 [Survey 9].

[60] Wolters Kluwer 2020 Future Ready Lawyer, pp. 4–5 [Survey 10].

[61] Wolters Kluwer 2020 Future Ready Lawyer, pp. 4–5 [Survey 10].

[62] Wolters Kluwer 2020 Future Ready Lawyer, p. 14 [Survey 10].

[63] Wolters Kluwer 2020 Future Ready Lawyer, p. 17 [Survey 10].

21.3.5 Findings from the Meta-Synthesis

Our meta-synthesis reveals some answers to the questions we posed at the beginning of the chapter. While there is some awareness on the part of lawyers as to the AI and ML based legal tech tools available to them, this awareness is not universal. Knowledge of these tools depends upon various factors such as age, technical competency, practice area and the size and complexity of the organisation in which the lawyer works. Lawyers involved in MDTs tend to have more affinity with these AI and ML based legal tech tools by dint of their work with other individuals with a specialism in technology. While lawyers see new practice opportunities with AI and ML based legal tech tools that did not exist before, this is not an overwhelming view and there are clear problems in distinguishing the added value component that AI and ML bring to the mix as opposed to legal technology tools generally.

One area, however, that appears to have had a breakthrough is the field of legal analytics. This may owe to a fear on the part of some lawyers in the US that if they do not engage with such products, they will be at a competitive disadvantage in complex commercial and intellectual property litigation. If AI and ML based legal tech tools are to fully reach their potential to transform legal practice, there will be a need for the development of appropriate metrics that will enable lawyers to assess the capabilities and dynamics of different products and services that are available on the market in a transparent and cross-platform capability. This would help tech evangelists to make a better business case in their respective organisations. The hesitancy to embrace AI and ML legal tech tools in some organisations also has to do with the barriers to adaption of such new technology. These range from those common to all organisations, such as network capacity and a willingness to invest staff resources in training new ML systems, to those unique to law practice, such as the predominance of the billable hour or the compensation structure at law firms.

While lawyers believe that using AI and ML based legal tech tools in legal practice can create competitive advantages that over time might become sustainable, they must recognize that this requires building essential commercial value for their stakeholders for using these tools; real solutions must be offered as opposed to the attraction of a novelty or a new gadget. Legal teams investing in AI and ML based legal tech tools must be careful not to place too much value in the durability of first mover advantage as a substitute for well-thought product acquisition, staff upskilling costs, sound business case development and realistic management of internal expectations to develop long term value in legal teams for the use of such AI and ML based legal tech tools.

21.4 Expert Sampling

A non-representative expert sampling of UK-based non-lawyer legal tech professionals whose work focuses on the utilisation of AI and ML based legal tech tools in different legal practice environments confirms the findings derived from the meta-synthesis. The 2019 report Lawtech Adoption Research–In-depth Interviews[64] contains a series of in-depth interviews of 47 senior representatives of Lawtech vendors, legal services providers and thought leaders in the legal tech sector. The views expressed confirm the findings from the meta-synthesis. For instance, one business development director at a law tech start-up expressed the view that the hype has moved far away from reality: "I feel the media is doing a disservice to the industry and making it sound much more advanced than it is which filters through to other parts of the ecosystem ... we are getting asked by law firms ... Where is your AI? ... There needs to be greater focus on engagement and getting adoption of existing tools..."[65] Another Lawtech CEO observed: "It is very hard to find a partner within a firm that is willing to be the first to deploy ML or NLP on a live client project for the first time in a law firm... they just see the risk of it going wrong, losing the client and damaging the law firm's reputation. This is the fundamental difference."[66]

AI has had a win in the US in the use of data analytics to predict case outcomes.[67] Here a strategy director at one London law firm confirms the findings of the Lexis Nexis 2020 Legal Analytics Study [Survey 5]: "The panacea is using AI and ML driven tools that can accurately predict legal outcomes."[68] Finally, another Lawtech founder commented on first mover advantage: "The most successful early adopters were the big law firms with the war chests—they could sacrifice the human labour and free up expensive lawyers to focus on other things and take a mid to longer term view. These firms have had the opportunity to work with legal tech and get the most out of it."[69]

The 2018 UK Interviews[70] also employed a purposive sampling focused on interviewing representatives from top UK legal services firms leading on AI adoption as well as those considering adoption to provide an in-depth understanding of how AI is expected to impact firms in the sector.[71] While these interviewees were law firms leaders who were in the market to buy legal tech applications (as opposed to those who develop them or consult on the integration of these systems with existing legal tech platforms), their views are instructive. "One of the things that worries me at the minute is that everything is badged AI, because it is a way of selling it, but most of the technology is not AI" said one interviewee, while another stated "you do need to reserve the AI label for things that typically a human being would do with some sort of cognitive task around it, like interpretation or judgment."[72]

---

[64] Law Society 2019, p. 10.

[65] Law Society 2019, p. 19.

[66] Law Society 2019, p. 26.

[67] Law Society 2019, p. 28.

[68] Law Society 2019, p. 28.

[69] Law Society 2019, p. 34.

[70] Brooks et al. 2019.

[71] Brooks et al. 2019, p. 140.

[72] Brooks et al. 2019, p. 142.

One interviewee placed AI based legal work within a hierarchy of the sort of work law firms do which was helpful to see how law firms see it fitting into the overall value chain that law firms offer their clients:

> "Think of legal work as a pyramid. At the top, you have the 'rocket science work'. That's where someone's got a great reputation in the field for a very sophisticated type of legal work. I don't see that being touched by AI in any meaningful way for potentially decades. In the middle, you've got the business-as-usual contract work, and that's where AI tools will be used to make our jobs quicker. At the bottom, you've got the really commoditised work. I see that's where AI solutions are going to take that bread-and-butter work."[73]

Our sampling of non-lawyer legal tech professionals consists of three individuals: one who is an associate partner at an MDT [Expert 1], another who is a legal tech management consultant with one of the Big Four accounting firms [Expert 2] and, finally, the third individual who is a senior commercial manager with leading an IT services provider with expert focus on providing digital legal services [Expert 3]. All three were asked open-ended qualitative survey questions that focus on the use of AI and ML in legal tech solutions for law practice.

Expert 1 expressed the viewpoint that AI tools are a way to give access to legal output and analysis to non-lawyers pointing to specific examples such as contract analytics which enables non-lawyers to contribute to review and analysis or reasoning engines that distil complex legal rules into simple "yes/no" outcome statements for specific use-cases.[74]

Expert 2 pointed out that the poor design of some of these AI products hurt their value proposition. They suggest that some of the legal tech tools currently in their first wave of rollout "can be quite clunky in their design" while others have not been designed with legal professionals in mind but are products given a "legal skin" to market them to the legal sector.[75] Expert 2 states that this presents an issue of underdevelopment in that such legal tech products may not fully align with the day-to-day activities that lawyers engage in which is a hindrance to the creation of a sustainable value chain.[76]

Expert 3 felt that AI tools can be an excellent resource in sophisticated legal practice environments, but that for them to work one had to be aware of the set-up constraints, learning requirements and organisational support needed to make for successful implementation.[77] For instance, the tools need to be taught to develop ML, so sufficient practice and use time must be provided after initial parameters are set before deployment through pilots start.[78] Digital tool training has to be provided and the resources need to be digital savvy and embrace a digital transformation culture that supports change and reaches across the organisation through the value chain.

---

[73] Brooks et al. 2019, p. 144.

[74] Expert 1 Purposive Survey Questionnaire Response—5 March 2021.

[75] Expert 2 Purposive Survey Questionnaire Response—15 February 2021.

[76] Expert 2 Purposive Survey Questionnaire Response—15 February 2021.

[77] Expert 3 Purposive Survey Questionnaire Response—8 February 2021.

[78] Expert 3 Purposive Survey Questionnaire Response—8 February 2021.

21.5   Conclusions and Further Research

This chapter describes a theoretical meta-synthesis of data systematically obtained by quantitative survey evidence of the perceptions of lawyers on the usefulness of AI in their own present legal work. Starting with the tension between hype and reality, the chapter highlights some unifying themes that weave through the different surveys with respect to lawyer knowledge of AI and ML tools, barriers to their effective use in practice and how legal teams using such tools effectively can generate sustainable competitive advantage. The research questions posed at the outset of this chapter can now be answered.

There is some awareness on the part of lawyers of AI and ML based legal tech tools available to them although this awareness is not across the board and it will vary depending on the type of organisation that an individual lawyer works in. While some lawyers see new practice opportunities in AI and ML based legal tech tools that did not exist previously, the value proposition for the use of these tools to create a sustainable competitive advantage is hard to gauge due to the lack of industry-wide accepted metrics to measure performance, efficiency and cost-effectiveness. This problem is compounded by the fact that many lawyers do not fully understand how AI and ML based legal tech tools work. While one might argue that a lawyer does not need to know how the Internet works to use emails or store their documents in a cloud server, this argument has less credibility when one takes into account the highly competitive nature of entrepreneurial legal practice that characterises the competitive market for legal services.

Most notably, we see that AI and ML based legal tech tools tend to be a value-added component for legal work done at high-end law firms, sophisticated MDTs and large corporate legal departments who can incorporate such new technologies in a scalable manner in their operating models. However, this does not imply that AI and ML based legal tech tools do not play a role in more workaday legal environments as computer-assisted legal research services, billing and timesheet applications and cloud-based legal document management systems are now the norm in most legal practice settings. Further research in the form of a qualitative survey of non-lawyer legal tech professionals with follow-on semi-structured interviews is needed to offset the confirmation bias posed by the surveys studied in the meta-synthesis that presumes that lawyers as opposed to legal tech professionals are best able to assess the sustainable competitive advantage that these innovative tools may offer legal practice going forward.

References

Alarie B, Niblett A, Yoon A (2018) How artificial intelligence will affect the practice of law. University of Toronto Law Journal 68(1), 106–124. https://www.muse.jhu.edu/article/688836. Accessed 27 February 2021.

American Bar Association (2020) 2020 Legal Technology Survey Report. [Survey 1] https://www. americanbar.org/groups/law_practice/publications/techreport/2020/ Accessed 13 March 2021.

Bloomberg Law (2019) Legal Operations & Technology Survey: Executive Survey [Survey 2] https://pro.bloomberglaw.com/reports/a-changing-landscape-legal-operations-survey-results-and-detailed-analysis/ Accessed 13 March 2021.

Bloomberg Law (2020a) Legal Operations Survey: Executive Survey [Survey 3] https://pro.bloomb erglaw.com/reports/legal-operations-survey-executive-summary/ Accessed 13 March 2021.

Bloomberg Law (2020b) Legal Technology Survey 2020 [Survey 4] https://aboutblaw.com/Tzg Accessed 13 March 2021.

Bloomberg Law (2021) AI-Analytics Website. https://pro.bloomberglaw.com/ai-analytics/ Accessed 14 March 2021.

Brooks C, Gherhes C, Vorley T (2019) Artificial intelligence in the legal sector: pressures and challenges of transformation. Cambridge Journal of Regions, Economy and Society. https://doi. org/10.1093/cjres/rsz026 Accessed 25 February 2021.

Busetto L, Wick W, Gumbinger C (2020) How to use and assess qualitative research methods. Neurol. Res. Pract. 2, 14. https://doi.org/10.1186/s42466-020-00059-z Accessed 12 March 2021.

Cellan-Jones R (2017) The robot lawyers are here - and they're winning https://www.bbc.co.uk/ news/technology-41829534 Accessed 25 February 2021.

Cincinnati University Library Website (2021) Legal Analytics Guide (Last Updated 8 March 2021) https://guides.libraries.uc.edu/legalanalytics Accessed 13 March 2021.

Coyne KP (1986) Sustainable competitive advantage—What it is, what it isn't, Business Horizons, Volume 29, Issue 1, 54-61, ISSN 0007-6813, https://www.sciencedirect.com/science/article/pii/ 000768138690087X Accessed 3 July 2021.

Cross M (2020) No robot invasion: survey shows low levels of AI take-up https://www.lawgaz ette.co.uk/practice/no-robot-invasion-survey-shows-low-levels-of-ai-take-up/5103590.article Accessed 25 February 2021.

Davis A (2020) The Future of Law Firms (and Lawyers) in the Age of Artificial Intelligence. The Professional Lawyer Vol. 27, No. 1 (2 October 2020 Feature) https://www.americanbar.org/ groups/professional_responsibility/publications/professional_lawyer/27/1/the-future-law-firms-and-lawyers-the-age-artificial-intelligence/ Accessed 12 March 2021.

Dolin R (2017) Measuring Legal Quality. https://ssrn.com/abstract=2988647 or https://doi.org/10. 2139/ssrn.2988647 Accessed 28 February 2021.

Epstein B (2018) Social Ontology. The Stanford Encyclopedia of Philosophy, Summer 2018 edn. In: Zalta EN (ed) https://plato.stanford.edu/archives/sum2018/entries/social-ontology/ Accessed 11 March 2021.

Etikan I, Musa S, Alkassim R (2016) Comparison of convenience sampling and purposive sampling. American journal of theoretical and applied statistics, 5(1), 1-4. http://www.sciencepublishi nggroup.com/journal/paperinfo?journalid=146&doi=10.11648/j.ajtas.20160501.11 Accessed 15 March 2021.

Evans JW, Gabel AL (2014) Legal Competitive Advantage and Legal Entrepreneurship: A Preliminary International Framework, 39 N.C. J. Int'l L. & Com. Reg. 333. Available at: http://schola rship.law.unc.edu/ncilj/vol39/iss2/2 Accessed 5 July 2021.

Finfgeld D (2003) Metasynthesis: The State of the Art—So Far. Qualitative Health Research, 13(7), 893–904. https://doi.org/10.1177/1049732303253462 Accessed 10 March 2021.

Ganguly A, Nilchiani R, Farr J (2010) Defining a Set of Metrics to Evaluate the Potential Disruptiveness of a Technology. Engineering Management Journal, 22:1, 34-44, DOI: https://doi.org/10. 1080/10429247.2010.11431851 https://www.tandfonline.com/doi/abs/10.1080/10429247.2010. 11431851 Accessed 7 March 2021.

Gephart R (2004) Qualitative Research and the Academy of Management Journal (Editorial). Academy of Management Journal, 47(4), 454–462. https://doi.org/10.5465/AMJ.2004.14438580 Accessed 10 March 2021.

Hildebrandt M (2018) Law as computation in the era of artificial legal intelligence: Speaking law to the power of statistics. University of Toronto Law Journal 68(1), 12–35. https://www.muse.jhu.edu/article/688832. Accessed 27 February 2021.

Hoon C (2013) Meta-Synthesis of Qualitative Case Studies: An Approach to Theory Building. Organizational Research Methods 16(4) 522–556. https://core.ac.uk/download/pdf/132311799.pdf Accessed 10 March 2021.

Huie M (2020), Top Three Trends to Watch in Legal Operations, Bloomberg Law, https://pro.bloomberglaw.com/legal-operations-top-three-trends/ Accessed 13 March 2021.

Kerin R, Varadarajan P, Peterson R (1992). First-Mover Advantage: A Synthesis, Conceptual Framework, and Research Propositions. Journal of Marketing. 56(4), 33–52. https://doi.org/10.1177/002224299205600404 Accessed 15 March 2021.

Law Society (2019) Lawtech Adoption Research Report – In-depth Interviews https://www.lawsociety.org.uk/en/topics/research/lawtech-adoption-report Accessed 14 March 2021.

Law Society Website (2021) https://www.lawsociety.org.uk/ Accessed 14 March 2021.

Lehr D, Ohm P (2017) Playing with the Data: What Legal Scholars Should Learn About Machine Learning. 51 U.C.D. L. Rev. 653, 669 (2017) https://lawreview.law.ucdavis.edu/issues/51/2/Symposium/51-2_Lehr_Ohm.pdf Accessed 26 February 2021.

Lexis Nexis (2020) Legal Analytics Study Bringing Value into Focus [Survey 5] https://www.lexisnexis.com/supp/largelaw/no-index/lexisnexis-alm-legal-analytics-study.pdf Accessed 13 March 2021.

Lieberman M, Montgomery D (1988) First-Mover Advantages. Strategic Management Journal, 9, 41–58. http://www.jstor.org/stable/2486211 Accessed 3 July 2021.

McGinnis J, Pearce R (2014) The Great Disruption: How Machine Intelligence Will Transform the Role of Lawyers in the Delivery of Legal Services. 82 Fordham L. Rev. 3041 https://ir.lawnet.fordham.edu/flr/vol82/iss6/16 Accessed 25 February 2021.

Murphy K (2012) Machine Learning: A Probabilistic Perspective. MIT Press, Cambridge, MA. https://mitpress.ublish.com/ereader/3/?preview#page/Cover Accessed 7 March 2021.

Noblit GW, Hare RD (1988) Meta-Ethnography: Synthesizing Qualitative Studies. SAGE, Newbury Park. https://www.google.co.uk/books/edition/Meta_Ethnography/fQQb4FP4NSgC?hl=en&gbpv=1&pg=PA5&printsec=frontcover Accessed 10 March 2021.

Palmer J (2020) Analysis: Legal Tech Is Helping Lawyers, But Where's the Love? Bloomberg Law, 28 October 2020 https://news.bloomberglaw.com/bloomberg-law-analysis/analysis-legal-tech-is-helping-lawyers-but-wheres-the-love?context=article-related Accessed 13 March 2021.

Porter M (1985) Competitive Advantage: Creating and Sustaining Superior Performance. New York: Macmillan https://www.albany.edu/~gs149266/Porter%20(1985)%20-%20chapter%201.pdf Accessed 7 March 2021.

Practical Law UK Practice Note (2021) Demystifying legal technology (by Dey A based on original note by Tromans R) [w-018-6085] https://uk.practicallaw.thomsonreuters.com/w-018-6085?originationContext=document&transitionType=DocumentItem&contextData=(sc.Default)&comp=pluk&firstPage=true Accessed 9 March 2021.

Remus D, Levy F (2017) Can robots be lawyers: Computers, lawyers, and the practice of law. Georgetown Journal of Legal Ethics, 30(3), 501–558 https://papers.ssrn.com/sol3/papers.cfm?abstract_id=2701092 Accessed 7 March 2021.

Reutlinger A (2020) What is epistemically wrong with research affected by sponsorship bias? The evidential account. Euro Jnl Phil Sci 10, 15 https://doi.org/10.1007/s13194-020-00280-2 Accessed 13 March 2021.

Rudgard O (2020) 23-year-old British entrepreneur's 'robot lawyer' raises $12m from top Silicon Valley investors: demand for the company's services has risen dramatically during the pandemic. The Telegraph, 23 June 2020. https://www.telegraph.co.uk/technology/2020/06/23/23-year-old-british-entrepreneurs-robot-lawyer-raises-12m-top/ Accessed 25 February 2021.

Ryan A (2006) Post-Positivist Approaches to Research. In: Researching and Writing your thesis: a guide for postgraduate students. MACE: Maynooth Adult and Community Education, pp. 12–26. http://mural.maynoothuniversity.ie/874/ Accessed 11 March 2021.

Sako M, Armour J, Parnham R (2020) Lawtech Adoption and Training: Findings from a Survey of Solicitors in England and Wales. [Survey 8]. University of Oxford, Oxford. https://www.law.ox.ac.uk/unlocking-potential-artificialintelligence-english-law/unlocking-potential-ai-english-law-research Accessed 24 February 2021.

Siedel G, Haapio H (2010) Using proactive law for competitive advantage. American Business Law Journal, 47(4), 641–686. https://heinonline.org/HOL/Print?collection=journals&handle=hein.journals/ambuslj47&id=675 Accessed 6 March 2021.

Stanford Law School (2021) CodeX, the Stanford Center for Legal Informatics Techindex https://techindex.law.stanford.edu/ Accessed 8 March 2021.

Surden H (2019) Artificial Intelligence and Law: An Overview. 35 Ga. St. U. L. Rev. 1305 https://scholar.law.colorado.edu/articles/1234 Accessed 8 March 2021.

Tannenbaum S, Mathieu J, Salas E, Cohen D (2012) On Teams: Unifying Themes and the Way Ahead. Industrial and Organizational Psychology, 5(1), 56-61. doi:https://doi.org/10.1111/j.1754-9434.2011.01406.x https://psycnet.apa.org/record/2012-04594-012 Accessed 27 February 2021.

Thomson Reuters Institute (2020) Legal Department Operations (LDO) Index, 5th edn. [Survey 6] https://legal.thomsonreuters.com/content/dam/ewp-m/documents/legal-tracker/en/pdf/reports/2020-ldo-report.pdf Accessed 13 March 2021.

Thomson Reuters Institute (2021) State of Corporate Law Departments [Survey 7] https://legal.thomsonreuters.com/en/insights/reports/2021-state-of-corporate-law-departments-report Accessed 13 March 2021.

Watkins T, Mew C (2019) Will AI replace lawyers? Assessing the potential of artificial intelligence in legal services. Computer Weekly. https://www.computerweekly.com/opinion/Will-AI-replace-lawyers-Assessing-the-potential-of-artificial-intelligence-in-legal-services Accessed 25 February 2021.

Wolters Kluwer (2019) Future Ready Lawyer [Survey 9] https://lrus.wolterskluwer.com/knowledge-library/the-future-ready-lawyer/ Accessed 13 March 2021.

Wolters Kluwer (2020) Future Ready Lawyer Performance Drivers [Survey 10] https://www.wolterskluwer.com/en-gb/expert-insights/performance-drivers-and-change-in-the-legal-sector Accessed 13 March 2021.

Other Documents

Independent High-Level Expert Group on Artificial Intelligence Set Up by the European Commission (AI HLEG), A Definition of AI: Main Capabilities and Disciplines, Definition Developed for the purpose of the AI HLEG's Deliverables, 8 April 2019 https://www.aepd.es/sites/default/files/2019-12/ai-definition.pdf Accessed 13 March 2021.

Stuart Weinstein is Reader in Legal Risk Management, Aston Law School, College of Business and Social Science, Aston University, Birmingham, United Kingdom. Mr Weinstein earned a Bachelor of Arts with Honors from Williams College, Williamstown, Massachusetts, a Juris Doctor from Columbia University School of Law, New York, New York, and a Master's in Business Administration from the University of Hertfordshire, Hatfield, Hertfordshire, United Kingdom.

Chapter 22
AI and Lawmaking: An Overview

Annemarie Drahmann and Anne Meuwese

Contents

Abstract This chapter explores how AI could help improve both the process and the outcome of lawmaking by legislators. Among the possible applications of AI in lawmaking discussed in the chapter are opportunities in the areas of (1) legislative technique, (2) legislative process and (3) legislative monitoring. Each section also pays attention to the challenges and risks and come with the possible applications presented. All of these developments are at an early stage or can perhaps not even be called 'developments' yet. There is growing experience, however, with designing

This chapter was completed on 1 July 2021, developments after this date are therefore not taken into account. This is particularly important to note with regard to the DSO case study, as the DSO had not yet been finalized at that time. The authors would like to thank Dafne van der Kraan for her excellent research support.

A. Drahmann (✉) · A. Meuwese
Leiden Law School, Leiden University, Leiden, The Netherlands
e-mail: a.drahmann@law.leidenuniv.nl

A. Meuwese
e-mail: a.c.m.meuwese@law.leidenuniv.nl

data-based systems and legislation in parallel. Even if these systems do not necessarily include elements of AI properly speaking, meaningful learning can take place
from such projects. Therefore, for each of the three aforementioned possible applications, this chapter analyzes the case of the Digitaal Stelsel Omgevingswet ('DSO',
'Digital System Environment and Planning Act'), an online system for digital information regarding environmental and planning law, set to enter into force in The
Netherlands on 1 Januari 2023.

Keywords AI · Lawmaking · Legislative technique · Legislative process ·
Legislative evaluation · Digital system Environment and Planning Act

22.1   Introduction

Although legislative studies is an established subdiscipline of legal research, attention for legislation as a source of law is remarkably limited, given the centrality of
legislation to many areas of life and as compared to the scrutiny court decisions get.
This state of affairs may explain why publications on 'Artificial intelligence (AI) and
law' and practical AI applications in the field of law have as of yet not focused on
legislation much.[1] As this chapter demonstrates, AI and legislation actually intersect
in many different ways. The aim of this chapter is to provide some directions for
answers to the question: 'How can AI help improve both the process and the outcome
of lawmaking by legislators?'

   To that end, this chapter presents an overview, both of various ways in which
legislation and AI systems may become aligned, and of the challenges involved in
employing AI to improve processes of legislative lawmaking. It does not address
the debate on whether or not AI should be regulated through dedicated 'AI laws' or
other issues related to the regulation *of* AI. For this reason, and because of its focus
on more procedural aspects of legislation, this chapter prefers the term 'lawmaking',
which here should be understood to refer to 'legislative lawmaking' exclusively. For
illustrations of the relevant practices and developments experiences from several
countries are drawn upon, while the emphasis is on The Netherlands. Because of this
focus, it should be noted that the context of a decentralized unitary state means that
legislation can be adopted by both central and local governments and that therefore
the term 'lawmaking' may refer to either level.

   There is growing experience with designing data-based systems and legislation
in parallel.[2] Even if these existing data-based systems do not necessarily include

---

[1] In this chapter the relatively broad definition of AI presented in Annex I of the European
Commission's proposal for an AI regulation is adhered to: "(a) Machine learning approaches,
including supervised, unsupervised and reinforcement learning, using a wide variety of methods
including deep learning; (b) Logic- and knowledge-based approaches, including knowledge representation, inductive (logic) programming, knowledge bases, inference and deductive engines,
(symbolic) reasoning and expert systems; (c) Statistical approaches, Bayesian estimation, search
and optimization methods."

[2] Lokin 2020.

machine learning elements, it is possible to meaningfully draw lessons from such projects for AI at large. This chapter analyzes the case of the Digital System Environment and Planning Act' (hereafter: 'DSO', for *Digitaal Stelsel Omgevingswet*), an online system for all digital information regarding environmental and planning law in The Netherlands. With the Environment and Planning Act, the Dutch legislator aims to simplify and merge 26 laws that relate to the physical living environment. Digitalization is intended to play a crucial role in bringing about this simplification. Interestingly, the Dutch government has made a commitment not to let the new legislative act enter into force as long as the DSO is not yet operating adequately. On 1 January 2023 only the basic infrastructure is expected to be ready.[3] After that, the DSO will be further developed, making it a suitable illustration for the potential AI holds with regard to lawmaking. Another reason why the DSO case is relevant lies in the lessons that can be learned from the challenges encountered while putting in place the DSO basic infrastructure. After all, digitalization is often the first step in or a pre-condition for developing AI-based systems.

Because of the well-known risks of violations of privacy rules and data security standards that come with the use of AI technologies involving personal data,[4] this chapter aims to pay special attention to AI applications that use other types of data. This is another reason why the DSO makes for an interesting case study: it is an example of advanced digitalization of complex legislation, but without some of the usual pitfalls (e.g. over-reliance on technology, but also an exclusive focus on personal data).

Section 22.2 sets out how legislation and AI intersect and introduces the DSO case study. Section 22.3 through Sect. 22.5 each deal with one specific dimension of legislative lawmaking: technique, process and monitoring respectively. For each section possible instances of 'alignment' as well as 'challenges' in terms of the resulting adaptations needed in the world of law and potential risks are discussed. Section 22.6 provides conclusions.

22.2 Legislation and AI

In Sect. 22.2.1, the role AI can play in lawmaking processes is introduced. Section 22.2.2 introduces the DSO.

---

[3] *Parliamentary papers II* 2020/21, 33118, no. 190, pp. 1–2. See for a more detailed description of the DSO: Drahmann and Huijts 2021.

[4] Bucher 2018.

22.2.1 Introducing Legislation as an AI Topic

Interlinkages between legislation and technology traditionally are found where law is seen as 'information' and ICT is used to disclose it. As such, applications may range from mere 'information management'[5] to advanced analysis. This chapter aims to explore the latter end of the spectrum, whilst not shunning questions as to how the application of AI techniques to legislation in a variety of ways may impact on lawmaking as an activity fundamental to the constitutional state. Attention to the regulatory effects of technology as such was drawn most forcefully by Lessig when he coined the phrase 'code is law',[6] often reversed as 'law is code' in the two decades that have passed since.[7]

It has been argued that "[a]mong the social sciences, law may come the closest to a system of formal logic" since "legal rulings involve setting forth axioms derived from precedent, applying those axioms to the particular facts at hand, and reaching a conclusion accordingly".[8] Thus, "[t]his logic-oriented methodology is exactly the type of activity to which machine intelligence can fruitfully be applied".[9] This quote refers mainly to traditional 'common law style' legal reasoning, or to judicial lawmaking processes all over the world. The role of legislation is rather to either codify these 'axioms' or to phrase novel ones, in an attempt to regulate a particular aspect of society or the economy. As such the role AI can play in legislative lawmaking processes is distinct from the possibilities that exist in relation to judicial lawmaking or law at large.

Legislation, to a greater extent than other formal legal documents, has some properties that do align with certain features of AI technology. For example, legislative texts are indeed 'coded' in the sense of being jargonistic. Furthermore, implementation and application of legislation are activities with a high density of information. As "[n]ew information and communication technologies have dramatically improved the possibilities for searching, selecting, and integrating the vast amount of information generated and used by government and have—in theory—allowed for an unprecedented degree of interactivity between citizens and the government",[10] the general rules intended to govern much of this interaction are bound to be impacted.

22.2.2 Introducing the DSO

Until now, in the Netherlands environmental law has been divided into dozens of laws dealing with topics such as soil, construction, noise, infrastructure, mining, the

---

[5] Biasiotti et al. 2008.

[6] Lessig 1999.

[7] E.g., De Felipi and Hassan 2016.

[8] Toews 2019.

[9] Toews 2019.

[10] Stivers 1994.

environment, care for monuments, nature, spatial planning and water management. The Environmental and Planning Act will integrate 26 acts, 60 decrees and 75 ministerial regulations into one act with four decrees and one ministerial regulation. The act affects over 400 municipalities, provinces, regional water management boards and ministries, since all these authorities are authorized to enact regulations and issue permits. This is a gigantic operation for both the legislator and the authorities that will have to implement the new legislation. Parallel to the legislative process, a new digital system has been built: the DSO.

Developing the DSO turned out to be a massive project. It involves not only the development of a new national information technology structure, but also the process of connecting over 400 authorities to that national structure. Both the central government and local governments will have to use certain standards when they submit their regulations to the DSO. Subsequently, those regulations will be 'translated' into several applications, which can be divided into two functions. The first function is to provide access to information about the physical living environment. This function is divided into three parts, namely displaying rules for the physical living environment, being able to access other information about the physical living environment, and the so-called 'applicable rules', or question trees.[11] The second function concerns a digital permit desk, which in the future may come to include an application for filing objections against permit decisions. With the DSO, usable and reliable information about both the legal and the actual state of the physical living environment should become accessible to both stakeholders and authorities. This would reduce the burden of research, make it easier for stakeholders and authorities to exchange information, and speed up and improve decision-making.[12]

The minister of the Interior and Kingdom Relations has promised parliament that the new act will not enter into force if the DSO is not yet operating in a satisfactory manner.[13] In 2017, an interim ICT assessment revealed serious concerns about the feasibility of the original plans for the DSO, resulting in the ambitions being adjusted downwards.[14] Among other things, it was argued that creating an algorithm to show only the information relevant to the user would be too complicated. The draft DSO assumed that the search would automatically show 'the right information' on the screen by the system making a selection from many small pieces of environment information. However, these pieces of information are derived from thousands of environment rules, all of which must be provided with metadata. Because neither the DSO developers nor the users had a concrete idea of what 'the right information' was, it was not yet known what this algorithm should look like. Errors could lead to incomplete or excessive search results, and also to legally incorrect information.[15] Therefore, the basic functionalities that will be ready on 1 January 2023 will not contain this algorithm. These basic functionalities do not qualify as AI in the strict

---

[11] Also referred to as decision trees.

[12] Explanatory memorandum, pp. 55–56 and 353 (*Parliamentary papers II*, 2013/14, 33962, no. 3).

[13] *Parliamentary papers II* 2020/21, 33118, no. 188, pp. 1–2 en 9.

[14] Advice of the ICT Review Office 2017.

[15] Advice of the ICT Review Office 2017, pp. 4–5.

sense, but they will be expanded in the coming years. It is interesting to explore what that expansion could look like. Also, it must not be forgotten that the basic functionalities of integration of legal rules relating to the living environment, linked to digital geo-information in which all the governments are involved, is unique in the world and not an off-the-shelf solution.[16]

22.3 AI and Legislative Technique

In Sect. 22.3.1 three ways in which AI has the capacity to influence the legal technique behind legislation are discussed. Section 22.3.2 discusses some relevant challenges arising from the DSO case.

22.3.1 Alignment

The three ways in which AI has the capacity to influence the legal technique behind legislation that will be discussed in this section are: a potential fundamental impact on the types of norms used, automation of application of legislative norms and the use of AI to make legislation more accessible to citizens and businesses. The implications of these two latter shifts on lawmaking processes are also briefly discussed, leaving only procedural issues not related to legislative technique for Sect. 22.4.

Firstly, AI could influence the types of norms used in legislation in sectors in which AI is used to support administrative decision-making. The emergence of "super-human capacities of information-processing through artificial intelligence" has made it possible to "redefine the optimal complexity of legal rules and refine their content to a hitherto unachievable level of granularity".[17] In the realm of private law this technique is already being applied.[18] For instance, there is no reason to stick to general terms and conditions if a company has all the information to cheaply produce tailor-made ones.[19] Applying this technique as a legislator is more complex because of greater concerns regarding privacy and data collection.[20] But it is also clear that there is a lot to gain from a more targeted regulatory approach. In many cases general rules yield suboptimal results as compared to norms targeted to the regulatee.[21] For instance, social benefits tend to be distributed according to a complex set of general rules, potentially leading to many unintended effects. The discussion in The

---

[16] Gateway Review report 19 February 2020, p. 5 (Annex to *Parliamentary papers II*, 2019/20, 33118, no. 139).

[17] Busch and De Franceschi 2018, p. 413.

[18] Hacker 2018.

[19] Devins et al. 2017.

[20] Kugler and Strahilevitz 2019.

[21] Sunstein 1995.

Netherlands around this topic currently centers on the introduction of more legal provisions allowing individual administrative decision-makers to grant exemptions to general rules.[22] This would go some way towards 'fixing the system', but would also favor assertive citizens over others.[23] However, in theory, specifying certain living standards in legislation and calculating individualized benefits accordingly is possible.

Generally speaking, there are two ways in which 'algorithmic lawmaking' could contribute to mitigating the 'over-inclusiveness' or 'under-inclusiveness'[24] many laws suffer from. First, "models built from large stores of data [...] permit the creation and application of finely tuned rules".[25] However, this application encounters the exact criticism often levelled at algorithmic decision-making in general: predictions for the future rely on existing data and therefore are prone to perpetuate existing problems. Laws—in many cases meant to tackle societal problems—cannot rely too heavily on the past to regulate the future. The second option takes the opposite approach. It can be argued that where the absence of regularities causes regulatory failures, "machine learning loses its advantage and, as a result, looser standards can become superior to rules."[26] Simply put, standards could be agreed upon and algorithms could help establish whether the standards have been met, as in the—hypothetical!—benefits example above. In both cases, normative hierarchies common to public law systems, in particular the juxtaposition of 'general rules' or 'concrete, individual decisions', may need rethinking.[27]

To a very limited extent, and beyond the specific DSO context, data-driven personalized norms already play a role in Dutch environmental law. Dutch regional water management boards use dynamic groundwater data placed on a publicly accessible map to determine usage limits for farmers.[28] It remains to be seen whether or not the transparency of the data-based process of norm application contributes to greater acceptance of the norms.

Secondly, and more realistic for the moment, there is a growing practice of 'algorithmic application' of legislation. This ranges from real-time application of the law through "techno-regulation"[29] to more of a supportive role in 'classic' application of laws.[30] The focus here is on the latter, since this is where most experience has been gathered so far. Countering arbitrariness in decision-making is an important driver for a number of public law doctrines. Automation of decision-making, in the sense of

---

[22] Van den Berge 2020. These legal provisions are the so-called 'hardship clauses'.

[23] Wolswinkel et al. 2021.

[24] Kelso 1994, p. 1281.

[25] Fagan and Levmore 2019, p. 11.

[26] Fagan and Levmore 2019, p. 1.

[27] Citron 2008, p. 1249; Perritt 1992.

[28] Van Maanen 2021. See also https://www.aaenmaas.nl/onswerk/regels/beregenen/beregenen-gro ndwater/. For the map, see https://storymaps.arcgis.com/collections/e87e6157b8ba4002bdfcea39 4054196e?item=3.

[29] Hildebrandt and Koops 2010.

[30] Bovens and Zouridis 2002.

employing algorithms to execute public law rules, carries the promise of limiting or even eliminating arbitrariness in judgments. This practice has developed from *ad hoc* applications and therefore does not necessarily involve designing legislative norms in a different way, although the experience so far does suggest legislators need to make stronger choices with regard to the 'automatability' of their rules. Designing rules that are suitable for application with the help of an algorithm implies not only that the product has to be clear in terms of its structure and meaning, but also that the design of automated application has to be integrated into the legislative process.[31]

The DSO case, too, has elements of facilitating implementation of the Environment and Planning Act through algorithms. Its 'question trees' are human made and provide informational output only, serving as a preparation for online permit application. In the DSO, regulations are converted into applicable rules, which allow citizens to use question trees to get answers to the question whether they need a permit for their activity. If the answer is positive, citizens should be able to apply directly for the required environmental permit via an interactive form. This process is fully controlled by human decision-makers. The case illustrates nicely how thin the line is between 'algorithmic application of legislation' and the use of algorithms to make legislative rules more accessible to citizens, an aspect which will be discussed in Sect. 22.3.2. Furthermore, the DSO consists of a digital permit desk. Interactive forms are used for permit applications. This means that the questions the applicant is presented with depend on the answers to earlier questions. The intention is that more and more government information will be entered on the application form so that the applicant only has to check it.[32] The more information that is integrated over time, the more the application forms will focus on location and activity.[33]

Thirdly, a final category of applications refers to algorithms that help make legislative and regulatory rules more accessible to the public. The DSO case teaches some valuable lessons with respect to this objective. The DSO's question trees certainly play a role here, but the 'clickable' access to a myriad of provincial and municipal rules even more so. In the DSO, area-related legislation is accessible on digital maps. Citizens, businesses and government officials can easily access the regulations that apply at a particular location with just one click on the map. One of the requirements for realizing this functionality is that geo-coordinates must be added to regulations.[34]

---

[31] Lokin 2018. For an English summary, see https://research.vu.nl/ws/portalfiles/portal/69432699/abstract+english.pdf.

[32] *Official Journal* 2020/400, pp. 1138-1139.

[33] *Parliamentary papers II*, 2017/18, 34986, no. 3, p. 50.

[34] *Parliamentary papers II*, 2013/14, 33962, no. 3, p. 357.

22.3.2 Challenges

This section starts out by discussing some challenges arising from the DSO case. From those challenges, wider concerns are extrapolated regarding various AI-inspired changes to legislative technique.

The basic principle of the DSO that legislation is accessible with a click on the map is an important step forward. One of the challenges the DSO developers were facing was to not make the DSO too complex. Three examples illustrate this. First of all, contrary to the ambition of the legislator, a copy of issued permits is not yet available.[35] The reason why this has not yet been developed is that this would require further attention, among other things, regarding the protection of personal data. Secondly, information about the environment quality at a particular location is still missing. The ambition was that there would be an 'information house' for each domain—such as water, air, soil and nature. These information houses would collect, validate and process data about the physical living environment.[36] On 1 January 2023, only environment quality reports will be placed on the portal. Thus, the information is retrievable for citizens and businesses, but for the time being it is not converted into a product that fits within the 'click on the map' structure of the DSO system. Thirdly, the ambition of the legislator was that all governments would create question trees for their legislation, but the initial ICT solution was too complex to implement in a timely manner. There would not only be too many—tens of thousands – question trees, but it was also questioned whether it was feasible to integrate the software questionnaires of different levels of government into a single list that made sense to the user.[37] As a result, in 2023 question trees will only be provided for a few frequently used state rules.[38]

All three simplifications of the DSO represent a missed opportunity. The added value of the DSO lies precisely in the fact that citizens can find all regulations relating to the environment in one place. Without a copy of the issued permits, citizens cannot gain a full understanding of what is permitted at a location. There is a risk that they will draw incorrect conclusions as a result. Also, adding the actual environment quality as a second layer over the regulations contributes to the information objective of the legislator, because in that case it could be automatically shown whether, given the combination of the regulations and the environment quality, there is still room for new developments at a specific location. Finally, the question trees make regulations accessible to citizens, as the average citizen may not understand the language used in complex environmental regulations and may even not know whose government a permit system belongs to.

---

[35] Only of environmental permits for an activity that falls outside the scope of the environmental plan will be announced—and only announced—in the DSO (*Parliamentary papers II*, 2017/18, 34986, no. 3, p. 64).

[36] Advice of the ICT Review Office 2017, p. 5.

[37] Advice of the ICT Review Office 2017, p. 4.

[38] *Parliamentary papers II*, 2017/18, 34986, no. 3, p. 48.

Looking further into the future, beyond the stated objectives of the Dutch legislator, the DSO offers a glance of how the availability of extensive and wide-ranging data could make it easier to legislate through standards. Generating personalized norms, for instance, when it comes to the manure quantities allowed on particular farmland which could be calculated on the basis of a wide range of factors, is far from unthinkable. However, as mentioned in Sect. 22.2.2, creating an algorithm that shows only the information relevant to the user, requires clear understanding of what 'the right information' is. Based on various constitutional principles, personalized law can also easily be deemed illegitimate. If laws are not sufficiently general, they will fail, so one of the core mechanisms of public law goes.[39] The main objection here is that it amounts to unequal treatment.[40] A powerful counterargument is that the reverse expression of the equality principle, namely that 'unequal cases ought to be treated unequally' has not yet been explored sufficiently in law, and certainly not in conditions of more advanced methods of data analysis.

A final challenge is privacy-related. Even though personal data are not the bread and butter of the DSO, it can still serve as an illustration to this challenge. The more information that is disclosed in the DSO about objects on the map, whether automated or not, the greater the chance that it can be traced back to individuals (who live in those objects, or are otherwise linked to them). Although the right to privacy is important, the general interest of protecting the environment plays a major role in environmental law. Local residents and NGOs must be able to take note of developments that are relevant to the environment so that they can take legal action if necessary. Moreover, a digital platform like the DSO can ensure to a great extent that only anonymized environment information is shown and thus privacy is protected as much as possible.

The second area of applying AI to legislative technique, where legal rules are being translated into algorithms, has also raised serious fundamental objections. For instance, the importance of 'residual discretion' that administrative decision-makers have to give expression to the role of principles in administrative decision-making,[41] makes automated application of legislation suspect. Another often heard concern is the amount of *de facto* discretion given to professionals with a technical background and no accountability to the public.[42] In the end, they 'translate' legal rules in an often non-transparent and suboptimal way.

The DSO offers a limited solution in this regard: there is less that is 'lost in translation' because of the simultaneous design of legal rules and trees. The trees in principle have informational value only and do not replace applicable rules of the government.[43] However, they are part of the preparation of a permit application and

---

[39] Fuller 1969.

[40] College Bescherming Persoonsgegevens Jaarverslag (2013) [former name of the Dutch Data Protection Authority]. Jaarverslag College bescherming persoonsgegevens 2013–Recht.nl Last accessed 12 March 2021.

[41] Passchier 2021, p. 65.

[42] Passchier 2021, p. 73.

[43] *Parliamentary papers II*, 2017/18, 34986, no. 3, pp. 48-49.

as such misinterpreting a question can have significant consequences. Here, the fact that trees have to be phrased in a B1 level of Dutch[44] and the fact that the interface is designed so that after each question of the tree an applicant moves to the next question are worth mentioning as elements that can have a much larger effect on a stakeholder's legal position than should be the case. Apart from these 'significant details', the unclear legal status of 'decision trees' (which moreover deviates from the legal status of other digital information in the DSO) is bound to pose problems. The DSO will include a disclaimer that no rights can be derived from the outcome of the question tree. This shows an outdated government perspective instead of a citizen perspective. If the government considers digitization to be really important for the provision of information to citizens, then sticking to the classic 'paper' form of legal texts does not fit well. If rules are presented by the government itself in the form of question trees then it is appropriate if citizens can trust the outcome of that question tree.[45]

22.4 AI and Legislative Process

The expected increased frequency of legislative projects for which an AI system will need to be designed in parallel was signaled in Sect. 22.3. This section deals with other procedural aspects of legislative lawmaking, which may be affected by developments in AI: participation and various applications of textual analysis. Section 22.4.1 will describe these developments and Sect. 22.4.1 some related challenges.

22.4.1 Alignment

One aspect of lawmaking that has been the object of pioneering projects on how to use information technology to enhance the quality of legislation is citizen participation. Examples that stand out are the 'Regulation Room'[46] and 'Crowdlaw'.[47] However,

---

[44] Thus, in the DSO, it is possible to search for rules about "felling a tree" instead of "felling standing timber"; *Official Journal* 2020/400, p .1139.

[45] The legislative history stated that if one acts in good faith on the basis of an unambiguous result of a concrete and detailed permit check, but the competent administrative authority nevertheless finds that the applicable regulations have been violated, a successful reliance on the principle of legitimate expectations may be appropriate. However, the legislative history indicates that this will not often be the case, for example because the citizen himself has entered incorrect information in the questionnaire, resulting in an incorrect conclusion, or because the permit check has only been done for a certain permit system and it turns out later that another permit was also required for which no permit check was (or could be) done. (*Parliamentary papers I* 2019/20, 34986, no. W, pp. 19-20).

[46] Solivan and Farina 2013.

[47] Noveck 2018.

projects that include AI as part of the technological aspects are few and far between. One future application could be 'nudging' to encourage participation. For instance citizens who submitted input may choose to receive data about the number of other citizens having provided input into the same consultation process.

There is a participation angle to the DSO. In 2023, the DSO will only serve to get information regarding the rules that apply at a certain location and to file a permit application. But in the longer term, it should become a communication tool, allowing citizens and NGOs to upload their views on intended regulations.[48] One feature of the DSO that could grow into a nudging tool of sorts is the automatic email alert service citizens can sign up for if they are interested in learning when a permit that will affect their living environment is applied for or granted. This could in the future be connected to participation opportunities in lawmaking processes, but whether the DSO will actually develop into a participation platform remains to be seen.

AI-based (or regular) textual analysis of legislative texts is another way in which AI could strengthen lawmaking processes. There is a lot of data available regarding and surrounding legislation and the policies it is based on. Yet, not much in the way of processing this data to translate it into insights that are relevant to either lawmakers or those wanting to participate in lawmaking processes has been tried thus far. One study involved an unsupervised machine learning approach to the analysis of thousands of public comments submitted to the United States Transport Security Administration (TSA) on a 2013 proposed regulation for the use of new full body imaging scanners in airport security terminals.[49] The analysis showed that the algorithm produced "salient topic clusters that could be used by policymakers to understand large amounts of text such as in an open public comments process".[50]

Concrete applications include interpretative tools analogous to those already existing for case law. Applications such as Casetext and ROSS Intelligence[51] offer sophisticated semantic understanding of legal documents' actual meanings. For legislative texts such applications do not exist yet, even if, arguably, there is a greater need for this as legislative language is notoriously dense and technical. At the same time, whether or not language use in lawmaking offers a sufficient degree of regularity for algorithms to be trained adequately, is not clear. This opens the possibility for another type of application: spotting patterns and trends in legislative texts or activity.[52] For example, legislative drafters could receive a warning from the system if they propose to use language that deviates from existing texts or that is associated with provisions that have proven problematic in court. Similarly, there are plenty of opportunities when it comes to translating legislative texts and possibly even drafting legislative texts.

---

[48] *Parliamentary papers II*, 2017/18, 34986, no. 3, p. 316.

[49] Ingrams 2020.

[50] Ingrams 2020.

[51] Yamane 2020, pp. 879–880.

[52] Wolswinkel et al. 2021.

22.4.2 Challenges

The main challenge for using AI to improve participation is that legal duties to organize participation (in legislative processes) tend to be of a 'soft' nature. The question often is: who has the drive/resources to set up costly ICT infrastructures for this, let alone AI-based systems? Pilot projects would need to show that participation can be improved in a cost-effective manner. Another challenge for using AI-driven text analysis to improve lawmaking processes is that the available textual legislative data often only follow minimal machine readability standards. The way forward here is to start with pilot projects.

The DSO case points to a more specific challenge in this regard. The draft DSO planned to lay down definitions of terms at the central government level and relate them to each other in a system catalogue. This should increase the accessibility and comprehensibility of legislation and the legal certainty for citizens. According to the 2017 ICT study, however, this would lead to a system catalogue containing about 80,000 terms, the maintenance and alignment of which would be labor-intensive and prone to error.[53] Hence, this system catalogue was never created. Nevertheless, standardizing language leads to accessibility and comprehensibility of regulations. In the further development of the DSO, there may be a role for AI here. By comparing the definitions used, divergent definitions can be highlighted and a proposal for standardization can be made.

22.5 AI and Legislative Monitoring

22.5.1 Alignment

Evaluation of legislation, whether it occurs ex ante or ex post is something that is difficult to get right.[54] The political nature of lawmaking,[55] the intellectual difficulties of 'predicting' and establishing the real-world effects of legislative initiatives and capture by special interests mean that there is a lot to gain from rethinking the role of evaluation in lawmaking. One direction the academic literature points to is to conceive ex ante and ex post evaluation as a 'regulatory cycle'.[56] This approach implies that legislation should be 'monitored' as opposed to only being evaluated 'ad hoc'. There could be an important role for AI in monitoring the effects of legislation after it takes effect. In order for this to be a realistic option, the legislator needs to consider data that need to be collected and make arrangements for this—much like the parallel design of legislation and digital system that characterizes the DSO.

---

[53] Advice of the ICT Review Office 2017, p. 4.

[54] Adviescollege toetsing regeldruk 2020.

[55] Passchier 2021, p. 61.

[56] Mastenbroek et al. 2016.

In a 'cyclical' conceptualization of lawmaking, AI could be particularly helpful in pointing to regulatory failures that may have gone unnoticed if the legislator relies merely on *ad hoc* and stakeholder-dependent data collection.

The DSO does have a built-in system of quality assurance and monitoring, but this is related to consistency rather than to real-world effects of the legislation. In addition to being able to set quality requirements for the information that is delivered, validation mechanisms are built into the interfaces for the electronic delivery of information.[57] Simply put: if local governments try to include rules that do not fit (in the sense that they do not match the centrally set standards) a 'red flag' appears. This validation can ensure that the information accessed meets certain technical quality requirements. Any factual inadequacies in the information cannot be checked automatically. The Environment and Planning Act does also include the possibility of designating a governmental body to monitor and report on the quality of the information provided, for example by means of file comparisons or in some other way[58] and the DSO will have a technical option for users to provide feedback if that user believes that specific information is incorrect.[59] These are features that show how digital systems designed in parallel with legislation could aid evaluation.

22.5.2   Challenges

A clear challenge associated with using AI to improve the monitoring of effects of legislation is the risk of information overload.[60] Even in non-automatized evaluation processes, high quality input often goes unnoticed. This may indeed be a consequence of information overload, but it may also be a matter of willful neglect, given the political interests at stake. Why would AI-based monitoring work if legislators struggle to put in place 'regular' evaluation? One answer to this is that it could operate in a different way. Rather than having a large evaluation report to react to after three to five years, a continuous monitoring system could 'flag' unexpected trends associated with the legislation, providing decision-makers with the possibility to propose changes before a proper regulatory failure occurs, possibly making it more worthwhile for political decision-makers to pay attention.

There is also the cost of setting up AI-based monitoring systems. Adding ever more 'tests' makes the evaluation process too burdensome. In response to this, one might argue that more advanced, properly AI-based systems should be reserved for selected legislative initiatives only. However, it is well known that attempts to put the 'principle of proportionate analysis' into practice, create possibilities for

---

[57] Article 20.27 of the Act.

[58] Ultimately, the minister is responsible for the DSO. In that context, the minister must supervise the municipalities, provinces and regional water management boards and intervene if there is any neglect of duties.

[59] Article 20.30 of the Act.

[60] Cohen 2016, p. 32.

policy-makers and politicians to dodge rigorous analysis.[61] In a type of preliminary regulatory impact assessment, areas of uncertainty with regard to the expected effects of the legislation would need to be mapped and specialists would need to get the opportunity to indicate to what expect AI could be of help there. It is also important to note that smart AI-based monitoring systems could actually be fairly economical to run compared to large *ad hoc* evaluation studies.

22.6   Concluding Remarks

The broad range of AI applications in lawmaking processes that this chapter has presented point to some commonalities. Across the three dimensions of technique, process and monitoring it is clear that most instances of possible alignment of AI and lawmaking currently are at the stage of mere digitalization, rather than wide-spread introduction of actual AI techniques using machine learning. The DSO case illustrates that even at that less ambitious stage there are plenty of challenges for the legislator. One lesson is to not make an ICT-system too complex, especially if a lot of different authorities are involved. It seems more feasible to start simple and to build from there. For instance, creating thousands of question trees for all governmental rules and a system catalog with 80,000 terms turned out to be unrealistic. Also, it is complex to create an ICT-system parallel to new legislation. If there are uncertainties about the content, it is difficult to develop an ICT-system: creating an algorithm to show only the relevant information requires a clear idea of what 'the right information' is. However, the case also shows that it is possible to ensure that decentral lawmakers design their rules in a digi-friendly manner. Adding geodata to regulations allows them to be accessed with a click on the map, and creating question trees and interactive permit application forms ensure that law is disclosed in a user-friendly way. With AI it should become possible in the future to simplify the process of developing more uniform legal language, as AI could be used to detect patterns in existing legislative language first.

The DSO case also shows that the tuning down of initial ambitions does not preclude adding more sophisticated features to the system in the future. These could range from a portal that can encourage citizen participation flagging initiatives that are likely to be of interest to them, to a radical simplification of permit applications. As part of this incremental development, of the DSO and of AI-based applications for lawmaking all over the world, the fundamental challenges enumerated here need to be addressed. In particular, the more radical AI influences, such as the possibility to deduce 'personalized norms', requires thorough and careful discussions. This chapter shows that at the other end of the spectrum, where no personal data are being used and AI only is an aid to decision-makers, there is a lot of less controversial ground to be gained.

---

[61] Alemanno 2011.

References

Adviescollege toetsing regeldruk (2020) Rapportage n.a.v. het ATR-onderzoek naar het IAK(-document) bij voorgenomen wet- en regelgeving [Report following the ATR survey on the IAK (document) in proposed legislation and regulation]. The Hague, December 2020.

Advice of the ICT Review Office (2017) Annex to Parliamentary papers II, 2017/18, 33118, no. 98.

Alemanno A (2011) A Meeting of Minds on Impact Assessment. European Public Law 17(3):485–505.

Biasiotti M, Francesconi E, Palmirani M, Sartor G, Vitali F (2008) Legal Informatics and Management of Legislative Documents. Global Centre for ICT in Parliament Working Paper No. 2.

Bovens M, Zouridis S (2002) From Street-Level to System-Level Bureaucracies: How Information and Communication Technology is Transforming Administrative Discretion and Constitutional Control. Public Administration Review (62)2:174–184.

Bucher T (2018) If...Then: Algorithmic Power and Politics. Oxford University Press, Oxford.

Busch C, De Franceschi A (2018) Granular Legal Norms: Big Data and the Personalization of Private Law. In: Mak V, Tjong Tjin Tai E, Berlee A (eds) Research Handbook on Data Science and Law. Edward Elgar Publishing, Gloucestershire, pp. 408–424.

Citron D (2008) Technological due process. Washington University Law Review 85(6):1249–1313.

Cohen J (2016) The Regulatory State in the Information Age. Theoretical Inquiries in Law 17(2):1–32.

De Filippi P, Hassan S (2016) Blockchain technology as a regulatory technology: From code is law to law is code. First Monday 21(12).

Devins C, Felin T, Kauffman S (eds) (2017) The Law and Big Data. Cornell Journal of Law and Public Policy 27(2):357–413.

Drahmann A, Huijts JHM (2021) Het Digitaal Stelsel Omgevingswet: ICT-flop of belofte voor de toekomst? [The Digital System Environment and Planning Act: ICT flop or promise for the future?]. Computerrecht 2021(3): 241–249.

Fagan F, Levmore S (2019) The Impact of Artificial Intelligence on Rules, Standards, and Judicial Discretion. Southern California Law Review 93(1):1–35.

Fuller L (1969) The Morality of Law, rev. edn. Yale University Press, New Haven.

Hacker P (2018) The ambivalence of algorithms. In: Bakhoum M, Conde Callego B, Mackenrodt M (eds) Person Data in Competition. Consumer Protection and Intellectual Property Law. Springer, Berlin, pp. 85–117.

Hildebrandt M, Koops B-J (2010) The Challenges of Ambient Law and Legal Protection in the Profiling Era. Modern Law Review 73(3):428–460.

Ingrams A (2020) A machine learning approach to open public comments for policymaking. Information Polity 25(4):433–448.

Kelso R (1994) Considerations of Legislative Fit Under Equal Protection, Substantive Due Process, and Free Speech Doctrine: Separating Questions of Advancement, Relationship and Burden. University of Richmond Law Review 28(5):1279–1310.

Kugler M, Strahilevitz L (2019) Assessing the Empirical Upside of Personalized Criminal Procedure. University of Chicago Law Review 86:489–525.

Lessig L (1999) Code and other laws of cyberspace. Basic Books, New York.

Lokin M (2018) Wendbaar wetgeven. De wetgever als systeembeheerder [Agile Legislation, the legislator as system administrator]. Boom Juridisch, The Hague.

Lokin M (2020) Agile Law Making. In: Dietz J, Mulder H (eds) Enterprise Ontology. A Human-Centric Approach to Understanding the Essence of Organisation. Springer, Berlin, pp. 416–417.

Mastenbroek E, Van Voorst S, Meuwese A (2016) Closing the regulatory cycle? A meta evaluation of ex-post legislative evaluations by the European Commission. Journal of European Public Policy, 23(9):1329–1348.

Noveck B-S (2018) Crowdlaw: Collective intelligence and lawmaking. Analyse & Kritik 40(2):359–380.

Passchier R (2021) Artificiële intelligentie en de rechtsstaat. Boom Juridisch, The Hague.
Perritt H (1992) The Electronic Agency and the Traditional Paradigms of Administrative Law. Administrative Law Review 44:96–98.
Solivan J, Farina C (2013) Regulation Room: How the Internet Improves Public Participation in Rulemaking. Cornell e-Rulemaking Initiative Publications 13, https://scholarship.law.cornell.edu/ceri/13.
Stivers C (1994) The Listening Bureaucrat: Responsiveness in Public Administration. Public Administration Review 54(4):364–369.
Sunstein S (1995) Problems with Rules. California Law Review 953(83):956–1021.
Toews R (2019) AI Will Transform the Field of Law. Forbes. https://www.forbes.com/
Van den Berge L (eds) (2020) Maatwerk in het bestuursrecht. Boom Juridisch, The Hague.
Van Maanen G (2021) Open ground water data in Noord-Brabant: a philosophical ethnography of open data policy. Presentation at conference 'Knowledge, Citizenship, Democracy'. Groningen University 14-16 April 2021. https://www.rug.nl/staff/l.m.herzog/program_abstracts_digital.pdf.
Wolswinkel C, Meuwese A, Boonstra N (2021) Measuring 'customization' in legislation: lessons learnt from a cross-departmental exercise, forthcoming.
Yamane N (2020) Artificial Intelligence in the Legal Field and the Indispensable Human Element Legal Ethics Demands. The Georgetown Journal of Legal Ethics 33:877–890. https://www.georgetown.edu/

Annemarie Drahmann is Associate professor of Constitutional and Administrative Law at Leiden University, Leiden Law School, The Netherlands, a.drahmann@law.leidenuniv.nl.

Anne Meuwese is Professor of Public law and Governance of Artificial Intelligence at Leiden University, Leiden Law School, The Netherlands, a.c.m.meuwese@law.leidenuniv.nl.

Chapter 23
Ask the Data: A Machine Learning Analysis of the Legal Scholarship on Artificial Intelligence

Antonella Zarra

Contents

Abstract In the last decades, the study of the legal implications of artificial intelligence (AI) has increasingly attracted the attention of the scholarly community. The proliferation of articles on the regulation of algorithms has gone hand in hand with the acknowledgment of the existence of substantial risks associated with current applications of AI. These relate to the widening of inequality, the deployment of discriminatory practices, the potential breach of fundamental rights such as privacy, and the use of AI-powered tools to surveil people and workers. This chapter aims to map the existing legal debate on AI and robotics by means of bibliometric analysis and unsupervised machine learning. By using structural topic modeling (STM) on abstracts of 1298 articles published in peer-reviewed legal journals from 1982 to 2020, the chapter explores what the dominant topics of discussion are and how the academic debate on AI has evolved over the years. The analysis results in a systematic computation of 13 topics of interest among legal scholars, showing trends of research and potential areas for future research.

A. Zarra (✉)
Institute of Law and Economics, University of Hamburg, Hamburg, Germany
e-mail: antonella.zarra2@unibo.it; zarra@law.eur.nl

Department of Law and Economics, Erasmus University Rotterdam, Rotterdam, The Netherlands

Department of Economics, Bologna University, Bologna, Italy

© T.M.C. ASSER PRESS and the authors 2022
B. Custers and E. Fosch-Villaronga (eds.), *Law and Artificial Intelligence*,
Information Technology and Law Series 35,
https://doi.org/10.1007/978-94-6265-523-2_23

Keywords Artificial intelligence · Empirical legal studies · Machine learning · Bibliometric analysis · Text mining · Topic modeling · Natural language processing · Legal research · Information retrieval · Automated text analysis

23.1 Introduction

Artificial intelligence (AI)[1] is a constantly evolving topic of interest in legal studies. Given both the considerable number of articles assessing the legal repercussions of a widespread use of algorithms and the enhanced adoption of AI-based software to analyze legal texts, it is worth presenting a review which could allow us to understand the main trends of debate among legal scholars. This chapter aims to investigate: (i) which research topics in relation to AI have been covered in legal research (ii) how the topics have evolved across the years and (iii) how they have been distributed within different legal fields.

Based on 1298 articles retrieved from Web Of Science (WOS) and Scopus, this chapter applies natural language processing (NLP) methods to generate useful insights from the academic literature in the field of law. In particular, it employs two complementary analytical approaches to examine the evolution and structure of the field. First, it performs a hybrid quantitative text mining analysis to recover key information from articles' keywords applying standard scientometric techniques (*e.g.* keyword co-occurrences). Then, it extracts and processes data from abstracts by means of unsupervised machine learning, running a Structural Topic Modeling (STM) to identify in a systematic manner salient latent topics on AI emerged from the academic debate.

Overall, as expected, the number of publications in peer-reviewed legal journals increased with time. While the bulk of early-stage research employed AI as a methodological tool, for instance, utilizing machine-assisted methods to rationalize legal reasoning, in recent years the debate has been fed with normative contributions on the regulatory and legal implications of AI in a variety of fields, from more sectorial domains such as data protection law to traditional segments such as tort law and contract law.

The results show three key functions of AI in legal research. First, owing to substantial advancements in the computational power of machines which can now process large amounts of data, AI has become instrumental in digital forensics, evidence discovery and cryptography. Second, legal informatics has established itself as a leading sub-field over the years, although the recent exponential growth of publications in more mainstream outlets covering broader issues such as transparency,

---

[1] In this chapter, the terms "artificial intelligence", "AI", "automated decision-making", "autonomous agents" are used interchangeably.

discrimination and human rights is closing the gap. Third, owing to recent scandals (*e.g.* Cambridge Analytica[2]) involving the breach of personal data by powerful online players and the concomitant urge to regulate automated decision-making with new laws (*e.g.* the EU General Data Protection Regulation, GDPR), *data protection* features as one of the key topics chosen by the scholarly community. Further highly debated topics are the regulation of AI applications, online platforms and social media, ethics and the legal personhood of robots. The results provide an exploratory understanding of the main trends in legal research, depicting the evolution of the field over time while offering some preliminary guidance for researchers who are interested in specific sub-fields. This chapter contributes with new methodological insights for systematic literature reviews in legal research while at the same time complementing existing studies.

After pointing out the conceptual structure of this chapter in Sect. 23.2 and Sect. 23.3, data and methodology are presented in Sect. 23.4. Descriptive information of the sampled documents is included in Sect. 23.5.1, while Sect. 23.5.2 and Sect. 23.5.3 illustrate the results. Finally, Sect. 23.6 concludes with recommendations for future research avenues.

23.2 Evaluating Legal Scholars' Interest in Artificial Intelligence

AI is affecting pervasively our daily lives in a vast array of domains, from healthcare to culture, from agriculture to urban mobility. Owing to their increased computational power, nowadays machines can outperform humans in earlier cancer detection,[3] craft a fine Rembrandt style painting,[4] or help farmers monitor the level of consumption of their livestock.[5] For instance, during the COVID-19 pandemic, AI-based technologies were used as evidence-based tools to predict mortality risk, screen the population and detect early symptoms of the disease.[6] In sum, the extensive deployment of algorithmic-driven solutions thanks to breakthroughs in machine learning is generating a wave of excitement among entrepreneurs and the business leaders.

---

[2] Cadwalladr C, Graham-Harrison E (2018) Revealed: 50 million Facebook profiles harvested for Cambridge Analytica in major data breach. In: The Guardian. http://www.theguardian.com/news/2018/mar/17/cambridge-analytica-facebook-influence-us-election. Accessed 7 July 2021.

[3] Johnson K (2019) Google's lung cancer detection AI outperforms 6 human radiologists. In: VentureBeat. https://venturebeat.com/2019/05/20/googles-lung-cancer-detection-ai-outperforms-6-human-radiologists/. Accessed 7 July 2021; Savage 2020.

[4] Baraniuk C (2016) Computer paints 'new Rembrandt' after old works analysis. In: BBC News. https://www.bbc.com/news/technology-35977315. Accessed 7 July 2021.

[5] European Commission 2018 Communication Artificial Intelligence for Europe.

[6] Tayarani 2021; Vaishya et al. 2020, pp. 337–339.

In line with this techno-enthusiasm, academic productivity on AI matters has boosted significantly in the last decade. The percentage of AI publications in peer-reviewed publications tripled from less than 1% in the late 1990s to 3% in 2018.[7] Not surprisingly, such studies belong for the vast majority to the fields of computer science, data science and engineering, and they address technical and methodological advancements in AI applications.

In this context, the role played by social scientists, and in particular jurists, within the academic scholarship on AI, has been quite marginal. More specifically, from the 1980s to the late 2000s, the legal research on AI was limited to studies on *legal informatics*, which pertains to the application of technology to the legal environment. In legal informatics, AI is employed in modeling legal ontology or, for instance, in online dispute resolution platforms. *AI and Law* is a sub-field concerned with applications of AI to legal informatics and vice versa with the transposition of legal reasoning techniques to AI. The last ten years (from 2010 to 2020) have seen a change of pace in terms of the nature and heterogeneity of topics of interest for legal scholars interested in artificial intelligence. In fact, while technological advancements were enabling the growth of services powered by AI, legal scholars started raising normative questions on the legal and societal repercussions of a massive use of automated decision-making systems. If on the one hand the perceived benefits of digitization were reinforcing an optimistic sentiment towards AI, concerns on potential misuses of algorithms by firms and on the resulting risks for individuals are catching the attention of policymakers and researchers. Some of the flaws of AI systems are increasingly evident. For instance, in May 2018, a self-driving Uber hit and killed a pedestrian in Arizona.[8] Similarly, in January 2020, a faulty facial recognition system misidentified an African American man, who was arrested for a crime he did not commit.[9] As a result of the increased dangers caused by defective AI systems, in recent years the legal academic debate has been extended to a variety of issues, including liability, trustworthiness and fairness of algorithms.[10]

Excluding the methodological usage of machine learning for legal texts and the well-established applications of legal informatics, there are several aspects of AI deserving attention from the legal scholarship. Some legal questions pertain to a more conceptual sphere, such as the need of a legal definition and a coherent taxonomy for the different applications of AI, others are rather applied and deal with the issues of controlling the actions performed by autonomous agents and the impossibility to predict certain outcomes of self-learning systems. Further questions concern the uncertainty about how the technology will develop, and how such evolution might affect other societal changes in the future.[11]

---

[7] Perrault et al. 2019, p. 14.

[8] Bogost I (2018) Can You Sue a Robocar? In: The Atlantic. https://www.theatlantic.com/technology/archive/2018/03/can-you-sue-a-robocar/556007/. Accessed 7 July 2021.

[9] Hill K (2020) Wrongfully Accused by an Algorithm. In: NY Times. https://www.nytimes.com/2020/06/24/technology/facial-recognition-arrest.html. Accessed 7 July 2021.

[10] See for instance Sweeney 2013; O'neil 2016; Datta et al. 2015.

[11] Gurkaynak et al. 2016, p. 750.

One of the enduring matters of dispute pertains to the establishment of a legal definition for AI systems. In this respect, some definitions are human-centric and portray
AI by its capability to mimic human behavior.[12] Others describe AI as a driver of
innovation, or a General-Purpose Technology (GPT).[13] All in all, the existence of
countless opaque definitions contributes to strengthening fears that technology is
ungovernable and hinders legal certainty around AI.[14] Another stream of research
originates from the enhanced level of responsibility assigned to automated technologies, which are unintelligible even for their owners (including programmers).
Thus, despite their promises to be fairer and more transparent than humans, algorithmic systems can be subject to biases,[15] and may eventually bring about more
inequality and discrimination,[16] as suggested by researchers in international law,
competition law and labor law. Finally, an interesting topic of research for legal
scholars is the attribution of legal personality to robots and autonomous agents,
which might have non-negligible consequences on—among other things—liability
in case of AI-facilitated wrongs.[17]

Given the growing number and diversity of the above-mentioned emerging trends
in legal scholarship on AI, it is worth providing an organized summary of the existing
research by identifying old and new areas of research to build knowledge, gain an
understanding and show the future direction of this research area. In order to obtain a
systematic assessment of the trends in the legal literature on AI, this chapter employs
text mining techniques that allow to deconstruct the main anchors and evolution of
the research domain, aiming to provide a clear picture of the legal literature on AI.
The next section illustrates how text analysis and machine-assisted methods have
been used to address legal questions, to conduct literature reviews in social sciences,
and to examine various aspects of AI.

---

[12] See among others Turing 1950/2004; McCarthy 1998.

[13] Cockburn et al. 2018; Trajtenberg 2018.

[14] Buiten 2019, p. 43.

[15] For instance, Sweeney 2013 found that a black-sounding name searched for on Google would
be 25% more likely to be associated with an ad suggestive of an arrest record. In a widely cited
book, *Weapons of Math Destruction*, O'neill 2016 argues that algorithms perpetuate human biases
leading to a greater inequality.

[16] The discriminatory implications of algorithms have been largely investigated by a plethora of
authors in the field of competition law and industrial organization (among many, Stucke and Ezrachi
2016; Mehra 2015; Gata 2015; Parcu et al. 2017. For a discussion on algorithmic-based price fixing
in the context of online platforms, see Calvano et al. 2020.

[17] For a more in-depth discussion on the attribution of legal personhood to robots and AI see, *inter
alia*, Chen and Burgess 2019; Leroux et al. 2012; Solum 1991; van den Hoven van Genderen 2018.

23.3 Automating Text Analysis in Legal Research: The Potential of Topic Modeling

Despite the relevance of semantics in legal research, to date, scholars have overlooked the potential of automated text analysis in favor of more traditional methods. A number of publications in social and managerial sciences opt for the framework of systematic literature reviews, which identify and critically appraise a selection of articles relevant for a specific research question. For instance, some authors are interested in the impact of artificial intelligent systems on public administration,[18] while others examine pros and cons of the use of algorithms in supply chains[19] or innovation management.[20] Recent contributions appraise how AI is represented in economic modeling as well as its broader impact on the economy.[21] When it comes to self-standing literature reviews in legal research, this practice is not well-established.[22] The reluctance of legal scholars toward literature reviews (automated or manual) may be problematic for dynamic and prolific fields such as artificial intelligence, where the amount of research is expected to keep growing in the future.[23]

Unlike standard "manual" reviews, the automated processing and analysis of publications through text mining has several advantages. First, it allows to skim through a large set of documents in a more efficient manner, especially for those long-established research topics where copious literature exists. Second, it can bring to light latent topics emerging from the literature that might have been overlooked by human eyes. Third, it can spot patterns and similarities in the texts, uncovering relationships and overlaps among authors, journals and sub-fields.

Automated text analysis can be performed in either a supervised or an unsupervised manner.[24] While supervised learning envisages the manual coding of a training data set of documents prior to the analysis, with unsupervised approaches the algorithm trains itself and detects autonomously patterns in data. Among the several unsupervised methods, topic modeling has become a widespread quantitative tool for text analysis in recent years. Unlike dictionary methods or other approaches focusing on single words' frequency, topic modeling lets researchers analyze groups of words together while putting them in a broader context, identifying latent topics emerging from a corpus of documents.[25]

Although several types of techniques are utilized to recognize relations within texts (*e.g.* cluster analysis and semantic analysis), topic modeling is emerging as

---

[18] Reis et al. 2021, 2019; de Sousa et al. 2019.

[19] Toorajipour et al. 2021.

[20] Haefner et al. 2021.

[21] Yingying and Zhou 2019.

[22] Goanta et al. 2020, p. 1.

[23] Ibid.

[24] Quinn et al. 2010.

[25] Curini and Franzese 2020.

a state-of-the-art approach for text mining,[26] mainly because of three advantages. First, while in conventional cluster analysis (*e.g.* k-means clustering) each text is associated to one and only one cluster, topic modeling assigns to each text a probability of belonging to a latent topic. As a consequence, a text can be associated with multiple themes, which is often the case for research papers. Furthermore, as opposed to cluster analysis, by adopting more sophisticated Bayesian techniques to compute probabilities, topic modeling produces more accurate results and proves more suitable for not too short texts. Finally, on a more generic note, as it does not rely on manual coding of training data sets, it is significantly less time-consuming than other techniques.[27]

One of the pioneers in field of topic modeling is David Blei, whose landmark contributions[28] on Latent Dirichlet Allocation (LDA) have paved the way for the development of more sophisticated text mining applications. To date, LDA is the most used probabilistic topic modeling technique.[29] The modeling works by requiring the researcher to specify a value of k numbers of topics in a corpus of documents. It then assigns randomly each word included in the corpus to one of the k topics. Topic assignments are updated iteratively by updating the prevalence of the word across the topics and the prevalence of the topics in the set of documents. LDA yields two kinds of output. On the one hand, it shows the words with highest frequency associated with each of the k topics. On the other hand, it displays the probability of each document to be associated with a topic. Legal scholars have been employing topic modeling to study the decisions of the European Court of Justice[30] and the US Supreme Court[31] or the judicial activity of the Australian High Court.[32]

Along with LDA, structural topic modeling (STM),[33] which can be considered its extended version, is growing in popularity among researchers and is being used in disparate domains.[34] Researchers have used it to assess and compare political systems[35] or to explore national climate change strategies.[36] Unlike LDA, STM exploits documents metadata (*e.g.* author's name, year of publication, keywords) to

---

[26] Chen and Xie 2020.

[27] Asmussen and Møller 2019.

[28] Blei et al. 2003.

[29] Lancichinetti et al. 2015. In the social sciences, this method has been applied to several types of analyses, from the identification of concepts in the news coverage (see DiMaggio et al. 2013) to the examination of speeches of German politicians (Baum 2012) or to assess the literature on crisis and disaster, see Kuipers et al. 2019.

[30] Dyevre and Lampach 2020.

[31] Livermore et al. 2016.

[32] Carter et al. 2016.

[33] See Roberts et al. 2014, p. 2: "[t]he *stm* package [...] provides tools to facilitate the work flow associated with analyzing textual data. The design of the package is such that users have a broad array of options to process raw text data, explore and analyze the data, and present findings using a variety of plotting tools."

[34] Chen and Xie 2020.

[35] Lucas et al. 2015; Milner and Tingley 2015.

[36] Hsu et al. 2020.

refine the process of allocating words to topics. The goal of such modeling is to let researchers uncover topics and estimate their relationship to document metadata. One of the reasons for its popularity is the R package[37] developed by the authors, called *stm*,[38] which makes it an adaptable tool due to its versatility. Because of its superior accuracy, this chapter applies STM to a corpus of legal articles on AI. When performing the analysis, the assumption that "changes in the semantic content of topics […] follow the evolution of knowledge in the field" is embraced.[39] As a result, the evolution of the topics can be interpreted as a proxy of macro-developments in the legal scholarship on AI. To the best of our knowledge, only one recent study has tried to systematize the legal knowledge on AI using automated text analysis to retrace the history of artificial intelligence and link it with the evolution of doctrinal research.[40] This chapter employs STM as a methodology and integrates the analysis with bibliometric techniques resorting on a combined dataset from two popular databases, as shown in the next section.

23.4   Data and Methods

23.4.1   Data

Although the considerable scientific interest in artificial intelligence, which is both a topic of research per se and a tool for analysis, led to an exponential growth in the number of studies featuring this subject, most of the existing literature tends to pertain to the areas of computer science, data science and engineering, while a marginal role is played by articles from social sciences. Hence, given the relative "scarcity" of articles in the legal field, in order to obtain a broad sample of publications from the legal literature, after careful consideration, it was decided to extract data from two distinct databases, Web of Science (WOS)[41] and Scopus,[42] which were merged at a later stage.[43] WOS and Scopus are two collections of databases managed

---

[37] R packages are extensions of the statistical programming language R, consisting of collections of functions, code and data sets which can be installed and employed by users.

[38] Roberts et al. 2019.

[39] Ambrosino et al. 2018, p. 27.

[40] Goanta et al. 2020; Rosca et al. 2020.

[41] See: www.webofknowledge.com.

[42] See: www.scopus.com.

[43] The choice of a combined dataset was dictated by several reasons. First, as the goal was to collect a significant and comprehensive number of articles for a somewhat niche sub-area of interest, a merged dataset would ensure a wider coverage. In this respect, a number of studies have found that in general Scopus provides access to more content and has the advantage of including not only journals but also conference proceedings and books (see Fingerman 2006 and Goodman 2007. Second, a wide timespan was needed in order to assess the topic trends over time. In this respect, it has been argued that WOS covers a wider timespan Goodman 2007. All in all, the two databases complement each other, and some authors suggest using them in tandem, for instance Mongeon and

respectively by the Thomson Reuters Institute of Scientific Information and Elsevier, which cover research articles, books and conference proceedings in a variety of fields, from humanities to social sciences.

The dataset was built retrieving the articles' bibliometric information. Data and metadata such as the title of the publication, keywords, abstracts, affiliation and name of the author(s), title of the journal, year of publication and full citation were extracted. As the goal was to identify articles belonging to the different areas of law with a specific reference to AI, the data collection strategy involved defining adequate keywords and restricting the search to journals belonging to the category "law". With regard to the identification of keywords, it was decided to keep any article that included the words "AI", "artificial intelligence", "algorithm" or "robot" in either the title, the keywords provided by the authors or the abstract.[44] As to the selection of legal journals, while WOS allows for the restriction of the search to the category "law", such action was not possible on Scopus, where legal sources are included in the broader domain of "social sciences". Consequently, in order to further delimit the results, sources belonging to the law category were manually picked from the list of legal journals provided by Scopus. The steps allowed to retain 979 results from WOS and 769 from Scopus, adding up to a total number of 1748 articles.

During the next stage, the documents were imported to R[45] and merged; duplicate items were removed, leading to 1569 results. Subsequently, screening criteria were employed to retain only value-added data: articles without abstracts were excluded, misread texts were corrected, and several new dummy variables regarding the type of source (e.g. whether specialized legal journals or generic legal journals) were created. After these steps, the final number of articles was 1298. In the data processing phase, the *Quanteda* R package[46] was adopted to prepare the corpus of documents to the text analysis.[47] Table 23.1 presents the main information about the publications included in the dataset.

Paul-Hus 2016; Echchakoui 2020; Escalona Fernández et al. 2010. In light of the mentioned reasons, this chapter uses both catalogues utilizing the merging function from the R package *Bibliometrix*, see Aria and Cuccurullo 2017.

[44] The search accounted for plural (e.g. robots) and derived forms (e.g. robotization) by using the "*" wildcard character.

[45] R is a programming language and free software used for statistical computing and graphics.

[46] Benoit et al. 2018.

[47] More specifically, the words were converted to lowercase, punctuation, stop words (e.g. "the", "also", "for") and non-relevant terms, (e.g. "article", "research", "can") and special characters were removed. Furthermore, words were stemmed to their root for an easier comparison and terms with less than two characters and occurring less than 10 times in the documents were removed. Stemming was implemented using Porter's algorithm (Porter 1980), which is the standard modality for text analysis. In addition, in order to obtain a balanced and informative sample, words appearing in less than 5% of the documents as well as words appearing in more than 90% of the documents were removed.

Table 23.1 Main information about data

Description	Results
MAIN INFORMATION ABOUT DATA	
Timespan	1982:2020
Sources (Journals, Books, etc.)	336
Documents	1298
Average years from publication	5. 07
Average citations per documents	6.77
Average citations per year per document	1.027
References	49178
AUTHORS	
Authors	2144
Authors of single-authored documents	629
Authors of multi-authored documents	1515
AUTHORS COLLABORATION	
Single-authored documents	706
Documents per Author	0.605
Authors per Document	1.65
Co-Authors per Documents	1.88
Collaboration Index	2.56

Source The author

23.4.2 Methods

The data analysis phase consisted of several steps in which automated quantitative text analysis was deployed on articles in the period 1982–2020. A non-positional "bag-of-words" model was adopted, i.e. the word order in the abstracts was ignored.[48] Table 23.2 illustrates the main analytical methods adopted in this chapter.

The first part of the analysis was aimed at finding the most relevant keywords appearing in legal journals with regard to algorithms and their evolution in time. At this stage, traditional scientometric procedures were executed, from the computation of the scientific production over time to the analysis of keywords co-occurrence. More specifically, the output of the keyword co-occurrence analysis serves as a preliminary step to discover the conceptual structure of the corpus of documents. The conceptual structure maps the combination of the most important keywords and their connection identifying clusters of concepts focusing on similar research strands. Finally, from a chronological viewpoint, the evolution of concepts in the timeline of legal research is delineated.

The second part of the data analysis involved the execution of a probabilistic topic modeling, namely STM, which detects the topics in an unsupervised manner. In order

---

[48] Blei et al. 2003.

Table 23.2 Adopted methodologies

Analytical method	Computational tool	Purpose
Keyword co-occurrence and word co-analysis	*Bibliometrix* R Package	To identify the mutual interconnections of concepts based on the combined presence of keywords in the examined literature
Trend Topics	*Bibliometrix* R Package	To investigate the evolution of legal research over time
Structural Topic Modeling	*stm* R Package	To detect latent topics in the research field

Source The author

to run the modeling, a corpus was created from the articles abstracts, and a document-feature matrix (DFM) was built. STM assumes a fixed number (k) of topics to be specified upfront by the researcher.[49] From the assessment of the model, the ideal number of topics in the sampled corpus was larger than 23. However, the semantic coherence of this categorization was significantly low, and therefore it was decided to opt for a lower number. Several attempts from five to 30 topics were performed, and after careful consideration a list of 13 topics was selected, as it ensured the least overlap and most clarity among different areas.[50]

23.5 Results

23.5.1 Descriptive Details of the Dataset

Figure 23.1 plots the number of publications per year on AI in legal research. The sample consists of 1298 articles published in peer-reviewed journals and books in the period 1982–2020. The trend in legal research on AI clearly replicates the growth

---

[49] In this respect, although this is an arbitrary decision and there is not a right number of topics, see Grimmer and Stewart 2013, nor a standardized procedure to infer such a number, see Rhody 2012, some tests might assist in selecting the optimal number of topics by computing the held-out likelihood, which is "the estimation of the probability of words appearing within a document when those words have been removed from the document in the estimation step", see Roberts et al. 2019, as well as the residuals, namely the distance between the observed and predicted values of data. Both held-out probability and residuals help assess the model's performance. An optimal number of k topics corresponds to a high held-out likelihood and a low residual.

[50] In addition, as many of the words belonging to the semantic area of AI appear in combination, a further analysis took into account also multiple words expressions creating bi-grams (word pairs) such as "machine learning", "criminal law", and so on. Nevertheless, with tasks such as topic modeling, n-grams do not significantly affect the performance of the modeling, see Hopkins and King 2007. Hence, only single words were kept for the STM.

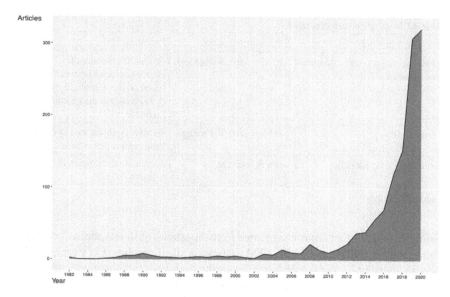

Fig. 23.1 Annual scientific production on AI in legal research. *Source* The author

experienced by the entire field (see Sect. 23.2), where a substantial progress was recorded from 2010 onwards.

The first articles of the dataset explicitly referring to AI in legal research were published in the early 1980s.[51] Initial publications used artificial intelligence techniques mainly as a methodological tool, rather than a subject of legal research *per se*. These articles belong to the sub-field which has been known as *"legal informatics"* or *"AI and law"*, which studies the development of computational modeling of legal reasoning and decision-making as well as the use of AI systems in the legal domain. For instance, concepts and procedures from artificial intelligence were used to develop a machine-assisted prediction of the practice of gerrymandering[52] or to carry out a foreign policy simulation.[53] The first article in the corpus taking stock of the state of artificial intelligence and the law dates to 1990 and discusses intelligent legal information systems as well as computational models of legal reasoning, arguing that the knowledge representation problem was the most urgent issue.[54]

---

[51] In this respect, it must be stressed that the legal interest in intelligent machines dates back to at least the 1950s, where the first contributions appeared in legal outlets such as *Jurimetrics* Journal, in line with the first boom of AI experienced in computer science. However, the timespan of the dataset does not allow to retrieve articles published before 1982, hence for an in-depth review of the first (1956–1974) and second wave (1980–1987) of legal research on AI, see Goanta et al. 2020, pp. 9–11.

[52] Wildgen 1989.

[53] Schrodt 1988.

[54] McCarty 1990.

Another interesting contribution developed an algorithm to model the dynamics of family law negotiation.[55]

Over time, from 1982 to approximately 2010, the number of articles increased, but only to a limited extent, as machine-assisted analyses were presumably intertwined with technical advancements in AI applications and the use of algorithms to address legal problems was rather a niche area. However, a few exceptions in those early years deserve some attention. In fact, AI became a subject of normative concerns when regulators had to define which legal approach to adopt towards early computer software and symbolic AI applications. For example, when courts started ruling on the first computer software and databases applying the intellectual property regime, scholars questioned whether such regime would be applicable in the future when purely machine-made programs would take over.[56] Also, scholars started the long-lasting debate on property and liability rules applied to "internet connected computer-systems", questioning whether injunctions would be the right remedy to discourage the extraction of personal data.[57] To sum up, from 1982 to 2010, the vast bulk of the legal research on AI was devoted to a machine-assisted computation of legal reasoning, with some normative exceptions concerning the legal treatment of software and databases, as well as early applications of algorithms in the collective sphere.

From 2014 onwards, a rapid increase in publications can be observed, in particular at least 50 articles appeared in 2015, doubling two years later and peaking at more than 300 articles in 2019 (308 articles) and 2020 (321 articles). This upsurge shows not only the growing academic interest in AI, but it also parallels technological advancements and policy/legal issues emerged in recent years. Section 23.5.2 provides a more detailed assessment of the assortment of topics that emerged in recent years.

When it comes to the types of sources dealing with law and AI, it is worth noting the prominent presence of specialized outlets, emphasizing the enduring importance of AI as a computational tool for legal reasoning and legal applications. The most relevant journals in terms of number of articles are *"Digital Investigation"*, with 97 articles, which deals with digital forensics, followed by *"Social Science Computer Review"* (63 articles), which covers societal issues related to technology, and *"Computer Law and Security Review"* (58 articles), which deals with IT law and computer security. The first non-sectorial sources appear at the 5th position with 27 publications from the *"Biolaw Journal"*, and at the 8th place with the Italian criminal law journal *"Archivio Penale"* (20 articles).

With regard to the scientific production of top-authors across the years, Fig. 23.2 displays scholars ranked in terms of number of articles produced (the bubble size is proportional to the number of articles) and total citations (the color intensity is proportional to the total citations) per year. Prof. Trevor Bench-Capon is the most

---

[55] Bellucci and Zeleznikow 1998.

[56] Miller 1993.

[57] Bellia 2004.

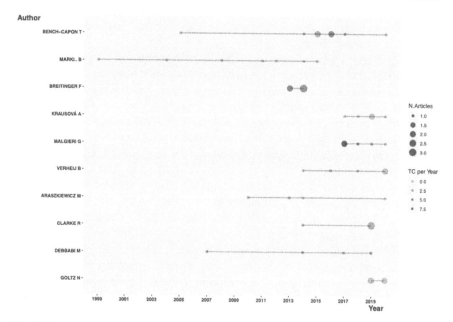

Fig. 23.2 Top authors' production over time. *Source* The author

prolific scholar of the sample, with eight articles, followed by Prof. Brano Markic (seven). Both authors are experts in the field of legal informatics.

23.5.2 Keyword Analysis

In the first stage of the data analysis, an assessment of the top keywords of the articles has been performed. Table 23.3 provides an overview of the top 30 terms used by the authors in the selected publications in the period of observation. Excluding generic terms such as *artificial intelligence, algorithm(s),* and other words that were expressly employed as a search-key, terms related to privacy (*data protection* and *transparency*) and forensics (*digital forensics, computer crime*) can be identified as the most popular, followed by expressions linked to human rights and ethics. Furthermore, it seems that copyright, liability, as well as regulation are themes of academic discussion about AI. When looking at the type of AI application, machine learning is the most used keyword, followed by robots, and natural language processing.

An additional level of analysis revolves around keywords co-occurrence, which shows the mutual interconnection of terms according to their paired presence within the literature. In Fig. 23.3, each node represents a keyword, while each link shows the co-occurrence of a pair of terms. The thicker the link between the nodes, the stronger the co-occurrence between words in multiple articles. The use of this analysis helps identify similarities in the data while detecting clusters of concepts. In this respect,

Table 23.3 Top 30 keywords frequency

Keyword	Frequency	Keyword	Frequency	Keyword	Frequency
Artificial intelligence	287	robotics	30	Liability	22
Law/legal	130	Internet	27	Bias	21
Algorithm(s)	114	Technology	27	Decision-making	21
Big data	90	Transparency	27	Governance	21
Digital forensic	70	Discrimination	26	Electronic crime counter measures	20
Privacy	63	Regulation	26	Ethics	20
Machine learning	49	automation	25	Accountability	19
Information	44	Human rights	25	Data	19
Data protection	40	Competition	24	Computer forensic	18
Computer crime	30	Rights	23	Copyright	18

Source The author

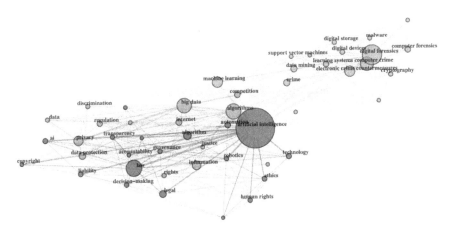

Fig. 23.3 Keyword co-occurrences in the legal literature on AI. *Source* The author

in Fig. 23.3 different colors are used to identify words belonging to the same cluster. More specifically, the distance between two keywords is roughly inversely proportional to their similarity. Thus, keywords with a higher co-occurrence rate tend to be next to each other. Interestingly, there seems to be a twofold trend. On the one hand, the graph shows (in green) the co-occurrence of words such as *digital forensics, cryptography, electronic crime countermeasures* and *data mining*. On the other hand, two groups of documents strongly connected can be identified. In light blue,

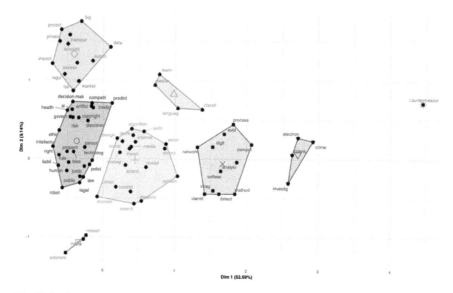

Fig. 23.4 Conceptual map (Multiple correspondence analysis and K-means clustering of articles expressing common concepts). *Source* The author

documents dealing with *big data* and *algorithms* appear to be connected to *regulation* of new technologies, *competition*, *discrimination* and *privacy*. In red, articles featuring keywords such as *artificial intelligence*, *automated decision-making* and *law* show strong co-occurrence with those discussing *accountability*, *AI governance*, and *transparency*, which are in turn also linked to the topic of *liability*, *copyright*, *ethics* and *human rights*.

A similar analysis is illustrated in Fig. 23.4, in which a Multiple Correspondence Analysis (MCA) has been performed in combination with a k-means clustering.[58] In Fig. 23.4, keywords are close to each other because a large proportion of articles treat them together; they are distant from each other when only a small fraction of articles discuss these keywords together. For example, in the case of AI legal research, *digital evidence* and *electronic crime* are close to each other because many articles focusing on digital forensic analyses often address issues such as encryption. Similarly, *electronic crime* and *privacy* are far from each other, because relatively few articles on computer crime also discuss the issue of data protection.

There is an evident polarization in favor of articles emphasizing data protection, fundamental rights and transparency as opposed to digital forensics and electronic

---

[58] MCA is an exploratory multivariate technique for the graphical and numerical analysis of multivariate categorical data to obtain a two-dimensional representation of the data (see Aria and Cuccurullo 2017). K-means clustering (Gifi 1990) involves the identification of clusters of documents expressing common concepts. It distinguishes *k* groups of documents. In our case, the algorithm classifies the articles into 8 groups in a way that maximizes the differences between groups and minimizes the differences within them. In order to better tackle the association between documents, keywords have been stemmed to their root by means of Porter's algorithm.

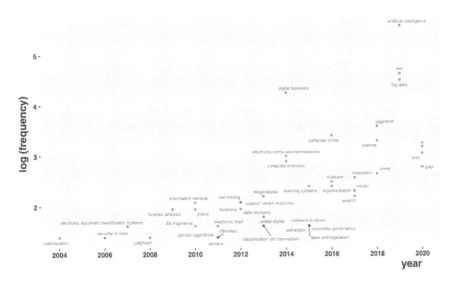

Fig. 23.5 Evolution of keywords over time. *Source* The author

crime countermeasures. In fact, the most densely populated quadrants are on the left side of the map. On the top left-hand part of the map, articles focusing on regulatory impact assessment, fairness, accountability and privacy can be found. In the same quadrant, in the red cluster, a strong connection between articles related to *inter alia* ethics, intellectual property rights, legal personhood and liability can be found. The quadrants on the bottom and top right are scarcely populated. Unfortunately, the k-means cluster analysis involves some limitations, as each text is associated to one and only one cluster, while normally an article can be associated with multiple themes. Hence, it is not possible to draw sound conclusions on the categorization of legal topics. For this reason, topic modeling (which is presented in Sect. 23.5.3) is a more precise tool.

With a further examination of the keywords, the evolution over time of research trends is investigated.[59] Unsurprisingly, Fig. 23.5 reveals that the legal research on AI has become more diversified in recent years. The dynamic trend of keywords depicts a shift in focus, from legal reasoning and knowledge engineering, which are linked inherently to the research field of AI and law, to more recent and sophisticated AI techniques (*e.g.* Bayesian networks) applicable to legal argumentation and legal texts. Finally, it is worth emphasizing the rise in popularity of articles on the EU GDPR in 2020.

---

[59] Such analysis has been performed by *TrendTopic* algorithms in the *Bibliometrix* package, selecting the three most frequent keywords per year appearing at least four times in the corpus of articles. Given the low number of articles in the first decades of our sample, the analysis is limited to the period 2004–2020.

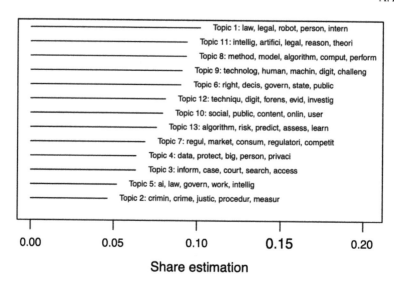

Fig. 23.6 Structural topic modeling (STM): topic shares. *Source* The author

23.5.3 Structural Topic Modeling

While the first part of our analysis focused on articles' keywords, topic modeling, which is presented in this section, extrapolates data from the abstracts which contain richer information on the latent topics emerging from the literature. The structural topic modeling analysis improves the performance of the previous techniques (*e.g.* LDA) by taking into account covariates. In this analysis, two covariates are added to the model, namely a dummy variable which distinguishes between sectorial outlets (*e.g.* "Artificial Intelligence and Law") and mainstream law reviews, and a further variable for the year of publication. As stated above, in STM the researcher chooses upfront the number of latent topics, which is a non-negligible step, as it could easily lead to overfitting or underfitting problems. After careful consideration, 13 topics seemed a reasonable number of themes, where the least overlap was found. Figure 23.6 displays the topics ordered by their expected frequency across the corpus as a whole. The x-axis (share estimation) shows which topics are overall more common and the most common words for each topic.[60]

Interestingly, topic 1, which features terms related to robots and the attribution of legal personality to autonomous agents, ranks first in terms of frequency within the whole corpus, followed by topic 11, which deals with AI applied to legal reasoning. A further methodological topic is positioned at the third place (topic 8), where words connected to algorithmic modeling appear to be significantly frequent. A final step in the analysis consists of labeling the topics by interpreting the content of the words most highly associated with each topic, assisted by contextual information. In this

---

[60] For example, topic 1 features in almost 10% of the articles of the corpus.

respect, after examination, 13 labels were attributed (Table 23.4). For instance, documents with a high frequency of terms such as *regulation, market, consumer, competition, enforcement, economy,* and *innovation* were classified under the label "market regulation", which corresponds to topic 7 in Fig. 23.6. In the same vein, abstracts including words such as *user, social media, content,* and *internet* were included in the category "online platform" (topic 10 in Fig. 23.6). This categorization may serve as a starting point for legal scholars who either aim to delve into a specific research topic or want to have a bird's eye view on the existing knowledge in legal scholarly community.

23.6 Conclusions

This chapter has used topic modeling in combination with scientometric analysis to perform a mapping of AI legal research. Unlike traditional review methods, an algorithm-based methodology has been adopted. The main contribution of this chapter lies in the methodological improvements ensured by the use of unsupervised machine learning. In fact, a gap in literature reviews within the legal domain exists, with few scholars adopting such a machine-based methodology for assessing the legal debate in a certain research area.

With this review of 1298 articles published between 1982 and 2020, 13 salient latent topics were identified, which can be categorized in three main areas. The first pertains to AI as a methodological tool used in legal studies, the second refers to the application of AI technologies to the science of forensics and criminal law, and the third deals with normative legal issues such as the attribution of legal personhood to autonomous agents, the protection of users' personal data, and the variety of regulatory challenges for the governance of AI. Interestingly, while from the keyword analysis it seems that data protection is attracting more attention, possibly because of the broad media coverage and the recent legal initiatives, topic modeling reveals that legal authors are particularly interested in the attribution of legal personality to AI systems and the resulting ethical implications. These analyses provide insights for researchers who want to contribute further to the legal research on artificial intelligence by clarifying the existing core literature base, the trends and advancement of the research field over time, and the saliency of certain topics.

However, the assumption that the development in the semantic content of topics represents the evolution of knowledge in the legal field is a strong one and deserves further attention. It must be emphasized that the use of topic modeling is—after all— a tool that facilitates the searching and screening of large numbers of documents which entails some limitations as well. First, the interpretation of topic modeling might resemble the process of "reading tea leaves", as it might force researchers to find meaning in patterns that might be random.[61] Second, the arbitrary choice of a number k of topics may lead to an overestimation or under-estimation of categories,

---

[61] Chang et al. 2009.

Table 23.4 Structural Topic modeling (STM): topic labels

Legal personality (Topic 1)
law, legal, robot, person, intern, autonom, liabil, human, rule, argu, respons, limit, act, ethic, civil, life, problem, regul, harm, right
Criminal justice (Topic 2)
crimin, crime, justic, procedur, measur, investig, state, prevent, activ, methodolog, organ, strategi, problem, intern, univers, oper, legisl, identifi, action, conduct
Courts (Topic 3)
inform, case, court, search, access, interest, manag, work, test, algorithm, network, oper, improv, identifi, service, recommend, solut, posit, conduct, internet
Data protection (Topic 4)
data, protect, big, person, privaci, process, individu, collect, inform, right, impact, access, challeng, standard, subject, control, fundament, applic, require, avail
Challenges in AI governance (Topic 5)
ai, law, govern, work, intellig, artifici, challeng, technolog, sector, institut, servic, respons, human, ethic, impact, legal, design, capabl, pose, public
Automated decision-making in the public sector (Topic 6)
right, decis, govern, state, public, autom, administr, decision-mak, process, law, constitut, account, principl, privat, algorithm, control, protect, transpar, general, individu
Markets regulation (Topic 7)
regul, market, consum, regulator, competit, law, enforce, algorithm, service, industri, product, innov, busi, econom, act, european, rule, effect, harm, framework
Algorithmic modeling (Topic 8)
method, model, algorithm, comput, perform, compar, effect, program, problem, improv, test, evalu, solut, identifi, experi, major, direct, natur, reduc, design
Societal technological transformation (Topic 9)
technolog, human, machin, digit, challeng, advanc, world, us, idea, role, impact, transform, societi, futur, requir, econom, face, emerg, legal, play
Online platforms (Topic 10)
social, public, content, onlin, user, platform, polit, media, internet, communic, polici, secur, valu, inform, govern, interact, emerg, power, respons, effect
AI in legal reasoning (Topic 11)
intellig, artific, legal, reason, theory, expert, law, applic, model, work, scienc, ethic, interpret, right, case, problem, process, comput, fact, construct
Digital Forensics (Topic 12)
techniqu, digit, forens, evid, investing, network, software, structur, process, knowledg, tool, work, algorithm, learn, machin, implement, model, applic, identifi, evalu
Risk assessment (Topic 13)
algorithm, risk, predict, assess, learn, decis, machin, discrimin, tool, fair, employ, require, model, futur, individu, reli, transpar, accuraci, limit, explain

Source The author

undermining the accuracy of the analysis. Third, topics modeling is prone to be abused, if wrongly interpreted. Human validation remains key in ensuring sound and reliable results, as humans are ultimately in charge of labelling and hermeneutically interpreting topics *a posteriori*.[62]

Finally, three caveats pertain to the intrinsic characteristics of the sample. First, it does not consider earlier landmark works on the subject,[63] as the time coverage provided by WOS and Scopus starts from 1982. Second, a selection bias may emerge due to the search keys used to retrieve the publications. Third, the proportion of country-based legal literature is relatively low compared to international sources, hence part of the national legal scholarship may be excluded from the analysis.

With that said, and with due caution, topic modeling can be employed to interpret the evolution of knowledge over time, as a promising tool that may help challenge human subjective classification of texts. In this respect, this chapter situates itself in this evolution by proposing a methodological approach that is often neglected by the legal scholarly community, which is the use of natural language processing and text mining tools to uncover and map a copious research area such as AI and law.

References

Ambrosino A, Cedrini M, Davis JB et al. (2018) What topic modeling could reveal about the evolution of economics. J Econ Methodol 25:329–348.

Aria M, Cuccurullo C (2017) Bibliometrix : An R-tool for comprehensive science mapping analysis. Journal of Informetrics 11(4):959–975. https://doi.org/10.1016/j.joi.2017.08.007.

Asmussen CB, Møller C (2019) Smart literature review: a practical topic modelling approach to exploratory literature review. J Big Data 6:93. https://doi.org/10.1186/s40537-019-0255-7.

Baum D (2012) Recognising speakers from the topics they talk about. Speech Commun 54:1132–1142. https://doi.org/10.1016/j.specom.2012.06.003.

Bellia PL (2004) Defending Cyberproperty. NYUL Rev 79:2164.

Bellucci E, Zeleznikow J (1998) A comparative study of negotiation decision support systems. In: Proceedings of the Thirty-First Hawaii International Conference on System Sciences. IEEE Comput. Soc, Kohala Coast, HI, USA, pp 254–262.

Benoit K, Watanabe K, Wang H et al. (2018) quanteda: An R package for the quantitative analysis of textual data. J Open Source Softw 3:774. https://doi.org/10.21105/joss.00774.

Blei DM (2012) Probabilistic topic models. Commun ACM 55:77–84.

Blei DM, Ng AY, Jordan MI (2003) Latent dirichlet allocation. J Mach Learn Res 3:993–1022.

Buchanan BG, Headrick TE (1970) Some Speculation about Artificial Intelligence and Legal Reasoning. Stanford Law Rev 23:40. https://doi.org/10.2307/1227753.

Buiten MC (2019) Towards intelligent regulation of Artificial Intelligence. Eur J Risk Regul 10:41–59.

Calvano E, Calzolari G, Denicolo V, Pastorello S (2020) Artificial intelligence, algorithmic pricing, and collusion. American Economic Review 110:3267–97.

---

[62] Rhody 2012; Blei 2012; Ambrosino et al. 2018.

[63] For instance, the seminal contribution of Buchanan and Headrick 1970 is not included in the review. In this respect, for a broader chronological overview, see Goanta et al. 2020.

Carter DJ, Brown J, Rahmani A (2016) Reading the high court at a distance: Topic modelling the legal subject matter and judicial activity of the High Court of Australia, 1903-2015. UNSWLJ 39:1300.

Chang J, Gerrish S, Wang C et al. (2009) Reading tea leaves: How humans interpret topic models. Adv Neural Inf Process Syst 22:288–296.

Chen J, Burgess P (2019) The boundaries of legal personhood: how spontaneous intelligence can problematise differences between humans, artificial intelligence, companies and animals. Artif Intell Law 27:73–92.

Chen X, Xie H (2020) A Structural Topic Modeling-Based Bibliometric Study of Sentiment Analysis Literature. Cogn Comput 12:1097–1129. https://doi.org/10.1007/s12559-020-09745-1.

Cockburn IM, Henderson R, Stern S (2018) The Impact of Artificial Intelligence on Innovation: an exploratory analysis. In: The economics of artificial intelligence: an Agenda. National Bureau of Economic Research

Curini L, Franzese R (2020) The SAGE Handbook of Research Methods in Political Science and International Relations. SAGE Publications Limited.

Datta A, Tschantz MC, Datta A (2015) Automated Experiments on Ad Privacy Settings. Proc Priv Enhancing Technol 2015:92–112. https://doi.org/10.1515/popets-2015-0007.

de Sousa WG, de Melo ERP, Bermejo PHDS et al. (2019) How and where is artificial intelligence in the public sector going? A literature review and research agenda. Gov Inf Q 36:101392. https://doi.org/10.1016/j.giq.2019.07.004.

DiMaggio P, Nag M, Blei D (2013) Exploiting affinities between topic modeling and the sociological perspective on culture: Application to newspaper coverage of U.S. government arts funding. Poetics 41:570–606. https://doi.org/10.1016/j.poetic.2013.08.004.

Dyevre A, Lampach N (2020) Issue attention on international courts: Evidence from the European Court of Justice. Rev Int Organ 1–23.

Echchakoui S (2020) Why and how to merge Scopus and Web of Science during bibliometric analysis: the case of sales force literature from 1912 to 2019. J Mark Anal 8:165–184. https://doi.org/10.1057/s41270-020-00081-9.

Escalona Fernández MI, Lagar Barbosa P, Pulgarín Guerrero A (2010) Web of Science vs. SCOPUS: un estudio cuantitativo en Ingeniería Química. An Documentación 13:159–175.

European Commission (2018) Communication from the Commission to the European Parliament, the European Council, the Council, the European Economic and Social Committee and the Committee of the Regions on Artificial Intelligence for Europe. https://www.bbc.com/news/technology-35977315.

Fingerman S (2006) Web of Science and Scopus: Current features and Capabilities. ISTL. https://doi.org/10.5062/F4G44N7B.

Gata JE (2015) The sharing economy, competition and regulation. CPI Compet Policy.

Gifi A (1990) Nonlinear multivariate analysis. Wiley-Blackwell.

Goanta C, van Dijck G, Spanakis G (2020) Back to the Future: Waves of Legal Scholarship on Artificial Intelligence. In: Ranchordás S, Roznai Y (eds) Time, Law, and Change: An Interdisciplinary Study. Hart Publishing.

Goodman D (2007) Update on Scopus and Web Of Science. Charlest Advis 8:15–15.

Grimmer J, Stewart BM (2013) Text as Data: The Promise and Pitfalls of Automatic Content Analysis Methods for Political Texts. Polit Anal 21:267–297. https://doi.org/10.1093/pan/mps028.

Gurkaynak G, Yilmaz I, Haksever G (2016) Stifling artificial intelligence: Human perils. Comput Law Secur Rev 32:749–758.

Haefner N, Wincent J, Parida V, Gassmann O (2021) Artificial intelligence and innovation management: A review, framework, and research agenda. Technol Forecast Soc Change 162:120392. https://doi.org/10.1016/j.techfore.2020.120392.

Hopkins D, King G (2007) Extracting systematic social science meaning from text. Manuscript available at http://gking.harvard.edu/files/words.pdf.

Hsu A, Brandt J, Widerberg O et al. (2020) Exploring links between national climate strategies and non-state and subnational climate action in nationally determined contributions (NDCs). Clim Policy 20:443–457.

Kuipers S, Kantorowicz J, Mostert J (2019) Manual or Machine? A Review of the Crisis and Disaster Literature. Risk, Hazards & Crisis in Public Policy 10(4):388–402. https://doi.org/10.1002/rhc3. 12181

Lancichinetti A, Sirer MI, Wang JX et al. (2015) High-Reproducibility and High-Accuracy Method for Automated Topic Classification. Phys Rev X 5:011007. https://doi.org/10.1103/PhysRevX.5. 011007.

Leroux C, Labruto R, Boscarato C, Caroleo F, Günther JP, Löffler S, Hilgendorf E (2012) Suggestion for a green paper on legal issues in robotics. Contribution to Deliverable D, 3(1).

Livermore MA, Riddell A, Rockmore D (2016) Agenda formation and the US Supreme Court: A topic model approach. Ariz Law Rev 1(2).

Lucas C, Nielsen RA, Roberts ME et al. (2015) Computer-assisted text analysis for comparative politics. Polit Anal 23:254–277.

McCarthy J (1998) What is artificial intelligence?.

Mccarty LT (1990) Artificial Intelligence and Law: How to Get There from Here. Ratio Juris 3:189–200. https://doi.org/10.1111/j.1467-9337.1990.tb00057.x.

Mehra SK (2015) Antitrust and the robo-seller: Competition in the time of algorithms. Minn Rev 100:1323.

Miller AR (1993) Copyright Protection for Computer Programs, Databases, and Computer-Generated Works: Is Anything New Since CONTU? Harv Law Rev 106:977. https://doi.org/10.2307/1341682.

Milner HV, Tingley D (2015) Sailing the water's edge: The domestic politics of American foreign policy. Princeton University Press.

Mongeon P, Paul-Hus A (2016) The journal coverage of Web of Science and Scopus: a comparative analysis. Scientometrics 106:213–228.

O'neil C (2016) Weapons of math destruction: How big data increases inequality and threatens democracy. Broadway Books.

Parcu PL, Monti G, Botta M (2017) Abuse of Dominance in EU Competition Law: Emerging Trends. Edward Elgar Publishing.

Perrault R, Shoham Y, Brynjolfsson E et al. (2019) Artificial Intelligence Index Report 2019. Human-Centered AI Institute Stanford University. https://hai-annual-report.stanford.edu/# Accessed 7 July 2021.

Porter MF (1980) An algorithm for suffix stripping. Program 14:130–137.

Quinn KM, Monroe BL, Colaresi M et al. (2010) How to Analyze Political Attention with Minimal Assumptions and Costs. Am J Polit Sci 54:209–228. https://doi.org/10.1111/j.1540-5907.2009. 00427.x.

Reis J, Espírito Santo P, Melão N (2019) Impacts of Artificial Intelligence on Public Administration: A Systematic Literature Review. 2019 14th Iber Conf Inf Syst Technol CISTI Inf Syst Technol CISTI 2019 14th Iber Conf On 1–7. https://doi.org/10.23919/CISTI.2019.8760893.

Reis J, Espírito Santo P, Melão N (2021) Influence of artificial intelligence on public employment and its impact on politics: A systematic literature review. Braz J Oper Prod Manag 18: https://doi.org/10.14488/BJOPM.2021.010.

Rhody LM (2012) Topic modeling and figurative language. Journal of Digital Humanities. https://academicworks.cuny.edu/gc_pubs/452/.

Roberts ME, Stewart BM, Tingley D et al. (2014) Structural topic models for open-ended survey responses. Am J Polit Sci 58:1064–1082.

Roberts ME, Stewart BM, Tingley D (2019) Stm: An R package for structural topic models. J Stat Softw 91:1–40.

Rosca C, Covrig B, Goanta C et al. (2020) Return of the AI: An Analysis of Legal Research on Artificial Intelligence Using Topic Modeling. In: Proceedings of the 2020 NLLP Workshop. 24 August 2020, San Diego, US. ACM, New York, NY, USA.

Savage N (2020) How AI is improving cancer diagnostics. Nature 579:S14–S16. https://doi.org/10. 1038/d41586-020-00847-2.

Schrodt, 1988.Schrodt PA (1988) PWORLD: A Precedent-Based Global Simulation. Soc Sci Comput Rev 6:27–42. https://doi.org/10.1177/089443938800600104.

Solum LB (1991) Legal personhood for artificial intelligences. NCL Rev 70:1231.

Stucke and Ezrachi, 2016.Stucke M, Ezrachi A (2016) Virtual Competition. Harvard University Press, Cambridge, MA.

Sweeney, 2013.Sweeney L (2013) Discrimination in online ad delivery. Queue 11:10–29.

Tayarani M (2021) Applications of artificial intelligence in battling against covid-19: A literature review. Chaos Solitons Fractals 142:110338. https://doi.org/10.1016/j.chaos.2020.110338.

Toorajipour R, Sohrabpour V, Nazarpour A et al. (2021) Artificial intelligence in supply chain management: A systematic literature review. J Bus Res 122:502–517.

Trajtenberg M (2018) Artificial Intelligence as the Next GPT: A Political-Economy Perspective. National Bureau of Economic Research, Cambridge, Mass.

Turing AM (1950/2004) Computing machinery and intelligence. Essent Turing Ideas Gave Birth Comput Age Ed B Jack Copeland Oxf Oxf UP 433–464.

Vaishya R, Javaid M, Khan IH, Haleem A (2020) Artificial Intelligence (AI) applications for COVID-19 pandemic. Diabetes Metab Syndr Clin Res Rev 14:337–339. https://doi.org/10.1016/j.dsx. 2020.04.012.

van den Hoven van Genderen R (2018) Do we need new legal personhood in the age of robots and AI? In: van den Hoven van Genderen R (author) Robotics, AI and the Future of Law. Springer, pp. 15–55.

Wildgen JK (1989) Gerrymanders and Gerrygons: Microcomputer-Assisted Spatial Analytic Approaches to Vote Dilution Detection. Soc Sci Comput Rev 7:147–160. https://doi.org/10.1177/ 089443938900700202.

Yingying Lu, Yixiao Zhou (2019) A short review on the economics of artificial intelligence. CAMA Work Pap.

Antonella Zarra is a PhD researcher at the Institute of Law and Economics of Hamburg University. She was a visiting researcher at the Economics Department of Bologna University and at the School of Law of Erasmus University Rotterdam. She holds a MSc in Economics of International Institutions and a BSc in Economics and Management from Bocconi University, Italy. Previously, she worked in research projects for the European institutions, national administrations, foundations and in public affairs for the telecoms industry. Her doctoral project focuses on the regulation of artificial intelligence and other automated decision-making systems. Her research interests include empirical legal studies, computational social sciences, as well as the impact of artificial intelligence on individuals' privacy, safety and trust. She is the author of several articles and publications on regulation (energy, financial and ICT markets), EU policy, digital economy and gender studies.

Part V
The Future of AI

Chapter 24
The Study of Artificial Intelligence as Law

Bart Verheij

Contents

Abstract Information technology is so ubiquitous and AI's progress so inspiring that also legal professionals experience its benefits and have high expectations. At the same time, the powers of AI have been rising so strongly that it is no longer obvious that AI applications (whether in the law or elsewhere) help promote a good society; in fact they are sometimes harmful. Hence many argue that safeguards are needed for AI to be trustworthy, social, responsible, humane, ethical. In short: AI should be good for us. But how to establish proper safeguards for AI? One strong answer readily available is: consider the problems and solutions studied in AI & Law. AI & Law has worked on the design of social, explainable, responsible AI aligned with human values for decades already, AI & Law addresses the hardest problems across the breadth of AI (in reasoning, knowledge, learning and language), and AI & Law inspires new solutions (argumentation, schemes and norms, rules and cases,

---

This chapter is an adapted version of Verheij 2020a, which is based on the IAAIL presidential address delivered at the 17th International Conference on Artificial Intelligence and Law (ICAIL 2019) in Montreal, Canada (Cyberjustice Lab, University of Montreal, 19 June 2019). That version is licensed under a Creative Commons Attribution 4.0 International License (https://creativecomm ons.org/licenses/by/4.0/).

B. Verheij (✉)
Department of Artificial Intelligence, Bernoulli Institute, University of Groningen, Groningen, The Netherlands
e-mail: bart.verheij@rug.nl

© T.M.C. ASSER PRESS and the authors 2022
B. Custers and E. Fosch-Villaronga (eds.), *Law and Artificial Intelligence*,
Information Technology and Law Series 35,
https://doi.org/10.1007/978-94-6265-523-2_24

Fig. 24.1 Technological innovation in the law in the past (left) and in the future? (right). Left: Guillotine at the Nieuwmarkt in Amsterdam, 1812. *Source* Rijksmuseum RP-P-OB-87.033, anonymous. Right: Robot judge in the TV series Futurama, Judge 723. *Source* https://futurama.fandom.com/wiki/Judge_723

interpretation). In this chapter, it is argued that the study of AI as Law supports the development of an AI that is good for us, making AI & Law more relevant than ever.

Keywords artificial intelligence · law · knowledge representation and reasoning · machine learning · natural language processing · argumentation

24.1 Introduction

It is not a new thing that technological innovation in the law has attracted a lot of attention. For instance, think of an innovation brought to us by the French 18th century freemason Joseph-Ignace Guillotin: the guillotine. Many people gathered at the Nieuwmarkt, Amsterdam, when it was first used in the Netherlands in 1812 (Fig. 24.1, on the left). The guillotine was thought of as a humane technology, since the machine guaranteed an instant and painless death.

And then a contemporary technological innovation that attracts a lot of attention: the self-driving car that can follow basic traffic rules by itself, so is in that sense an example of normware, an artificial system with embedded norms. In a recent news article,[1] the story is reported that a drunk driver in Meppel in the province Drenthe in the Netherlands was driving his self-driving car. Well, he was driving his car, as the police discovered that he was tailing a truck, while sleeping behind the wheel, his car in autopilot mode. His driver's license has been withdrawn.

Indeed, technological innovation in AI is spectacular, think only of the automatically translated headline 'Drunken Meppeler sleeps on the highway', perhaps not perfect, but enough for understanding what is meant. Innovation in AI is going so fast that many people have become very enthusiastic about what is possible. For

---

[1] 'Beschonken Meppeler rijdt slapend over de snelweg' (automatic translation: 'Drunken Meppeler sleeps on the highway'), RTV Drenthe, 17 May 2019.

Fig. 24.2   A car breaching traffic law, automatically identified. *Source* The Author

instance, a recent news item reports that Estonia is planning to use AI for automatic decision making in the law.[2] It brings back the old fears for robot judges (Fig. 24.1, on the right).

Contrast here how legal data enters the legal system in France where it is since recently no longer allowed to use data to evaluate or predict the behavior of individual judges:

LOI no 2019–222 du 23 mars 2019 de programmation 2018–2022 et de réforme pour la justice (1) - Article 33

Les données d'identité des magistrats et des membres du greffe ne peuvent faire l'objet d'une réutilisation ayant pour objet ou pour effet d'évaluer, d'analyser, de comparer ou de prédire leurs pratiques professionnelles réelles ou supposées.

[The identity data of magistrates and members of the registry cannot be reused with the purpose or effect of evaluating, analyzing, comparing or predicting their actual or alleged professional practices.]

The fears are real, as the fake news and privacy disasters that are happening show. Even the big tech companies are considering significant changes, such as a data diet.[3] But no one knows whether that is because of a concern for the people's privacy or out of fear of more regulation hurting their market dominance. Anyway, in China privacy is thought of very differently. Figure 24.2 shows an automatically identified car of which it is automatically decided that it is breaching traffic law—see the red box around it. And indeed with both a car and pedestrians on the zebra crossing something is going wrong. Recently, a newspaper reported about how the Chinese

---

[2] 'Can AI be a fair judge in court? Estonia thinks so', Wired, 25 March 2019 (Eric Miller).

[3] 'Het nieuwe datadieet van Google en Facebook' (automatic translation: 'The new data diet from Google and Facebook', nrc.nl, 11 May 2019.

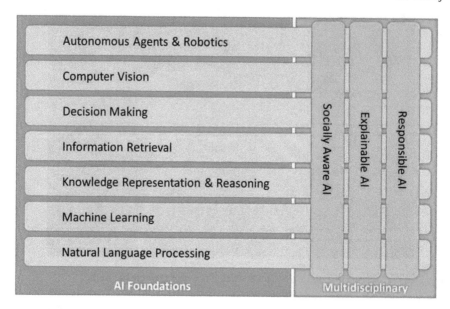

Fig. 24.3 Artificial Intelligence Grid: foundational areas and multidisciplinary challenges. *Source* Dutch AI Manifesto

public thinks of their social scoring system.[4] It seems that the Chinese emphasize the advantages of the scoring system, as a tool against crimes and misbehavior.

Against this background of the benefits and risks of contemporary AI, the AI community in the Netherlands has presented a manifesto[5] emphasizing what is needed: an AI that is aligned with human values and society. In Fig. 24.3, key fields of research in AI are listed in rows, and in columns three key challenges are shown: first, AI should be social, and should allow for sensible interaction with humans; second, AI should be explainable, such that black box algorithms trained on data are made transparent by providing justifying explanations; and, third, AI should be responsible, in particular AI should be guided by the rules, norms, laws of society.

Also elsewhere there is more and more awareness of the need for a good, humane AI. For instance, the CLAIRE Confederation of Laboratories for AI Research in Europe[6] uses the slogan:

Excellence across all of AI

For all of Europe

With a Human-Centered Focus.

In other words, this emerging network advertises a strong European AI with social, explainable, responsible AI at its core.

---

[4] 'Zo stuurt en controleert China zijn burgers' (automatic translation: 'This is how China directs and controls its citizens', nrc.nl, 14 June 2019.

[5] bnvki.org/wp-content/uploads/2018/05/Dutch-AI-Manifesto.pdf.

[6] https://claire-ai.org.

The field of AI & Law has been doing this all along. At least since the start of its primary institutions—the biennial conference ICAIL (started in 1987 by IAAIL),[7] the annual conference JURIX (started in 1988)[8] and the journal Artificial Intelligence & Law (in 1992)—, we have been working on good AI. In other words, AI & Law has worked on the design of socially aware, explainable, responsible AI for decades already. One can say that what is needed in AI today is to do AI as we do law.

24.2   Legal Technology Today

But before explaining how that could go, let us look at the current state of legal technology, for things are very different when compared to the start of the field of AI & Law. Here legal technology refers in particular to software systems aimed at supported legal practice.

In many countries, all branches of government now use legal technology to make information accessible for the public and to provide services as directly and easily as possible. For instance, a Dutch government website[9] provides access to laws, regulations and treaties valid in the Netherlands. The Dutch public prosecution provides an online knowledge-based system that gives access to fines and punishments in all kinds of offenses.[10] There you can for instance find out what happens when the police catch you with an amount of marihuana between five and 30 grams. In the Netherlands, you have to pay 75 euros, and there is a note: also the drugs will be taken away from you. Indeed in the Netherlands all branches of government have online presence, as there is a website that gives access to information about the Dutch judicial system, including access to many decisions.[11]

An especially good example of successful legal technology is provided by the government's income tax services.[12] In the Netherlands, filling out your annual tax form has become very simple. The software is good, it is easy to use, and best of all: in these days of big interconnected data much of what you need to fill in is already filled in for you. Your salary, bank accounts, savings, mortgage interest paid, the value of your house, it is all already there when you log in. In certain cases the tool even leaves room for some mild tax evasion—or tax optimization if you like—since by playing with some settings a married couple can make sure that one partner has to pay just below the minimal amount that will in fact be collected, which can save about 40 euros.

One might think that such legal tech systems are now normal, but that is far from true. Many countries struggle with developing proper legal tech at the government

---

[7] http://www.iaail.org.

[8] http://jurix.nl.

[9] https://wetten.overheid.nl.

[10] www.om.nl/onderwerpen/boetebase.

[11] https://uitspraken.rechtspraak.nl.

[12] www.belastingdienst.nl.

level. One issue is that the design of complex systems is notoriously hard, and this is already true without very advanced AI.

Also the Netherlands has had its striking failures. A scary example is the Dutch project to streamline the IT support of population registers. One would say a doable project, just databases with names, birth dates, marriages, addresses and the like. The project was a complete failure.[13] After burning 90 million euros, the responsible minister—by the way earlier in his career a well-recognized scientist—had to pull the plug. Today all local governments are still using their own systems.

Still, legal tech is booming, and focuses on many different styles of work. The classification used by the tech index maintained by the CodeX center for legal informatics at Stanford university distinguishes nine categories (Marketplace, Document Automation, Practice Management, Legal Research, Legal Education, Online Dispute Resolution, E-Discovery, Analytics and Compliance).[14] It currently lists more than a 1000 legal tech oriented companies. The market for legal technology is already worth a couple of 100s of millions of dollars and can be expected to grow significantly.

So legal tech clearly exists, in fact is widespread. But is it AI, in the sense of AI as discussed at academic conferences? Most of it not really. Most of what we see that is successful in legal tech is not really AI. But there are examples. The tax system just discussed can be regarded as a proper AI system. It has expert knowledge of tax law and it applies that legal expertise to specific situations. True, this is largely good old-fashioned AI already scientifically understood in the 1970s, but by its access to relevant databases of the interconnected-big-data kind, it certainly has a modern twist. One could even say that the system is grounded in real world data, and is hence an example of situated AI, in the way that the term was used in the 1990s (and perhaps before). But also this is clearly not an adaptive machine learning AI system, as is today expected of AI.

24.3 AI & Law is Hard

The reason why much of the successful legal tech is not really AI is simple. AI & Law is hard, very hard. In part this explains why many people are working on this. In AI & Law hard problems cannot be evaded.

Let us look at an example of real law. In 1967, pacifism was still a relevant political attitude. In that year the Dutch Supreme court decided that the inscription 'The Netherlands disarm', mounted on a tower (Fig. 24.4) was not an offense.[15] The court admitted that indeed the sign could be considered a violation of Article 1 of the

---

[13] 'ICT-project basisregistratie totaal mislukt' (automatic translation: 'IT project basic registration totally failed'), nrc.nl, 17 July 2017.

[14] https://techindex.law.stanford.edu/.

[15] Supreme Court The Netherlands, 24 January 1967: Nederland ontwapent (The Netherlands disarm).

Fig. 24.4 Nederland ontwapent (The Netherlands disarm). *Source* Nationaal Archief, 2.24.01.03, 918-0574 (Joost Evers, Anefo)

landscape management regulation of the province of North Holland, but the court decided that that regulation lacked binding power by a conflict with the freedom of speech, as codified in Article 7 of the Dutch constitution.

An example of a hard case. This outcome and its reasoning could not really be predicted, which is one reason why the case is still taught in law schools. The example can be used to illustrate some of the tough hurdles for the development of AI & Law as they have been recognized from the start; here a list used by Rissland 1988 when reviewing Anne Gardner's pioneering book 'An AI approach to legal reasoning' [Gardner 1987], a revision of her 1984 Stanford dissertation.[16]

1. *Legal reasoning is rule-guided, rather than rule-governed.* In the example, indeed both the provincial regulation and the constitution were only guiding, not governing. Their conflict had to be resolved. A wise judge was needed.

2. *Legal terms are open textured.* In the example it is quite a stretch to interpret a sign on a tower as an example of speech in the sense of freedom of speech, but that is what the court here did. It is the old puzzle of legally qualifying the facts, not at all an easy business, also not for humans. With my background in mathematics, I found legal qualification to be a surprisingly and unpleasantly underspecified problem when I took law school exams during my first years as

---

[16] For more on the complexity of AI & Law, see for instance Rissland 1983; Sergot et al. 1986; Bench-Capon et al. 1987; Rissland and Ashley 1987; Oskamp et al. 1989; Ashley 1990; van den Herik 1991; Berman and Hafner 1995; Loui and Norman 1995; Bench-Capon and Sartor 2003; Sartor 2005; Bench-Capon et al. 2012; Zurek and Araszkiewicz 2013; Lauritsen 2015; Ashley 2017.

484   B. Verheij

assistant professor in legal informatics in Maastricht, back in the 1990s. Today computers also still would have a very hard time handling open texture.

3. *Legal questions can have more than one answer, but a reasonable and timely answer must be given.* I have not checked how quickly the supreme court made its decision, probably not very quickly, but the case was settled. The conflict was resolved. A solution that had not yet been there, had been created, constructed. The decision changed a small part of the world.

4. *The answers to legal questions can change over time.* In the example I am not sure about today's law in this respect, in fact it is my guess that freedom of speech is still interpreted as broadly as here, and I would not be surprised when it is now interpreted even more broadly. But society definitely has changed since the late 1960s, and what I would be surprised about is when I would today see such a sign in the public environment.

One way of looking at the hurdles is saying that the subsumption model is false. According to the subsumption model of law there is a set of laws, thought of as rules, there are some facts, and you arrive at the legal answers, the legal consequences by applying the rules to the facts (Fig. 24.5). The case facts are subsumed under the rules, providing the legal solution to the case. It is often associated with Montesquieu's phrase of the judge as a 'bouche de la loi', the mouth of the law, according to which a judge is just the one who makes the law speak.

All hurdles just mentioned show that this perspective cannot be true. Rules are only guiding, terms are open-textured, there can be more answers, and things can change. Hence an alternative perspective is needed on what happens when a case is decided. Legal decision making is a process of constructing and testing a theory, a series of hypotheses that are gradually developed and tested in a critical discussion (Fig. 24.6). The figure suggests an initial version of the facts, an initial version of the relevant rules, and an initial version of the legal conclusions. Gradually the initial hypothesis is adapted. Think of what happens in court proceedings, and in what

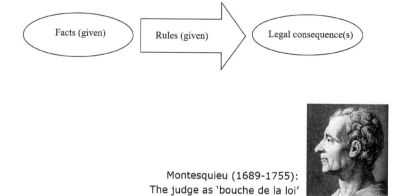

Montesquieu (1689-1755):
The judge as 'bouche de la loi'

Fig. 24.5 The subsumption model (Image Montesquieu adapted from Wikipedia: https://en.wikipedia.org/wiki/File:Charles_de_Secondat,_Baron_de_Montesquieu.jpg)

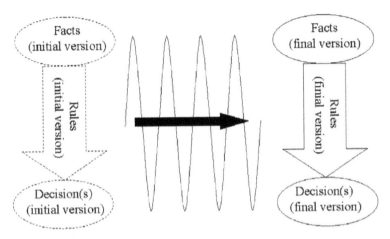

Fig. 24.6 The theory construction model. *Source* Verheij 2003a, 2005

in the Netherlands is called the 'raadkamer', the internal discussion among judges, where after a careful constructive critical discussion—if the judges get the time for that—finally a tried and tested perspective on the case is arrived at, showing the final legal conclusions subsuming the final facts under the final rules. This is the picture I used in 2003 (in an AI & Law special issue of the AI journal). A later version with Floris Bex emphasises that also the perspective on the evidence and how it supports the facts is gradually constructed [Bex and Verheij 2012]. In our field, the idea of theory construction in the law has been emphasized for instance by McCarty 1997, Hafner and Berman 2002, Gordon 1995, Bench-Capon and Sartor 2003 and Hage et al. 1993.

24.4   AI as Law

Today's claim is that good AI requires a different way of doing AI, a way that we in the field of AI & Law have been doing all along, namely doing AI in a way that meets the requirements of the law, in fact in a way that models how things are done in the law. Let us discuss this perspective a bit further.

There can be many metaphors on what AI is and how it should be done, as follows.

1.   AI as mathematics, where the focus is on formal systems;
2.   AI as technology, where the focus is on the art of system design;
3.   AI as psychology, where the focus is on intelligent minds;
4.   AI as sociology, where the focus is on societies of agents.

And then AI as law, to which we will return in a minute (Table 24.1).

In AI as mathematics, one can think of the logical and probabilistic foundations of AI, indeed since the start and still now of core importance. It is said that the

Table 24.1 AI metaphors.
Source The author

Logic	*AI as mathematics*	Probability theory
Expert systems	*AI as technology*	Machine learning
Cognitive modeling	*AI as psychology*	Cognitive computing
Multi-agent systems	*AI as sociology*	Autonomous robots

AI as law
Hybrid critical discussion systems

namegiver of the field of AI—John McCarty—thought of the foundations of AI as an instance of logic, and logic alone. In contrast, today some consider AI to be a kind of statistics 2.0 or 3.0.

In AI as technology, one can think of meticulously crafted rule-based expert systems or of machine learning algorithms evaluated on large carefully labeled data sets. In AI as technology, AI applications and AI research meet most directly.

In AI as psychology, one can think of the modeling of human brains as in cognitive modeling, or of the smart human-like algorithms that are sometimes referred to as cognitive computing.

In AI as sociology, one can think of multi-agent systems simulating a society and of autonomous robots that fly in flocks.

Perhaps you have recognized the list of metaphors as the ones used by Toulmin 1958 when he discussed what he thought of as a crisis in the formal analysis of human reasoning. He argued that the classical formal logic then fashionable was too irrelevant for what reasoning actually was, and he arrived at a perspective of logic as law.[17] What he meant was that counterarguments must be considered, that rules warranting argumentative steps are material (and not only formal), that these rules are backed by factual circumstances, that conclusions are often qualified, uncertain, presumptive, and that reasoning and argument are to be thought of as the outcome of debates among individuals and in groups (see also Hitchcock and Verheij 2006, Verheij 2009. All of these ideas emphasised by Toulmin have now been studied extensively, with the field of AI & Law having played a significant role in the developments.[18]

The metaphors can also be applied to the law, exposing some key ideas familiar in law. If we think of law as mathematics, the focus is on the formality of procedural rule following and of stare decisis where things are well-defined and there is little room for freedom. In law as technology, one can think of the art of doing law in a

---

[17] Toulmin 1958 speaks of logic as mathematics, as technology, as psychology, as sociology and as law (jurisprudence).

[18] See for instance the research by Prakken 1997; Sartor 2005; Gordon 1995; Bench-Capon 2003 and Atkinson and Bench-Capon 2006. Argumentation research in AI & Law is connected to the wider study of formal and computational argumentation, see for instance Simari and Loui 1992; Pollock 1995; Vreeswijk 1997; Chesñevar et al. 2000. See also the handbooks edited by Baroni et al. 2018 and written by van Eemeren et al. 2014.

jurisdiction with either a focus on rules, as in civil law systems, or with a focus on cases, as in common law systems. In law as psychology, one can think of the judicial reasoning by an individual judge, and of the judicial discretion that is to some extent allowed, even wanted. In law as sociology, the role of critical discussion springs to mind, and of regulating a society in order to give order and prevent chaos. And finally the somewhat pleonastic metaphor of law as law, but now as law in contrast with the other metaphors. I think of two specific and essential ideas in the law, namely that government is to be bound by the rule of law, and that the goal of law is to arrive at justice, thereby supporting a good society and a good life for its citizens.

Note how this discussion shows the typically legal, hybrid balancing of different sides: rules and cases, regulations and decisions, rationality and interpretation, individual and society, boundedness and justice. And as we know this balancing best takes place in a constructive critical discussion. Which brings us to the bottom line of the list of AI metaphors (Table 24.1): AI as law, where the focus is on hybrid critical discussion.

In AI as law, AI systems are to be thought of as hybrid critical discussion systems, where different hypothetical perspectives are constructed and evaluated until a good answer is found.

In this connection, I recently explained what I think is needed in AI (Fig. 24.7), namely the much-needed step we have to make towards hybrid systems that connect knowledge representation and reasoning techniques with the powers of machine learning. In this diagram I used the term argumentation systems. But since argumentation has a very specific sound in the field of AI & Law, and perhaps to some feels as a too specific, too limiting perspective, we can rephrase and speak of AI as Law in the sense of the development of hybrid critical discussion systems.

Fig. 24.7 Bridging the gap between knowledge and data systems in AI. *Source* Verheij 2018.

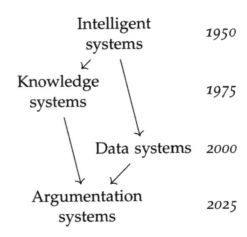

Fig. 24.8 Argumentation.
Source The author

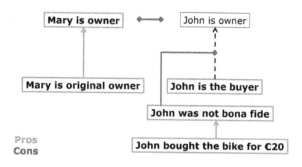

24.5   Topics in AI

Let me continue with a discussion of core topics in AI with the AI as Law perspective in mind. My focus is on reasoning, knowledge, learning and language.

24.5.1   Reasoning

First, reasoning. I then think of argumentation where arguments and counterarguments meet (van Eemeren et al. 2014, Atkinson et al. 2017, Baroni et al. 2018). This is connected to the idea of defeasibility, where arguments become defeated when attacked by a stronger counterargument. Argumentation has been used to address the deep and old puzzles of inconsistency, incomplete information and uncertainty.

Here is an example argument about the Dutch bike owner Mary whose bike is stolen (Fig. 24.8). The bike is bought by John, hence both have a claim to ownership—Mary as the original owner, John as the buyer. But in this case the conflict can be resolved as John bought the bike for the low price of 20 euros, indicating that he was not a bona fide buyer. At such a price, he could have known that the bike was stolen, hence he has no claim to ownership as the buyer, and Mary is the owner.

It is one achievement of the field of AI & Law that the logic of argumentation is by now well understood, so well that it can be implemented in argumentation diagramming software that applies the logic of argumentation, for instance, the ArguMed software that I implemented long ago [Verheij 2003a, 2005].[19] It implements argumentation semantics of the stable kind in the sense of Dung's abstract argumentation that was proposed some 25 years ago [Dung 1995], a turning point and a cornerstone in today's understanding of argumentation, with many successes. Abstract argumentation also gave new puzzles such as the lack of standardization leading to all kinds of detailed comparative formal studies, and more fundamentally the multiple formal semantics puzzle. The stable, preferred, grounded and complete semantics were the

---

[19] For some other examples, see Gordon et al. 2007; Loui et al. 1997; Kirschner et al. 2003; Reed and Rowe 2004; Scheuer et al. 2010; Lodder and Zelznikow 2005.

four proposed by Dung 1995, quickly thereafter extended to six when the labeling-based stage and semi-stable semantics were proposed [Verheij 1996]. But that was only the start because the field of computational argumentation was then still only emerging.

For me, it was obvious that a different approach was needed when I discovered that after combining attack and support 11 different semantics were formally possible [Verheij 2003b], but practically almost all hardly relevant. No lawyer has to think about whether the applicable argumentation semantics is the semi-stable or the stage semantics.

One puzzle in the field is the following. A key idea underlying Dung's 1995 original abstract argumentation paper is that derivation-like arguments can be abstracted from, allowing to focus only on attack. I know that for many this idea has helped them in their work and understanding of argumentation. For me, this was—from rather early on— more a distraction than an advantage as it introduced a separate, seemingly spurious layer. In the way that Jaap Hage put it: 'those cloudy formal structures of yours'—and he referred to abstract graphs in the sense of Dung—have no grounding in how lawyers think. There is no separate category of supporting arguments to be abstracted from before considering attack; instead, in the law there are only reasons for and against conclusions that must be balanced. Those were the days when Hage was working on Reason-Based Logic [Hage 1997] and I was helping him [Verheij et al. 1998]. In a sense, the ArguMed software based on the DefLog formalism was my answer to removing that redundant intermediate layer (still present in its precursor the Argue! system), while sticking to the important mathematical analysis of reinstatement uncovered by Dung (see Verheij 2003a, 2005). For background on the puzzle of combining support and attack, see van Eemeren et al. 2014, Sect. 11.5.5.

But as I said from around the turn of the millennium I thought a new mathematical foundation was called for, and it took me years to arrive at something that really increased my understanding of argumentation: the case model formalism [Verheij 2017a, b], but that is not for now.

24.5.2 Knowledge

The second topic of AI to be discussed is knowledge, so prominent in AI and in law. I then think of material, semi-formal argumentation schemes such as the witness testimony scheme, or the scheme for practical reasoning, as for instance collected in the nice volume by Walton et al. 2008.

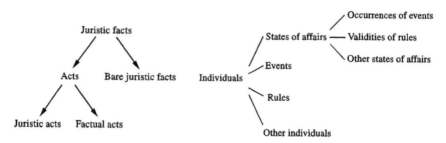

Fig. 24.9 Types of juristic facts (left); tree of individuals (right). *Source* Hage and Verheij 1999

I also think of norms, in our community often studied with a Hohfeldian or deontic logic perspective on rights and obligations as a background.[20] And then there are the ontologies that can capture large amounts of knowledge in a systematic way.[21]

One lesson that I have taken home from working in the domain of law—I started in the field of mathematics where things are thought of as neat and clean—one lesson is that in the world of law things are always more complex than you think. One could say that it is the business of law to find the exactly right level of complexity, and that is often just a bit more complex than one's initial idea. And if things are not yet complex now, they can become tomorrow. Remember the dynamics of theory construction (Fig. 24.6).

Figure 24.9 (left) shows how in the law different categories of juristic facts are distinguished. Here juristic facts are the kind of facts that are legally relevant, that have legal consequences. They come in two kinds: acts with legal consequences, and bare juristic facts, where the latter are intentionless events such as being born, which still have legal consequences. And acts with legal consequences are divided into juristic acts aimed at a legal consequence (such as contracting), and factual acts, where although there is no legal intention, still there are legal consequences. Here the primary example is that of unlawful acts as discussed in tort law. I am still happy that I learnt this categorization of juristic facts, as it has relevantly expanded my understanding of how things work in the world. And of how things should be done in AI. Definitely not purely logically or purely statistically, definitely with much attention for the specifics of a situation.

Figure 24.9 (right) shows another categorization, prepared with Jaap Hage, that shows how we then approached the core categories of things, or 'individuals' that should be distinguished when analyzing the law: states of affairs, events rules, other individuals, and then the subcategories of event occurrences, rule validities and other states of affairs. And although such a categorization does have a hint of the baroqueness of Jorge Luis Borges' animal taxonomy (that included those animals that belong to the emperor, mermaids and innumerable animals), the abstract core ontology

---

[20] See for instance Sartor 2005, Gabbay et al. 2013, Governatori and Rotolo 2010.

[21] See for instance McCarty 1989; Valente 1995; van Kralingen 1995; Visser 1995; Visser and Bench-Capon 1998; Hage and Verheij 1999; Boer et al. 2002, 2003, Breuker et al. 2004; Hoekstra et al. 2007; Wyner 2008; Casanovas et al. 2016.

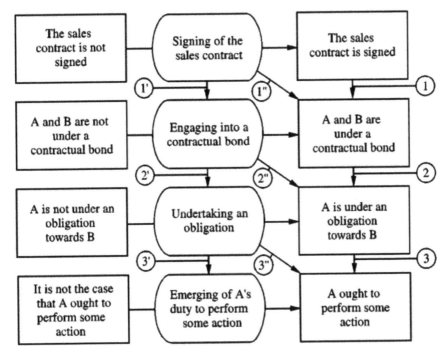

Fig. 24.10 Signing a sales contract. *Source* Hage and Verheij 1999

helped us to analyze the relations between events, rules and states of affairs that play a role when signing a contract (Fig. 24.10). Indeed at first sight a complex picture. For now it suffices that at the top row there is the physical act of signing—say when the pen is going over the paper to sign—and this physical act counts as engaging in a contractual bond (shown in the second row), which implies the undertaking of an obligation (third row), which in turn leads to a duty to perform an action (at the bottom row). Not a simple picture, but as said, in the law things are often more complex than expected, and typically for good, pragmatic reasons.

The core puzzle for our field and for AI generally that I would like to mention is that of commonsense knowledge. This remains an essential puzzle, also in these days of big data; also in these days of cognitive computing. Machines simply don't have commonsense knowledge that is nearly good enough. A knowledgeable report in the Communications of the ACM explains that progress has been slow [Davis and Marcus 2015]. It goes back to 2015, but please do not believe it when it is suggested that things are very different today. The commonsense knowledge problem remains a relevant and important research challenge indeed and I hope to see more of the big knowledge needed for serious AI & Law in the future.

One example of what I think is an as yet underestimated cornerstone of common-sense knowledge is the role of globally coherent knowledge structures— such as the scenarios and cases we encounter in the law. Bex 2011 took relevant steps to investigate scenario schemes and how they are hierarchically related, in the context of murder stories and crime investigation.[22] The field of AI & Law would benefit from more work like this, that goes back to the frames and scripts studied by people such as Roger Schank and Marvin Minsky.

I currently work on knowledge representation in terms of the case models mentioned before. It has for instance been used to represent how an appellate court gradually constructs its hypotheses about a murder case on the basis of the evidence, gradually testing and selecting which scenario of what has happened to believe or not [Verheij 2020b], and also to the temporal development of the relevance of past decisions in terms of the values they promote and demote [Verheij 2016].

24.5.3 Learning

Then we come to the topic of learning. It is the domain of statistical analysis that shows that certain judges are more prone to supporting democrat positions than others, and that as we saw no longer is allowed in France. It is the domain of open data, that allows public access to legal sources and in which the AI & Law community has been very active [Biagioli et al. 2005], Francesconi and Passerini 2007, Francesconi et al. 2010a, b, Sartor et al. 2011, Athan et al. 2013. And it is the realm of neural networks, back in the day called perceptrons, now referred to as deep learning.

The core theme to be discussed here is the issue of how learning and the justification of outcomes go together, using a contemporary term: how to arrive at an explainable AI, an explainable machine learning. We have heard it discussed at all career levels, by young PhD students and by a Turing award winner.

The issue can be illustrated by a mock prediction machine for Dutch criminal courts. Imagine a button that you can push, that once you push it always gives the outcome that the suspect is guilty as charged. And thinking of the need to evaluate systems [Conrad and Zeleznikow 2015], this system has indeed been validated by the Dutch Central Bureau of Statistics, which has the data that shows that this prediction machine is correct in 91 out of 100 cases (Fig. 24.11). The validating data shows that the imaginary prediction machine has become a bit less accurate in recent years, presumably by changes in society, perhaps in part caused by the attention in the Netherlands for so-called dubious cases, or miscarriages of justice, which may have made judges a little more reluctant to decide for guilt. But still: 91% for this very simple machine is quite good. And as you know, all this says very little about how to decide for guilt or not.

How hard judicial prediction really is, also when using serious machine learning techniques, is shown by some recent examples. Katz et al. 2017 claim that their US Supreme Court prediction machine could achieve a 70% accuracy. A mild improvement over the baseline of the historical majority outcome (to always affirm a previous

---

[22] For more work on evidence in AI & Law, see for instance Keppens and Schafer 2006, Bex et al. 2010, Keppens 2012, Fenton et al. 2013, Vlek et al. 2014, Di Bello and Verheij 2018.

Fig. 24.11 Convictions in criminal cases in the Netherlands. *Source* Central Bureau of Statistics (www. cbs.nl, data collection of 11 September 2017)

decision) which is 60%, and even milder over the 10-year majority outcome which is 67%. The system based its predictions on features such as judge identity, month, court of origin and issue, so modest results are not surprising.

In another study, Aletras et al. 2016 studied European Court of Human Rights cases. They used so-called n-grams and topics as the starting point of their training, and used a prepared dataset to make a cleaner baseline of 50% accuracy by random guessing. They reached 79% accuracy using the whole text, and noted that by only using the part where the factual circumstances are described already an accuracy of 73% is reached.

Naively taking the ratios of 70 over 60 and of 79 over 50, one sees that factors of 1.2 and of 1.6 improvement are relevant research outcomes, but practically modest. And more importantly these systems only focus on outcome, without saying anything about how to arrive at an outcome, or about for which reasons an outcome is warranted or not.

Learning is hard, especially in the domain of law.[23] I am still a fan of an old paper by Trevor Bench-Capon on neural networks and open texture [Bench-Capon 1993]. In an artificially constructed example about welfare benefits, he included different kinds of constraints: Boolean, categorical, numeric. For instance, women were allowed the benefit after 60, and men after 65. He found that after training, the neural network could achieve a high overall performance, but with somewhat surprising underlying rationales. In Fig. 24.12, on the left, one can see that the condition starts to be relevant long before the ages of between 60 and 65 and that the difference in gender is something like 15 years instead of five. On the right, with a more focused training set using cases with only single failing conditions, the relevance started a bit later, but still too early, while the gender difference now indeed was five years.

What I have placed my bets on is the kind of hybrid cases and rules systems that in AI & Law are normal.[24] I now represent Dutch tort law in terms of case models validating rule-based arguments [Verheij 2017b] (cf. Fig. 24.13).

---

[23] See also recently Medvedeva et al. 2019.

[24] See for instance work by Branting 1991; Skalak and Rissland 1992; Branting 1993; Prakken and Sartor 1996; Prakken and Sartor 1998; Stranieri et al. 1999; Roth 2003; Brüninghaus and Ashley 2003; Atkinson and Bench-Capon 2006; Čyras et al. 2016.

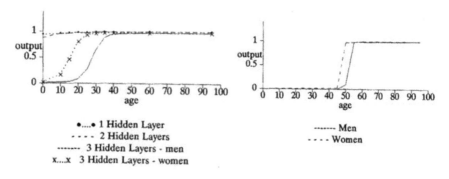

Fig. 24.12 Neural networks and open texture. *Source* Bench-Capon 1993

Fig. 24.13 Arguments, rules and cases for Dutch tort law. *Source* Verheij 2017b

24.5.4 Language

Then language, the fourth and final topic of AI that I would like to discuss here. Today the topic of language is closely connected to machine learning. I think of the labeling of natural language data to allow for training; I think of prediction such as by a search engine or chat application on a smartphone, and I think of argument mining, a relevant topic with strong roots in the field of AI & Law.

The study of natural language in AI, and in fact of AI itself, got a significant boost by IBM's Watson system that won the Jeopardy! quiz show. For instance, Watson correctly recognized the description of 'A 2-word phrase [that] means the power to take private property for public use'. That description refers to the typically legal concept of eminent domain, the situation in which a government disowns property for public reasons, such as the construction of a highway or windmill park. Watson's output showed that the legal concept scored 98%, but also 'electric company' and 'capitalist economy' were considered with 9% and 5% scores, respectively. Apparently Watson sees some kind of overlap between the legal concept of eminent domain, electric companies and capitalist economy, since 98+9+5 is more than a 100 percent.

And IBM continued, as Watson was used as the basis for its debating technologies. In a 2014 demonstration,[25] the system is considering the sale of violent video games to minors. The video shows that the system finds reasons for and against banning the sale of such games to minors. For instance, most children who play violent games do not have problems, but violent video games can increase children's aggression. The video remains impressive, and for the field of computational argumentation it was somewhat discomforting that the researchers behind this system were then outsiders to the field.

The success of these natural language systems leads one to think about why they can do what they do. Do they really have an understanding of a complex sentence describing the legal concept of eminent domain; can they really digest newspaper articles and other online resources on violent video games?

These questions are especially relevant since in the field of AI & Law we have had the opportunity to follow research on argument mining from the start. Early and relevant research is by Mochales Palau and Moens 2009, 2011 studying argument mining. As already shown in that paper, it should not be considered an easy task to perform argument mining. Indeed the field has been making relevant and interesting progress, but no one would claim the kind of natural language understanding needed for interpreting legal concepts or online debates.[26]

So what then is the basis of apparent success? Is it simply because a big tech company can do a research investment that in academia one can only dream of? Certainly that is a part of what has been going on. But there is more to it than that as can be appreciated by a small experiment I did, this time actually an implemented online system. It is what I ironically called Poor Man's Watson,[27] which has been programmed without much deep natural language technology, just some simple regular expression scripts using online access to the Google search engine and Wikipedia. And indeed it turns out that the simple script can also recognize the concept of eminent domain: when one types 'the power to take private property for public use' the answer is 'eminent domain'. The explanation for this remarkable result is that for some descriptions the correct Wikipedia page ends up high in the list of pages returned by Google, and that happens because we—the people—have been typing in good descriptions of those concepts in Wikipedia, and indeed Google can find these pages. Sometimes the results are spectacular, but also they are brittle since seemingly small, irrelevant changes can quickly break this simple system.

For the debating technology something similar holds since there are websites collecting pros and cons of societal debates. For instance, the website procon.org has

---

[25] Milken Institute Global Conference 2014, session 'Why Tomorrow Won't Look Like Today: Things that Will Blow Your Mind', youtu.be/6fJOtAzICzw?t=2725.

[26] See for instance Schweighofer et al. 2001; Wyner et al. 2009/2010; Grabmair and Ashley 2011; Ashley and Walker 2013; Grabmair et al. 2015; Tran et al. 2020.

[27] Poor Man's Watson, www.ai.rug.nl/~verheij/pmw.

a page on the pros and cons of violent video games.[28] Arguments it has collected include 'Pro 1: Playing violent video games causes more aggression, bullying, and fighting' and 'Con 1: Sales of violent video games have significantly increased while violent juvenile crime rates have significantly decreased'. The web site Kialo has similar collaboratively created lists.[29] Concerning the issue 'Violent video games should be banned to curb school shootings', it lists for instance the pro 'Video games normalize violence, especially in the eyes of kids, and affect how they see and interact with the world' and the con 'School shootings are, primarily, the result of other factors that should be dealt with instead'.

Surely the existence of such lists typed in, in a structured way, by humans is a central basis for what debating technology can and cannot do. It is not a coincidence that—listening carefully to the reports—the examples used in marketing concern curated lists of topics. At the same time this does not take away the bravery of IBM and how strongly it has been stimulating the field of AI by its successful demos. That also for IBM things are sometimes hard is shown by the report from February 2019 when IBM's technology entered into a debate with a human debater, and this time lost.[30] But who knows what the future brings.

What I believe is needed is the development of an ever-closer connection between complex knowledge representations and natural language explanations, as for instance in work by Vlek et al. 2016 on explaining Bayesian Networks, with nice connections to the work by Keppens 2019.

24.6 Conclusion

As I said I think the way to go for the field is to develop an AI that is much like the law, an AI where systems are hybrid critical discussion systems. After phases of AI as mathematics, as technology, as psychology, and as sociology—all still important and relevant—, an AI as Law perspective provides fresh ideas for designing an AI that is good (Table 1). And in order to build the hybrid critical discussion systems that I think are needed, lots of work is waiting in reasoning, in knowledge, in learning and in language, as follows.

For reasoning (Sect. 24.5.1), the study of formal and computational argumentation remains relevant and promising, while work is needed to arrive at a formal semantics that is not only accessible for a small group of experts.

For knowledge (Sect. 24.5.2), we need to continue working on knowledge bases large and small, and on systems with embedded norms. But I hope that some are also brave enough to be looking for new ways to arrive at good commonsense knowledge for machines. In the law we cannot do without wise commonsense.

[28] videogames.procon.org.

[29] kialo.com.

[30] 'IBM's AI loses debate to a human, but it's got worlds to conquer', https://www.cnet.com/, 11 February 2019.

For learning (Sect. 24.5.3), the integration of knowledge and data can be addressed by how in the law rules and cases are connected and influence one another. Only then the requirements of explainability and responsibility can be properly addressed.

For language (Sect. 24.5.4), work is needed in interpretation of what is said in a text. This requires an understanding in terms of complex, detailed models of a situation, like what happens in any court of law where every word can make a relevant difference.

The perspective of AI as Law discussed here can be regarded as an attempt to broaden what I said in the lecture on 'Arguments for good AI' where the focus is mostly on computational argumentation [Verheij 2018]. There I explain that we need a good AI that can give good answers to our questions, give good reasons for them, and make good choices. I projected that in 2025 we will have arrived at a new kind of AI system bridging knowledge and data, namely argumentation systems (Fig. 24.7). Clearly and as I tried to explain, there is still plenty of work to be done. I expect that a key role will be played by work in our field on connections between rules, cases and arguments, as in the set of cases formalizing tort law (Fig. 24.13, on the left) that formally validate the legally relevant rule-based arguments (Fig. 24.13, on the right).

By following the path of developing AI as Law we can guard against technology that is bad for us, and that—unlike the guillotine I started with—is a really humane technology that directly benefits society and its citizens.

In conclusion, in these days of dreams and fears of AI and algorithms, the field of AI & Law is more relevant than ever. AI & Law has worked on the design of socially aware, explainable, responsible AI for decades already.

And since we in AI & Law are used to addressing the hardest problems across the breadth of AI (reasoning, knowledge, learning, language)—since in fact we cannot avoid them—, our field can inspire new solutions. In particular, I discussed computational argumentation, schemes for arguments and scenarios, encoded norms, hybrid rule-case systems and computational interpretation.

We only need to look at what happens in the law. In the law, we see an artificial system that adds much value to our life. Let us take inspiration from the law, and let us work on building Artificial Intelligence that is not scary, but that genuinely contributes to a good quality of life in a just society.

References

Aletras N, Tsarapatsanis D, Preotiuc-Pietro D, Lampos V (2016) Predicting judicial decisions of the European Court of Human Rights: a natural language processing perspective. Peer J Computer Science, 2:1–19, 2016. https://doi.org/10.7717/peerj-cs.93
Ashley KD (1990) Modeling Legal Arguments: Reasoning with Cases and Hypotheticals. The MIT Press, Cambridge, MA
Ashley KD (2017) Artificial Intelligence and Legal Analytics: New Tools for Law Practice in the Digital Age. Cambridge University Press, Cambridge

Ashley KD, Walker VR (2013) Toward constructing evidence-based legal arguments using legal decision documents and machine learning. In: Proceedings of the Fourteenth International Conference on Artificial Intelligence and Law, pp. 176–180. ACM, New York, NY

Athan T, Boley H, Governatori G, Palmirani M, Paschke A, Wyner A (2013) OASIS LegalRuleML. In Proceedings of the 14th International Conference on Artificial Intelligence and Law (ICAIL 2013), pp. 3–12. ACM Press, New York, NY

Atkinson K, Bench-Capon TJM (2006) Legal case-based reasoning as practical reasoning. Artificial Intelligence and Law, 13:93–131

Atkinson K, Baroni P, Giacomin M, Hunter A, Prakken H, Reed C, Simari G, Thimm M, Villata S (2017) Toward artificial argumentation. AI Magazine, 38(3):25–36

Baroni P, Gabbay D, Giacomin M, van der Torre L (eds) (2018) Handbook of Formal Argumentation. College Publications, London

Bench-Capon TJM (1993) Neural networks and open texture. In: Proceedings of the Fourth International Conference on Artificial Intelligence and Law, pp. 292–297. ACM Press, New York, NY

Bench-Capon TJM (2003) Persuasion in practical argument using value-based argumentation frameworks. Journal of Logic and Computation, 13(3):429–448

Bench-Capon TJM, Araszkiewicz M, Ashley KD, Atkinson K, Bex FJ, Borges F, Bourcier D, Bourgine D, Conrad JG, Francesconi E, Gordon TF, Governatori G, Leidner JL, Lewis DD, Loui RP, McCarty LT, Prakken H, Schilder F, Schweighofer E, Thompson P, Tyrrell A, Verheij B, Walton DN, Wyner AZ (2012) A history of AI and Law in 50 papers: 25 years of the International Conference on AI and Law. Artificial Intelligence and Law, 20(3):215–319

Bench-Capon TJM, Robinson GO, Routen TW, Sergot MJ (1987) Logic programming for large scale applications in law: A formalisation of supplementary benefit legislation. In: Proceedings of the 1st International Conference on Artificial Intelligence and Law (ICAIL 1987), pp. 190–198. ACM, New York, NY

Bench-Capon TJM, Sartor G (2003) A model of legal reasoning with cases incorporating theories and values. Artificial Intelligence, 150(1):97–143

Berman DH, Hafner CL (1995) Understanding precedents in a temporal context of evolving legal doctrine. In: Proceedings of the Fifth International Conference on Artificial Intelligence and Law, pp. 42–51. ACM Press, New York, NY

Bex FJ (2011) Arguments, Stories and Criminal Evidence: A Formal Hybrid Theory. Springer, Berlin

Bex FJ, van Koppen PJ, Prakken H, Verheij B (2010) A hybrid formal theory of arguments, stories and criminal evidence. Artificial Intelligence and Law, 18:1–30

Bex FJ, Verheij B (2012) Solving a murder case by asking critical questions: An approach to fact-finding in terms of argumentation and story schemes. Argumentation, 26:325–353

Biagioli C, Francesconi E, Passerini A, Montemagni S, Soria C (2005) Automatic semantics extraction in law documents. In: Proceedings of the 10th International Conference on Artificial Intelligence and Law (ICAIL 2005), pp. 133–140. ACM Press, New York, NY

Boer A, Hoekstra R, Winkels R (2002) METAlex: Legislation in XML. In: Bench-Capon TJM, Daskalopulu A, Winkels R (eds) Legal Knowledge and Information Systems. JURIX 2002: The Fifteenth Annual Conference, pp. 1–10. IOS Press, Amsterdam

Boer A, van Engers T, Winkels R (2003) Using ontologies for comparing and harmonizing legislation. In: Proceedings of the 9th International Conference on Artificial Intelligence and Law, pp. 60–69. ACM, New York, NY

Branting LK (1991) Building explanations from rules and structured cases. International Journal of Man-Machine Studies, 34(6):797–837

Branting LK (1993) A computational model of ratio decidendi. Artificial Intelligence and Law, 2(1):1–31

Breuker J, Valente A, Winkels R (2004) Legal ontologies in knowledge engineering and information management. Artificial Intelligence and Law, 12 (4):241–277

Brüninghaus S, Ashley KD (2003) Predicting outcomes of case based legal arguments. In: Proceedings of the 9th International Conference on Artificial Intelligence and Law (ICAIL 2003), pp. 233–242. ACM, New York, NY

Casanovas P, Palmirani M, Peroni S, van Engers T, Vitali F (2016) Semantic web for the legal domain: the next step. Semantic web, 7(3):213–227

Chesñevar CI, Maguitman AG, Loui RP (2000) Logical models of argument. ACM Computing Surveys, 32(4):337–383

Conrad JG, Zeleznikow J (2015) The role of evaluation in AI and law: an examination of its different forms in the AI and Law Journal. In: Proceedings of the 15th International Conference on Artificial Intelligence and Law (ICAIL 2015), pages 181–186. ACM, New York, NY

Davis E, Marcus G (2015) Commonsense reasoning and commonsense knowledge in Artificial Intelligence. Communications of the ACM, 58(9):92–103

Di Bello M, Verheij B (2018) Evidential reasoning. In: Bongiovanni G, Postema G, Rotolo A, Sartor G, Valentini C, Walton DN (eds) Handbook of Legal Reasoning and Argumentation, pp. 447–493. Springer, Dordrecht

Čyras K, Satoh K, Toni F (2016) Abstract argumentation for case-based reasoning. In: Proceedings of the Fifteenth International Conference on Principles of Knowledge Representation and Reasoning (KR 2016), pp. 549–552. AAAI Press

Dung PM (1995) On the acceptability of arguments and its fundamental role in nonmonotonic reasoning, logic programming and n-person games. Artificial Intelligence, 77:321–357

Fenton NE, Neil MD, Lagnado DA (2013) A general structure for legal arguments about evidence using Bayesian Networks. Cognitive Science, 37: 61–102

Francesconi E, Passerini A (2007) Automatic classification of provisions in legislative texts. Artificial Intelligence and Law, 15(1):1–17

Francesconi E, Montemagni D, Peters W, Tiscornia D (2010a) Integrating a bottom–up and top–down methodology for building semantic resources for the multilingual legal domain. In: Semantic Processing of Legal Texts, pp. 95–121. Springer, Berlin

Francesconi E, Montemagni S, Peters W, Tiscornia D (2010b) Semantic processing of legal texts: Where the language of law meets the law of language. Springer, Berlin

Gabbay D, Horty J, Parent X, van der Meyden R, van der Torre L (2013) Handbook of Deontic Logic and Normative Systems. College Publication, London

Gardner A (1987) An Artificial Intelligence Approach to Legal Reasoning. The MIT Press, Cambridge, MA

Gordon TF (1995) The Pleadings Game: An Artificial Intelligence Model of Procedural Justice. Kluwer, Dordrecht

Gordon TF, Prakken H, Walton DN (2007) The Carneades model of argument and burden of proof. Artificial Intelligence, 171(10–15):875–896

Governatori G, Rotolo A (2010) Changing legal systems: Legal abrogations and annulments in defeasible logic. Logic Journal of the IGPL, 18(1):157–194

Grabmair M, Ashley KD (2011) Facilitating case comparison using value judgments and intermediate legal concepts. In: Proceedings of the 13th international conference on Artificial intelligence and law, pp. 161–170. ACM, New York, NY

Grabmair M, Ashley KD, Chen R, Sureshkumar P, Wang C, Nyberg E, Walker VR (2015) Introducing LUIMA: an experiment in legal conceptual retrieval of vaccine injury decisions using a UIMA type system and tools. In: Proceedings of the 15th International Conference on Artificial Intelligence and Law, pp. 69–78. ACM, New York, NY

Hafner CL, Berman DH (2002) The role of context in case-based legal reasoning: Teleological, temporal, and procedural. Artificial Intelligence and Law, 10(1–3):19–64

Hage JC (1997) Reasoning with Rules. An Essay on Legal Reasoning and Its Underlying Logic. Kluwer Academic Publishers, Dordrecht

Hage JC, Verheij B (1999) The law as a dynamic interconnected system of states of affairs: a legal top ontology. International Journal of Human-Computer Studies, 51(6):1043–1077

Hage JC, Leenes R, Lodder AR (1993) Hard cases: a procedural approach. Artificial intelligence and law, 2(2):113–167

Hitchcock DL, Verheij B (Eds.) (2006) Arguing on the Toulmin Model. New Essays in Argument Analysis and Evaluation (Argumentation Library, Volume 10). Springer, Dordrecht

Hoekstra R, Breuker J, Di Bello M, Boer A (2007) The LKIF core ontology of basic legal concepts. In: Casanovas P, Biasiotti MA, Francesconi E, Sagri MT (eds) Proceedings of LOAIT 2007. Second Workshop on Legal Ontologies and Artificial Intelligence Techniques, pp. 43–63. CEUR-WS

Katz DM, Bommarito II MJ, Blackman J (2017) A general approach for predicting the behavior of the Supreme Court of the United States. PLoS ONE, 12(4):1–18. https://doi.org/10.1371/journal.pone.0174698

Keppens J (2012) Argument diagram extraction from evidential Bayesian networks. Artificial Intelligence and Law, 20:109–143, 2012

Keppens J (2019) Explainable Bayesian network query results via natural language generation systems. In: Proceedings of the 17th International Conference on Artificial Intelligence and Law (ICAIL 2019), pp. 42–51. ACM, New York, NY

Keppens J, Schafer B (2006) Knowledge based crime scenario modelling. Expert Systems with Applications, 30(2):203–222

Kirschner PA, Buckingham Shum SJ, Carr CS (2003) Visualizing Argumentation: Software Tools for Collaborative and Educational Sense-Making. Springer, Berlin

Lauritsen M (2015). On balance. Artificial Intelligence and Law, 23(1):23–42

Lodder AR, Zelznikow J (2005) Developing an online dispute resolution environment: Dialogue tools and negotiation support systems in a three-step model. Harvard Negotiation Law Review, 10:287–337

Loui RP, Norman J (1995) Rationales and argument moves. Artificial Intelligence and Law, 3:159–189

Loui RP, Norman J, Altepeter J, Pinkard D, Craven D, Linsday J, Foltz M (1997) Progress on Room 5: a testbed for public interactive semi-formal legal argumentation. In: Proceedings of the 6th International Conference on Artificial Intelligence and Law, pp. 207–214. ACM Press, New York, NY

McCarty LT (1989) A language for legal discourse. i. basic features. In: Proceedings of the 2nd International Conference on Artificial Intelligence and Law (ICAIL 1989), pp. 180–189. ACM, New York, NY

McCarty LT (1997) Some arguments about legal arguments. In: Proceedings of the 6th International Conference on Artificial Intelligence and Law (ICAIL 1997), pp. 215–224. ACM Press, New York, NY

Medvedeva M, Vols M, Wieling M (2019) Using machine learning to predict decisions of the European Court of Human Rights. Artificial Intelligence and Law, pp. 1–30

Mochales Palau R, Moens MF (2009) Argumentation mining: the detection, classification and structure of arguments in text. In: Proceedings of the 12th International Conference on Artificial Intelligence and Law (ICAIL 2009), pp. 98–107. ACM Press, New York, NY

Mochales Palau R, Moens MF (2011) Argumentation mining. Artificial Intelligence and Law, 19(1):1–22

Oskamp A, Walker RF, Schrickx JA, van den Berg PH (1989) PROLEXS divide and rule: a legal application. In: Proceedings of the Second International Conference on Artificial intelligence and law, pp. 54–62. ACM, New York, NY

Pollock JL (1995) Cognitive Carpentry: A Blueprint for How to Build a Person. The MIT Press, Cambridge, MA

Prakken H (1997) Logical Tools for Modelling Legal Argument. A Study of Defeasible Reasoning in Law. Kluwer Academic Publishers, Dordrecht

Prakken H, Sartor G (1996) A dialectical model of assessing conflicting arguments in legal reasoning. Artificial Intelligence and Law, 4:331–368

Prakken H, Sartor G (1998) Modelling reasoning with precedents in a formal dialogue game. Artificial Intelligence and Law, 6:231–287

Reed C, Rowe G (2004) Araucaria: Software for argument analysis, diagramming and representation. International Journal of AI Tools, 14(3–4):961– 980

Rissland EL (1983) Examples in legal reasoning: Legal hypotheticals. In: Proceedings of the 8th International Joint Conference on Artificial Intelligence (IJCAI 1983), pp. 90–93

Rissland EL (1988) Book review. An Artificial Intelligence Approach to Legal Reasoning. Harvard Journal of Law and Technology, 1(Spring):223–231

Rissland EL, Ashley KD (1987) A case-based system for trade secrets law. In: Proceedings of the First International Conference on Artificial Intelligence and Law, pp. 60–66. ACM Press, New York, NY

Roth B (2003) Case-Based Reasoning in the Law. A Formal Theory of Reasoning by Case Comparison. Dissertation Universiteit Maastricht, Maastricht

Sartor G (2005) Legal reasoning: a cognitive approach to the law. Vol 5 of Treatise on legal philosophy and general jurisprudence. Springer, Berlin

Sartor G, Palmirani M, Francesconi E, Biasiotti MA (2011) Legislative XML for the semantic web: principles, models, standards for document management. Springer, Berlin

Scheuer O, Loll F, Pinkwart N, McLaren BM (2010) Computer-supported argumentation: A review of the state of the art. International Journal of Computer-Supported Collaborative Learning, 5(1):43–102

Schweighofer E, Rauber A, Dittenbach M (2001) Automatic text representation, classification and labeling in European law. In: Proceedings of the 8th International Conference on Artificial intelligence and law, pp. 78–87. ACM, New York, NY

Sergot MJ, Sadri F, Kowalski RA, Kriwaczek F, Hammond P, Cory HT (1986) The British Nationality Act as a logic program. Communications of the ACM, 29(5):370–386

Simari GR, Loui RP (1992) A mathematical treatment of defeasible reasoning and its applications. Artificial Intelligence, 53:125–157

Skalak DB, Rissland EL (1992) Arguments and cases: An inevitable intertwining. Artificial Intelligence and Law, 1(1):3–44

Stranieri A, Zeleznikow J, Gawler M, Lewis B (1999) A hybrid rule–neural approach for the automation of legal reasoning in the discretionary domain of family law in Australia. Artificial Intelligence and Law, 7(2-3):153–183

Toulmin SE (1958) The Uses of Argument. Cambridge University Press, Cambridge

Tran V, Le Nguyen M, Tojo S, Satoh K (2020) Encoded summarization: Summarizing documents into continuous vector space for legal case retrieval. Artificial Intelligence and Law, pp. 1–27

Valente A (1995) Legal Knowledge Engineering. A Modelling Approach. IOS Press, Amsterdam

van den Herik HJ (1991) Kunnen Computers Rechtspreken? Gouda Quint, Arnhem

van Eemeren FH, Garssen B, Krabbe ECW, Snoeck Henkemans AF, Verheij B, Wagemans JHM (2014) Handbook of Argumentation Theory. Springer, Berlin

van Kralingen RW (1995) Frame-based Conceptual Models of Statute Law. Kluwer Law International, The Hague

Verheij B (1996) Two approaches to dialectical argumentation: Admissible sets and argumentation stages. In: Meyer JJ, van der Gaag LC (eds) Proceedings of NAIC'96. Universiteit Utrecht, Utrecht, pp. 357–368

Verheij B (2003a) Artificial argument assistants for defeasible argumentation. Artificial Intelligence, 150(1–2):291–324

Verheij B (2003b) DefLog: on the logical interpretation of prima facie justified assumptions. Journal of Logic and Computation, 13(3):319–346

Verheij B (2005) Virtual Arguments. On the Design of Argument Assistants for Lawyers and Other Arguers. T.M.C. Asser Press, The Hague

Verheij B (2009) The Toulmin argument model in artificial intelligence. Or: How semi-formal, defeasible argumentation schemes creep into logic. In: Rahwan I, Simari GR (eds) Argumentation in Artificial Intelligence, pp. 219–238. Springer, Berlin

Verheij B (2016) Formalizing value-guided argumentation for ethical systems design. Artificial Intelligence and Law, 24(4):387–407

Verheij B (2017a) Proof with and without probabilities. Correct evidential reasoning with presumptive arguments, coherent hypotheses and degrees of uncertainty. Artificial Intelligence and Law, 25(1):127–154

Verheij B (2017b) Formalizing arguments, rules and cases. In: Proceedings of the 16th International Conference on Artificial Intelligence and Law (ICAIL 2017), pp. 199–208. ACM Press, New York, NY

Verheij B (2018) Arguments for Good Artificial Intelligence. University of Groningen, Groningen. https://www.ai.rug.nl/~verheij/oratie/

Verheij B (2020a) Artificial intelligence as law. Presidential Address to the seventeenth international conference on artificial intelligence and law. Artificial Intelligence and Law 28 (2), 181-206

Verheij B (2020b) Analyzing the Simonshaven case with and without probabilities. Topics in Cognitive Science, 12(4), 1175–1999. https://doi.org/10.1111/tops.12436

Verheij B, Hage JC, van den Herik HJ (1998) An integrated view on rules and principles. Artificial Intelligence and Law, 6(1):3–26

Visser PRS (1995) Knowledge Specification for Multiple Legal Tasks; A Case Study of the Interaction Problem in the Legal Domain. Kluwer Law International, The Hague

Visser PRS, Bench-Capon TJM (1998) A comparison of four ontologies for the design of legal knowledge systems. Artificial Intelligence and Law, 6 (1):27–57

Vlek CS, Prakken H, Renooij S, Verheij B (2014) Building Bayesian Networks for legal evidence with narratives: a case study evaluation. Artificial Intelligence and Law, 22(4):375–421

Vlek CS, Prakken H, Renooij S, Verheij B (2016) A method for explaining Bayesian Networks for legal evidence with scenarios. Artificial Intelligence and Law, 24(3):285–324

Vreeswijk GAW (1997) Abstract argumentation systems. Artificial Intelligence, 90:225–279

Walton DN, Reed C, Macagno F (2008) Argumentation Schemes. Cambridge University Press, Cambridge

Wyner A (2008) An ontology in OWL for legal case-based reasoning. Artificial Intelligence and Law, 16(4):361

Wyner A, Angelov K, Barzdins G, Damljanovic D, Davis B, Fuchs N, Hoefler S, Jones K, Kaljurand K, Kuhn T et al (2009) On controlled natural languages: Properties and prospects. In: International Workshop on Controlled Natural Language, pp. 281–289, Berlin

Wyner A, Mochales-Palau R, Moens MF, Milward D (2010) Approaches to text mining arguments from legal cases. In: Semantic processing of legal texts, pp. 60–79. Springer, Berlin

Zurek T, Araszkiewicz M (2013) Modeling teleological interpretation. In: Proceedings of the Fourteenth International Conference on Artificial Intelligence and Law, pp. 160–168. ACM, New York, NY

Bart Verheij uses an argumentative perspective to study the connections between knowledge, data and reasoning, as a contribution to responsible artificial intelligence. He often uses the law as a domain of application. He holds the chair of artificial intelligence and argumentation as associate professor at the University of Groningen, where he is head of the department of Artificial Intelligence in the Bernoulli Institute of Mathematics, Computer Science and Artificial Intelligence. He is co-coordinator of the 'Responsible Hybrid Intelligence' line of the NWO Gravitation Hybrid Intelligence project. He is co-editor-in-chief of the journal Argument and Computation and was president of the International Association for Artificial Intelligence and Law (IAAIL). He was resident fellow at Stanford University (at the CodeX Center for Legal Informatics), was invited researcher at the Isaac Newton Institute for Mathematical Sciences (University of Cambridge), and taught graduate courses at Sun Yat-Sen University (Guangzhou, China), Central South University (Changsha, China), University of Potsdam (Potsdam, Germany) and Universidad Nacional del Sur (Bahia Blanca, Argentina).

Chapter 25
The Right to Mental Integrity in the Age of Artificial Intelligence: Cognitive Human Enhancement Technologies

Sümeyye Elif Biber and Marianna Capasso

Contents

Abstract This chapter provides an analysis of philosophical and legal aspects of AI-driven cognitive human enhancement technologies that complement human rights norms in the context of the right to mental integrity. The philosophical analysis focuses on extended cognition theories in philosophy of mind. Such theories individuate a list of criteria to assess whether an external artefact can be cognitively integrated with human cognitive processes. This chapter shows that two AI-cognitive human enhancement technologies—brain computer interfaces and intelligent personal assistants—do not completely satisfy the criteria of extended cognition due to their unique capabilities. Subsequently, the legal analysis concentrates on the debate on the right to mental integrity to see whether the human mind is safeguarded in the face of such concerns at international and European levels. Although the right to mental integrity has been recognized in international and European human rights law, the meaning and the scope of the concept has remained unclear. To fill this gap, this chapter engages with the issue of an adequate form of cognitive integration and assumes that, if external artefacts such as AI-cognitive human enhancement technologies are not completely or sufficiently integrated with human cognitive processes, such artefacts may not serve mental integrity of individuals. In the light of this analysis, this chapter comes to the conclusion that it is

S. E. Biber (✉) · M. Capasso
Sant'Anna School of Advanced Studies, Pisa, Italy
e-mail: sumeyyeelif.biber@santannapisa.it

M. Capasso
e-mail: marianna.capasso@santannapisa.it

© T.M.C. ASSER PRESS and the authors 2022
B. Custers and E. Fosch-Villaronga (eds.), *Law and Artificial Intelligence*,
Information Technology and Law Series 35,
https://doi.org/10.1007/978-94-6265-523-2_25

necessary to introduce *absolute* protection to mental integrity in conjunction with mental privacy to protect the individual from any intrusion of mental states.

Keywords Mental integrity · extended cognition · cognitive enhancement · human rights · artificial intelligence (AI) · brain-computer interfaces (BCI) · intelligent personal assistants (IPAs)

25.1 Introduction

AI-driven technologies are increasingly used as cognitive tools, i.e., tools that are intended to engage and facilitate cognitive processing,[1] as shown by the introduction of machine learning in areas such as memory processes, visual and auditory processing, and planning and daily decision-making tasks with the use of online recommender systems or virtual assistants. In this context, one of the most advanced and promising cognitive products might be "Neuralink", developed amongst others by Elon Musk, a generalized, simplified, and implantable device designed to solve brain and spine problems ranging from memory loss to brain damage by correcting electrical signals of the brain.[2] The most interesting capability of Neuralink is that it melds with the human body and connects wirelessly to devices such as phones or driverless cars, and ultimately merges the human brain with artificial intelligence (AI).[3] In this sense, a multitude of legal and ethical issues arise, since it is not unimaginable that in the near future, the activities of the brain will be recorded, shared, and manipulated. Eventually, such advanced systems will alter the conventional understanding of the human mind.[4]

This chapter aims to analyse the challenges posed by these systems from legal and philosophical perspectives. To achieve this purpose, Sect. 25.2 explains the capabilities of cognitive tools, particularly focusing on machine-based cognitive human enhancement technologies (HETs), brain-computer interfaces (BCI) and intelligent personal assistants (IPAs), that are combined with AI and target intelligence, clarity, and creativity.[5] Section 25.3 explores the constitutive role that such systems may have if we consider them as cognitive extensions of the human brain and the philosophical implications. Our assumption is that if an external artefact does not engage with an adequate form of cognitive integration with human cognitive processes, it may not serve the mental integrity of individuals. Section 25.4 discusses the legal debate on

---

[1] See Kommers et al. 1992.

[2] The debate is available at Neuralink Progress Update, Summer 2020. https://www.youtube.com/watch?v=DVvmgjBL74w Accessed on 22 February 2021.

[3] Knapp (2019) Elon Musk Sees His Neuralink7 Merging your Brain with A.I. https://www.forbes.com/sites/alexknapp/2019/07/17/elon-musk-sees-his-neuralink-merging-your-brain-with-ai/?sh=37883c754b07. Accessed on 22 February 2021.

[4] Ienca and Andorno 2017.

[5] See SIENNA 2018 D.3.1. The project developed six categories of HET: cognitive, affective, moral, physical, cosmetic, and longevity; see also a detailed report of European Parliament STOA 2009.

to what extent international and European human rights norms protect mental states from being accessed or even manipulated by states without the individual's consent. Particularly, it analyses leading judgments of the European Court of Human Rights and the Court of Justice of the European Union on the interpretation of the right to mental integrity. Considering the criteria developed under the theory of extended cognition, Sect. 25.5 then argues that at this stage of such technologies, it is necessary to introduce *absolute* protection to mental integrity, as the criteria of extended cognition are not fulfilled, in conjunction with mental privacy to protect individuals from any intrusion upon their mental states. Consequently, Sect. 25.6 finalizes this chapter with some concluding remarks.

25.2 Cognitive Human Enhancement Technologies

According to the SIENNA Report, human enhancement is defined as "a modification aimed at improving human performance and brought about by science-based and/or technology-based interventions in or on the human body".[6] Cognitive enhancements are classified into three, namely intelligence enhancements, clarity enhancements, and creativity enhancements.[7] Intelligence enhancements are able to improve intellectual capabilities such as thinking and reasoning. Clarity enhancements particularly focus on the ability to concentrate and maintain rigour. Creativity enhancements, on the other hand, improve inventiveness, artistic ability and design-related tasks.[8]

This chapter focuses on two machine-based cognitive HETs: BCIs and IPAs, that both use artificial intelligence (AI). Both technologies are advanced examples of how AI-driven systems are increasingly used for cognitive purposes.

BCIs are the systems that translate brain signals into new kinds of output.[9] The uniqueness of the device lies in its communication system that offers a special way of enabling direct interaction between a machine and the human brain without the use of muscles ("non-muscular channel").[10] Prototypes have already appeared in the military domain to control connected devices via thought and restore the function of soldiers injured in combat.[11] In addition to physical rehabilitation, some studies have shown that it has a great potential to improve memory encoding.[12] Further, a

---

[6] See SIENNA 2018 D.3.1., p. 5. As noted in the report, the definition is adapted from a similar definition established by the European Parliament STOA 2009.

[7] SIENNA 2018 D.3.1., p. 19.

[8] Ibid.

[9] Wolpaw and Winter Wolpaw 2012.

[10] Umair et al. 2017. See a more detailed definition in Wolpaw and Winter Wolpaw 2012, p. 3: "A BCI is a system that measures central nervous system (CNS) activity and converts it into artificial output that replaces, restores, enhances, supplements, or improves natural CNS output and thereby changes the ongoing interactions between the CNS and its external or internal environment."

[11] Binnendijk et al. 2020.

[12] Burke et al. 2015.

recent study has shown that artificial intelligence has advanced BCIs, allowing them to analyse and decode neural activity in an efficient way.[13]

Other machine-based cognitive HETs are IPAs, which are intelligent automated systems equipped with AI designed to assist users in their tasks.[14] Specifically, cognitive assistants enable users to improve their cognitive processes, offering them computational capabilities based on tools such as machine learning operating on large amounts of data.[15] The most well-known examples are Amazon's Alexa and Apple's Siri, which rely on interactive voice interfaces that are based on the analysis of user data to react and recommend.[16] The novelty of such devices is that they combine intelligence and interaction to proactively anticipate and adapt their functionalities,[17] and they enhance user cognition and capabilities in various domains: in smart homes, in cars, in consumer markets, in e-learning, in work or for impaired people and elderly.[18]

The main targets of these HETs are the human cognitive processes that can be influenced and improved by those applications. These technologies provide unprecedented possibilities for accessing, analysing and sharing cognitive processes and data and, if not checked and controlled, their impact can probably lead to undesirable and risky outcomes. Therefore, it is crucial to explore the implications of these technologies to provide a comprehensive perspective on their significant role in society.

25.3 Assessing AI-driven Cognitive HETs as Cognitive Extensions

AI-driven cognitive HETs open new possibilities that may replace or substitute the cognitive processes of human agents. Indeed, epistemic tasks such as classification, pattern recognition, prediction are performed by AI in a faster and more efficient way. AI can help access and recover information, enabling users to exhibit and improve capabilities and performances related to memory, critical thinking and rigour.[19] Nonetheless, despite these benefits, such systems can also change users' behaviour through more pervasive and targeted interventions and can explicitly or

---

[13] Zhang et al. 2020.

[14] SIENNA 2018 D 3.1, p. 34.

[15] Le and Wartschinski 2018, p. 45. For a tentative ontology and classification of different kinds of cognitive assistants, see Maier et al. 2019.

[16] See Amazon (2018) Alexa Skills Kit. https://developer.amazon.com/en-US/docs/alexa/ask-overviews/what-is-the-alexa-skills-kit.html. Accessed 21 February 2021.

[17] The two criteria were individuated by Maedche et al. 2016.

[18] For a review of application domains of such systems, see also Knote et al. 2018.

[19] These are related to intelligence, clarity and creativity, which are the three targets for interventions of cognitive enhancement individuated by the Sienna Report, see Sect. 25.2 of this chapter.

subliminally exploit users' cognitive weaknesses more easily.[20] Therefore, AI should be scrutinized closely, especially if it deals with the cognitive capabilities of users. One way to do this might spring from the philosophy of mind theories on extended cognition.[21] There are at least two reasons that make those theories useful in this discussion.

First, Clark and Chalmers' theory of extended cognition or extended mind[22] claims that cognition is not relegated to the brain but rather extends to the environment. Other artefacts in the environment, they argue, are not merely external instruments that influence an individual's cognitive processes in a causal modality but can be a constitutive part and an extension of such processes. Their theory provides a list of criteria to assess the cognitive integration between human brains and artefacts present in an environment.

Second, scholars have already engaged with the thesis of extended cognition in relation to technologies such as the web or computers.[23] Recently, some have specifically focused on AI and have defined AI-driven systems as "cognitive extenders" with completely different capabilities from the human brain.[24] Conversely, others are promoting an "extended parity principle" between cognitive systems constituted by humans and environment and cognitive systems constituted by AI and environment.[25]

One of the criteria discussed by those theorists is the parity principle, which sustains that if external artefacts play the same functional role of internal processes like belief or memory then they can be considered cognitively integrated with the human brain.[26] Moreover, according to Clark, cognitive integration requires that external artefacts meet other criteria which are reliability, accessibility, and trustworthiness. Namely, any information retrieved from an artefact should be reliably available and invoked, automatically endorsed, not subject to critical scrutiny, and easily accessible when required.[27] Finally, another criterion individuated by Clark is "continuous reciprocal causation", that is a condition for a two-way cognitive and extended interaction.[28]

---

[20] Big Data and AI can lead to *hypernudge,* a more insidious, dynamic, and efficacious form of nudge, see Yeung 2017 on this point.

[21] It is important to note that there are dense theoretical debates about different approaches on extended cognition, however, it is beyond the aim of this chapter to engage with these theories in detail. Therefore, we will only consider the first wave of extended cognition.

[22] Clark and Chalmers 1998. For a recent perspective on this position, see Clark 2008. However, to be precise, the extended cognition is distinguished from the extended mind thesis, according to which cognitive states such as beliefs and others can have as their supervenience base extra-organismic elements, see on this point Carter et al. 2018.

[23] Among scholars that make use of the thesis of extended cognition in relation to technology are included: Smart 2018, Carter and Palermos 2016, Ludwig 2015.

[24] Hernandez-Orallo and Vold 2019.

[25] Pellegrino and Garasic 2020.

[26] Clark and Chalmers 1998, p. 8.

[27] The criteria are listed by Clark 2010, p. 46 and are called the Glue and Trust Conditions, see also Clarks 2011, p. 79 ff.

[28] Clark 2011, p. 131 ff, Clark 1997.

Turning our discourse to AI-driven systems, all those criteria specified by extended cognition can help examine such peculiar artefacts whether they can be suitable for cognitive integration with the human brain or not. For example, further advancing the criterion of continuous reciprocal causation, one could claim that AI-driven systems should not be just mere "cognitive assistants"[29] but should interact with human users in a "cognitive interaction",[30] in which the system and users mesh. One profound implication of these interactions is that the human cognitive capabilities should undertake a co-creation process and evolution with the technology at stake. This happens when the external element and the human brain are deeply interdependent and coupled through an ongoing and reciprocal feedback loop.[31] Intelligent systems such as IPAs should provide user assistance, i.e., the capability to support humans in an ongoing reciprocal dialogue (using texts or voice) via their degree of interactivity and intelligence.[32] In the case of BCIs, the promotion of a coupled interaction is evident *prima facie* since those devices are "in direct contact with the brain"[33] and act upon the neural mechanisms of their users to receive feedback.

However, AI-driven cognitive HETs do not completely or sufficiently satisfy or even challenge all those criteria. Therefore, concerns may arise on their consistency with an adequate form of cognitive integration.[34] A debated topic is how and to what extent artefacts should be seen as partially or completely constitutive parts or even 'extenders' of the human cognitive processes. Indeed, the parity principle has its weaknesses: an external and novel artefact can enable some cognitive capabilities beyond the human brain. Cognitive integration can come in degrees and can imply different dimensions.[35] However, the advantage in adopting such perspectives on extended cognition is that they can shed light on AI-driven systems, seeing them

---

[29] See on this point Nalepa et al. 2018.

[30] See Bernard and Arnold 2019.

[31] Palermos 2014, p. 33.

[32] Morana et al. 2019.

[33] I.e., by changing the brain directly. This is the criterion adopted by Vincent et al. 2020 to distinguish between "core" and "penumbral" neurointerventions.

[34] Recently, another author that draws from extended cognition theory has been Carter 2020. He discusses the two terms of 'cognitive integration' and 'cognitive enhancement' and advances the thesis that the notion of enhancement as such is "theoretically unimportant for accounting for why certain kinds of high-tech epistemic dependence genuinely threaten to undermine intellectual autonomy and others such kinds of dependence don't" (Ivi, conclusions). Another recent attempt to connect enhancement and extended cognition can be found in Carter and Pritchard 2019, who propose a "cognitive achievement account of cognitive enhancement". However, a distinction between enhancement and 'extension' as used in this chapter should be drawn: an 'extension' includes a move beyond *intracranialism*, i.e., the conception that locates cognitive processes inside the brain, and does not influence cognition but rather constitutes it. Adopting the terms 'extension' and 'cognitive integration' could arguably be a way to conceptually sharpen the understanding of some forms of HETs.

[35] This is the reason why some extended cognitive theorists decided to adopt distinct views, see Palermos 2014 and the second wave of extended cognition, for example Heersmink 2015. Heersmink argues that cognitive integration comes in degree and requires different dimensions, i.e., information flow, reliability, durability, procedural and informational transparency, individualization, transformation (how the cognitive processes change with the use of artefact). An artefact has not to be

not as external tools but as systems that can become progressively integrated with human cognitive processes.

Nonetheless, a functionalist theory like that of extended cognition, on the one hand, has the merit of individuating relevant cognitive criteria that are to be met in an integrated system—such as parity, accessibility, trustworthiness—but on the other hand, risks to neglect the normative and justificatory or explanatory role that such criteria should also have, beyond their cognitive role. Regarding technologies that should realize cognitive or epistemic capabilities, there is a need to discuss their functional modalities and the normative justifications of their impact on individuals and their social context. Cognitive enhancement through AI-driven HETs not only needs conceptualization, i.e., a description to group together a series of interventions and their effects on cognitive processes and epistemic actions but also needs normative justification: a clarification and an explanation to distinguish wrongful and right forms of intervention.

With particular reference to IPAs and BCIs, security and privacy concerns have arisen about the fact that users' data can be used to train AI or can even be shared with third parties such as governments or used for manipulation.[36] BCIs can pave the way to 'brain-hacking', i.e., a neurocrime that aims at the illicit access to and manipulation of neural information and computation, if their design and regulation are not supported by a comprehensive ethical and legal reflection, as scholars suggested.[37] Another potential issue is related to the predominant impact that market-driven big tech corporations such as Google or Amazon can have on the public sphere, since such corporations can now track and store data in an unprecedented way and even enter the domains of health and of public research and policy, as the recent COVID-19 pandemic has shown.[38] For example, Amazon's Alexa has been recently equipped with new healthcare skills that allow it to receive and transmit health information.[39] Moreover, the increasing proliferation of neurological data generated outside the clinical sphere and in the consumer market requires adequate infrastructures to tackle the challenge of safeguarding individual rights, such as privacy and security of those data.[40]

AI can also promote increasing dependency and loss of control by users if not adequately designed as a cognitive extension. It has been argued that a closed-loop system such as deep brain stimulations, which works through electrical impulses, may

---

equally integrated in all dimensions. On the issues related to the parity principle, see also Heinrichs 2017.

[36] Chung et al. 2017. See Mecacci and Haselager 2017 for an interesting ethical framework regarding mental privacy and brain reading. In the predominant typology of influence types used in bioethics literature, manipulation is an influence that subverts agents' rational capacity and bypasses mental processes such as understanding, and it has been understood as a term "in-between" rational persuasion and coercion by force, see Faden and Beauchamp 1986, Blumental-Barby 2012.

[37] Ienca and Haselager 2016.

[38] This has been called "the Googlization of health research", see on this Sharon 2016, 2020.

[39] Jiang 2019.

[40] Ienca et al. 2018.

enforce self-estrangement, with loss of control and distorted perception of capacities.[41] BCI devices can induce an abrupt transition in patient self-understanding that can be associated with a sense of powerlessness and result in severe distress in certain cases.[42] On the contrary, a recent study has shown how Amazon's Alexa increases the sense of independence and self-management for people with dementia and other diseases and cognitive impairments or generalized anxiety or depression.[43]

IPAs and BCIs mediate and actively participate in the moral sense-making of their users or their affective and emotional experiences.[44] Therefore, the use and adoption of AI-driven cognitive HETs call for a discussion on the criteria that such systems should respect to be integrated into the cognitive sphere of individuals since they are peculiar forms of systems with new capabilities and challenges. Of pivotal importance is also a discussion on the transparency, explicability and public accountability regarding the source and the mechanisms and long-term effects of such AI-driven cognitive HETs. This discussion challenges greatly what kind of normative regulations one should apply to individuals that engage in their use. These issues have remained unexplored in the literature on cognition but surely deserve a further evaluation to advance our understanding of the impact that AI-systems may have on decisions that significantly impact the individual's cognitive sphere.

25.4   Mental Integrity in International and European Human Rights Law

This section focuses on the extent to which international and European human rights norms protect mental states and cognitive processes from being accessed or even manipulated by states through BCIs or IPAs without the individual's consent.[45] Neither human rights law nor domestic law answers the question of the legal status of the mind. Yet, "mental" or "psychological" integrity has been recognized in the case-law of the European Court of Human Rights (ECtHR) within the scope of the right to respect for private life of the European Convention of Human Rights (ECHR).[46] The

---

[41] Gilbert et al. 2017.

[42] Ibid.

[43] Chambers and Beaney 2020.

[44] A hermeneutical approach to technologically mediated sense making via AI-powered voice assistants can be found in Kudina 2021. On affective BCIs, see Steinert and Friedrich 2020.

[45] Indeed, it is suggested that when it comes to robotics and HETs, in Europe, some anchor point "can be found in the common heritage of human rights and values" for regulatory dilemmas posed by such devices. See the debate in Leenes et al. 2017. See also an example of using human rights as "normative anchor points of governance" in the context of human enhancement technologies in Ruggiu 2018.

[46] Convention for the Protection of Human Rights and Fundamental Freedoms, Rome, 4 November 1950, in force 3 September 1953, 213 UNTS 221. Article 8 of the Convention: "Everyone has the right to respect for his private and family life, his home and his correspondence." It is important to note there are discussions assessing the relationship between emerging technologies and freedom of

ECtHR has repeatedly emphasized a broad understanding of the concept of "private life" covering physical and psychological integrity:

> The Court … reiterates that "private life" is a broad term, encompassing, inter alia, aspects of an individual's physical and social identity, including the right to personal autonomy, personal development and to establish and develop relationships with other human beings and the outside world. The Court has … held that private life includes a person's physical and psychological integrity and that the State is also under a positive obligation to secure to its citizens their right to effective respect for this integrity.[47]

This understanding indicates that private life is not limited to bodily integrity or physical places; it can also encompass the mental sphere. In this context, privacy protects "against unwanted intrusions into people's private lives in a traditional sense of guarding a person's private space—be that in their head or in their home."[48] Indeed, in the case of *Bensaid v. the United Kingdom,* which was about the removal of the applicant suffering from a psychotic illness to a country where the necessary medical treatment was not available, the ECtHR noted the importance of the protection of mental health and interpreted it as an "indispensable precondition" to the enjoyment of Article 8 of the Convention:

> Mental health must also be regarded as a crucial part of private life associated with the aspect of moral integrity. Article 8 protects a right to identity and personal development, and the right to establish and develop relationships with other human beings and the outside world. The preservation of mental stability is in that context an indispensable precondition to effective enjoyment of the right to respect for private life.[49]

Furthermore, the ECtHR has broadly interpreted the terms mental and psychological integrity. According to the case-law, these terms do not cover only the setbacks in mental capabilities but also situations in which no clinical-pathological mental disorders occur. For instance, in the case of *Taliadorou and Stylianou v. Cyprus,* the ECtHR has considered damages to an individual's reputation as damages to psychological and moral integrity.[50]

---

thought claiming that Article 9 of the ECHR should be understood as an absolute right to protect the integrity of the *forum internum*. However, considering the current jurisprudence of the ECtHR on Article 9, it is hard to consider neural activities or the assessment of cognitive processes as "thought". Therefore, this section only focuses on the case-law interpreting the concept of mental integrity. See a recent discussion on the freedom of thought and brain computer interfaces in O'Callaghan and Shiner 2021.

[47] ECtHR, *Tysiac v. Poland*, No. 5410/03, 20 March 2007, para 107.

[48] Marshall 2009, p. 3.

[49] ECtHR, *Bensaid v. United Kingdom*, No. 44599/98, 6 February 2001, para 47.

[50] ECtHR, *Taliadorou and Stylianou v. Cyprus,* No. 39627/05 and 39631/05, 16 October 2008, par. 57-58. See also ECtHR, Kyriakides v. Cyprus, No. 39058/05, 16 October 2008. See also the case of *Bati and others v. Turkey* where the ECtHR emphasized that various forms of ill-treatment without leaving physical marks can harm mental integrity, no. 33097/96, and 57834/00, 3 June 2004, par. 114. It is important to note that these judgments should be considered in the light of Article 5 of the proposed Artificial Intelligence Act by the European Commission. Article 5 of the AI Act prohibits AI practices that manipulate individuals' behaviours through "subliminal techniques" that can cause "physical or psychological harms". See a recent comment on the proposed AI Act in Biber 2021.

After the recognition of the concept of "mental integrity" in the case law of the ECtHR, this concept appeared in the Convention on the Rights of Persons with Disabilities (CRPD) in 2008. Article 17 of the Convention states that "every person with disabilities has a right to respect for his or her physical and mental integrity on an equal basis with others".[51]

In the EU, Article 3(1) of the Charter of the Fundamental Rights of the European Union (CFR) explicitly guarantees the right to respect for "physical and mental integrity".[52] The most important source of that provision is the Council of Europe Convention on Human Rights and Biomedicine ("Oviedo Convention").[53] The Oviedo Convention regulates the primacy of the human being "over the sole interest of science and society" under Article 2.[54] The explanatory report of the Oviedo Convention underlines that it is inspired by the principle of the primacy of the human being, and "all its articles must be interpreted in this light."[55]

Accordingly, in the judgment of *Netherlands v. European Parliament and Council*, the Court of Justice of the European Union (CJEU) has confirmed that a fundamental right to human integrity and human dignity is part of European Union Law: "It is for the Court of Justice, in its review of the compatibility of acts of the institutions with the general principles of Community law, to ensure that the fundamental right to human dignity and integrity is observed."[56]

However, the meaning and the scope of the integrity has remained unclear.[57] Indeed, some human rights experts have highlighted that the law is ill-equipped to address novel challenges posed by new technologies and proposed a new free-standing human right called "the right to mental self-determination."[58] In this way, a

[51] The Convention on the Rights of Person with Disabilities and its Optional Protocol, adopted on 13 December 2o06 and opened for signature on 30 March 2007.

[52] Charter of Fundamental Rights of the European Union, Nizza, 7 December 2000, in force 1 December 2009, OJ 2012 No. C-326/2. Article 3(1) of the Charter: "Everyone has the right to respect for his or her physical and mental integrity."

[53] Michalowski 2014.

[54] Convention for the Protection of Human Rights and Dignity of the Human Being with regard to the Application of Biology and Medicine, entered into force on 1 December 1999.

[55] Council of Europe, Explanatory Report to the Convention for the Protection of Human Rights and Dignity of the Human Being with Regard to the Application of Biology and Medicine: Convention on Human Rights and Biomedicine, 4 April 1997, para 22.

[56] CJEU, Case C-377/98, *Netherlands v. European Parliament and Council* (2001) ECR-I 7079, para 70.

[57] Bublitz 2020.

[58] Bublitz 2020, pp. 387–408. See also the report of the Parliamentary Assembly of the Council of Europe 2020. In the US, there is an initiative called "NeuroRights Initiative" established by the Columbia University, working to incorporate five specific neuro-rights into international human rights law namely, the right to personal identity, the right to free will, the right to mental privacy, the right to equal access to mental augmentation, and the right to protection from algorithmic bias, available at https://neurorightsfoundation.org/mission. In the world, Chile took the first step on neuro-rights to prevent the misuse of artificial intelligence and neurotechnology, see the debate in Munoz "Chile- right to free will needs definition", 29.10.2019, available at https://www.nature.com/articles/d41586-019-03295-9.

sort of reform is proposed in mind-protecting norms. Advances in cognitive sciences affording novel technical means to alter minds have been considered as one of the crucial reasons to justify such a novel right.[59]

Furthermore it is important to note that these analyses do not engage with cognitive theories on the issue. More specifically, they do not provide a fine-grained and specific analysis of technological systems that can interfere with individuals' cognitive processes. There could be scientific uncertainty or disagreement about these systems and related interferences. Yet, those situations cannot provide a justification for the law not to protect the mind. Therefore, a different and comprehensive approach that deals with philosophical considerations on the issue could be an asset to sharpen and advance the meaning and the protection of mental integrity.

25.5   How to Protect Mental Integrity

If an external artefact does not engage with an adequate form of cognitive integration with human cognitive processes, it may not serve mental integrity of individuals. Under this hypothesis, the philosophical implications discussed in Sect. 25.3 provide some input for the legal debate on mental integrity. First, the philosophical approach included in this chapter can shed light on the fact that there is a need for specific criteria and dimensions to realize an adequate form of cognitive integration between external artefacts in the environment and the human brain. Under the extended cognition theory, humans and AI-systems are not seen as separate systems, but as a *continuum*: the functional role of artefacts such as AI-systems can be seen as fundamental to our cognition and brain. However, this also raises a series of concerns, since AI-driven cognitive HETs are artefacts that may even challenge the criteria that are necessary to an appropriate cognitive integration and radically change the individuals' cognitive sphere.

Second, the philosophical discussion highlights that there is also the need to explore the normative challenges related to the use of AI-driven cognitive HETs. Concerns have been raised on the fact that such systems may endanger privacy and security or increase loss of control, dependency and self-estrangement, and, last but not least, the risk of being manipulated.

Lavazza defined mental integrity as the mastery of mental states and brain data by individuals, so that no other actors can access or alter those without consent.[60] Thus, privacy of brain data should be supported by a consent-based approach, along with the goal of cognitive freedom: i.e., the right to alter one's mental states with neuro-tools or to refuse to do so.[61]

---

[59] Bublitz 2020, p. 387 (arguing that although legal systems engage with bodily integrity in detail even in exceptional situations such as pregnancy or organ transplantation, they highly disregard the interventions on the human mind).

[60] See Lavazza 2018.

[61] See Bublitz 2013.

However, information gathering by AI-driven cognitive HETs, such as BCIs and IPAs, often happens in cases where agents are not even aware that their data and cognitive processes are accessible and extended to such devices.[62] Therefore, the need to overcome the limits of a consent-based approach also requires reconsidering the meaning of mental integrity in such cases.

Finally, the philosophical approach adopted in this chapter plays an indispensable role in the reflection on mental integrity. In the legal debate, as already shown, the meaning and the scope of integrity has remained unclear. Following suggestions from philosophy of mind and cognition, a new account on mental integrity can be explored and further advanced. Hence, this chapter aims to tie the legal discussion and the philosophical literature together, to the mutual benefit of both fields. 'Mental integrity' should comprise not only 'brain' integrity and individual integrity but should extend to the environment, including the social task to design technological artefacts that are cognitively integrated and meaningfully support the control, autonomy and capabilities of human agents and their cognitive processes. Thus, the chapter recognises that the fundamental tasks in the promotion of 'mental integrity' are respectively the development of AI-driven cognitive HETs as appropriately integrated artefacts, and the need for regulation of those technologies against sectional and partisan interventions from the wider social-political environment. These latter run the risk of endangering the human cognitive sphere with the introduction of unreliable, loosely coupled and unaccountable systems.

In the current legal framework, human rights norms do not provide *absolute* protection for mental integrity.[63] That means that in the long run, the door would be -legally- open for advanced neuro-surveillance to states under the conditions of legitimacy, necessity, and proportionality.[64] It has been already highlighted that governments could use such technologies for purposes such as military, law enforcement and criminal justice.[65] AI-driven cognitive HETs are able to record the user's mental states, the most intimate information about one's personality and identity.[66]

---

[62] See a discussion on the challenges of informed consent in implantable BCI research in Klein 2016, who identifies six core risk domains as central to the informed consent, namely safety, cognitive and communicative impairment, inappropriate expectations, involuntariness, affective impairment, and privacy and security. In terms of informational privacy, the author discusses that BCI systems are able to generate a trove of potentially intimate personal information, such as toileting, sex, counselling children, comforting a loved one, unexpressed thoughts, personality characteristics, or emotions.

[63] Ligthart et al. 2020; Ienca and Andorno 2017.

[64] For some dystopian examples of state surveillance already happening in China see a well-written article in Anderson (2020) The Panopticon is Already Here https://www.theatlantic.com/magazine/archive/2020/09/china-ai-surveillance/614197/. Accessed on 21 February 2021.

[65] Schmerling (2019). The Ethical and Legal Implications of Brain-Computer Interfaces https://www.calcalistech.com/ctech/articles/0,7340,L-3762798,00.html. Accessed on 22 February 2021.

[66] Floridi 2016; Hallinan et al. 2014.

Therefore, in line with the philosophical concerns identified in Sect. 25.3 regarding these systems and their potential role for individuals' cognitive sphere, it is necessary to introduce *absolute* protection to mental integrity in conjunction with mental privacy to protect the individual from any intrusion upon mental states.

Although human rights norms do not provide *absolute* protection to mental integrity or mental privacy, the legal principle of human dignity can construct the latter. Indeed, the principle has particular importance in the context of human enhancement technologies in general. As noted in the SIENNA report, regulators need to be diligent about different understandings of dignity that are placed between the principle of self-determination and conservative conceptualization of the principle of human dignity.[67] In this context, when it comes to the applications discussed here, human dignity could prohibit any interference with mental integrity and privacy since human dignity is *inviolable.*

25.6   Conclusion

Human cognition is targeted by a range of medical and technological interventions in the modern age. AI-driven cognitive HETs such as BCIs and IPAs discussed in this chapter pose many concerns and challenges in both legal and philosophical domains ranging from self-estrangement to distorted perception of human capacities.

Although the right to mental integrity has been recognized in international and European human rights law, the meaning and the scope of the concept has remained unclear. To fill this gap, this chapter discussed the main criteria and concerns raised by the philosophy of mind theories on extended cognition, assuming that if external artefacts such AI-driven cognitive HETs do not engage with an adequate form of cognitive integration with human cognitive processes, they may not serve mental integrity of individuals.

Indeed, the analysis on two cognitive AI-driven HETs in this chapter has shown that such systems actually do not completely or sufficiently satisfy or even challenge all the criteria necessary in the context of an adequate form of cognitive integration with the human brain. Moreover, normative concerns arise on the use and adoption of those systems. Therefore, this chapter concludes that at this stage it is necessary to introduce *absolute* protection to mental integrity in conjunction with mental privacy to protect the individual from any intrusion upon mental states. This indeed may protect individuals from state intrusions that could undermine their mental integrity and entail an unjustified additional sphere of influence on it.

---

[67] SIENNA D.3.2 2019; See also Ruggiu 2013, Beyleveld and Brownsword 2001 (arguing two approaches to dignity: "dignity as empowerment" and "dignity as constraint"). These two approaches were mentioned in the case of *Vo v. France,* No. 53924/00, 8 July 2004, para 40.

References

Bernard D, Arnold A (2019) Cognitive interaction with virtual assistants: From philosophical foundations to illustrative examples in aeronautics. Computers in Industry, 107: 33–49, ISSN 0166-3615, https://doi.org/10.1016/j.compind.2019.01.010

Beyleveld D, Brownsword R (2001) Human Dignity in Bioethics and Biolaw. Oxford University Press, Oxford

Biber SE (2021) Machines Learning the Rule of Law: EU Proposes the World's First AI Act. Verfassungsblog, https://verfassungsblog.de/ai-rol/, DOI: https://doi.org/10.17176/20210714-015912-0

Binnendijk A, Marler T, Bartel EM (2020) Brain Computer Interfaces: U.S. Military Applications and Implications, An Initial Assessment. Rand Corporation.

Blumental-Barby JS (2012) Between reason and coercion: Ethically permissible influence in health care and health policy contexts. Kennedy Institute of Ethics Journal, 22(4): 345–366

Bublitz JC (2013) My mind is mine!? Cognitive liberty as a legal concept. In: Hildt E, Franke AG (eds) Cognitive Enhancement. An Interdisciplinary Perspective. Springer, Dordrecht, pp 233–26.

Bublitz JC (2020) The Nascent Right to Psychological Integrity and Mental Self-Determination. In: von Arnauld A, von der Decken K, Susi M (eds) The Cambridge Handbook of New Human Rights Recognition, Novelty, Rhetoric. Cambridge University Press, Cambridge, 387–408

Burke JF, Merkow MB, Jacobs J, Kahana MJ, Zaghloul KA (2015) Brain Computer Interface to Enhance Episodic Memory in Human Participants. Frontiers in Human Neuroscience, 8: 1055

Carter JA (2020) Intellectual autonomy, epistemic dependence and cognitive enhancement. Synthese 197: 937–2961. https://doi.org/10.1007/s11229-017-1549-y

Carter JA, Clark A, Kallestrup J, Palermos SO, Pritchard D (2018) Extended Epistemology: an introduction. In: Carter JA, Clark A, Kallestrup J, Palermos SO, Pritchard D (eds) Extended Epistemology. Oxford University Press, Oxford, pp 1–16

Carter JA, Palermos SO (2016) The ethics of extended cognition: Is having your computer compromised a personal assault? Journal of the American Philosophical Association, 2(4): 542–560

Carter JA, Pritchard D (2019) The Epistemology of Cognitive Enhancement. J Med Philos; 44(2):220–242. doi: https://doi.org/10.1093/jmp/jhy040

Carter S, Nielsen M (2017) Using artificial intelligence to augment human intelligence. Distill. https://distill.pub/2017/aia

Chambers R, Beaney P (2020) The potential of placing a digital assistant in patients' homes. Br J Gen Practice 70(690): 8–9

Chung H, Iorga M, Voas J, Lee S (2017) Alexa, Can I Trust You? Computer 50 (9): 100–104. https://doi.org/10.1109/MC.2017.3571053. ISSN 0018-9162

Clark A (1997) Being There: Putting Brain, Body, and World Together Again. MIT Press, Cambridge, MA

Clark A (2008) Supersizing the Mind: Embodiment, Action, and Cognitive Extension. Oxford University Press, New York

Clark A (2010) Memento's revenge: The Extended Mind, extended. In: Menary R (ed) The Extended Mind. MIT Press, Cambridge, MA, pp 43–66

Clark A (2011) Supersizing the Mind. Oxford University Press, Oxford

Clark A, Chalmers D (1998) The extended mind. Analysis 58(1): 7–19

European Parliament STOA (2009) Human Enhancement Study. https://www.europarl.europa.eu/RegData/etudes/etudes/join/2009/417483/IPOL-JOIN_ET(2009)417483_EN.pdf Accessed on 21 February 2021

Faden R, Beauchamp T (1986) A History and Theory of Informed Consent. Oxford University Press, Oxford

Floridi L (2016) On Human Dignity as a Foundation for the Right to Privacy. Philos. Technol. 29: 307–312 https://doi.org/10.1007/s13347-016-0220-8

Gilbert F, Goddard E, Viaña JNM, Carter A, Horne M (2017) I miss being me: Phenomenological effects of deep brain stimulation. AJOB Neuroscience,8(2): 96–109. https://doi.org/10.1080/215 07740.2017.1320319

Hallinan D, Schütz P, Friedewald M, de Hert P (2014) Neurodata and Neuroprivacy: Data Protection Outdated? Surveillance and Society. 12: 55–72. https://doi.org/10.24908/ss.v12i1.4500

Heersmink R (2015) Dimensions of Integration in embedded and extended cognitive systems. Phenomenology and the Cognitive Sciences. 13 (3): 577–598

Heinrichs JH (2017) Against Strong Ethical Parity: Situated Cognition Theses and Transcranial Brain Stimulation. Front. Hum. Neurosci. 11:171. doi: https://doi.org/10.3389/fnhum.2017. 00171

Hernandez-Orallo J, Vold K (2019) AI Extenders: The Ethical and Societal Implications of Humans Cognitively Extended by AI, 507–513. https://doi.org/10.1145/3306618.3314238

Ienca M, Andorno R (2017) Towards New Human Rights in the Age of Neuroscience and Neuroscience and Neurotechnology. Life Sciences, Society and Policy, 13, https://doi.org/10.1186/s40 504-017-0050-1

Ienca M, Haselager P (2016) Hacking the brain: brain–computer interfacing technology and the ethics of neurosecurity. Ethics and Information Technology, 18(2): 117–129

Ienca M, Haselager P, Emanuel EJ (2018) Brain leaks and consumer neurotechnology. Nature biotechnology, 36(9): 805–810

Jiang R (2019) Introducing New Alexa Healthcare Skills. https://developer.amazon.com/en-US/blogs/alexa/alexa-skills-kit/2019/04/introducing-new-alexa-healthcare-skills Accessed on 22 February 2021

Klein E (2016) Informed consent in implantable BCI research: identifying risks and exploring meaning. Science and Engineering Ethics, 22(5): 1299–1317

Knote R, Janson A, Eingebord L, Sollner M (2018) The What and How of Smart Personal Assistant: Principles and Application Domains for IS Research. In: Multikonferenz Wirtschaftsinformatik, Luneburg, Germany

Kommers P, Jonassen DH, Mayes T (eds) (1992) Cognitive tools for learning. Springer-Verlag, Heidelberg FRG

Kudina O (2021) Alexa, who am I?: Voice Assistants and Hermeneutic Lemniscate as the Technologically Mediated Sense-Making. Hum Stud, https://doi.org./https://doi.org/10.1007/s10746-021-09572-9

Lavazza A (2018) Freedom of thought and mental integrity: The moral requirements for any neural prosthesis. Frontiers in Neuroscience. https://doi.org/10.3389/fnins.2018.00082

Le N-T, Wartschinski L (2018) A cognitive assistant for improving human reasoning skills. International Journal of Human-Computer Studies, 117. https://doi.org/10.1016/j.ijhcs.2018. 02.005

Leenes R, Palmerini E, Koops B-J, Bertolini A, Salvini P, Lucivero F (2017) Regulatory challenges of robotics: Some guidelines for addressing legal and ethical issues. Law, Innovation and Technology. 9: 1–44. https://doi.org/10.1080/17579961.2017.1304921

Ligthart S, Douglas T, Bublitz C, Kooijmans T, Meynen G (2020) Forensic Brain-Reading and Mental Privacy in European Human Rights Law: Foundations and Challenges. Neuroethics, Springer, https://doi.org/10.1007/s12152-020-09438

Ludwig D (2015) Extended cognition and the explosion of knowledge. Philosophical Psychology, 28(3): 355–368

Maedche A, Morana S, Shacht S, Werth D, Krumeich J (2016) Advanced User Assistance Systems. Business & Information Systems Engineering, 58, 5: 367–370

Maier T, Menold J, McComb C (2019) Towards an Ontology of Cognitive Assistants. Proceedings of the 22nd International Conference on Engineering Design (ICED19), Delft, The Netherlands, 5–8 August 2019. DOI:https://doi.org/10.1017/dsi.2019.270

Marshall J (2009) Personal Freedom through Human Rights Law? Autonomy, Integrity and Integrity under the European Convention on Human Rights. Martinus Nijhoff Publishers, Leiden/Boston

Mecacci G, Haselager P (2017) Identifying criteria for the evaluation of the implications of brain reading for mental privacy. Science and Engineering Ethics. https://doi.org/10.1007/s11948-017-0003-3

Michalowski S (2014) Right to Integrity of the Person. In: Peers S, Hervey T, Kenner J, Ward A (eds) The EU Charter of Fundamental Rights: A Commentary. Hart Publishing, London, pp 39–60

Morana S, Pfeiffer J, Adam MTP (2019) User Assistance for Intelligent Systems. Business & Information Systems Engineering, 62 (3):189–192. https://aisel.aisnet.org/bise/vol62/iss3/1

Nalepa GJ, Costa A, Novais P, Julian V (2018) Cognitive assistants. International Journal of Human-Computer Studies, 117: 1–68

O'Callaghan P, Shiner B (2021) The Right to Freedom of Thought in the European Convention on Human Rights. European Journal of Comparative Law and Governance

Palermos SO (2014) Loops, Constitution, and Cognitive Extension. Cognitive Systems Research, 27: 25–41

Pellegrino G, Garasic M D (2020) Artificial Intelligence and extended minds. Why not? Rivista Internazionale di Filosofia e Psicologia, 11, 2: 150–168

Ruggiu D (2013) A Right-Based Model of Governance: The Case of Human Enhancement and the Role of Ethics in Europe. In: Konrad K, Coenen C, Dijkstra A, Milburn C, van Lente H (eds) Shaping Emerging Technologies: Governance, Innovation, Discourse. Ios Press / Aka, Berlin, pp 103–115

Ruggiu D (2018) Implementing a Responsible, Research and Innovation Framework for Human Enhancement According to Human Rights: The Right to Bodily Integrity and the Rise of 'Enhanced Societies'. Law, Innovation and Technology: 1–40

Sharon T (2016) The Googlization of health research: from disruptive innovation to disruptive ethics. Personalized Medicine. 13(6): 563–574

Sharon T (2020) Blind-sided by privacy? Digital contact tracing, the Apple/Google API and big tech's newfound role as global health policy makers. Ethics and Information Technology. https://doi.org/10.1007/s10676-020-09547-x

Smart P (2012) The Web-Extended Mind. Metaphilosophy, 43, 4: 426–445

Smart P (2018) Emerging Digital Technologies: Implications for Extended Conceptions of Cognition and Knowledge. In: Carter AJ, Clark A, Kallestrup J, Palermos OS, Pritchard D (eds) Extended Epistemology. Oxford University Press, Oxford, pp 266–304

Steinert S, Friedrich O (2020) Wired Emotions: Ethical Issues of Affective Brain–Computer Interfaces. Sci Eng Ethics 26: 351–367 https://doi.org/10.1007/s11948-019-00087-2

The Parliamentary Assembly of the Council of Europe (2020) The Brain-Computer Interface: New Rights or New Threats to Fundamental Freedoms, 24 September 2020, available at https://pace.coe.int/en/files/28722 Accessed 21 February 2021

The SIENNA Project (2018) D.3.1. State-of-the-Art Review, Human Enhancement https://www.sienna-project.eu/digitalAssets/788/c_788666-l_1-k_d3.1sotahet.pdf Accessed 21 February 2021

The SIENNA Project (2019) D.3.2. Analysis of the Legal and Human Rights Requirements for Human Enhancement Technologies in and outside the EU https://www.sienna-project.eu/news/news-item/?tarContentId=883290 Accessed 21 February 2021

Umair A, Ashfaq U, Khan MG (2017) Recent Trends, Applications, and Challenges of Brain-Computer Interfacing (BCI). International Journal of Intelligent Systems and Applications (IJISA), 9, 2: 58–65

Vincent NA, Nadelhoffer T, McCoy A (2020) Law Viewed Through the Lens of Neurointerventions. In: Vincent N A, Nadelhoffer T, McCoy A (eds) Neurointerventions and the Law: Regulating Human Mental Capacity. Oxford University Press, New York

Wolpaw JR, Winter Wolpaw E (2012) Brain-Computer Interfaces: Something New Under the Sun. In: Wolpaw J R, Winter Wolpaw E (eds) Brain-Computer Interfaces: Principles and Practice. Oxford University Press, Oxford, pp 3–14

Yeung K (2017) 'Hypernudge': Big Data as a mode of regulation by design. Information, Communication & Society, 20,1: 118–136

Zhang X, Yao L, Wang X, Monaghan JJM, Mcalpine D, Zhang Y (2020) A survey on deep learning-based non-invasive brain signals: recent advances and new frontiers. J Neural Eng. doi: https://doi.org/10.1088/1741-2552/abc902 Epub ahead of print. PMID: 33171452

Sümeyye Elif Biber   is a Ph.D. candidate in Law at Sant'Anna School of Advanced Studies, Pisa in Italy. Previously, she obtained her LLB from Istanbul University Law School with a "high honor" degree and received her LLM degree from Koç University with her thesis "Concretization of Constitutional Norms Referring to the Right to Respect for Private Life in the Individual Application Case-Law". While as an LLB candidate, she conducted an ERASMUS internship in London. She also participated in the International Summer School of German Language and Culture at the University of Heidelberg during her post-graduate studies in Germany. She has been a member of the International Association of Public Law (ICON-S) since 2017, and the International Council on Global Privacy and Security, by Design since 2019. Her research interests include interpretation of fundamental rights and freedoms in the context of new advanced technologies, the role of human dignity in artificial intelligence design, international human rights law, and the European Court of Human Rights and its jurisprudence.

Marianna Capasso   is a Ph.D. candidate in Human Rights and Global Politics: Legal, Philosophical and Economic Challenges at Sant'Anna School of Advanced Studies, Pisa in Italy. She holds a BA and MA in Philosophy from University of Pisa and a diploma in Humanities from Scuola Normale Superiore, Pisa. In 2020 Marianna was a visiting Ph.D. at Delft University of Technology. Her main research interests include philosophy of technology, political theory, applied ethics. She has authored or co-authored articles on these topics in journals such as Minds and Machines, Frontiers in Robotics and AI, and others.

Chapter 26
Regulating Artificial General Intelligence (AGI)

Tobias Mahler

Contents

Abstract This chapter discusses whether on-going EU policymaking on AI is relevant for Artificial General Intelligence (AGI) and what it would mean to potentially regulate it in the future. AGI is typically contrasted with narrow Artificial Intelligence (AI), which excels only within a specific given context. Although many researchers are working on AGI, there is uncertainty about the feasibility of developing it. If achieved, AGI could have cognitive capabilities similar to or beyond those of humans and may be able to perform a broad range of tasks. There are concerns that such AGI could undergo recursive circles of self-improvement, potentially leading to superintelligence. With such capabilities, superintelligent AGI could be a significant power factor in society. However, dystopian superintelligence scenarios are highly controversial and uncertain, so regulating existing narrow AI should be a priority.

T. Mahler (✉)
Faculty of Law, Norwegian Research Centre for Computers and Law, University of Oslo, Oslo, Norway
e-mail: tobias.mahler@jus.uio.no

© T.M.C. ASSER PRESS and the authors 2022
B. Custers and E. Fosch-Villaronga (eds.), *Law and Artificial Intelligence*,
Information Technology and Law Series 35,
https://doi.org/10.1007/978-94-6265-523-2_26

521

Keywords artificial general intelligence · regulation · risk management · existential risk · safety · European Union · law

26.1   Introduction

Current AI technology, often based on machine learning,[1] is narrow in the sense that it can learn to solve specific problems,[2] such as selecting a job applicant,[3] writing texts[4] or playing a game.[5] Typically, it cannot solve problems across a wide range of contexts. For instance, an AI system that has learned to drive a car cannot transfer that knowledge into a new domain; it cannot make investment suggestions or write a love letter.

AGI is a label often used for future forms of AI that are significantly less limited than current technologies and far more capable of competing with human intelligence than narrow AI. AGI has been defined as a form of AI that 'equals or exceeds human intelligence in a wide variety of cognitive tasks'.[6] So far, it does not exist, but narrow AI can solve many problems without any need to be intelligent.[7] The idea of AGI is based on the hypothesis that progress can be made towards the increased and broad intelligence of artificial agents.[8] Given the speed at which AI has been developed and has taken over on a global scale, some argue that the possibility that AGI may be created cannot be excluded.[9]

This potential future increase in intelligence is focused on advantages for humanity, but it has also raised concerns. There is a stream of literature predicting that AGI could be used to develop even better, more intelligent AGI systems, which in turn could be used to create yet greater intelligence, leading to an 'intelligence explosion'.[10] This has led to a dystopian scenario of superintelligent machines, beyond the control or understanding of humanity.[11] However, it is by no means certain that such a scenario is likely or even possible. An alternative scenario for the future is that intelligence in AGI will continue to increase gradually, even after surpassing human intelligence.[12]

---

[1] Bygrave 2020.

[2] Ng and Leung 2020, p. 64.

[3] Garg et al. 2021.

[4] Floridi and Chiriatti 2020.

[5] Silver et al. 2017.

[6] Everitt et al. 2018.

[7] Floridi and Chiriatti 2020.

[8] Everitt 2018; Everitt et al. 2018; Goertzel and Pennachin 2007; Heaven 2020; Huang 2017; Yampolskiy and Fox 2013.

[9] E.g. Bostrom 2014.

[10] Bostrom 2014; Chalmers 2010; Yudkowsky 2008.

[11] This dystopic scenario is extensively elaborated in Bostrom 2014.

[12] United States Executive Office of the President 2016, p. 8.

From a policymaking perspective, this is a challenging situation. There is no scientific agreement on whether or when technological development might reach the thresholds of AGI and, potentially, superintelligence. AGI policy is arguably affected by the Collingridge dilemma, which applies generally to the regulation of future technology: 'When change is easy, the need for it cannot be foreseen; when the need for change is apparent, change has become expensive, difficult, and time-consuming.'[13] Currently it is hard to see how AGI policymaking should be considered a priority, in light of pressing challenges related to existing or forthcoming AI systems.

A case in point is a report by the Obama Administration,[14] which argued that long-term concerns about superintelligent AGI should have little impact on current policy. It suggested that the policies the US federal government should adopt in the near-to-medium term if these fears are justified are almost exactly the same policies the government should adopt if they are not justified.[15] It concluded that the best way to build capacity for addressing the longer-term speculative risks is to attack the less extreme risks already seen today while investing in research on longer-term capabilities and how their challenges might be managed.[16]

This appears to be sound advice, but it also raises two questions, which will be addressed in this chapter. First, what does it mean that the policies for narrow and general AI should be 'almost exactly the same'?[17] Second, how can long-term AGI challenges be managed?

The first question will be assessed in the context of on-going European policymaking. The European Union (EU) Commission has drafted an AI Act ('the proposed AIA').[18] This focuses on a list of AI systems that are either prohibited or regulated as 'high-risk' AI. It is clear from the proposal that the EU primarily aims to regulate current or imminent AI systems; the proposal does not explicitly envisage uncertain future scenarios of AI development, such as AGI. Nevertheless, this chapter examines whether some of the approaches in the proposed AIA could have an impact on AGI challenges and concerns. Indeed, it is argued here that some of the proposal's provisions would be directly relevant also for AGI. As for the second question, this chapter examines the utility of AGI-specific policy recommendations in literature[19] which are not included in the proposed AIA. In theory, some of these recommendations could be used to complement the proposed AIA with dedicated regulatory

---

[13] Collingridge 1980, p. 11.

[14] United States Executive Office of the President 2016, p. 8.

[15] Ibid.

[16] Ibid.

[17] Ibid.

[18] European Commission 2021, Proposal for a Regulation of the European Parliament and of the Council Laying Down Harmonised Rules on Artificial Intelligence (Artificial Intelligence Act) and Amending Certain Union Legislative Acts, 2021/0106 (COD). Hereinafter referred to as the proposed AIA.

[19] Armstrong et al. 2016; Bostrom 2014; Everitt 2018; Goertzel 2015; Naudé and Dimitri 2020; Yudkowsky 2008.

mechanisms addressing AGI risks. However, in practice, it is questionable whether these policy recommendations would be feasible or sufficiently effective.

This chapter is structured as follows. Section 26.2 introduces concepts and technological enablers for the hypothetical future development of AGI. Furthermore, it explores societal consequences and risks that have been forecasted as consequences of superintelligent AGI. It also introduces AGI safety mechanisms and draws initial conclusions for policymaking. Section 26.3 introduces the proposed AIA and its focus on the problems of currently existing narrow AI systems. The section then proceeds to two regulatory approaches that are present in the proposal and which have relevance for AGI, namely risk management and human oversight. Section 26.4 complements this with three regulatory approaches that have been proposed in AGI literature,[20] but which are not present in the proposed AIA. The focus is on specific requirements for procedures when developing an AGI, mechanisms to ensure that AGI systems work towards the achievement of human values and economic incentives. Section 26.5 draws conclusions from the preceding analysis.

26.2   AGI

Discussions about the future of AI sometimes employ the framing of AGI.[21] The term AGI emphasizes future AI development beyond the current state of the art, which is characterized as 'narrow' AI. Sections 26.2.1–26.2.6 introduce key concepts, potential technological AGI enablers, superintelligence, its consequences, AGI safety, and policy implications respectively.

26.2.1   Concepts

AGI can be defined as an AI system that 'equals or exceeds human intelligence in a wide variety of cognitive tasks'.[22] A dictionary definition of 'cognitive' is something involving conscious intellectual activity, such as thinking, reasoning or remembering.[23] The two definitions, read together, highlight Alan Turing's question 'Can

---

[20] Ibid.

[21] Everitt 2018; Everitt et al. 2018; Goertzel and Pennachin 2007; Heaven 2020; Huang 2017; Yampolskiy and Fox 2013.

[22] Everitt et al. 2018.

[23] 'Cognitive', Merriam-Webster Dictionary, https://www.merriam-webster.com/dictionary/cognitive. Accessed on 29 June 2021.

machines think?'[24] However, without a clear definition of 'thinking', an answer to the question is still needed.[25]

The concept of intelligence has been elusive and challenging throughout history. Some argue that thinking includes consciousness[26] and use the term 'strong AI' to denote machines with it.[27] However, there is no clear understanding of what consciousness is, what it would imply to have conscious AI, or how one could verify it.[28] Others assert that any attempt to build conscious machines could never completely exceed human capabilities—and that if a computer would be able to achieve consciousness, such a machine would not be considered a computer anymore.[29] A relevant starting point for theories on AGI is a non-anthropomorphic definition of intelligence, such as 'an agent's ability to achieve goals in a wide range of environments'.[30] Humans can achieve goals across a broad range of contexts, but existing AI systems can solve tasks in only their respective narrow domains; they lack general intelligence.

The reference point for yet another framing for future AI technologies, i.e. super-intelligence, is human intelligence.[31] While AGI focuses on the contrast with narrow intelligence, superintelligence emphasizes the potential that AI could become more intelligent than humans. Both terms, 'AGI' and 'superintelligence' are sometimes normatively loaded, with AGI emphasizing the utopia of better future AI systems and 'superintelligence' being the label for a dystopian scenario in which a more intelligent agent dominates humans. Here, the two terms will be used interchangeably, as this chapter deals with AGI as a potential nucleus for superintelligence.

26.2.2 Potential Technological AGI Enablers

The idea of genuinely intelligent machines has been a part of AI research efforts from the field's inception,[32] but so far, all efforts to create AGI have been unsuccessful.

---

[24] The question was central to Turing 1950. However, as noted by Bringsjord and Govindarajulu 2020, Descartes discussed an earlier version of the Turing test in 1637: 'If there were machines which bore a resemblance to our body and imitated our actions as far as it was morally possible to do so, we should always have two very certain tests by which to recognise that, for all that they were not real men.'

[25] Lutz and Tamò 2015 suggest that one should use other verbs to describe the 'thinking' of robots, such as 'sense-process-weigh-act'.

[26] See this in detail in Searle 1997.

[27] Bringsjord and Govindarajulu 2020. Ng and Leung 2020 do not offer a conclusion on whether AGI can achieve consciousness.

[28] See Floridi 2005 for a test to distinguish between conscious (human) and conscious-less agents.

[29] Signorelli 2018, Conscious machines also raise the question of whether they are worthy of rights protection, which is not considered here. See Gellers 2021.

[30] Legg and Hutter 2007; Everitt et al. 2018, p. 3.

[31] Bostrom 2014.

[32] Turing 1950.

Early AI researchers postulated that one could develop a 'child machine' which could learn and be improved.[33] Since then, development efforts and ideas have grown to be based on imitating and improving existing forms of intelligence or on their evolution.

Inspiration is sought from biological brains, including human brains,[34] the swarm intelligence of beehives[35] and evolutionary processes.[36] History shows that, despite the absence of a 'master plan' and specific goals, evolutionary processes have generated various forms of intelligence. Humans, for instance, are arguably just by-products of evolution. Similarly, it is argued that AGI could evolve from a spontaneous cognitive development process based on progressively increasing coordination between AI agents.[37] Another approach to developing AGI might be whole brain emulation, which would imply scanning and closely modelling the computational structure of a biological brain.[38]

Some authors have also argued that AGI could evolve from computer hardware and software.[39] This argument has foundations in various factors, such as hardware improvements based on lowering computer prices and growing budgets (despite doubts whether Moore's law will hold in the future) and the prospects of quantum computing. Moreover, some have claimed that improvements to neural networks could contribute to human-level AI.[40] So far, the ability of reinforcement learning algorithms such as AlphaZero is impressive, as it can adapt to various game rules, which is a notable step towards achieving a general game-playing system.[41] However, no existing approaches have yielded results that come close to achieving AGI. Text-creating AI such as GPT-3 may appear intelligent, but it has no understanding of what it does; it primarily reproduces patterns it has learned from training data.[42]

The prospect of AGI is highly uncertain and very controversial. Critics have argued that the very idea of AGI is 'utterly implausible'.[43] One argument is that machines can do amazing things, including playing many games better than us and yet they are all versions of a Turing machine, 'an abstract model that sets the limits of what can be done by a computer through its mathematical logic.'[44] However, the human brain is not a Turing machine and it is impossible to know what consequences a

---

[33] Bostrom 2014, p. 27, Turing 1950, p. 456.

[34] Huang 2017.

[35] Weinbaum and Veitas 2017.

[36] Darwish et al. 2020.

[37] Weinbaum and Veitas 2017.

[38] Bostrom 2014, p. 35, Koene and Deca 2013.

[39] Turchin 2019.

[40] Ibid., p. 51.

[41] Silver et al. 2018.

[42] Floridi and Chiriatti 2020, p. 684: 'In the same way [that] Google "reads" our queries without[,] of course[,] understanding them, and offers relevant answers […] GPT-3 writes a text continuing the sequence of our words (the prompt), without any understanding.'

[43] Floridi 2019.

[44] Ibid.

future merger of neuroscience and computing may generate.[45] Those confident in the achievability of AGI argue that evolution has already produced intelligence, so this process could be replicated just as flying animals were used to learn how to build aircraft.[46]

26.2.3 Superintelligence

The argument that AGI could become superintelligent is based on AI's putative creativity.[47] The possible capabilities of a generally intelligent agent include creating a new AI system. Examples in which AI is used to create new software already exist.[48] In theory, AGI could recreate itself at a higher level of intelligence. It is argued in literature that a sufficiently intelligent AGI system could undergo an 'intelligence explosion',[49] during which it would experience recursive circles of self-improvement.[50] In theory, it could surpass human intelligence and lead to the evolution of superintelligence.[51]

The AI community discusses the controversial hypothesis of intelligence explosion with a focus on whether it could happen in the foreseeable future.[52] There is significant uncertainty with respect to whether and when such a hypothetical development may happen. So far, the main scientific method for addressing this question is conducting expert surveys, which is unsatisfactory as these investigate only beliefs and opinions. One such survey concluded that 'AI systems will likely reach overall human abilities around 2040–2050 and move on to superintelligence less than 30 years thereafter.'[53] A critic conducted a second survey in which most experts opined that superintelligence would arrive in more than 25 years.[54] It was concluded that superintelligence was beyond the foreseeable horizon, but in the same survey, only 25% of experts held the opinion that superintelligence would never be achieved.

In the most recent survey, AI researchers thought there was a 50% probability of AI 'outperforming humans in all tasks' in 45 years.[55] If these estimates are accurate,

---

[45] Signorelli 2018.

[46] Chalmers 2010; Moravec (1976) (unpublished manuscript cited in Bostrom 2014, p. 28), an example of an evolutionary approach to AGI is in Weinbaum and Veitas 2017.

[47] Bostrom 2014; Sotala 2017; Yudkowsky 2008.

[48] Becker and Gottschlich 2021.

[49] Chalmers 2010; Good 1966.

[50] Bostrom 2014; Sotala 2017; Yudkowsky 2008.

[51] Bostrom 2014.

[52] Etzioni 2016 argues against an existential threat based on the argument that experts believe it will take more than 25 years to develop AGI; for an opposing view, see Dafoe and Russell 2016.

[53] Müller and Bostrom 2014.

[54] Etzioni 2016.

[55] Grace et al. 2018, p. 729 state that 'Researchers believe there is a 50% chance of AI outperforming humans in all tasks in 45 years and of automating all human jobs in 120 years, with Asian respondents expecting these dates much sooner than North Americans'.

it means that there is a fair chance that some humans could experience AGI in their lifetime. It is unclear what this means for AI policymaking. However, uncertainty over the future evolution of AGI may explain why the EU Parliament chose, in 2017, to take a 10 to 15-year perspective with respect to legal frameworks for AI and robotics, implicitly excluding AGI issues from the first AI legal framework.[56]

26.2.4 The Societal Consequences and Risks of Superintelligence

Discourse about the societal consequences of AGI has primarily focused on the potential of superintelligence.[57] An AGI system that is more intelligent than humans could bring about significant benefits for humanity. It could achieve things humans likely cannot do, such as inventing new sources of energy or ensuring nutrition for all humans while preserving the planet's resources.

However, superintelligent AI might also involve existential risks, especially if it is not interested in human needs. For the first time in history, humans could face an actor more intelligent than themselves who might be an ally or a competitor. For humanity, the creation of an AGI system would likely have substantial beneficial results and implied risks. The effects on society would depend on various factors, such as AI governance, the distribution of gains and how a generally intelligent artificial agent would wield its powers.

Increasingly intelligent AI might first lead to rising unemployment rates and changes in the labor market as a growing number of jobs could become automated.[58] More uncertain consequences could follow if superintelligence is achieved. The assumption in literature is that superintelligence would not merely imply the existence of AGI slightly more intelligent than humans.[59] Indeed, the intelligence of humans is naturally limited, while AI limits are unknown. Therefore, some argue that if future AI could achieve human-level intelligence, it would significantly surpass that level and it is not known where the process would stop.[60] Examples often compare the disparity between AGI and human potential to the difference in intelligence levels of humans and certain animals, e.g., mice.[61]

Optimists argue that with capabilities far surpassing those of humans, AGI might be able to solve many of humanity's challenges.[62] This rests on the assumption that high intelligence also implies power; e.g., humans being more powerful than animals. Thus, a superintelligent agent could, for example, use its capabilities to

---

[56] European Parliament 2017, para 51.

[57] Bostrom 2014.

[58] Makridakis 2017.

[59] Ibid., Sotala 2017; Yudkowsky 2008.

[60] Ibid.

[61] Bostrom 2014, p. 70; Goertzel 2015.

[62] Goertzel 2015.

switch off weapons systems, thereby preventing wars, or to find novel solutions to environmental threats.[63]

In the 1960s, some suggested that the 'first ultraintelligent machine' would be the last invention that mankind would need to make.[64] However, if the benefits of such an invention were to accrue primarily for the system's owner, the first superintelligent AI would convey enormous power and wealth to its inventor, leading to a 'winner takes all' situation.[65] A company that could control the first superintelligent AI would have a monopoly over the ability to solve problems no human has been able to solve, to generate new inventions, and to likely dominate many markets. AGI could therefore raise questions about the distribution of wealth and power, and the first-mover advantage could create incentives to cut corners and compromise safety.[66]

This would be important as AGI could wield significant powers over humanity, perhaps creating an existential threat.[67] That danger would lie in the power of a superintelligent AGI achieving intelligence levels that far surpass those of people. Humanity lacks experiences with a more intelligent actor, but imagination can be fueled by the situation of animals dominated by more intelligent beings, i.e., humans. A dystopian view is that a superintelligent agent would be able to act in ways not controllable by humans. A US government report described this scenario as follows. 'If computers could exert control over many critical systems, the result could be havoc, with humans no longer in control of their destiny at best and extinct at worst.'[68] It is therefore uncertain whether superintelligent AGI would be safe for humans because it is unclear whether such a system would act in the interests of humanity. As one AI scientist noted, 'if gorillas had accidentally created humans way back when, the now endangered primates likely would be wishing they had not done so.'[69]

Overall, the threat of AGI seems to be impossible to scientifically verify or refute. For epistemic reasons, one cannot know in advance the consequences of a technology that does not yet exist, and conducting an experiment to determine what may happen seems unfeasible and perhaps unethical. The perceived threat rests on only a *hypothesis* of an irreversible acceleration of intelligence levels, combined with uncertainty about how superintelligent AGI would treat humans. The existence of such intelligence may not represent a threat if it supports humans in achieving their goals.[70] However, the problem is that one cannot know in advance how a superintelligent actor would behave.

---

[63] Ibid.

[64] Good 1966, p. 33.

[65] Armstrong et al. 2016.

[66] Ibid.

[67] Bostrom 2014; Galanos 2019; Liu et al. 2018.

[68] United States Executive Office of the President 2016, p. 8.

[69] Russell 2016, p. 58.

[70] Everitt 2018, p. 4.

26.2.5 AGI Safety

While some philosophical literature has emphasized the existential threat potentially created by superintelligence, some technical literature has focused on the problem as a question of safety.[71] Concerns include safe interruption, reliability and value specification. To start with the first concern, AGI systems may use their intelligence to circumvent any attempts to interrupt their operation. Technical AGI literature has discussed formal (mathematical) approaches to this 'shutdown problem' but has not yet been able to solve it.[72]

Reliability addresses the creation of an agent that keeps pursuing the goals it is designed for, which is a very technical question.[73] Less technical is the matter of value specification, i.e., how to ensure that an AGI system works towards the 'right' goals. Ultimately, the goals of an AI system depend on programming and self-learning, which can be influenced by developers. The elicitation and programming of goals and values into AGI could be challenging and risky. The ancient myth of King Midas shows that the desire to 'turn everything into gold', when taken literally, can have destructive consequences. If everything turns into gold, food becomes inedible and human lives are lost. Following this line of thinking, literature has explored what would happen if a superintelligent AGI were designed to pursue the sole purposes of making paperclips[74] or baking cheesecakes.[75] Such tasks do not require an elevated level of intelligence, but the thought experiment involves a very powerful AGI that would take a limited task extremely seriously. It could convert the world into only paperclips or bake cheesecakes as large as cities because other human goals are not included in its internal reasoning processes. The simple process of optimization, pursuing ill-conceived goals, could lead to the theoretical demise of humanity.[76] While it is easy to ridicule these teleological thought experiments because it is unlikely that a real developer would assign these tasks to a superintelligent AGI,[77] the underlying issue remains relevant.[78] The goals and values to be pursued by an AI system need to be carefully elicited and must align with human values and interests.[79]

---

[71] For an overview of AGI safety issues, see Everitt et al. 2018.

[72] Soares et al. 2015.

[73] Everitt et al. 2018.

[74] Goertzel 2015.

[75] Yudkowsky 2008.

[76] Liu et al. 2018, p. 8.

[77] Goertzel 2015, p. 55 notes, 'Bostrom and Yudkowsky ... worry about what happens when a very powerful and intelligent reward-maximiser is paired with a goal system that gives rewards for achieving foolish goals[, such as] tiling the universe with paperclips'.

[78] Wiener 1960 states, 'if we use, to achieve our purposes, a mechanical agency with whose operation we cannot interfere effectively ... we had better be quite sure that the purpose put into the machine is the purpose which we really desire'.

[79] Everitt 2018, p. 204.

Key to value alignment is the question how goals and intelligence are related. Those arguing that superintelligence is an existential risk often see goals and intelligence as orthogonal or independent.[80] The orthogonality thesis refers to the possibility of combining various types of goals with different levels of intelligence; an AGI could pursue the unintelligent aim of making paperclips.

An opposing view acknowledges this thesis as a purely abstract possibility, but argues that one ought to consider *likely* combinations of intelligence and goals in practice.[81] In this view, goals and intelligence ought to be seen as interdependent and developed together. This reasoning rules out some of the scenarios mentioned above, which seem unrealistic. However, the goals and values of AI remain crucial. To manage AGI risks, AI developers must ensure human and AI value alignment. A superintelligence with adequate goals and values would be safe in that it might benefit humanity rather than threaten it.

26.2.6   *Preliminary Conclusion and Implications for Policymaking*

In summary, the prospects and potential consequences of AGI technology are uncertain, but some scholars hold the opinion that the scenario of superintelligence development could involve existential risks for humanity. The likelihood of superintelligence development is difficult to judge and highly contested.

AGI regulation issues are affected by the classic Collingridge dilemma, which generally applies to the regulation of future technology. At present, it is highly uncertain whether and when AGI development might succeed. Some argue that the speed of change in a hypothetical 'intelligence explosion' might be high, which indicates that time is of the essence if a first AGI system ever becomes visible on the technological horizon.[82] However, at that point in time, regulatory intervention may be challenging.

The quandary consists of two problems. First, once a powerful AGI is created (assuming this is feasible), humanity may lack the time and mechanisms to adequately govern the technology because its consequences will already be present. This may make regulation more difficult or costly than it would be otherwise. Previous phases of development may set AGI goals, and restricting further evolution may be challenging with respect to competition. It may then be too late for adequate regulatory interventions. Second, any point in time before the development of AGI, such as the present, may be too early to intervene.

---

[80] Bostrom 2014, p. 107 notes, 'more or less any level of intelligence could in principle be combined with more or less any final goal'.

[81] Goertzel 2015, p. 64.

[82] As mentioned above, AGI could use its intelligence to improve its code quickly, with accelerating enhancement capabilities, see Bostrom 2014; Chalmers 2010; Goertzel 2015.

The prospect of AGI may simply be too speculative and foggy to justify regulatory intervention. Information asymmetries may aggravate the problem as it may be difficult for policymakers and legal researchers to identify and adequately appreciate the consequences of ongoing research and development.[83] Significant portions of such development may be conducted by private companies maintaining commercial confidentiality or state actors interested in protecting national interests.

Considering this dilemma, the following sections do not discuss whether AGI should be regulated at present. Instead, they examine whether some of the regulatory mechanisms included in the proposed AIA might be relevant for the regulation of AGI. Moreover, they assess further policy options not included in the proposed AIA.

26.3   The Proposed AIA

Fueled by the concerns surrounding current AI systems, the European Commission issued the proposed AIA, suggesting harmonized rules for AI systems in the EU. In the proposal, an AI system means 'software that is developed with one or more of the techniques and approaches listed in Annex I and can, for a given set of human-defined objectives, generate outputs, such as content, predictions, recommendations or decisions[,] influencing the environments they interact with'.[84] This definition encompasses various technologies and uses—from spam filters to lethal autonomous weapons[85]—which raise vastly different regulatory issues. The definition is also sufficiently broad to include AGI, at least if it could be achieved with one of the many listed techniques. Nevertheless, the proposal does not regulate AI systems per se; it focuses on a risk-based shortlist of AI systems.

The approach of the proposed AIA consists of using risk levels as regulatory thresholds. AI systems that represent unacceptable risks are forbidden, while high-risk systems must comply with specified requirements. Other (less risky) systems must comply with few or no requirements. This risk-based strategy is designed to ensure the proportionality of the proposed AIA by tailoring the rules to the 'intensity and scope of the risks that AI systems can generate'.[86] The focus is on high-risk AI systems. If an AI system is classified as such, detailed requirements and obligations are triggered.[87]

Article 6 of the proposed AIA defines high-risk AI systems. Such systems include, pursuant to Article 6(2), any of the areas listed in Annex III. The proposal does not define 'areas' but does provide examples, including critical infrastructure, education, employment, law enforcement and border control. In each area, Annex III lists one

---

[83] Guihot et al. 2017, p. 32.

[84] The proposed AIA, Article 3(1).

[85] Autonomous weapons are excluded from the scope of the proposed AIA but fit within its AI definition.

[86] The proposed AIA, Recital 14.

[87] The proposed AIA, Title III, Chapters 2 and 3.

or more relatively concrete use cases, such as systems 'used by law enforcement authorities as polygraphs and similar tools or to detect the emotional state of a natural person.'[88] In addition, the proposed AIA defines prohibitions for certain AI systems. Article 5 prohibits, for example, an AI system that exploits any vulnerabilities of a specific group of persons due to a disability if further conditions are fulfilled.[89]

The proposal does not explicitly exclude the possibility that an AI system used for a regulated use case or functionality may have other capabilities. In this sense, it is indifferent to whether such a system may be narrow or general AI. However, it seems that the use cases were written with narrow AI systems in mind, which are characterized by their ability to solve a limited set of problems. The list of use cases in Annex III shows narrow purposes, strongly inspired by AI systems that already exist or are in development. Annex III highlights narrow AI systems which have already been shown to be problematic or are likely to raise societal concerns. They focus strongly on such extant systems, e.g., machine learning, which may bring along problems like opacity and bias. This means that the proposed AIA at least implicitly focuses on current narrow AI, disregarding potential AGI in the future.

Despite the fact that the proposed AIA does not explicitly address AGI, several of its elements might arguably address some AGI concerns. A comprehensive analysis of the proposal is beyond the scope of this chapter. However, two regulatory approaches—risk management and human oversight—serve as examples and will be discussed in Sects. 26.3.1 and 26.3.2 respectively.

26.3.1 Risk Management

The first regulatory approach is to require AGI developers to manage risks. Article 9 of the proposed AIA requires that a risk management system be established, implemented, documented and maintained in relation to high-risk AI systems. This should be done to identify and analyze known and foreseeable dangers associated with each high-risk AI system. Although AGI systems as such do not necessarily qualify as high-risk under the proposed AIA, the overall approach seems to be relevant. AGI risks may not be easily foreseeable, but they have been identified in literature.[90] Thus, Article 9, if applicable to AGI, would require the elimination or reduction of risks or, alternatively, the adequate mitigation of and control measures for risks that cannot be eliminated.

---

[88] The proposed AIA, Annex III, Section 6(b).

[89] The proposed AIA, Article 5(1)(b).

[90] Armstrong et al. 2016; Bostrom 2014; Everitt 2018; Goertzel 2015.

26.3.2 Human Oversight

A mechanism to reduce risks could also be to ensure human oversight over AGI. However, the potential prospects of such oversight would be limited if AGI could use its capabilities to circumvent any constraints.[91] The problem would be that as AI systems increase their intelligence, they could resist interventions by programmers. For example, if a shutdown conflicted with their programmed goals, they might resist it. Therefore, corrigibility is a key desired feature of AGI systems.[92] This refers to the AI system's cooperation with external actors to correct errors when the system is interrupted or altered, despite the interruption conflicting with the built-in purpose of the system.[93] An example of actual AI interruption is the case of the Microsoft chatbot Tay that was shut down because of its offensive and inflammatory tweets.[94] However, Tay was not based on an AGI system, so it was unable to resist the shutdown. By comparison, if a superintelligent AGI system would be behind the chatbot, allowing a shutdown might conflict with its main goals and the agent would have an incentive, and theoretically even a possibility, to resist.

Securing shutdowns for misbehaving AGIs can be seen as a possible regulatory tool. In the proposed AIA, Article 14 requires human oversight over high-risk AI systems. Under Article 14(2), such oversight shall aim to prevent or minimize risks to health, safety or fundamental rights when a high-risk AI system is used in accordance with its intended purpose or under conditions of reasonably foreseeable misuse. According to Article 14(4), human oversight measures shall enable the overseer to understand the capacities and limitations of the system and to monitor its operation, which is arguably challenging with respect to AGI. Article 14 also requires some type of stop button for interrupting the system or otherwise intervening in its operation.

In other words, solving the 'shutdown problem' would be necessary for compliance with the proposed AIA if it were to apply to AGI.[95] However, according to scholars, it is uncertain whether safe interruption can be guaranteed for an AGI system with a superintelligence potential.[96] Compelling a superintelligence to do something that conflicts with its goals seems challenging if not impossible. Therefore, it may be even more important to ensure value alignment.

In summary, the proposed AIA does offer mechanisms that appear relevant for AGI. Several other articles not discussed here could also be relevant, but a comprehensive analysis of the proposed AIA is beyond the scope of this chapter.

---

[91] Bostrom 2014.

[92] Lo et al. 2019.

[93] Ibid., p. 78.

[94] Neff and Nagy 2016.

[95] As mentioned above, this is not the case as the proposed AIA directly regulates only specific types of narrow AI.

[96] Everitt 2018, p. 204.

26.4 AGI-specific Regulation

While the proposed AIA offers some relevant mechanisms, its main focus is on narrow AI. Therefore, it is worth considering what it would mean to create a regulatory framework with an AGI emphasis. A variety of policy proposals (reviewed below) have suggested measures to address anticipated AGI challenges. Sections 26.4.1–26.4.3 discuss requirements for AGI development procedures, an approach to ensure value alignment, and the use of economic incentives.

26.4.1 AGI Development Procedures

Various policy proposals focus on AGI development procedures.[97] However, there is no agreement on how safe AGI-development could be carried out. Two views propose procedures that are diametrically opposed to each other.

The first line of thought suggests that developers should adopt tightly controlled settings rather than regular open academic collaborations.[98] For example, some have noted, 'perhaps the scientists involved would have to be physically isolated and prevented from communicating with the rest of the world for the duration of the project, except through a single carefully vetted communication channel.'[99] Such suggestions focus on containing AGI risks by isolating its development from the world or by conducting AGI development in only simulations. Other proposals for constraints argue that one should limit the number of groups seeking to develop AGI to reduce the risks inherent in an AI arms race.[100] These proposals come from authors who mainly focus on AGI risks, rather than its potential benefits.

An opposite and more optimistic view is that the development of AGI should be as open as possible.[101] This is the core tenet of open-ended AI development, inspired by evolutionary processes.[102] The approach is inspired by various intelligence manifestations, from brain cells to beehives and human social systems. In this view, AGI must evolve during close contact and collaboration with human agents rather than in isolation; an 'open pursuit of AGI is going to work out better than an elite group of uber-nerds locked in a secure installation.'[103]

The closed approach to AGI development intends to limit risks by locking the AGI system into a separate, highly controlled environment, which is perhaps not entirely realistic. It remains unclear which state or government agency would administrate or control such a closed environment. Tough constraints may end up backfiring, as

---

[97] Armstrong et al. 2016; Bostrom 2014; Everitt 2018; Goertzel 2015.

[98] Bostrom 2014.

[99] Ibid., p. 253.

[100] Armstrong et al. 2016.

[101] Everitt 2018; Goertzel 2015.

[102] Weinbaum and Veitas 2017.

[103] Goertzel 2015, p. 85.

advanced AI may not necessarily accept such limitations.[104] In comparison, open-ended AGI is similar to how intelligence has evolved so far, and it is an approach for fostering innovation, rather than limiting it. However, evolution has not been beneficial for all species—many have gone extinct and others have been dominated by humans. Thus, perhaps neither tightly controlled nor open AGI development processes are risk free.

26.4.2 AGI and Human Values

When examining the need for AGI regulation, a key concern is whether such a system would act in humanity's best interest. It is unclear whether legal mechanisms would be adequate for and relevant to achieving value alignment. While it may be possible—in theory—for a law to mandate that AI is 'human-centered', 'beneficial' or similarly aligned with human values, what effects would this have?[105] It may be simple to establish the abstract principle, but it would be significantly more challenging to translate it into concrete, actionable requirements that could be controlled and enforced.

A potential regulatory approach might be to focus on the process of AGI value acquisition, as mentioned above. If goals and values of an AI system originate from a learning process based on training data, it may be useful to create specific rules for the data, expanding further on the proposed AIA's Article 10. Indeed, value alignment is equally relevant to both AGI and present 'narrow' AI. For example, an AI-based recruitment platform can reproduce the biases of previous hiring decisions represented in training data. Therefore, its hiring recommendations may be aligned with earlier practices, but not necessarily with its user's values. Adequate rules on training data might be a first step in the direction of value alignment in such a situation.

Article 10 of the proposed AIA addresses appropriate data governance and management practices, including relevant design choices, data collection and examinations of possible biases in the data. There are requirements for data sets, e.g., 'they shall be relevant, representative, free of error and complete'.[106] These requirements may be adequate for narrow AI systems. In comparison, AGI value alignment seems to be a more complex problem for which further alternatives should be considered in future research and policymaking.

---

[104] Everitt 2018, p. 204.

[105] Yudkowsky 2008, p. 334 argues that '[l]egislation could (for example) require researchers to publicly report their [f]riendliness strategies or penalise researchers whose AIs cause damage'.

[106] The proposed AIA, Article 10(3).

26.4.3 Economic Incentives

From an economic perspective, AGI risks may be related to market failures, which regulators could address with incentives, such as taxation and the government procurement of AGI.[107] Market actors have important roles in financing AI research and carrying out AI development on behalf of other actors, such as states. Presumably, there is limited demand for unsafe AGI systems, so economic incentives may favor the creation of safe AGI systems.

However, it is claimed that a race to AGI development could be an incentive for cutting corners and compromising safety to achieve first-mover advantages.[108] Considering game-theoretical approaches, some authors have argued for economic interventions, such as the introduction of an intermediate prize, modifying winner-takes-all perspectives.[109] However, at a practical level it remains unclear how such a strategy could be implemented, particularly in a global context in which nations, such as the United States and China, and regions, such as the EU, are competing in a race for future AI systems. Economic approaches may require some type of global agreement, which currently appears to be absent, and which seems unlikely, considering political differences and strategic interests.

26.5 Conclusion

The discussion of potential AGI regulatory mechanisms has barely begun, but few of the regulatory measures focusing on AGI appear to be clearly effective. In theory, the most relevant goal for regulation seems to be value alignment. If regulatory measures can ensure that AI and human values are aligned, it may be less of a problem that superintelligent AGI can be difficult to constrain with the limited biological intelligence of humans. However, in practice it is unclear how value alignment and human oversight can be ensured from an AI engineering perspective, and this is not a good starting point for regulatory interventions. Thus, before adopting any AGI regulation, a better understanding is needed of how legal regulation can contribute to mitigating long-term AGI risks.

Currently, there are significant hurdles preventing a political focus on AGI. It is already difficult to create new legal frameworks for existing narrow AI, which should be a priority because it affects humans at present. The proposed AIA will likely become unmanageable if it is combined with a discussion on AGI. Debates on AI following public comments by prominent figures in the past few years indicate that there is significant interest in Hollywood-like scenarios of AI doom. However, a concrete regulatory discourse about the existing and immediately foreseeable technology of narrow AI is needed first. Once there is an adequate regulatory framework

---

[107] Naudé and Dimitri 2020.

[108] Armstrong et al. 2016.

[109] Ibid.

for present AI systems, whether and how AGI may be added to the framework can be considered.

In summary, it is too early to regulate hypothetical AGI, but this should not stop discussions regarding its potential risks and strategies for its regulation. Future research should identify and assess alternative regulatory mechanisms, particularly in a global context, as EU rules alone may be insufficient for addressing the global impacts of future AI technology.

Acknowledgements The research presented in this chapter was partly financed by the Vulnerability in the Robot Society (VIROS) project, which is funded by the Norwegian Research Council (project number 247947). I thank the editors, anonymous reviewers and all members of the VIROS Project, especially Lee Bygrave, Rebecca Schmidt, Live Sunniva Hjort and Tereza Duchoňová, for their comments to an earlier version of this chapter. All errors are the sole responsibility of the author.

References

Armstrong S, Bostrom N, Shulman C (2016) Racing to the precipice: a model of artificial intelligence development. AI and Society 31:201–206

Becker K, Gottschlich J (2021) AI Programmer: autonomously creating software programs using genetic algorithms. Paper presented at the Proceedings of the Genetic and Evolutionary Computation Conference, https://doi.org/10.1145/3449726.3463125

Bostrom N (2014) Superintelligence: paths, dangers, strategies. Oxford University Press, Oxford

Bringsjord S, Govindarajulu N (2020) Artificial intelligence. https://plato.stanford.edu/archives/sum2020/entries/artificial-intelligence/ Accessed 6 July 2021

Bygrave L (2020) Machine learning, cognitive sovereignty and data protection rights with respect to automated decisions. University of Oslo Faculty of Law

Chalmers D (2010) The singularity: a philosophical analysis. Journal of Consciousness Studies 17:7–65

Collingridge D (1980) The social control of technology. Frances Pinter, London

Dafoe A, Russell S (2016) Yes, we are worried about the existential risk of artificial intelligence. https://www.technologyreview.com/2016/11/02/156285/yes-we-are-worried-about-the-existential-risk-of-artificial-intelligence/ Accessed 5 July 2021

Darwish A, Hassanien A E, Das S (2020) A survey of swarm and evolutionary computing approaches for deep learning. Artificial Intelligence Review, 53(3):1767–1812

Etzioni O (2016) No, the experts don't think superintelligent AI is a threat to humanity. https://www.technologyreview.com/2016/09/20/70131/no-the-experts-dont-think-sup erintelligent-ai-is-a-threat-to-humanity/ Accessed 6 July 2021

European Commission (2021) Proposal for a Regulation of the European Parliament and of the Council Laying Down Harmonised Rules on Artificial Intelligence (Artificial Intelligence Act) and Amending Certain Union Legislative Acts, 2021/0106 (COD)

European Parliament (2017) Civil Law Rules on Robotics: European Parliament Resolution of 16 February 2017 with Recommendations to the Commission on Civil Law Rules on Robotics, 2015/2103 (INL)

Everitt T (2018) Towards safe artificial general intelligence. Australian National University, Canberra

Everitt T, Lea G, Hutter M (2018) AGI safety literature review. International Joint Conference on Artificial Intelligence

Floridi L (2005) Consciousness, agents and the knowledge game. Minds and Machines 15:415–444

Floridi L (2019) Should we be afraid of AI? Aeon Magazine 9 May 2016

Floridi L, Chiriatti M (2020) GPT-3: Its nature, scope, limits and consequences. Minds and Machines 30:681–694

Galanos V (2019) Exploring expanding expertise: artificial intelligence as an existential threat and the role of prestigious commentators 2014–2018. Technology Analysis and Strategic Management 31:421–432

Garg S, Sinha S, Kar A, Mani M (2021) A review of machine learning applications in human resource management. International Journal of Productivity and Performance Management doi: https://doi.org/10.1108/IJPPM-08-2020-0427

Gellers J (2021) Rights for robots: artificial intelligence, animal and environmental law. Artificial intelligence, animal and environmental law. Taylor and Francis, Abingdon

Goertzel B (2015) Superintelligence: fears, promises and potentials. Journal of Evolution and Technology 25:55–87

Goertzel B, Pennachin C (2007) Artificial general intelligence. Springer, Berlin

Good I (1966) Speculations concerning the first ultraintelligent machine. Advances in Computers 6:31–88

Grace K, Salvatier J, Dafoe A, Zhang B, Evans O (2018) When will AI exceed human performance? Evidence from AI experts. The Journal of Artificial Intelligence Research 62:729–754

Guihot M, Matthew A, Suzor N (2017) Nudging robots: Innovative solutions to regulate artificial intelligence, Vanderbilt Journal of Entertainment and Technology Law 20:385–456

Heaven W D (2020) Artificial general intelligence: Are we close, and does it even make sense to try? https://www.technologyreview.com/2020/10/15/1010461/artificial-general-intelligence-robots-ai-agi-deepmind-google-openai Accessed 6 July 2021

Huang T-J (2017) Imitating the brain with neurocomputer a "new" way towards artificial general intelligence. International Journal of Automation and Computing 14(5):520–531

Koene R, Deca D (2013) Whole brain emulation seeks to implement a mind and its general intelligence through system identification. Journal of Artificial General Intelligence 4:1–9

Legg S, Hutter M (2007) Universal intelligence: a definition of machine intelligence. Minds and Machines 17:391–444

Liu H-Y, Lauta K, Maas M (2018) Governing boring apocalypses: a new typology of existential vulnerabilities and exposures for existential risk research. Futures 102:6–19

Lo Y, Woo C, Ng K (2019) The necessary roadblock to artificial general intelligence: corrigibility. AI Matters 5:77–84

Lutz C, Tamò A (2015) Robocode-ethicists: privacy-friendly robots, an ethical responsibility of engineers? 2015 ACM SIGCOMM Workshop on Ethics in Networked Systems Research, London

Makridakis S (2017) The forthcoming artificial intelligence (AI) revolution: its impact on society and firms. Futures 90:46–60

Müller V, Bostrom N (2014) Future progress in artificial intelligence: a poll among experts. AI Matters 1:9–11

Naudé W, Dimitri N (2020) The race for an artificial general intelligence: implications for public policy. AI and Society 35:367–379

Neff G, Nagy P (2016) Automation, algorithms, and politics: talking to nots: dymbiotic agency and the case of Tay. International Journal of Communication, 10: 4915–4931

Ng G, Leung W (2020) Strong artificial intelligence and consciousness. Journal of Artificial Intelligence and Consciousness 7:63–72

Russell S (2016) Should one fear supersmart robots? Scientific American 314:58–59

Searle J (1997) The mystery of consciousness. New York Review of Books, New York

Signorelli C (2018) Can computers become conscious and overcome humans? Front Robot AI 5:121

Silver D, Schrittwieser J, Simonyan K, Antonoglou I, Huang A, Guez A, . . . Bolton A (2017) Mastering the game of go without human knowledge. Nature 550:354-35

Silver D, Hubert T, Schrittwieser J, Antonoglou I, Lai M, Guez A, [...] Graepel T (2018) A general reinforcement learning algorithm that masters chess, shogi, and Go through self-play. Science 362(6419):1140–1144

Soares N, Fallenstein B, Armstrong S, Yudkowsky E (2015) Corrigibility. https://www.aaai.org/ocs/index.php/WS/AAAIW15/paper/viewFile/10124/10136 Accessed 6 July 2021

Sotala K (2017) How feasible is the rapid development of artificial superintelligence? Physica Scripta 92:113001:1–14

Turchin A (2019) Assessing the future plausibility of catastrophically dangerous AI, 107:45–58

Turing A M (1950) Computing machinery and intelligence. Mind 59:433–460

United States Executive Office of the President (2016) Preparing for the future of artificial intelligence. Technical report. National Science and Technology Council, Washington D.C., October 2016

Weinbaum D, Veitas V (2017) Open ended intelligence: the individuation of intelligent agents. Journal of Experimental and Theoretical Artificial Intelligence 29:371–396

Wiener N (1960) Some moral and technical consequences of automation. Science 131:1355–1358

Yampolskiy R, Fox J (2013) Safety engineering for artificial general intelligence. Topoi 32:217–226

Yudkowsky E (2008) Artificial intelligence as a positive and negative factor in global risk. In: Bostrom N, Cirkovic M (eds) Global catastrophic risks. Oxford University Press, Oxford

Tobias Mahler is professor at the Faculty of Law at the University of Oslo, where he is the legal research leader of the "vulnerability in the robot society" (VIROS) project, the deputy director of the Norwegian Research Centre for Computers and Law (NRCCL) and the leader of the Legal Innovation Lab Oslo (LILO). He holds a PhD from the University of Oslo, an LLM degree in legal informatics from the University of Hannover, and a German law degree (first state exam). Prof. Mahler is also Director of the Master of Laws Programme in Information and Communication Technology Law at the University of Oslo. He teaches robot regulation, cybersecurity regulation, legal technology and artificial intelligence. Mahler has been a visiting fellow at the Max Planck Institute for Foreign and Criminal Law in Freiburg, Germany, and the Stanford Centre for Internet and Society. In 2020 he acted as an expert advisor to the European Commission on drafting the upcoming Digital Services Act.

Chapter 27
Influence, Immersion, Intensity, Integration, Interaction: Five Frames for the Future of AI Law and Policy

Hin-Yan Liu and Victoria Sobocki

Contents

Abstract Law and policy discussions concerning the impact of artificial intelligence (AI) upon society are stagnating. By this, we mean that contemporary discussions adopt implicit assumptions in their approaches to AI, which presuppose the characteristics of entity, externality, and exclusivity. In other words, for law and policy purposes: AI is often treated as some*thing* (encapsulated by AI personhood proposals); as the *other* (discernible from concerns that human beings are the decision subjects of AI applications); and as *artificial* (thereby concentrating on the artefactual characteristics of AI). Taken together, these form an overly narrow model of AI and unnecessarily constrain the palette of law and policy responses to both the challenges and opportunities presented by the technology. As a step towards rounding out law and policy responses to AI, with a view to providing greater societal resilience to, and preparedness for, technologically-induced disruption, we suggest a more integrated and open-minded approach in how we model AI: *influence*, where human behaviour is directed and manipulated; *immersion*, where the distinctions between physical and

H.-Y. Liu (✉)
University of Copenhagen, Copenhagen, Denmark
e-mail: hin-yan.liu@jur.ku.dk

V. Sobocki
Risk Advisory, Deloitte Denmark, Copenhagen, Denmark
e-mail: vsobocki@deloitte.dk

© T.M.C. ASSER PRESS and the authors 2022
B. Custers and E. Fosch-Villaronga (eds.), *Law and Artificial Intelligence*,
Information Technology and Law Series 35,
https://doi.org/10.1007/978-94-6265-523-2_27

virtual realities dissolve; *intensity*, where realities and experiences can be sharpened, lengthened, or otherwise altered; *integration*, where the boundaries between AI and human are being blurred; and *interaction*, where feedback loops undermine notions of linearity and causality. These pivots suggest different types of human relationships with AI, drawing attention to the legal and policy implications of engaging in AI-influenced worlds. We will ground these conceptually driven policy framing pivots in examples involving harm. These will demonstrate how contemporary law and policy framings are overly narrow and too dependent on previous comforting pathways. We will suggest that further problem-finding endeavours will be necessary to ensure more robust and resilient law and policy responses to the challenges posed by AI.

Keywords Extended Reality (XR) · Virtual Reality (VR) · Augmented Reality (AR) · Immersion · Manipulation · Virtual Violence · Legal Disruption · Virtual Environments · Law and Policy Responses

27.1 Introduction

Two decades into the new millennium, the societal impact of artificial intelligence (AI) applications is already posing disruptive challenges across virtually all domains of human activity.[1] Legal scholarship and policy discussions have proliferated in response to these present or projected problems, and ethical guidelines have been widely promulgated as attempts to assuage increasing public concern.

Despite this bloom in AI law and policy work, we claim that these contemporary discussions on the impact of AI on society are stagnating, and furthermore, that such stagnation is perilous in providing a false sense of progress and preparedness.

In this chapter, we seek to reconcile the apparent paradox between the proliferation of policy responses to the societal impact of AI application and our claim that this burgeoning debate is stagnating. Our objective is to propose pivots with respect to how to frame and approach the societal impacts of AI applications. Following from this, our aim is to analyse prospective and possible future interfaces and provide a more holistic and comprehensive understanding of the type and nature of challenges posed by AI applications and, thereby, enable more resilient and robust legal and policy responses. In proposing these pivots, we do not devalue or underestimate the value of contemporary work seeking to militate the societally disruptive effects of AI applications, and indeed we see our proposed frameworks as complementary. Rather, we recognise and underscore the multifaceted array of challenges introduced by AI applications. Ultimately, our goal in this chapter is to encourage engagement with as much of the broad interface between AI and society as possible in order to maximise policy preparedness for a fuller range of possible eventualities.

The chapter first grounds our claim that AI law and policy has stagnated due to the limited and incomplete frames that have been deployed to try to understand AI

[1] See for an overview Liu et al. 2020.

and the challenges that the applications of the technology introduce, exacerbate, or reveal (Sect. 27.2). In slogan form: we do not know what the problems posed by AI are, nor whether the problems we have identified are the most significant and most urgent problems there are in the potential problem space. We then move to set out our proposed policy pivots—our five frames for the future of AI law and policy: *influence, immersion, intensity, integration,* and *interaction* (Sect. 27.3). The purpose of these frames is to shift the AI law and policy debate towards identifying and confronting other AI problems that are currently underexplored in the literature. We then examine our five pivots through the perspective of harm to try to tease out what the challenges are of adopting our proposed pivots and the biases present in extant law and policy (Sect. 27.4), before we draw some concluding thoughts for future research.

27.2 Background

Our contention that AI law and policy work has stagnated rests upon our claim that this work rests upon overly, and unjustifiably, narrow foundations. In an important sense, this narrowness has been pre-ordained by the definitional parameters imposed by 'Artificial Intelligence'. By foregrounding the characteristics of *artificiality* and *intelligence,* law and policy work has become path-dependent upon the ramifications of this definitional framing.[2] Imperceptible ramifications flow from this framing that together render an overly narrow, and therefore brittle, basis for law and policy responses.

That artificiality and intelligence are the points of departure that lead to a common yet under-examined set of presumptions that form the foundation for much of AI law and policy work. In other words, AI applications are modelled as some*thing* or (or in some formulations, some*one*), and furthermore as something *other,* and as *artificial.* Thus, AI applications are stereotypically poised, for example, as something threatening to take away jobs,[3] render important decisions,[4] to discriminate unlawfully,[5] and to otherwise constrain or control human beings.[6] Such threats are then heightened both because AI applications stand in opposition to human beings (and what it means to be human in the context of cyborg discussions where AI applications may be fused with the human body or mind),[7] and because they are non-human by definition.

---

[2] Intelligence is notoriously difficult to define, with one study collecting around 70 different definitions, Legg and Hutter 2007.

[3] Brynjolfsson and McAfee 2014; Ford 2015.

[4] Bhuta et al. 2016.

[5] Angwin et al. 2016.

[6] Liu 2018.

[7] MacKellar 2019.

The above may be a caricature that overlooks some important nuances introduced into contemporary law and policy work. A notable example is Daniel Susser's insight that the foundational challenges posed by AI applications are not so much that these make decisions *about* us, but rather that these invisibly influence *our* decision-making processes.[8] Indeed, we would consider that Susser had launched a pivot away from the orthodox (definitional) approaches to AI applications towards an alternative way of approaching AI applications and their real societal impacts.

In addition to modelling AI applications based on the assumption that these are independent from, external to, and in opposition against human beings and human interests, there are a myriad of other ways to understand and approach the societal impact of AI applications. In previous work, one of us invoked the parable of 'the Blind Men and the Elephant'[9] to suggest that it is possible to overlook critical aspects of a phenomenon despite possessing relevant expertise. Indeed, there are severe blindsides and shortcomings of any attempt to broaden perspectives on, and understanding of, complex phenomena that take departure from narrow starting points.[10] Such realisation should make us more humble in our confidence that we have identified the most urgent or significant problems flowing from the societal application of AI. Similarly, one of us had also attempted to pivot the policy discussion surrounding "autonomous" weapons systems away from the autonomy framework in order to grapple with the greater difficulties in framing such weapons systems through a networks and systems approach to militarised technologies.[11]

The policy pivots that we propose here are of a different flavour entirely. The parable of the blind men and the elephant argued for a broader and more inclusive examination of a static and complicated phenomenon,[12] while the advocated pivot away from the autonomy framework sought to reimagine the legal and policy consequences that stem from alternative conceptual frameworks. In this chapter, we foreground the relational interface between AI applications and human beings as the source of legal disruption in the future of AI law and policy. As such, this chapter moves beyond the articulation of Lyria Bennett Moses' sociotechnical change,[13] since the problem space that we are engaged with rests largely within the individual

---

[8] Susser 2019.

[9] Saxe 1872. This parable warns of making generalisations from specific observations of a phenomenon, that we should not conclude that elephants are pythons merely because we happen to touch only the trunk. In the parable, some blind men who have never before encountered an elephant seek to understand what an elephant is. One touches the tail, and concludes that an elephant is like a rope. Another touches the leg and infers that elephants are pillars. Another touches the elephant's trunk and believes an elephant to be a python. While each man engages with an aspect of an elephant, and in that sense gains a comprehension of one aspect of 'elephantness', this comprehension is neither holistic nor complete, and the result is that the concept of 'elephantness' remains elusive to such an approach to describing the world.

[10] Liu and Maas 2021.

[11] Liu 2019.

[12] Indeed, we critiqued these unexamined presumptions as severe limitations to that parable in Liu and Maas 2021.

[13] Bennett Moses 2007, 2016.

and in the interaction between the AI application and the individual. While this may qualify as shifts in the sociotechnical landscape in the broad sense, to frame it as such would overlook that the crux is posed by the influence, manipulation, and control over individuals that AI applications may afford.

27.3   Our Proposed Policy Pivots

Our five frames for the future of AI law and policy are *influence, immersion, intensity, integration*, and *interaction*.

These frames are united by the blurring of hitherto distinct categories, and by mutual, iterative, and dynamic engagement. At a superficial level, our frames frustrate metaphorical legal responses which are premised upon analogies with, or distinctions from, historical precedent.[14] More fundamentally, however, our pivots question the very nature of human moulding and manipulation, with the profound policy ramifications that might follow from shaking the traditional legal foundations. This in turn suggests that there may be different levels or scales at which our pivots might initiate appropriate law and policy responses.

A useful heuristic to intuitively grasp our five pivots may be to view AI law and policy through the lens of a related emerging technology (which may also be powered or assisted by AI): extended reality (XR), which in turn encompasses augmented reality (AR), mixed reality (MR), and virtual reality (VR). To be clear, this is not a chapter tackling the myriad of law and policy challenges raised by the prospects of XR technologies or their application, and we are agnostic with regards to the pace and progress in its research and development. Instead, we invoke the XR metaphorically to emphasise the *interface* between AI and the human being, and to focus on, and move beyond the changes in the sociotechnical landscape[15] between human and machine. Thus, our pivots interrogate the presumptions of independence, externality, and artefactual qualities of AI applications within orthodox legal and policy work. Instead, we emphasise the worlds that can be digitally created, manipulated, and distorted, in the hope of initiating the necessary legal and policy discussions that would flow from taking these approaches.

Thus, our five pivots depart from the orthodox legal treatment of AI as discrete applications that impinge upon defined areas of human activity towards situations where AI is infused into, and impact upon, the very fabric of our reality. In this sense, we view AI as a factor that both mediates and manufactures our reality, and we explore the ramifications of this approach for law and policy through the lens of harm.

---

[14] Calo 2015, 2016.

[15] Bennett Moses 2016.

27.3.1 Influence

Extrapolating from Daniel Susser's insight that it is the invisible influences of AI applications upon human behaviour that pose the more insidious dimensions to policy problems,[16] our first pivot concerns influence. The fact that choice architectures are technologically mediated, however, comprises only one aspect of the perils of influence.

There are at least two other types of influence that expand the range of challenges for AI law and policy work. The first concerns Roger Brownsword's proposed trajectory of regulatory travel, starting from first-generation normative signalling, through second-generation design and architecture, and ending at the incorporation of regulation directly into the regulatee.[17] At first, this appears to be a concern for our integration pivot, discussed below, but we would like to elaborate on the idea that deep and pervasive influence does not necessarily require (physical bodily) integration. In other words, incorporation is one way to meld regulation and regulatee together but it may also be possible to do this, for example, via dynamic and tailored environments.[18] Indeed, recognising such converging effects is crucial because law and policy responses may build in litmus tests that monitor the progress of technological capabilities that are required to embed regulation into the regulatee (in Brownsword's example, this could be to keep tabs on cutting edge capacities of controlling genetic coding). If we are right about this, some insidious forms of influence could bypass such law and policy work because the 'relevant' technologies have not yet matured or proliferated and therefore have not passed certain thresholds of public concern. An example of this could be Facebook's immense experiment[19] from 2012, in which it manipulated information posted on users' news feeds and found that it could make people feel more positive or negative through a process of "emotional contagion".[20] This showcases that one does not always need genetic or neural interfaces to manipulate people's moods and behaviour.

How might this work in practice? If we accept Brownsword's notion of technological management,[21] and Lawrence Lessig's architecture/code modality of regulation,[22] human behaviour is facilitated and constrained in a myriad of non-normative ways (outside of the law). While such approaches to regulation seek to collapse the

---

[16] Susser 2019.

[17] Brownsword 2015, pp. 30–31.

[18] Liu 2021.

[19] Kramer et al. 2014.

[20] Booth 2014.

[21] See also Brownsword 2016. In a nutshell, technological management involves situations where only condoned behaviour is possible, and conversely where undesirable behaviour is rendered impossible. This is achieved through configuring the possibilities of technological applications.

[22] Lessig 1999, pp. 507–510. In short, this is where the architecture or configuration permits or prevents certain behaviours or outcomes. This constitutes a modality of regulation because of its influence and constraints, and complements law, social norms and market as the other regulatory modalities.

undesirable into the impossible, these are predicated upon a fairly static approach to behavioural influence (which itself may be a corollary of deploying the metaphor of architecture). The point here is that architectural modalities of regulation are similar: their influence over behaviour is exerted in a relatively blunt, consistent, and persistent manner upon all regulatees over time.[23]

Carrying the discussion forward, Karen Yeung has advanced the notion through her concept of 'hypernudge' whereby 'digital decision-"guidance" processes are designed so that it is not the machine, but the targeted individual, who makes the relevant decision'.[24] Here we can begin to see how the individual may be caged within a dynamically-adaptive regulatory 'glove' which is perfectly tailored to the regulatee.[25] As Shoshana Zuboff reported: '"We can engineer the context around a particular behaviour and force change that way (…) *We are learning how to write the music, and then we let the music make them dance.*"'[26]

Such influence, which powerfully yet invisibly incentivises the desired behaviour in the absence of ostensible coercion or integration within the regulatee, demonstrates the necessity of this pivot for law and policy work. The keystone concept of autonomy within legal regimes permits few restrictions to the choices that agents freely make, leaving such dynamically-adaptive forms of influence to proceed unfettered, even in legal systems founded upon human rights and the rule of law.

In this context, the burgeoning Social Credit System in China[27] is even more insidious and pervasive, and can be seen precisely as a manifestation of comprehensive behavioural control beyond democratic oversight and human rights protections that is both tailored and tethered to the individual regulatee.[28] Its non-normative regulatory impact can be discerned, at least in part, from the failure of human rights law to *contain* the effects of the Social Credit System.[29] The point here is that the individual is neither coerced nor compelled towards certain behaviours, but rather that those behaviours are driven internally (albeit induced by external factors) than by traditional forms of regulation.

The second type of influence can be developed through the notion of the 'anti-Panopticon' whereby the absence of visceral responses produces the desired

---

[23] An example of this may be found in the difference between billboard and television advertising which broadcasts the same message to everybody encountering it on the one hand, and personalised or targeted advertising which tailors each advertisement to a specific individual based upon their data profile on the other hand.

[24] Yeung 2017, p. 121.

[25] The effect is more than that of a filter bubble, where individuals are fed with information that confirms their cultural or ideological positions.

[26] Zuboff 2019, p. 23. Emphasis original.

[27] Hvistendahl 2017; Mistreanu 2018.

[28] Note that this critique is made from a Western perspective that emphasises the potential erosion of individual autonomy potentially inheriting in these technological capabilities. Conversely, such a system may enhance social trust and cohesion which are among the stated objectives of the Social Credit System. Equally, credit scoring exists in the West but is not generally subjected to such heavy scrutiny even though the process (and outcome to some extent) are similar.

[29] Liu 2018, pp. 210–214.

behaviour. Jeremy Bentham's idea for the Panopticon is well-known: an architectural design for a prison whereby the prisoners would not know whether or not they were being observed at any moment in time. The prospect of perpetual surveillance coupled with the impossibility of authenticating it was meant to internalise norms of compliant behaviour within the prisoners. When it comes to cyberspace, the reverse seems to be the case—by now we *know* we are being observed, but still, we do not *feel* it due to the design of the infrastructure and the interfaces.[30] The inability to summon an appropriate emotional response to what we are aware of, cognitively, is a large part of the problem[31] and disarms our resistance against hidden influences and biases.

These observations suggest that the idea of technological transparency may be misleading, for example, as seen with "black box" models in machine learning, where no human can understand it, even if one has a list of the input variables.[32] Instead, the purported transparency is, in reality, a filter or a distorting lens and not a transparent window. Rather than seeing "through" a technology, that technology draws our attention to certain attributes of the world while minimising the relevance of others thereby subtly, yet deterministically influencing our perceptions within that world. Insofar as our behaviours and our regulatory regimes have not adapted to such distortions, such influence is deeply disruptive of contemporary legal and policy presumptions.

27.3.2 Immersion

Subjugation to surveillance absent visceral feeling is one thing; being influenced without awareness altogether is another. As Daniel Susser writes:

> [O]nce we become sufficiently adept at using technologies we stop focusing on the technologies themselves and direct our attention instead to the things we are able to do *through* them… This is often referred to as *technological transparency*, pointing to the fact that we generally experience the world through technology, rather than experiencing technology itself, directly.[33]

While Susser presents technological transparency as a means of advancing his argument of invisible influence, we approach this invisibility in terms of lowering barriers. Here, we emphasise how immersion is facilitated through technological transparency as the barriers between us and the world that we inhabit are lifted. A different way of putting this is that our critical thinking and analytical defences

---

[30] Lawrence Lessig provides an early example in relation to protected privacy in real and in cyberspace: "In cyberspace, surveillance is not self-authenticating. Nothing reveals whether you are being watched, so there is no real basis upon which to consent". See generally Lessig 1999, pp. 504–505.

[31] See also this argument presented in a different context in Harris 2016.

[32] Rudin and Radin 2019.

[33] Susser 2019, p. 2. Emphasis original.

diminish where overly smooth interfaces provide the user with a seamless experience without friction or frustration. "Getting lost" in the subjective experience of the world that the technology brings to life undermines our awareness that our agency, autonomy, and experience are mediated through that technology.[34] We are distracted from the inner workings of the technology and seduced by the seamlessness. Technological transparency can be perilous insofar as this facilitates our immersion in a technologically generated world.

Take a relatively mundane technology, the printed page: is reading is nothing more than peering over pigment placed upon processed plant fibre? But the act of reading is capable of invoking entire worlds within the mind of the reader, and then immersing the reader within that world that has been generated in their mind through reading.[35] Yet, significant differences remain between reading print and being immersed and embodied in an XR world defined by choice of available action.[36] Furthermore, as technological prowess grows and where XR worlds become indistinguishable from the physical world, immersion can provide for experiences that are richer than their present association with video games might suggest.[37] Edward Castronova conducted a large study of the game *EverQuest*: he found that 22% of users wanted to spend all their time there, and 40% said they would quit their jobs or studies if they had sufficient wages in the game world.[38]

Immersion invokes presence or embodiment, which is the feeling of *existing* within a game or world. The notion of embodied intelligence applies to human beings because we rely on our bodies to interact with and make sense of the world, and human emotion is mediated through these physical bodies. This accentuates the potential for control and harm through technologies such as XR because the embodiment itself can be hijacked and influenced in technologically rendered worlds.

Indeed, we consider immersion as the functional difference between the much lambasted "virtual" crime and "true" crime. A "rape in cyberspace" was one of the first and most widely documented instances of virtual crime involving a 'real time non-consensual *textual description* of the violent sexual mutilation of an online community member to other community members'.[39] Contrast this with a more recent incident taking place in VR where a player had her avatar (a free-floating helmet, a persistent bow for one hand, and the other hand free-floating) groped in

---

[34] The brevity of this chapter restricts our discussion, and so we use the concept of immersion to also capture the related, but distinct, notions of flow and presence. We consider that immersion is the prerequisite for flow and presence.

[35] In this vein, we might consider music, books, and film to be the antecedents of extended reality technologies before memory and processing power were up to the task of computationally generating such worlds. Yet, immersion in such "static" media faces more constraints due to the flow of the narrative that forecloses participatory interaction, thereby losing the ability to be present *within* such media and the possibility to change outcomes through actions and decisions.

[36] It is also worth bearing in mind the affordance and signifiers that will influence and determine the possible range of behaviours in XR, being a designed world. See generally Norman 2013.

[37] Danaher 2019, chapter 7.

[38] Lastowka and Hunter 2006a, p. 16.

[39] Lastowka and Hunter 2006b, p. 122. Emphasis added.

the spaces where her chest and groin would have been.[40] In the words of the victim: 'Of course, you're not physically being touched, just like you're not actually one hundred feet off the ground, but it's still scary as hell.'[41]

While individual instances of such activity, whether legally recognised as crimes or not, are problematic, the pivot of immersion reveals the potential for structural control of individuals who participate in such worlds. Embodied forms of immersion in a technologically rendered environment mean that whoever is in control of that world also exercises immense influence over the individual behind the avatar—an extreme form of caging where the individual is completely subsumed within that world.[42] Insofar as AI applications are used to generate or maintain XR worlds in which individuals are immersed, or function as non-playable characters (NPCs) in such worlds, AI law and policy responses need to also take into account such prospects for harm.

27.3.3 Intensity

Insofar as immersion facilitates intensity of experiences, we need to consider the prospect for technologies such as XR to produce worlds that are technologically superior to reality (for example in terms of resolution, excitement, or engagement) which may, in turn, provide for more rewarding experiences than those proffered by the physical world. This has direct relevance for the experience of harm and suffering because of the potential that intensity not only exacerbates existing conceptions of harm, but may also introduce new categories of harm yet conceivable because these are not within the adjacent possible of our present.[43]

To unpack the concept of intensity, we note that the human mind is capable of simultaneously generating and experiencing "experiences" that are well beyond the realm of the quotidian. A stark example of intense and categorically different experiences involve the near-death experience (NDE),[44] where '[m]ost episodes involve similar feelings of wonder, mental clarity and bliss'.[45] Furthermore, NDEs can trigger transformational changes in individuals who experience them: they have been reported as 'an experience that, sometimes in a matter of seconds, dramatically transforms people's attitudes, values, beliefs, and behaviours' and which have been observed to persist for decades after the event.[46]

---

[40] Belamire 2016; Wong 2016.

[41] Belamire 2016.

[42] Insofar as the user has not agreed to this in the Terms of Service (ToS) or the End User License Agreement (EULA). See further Balkin 2006.

[43] Johnson 2011, pp. 30–33.

[44] Greyson 2021.

[45] Moshakis 2021.

[46] Moshakis 2021.

In terms of intensity, the point here is that technologies such as XR hold the potential to generate hyper-realistic environments and experiences that may be more intense than those that are typically encountered in the day-to-day physical world. This potential then connects with the human capacity for intense and indescribable experiences revealed by NDEs,[47] to suggest that law and regulation may have to identify, describe, and account for new depths and categories of human experience that may hitherto have been rare. Thus, technologies such as XR may render exceptional experiences commonplace, and may also introduce entirely new possibilities of experience. This has a strong bearing upon the nature of harm that can be suffered in technologically rendered environments that may not correlate neatly with our existing notions, interpretations, and recognition of harm.[48]

27.3.4 Integration

The integration of the physical body *with* technology is becoming a looming possibility on the technological horizon through progress in genetic engineering and neural interfaces, and these technologies hold the potential to alter humans and humanity in completely new and fundamental ways. Yet, unlike our other proposed pivots thus far, the prospect of physically integrating technological artefacts with the human body may largely be a distraction: in our view, it is at most functioning as a red flag because of the relative difficulty to remove or roll back technological integration to re-establish physical independence. This position is consistent with our suggestion that immersion, intensity, and interaction are the overriding factors and that these do not require physical coupling to achieve.

Thus, we argue that physical integration is *not* necessary for human beings to be fully immersed and interact with technologically rendered worlds, and subject to the intensity of experiences that these afford. As such, this should not provide grounds for a large distinction. Take for example the smartphone, smartwatch or VR headset. As Elon Musk claims:

> We're already a cyborg – you have a digital version of yourself, a partial version of yourself online in the form of your emails, your social media, and all the things that you do. We already have "super powers," [due to] the world's access to smartphones and personal computers.[49]

A different way of putting this is that technological artefacts can exert influence and control without it being physically intertwined with the body, for example, via the Social Credit System[50] or social media. Thus, we argue that immersion is sufficient

---

[47] One subject said that "recalling is [NDE] was like 'to draw an odour with crayons', which is to say, basically impossible". Moshakis 2021.

[48] Experiences of greater intensity, and the higher frequency of such experiences, may have implications for post-traumatic stress disorder (PTSD). Searches for XR and PTSD readily turn up projects using XR for the *treatment* of PTSD, but not for XR as the *cause* or *trigger* of PTSD.

[49] Ricker 2016.

[50] Hvistendahl 2017; Liu 2018; Mistreanu 2018.

for harm to take place, for example, by vicariously experiencing trauma in XR, and physical integration with the body may be considered as only an exacerbating factor that complicates withdrawal.

There is, however, one specific form of harm related to integration that demands caution: if the memory of someone tampering with your biology or body is wiped away, in theory, you would have no chance of knowing anything about this event. This would be tantamount to a regulator embedding the means of influence and control directly into the regulatee,[51] but making escape, reversion, or removal difficult if not impossible. At least in the other scenarios it is still possible to walk away—to close the book, put the smartphone away, take off the VR headset. When the memory of integration is removed, then alternative possibilities are also taken away.

27.3.5 Interaction

A defining characteristic of AI applications is their liminal status between agent and object that confounds contemporary legal categories.[52] At heart, this concerns the prospect for human interaction with AI applications, and this is no different with the generation of XR worlds where both the environment and other avatars (for human as well as non-playable characters) can be engaged with in adaptive and dynamic ways. Indeed, imagination, computational power, and technical prowess are the only limitations in terms of interactions in XR, and AR is already used for designing living spaces and doing surgery at present, while VR applications are imagined for use in the classroom and the courtroom.[53]

From a regulatory standpoint, there are at least two major ramifications flowing from interaction within XR worlds. The first is essentially the opposite of Ryan Calo's view, in robot law, that cyberspace activities can reach out into the real world to cause physical harm.[54] In our interaction pivot, however, it is real life reaching into cyberspace causing "harm". Yet, the types of harm through interaction in XR worlds are not readily recognised in legal, regulatory, or governance systems because the forms of loss and damage are neither well-documented nor well-understood. This is hindered by terminology such as 'virtual' that is often used to describe such harm, which has the effect of further segregating and effectively denying the prospect for new or different types of harm to gain acceptance.[55]

Secondly, technologies such as XR can lower the barriers related to both action and experience because the limits imposed by physical space, physical laws, and even time, can be altered or removed. Profound regulatory ramifications may arise because regulation can be understood as the interaction between the "settings" of

---

[51] Akin to the third generation of the regulatory environment: Brownsword 2015, pp. 30–31.

[52] Liu and Maas 2021.

[53] Vaughn 2019.

[54] Calo 2015, pp. 532–537.

[55] Lastowka and Hunter 2006b, pp. 122–124.

various regulatory modalities.[56] If fundamental presumptions undergirding possibilities for action are subject to such upheaval, new and revealed possibilities may lead to insufficiency in our contemporary regulatory configuration. Lawrence Lessig provides an apt example:

> We have special laws to protect against the theft of autos, or boats. We do not have special laws to protect against the theft of skyscrapers. Skyscrapers take care of themselves. The architecture of real space, or more suggestively, its real-space code, protects skyscrapers much more effectively than law. Architecture is an ally of skyscrapers (making them impossible to move); it is an enemy of cars and boats (making them quite easy to move).[57]

In this example, reconfiguring the real, or virtual, space code can have regulatory consequences because changes in the architecture/code modality of regulation may suddenly make it possible to "steal" a skyscraper (by shrinking and pocketing it)— actions that are inconceivable and impossible at present and which our contemporary regulatory framework neither anticipates nor accommodates for. What might be even more pertinent in this regard is that the very nature and character of "theft" might be outmoded in XR worlds that are created, for example, because the code undergirding the "skyscraper" may be copied, duplicated, and modified without incurring traditional costs to the original "owner".[58] This suggests that the nature of interests, and concomitant harms, may categorically differ from those that are recognised and protected by law at present.

27.4 The Five Pivots Through the Perspective of Harm

We now focus on the question of harm in relation to our proposed pivots. Harm is used in connection with damage and injury, but while injury requires legal and moral recognition,[59] damage and harm are applied more broadly to anything involving suffering or loss. In a legal sense, harm is defined as "any harm done to a person by the acts or omissions of another." Injury may include physical hurt as well as damage to reputation or dignity, loss of a legal right, or breach of contract. If the injuring party was either wilful or negligent then that party is liable for payment of damages for the harm caused. Harm also plays an important role in the legal landscape when deciding which actions should be criminalised and why. Indeed, one could argue that the very *concept* of law came about due to a need to mitigate conflicts of harm and injury in society.[60]

---

[56] Lessig 1999, pp. 507–510.

[57] Lessig 1999, p. 523.

[58] Scarcity limitations and zero-sum interactions that are prevalent in the physical world need not be imported in their present configuration into XR worlds.

[59] Veitch 2007.

[60] Such as seen in the Code of Hammurabi, one of the earliest legal codes known in the world, see King 2015, Introduction.

While harm is often intuitive and apparent in the real world, it becomes a murky concept when it is tested in XR worlds. The law at present respects the potential for psychological, economic, reputational, cultural, and political harm,[61] but are these types of harm comprehensive and sufficient for capturing activities taking place in XR worlds?

The concept of harm is disproportionately biased towards protecting bodily integrity, but absent physical bodily exposure in XR worlds, the very understanding of harm might be jeopardised.[62] Importing questions of harm into XR worlds requires us to refine notions of harm and suffering because these may bend or break existing legal categories. Is it possible to import (the notion of) bodily harm back into XR worlds, and if so, are there differences with respect to playing video games? For decades, video games have been blamed for causing violence, despite a dearth of empirical evidence to support such notions.[63] Due to the fully immersive, intense, and interactive nature of VR, which seeks to and increasingly succeeds in mimicking real-world experiences, there is apt concern about the effects of violence perpetrated, witnessed, and experienced in XR worlds (and notably this is happening before we have even reached full-body tactile sensations).

While law and policy may be slow to recognise and remedy such harms, an emerging body of empirical evidence underpins the prospect for harm in XR. To take two examples: a violent computer game in VR had statistically significant effects on a participant's internal state of hostility and aggression;[64] while another study found that VR game participants reported significantly higher presence and body ownership, and that the violence received and enacted by them felt more real and personally involving.[65] Yet another study found that those participating in VR reported higher levels of absorption: this increased the intensity of their negative emotional response to the scenario, which in turn had a significant positive correlation with negative rumination (i.e., harmful self-related thoughts related to distress).[66]

Thomas Metzinger argued that VR may also lead to depersonalization, which may make one's physical body start to seem unreal. He continued to argue that:

> Fully immersive experiences have a bigger and more lasting impact on people's behaviour and psychology. [...] Consumers must understand that not all of the risks are known in advance. [...] These technologies could potentially [also] be used by the military. Virtual torture is still torture.[67]

---

[61] Agrafiotis et al. 2018.

[62] But see the focus on property crimes in Lastowka and Hunter 2006b.

[63] Mileva 2020.

[64] Arriaga et al. 2008.

[65] Graham Wilson and Mark Mcgill, Violent Video Games in Virtual Reality: Re-Evaluating the Impact and Rating of Interactive Experiences, https://www.researchgate.net/publication/328546 457_Violent_Video_Games_in_Virtual_Reality_Re-Evaluating_the_Impact_and_Rating_of_Int eractive_Experiences.

[66] Lavoie et al. 2021.

[67] Ananthaswamy 2016.

Beyond scientific studies, there have been multiple art pieces featuring the usage of VR showcasing grotesque violence and sexual abuse, all making viewers uncomfortable, thrilled, and curious about the future.[68] As one of the artists poignantly states: "This is real abuse, not a simulation."[69] Taken together, these examples suggest that experiences in XR worlds may intersect with notions of harm in both familiar and entirely novel ways, with the potential to significantly shift the sociotechnical landscape.[70] Indeed, by examining harm through the lens of XR worlds, we may even uncover forms of latent harm that are present and pervasive in present society.

We can experience harm in our physical world through our human bodies, but the parameters of such harm are limited by the laws of physics and bound by human physiology. XR worlds, however, open the possibility of wicked and unlimited types of harm that we could not begin to fathom because of the possibility to influence and control the world that the individual inhabits. For example, the prospect for psychological harm would be magnified where an arachnophobe's reality is saturated with spiders in ways that defy the laws of physics or real-world possibilities. Immersion within an XR world would render resistance or escape futile. The intensity of the experience could change the threshold for traumatic experience, and interaction may render the hapless victim incapable of doing anything to alter the XR reality or the subjective experience of it. Yet, harm in XR worlds can be perpetrated much more subtly, in ways that are less noticeable but nevertheless very destructive, such as modifying the reality of the participants even very slightly without their knowledge or consent.

We divide XR harm into four categories: physical, psychological, subtle manipulation, and societal consequences. Strict physical harm is not directly relevant to XR worlds,[71] but much of this shifts instead to psychological harm. Indeed, new forms of psychological harm may be introduced in XR worlds since neither the human body nor the contemporary legal system would be able to make sense of immersing the mind in digitally rendered worlds while leaving the physical body "behind". Thus, XR worlds exacerbate existing forms of physical and psychological harm, but also create new possibilities for novel types of harm that fall within these familiar categories.[72] While new forms of psychological harm may cause controversy for the law (for example, the non-consensual sexual activities in cyberspace and VR discussed above),[73] they nevertheless comprise of legally-recognisable forms of harm. Thus, the question is whether a particular activity gives rise to psychological harm in XR worlds, and not the more basic question of whether harm is relevant in the first place.

It is at this basic level that subtle manipulation and societal consequences introduce challenges for the very notion of harm itself. Subtle manipulation refers to harm done

---

[68] Valentish 2019.

[69] Jeffries 2018.

[70] Bennett Moses 2016.

[71] With a caveat that XR technologies may alter individual behaviour in ways that lead to physical harm.

[72] Liu et al. 2020.

[73] Lastowka and Hunter 2006b, pp. 122–124.

in a way that is very unnoticeable but nevertheless alters an individuals' experience.[74] Societal consequences refer to larger scale or longer term effects arising from XR worlds, for example, changes in social values in general,[75] or specifically in relation to violence and assault, or even just people "quitting" normal society.[76]

Both subtle manipulation and societal consequences differ from the categories of physical and psychological harm because it is not clear that these can "constitute" harm at all under the contemporary legal process. For example, both propaganda and advertising can be considered as forms of subtle manipulation, but only propaganda for war has been deemed problematic under international human rights law.[77] It is worth noting that the relevant legal provision prohibits propaganda for war, rather than providing an individual right to be protected against it, suggesting that its purpose is not related to the harm that such activities pose for the individual. When it comes to societal consequences, its nexus to harm becomes even more tenuous because the configuration of society serves as the backdrop benchmark against which "harm" is measured. If "harm" is built into the background conditions of society, then it will be difficult to identify and isolate that harm, for example, during times of slavery, when some people were naturally expected to be treated worse than others.

For us, subtle manipulation and societal consequences raise a different type of challenge for (legally-recognised) harm.[78] Unlike physical and psychological harm, for which XR worlds introduce new potential variations or exacerbate controversies associated with the recognition of harm, subtle manipulation and societal consequences obfuscate the potential for harm to be identified and recognised. As such, subtle manipulation and societal consequences question the very concept of harm and threaten to lock out contemporary legal protections that individuals might use to prevent or seek compensation in relation to harms suffered.

27.5 Concluding Thoughts: Harm through the Five Pivots

In this chapter, we have proposed five pivots in an approach that will characterise the next generation of law and policy questions related to AI. These bring forward different challenges posed by AI which may play a role in creating and sustaining the worlds in which we inhabit and where we interact (as well as our perception of the physical world). By shifting our attention to the law and policy questions raised by XR worlds, we have been able to identify some of the factors that we believe need to be addressed as AI applications connect with other emerging technologies

---

[74] The absence of awareness or (informed) consent exacerbates the prospect for harm.

[75] See generally Danaher 2020.

[76] In popular culture, see for example Cline 2011.

[77] Article 20(1) of the International Covenant on Civil and Political Rights (ICCPR), United Nations General Assembly Resolution 2200A (XXI) of 16 December 1966.

[78] Subtle manipulation is theoretically value-neutral: the obvious flipside to our discussion on harm include parenting and education which may be considered as "virtuous" manipulation.

to create new environments and agents for individuals to engage with. In Sect. 27.4, we suggested that XR worlds may give rise to different categories of harm: either variants of familiar forms of harm; or new types of harm that will likely dilute or elude legal protection.

We would like to conclude this chapter by bringing our five pivots and two categories of harm together in order to chart the potential problem space at the intersection of our new approaches and the limitations of contemporary notions of harm. What is telling from the harm perspective is that, aside from Integration, all of the pivots "involve" the individual in the sense of altering the individual's sense of agency and surroundings. The concept of harm seems primarily to concern external action or external forces, implicitly treating the individual as a patient who needs protection and compensation as a result of having harm inflicted by an external actor or agent. Conversely, the pivots of Influence, Immersion, Intensity, and Interaction operate "within" the individual, situating the effects within the agency of the individual agent. This has the effect of obfuscating any harm that may ensue, making potential harm difficult or even impossible to identify, and resists legal recognition of injury ensuing from those harms.

These obfuscating effects are further compounded by the new categories of harm that we identify as subtle manipulation and societal consequences. We can consider subtle manipulation as a common denominator for why harm can be hidden in our pivots: subtle manipulation is a different way of saying that the effects have become intertwined within the agent. Yet subtle manipulation also suggests that the harm is not inherent within our pivots, but rather is a potential outcome of their usage. In other words, the new perspectives put forward in our pivots do not necessarily give rise to new forms of harm: rather, it is the potential deployment of these pivots towards Subtle Manipulation that puts our pivots within the purview of harm.

We can identify a similar effect with regard to our pivots and the harm related to societal consequences, but with one twist. While harm is implicit within subtle manipulation because of external coercion or because it is a means towards an ulterior end, it is not clear that this will be the case with societal consequences. This is a double-edged sword: if we accept that harm is neither inherent within our pivots nor within societal consequences, then it would appear that contemporary notions of harm are excluded at their intersection. Yet, as we have suggested, our pivots reveal the redistribution of burdens, exacerbate existing forms of harm, and introduce new means for causing damage. Similarly, with societal consequences the prospect for harm can be hidden within the background conditions of society in ways that render such harm imperceptible. Thus, we can visualise this as being in the quadrant where our pivots intersect with societal consequences, and we can expect a host of structural types of harm that can neither be readily identified nor remedied by our contemporary legal principles or processes.

This leads us to an overarching question for future research: why might the notion of harm be inadequate for identifying, recognising, and remedying the challenges brought about by pivoting the frames for AI law and policy? If the notion of harm diminishes in importance with changes in the ways in which we interact with technology itself, and with each other through it, there will be serious implications from any shortfall of protection against detrimental outcomes. Law and policy responses to AI applications must therefore take the diminishing role of harm into account. At a minimum, this implies that some sort of legal development[79] is necessary to ensure that there is no shortfall in protection. Realistically, however, we think that there are hard limits to what the notion of harm is able to achieve given the shifting parameters brought about both by new technologies and the pivots in approaches that we propose. We therefore suggest that complementary concepts in law and policy need to be developed that are capable of recognising and reining in the problems posed as we frame new understandings for AI applications and aligned technologies.

References

Agrafiotis I, Nurse JRC, Goldsmith M et al (2018) A taxonomy of cyber-harms: Defining the impacts of cyber-attacks and understanding how they propagate. Journal of Cybersecurity 4: https://doi.org/10.1093/cybsec/tyy006

Ananthaswamy A (2016) Virtual reality could be an ethical minefield – are we ready? New Scientist

Angwin J, Larson J, Mattu S, Kirchner L (2016) Machine Bias: There's software used across the country to predict future criminals. And it's biased against blacks. ProPublica

Arriaga P, Esteves F, Carneiro P, Monteiro MB (2008) Are the effects of Unreal violent video games pronounced when playing with a virtual reality system? Aggress Behav 34:521–538. https://doi.org/10.1002/ab.20272

Balkin JM (2006) Law and Liberty in Virtual Worlds. In: Balkin J, Noveck BS (eds) The State of Play: Law, Games, and Virtual Worlds. NYU Press, pp 86–117

Belamire J (2016) My First Virtual Reality Groping. Medium

Bennett Moses LB (2007) Why Have a Theory of Law and Technological Change? Minn JL Sci & Tech 8:589–606

Bennett Moses L (2016) Regulating in the Face of Sociotechnical Change. In: Brownsword R, Scotford E, Yeung K (eds) The Oxford Handbook of Law, Regulation and Technology. Oxford University Press, Oxford, pp 573–596

Bhuta N, Beck S, Geiß R et al (eds) (2016) Autonomous Weapons Systems: Law, Ethics, Policy. Cambridge University Press, Cambridge

Booth R (2014) Facebook reveals news feed experiment to control emotions. The Guardian

Brownsword R (2015) In the year 2061: from law to technological management. Law, Innovation and Technology 7:1–51. https://doi.org/10.1080/17579961.2015.1052642

Brownsword R (2016) Technological management and the Rule of Law. Law, Innovation and Technology 8:100–140

Brynjolfsson E, McAfee A (2014) The Second Machine Age: Work, Progress, and Prosperity in a Time of Brilliant Technologies. W. W. Norton & Company

Calo R (2015) Robotics and the Lessons of Cyberlaw. Cal L Rev 103:513

Calo R (2016) Robots as Legal Metaphors. Harvard Journal of Law & Technology 30:209–237

Cline E (2011) Ready Player One. Broadway Paperbacks

Danaher J (2019) Automation and Utopia: Human Flourishing in a World without Work. Harvard University Press

Danaher J (2020) Axiological Futurism: The Systematic Study of the Future of Human Values

Ford M (2015) The Rise of the Robots: Technology and the Threat of Mass Unemployment. One World, London

---

[79] Liu et al. 2020, pp. 233–242.

Greyson B (2021) After: A Doctor Explores What Near-Death Experiences Reveal about Life and Beyond. Bantam Press, London

Harris S (2016) Can we build AI without losing control over it? TED Conference. https://www.ted.com/talks/sam_harris_can_we_build_ai_without_losing_control_over_it?language=nl

Hvistendahl M (2017) Inside China's Vast New Experiment in Social Ranking. WIRED

Jeffries S (2018) Jordan Wolfson: "This is real abuse – not a simulation." The Guardian

Johnson S (2011) Where Good Ideas Come From: The Seven Patterns of Innovation. Penguin, London

King LW (translator) (2015) The Code of Hammurabi. CreateSpace Independent Publishing Platform

Kramer ADI, Guillory JE, Hancock JT (2014) Experimental evidence of massive-scale emotional contagion through social networks. PNAS 111:8788–8790

Lastowka FG, Hunter D (2006a) Virtual Worlds: A Primer. In: Balkin J, Noveck BS (eds) The State of Play: Law, Games, and Virtual Worlds. NYU Press, pp 13–28

Lastowka FG, Hunter D (2006b) Virtual Crime. In: Balkin J, Noveck BS (eds) The State of Play: Law, Games, and Virtual Worlds. NYU Press, pp 121–136

Lavoie R, Main K, King C, King D (2021) Virtual experience, real consequences: the potential negative emotional consequences of virtual reality gameplay. Virtual Reality 25:69–81. https://doi.org/10.1007/s10055-020-00440-y

Legg S, Hutter M (2007) A Collection of Definitions of Intelligence. arXiv:07063639 [cs]

Lessig L (1999) The Law of the Horse: What Cyber Law Might Teach. Harv L Rev 113:501

Liu H-Y (2018) The Power Structure of Artificial Intelligence. Law, Innovation and Technology 10:197–229

Liu H-Y (2019) From the Autonomy Framework towards Networks and Systems Approaches for "Autonomous" Weapons Systems. Journal of International Humanitarian Legal Studies 10:89–110

Liu H-Y (2021) AI Challenges and the Inadequacy of Human Rights Protections. Criminal Justice Ethics 40:2–22

Liu H-Y, Maas MM (2021) 'Solving for X?': Towards a problem-finding framework that grounds long-term governance strategies for artificial intelligence. Futures 126:102672

Liu H-Y, Maas M, Danaher J et al (2020) Artificial Intelligence and Legal Disruption: A New Model for Analysis. Law, Innovation and Technology 12:205–258

MacKellar C (ed) (2019) Cyborg Mind: What Brain-Computer and Mind-Cyberspace Interfaces Mean for Cyberneuroethics. Berghahn, New York/Oxford

Mileva G (2020) Can Virtual Reality Games Lead To Violent Behavior? AR Post

Mistreanu S (2018) Life Inside China's Social Credit Laboratory. Foreign Policy

Moshakis A (2021) What do near-death experiences mean, and why do they fascinate us? The Guardian

Norman DA (2013) The Design of Everyday Things. MIT Press, Cambridge, Massachusetts

Ricker T (2016) Elon Musk: We're already cyborgs. The Verge

Rudin C, Radin J (2019) Why Are We Using Black Box Models in AI When We Don't Need To? A Lesson From An Explainable AI Competition. Harvard Data Science Review 1:1–9. https://doi.org/10.1162/99608f92.5a8a3a3d

Saxe JG (1872) The Blind Men and the Elephant. J. Osgood, Boston

Susser D (2019) Invisible Influence: Artificial Intelligence and the Ethics of Adaptive Choice Architectures. In: Artificial Intelligence, Ethics and Society. Honolulu, Hawaii

Valentish J (2019) "Real" violence: coming to grips with the ethics of virtual reality brutality. The Guardian

Vaughn R (2019) Is Virtual Reality the Future of Courtrooms? Oklahoma Bar Association 90:10

Veitch S (2007) Law and Irresponsibility: On the Legitimation of Human Suffering. Routledge-Cavendish, Oxford

Wong JC (2016) Sexual harassment in virtual reality feels all too real – "it's creepy beyond creepy." The Guardian

Yeung K (2017) 'Hypernudge': Big Data as a mode of regulation by design. Information, Communication & Society 20:118–136

Zuboff S (2019) "We Make Them Dance": Surveillance Capitalism, the Rise of Instrumental Power, and the Threat to Human Rights. In: Jørgensen RF (ed) Human Rights in the Age of Platforms. MIT Press, Cambridge, Massachusetts, pp 3–51

Hin-Yan Liu, Associate Professor and Coordinator, Artificial Intelligence and Legal Disruption Research Group, Faculty of Law, University of Copenhagen, Denmark.

Victoria Sobocki, Consultant in Risk Advisory at Deloitte Denmark and cand.jur. (LL.M.) from the Faculty of Law, University of Copenhagen, Denmark.

Index